Models of Madness

Models of Madness shows that hallucinations and delusions are under-standable reactions to life events and circumstances rather than symptoms of a supposed genetic predisposition or biological disturbance. International contributors:

- Critique the 'medical model' of madness
- Examine the dominance of the 'illness' approach to understanding madness from historical and economic perspectives
- Document the role of drug companies
- Outline the alternatives to drug-based solutions
- Identify the urgency and possibility of prevention of madness

Models of Madness promotes a more humane and effective response to treating severely distressed people that will prove essential reading for psychiatrists and clinical psychologists and of great interest to all those who work in the mental health service.

John Read, Director, Clinical Psychology, Psychology Department, The University of Auckland.
Loren R. Mosher, Clinical Professor of Psychiatry, University of California at San Diego.
Richard P. Bentall, Professor of Experimental Psychology, Manchester University.

The ISPS book series
Series editor: Brian Martindale

The ISPS (the International Society for the Psychological Treatments of Schizophrenia and other Psychoses) has a history stretching back some 50 years, during which it has witnessed the relentless pursuit of biological explanations for psychosis. The tide is now turning again. There is a welcome international resurgence in interest in a range of psychological factors in psychosis that have considerable explanatory power and also distinct therapeutic possibilities. Governments, professional groups, users and carers are increasingly expecting interventions that involve talking and listening as well as skilled practitioners in the main psychotherapeutic modalities as important components of the care of the seriously mentally ill.

The ISPS is a global society. It is composed of an increasing number of groups of professionals organized at national, regional and more local levels around the world. The society has started a range of activities intended to support professionals, users and carers. Such persons recognize the potential humanitarian and therapeutic potential of skilled psychological understanding and therapy in the field of psychosis. Our members cover a wide spectrum of interests from psychodynamic, systemic, cognitive and arts therapies to the need-adaptive approaches and to therapeutic institutions. We are most interested in establishing meaningful dialogue with those practitioners and researchers who are more familiar with biological based approaches. Our activities include regular international and national conferences, newsletters and email discussion groups in many countries across the world.

One of these activities is to facilitate the publication of quality books that cover the wide terrain that interests ISPS members and other mental health professionals, policy makers and implementers. We are delighted that Brunner-Routledge of the Taylor & Francis group have seen the importance and potential of such an endeavour and have agreed to publish an ISPS series of books.

We anticipate that some of the books will be controversial and will challenge certain aspects of current practice in some countries. Other books will promote ideas and authors well known in some countries but not familiar to others. Our overall aim is to encourage the dissemination of existing knowledge and ideas, promote healthy debate and encourage more research in a most important field whose secrets almost certainly do not all reside in the neurosciences.

For more information about the ISPS, email isps@isps.org or visit our website www.isps.org

Models of Madness

Psychological, social and biological
approaches to schizophrenia

Edited by
John Read, Loren R. Mosher and
Richard P. Bentall

Dedicated to Loren Mosher (1933 - 2004)

Brunner-Routledge
Taylor & Francis Group
HOVE AND NEW YORK

First published 2004 by Brunner-Routledge
27 Church Road, Hove, East Sussex BN3 2FA

Simultaneously published in the USA and Canada
by Brunner-Routledge
29 West 35th Street, New York, NY 10001

Reprinted 2004 Brunner-Routledge
27 Church Road, Hove, East Sussex, BN3 2FA
270 Madison Avenue, New York, NY 10016

Brunner-Routledge is part of the T & f Informa plc

© 2004 Selection and editorial matter, John Read, Loren R. Mosher
and Richard P. Bentall; individual chapters, the contributors

Typeset in Times by Mayhew Typesetting, Rhayader, Powys
Printed and bound in Great Britain by TJ International Ltd, Padstow,
Cornwall
Paperback cover design by Hybert Design

This publication has been produced with paper manufactured to strict
environmental standards and with pulp derived from sustainable
forests.

British Library Cataloguing in Publication Data
A catalogue record for this book is available from the British Library

Library of Congress Cataloging-in-Publication Data
Models of madness : psychological, social and biological approaches to
schizophrenia / edited by John Read, Loren R. Mosher, Richard P.
Bentall.– 1st ed.
        p. ; cm.
Includes bibliographical references and index.
        ISBN 1-58391-905-8 (hbk) – ISBN 1-58391-906-6 (pbk)
    1. Schizophrenia. 2. Schizophrenia–Social aspects.
    [DNLM: 1. Schizophrenia.   2. Schizophrenic Psychology. WM 203 M689
2004] I. Read, John, Dr. II. Mosher, Loren R., 1933– III. Bentall,
Richard P.

    RC514.M5485 2004
    616.89'8–dc21

                                                        2003017397

ISBN 1-58391-905-8 (hbk)
ISBN 1-58391-906-6 (pbk)

Contents

List of tables and figures

Tables

Figures

Editors' bibliographies

John Read is currently Director of Clinical Psychology at the University of Auckland in New Zealand. After obtaining his PhD in Clinical Psychology in the USA in 1983, he worked as a clinical psychologist and a manager of mental health services in the USA and the UK. Most of this work was with people diagnosed as 'psychotic', most recently at the Acute Psychiatric Inpatient Unit of Auckland Hospital. In 1994 he accepted a position at the University of Auckland where, apart from undergraduate teaching and coordinating the professional training of postgraduate clinical psychology students, he has published numerous research papers, with psychiatrists and other psychologists, documenting the link between childhood trauma and psychosis in general and hallucinations in particular. His other research publications include studies demonstrating that, contrary to the approach taken by most destigmatization programmes, biological causal beliefs about mental health problems are related to increased fear and prejudice. Dr Read is an active member of the International Society for the Psychological Treatments of Schizophrenia and other Psychoses (ISPS) and was a member of the ISPS Task Force that collated research evidence of the effectiveness of a range of psychological modalities in the treatment of psychosis. He is a frequent media commentator on a range of mental health issues, from the damaging role of the pharmaceutical industry and the over-medicalization of theory and practice to the need to ban electroconvulsive therapy. Dr Read was invited to deliver the 2004 Annual Frieda Fromm-Reichmann Memorial Lecture at the Washington School of Psychiatry.

Loren R. Mosher received his MD (with honours) from Harvard Medical School. He took his psychiatric training at Harvard and the National Institute of Mental Health's (NIMH) Intramural Research Program in Bethesda, Maryland. After a year as an Assistant Professor of Psychiatry at Yale, he left in 1968 to become the first Chief of the NIMH's Center for Studies of Schizophrenia. While there he founded the *Schizophrenia Bulletin*. In 1980 he became Professor of Psychiatry at the Uniformed Services University of the Health Sciences (USUHS) in Bethesda. He left USUHS to direct the Montgomery County Mental Health System in 1988. Between 1996 and 1998 he served as Clinical Director of the San Diego County Mental Health System. He remains a Clinical Professor of Psychiatry at the University of California at San Diego. As a researcher Mosher has studied residential alternatives to psychiatric hospitalization. The results from his two major projects, one focused on newly psychotic persons and the other on unselected mental health system users, indicate that 85–90% of persons deemed in need of psychiatric hospitalization can be effectively treated in small, home-like, relationship-focused, normalizing settings. He is author or co-author of four books and more than 100 journal articles.

Richard P. Bentall was born in Sheffield in 1956. He was an undergraduate at the University College of North Wales, Bangor, where he went on to do his PhD in experimental psychology. He obtained a qualification in clinical psychology at the University of Liverpool. He also later obtained an MA in philosophy applied to health care from University College Swansea. After a brief period as a National Health Service forensic psychologist, he returned to the Universty of Liverpool as a lecturer, where he eventually became a Professor of Clinical Psychology. In 1989 he received the British Psychological Society's May Davidson Award for his contributions to Clinical Psychology. In 1999 he became Professor of Experimental Clinical Psychology at the University of Manchester. Besides numerous research publications in scientific journals concerning cognitive models of understanding psychosis, Professor Bentall was the editor of *Reconstructing Schizophrenia* (Routledge, 1990) and is the author of *Madness Explained: Psychosis and Human Nature* (Penguin, 2003).

Editors and contributors

John Read (coordinator editor)
Director of Clinical Psychology, Psychology Department, The University of Auckland, Private Bag 92019, Auckland, New Zealand

j.read@auckland.ac.nz

www.psych.auckland.ac.nz/psych/staff/JohnRead.htm

Loren R. Mosher (co-editor)
Director, Soteria Associates, San Diego, CA 92122, USA
Clinical Professor of Psychiatry, School of Medicine, University of California, San Diego, CA, USA
Adjunct Professor of Psychiatry, Uniformed Services University of the Health Sciences, Bethesda, MD, USA

www.mosher-soteria.com

Richard P. Bentall (co-editor)
Professor, Experimental Psychology, Manchester University, Coupland 1 Building, Oxford Road, Manchester M13 9PL, UK

bentall@psy.man.ac.uk

Volkmar Aderhold
Klinik für Psychiatrie und Psychotherapie, Hamburg University, UKE, Martinstr. 52, D-20246 Hamburg, Germany

Sharon Beder
Professor, Science and Technology Studies, University of Wollongong, Wollongong, NSW 2522, Australia

Jim Burdett
Consumer Consultant, Mind and Body Consultants Ltd, 44b The Drive, Epsom, Auckland, New Zealand

Judi Chamberlin
Staff Associate, National Empowerment Centre, 599 Canal Street, Lawrence, MA 01840, USA

Emma Davies
Programme Leader – Children and Families, Institute of Public Policy, Auckland University of Technology, Auckland, New Zealand

Jim Geekie
Clinical Psychologist, St Luke's Community Mental Health Centre, 615 New North Road, Auckland, New Zealand

Lisa Goodman
Associate Professor, Department of Counselling and Developmental Psychology, Lynch School of Education, Boston College, Campion 310, Chestnut Hill, MA 02461, USA

Richard Gosden
1 Arbor Court, Lilli Pilli, NSW 2536, Australia

William H. Gottdiener
Post-Doctoral Fellow, National Development and Research Institute, 111 Hicks Street, #7N, Brooklyn, New York, NY 11201, USA

Evelyn Gottwalz
Klinik für Psychiatrie und Psychotherapie, Hamburg University, UKE, Martinstr. 52, D-20246 Hamburg, Germany

Nick Haslam
Senior Lecturer, Department of Psychology, The University of Melbourne, Melbourne, VIC 3010, Australia

Jan Olav Johannessen
President, International Society for the Psychological Treatment of Schizophrenia and Other Psychoses (ISPS), Rogaland Psykiatriske Sjukehus, Postboks 1163, Hillevag, 4095 Stavanger, Norway

Jay Joseph
Licensed Clinical Psychologist (State of California), PO Box 5653, Berkeley, CA 94705-5653, USA

Bertram Karon
Professor, Department of Psychology, Michigan State University, East Lansing, MI 48824, USA

Brian Koehler
Adjunct Professor, School of Social Work, New York University, One Washington Square North, New York, NY 10003, USA
Faculty and Supervisor, Psychoanalytic Psychotherapy Study Center, New York, NY, USA

Jeffrey Masson
6 Karaka Bay, Peacock Street, Glendowie, Auckland, New Zealand

Anthony P. Morrison
Department of Clinical Psychology, Mental Health Services of Salford, Bury New Road, Manchester M25 3BL, UK

Colin A. Ross
President, Colin A. Ross Institute for Psychological Trauma, 1701 Gateway, Suite 349, Richardson, TX 75080, USA

Fred Seymour
Associate Professor and Director, Professional Psychology Unit, Psychology Department, The University of Auckland, Auckland, New Zealand

Ann-Louise Silver
President, USA Chapter of ISPS, 4966 Reedy Brook Lane, Columbia, MD 21044-1514, USA

Preface

In June 2000 I was sitting outside my hotel in Stavanger, Norway, preparing the seminar about child abuse and schizophrenia that I was to give later in the day, to the 800 or so people who had come to the 13th International Symposium for the Psychological Treatments of Schizophrenia and other psychoses. I will be forever grateful to Jan Olav Johannessen (the ISPS President) for inviting me to Norway, not least because of what happened next. At a nearby table three people were talking about how hard it is to get psychiatrists to realize the obvious fact that people are driven crazy by bad things happening to them. I overcame my usual shyness to introduce myself with some comment about 'Now I won't need to give my seminar – I'll be preaching to the converted' or some such nonsense. The three were to become good friends of mine before the conference was over. One was Volkmar Aderhold, a German psychiatrist with whom, a year later, I would be exchanging Dad stories in his Hamburg apartment (his was in the weapons branch of the S.S., mine was a British fighter pilot – so we both understand the intergenerational effects of bad things happening). The second was Petra Hohn, who gave a remarkable talk the next day – full of warmth, humanity and common sense – about her work in Sweden with people diagnosed 'schizophrenic'. The third, by far the shortest despite his hat, was Loren Mosher. When he said his name I had to stifle one of those awful 'not *the* Loren Mosher?' comments (although Loren would have loved it!). For twenty years I had been citing his work to any poor sod who would listen, as evidence that people who go crazy need other people more than they need medical-sounding labels and tranquillizing drugs.

The point of this story is that after four days in Stavanger I plummeted from an enormous high (partly jet-lag, partly short Norwegian nights, but mostly the excitement of finding so many kindred spirits in such a short time) to an exhausted low in my one night Oslo hotel, missing my new friends already. (I was too old to get bi-polar disorder I remember thinking.) Anyway, the next morning I found the solution to my 'low affect'. I decided to try to capture the spirit of Stavanger in a book and laid out, over breakfast, the first of many subsequent outlines and possible authors.

Soon after Routledge contracted the book I met Richard Bentall in Manchester. Another hero from my younger days. His *Reconstructing Schizophrenia* (Routledge, 1990) was a gem. Richard was coming to the end of writing *Madness Explained: Psychosis and Human Nature* (Penguin, 2003), a magnificent wide-ranging and scholarly treatise – a draft of which he let me read. I was delighted when, a few months later in New Zealand, he agreed to come on board as a third editor, joining Loren Mosher and myself. A cooler head than either of ours, for sure. Now we had a Brit, a Yank and a Kiwi.

I am exhausted now, writing this last little bit of what has taken three years – mostly in two- or three-hour stretches between work (thank you Fred and co. in the clinical programme for being so understanding for so long) and being with my partner, Emma, and our two young children, Jessica and Ben. Well they were young when I started. They have missed out at times. And so have I.

In 1994 I had left behind twenty years of trying to help people through madness in the face of a system that often didn't want to know, and entered the no less bizarre world – to me – of a university. On a good day I really enjoy preparing the next generation of helpers. On a bad day it seems utterly futile. I know what they will be facing. So this book, in a way, is for them. The purpose of all these seemingly endless hours is to try and weaken the awful stranglehold that simplistic biological ideology has in the world of mental health, so that the thousands of people around the world trying to use their humanness to reach out, in the face of madness, to the humanness of others might be valued and nurtured in their work, rather than marginalized or scorned.

I end with three stories, from my very first mental health job, thirty years ago, as a nursing aide in a New York psychiatric hospital. I tell them to first-year undergraduate students so that they understand where my 'biases' come from (and probably to second- and third-year students as well, but they are too polite to tell me).

He had been on the ward for three days without opening his eyes. No mean feat. The doctors had been trying to figure this out, but 'eye-closed behaviour' just wasn't anywhere to be found in the *Diagnostic and Statistical Manual*. One night, about two in the morning, I asked him, more from boredom than clinical judgement, why he kept his eyes shut. He immediately opened them, put his face uncomfortably close to mine, and said, 'It's about fucking time one of you idiots asked me that! I was put in here to get "insight", so that's what I'm fucking well doing!'

Just before my very first chance to help run the weekly group therapy session an old woman approached me to explain that she wouldn't be talking in the group because she thought that whatever she had said in the past in the group had always been turned into a 'symptom' and used against her. She didn't want me to be offended by her silence, she explained

(I think she could see I was a little nervous). After the group I retreated to the staff team where the patients' performance in the group was evaluated. The woman's not speaking was taken as a sure sign of her paranoia.

I was 'specialing' a teenage girl. This meant being locked in with her in the 'quiet room' (usually the noisiest place on the ward) to make sure she didn't try to harm herself. She hadn't spoken for weeks. A catatonic schizophrenic. Having had no training I tried: 'It's OK if you don't want to talk, but if you want to I will listen'. Nothing. The next day she said one word: 'My'. The next day she said 'father'. The next day she didn't speak. The next day she said 'me'. The missing word, I learned later, was rape.

Thank you Emma for *all* the ways you have helped make this book possible. Thank you to all the people psychiatrists call 'schizophrenic' that I have known, for trusting me enough to teach me what being mad is like and about its many causes. Thank you to the many people ('patients', 'carers' and 'mental health staff'), including the wonderful contributors to this book, who, against all the odds, have not given up on the truth that when we are mad we need other people to be people.

John Read
Auckland, June 2003

Loren Mosher died, in Berlin, in July 2004. He was 70. His partner - Judy Schreiber, three children, and close friend Volkmar Aderhold, were with him at the end.

We are all saddened by the loss of such an ardent and articulate advocate of the values we have tried to promote in *Models of Madness*. Despite being painfully out of step with many in his chosen profession, Loren never gave up hope that mental health services could change direction to a more humane pathway based on compassionate relationships between people. To the end he travelled the world tirelessly promoting the ideals he had proven effective at Soteria House. His ideas and faith will live on with many people in many countries, and in his book, to be published posthumously, *Soteria: Through Madness to Deliverance*. Soon after Loren passed away Judy said that he was probably having his first drink with Ronnie Laing. I hope so.

We are honoured that Loren found the energy to help us with this book, which we now dedicate to him in loving memory. Goodbye Loren. Thank you for being you.

John Read
Auckland, July 2004

Foreword

Models of Madness was, for me, an immense joy to read. I don't usually enjoy reading psychology textbooks, indeed, I assiduously avoid reading them, because most of them are written in impenetrable prose drained of all human life. This book is written simply, clearly and, besides being well-documented, it throbs with the passionate concern of all the contributors for those millions of people who suffered and are suffering as victims of the psychiatric system. But even more than that, this book marks the tremendous advance in the understanding of mental distress that has been achieved since the 1960s. Much of this misery came not just from the many vicissitudes of life but from the psychiatric system that was supposed to relieve such misery.

My contact with the psychiatric system began in 1961 when I was working in Sydney as an educational psychologist with special responsibilities for emotionally disturbed children. Teachers who were concerned about a particular child would invite me to the school to see the child and often the child's family as well. Thus it was that on a number of occasions I was the first person to identify a child as being psychotic, after which I would refer the child to a child psychiatrist. To do this I would have to talk to the parents and other family members, usually seeing them in the family home. None of the children who were psychotic came from an ordinary, loving home. Often the parents were very loving, but they were troubled people with secrets to hide, all of which pre-dated the child's breakdown.

All the child psychiatrists I worked with saw their patients and their patients' families as people in their own right, not as walking cases each with a diagnostic label. There was no talk of genes or biochemical changes, only of the stresses and strains within each person's life. I took this to be what psychiatrists did. It was not until I went to England in 1968 and began working in a clinic attached to the Department of Psychiatry of Sheffield University that I realized how advanced in their thinking these Sydney psychiatrists had been.

The psychiatrists I worked with in Sheffield were no different from the rest of the psychiatrists across the UK. They believed without question that there were mental illnesses which had a physical cause. Comments by patients like 'I've been depressed since my father died' and 'I haven't spoken to my brother for twenty years', which would have been noted and discussed in case conferences in Sydney, were ignored by the British psychiatrists except to date the onset of an illness. If a zealous psychologist newly arrived from one of the colonies tried to draw their attention to the significance of such statements, she achieved nothing but to rouse the psychiatrists' ire.

I was now in contact with two kinds of psychotic people whom I had not met in Sydney. The first group were those people on the back wards of the 'bins', as we called the old psychiatric hospitals. Years of repeated high doses of anti-psychotic drugs and course after long course of electroconvulsive therapy had rotted their brains until they were no more than shambling automatons. The wards where they lived were disgusting, as was the rest of these hospitals. I couldn't understand why the nurses and doctors allowed such conditions to exist, but if I asked I was told, 'If you make the place too nice for them they won't want to go home'.

The other kind of psychotic people I met were young adults on their first admission. It was psychiatric dogma that psychotherapy would make schizophrenics worse, but no such dogma was applied to those people diagnosed with 'drug-induced psychosis'. Since most of these patients were students and this was the 1970s, drugs were likely to be seen as the cause of any young person's psychosis. Thus in Sheffield, and again in Lincolnshire where I'd gone to set up a department of psychology, I met many young people in various states of psychosis. I was also able to get to know the families of many of them. None of them came from ordinary families. Often the parents were very loving, but the family had a secret, troubled history, again pre-dating their child's breakdown. It was totally unrealistic to see the family's peculiarities as being caused by the child's mad behaviour. As with the depressed people I came to know extremely well, it was blindingly obvious that it was not necessary to hypothesize a gene or a biochemical change to explain their particular form of mental distress. All that was required was a human understanding of human behaviour.

But something was changing outside the psychiatric system. The 1970s saw the growth of the self-help movement in many different areas of concern. Many people had grown tired of waiting for the 'experts' to solve their problems and they took matters into their own hands. Some of these people had suffered greatly in the psychiatric system and they now protested. They called themselves 'survivors' of the psychiatric system, and this increasingly powerful group grew into the Users' Movement. Those who could write about their experiences did so, and produced a very important body of literature. In the Netherlands Patsy Hage took her psychiatrist, Marius Romme, to task for not listening to what she had to say about her voices, and out of this came the Hearing Voices Movement. However, dissent within the psychiatric system was punished, as Loren Mosher and Peter Breggin soon found to their cost. Less well known people, usually psychologists and nurses, had their careers impeded, if not lost, because they criticized the system or simply produced research results that did not fit with what the managers and psychiatrists wanted. I have written about some of this in the second edition of my book *Beyond Fear* (HarperCollins, 2002), but a full history of this particular fight against oppression still needs to be written.

Meanwhile, a widespread legion of researchers were building up a vast body of research, which, taken together, shows that mental distress is not best explained by hypothesizing a gene or some biochemical change as the cause. Nor is it true to say that schizophrenia and depression are inevitably life-long illnesses that must be managed by psychiatrists. The evidence is there and much of it is presented in this book. However, ideas within the psychiatric system and within the general public need to change. This book should be required reading for every person entering any of the professions involved in physical and mental health, and it should be on the reading list of everyone who is concerned with the causes and cure of mental distress.

Dorothy Rowe

Part I

The illness model of 'schizophrenia'

Chapter 1

'Schizophrenia' is not an illness

John Read, Loren R. Mosher and Richard P. Bentall

'Schizophrenia is a chronic, severe, and disabling brain disease'. In June 2003, this was the opening statement of the US government agency, the National Insititute for Mental Health, on its public information website (www.nimh.hih.gov/publicat/schizoph.pdf) about the topic of our book. Such an opinion can be found in most 'educational' material, from psychiatric textbooks to drug company sponsored pamphlets. We disagree.

The heightened sensitivity, unusual experiences, distress, despair, confusion and disorganization that are currently labelled 'schizophrenic' are *not* symptoms of a medical illness. The notion that 'mental illness is an illness like any other', promulgated by biological psychiatry and the pharmaceutical industry, is not supported by research and is extremely damaging to those with this most stigmatizing of psychiatric labels. The 'medical model' of schizophrenia has dominated efforts to understand and assist distressed and distressing people for far too long. It is responsible for unwarranted and destructive pessimism about the chances of 'recovery' and has ignored – or even actively discouraged discussion of – what is actually going on in these people's lives, in their families and in the societies in which they live. Simplistic and reductionistic genetic and biological theories have led, despite the high risks involved and the paucity of sound research proving effectiveness, to the lobotimizing, electroshocking or drugging of millions of people.

The research we have gathered together in this book supports our belief that our efforts to understand and assist people experiencing the 'symptoms of schizophrenia' will benefit greatly from a fundamental shift away from unsubstantiated bio-genetic ideologies and technologies to a more down-to-earth focus on asking people what has happened and what they need.

We have not attempted an even-handed, 'objective' approach. What is required, after a hundred years or more of the dominance of an approach that is unsupported scientifically and unhelpful in practice, is a *balancing* stance rather than a balanced one. The traditional viewpoint is omnipresent in textbooks, research journals and the media. Other views have had difficulty being heard. As responsible critics, we have included discussion of bio-genetic theories and the treatments they have spawned to show the methodological flaws involved in the research that purports to support those theories and treatments. Our main purpose, however, is to show that there are sound research-based psychosocial alternatives to both understanding the origins of and intervening with what is currently called 'schizophrenia'.

The three of us have worked with hundreds of people unfortunate enough to be labelled 'schizophrenic'. We have been saddened, and sometimes angered, by the readiness of some mental health professionals to believe that the complexities of human experience can be reduced to, and understood in terms of, a single, contextless, medical-sounding word. We have too often seen that instead of trying to find out how the individual – and their loved ones – understand what is going on and what might help, the only solution offered is a chemical or electrical one, usually delivered in a dehumanizing, prison-like 'hospital'. Together with the other contributors to this book, from six countries and a range of disciplines – including users of mental health services – we want to see a less ideological approach to understanding and treating 'madness'. We want to see a truly evidence-based range of possible explanations discussed when individuals and families come into contact with us, and a wider range of options offered in terms of what might be helpful.

Since the 1970s, the illusion of a balance, of an integration of models, has been created by the so-called 'bio-psycho-social' approach. An integral part of this has been the 'vulnerability-stress' idea that acknowledges a role for social stressors but only in those who already have a supposed genetic predisposition. Life events have been relegated to the role of 'triggers' of an underlying genetic time bomb. This is not an integration of models, it is a colonization of the psychological and social by the biological. The colonization has involved the ignoring, or vilification, of research showing the role of contextual factors such as stress, trauma (inside and beyond the family), poverty, racism, sexism, and so on in the aetiology of madness. The colonization even went so far as to invent the euphemism 'psycho-education' for programmes promulgating the illness ideology to individuals and families.

Perhaps most cruelly of all, the belief that because 'schizophrenia' is an illness and, therefore, life events and circumstances can play no role in its causation has led to the awful conclusion that nothing can be done to prevent it. Rather than lobby governments to fund primary prevention programmes that could improve the quality of life for children, adolescents and their families, biological psychiatry gives politicians a perfect excuse for doing nothing.

The majority of the public, many members of the mental health professions and most people labelled 'schizophrenic' understand that mental health difficulties originate in the life circumstances – past and present – of the individuals and families concerned. Only one very powerful branch of one profession, biological psychiatry, insists on overemphasizing biology and genetics. Its power is compounded by the support of the pharmaceutical industry. This book, then, has been written largely to bring together the body of evidence that will increase the confidence of the majority when faced with that misguided but powerful minority who proclaim with all the trappings of scientific and professional expertness: 'it's an illness – so you must take the drugs' by force if necessary.

This book is not only about the one in a hundred of us who attract the label 'schizophrenic'. Few families have no contact with someone who has been through the mental health system. The increasing medicalizing of human distress, ably abetted by drug company propaganda, knew no bounds in the latter part of the twentieth century. To market tranquillizers and antidepressants, what used to be called worrying and feeling sad are now 'anxiety disorders' and 'depressive illnesses'. Millions of our children are now on amphetamines to treat their difficulty concentrating and sitting still. Millions of older people sit tranquillized in 'homes'. Tens of thousands are still having electric shocks applied to their brains to cause convulsions in the name of 'psychiatric treatment'.

Beyond offering some alternatives and the evidence supporting those alternatives, this book examines the historical, economic and political contexts in which such simplistic bio-genetic ideology gained such a damaging supremacy. We do this lest we suffer illusions about the uphill struggle facing all of us determined to return mental health services to a more humane and effective pathway. Overcoming the obstacles will require that everyone – mental health professionals (including psychiatrists), people currently called 'schizophrenic', their loved ones, researchers, policy makers, service funders and managers, and politicians – play their part. For our part we have gathered together the research evidence that can be presented, in that struggle, to those whose minds are not forever closed to the rather simple ideas that human misery is largely inflicted by other people and that the solutions are best based on human – rather than chemical or electrical – interventions.

Our book is not the first to undertake such a task. For over 50 years, many others have documented the sterility and futility of trying to explain and treat 'madness' with the crude concepts and tools of biological psychiatry, and have offered alternatives. A selection of these is listed below. Our own contribution is partly an updating of the evidence, partly a resurrecting of forgotten or taboo research findings, and partly an introducing of newer approaches (such as understanding the role of childhood trauma, documenting that biological causal beliefs exacerbate stigma, and explaining how cognitive psychology can render the seemingly incomprehensible understandable). It is also a straightforward, unashamed wake-up call. Everyone involved should act, in whatever way your circumstances allow, to end this madness.

FURTHER READING

Adershold, V. *et al.* (2003). *Psychotherapie der Psychosen: Integrative Behandlong-sansdtze aus Skandinavien.* Gießen:Psychosozial Verlag.

Ballou, M. and Brown, L. (2002). *Rethinking Mental Health and Disorder: Feminist Perspectives.* New York: Guilford Press.

Bentall, R. (ed.) (1990). *Reconstructing Schizophrenia.* London: Routledge.

Bentall, R. (2003). *Madness Explained: Psychosis and Human Nature.* London: Penguin.

Bleuler, M. (1978). *The Schizophrenia Disorders* (translated by S. Clemens). New Haven, CT: Yale University Press.

Böker, W. and Brenner, H. (eds) (1996). *Integrative Therapie der Schizophrenie.* Bern: Huber.

Boyle, M. (1990). *Schizophrenia; A Scientific Delusion?* London: Routledge.

Breggin, P. (1991). *Toxic Psychiatry.* New York: St Martin's Press.

Breggin, P. (1997). *Brain Disabling Treatments in Psychiatry.* New York: Springer.

Brenner, M. (1973). *Mental Illness and the Economy.* Cambridge, MA: Harvard University Press.

Chamberlin, J. (1988). *On Our Own.* London: MIND.

Chesler, P. (1972). *Women and Madness.* New York: Avon.

Clark, I. (ed.) (2001). *Psychosis and Spirituality.* London: Whurr.

Cohen, D. (1988). *Forgotten Millions.* London: Paladin.

Cullberg, J. (forthcoming). *Psychosis.* Hove: Brunner-Routledge.

Fisher, S. and Greenberg, R. (1997). *From Placebo to Panacea: Putting Psychiatric Drugs to the Test.* New York: Wiley.

Foucault, M. (1965). *Madness and Civilization.* New York: Vintage.

Goldstein, M. *et al.* (eds) (1986). *Treatment of Schizophrenia: Family Assessment and Intervention.* Berlin: Springer.

Gosden, R. (2001). *Punishing the Patient: How Psychiatrists Misunderstand and Mistreat Schizophrenia.* Melbourne, VIC: Scribe.

Harris, M. and Landis, C. (eds) (1997). *Sexual Abuse in the Lives of Women Diagnosed with Serious Mental Illness.* Amsterdam: Harwood Academic.

Harrop, P. and Trower, C. (2003). *Why Does Schizophrenia Develop at Late Adolescence?* London: Wiley.

Jackson, M. (2001). *Weathering the Storms: Psychotherapy for Psychosis.* London: Karnac.

Johnstone, L. (2000). *Users and Abusers of Psychiatry,* 2nd edn. London: Routledge.

Joseph, J. (2003). *The Gene Illusion.* Ross-on-Wye: PCCS Books.

Karon, B. and vanden Bos, G. (1999). *Psychotherapy of Schizophrenia: The Treatment of Choice.* New York: Aronson.

Krausz, M. and Naber, D. (eds) (2000). *Integrative Schizophrenietherapie.* Freiburg: Karger.

Laing, R. (1959). *The Divided Self.* London: Tavistock.

Laing, R. (1967). *The Politics of Experience.* London: Penguin.

Laing, R. and Esterson, A. (1964). *Sanity, Madness and the Family.* London: Penguin.

Larkin, W. and Morrison, A. (forthcoming). *Understanding Trauma and Psychosis: New Horizons for Theory and Therapy*. Hove: Brunner-Routledge.

Lidz, T. *et al.* (1965). *Schizophrenia and the Family*. New York: International Universities Press.

Martindale, B. *et al.* (eds) (2000). *Psychosis: Psychological Approaches and their Effectiveness*. London: Gaskell.

Millett, K. (1990). *The Loony-bin Trip*. New York: Simon & Schuster.

Morrison, A. (ed.) (2002). *A Casebook of Cognitive Therapy for Psychosis*. Hove, UK: Brunner-Routledge.

Mosher, L. and Burti, L. (1994). *Community Mental Health: A Practical Guide*. London: Norton.

Newnes, C. *et al.* (eds) (1999). *This is Madness*. Ross-on-Wye: PCCS Books.

Newnes, C. *et al.* (eds) (2001). *This is Madness Too*. Ross-on-Wye: PCCS Books.

Rogers, A. *et al.* (1993). *Experiencing Psychiatry: Users' Views of Services*. Basingstoke: Macmillan.

Ross, C. (in press). *Schizophrenia: An Innovative Approach to Diagnosis and Treatment*. New York: Haworth Press.

Ross, C. and Pam, A. (1995). *Pseudoscience in Biological Psychiatry: Blaming the Body*. New York: Wiley.

Rowe, D. (2002). *Beyond Fear*. London: HarperCollins.

Sarbin, T. and Mancuso, J. (1980). *Schizophrenia: Medical Diagnosis or Moral Verdict?* New York: Pergamon Press.

Schwarz, F. and Maier, C. (eds) (2001). *Psychotherapie der Psychosen*. Stuttgart: Thieme.

Silver, A-L. (ed.) (1989). *Psychoanalysis and Psychosis*. Madison, CT: International Universities Press.

Sullivan, H. (1962). *Schizophrenia as a Human Process*. New York: Norton.

Thomas, P. (1997). *The Dialectics of Schizophrenia*. New York: Free Association Press.

Ussher, J. (1991). *Women's Madness: Misogyny or Mental Illness?* Hemel Hempstead: Harvester Wheatsheaf.

Valenstein, E. (1986). *Great and Desperate Cures*. New York: Basic Books.

Valenstein, E. (1998). *Blaming the Brain: The Truth about Drugs and Mental Health*. New York: Free Press.

Warner, R. (1985). *Recovery from Schizophrenia: Psychiatry and Political Economy*. London: Routledge.

Warner, R. (2000). *The Environment of Schizophrenia*. Hove: Brunner-Routledge.

Webart, A. and Cullberg, J. (eds) (1992). *Psychotherapy of Schizophrenia*. Oslo: Scandinavian University Press.

Whitaker. R. (2002). *Mad in America: Bad Science, Bad Medicine and the Enduring Mistreatment of the Mentally Ill*. Cambridge, MA: Perseus.

Wynne, L. *et al.* (eds) (1978). *The Nature of Schizophrenia*. New York: Wiley.

Chapter 2

A history of madness

John Read

We can understand our present situation better if we review the past. Others have undertaken this task in more detail than possible here (e.g. Bynum *et al.* 1985; Porter 2002). Historical vignettes have been selected to illustrate three themes in the hope that we may be less surprised to discover those themes in the present:

1   One of the functions of 'treatments' for people considered mad is to suppress behaviours, thoughts and feelings unacceptable or disturbing to those with the power to determine and enforce social norms.
2   The 'treatments' are frequently unhelpful and sometimes damaging and violent.
3   The experts of the day often camouflage the socio-political function, and the damaging nature, of the 'treatments' behind theories that the people concerned have personal defects that are ameliorated by the 'treatments'.

Past centuries have witnessed innumerable acts of genuine kindness and support, by layperson and expert, to those who are sufficiently odd to be rejected by the majority or who experience despair and disorientation. It is the contention of this book, however, that until we achieve a better integration of psycho-social perspectives into our theories and practice, the three themes of social control, unhelpful or damaging treatments and the camouflaging of these first two themes by simplistic theories, will continue to distort our understanding of, and efforts to assist, people considered mad.

GODS AND DEVILS

Four thousand years ago, personal intention was attributed to almost everything. Madness was understood as resulting from the evil influence of some enemy, real or imagined. Approaches to 'treatment' were the same as those used for other disturbing events: threats, bribery or submission in the case of human ill-wishers, and prayer or sacrifice in the case of more lofty adversaries (Alexander and Selesnick 1996: 9). The world-view in Mesopotamia around 2000 B.C. included the belief that evil demons were responsible for ailments and the source of recovery was the appropriate good god. To understand 'madness', this world-view was invoked in the form of Idta, the demon responsible. Idta was assisted by a collection of lesser demons and sorcerers and the whole department was answerable to Ishtar, the female deity supervising all witchcraft and evil (Alexander and Selesnick 1996). The Persians and Hindus also held evil gods – Ahriman and Siva, respectively – accountable for strange behaviours. They, too, believed that the treatment of choice was prayers to the adversaries of these divine mischief-makers, Ormuzd and Vishnu (Gordon 1949).

The earliest recorded attempts of the Hebrews to understand insanity also reflect the prevailing world-view (Miller 1975; Rosen 1964). Moses was clear about one cause: 'The Lord will smite thee with madness' (Deuteronomy 28: 28). Moses also came close to providing an early example of this book's central theme – that madness is caused by adverse life experiences: 'You shall be only oppressed and crushed continually; so that you shall be driven mad by the sight which your eyes shall see' (Deuteronomy 28: 34). The theory remains, however, one of divine punishment, since it is the Lord who does the oppressing and crushing. He does so, moreover, for breaking the code of social norms – the Commandments. So in this instance madness is a result of divine punishment for breaking norms rather than a term applied to people who break norms to justify their punishment.

Shemia, however, invoked today's prevailing attitude, that breaking norms is a consequence rather than a cause of madness. Faced with Jeremiah's unpalatable prophecy that Israelites would be permanently exiled, Shemia decreed that only a madman could utter such nonsense and prescribed a public beating (Rosen 1964). The world-view of the ancient Hebrews, in the Old Testament, included the notion that an efficient way to enforce conformity to social norms was to eliminate the person rather than just the behaviour: 'A man or woman who is a medium or a wizard shall be put to death; they shall be stoned with stones, their blood shall be upon them' (Leviticus 20: 27).

The reason given by Moses for punishing a long list of behaviours by death was: 'So you shall purge the evil from Israel'. If 'Israel' refers to race rather than country, this represents an early version of the genetic theory of unacceptable behaviour and the eugenic approach to eradicating madness via the creation of a genetically untainted race (see Chapter 4). The Old Testament was used for centuries as an expert theory justifying violence against those considered mad.

By the time of the first drafts of the Talmud (A.D. 70–200), the Hebrew world-view had changed. Now, to be punished for one's madness one must be considered responsible for it. While the Old Testament clearly held madness to be the direct result of sinning, the Talmud argues that the 'mad' are 'not responsible for the damage or the shame they produce'. They must, therefore, be helped rather than stoned or purged (Miller 1975; Rosen 1964).

THE INTRODUCTION OF REASON

Greece, too, had indulged in magical and religious theories. Homer, writing about 1000 B.C., provides an explanation consistent with the world-view at that time. Whether it was Ajax killing a flock of sheep believing it to be the enemy, or the daughters of Proteus believing they were cows and acting accordingly, there was a god to blame. If divine intervention was the cause, it must also be the cure. Accordingly, Aesculapius, originally a mere priest-physician, was promoted to godhood (Alexander and Selesnick 1996).

There followed in Greece what many describe as the most significant change in world-view that humanity has experienced. The 'Classical Era' was marked by the replacement of supernatural explanations with observation and reason. Priests were gradually replaced by physicians. The most famous doctor of all time, Hippocrates (460–377 B.C.), was among the first to promulgate the 'medical model' of madness. He produced the first of its endless and futile attempts to reduce the complexities of unusual, distressed or distressing human behaviours to a set of categories of illness, each with its own physiological cause:

> Men ought to know that from the brain and from the brain only arise our pleasures, joys, laughters and jests . . . Those who are mad through phlegm are quiet, and neither shout nor make a disturbance; those maddened through bile are noisy, evil-doers, and restless, always doing something inopportune.
>
> (Hippocrates 1931)

Terms such as 'phlegmatic' survive today. So do simplistic medical theories about why some people continue to be too noisy or too quiet. Hippocrates was just as convinced as biological psychiatry is today that he really was discovering the physical causes of illnesses, rather than promoting a simplistic theory that justifies and camouflages the social control of unacceptable or disturbing behaviour. The Dogmatist sect was certainly convinced. In the first of many such enterprises, it was dedicated to prohibiting any investigation beyond the biological ideology of the day, because Hippocrates had already discovered everything worth discovering.

Ducey and Simon (1975) offer an insight, still valuable today, into one motivation for simplistic biological theories. The Greeks were becoming aware of human conflicts; not only internal conflicts, such as the 'reasoning' versus 'desiring' dilemma identified by Plato (427–347 B.C.) 2300 years before Freud, but also conflicts between the individual and the demands of society. In the absence of religious instructions regarding such dilemmas, there was a need to identify other forces over which individuals had little control and for which they could not be held accountable:

> The Hippocratic model of mental illness and of its treatment may have provided an important source of relief of anxiety, guilt and responsibility, by translating inner conflicts and dissonances into physiological and physicalistic terms.
>
> (Ducey and Simon 1975: 19)

Hippocrates' treatments probably were effective in altering behaviour. I, for one, would have been less quiet or noisy, and would have agreed that my behaviour was biologically based, rather than face being forced to vomit or defecate uncontrollably, or to swallow hellebore – a poison now used in insecticides – especially if I knew that, if the emetics, purgatives and medicines failed, blood-letting was the treatment of last resort.

During this period there was a fading of an extreme male dominance that had included the feeding of boys at the expense of girls (Lacey 1968). When Plato wrote 'within the woman there is a wild, animalistic, Bicchantic, frenzied creature, who must be gratified, or else she goes beserk' (Ducey and Simon 1975: 21), he was not arguing that generations of oppression had led to pent-up anger, nor suggesting that such oppression can drive women mad. He was laying the foundations of a quite different type of theory of female madness, a theory in keeping with the physiological explanations of the time, one that could be used not to liberate women but to continue their suppression.

The invention of 'hysteria' is an early example of the repeated, and continuing, use of theories of madness to force women into the roles determined for them by men (see Chapter 12).

> Whenever the womb – which is an indwelling creature desirous of child-bearing – remains without fruits long beyond the due season, it is vexed and takes it ill; and by straying all ways through the body and blocking up the passages of the breath and preventing the respiration it casts the body into the uttermost distress, and causes, moreover, all kinds of maladies until the desires and love of the two sexes unite them.
>
> (Plato 1904: 916-c)

The treatments of choice for 'hysteria' were marriage and fumigation of the vagina. Although the experts told their 'patients' that the purpose of the 'treatment' was to attract the wandering uterus back to its rightful place, we can see with hindsight that it was the wandering of women from their subservient role that was the real concern.

A RETURN TO RELIGION

The social structure of the Roman Empire crumbled before an onslaught of epidemics and marauding barbaric tribes. The resulting insecurity facilitated a return to supernatural beliefs. By the fourth century A.D. Constantine had made Christianity the official religion, the Church and State having become an inseparable and immense power. In the field of madness, observation, reason and physiological theories were replaced with variations of old religious themes. In the New Testament Christ was venerated as the healer of the sick and the caster out of demons. Images of Aesculapius were now worshipped as images of Jesus, as the Church became protector of the infirm and insane.

In the search for some external, and preferably heavenly, force to explain frightening behaviour, it was thought that such behaviour was worse when people were alone at night. Obviously, the moon was responsible for craziness. Mad people have, ever since, been called 'lunatics'.

Another concept, more consistent with Christianity, explained almost any anxiety-provoking event, including epidemics, conflagrations and madness. The phenomenon of witchcraft offers one of the most horrifying examples of the extent of the violence that can be justified by theories about groups of people considered defective. The target group is typically that which best symbolizes the nature of a society's collective anxiety.

The extent to which cultural changes affect theories about whom or what is to blame for madness is well illustrated if we divide the Middle Ages into two periods. In the earlier period causal theories were influenced by the charitable aspects of Christianity. Care was relatively humane. Patients of the original Bethlem Hospital in London (later to degenerate into the Bedlam 'snake-pit') wore arm badges on pass. The response was so positive that people often counterfeited badges for themselves. People thought to be possessed by the Devil were not held responsible. The treatment of choice – exorcism – was not, therefore, a punitive process aimed at the individual, but a benevolent one directed against the real cause of the problem – the Devil.

However, from the eleventh century onwards, the breakdown of feudal structures, accompanied by insurrections, often aimed at the Church, demanded a set of scapegoats. Public trials and executions could deter other potential 'heretics'. Possessed women could not serve this purpose if they were not responsible for their actions. By the time Kraemer and Sprenger published their witch-hunting manual, *Malleus Maleficarum* (1486), it was discovered that witches voluntarily invite the Devil into their lives. The obvious treatment of choice was to annihilate the host.

Religious and social factors during this latter period of the Middle Ages had created an intense fear and hatred of women and a fiercely misogynist Church. Women were officially described as 'a foe to friendship, an unescapable punishment, a necessary evil, a natural temptation, a desirable calamity . . . an evil of nature painted with fair colours' (Kraemer and Sprenger 1486: 43).

The vast majority of people tortured and murdered were indeed women (Michelet 1939). Many of them were guilty of nothing more than being sought after for their healing skills. Their herbs and brews were a threat to the male priests' monopoly on healing. Others were guilty of no more than being female. The symptoms are listed in the diagnostic manual of the day:

> All witchcraft comes from carnal lust which is in women insatiable . . . Three general vices appear to have special dominion over wicked women, namely, infidelity, ambition and lust. Therefore they are more than others inclined toward witchcraft who more than others are given to these vices.
>
> (Kraemer and Sprenger 1486: 47)

The possession of too much phlegm or bile had been replaced, for political reasons, with possession by the Devil. While the various theories come and go, their purpose remains constant. Along with the mass murder of mental patients in Germany in the 1940s (see Chapter 4) and the political oppression of dissidents in KGB-managed Soviet 'psychiatric hospitals' (Bloch and Reddaway 1977), the Inquisition is a horrifically clear example of a well-organized programme of cruelty directed against those engaging in behaviours unacceptable or inconvenient to those in power. These programmes are always justified by theories disguising the violence as help for defective individuals. In the case of the murder of women diagnosed as witches, the help took the form of purifying their souls so they could enter heaven.

THE RETURN TO SCIENCE

During the return to observation and reason known as the Renaissance, religious views, while less influential, still held some sway. For instance, Johann Weyer (1515–1561) used observation in his relentless battle against the notion of witchery. He demonstrated that objects supposedly implanted in the stomach of an accused woman carried no signs of gastric juices. For this he earned himself the diagnosis 'Weirus Insanus'.

Increased emphasis on the psycho-social origins of madness were reflected in Shakespeare's *Hamlet* and Cervantes' *Don Quixote*. Thomas Sydenham, the famous English physician, contributed to psychological approaches by diagnosing on the basis of the individual's emotional circumstances at the time. Burton's *Anatomy of Melancholy* (1621), based partly on his need to understand his own chronic unhappiness, described one of the more popular diagnostic categories of this period. His theories were a blend of demonological and physiological. His treatments focused, like those of his contemporaries, on exercise, diets, drugs and, of course, purgatives. He adds, however, a lovely description of one non-medical treatment for his own personal malady:

> It is the best thing in the world . . . to get a trusted friend, to whom we may freely and sincerely pour out our secrets; nothing so delighteth and pleaseth the mind, as when we have a prepared bosom, to which our secrets may descend, of whose conscience we are assured as our own, whose speech may ease our succourless estate, counsel relief, mirth expel our mourning, and whose very sight may be acceptable unto us.
>
> (Burton 1621: 108–9)

Such a therapeutic experience was seldom enjoyed by thousands of Europeans who, under the guise of medical treatment, were being locked away, worked, purged and drugged. Soon after its opening in 1656, the Hôpital Général in Paris was 'treating' 6000 people. Typical of the view taken of this period by the modern historian of psychiatry is the opinion that:

> The Age of Reason marked a great leap forward. Through the efforts of the great scientists, philosophers, men of letters, and artists of the 17th century mental illness was further extricated from superstition and authoritarian error.
>
> (Alexander and Selesnick 1996: 104)

I suggest, however, that the direction being adopted would turn out to be a transition from error based on one form of authority (religion), to error based on an equally dangerous form of authority (simplistic and reductionist 'medical science'). The violence continued, masked by a different rationale.

CATEGORIZATION AND CONFINEMENT

From the latter part of the seventeenth century well into the eighteenth century the 'scientific' approach to understanding the world established the dominance it maintains today. During the 'Enlightenment' explanations of madness became dominated by categorization and physiology. Psychological and social factors were buried under the relentless drive to discover illnesses that would eventually lead to the invention of 'schizophrenia' (see Chapter 3). The illusion behind this quest, then as now, was that correct categorization would lead to the discovery of physiological causes. Actually, those rare instances where physiological origins of madness have been found – such as the effects of advanced syphilis – have been the cause, rather than the result, of a new classification. The Enlightenment's many attempts to find the imagined true categories of 'mental illness' led to no useful advances in physiological explanations. The categorizers simply remoulded the old theories to fit their new categories. The violent treatments continued.

Herman Boerhaave (1668–1738), for instance, justified continuation of blood-lettings and purgatives by discovering that 'melancholia' was caused by black juices. His invention of the rotating chair was more original. The theories used to portray this particular cruelty as a medical treatment varied. In Britain, Erazmus Darwin discovered that it reintroduced harmony to the 'disordered motions' of the nerves. Benjamin Rush, meanwhile, was convincing patients in North America that they were being spun into unconsciousness to unclog their congested blood, which, he had discovered, was the true cause of madness.

Even Cullen (1712–1790), who defined neuroses as ailments without localized pathology, was so influenced by the medical zeal of the times that he believed that neuroses were caused by the body's general physiological 'temperament' (Cullen 1812). Psychosocial explanations would not have justified his treatments. He added blistering of the forehead and cold dousings to the usual blood-letting, vomiting and purging (Alexander and Selesnick 1996).

The quest for localized brain pathology, still popular today, was well under way. At London's Bethlem asylum, John Haslem was already conducting autopsies (Alexander and Selesnick 1996). One wonders how many of these people had died as a result of the neglect and violence that was being justified by theories about disordered brains.

Who were these people? The 1656 Edict that founded the Hôpital Général defined its population as: 'the poor of Paris, of both sexes, of all ages and from all localities, of whatever breeding and birth, in whatever state they may be, able-bodied or invalid, sick or convalescent, curable or incurable' (Foucault 1965: 39). The mad were locked away not for being mad but for being poor.

The 'Great Confinement', as Foucault describes this period, served the economic function of forcing inmates to work at a fraction of the going rate, under the guise of exercise or 'occupational therapy'. It served the political function of suppressing, under the guise of help for the poor and sick, the increasing number of uprisings among the unemployed. It also bolstered a moral belief in hard work. The Edict established begging and idleness as the major causes of all disorders. The mad, Foucault argues, were being locked away all over Europe along with anyone else considered inconvenient or threatening to those in power, precisely because they were inconvenient or threatening. Calling the prisons hospitals concealed this.

The treatments behind the locked doors 'were physical cures whose meaning had been borrowed from a moral perception' (Foucault 1965: 159). Many were based on purification of the body, symbolizing the notion that mental illness was caused by moral contamination. Doublet suggested, in 1785, that if the traditional blood-lettings and purges failed, one should try abscesses and inoculation of scabies (Foucault 1965). This quest for the best purifying agent led to medical treatments such as force-feeding soluble tartar, chimney soot, woodlice and soap.

MORAL TREATMENT

Phillipe Pinel in France, William Tuke in England, Chiarugi in Italy and Muller and Reil in Germany are remembered for their humane treatment of mad people. Their various approaches have come to be known, accurately, as 'Moral Treatment' (Scull 1981). Pinel, renowned for unchaining the insane, found it impossible to differentiate the effects of madness from the effects of cruel treatments in hospitals. Unlike many of the experts before them, Pinel and his fellow reformers were honest about their being in the business of imposing society's moral code on deviant individuals. Pinel was particularly concerned to eradicate celibacy, promiscuity, apathy and laziness. Such a morality was a special goal for women because 'marriage constitutes for women a kind of preservative against the two sorts of insanity which are most inveterate and most often incurable' (Foucault 1965: 258).

Tuke founded the York retreat in 1792 on the values of his Quaker upbringing. His son Samuel, who succeeded him, believed that 'to encourage the influence of religious principles over the mind of the insane is considered of great consequence as a means of cure' (Tuke 1813: 121). Patients would be invited to tea parties with the staff to assess their social etiquette.

If the goals, for once, were less couched in medical terms, the means for imposing conformity remained the tools of social control. Samuel Tuke admitted what his predecessors had concealed behind the language of medicine when he wrote 'the principle of fear, which is rarely decreased by insanity, is considered of great importance in the management of patients' (Tuke 1813: 141). Pinel argued that:

> Considered as a means of repression, it often suffices to subject to the general law of manual labour a madman who is susceptible to it, in

order to conquer an obstinate refusal to take nourishment, and to subjugate insane persons.

(Foucault 1965: 266–7)

It is important to our understanding of the political function of modern psychiatry that we realize why the medic was invited into this new version of the asylum. The medic, who had played little part in the huge confining hospitals, entered now not as a medical expert but as an authority figure to add weight to the efforts of the attendants:

> The doctor's intervention is not made by virtue of a medical skill or power that he possesses in himself and that would be justified by a body of objective knowledge. It is not as a scientist that homomedicus has authority in the asylum, but as a wise man. If the medical profession is required, it is as a juridical and moral guarantee, not in the name of science.
>
> (Foucault 1965: 270)

Perhaps the authority of psychiatrists today still originates more from the political power we all bestow upon them than from any scientific expertise. Perhaps the source of this power is well disguised, even from themselves:

> In the time of Pinel and Tuke, this power had nothing extraordinary about it; it was explained and demonstrated in the efficacity, simply, of moral behaviour . . . But very soon the meaning of this moral practice escaped the physician to the very extent that he enclosed his knowledge in the norms of positivism; from the beginning of the 19th century, the psychiatrist no longer quite knew what was the nature of the power he had inherited from the great reformers.
>
> (Foucault 1965: 274)

Pinel understood the reason for introducing the medic into his asylums, and the difficulty in distinguishing medical treatment from social control:

> The doctrine in ethics of balancing the passions of men by others of equal or superior force, is not less applicable to the practice of medicine, than to the science of politics, and is probably not the only point of resemblance between the art of governing mankind and that of healing their diseases.
>
> (Pinel 1801: 228)

Whatever one's view of Moral Treatment (Chapter 15 offers a different slant), it had little impact on the stranglehold of biological theories about madness. The categorizations and the quest for physical explanations continued. Despite producing an important treatise on psychotherapy in 1803, Johann Reil, for instance, lumped together all silent patients into a single category, for which he prescribed the treatment of standing next to cannon fire – an early version of shock therapy.

The odd voice cried out in this medical wilderness. Falret (1794–1870) went beyond Pinel's questions about the effects of cruel treatment and wondered whether the concepts involved might be similarly damaging. He suggested replacing 'mental disease' with 'mental alienation'. He was drawing attention to the processes by which we can become disconnected from other people and from society as a whole, and also to the need to reframe the task facing those trying to help people reconnect, whom he named 'alienists'. Members of the medical profession were unimpressed and continued on their blinkered, scientific, re-categorizing way until one of their endless lists of categories included the terms 'dementia praecox' and 'schizophrenia'.

REFERENCES

Alexander, F. and Selesnick, S. (1996). *The History of Psychiatric Thought and Practice from Prehistoric Times to the Present.* New York: Harper & Row.

Bloch, S. and Reddaway, P. (1977). *Russia's Political Hospitals.* London: Gollancz.

Burton, R. ([1621] 1961). *The Anatomy of Melancholy*, Vol. 2 (edited by F. Dell and P. Jourdan-Smith). London: Dent.

Bynum, W. *et al.* (eds) (1985). *The Anatomy of Madness.* London: Tavistock.

Cullen, W. (1812). *First Lines of the Practice of Physic.* Edinburgh: Bell & Bradfute.

Ducey, C. and Simon, B. (1975). Ancient Greece and Rome. In J. Howells (ed.) *World History of Psychiatry.* New York: Brunner/Mazel.

Foucault, M. (1965). *Madness and Civilisation.* New York: Random House.

Gordon, B. (1949). *Medicine through Antiquity.* Philadelphia, PA: F.A. Davis.

Hippocrates (1931). *Sacred Heart* (translated by W. Jones). London: Heinemann.

Kraemer, M. and Sprenger, M. ([1486] 1941). *Malleus Maleficarum* (translated by J. Summer). London: Pushkin.

Lacey, W. (1968). *The Family in Classical Greece.* Ithaca, NY: Cornell University Press.

Michelet, J. (1939). *Satanism and Witchcraft.* Toronto: Citadel.

Miller, N. (1975). Israel and the Jews. In J. Howells (ed.) *World History of Psychiatry.* New York: Brunner/Mazel.

Pinel, P. (1801). *Traite Medic-philosphique sur L'Alientation Mentale.* Paris.

Plato (1904). *Timaeus* (translated by R. Bury). Cambridge, MA: Harvard University Press.

Porter, R. (2002). *Madness: A Brief History.* Oxford: Oxford University Press.

Reil, J. (1803). *Rhapsodien uber die Anwendung der Psychischen Curmethode auf Geisteszerruttungen.* Halle: Curt.

Rosen, G. (1964). *Madness in Society*. Chicago, IL: University of Chicago Press.
Scull, A. (1981). Moral treatment reconsidered. In A. Scull (ed.) *Madhouses, Maddoctors and Madmen*. Philadelphia, PA: University of Philadelphia Press.
Tuke, S. (1813). *Description of the Retreat*. York: Society of Friends.

Chapter 3

The invention of 'schizophrenia'

John Read

PSYCHIATRY IN CRISIS

Emil Kraepelin and Eugen Bleuler, two 'grandfathers' of modern psychiatry, were jointly responsible for the invention of 'schizophrenia'. Their contribution has been critiqued before (e.g. Bentall 1990, 2003; Boyle 1990). My intention here is to demonstrate how their invention represents a continuation of the historical themes, of social control and harmful treatments disguised by theories about help for defective individuals (see Chapter 2).

Throughout the nineteenth century, progress in medicine was impressive. The motivation to seek similar successes in relation to madness is understandable. New categorizations of madness were created, but psychiatry was still sufficiently committed to scientific process to abandon them when they proved worthless. Psychiatry could not afford, however, to abandon the quest for 'mental illnesses'. Its survival as a medical discipline depended on it.

In 1822, Bayle found a genuine physiological cause for one form of madness. His discovery, of brain damage in 'dementia paralytica', was later identified as syphilis. This fuelled hope that other 'mental illnesses' with physiological causes might be discovered. However, in the words of Bleuler (1924) himself: 'After Paresis was excluded . . . for 70 years theoretical psychiatry stood entirely helpless before the chaos of the most frequent mental diseases' (p. 372). By the end of the century, psychiatry had urgently needed a discovery.

A biographer has documented: 'Kraepelin's supremely controlling object was the furtherance of psychiatry' (Jelliffe 1932: 764). He secured financial backers for his mission:

> Kraepelin succeeded in obtaining from the Rockefeller Foundation the sum of $250,000 for his project, the first gift to be made by this organization to research work in Europe. A further gift from the Rockefeller Foundation increased the sum to $325,000 under the stipulation that

there should be strict adherence in the institute to Kraepelin's funda-mental idea.

(Jelliffe 1932: 768)

We will probably never know whether there was any connection between the Rockefellers' owning the petroleum industry, the discovery that petro-leum by-products could be used to produce medicines, and the stipulation in Kraepelin's contract.

EMIL KRAEPELIN

Outcomes

The task facing Kraepelin in Germany was the same one faced by all those classifiers who had tried and failed before him: to group together beha-viours that might all be caused by some physical pathology. In his first attempt in 1893, he claimed that he had discovered a group of people in whom deterioration began in adolescence and continued, inevitably, into a 'permanent state of psychological weakness'. Hence the name 'dementia praecox' ('praecox' meaning early).

Many of the behaviours he categorized as symptoms of dementia praecox had already been claimed by the inventors of two other illnesses, 'catatonia' and 'dementia paranoids'. He created a conglomerate illness by incor-porating and re-branding the other two. He did so despite the fact that the problems of many of the people labelled catatonic or paranoid neither began in adolescence nor resulted in dementia.

Some even got better. Kraepelin made no claim to have cured them. Either his invention did not exist or the people who got better didn't have dementia praecox. In 1913, he announced:

> The undoubted inadequacy of my former classification has led me once more to undertake the attempt to make a more natural grouping . . . Recovered cases were not taken into account because of the uncertainty which still exists, but only such cases as had led to profound dementia.
>
> (Kraepelin 1913: 89–90)

He claimed he had discovered an incurable, degenerative illness. When people whom he says have the illness get better, he says they haven't got the illness. He is then left with a group of people who don't get better, and uses them as evidence that the illness exists. This is circular logic or, less politely, nonsense. American psychiatrist Harry Sullivan (1927) complained: 'The Kraepelinian diagnosis by outcome has been a great handicap, leading to much retrospective distortion of data, instead of careful observation and induction' (p. 760).

Kraepelin repeatedly changed the rules for who has dementia praecox. Whenever he did so he claimed to have discovered 'a more natural grouping', creating the illusion of discovery where there is nothing more than yet another meaningless re-categorization.

Symptoms

Kraepelin couldn't wait for outcomes before making diagnoses. All he could do, like his predecessors, was make lists of behaviours and apply a medical sounding label. Then he claimed to have proved the existence of dementia praecox by showing that people who had it were exhibiting its symptoms.

His takeover of catatonia and paranoia had netted Kraepelin a total of 36 groups of 'psychic' symptoms and 19 types of bodily symptoms. One patient could have symptoms entirely different from a second, and totally the opposite to those of a third. They all supposedly had the same illness. Such constructs are known as 'dysjunctive' and fall outside meaningful scientific process (see Chapter 5).

Kraepelin (1913) asserted: 'We are justified in regarding the majority at least of the clinical pictures which are brought together here as the expression of a single morbid process, though outwardly they often diverge very far from one another' (p. 3). Having listed the most important features of his illness, he admitted that some patients did not show any of these:

> These features are certainly not demonstrable with full clearness in each individual case but still the general view over a great number of complete observations teaches that nowhere can a state be discovered which is not connected by imperceptible transitions with all the others.
>
> (Kraepelin 1913: 255)

So, if you can't see the features you're just not looking hard enough. Even if after strenuous efforts you still can't perceive 'the imperceptible', it doesn't mean it isn't there. He acknowledged that it can 'be very difficult, not only to judge correctly of the diagnostic significance of such deviations, but even to recognize their very existence' (p. 257).

Causes

Kraepelin needed to identify physical pathology to link to the symptoms. However, by his own admission, the causes 'are at the present time still wrapped in impenetrable darkness' (Kraepelin 1913: 224). The key words are 'at the present time'. The same words have been used ever since by researchers forever on the verge of finding the biological cause of schizophrenia.

Kraepelin (1913) began the eighth edition of his *Psychiatrica* (in which dementia praecox was not the only illness described) thus: 'A series of morbid pictures are here brought together under the term "endogenous dementias" merely for the purpose of preliminary enquiry' (p. 1). Psychiatry, however, urgently needed something more than 'preliminary enquiry' or 'impenetrable darkness'. Kraepelin suggested another, ingenious, re-branding exercise:

> If therefore the name . . . is to be replaced by another, it is to be hoped that it will not soon share the same fate of so many names of the kind, and of dementia praecox itself, in giving a view of the nature of the disease which will turn out to be doubtful or wrong.
>
> (Kraepelin 1913: 4)

He explicitly recommended that 'a name that as far as possible said nothing would be preferable' (p. 4). To claim to have discovered an illness without identifying any consistent symptoms, time of onset or outcome, and with no observable cause, contradicts the basic rules of medical science. To propose a meaningless name to avoid assumptions that might be tested places Kraepelin's work beyond the realms of science altogether.

EUGEN BLEULER

In 1911 Bleuler, working in Switzerland, published his famous *Dementia Praecox or the Group of Schizophrenias*. He divided Kraepelin's many-headed monster into several smaller beasts. He also expanded Kraepelin's invention, announcing that 'Today we include patients whom we would neither call "demented" nor exclusively victims of deterioration early in life' (Bleuler 1911: 7). He made explicit the criteria by which one knows whether a disease has been discovered:

> We must ask ourselves the questions: in what connection with other symptoms and anatomical findings, in what sort of course, as the result of which causes does the symptom appear? . . . Only the answers to these questions can provide us with the concept of the disease.
>
> (Bleuler 1911: 273)

Outcomes

Bleuler abandoned the idea that everyone with the disease ended up with 'dementia'. What did his search for some other consistent prognosis reveal?

It is impossible to describe all the variations which the course of schizophrenia may take.

(Bleuler 1911: 328)

What about the relationship between outcome and symptoms?

We have not discovered any correlation between the initial disease symptoms and the severity of the outcome or the illness.

(Bleuler 1911: 261)

Symptoms

Bleuler understood that merely naming or listing symptoms has little to do with discovering illnesses:

Such terms as acute paranoia, acute hallucinatory insanity, confusion mentale, as well as mania and melancholia . . . do not designate 'diseases' . . . Not only the names but the entire concepts were arbitrarily constructed by this or that observer, depending on which symptom he considered the most striking one . . . It would take me far too long if I were to say all the unpleasant things which I really ought to say about these notions . . . A symptom, regardless of whether it is psychic or physical is never a disease; neither is a symptom-complex.

(Bleuler 1911: 272–3)

Since a symptom-complex is not a disease, Bleuler had to demonstrate some connection between symptoms and causes. He admitted, however, that 'The anatomical findings do not correspond with the severity of the manifest symptoms' (p. 462). This is unsurprising, since 'We do not as yet know with certainty the primary symptoms of the schizophrenic cerebral disease' (p. 349). There had not even been any anatomical findings.

Causes

The pathology of schizophrenia gives us no indication as to where we should look for the causes of the disease. Direct investigation for specific cause or factors has also left us stranded.

(Bleuler 1911: 337)

We do not know what the schizophrenic process actually is.

(Bleuler 1911: 466)

Bleuler had failed to answer all of the questions he stated must be answered before the discovery of a disease can be claimed.

SYMPTOMS OF AN ILLNESS OR BROKEN SOCIAL NORMS?

If Kraepelin and Bleuler's invention is not a disease, what is it? A primary function of treatments for the mad has always been to control behaviour unacceptable to those with the power to determine and enforce social norms (see Chapter 2). Here is a sample of the hundreds of 'symptoms' of their 'illness'.

Behaviours

They conduct themselves in a free and easy way, laugh on serious occasions, are rude and impertinent towards their superiors, challenge them to duels, lose their deportment and personal dignity; they go about in untidy and dirty clothes, unwashed, unkempted, go with a lighted cigar into church.

(Kraepelin 1913: 34)

The loss of taste often makes itself felt in their choice of extraordinary combinations of colour and peculiar forms.

(Kraepelin 1913: 55)

The want of a feeling of shame expresses itself in regardless uncovering of their persons, in making sexual experience public, in obscene talk, improper advances, and in shameless masturbation.

(Kraepelin 1913: 34)

... more in girls, there is reported irritability, sensitiveness, excitability, nervousness, and along with these self-will and a tendency to bigotry ... [and] those patients, belonging rather more to the male sex, who were conspicuous by docility, good nature, anxious conscientiousness and diligence, and as patterns of goodness held themselves aloof from all childhood naughtiness.

(Kraepelin 1913: 236)

The patients sit about idle, trouble themselves about nothing, do not go to their work.

(Kraepelin 1913: 37)

Patients are in love with a ward-mate with complete disregard of sex, ugliness, or even repulsiveness.

(Bleuler 1911: 52)

It hardly makes any difference to the patient whether he is addressing a person in authority or someone more humbly-placed whether a man or a woman.

(Bleuler 1911: 49)

A hebephrenic, whose very speech was confusion, held the cigar-holder to the mouth of another patient suffering from muscular atrophy . . . He did this with a patience and indefatigability of which no normal person would ever be capable.

(Bleuler 1911: 48)

Perversions like homosexuality and similar anomalies are often indicated in the whole behaviour and in the dress of the patient.

(Bleuler 1924: 188)

Feelings

'Flat affect' and 'inappropriate affect' were primary symptoms of 'schizophrenia'. Being in touch with two opposing feelings was also abnormal, such 'ambivalence' being a defining characteristic of schizophrenia. Remembering too intensely was also a symptom:

Even decades later . . . nuances of sexual pleasure, embarrassment, pain or jealously, may emerge in all their vividness which we never find in the healthy when it is a question of recollecting the past.

(Bleuler 1911: 46)

Thoughts

Unusual thought processes are 'wrong pathways of thought' carrying 'the schizophrenic mark of the bizarre' (Bleuler 1911: 25). They are wrong because they are 'pathways deviating from experience' (p. 354). Since a thought is by definition part of one's experience, whose experience is it from which these thoughts are deviating?

Kraepelin (1913) defined 'incoherence of thought' in terms of whether psychiatrists can understand what is being said, highlighting 'that peculiarly bewildering incomprehensibility' (p. 20). Instead of recommending that understanding unusual thinking be included in psychiatric training programmes, he adds 'incomprehensibility' to his list of symptoms.

Bleuler (1911) found two specific types of thinking particularly bewildering or, in his terms, examples of 'disorders of association': 'Two ideas fortuitously encountered, are combined into one thought' and 'The inclination to cling to one idea to which the patient then returns again and again' (p. 14). (He relied heavily on these two types of thinking himself, combining lots of different unacceptable behaviours into one thought – 'schizophrenia' – and, despite all the contradictory evidence, returning again and again to that one idea.)

Bringing together ideas to form new ideas is the trademark of artists and philosophers. Holding steadfastly to one belief characterizes the religious or political enthusiast. Surely Bleuler, having excluded the inventors of non-existent diseases, would also exclude artists and enthusiasts? Not so:

> Poets and musicians must also be more sensitive than other people, a quality which is a hindrance to the daily tasks of life and often attains the significance of a disease.
>
> (Bleuler 1924: 172)

> Many schizophrenics display lively affect at least in certain directions. Among them are the active writers, the world improvers, the health fanatics, the founders of new religions.
>
> (Bleuler 1911: 41)

Bleuler appears to understand the difference between medical symptoms and deviance from social norms:

> Nowhere is the question: 'sick or not sick?' put so often in such an inexorable manner and with such heavy consequences as in the judgment of mental conditions. But the given question is false . . . Still more senseless is the question about well and sick where it is not a case of something added but of a plain deviation from the normal.
>
> (Bleuler 1924: 170)

Nevertheless, as a list of unacceptable behaviours and experiences, the writings of Kraepelin and Bleuler are frightening. What is left? What is considered healthy? We must be heterosexual, abide by rigid roles for males and females, obey our superiors, want to work, like certain colour combinations, not feel too much or too little, not get interested in new ideas, not show too much compassion for other people, be well-behaved (but, if male, not too well-behaved), not write too much poetry or play too much music, not try to change the world, and we must speak in a way that even psychiatrists can understand.

GENETICS

Kraepelin and Bleuler wanted to prove not only that all these behaviours were symptoms of a disease, but that the disease was genetically inherited.

They searched for evidence in the families of 'schizophrenics', extending their diagnostic net to catch an even wider range of behaviours:

> Among the brothers and sisters of the patients there are found striking personalities, criminals, queer individuals, prostitutes, suicides, vagrants, wrecked and ruined human beings, all being forms in which more or less well-developed dementia praecox may appear.
>
> (Kraepelin 1913: 234)

> Most frequently one finds in families schizoid characters, people who are shut-in, suspicious, incapable of discussion, people who are comfortably dull and at the same time sensitive, people who in a narrow manner pursue vague purposes, improvers of the universe, etc.
>
> (Bleuler 1911: 391)

With this broadened range of behaviours Bleuler found evidence of 'hereditary tainting' in 90% of the families concerned. Bleuler admitted that the same evidence of 'tainting' was found in 65% of people considered 'healthy'. 'Queer' parents having 'queer' children proves nothing about genetics, since any similarities are explainable in terms of learned behaviour and shared living conditions (see Chapter 7). Bleuler acknowledged:

> If someone cares to assume that the modifications of the psychic or physical factors produced by communal living produces such accumulations of disease in a given family group, we would be unable to produce any proof to the contrary.
>
> (Bleuler 1911: 337)

IGNORING THE SOCIAL CONTEXT

Any behaviour can be transformed into a symptom of mental illness simply by an expert decreeing it so. It helps, however, if the behaviour is portrayed as meaningless or bizarre. An effective way to do this is to ignore the social context.

Incarceration

One reality shared by most of the people whose behaviour was cited as evidence of schizophrenia was incarceration. Some people get upset when locked up. 'It is an everyday occurrence to see the patients soiling themselves or tearing their clothes, "because they won't let me go home"' (Bleuler 1911: 24). This is portrayed as paranoia:

> The 'persecuted' are dissatisfied with their environment, considering it the source of the persecution . . . Not quite on the same level is the indignation frequently met with in institutions, over lack of freedom, or other discomfort which the treatment inevitably brings in its wake.
>
> (Bleuler 1911: 48)

As an example of the symptom 'variability of attention', Bleuler (1924) cites 'Patients, who for a long time cannot give attention in any way, are suddenly capable of planning a complicated plan of escape' (p. 385). Only by ignoring what may be the most important reality in one's life could such sensible behaviour be turned into a symptom of 'schizophrenia'.

To illustrate 'disconnected, confused babble', Bleuler cites a letter:

> Here in this smith-house it doesn't go very well. This is indeed no parish-house or even a poor-house but in this place there is noise, anger, grumbling – sunny – heavenly-knells all year round. Many a small and large land owner, wind-bag or poor drunk from Thalweil, Addisweil, from Albis, from Salz, from Seen, from Rorbach, from Rorbas have never again returned to their own homes, etc, etc, etc. Greetings to all who are still alive. My own relatives no longer exist.
>
> (Bleuler 1911: 31)

If one remembers the social context, it seems to contain some under-standable statements:

- The institution is not what most people think it is.
- Many people here are angry.
- There are different kinds of people locked up here.
- Hope of release is minimal.
- One does not feel very alive when incarcerated.
- Since I have been here my family have all died, or I feel deserted by my family.

The psychiatrist

Another reality in psychiatric hospitals is powerful doctors who ask questions to establish your insanity. Only by ignoring this, and the resentment it can sometimes cause, can Kraepelin include the following in his list of symptoms:

> Often the patients refuse all information: 'That is their own affair', 'That is no one's business', 'People are cross-questioned in that way', 'They should not be there, did not require to give explanations'. One

patient first asked the physician to show him the diplomas that he might know with whom he had to do.

(Kraepelin 1913: 49)

Resistance to those in power is also a symptom:

When the patients should get up, they want to remain in bed: if they should remain in bed, they want to get up. Neither on command, nor in accordance with the rules of the hospital do they want to get dressed or undressed or come to meals or leave their meals; but if they can perform the same acts outside of the required time or somehow contrary to the will of the environment, they often do them.

(Bleuler 1924: 406)

Kraepelin comments:

There is another form of resistance to outside influences, which comes into existence wholly by impulse that is without foundation on ideas or emotions. Imperative negativism, the carrying out of action exactly contrary to that wished, scarcely allows for any other interpretation . . . When a patient begins to sing as soon as he is asked to be quiet, when he goes backward on being ordered to march, it is difficult to find an explanation in deliberation or emotional influences.

(Kraepelin 1913: 48)

An alternative interpretation is a deliberate, stubborn reaction to being told when to eat, sleep, get dressed, speak, be quiet and, finally (one wonders what place this one has in a hospital), to march.

There are other examples of specific behaviours by psychiatrists actually eliciting 'mad' behaviour:

The patients do not note contradictions when we take their negative answers for positive ones. I asked a patient: 'Do you hear voices?' He definitely denied it. I continued: 'What do they say to you?' 'Oh, all sorts of things'.

(Kraepelin 1913: 54)

One might conclude that the person asking the questions can't differentiate negative answers from positive ones (the latter perhaps resulting from trying to placate the powerful interrogator). One might cite this inability as a symptom of 'dementia psychiatrica'. Further evidence of this disease might be its consistent time of onset, around the time of entry into the psychiatric profession. It also tends to run in families and, therefore, is genetically inherited. But that would be silly.

Another example of apparently bizarre behaviour being explicable via specific actions of psychiatrists is the symptom 'waxy flexibility':

> This very striking disorder is plainly seen in the group in figure no. 3, which brings together a series of patients suffering from dementia praecox. They were put without difficulty in the peculiar positions and kept them, some with a sly laugh, others with rigid seriousness.
>
> (Kraepelin 1913: 53)

Despite admitting the patients were actually put in these peculiar positions by the psychiatrist (to see if they had the symptom of staying put), their maintaining those positions is perceived purely as a 'symptom' rather than a following of orders. Kraepelin asks them why they did it and is told 'It happens to order' and 'I do it because you wish it so'. 'I place myself according to what is commanded' (Kraepelin 1913: 38–9).

Here is an example of the symptom 'automatic obedience':

> He continues to put out his tongue when commanded to do so although one threatens to stab it, and causes him pain with a needle, as can be seen by the grimaces he makes.
>
> (Kraepelin 1913: 38)

Pressure to admit madness

Beyond the pressure – including specific instructions – to act crazy, there was also pressure to believe, or state, that you were mentally ill:

> An often discussed criterion of cure is that of the patients' insight into the nature of illness. People who speak of their delusions and their weird behaviour during the attack as being pathological phenomena . . . are not without reason easily considered as cured; whereas the opposite is thought of as being a rather certain sign of continuing disease.
>
> (Bleuler 1911: 257)

Furthermore, you had to admit that your problems were unrelated to whatever had happened in your life:

> They do not always locate the illness where the observer sees it to be. They realise, for example, the poor state of their nerves, the senselessness of their behaviour, but they insist that both are quite understandable reactions to stimuli and irritations of their environment.
>
> (Bleuler 1911: 257)

MEDICAL TREATMENT OR SOCIAL CONTROL?

A vital question, both before and since the invention of 'schizophrenia', is whether 'treatments' are best understood as attempts to cure an illness or as attempts to suppress socially unacceptable behaviour (see Chapter 2). Kraepelin (1913) devotes less than five of his 300 pages to *How to Combat It*. Apart from hospitalization he has little to suggest other than 'occupation' and various restraints including bed-rest and prolonged baths. The patients had doubts about their value:

> The patients do not remain in the bath, but always jump out again, perform neck-breaking gymnastics, roll about on the floor. The next thing now to be tried is to quiet the patients so far by a sedative, Nyoscine, Sulphonal, Trional, Veronal, that he may remain some hours in the bath.
>
> (Kraepelin 1913: 257)

At this point in the history of schizophrenia, the use of drugs was not seen as a medical treatment. The drugs were used to tranquillize and to get people to do as they were told. The same is true of another of Kraepelin's treatments. Leucocytosis consisted of injecting sodium nucleinate to cause fever. Kraepelin (1913) admits that from a medical point of view 'nothing was achieved'. He adds, however: 'Under the influence of a fever . . . negativistic patients appear more docile and obey medical orders' (pp. 281–2).

Bleuler (1911) lists various forms of restraint, chemical and otherwise. He admits, however, that 'we know of no measures which will cure the disease, as such, or even bring it to a halt' and 'treatment of schizophrenia by medication does not exist' (p. 485). Nevertheless, he recommends sedatives: 'Patients, who otherwise would not get accustomed to work, to their bed, to bathing, and to normal conditions, may gradually be trained, while under the effect of mild sedation' (p. 486). His discussion of a particularly nasty chemical which induces vomiting suggests, yet again, that what might appear to be medical treatment is actually elimination of unacceptable behaviour:

> Apomorphine is a chemical restraint of a special type. Some acute agitated states can be interrupted immediately by an injection of an emetic dose . . . Apomorphine is effective as a tool of education, in as much as the patient remains fully conscious while he calms down, and in this way can practice better behaviour. I cannot recommend it on ethical grounds; but then, again, I must ask whether it is not more unethical to permit a whole roomful of patients to be annoyed by a single agitated patient than to cause the offender to vomit.
>
> (Bleuler 1911: 486)

Not many psychiatrists today are as honest as Bleuler about the function of chemicals. Many genuinely believe that the medications used are treating the symptoms of an illness, rather than tranquillizing people into pacifity and compliance, partly or primarily for the convenience of others.

Bleuler is not remembered for delineating the criteria for discovering an illness, or for his honesty about the lack of evidence in relation to symptoms, outcome, cause or treatment. Long before his famous 1911 article was eventually translated into English (1950), the notion of a biogenetically based illness called 'schizophrenia' had been unquestioningly accepted by psychiatrists all over the 'developed' world as if it were scientific fact. The majority had not even read Bleuler's description of it.

Psychiatry survived its crisis. It did so at an appalling cost for the millions who for a century thereafter have been branded with the scientifically meaningless and socially devastating label 'schizophrenia'.

REFERENCES

Bentall, R. (ed.) (1990). *Reconstructing Schizophrenia*. London: Routledge.

Bentall, R. (2003). *Madness Explained: Psychosis and Human Nature*. London: Penguin.

Bleuler, E. ([1911] 1950). *Dementia Praecox or the Group of Schizophrenias* (translated by J. Zinkin). New York: International Universities Press.

Bleuler, E. (1924). *Textbook of Psychiatry* (translated by A. Brill). New York: Macmillan.

Boyle, M. (1990). *Schizophrenia: A Scientific Delusion?* London: Routledge.

Jelliffe, E. (1932). Emil Kraepelin. *Archives of Neurology and Psychiatry* 27: 759–72.

Kraepelin, E. ([1913] 1919). Dementia praecox. In E. Kraepelin, *Psychiatrica*, 8th edn (translated by R. Barclay). Melbourne, FL: Krieger.

Sullivan, H. (1927). Tentative criteria of malignancy in schizophrenia. *American Journal of Psychiatry* 84: 759–82.

Chapter 4

Genetics, eugenics and mass murder

John Read and Jeffrey Masson

In 1941, the staff of the Hadamer Psychiatric Institution were invited to a ceremony and each given a bottle of beer. The occasion was the murder of the ten thousandth mental patient.

Some might argue that what happened in Germany 60 years ago has nothing to do with how biological psychiatry operates today. We document these awful events, however, precisely because they so clearly illustrate, again, the three themes present throughout the history of the treatment of people considered mad: (1) social control in the interests of the powerful, (2) damaging and violent 'treatments', and (3) the ability of experts to generate theories camouflaging what is really happening (see Chapter 2).

The genetic theories that still dominate psychiatry today provided the motivation, and the camouflage, for what happened. It was psychiatrists who developed the theory that undesirable behaviour is genetically transmitted. It was this theory that was used to justify compulsory sterilization and murder. The inventors of schizophrenia paved the way. In 1913, Kraepelin, writing about 'dementia praecox', had stated 'Lomer has, it is true, proposed as a heroic profilactic measure bilateral castration as early as possible, but scarcely anyone will be found who will have the courage to follow him' (p. 278). It is not certain that 'profilactic' referred to prevention of reproduction. It is possible he thought castration might prevent deterioration of the individual. Bleuler, writing two years earlier, left no room for doubt: 'Lomer and von Rohe have again recommended castration, which, of course, is of no benefit to the patients themselves. However, it is to be hoped that sterilisation will soon be employed on a larger scale . . . for eugenic reasons' (Bleuler 1911: 473). His thoughts on keeping his patients alive were ominous:

> Most of our worst restraining measures would be unnecessary if we were not duty bound to preserve the patients' lives which, for them as well as for others, are only of negative value . . . Even if a few more killed themselves – does this reason justify the fact that we torture hundreds of patients and aggravate their disease? At the present time

we psychiatrists are burdened with the tragic responsibility of obeying the cruel views of society: but it is our responsibility to do our utmost to bring about a change in these views in the future.

(Bleuler 1911: 488)

The eugenics movement, aimed at improving 'race hygiene' by eliminating tainted genes, shared Bleuler's commitment. It was an international phenomenon. American scientific journals, such as *Eugenics Review* and *Eugenical News*, gave academic credibility to the sinister movement for twenty years before the sterilization and murder of mental patients began.

In 1920, Dr Alfred Hoche, professor of psychiatry at Freiberg, and Rudolf Binding, a law professor, wrote the book *Release and Destruction of Lives not Worth Living*. Continuing Bleuler's theme of lives 'of negative value', they wrote of 'those who are not capable of human feeling, those ballast lives, and empty human husks that fill our psychiatric institutions and can have no sense of the value of life. Theirs is not a life worth living; hence their destruction is not only tolerable, but humane' (p. 32).

In 1924, Eugen Bleuler recommended:

The more severely burdened should not propogate themselves . . . If we do nothing but make mental and physical cripples capable of propagating themselves, and the healthy stocks have to limit the number of their children because so much has to be done for the maintenance of others, if natural selection is generally suppressed, then unless we will get new measures our race must rapidly deteriorate.

(Bleuler 1924: 214)

Bleuler's plea for action was answered, in Germany, by the 1933 law allowing compulsory sterilization in cases of 'congenital mental defect, schizophrenia, manic-depressive psychosis, hereditary epilepsy, hereditary chorea, hereditary blindness, heredity deafness, severe physical deformity and severe alcoholism' (Muller-Hill 1988: 30). The primary author of the legislation was Ernst Rudin, professor of psychiatry at the Universities of Munich and Basel. Over 56,000 patients were sterilized in the first year. By 1939, about 350,000 had been sterilized. Other nations were also willing to use psychiatry's genetic theories to narrow the gene pool (Chapter 7). In the 1930s, eugenic sterilization laws were passed in Norway (Hansen 1936), Denmark (Hansen 1939) and Finland (Anonymous 1938). In Sweden, 63,000 people, mostly women displaying 'antisocial behaviour', were sterilized under eugenic legislation, starting in 1934 (Muller-Hill 1988). The German law 'was envied by the international eugenics movement' presumably because of its unequivocal endorsement of compulsion (Muller-Hill 1988: 201). However, the USA had been the first to translate genetic theories into eugenic programmes (Friedlander 1995; Gallagher 1990). By

1932, the Human Betterment Foundation reported that in California alone 10,000 eugenic sterilizations had been perpetrated, two-thirds of which were cases of 'insanity' (Gosney 1937).

By 1938 sterilization began, in Europe, to be replaced with murder. The psychiatrists, and other doctors, started with young children with psychological or physical abnormalities, at first starving them to death and later gassing them, in psychiatric institutions (Muller-Hill 1988). Despite the falsified death certificates issued to the parents, everyone was aware of what was happening; including the local communities, who could smell the cremations and knew who was in the buses arriving at the hospitals (Muller-Hill 1988). The child victims also knew. They played games with coffins (Dudley and Gale 2002).

In 1939, a plan to murder all mental patients was put into operation (Muller-Hill 1988). Those responsible for the plan and for 'selecting' who should die – from application forms submitted by all German psychiatric institutions – included the Chairs of Psychiatry at Cologne (Max de Crinis), Konigsberg and Munster (Frederich Mauz), Marburg and Breslau (Werner Villinger), Wurzburg (Werner Heyde), Dusseldorf (Friedrich Panse) and Bonn (Kurt Polisch), as well as Professor Carl Schneider, Chair of Psychiatry at the University of Heidelberg (the same prestigious position held a generation earlier by Emil Kraepelin).

The murders were called 'euthanasia', 'mercy killing' or 'help for the dying'. By September 1941, over 70,000 mental patients had been killed with carbon monoxide (suggested by Professor Heyde, a psychiatrist) in six specially adapted psychiatric hospitals. The total figure for Germany alone is well over a quarter of a million (Wertham 1966). The number killed elsewhere is unknown. Wertham estimated that of all the patients in German and Austrian mental hospitals in 1939, fewer than 15% remained by 1945. In three months during 1940, over 4000 were killed in Polish mental hospitals (Muller-Hill 1988). In French mental hospitals, 40,000 were starved to death (Koupernick 2001).

The possibility that the eminent psychiatrists who coordinated the murders (and the junior doctors who actually committed them) had convinced themselves that this treatment was beneficial to the recipients is raised by the omission of one category of patient. Jewish mental patients were excluded from 1939 to 1941 because 'they did not deserve the benefit of psychiatric euthanasia' (Wertham 1966: 159). Perhaps it had been decided that the Jewish race should be left to genetically degenerate while the Aryan race was cleansed of schizophrenic and other undesirable genetic material.

Towards the end of 1941, the gas chambers at psychiatric institutions were dismantled and shipped east to Belzec, Majdanke, Auschwitz, Trablinka and Sobidor to kill Jews. The doctors and nurses often accompanied the equipment (Muller-Hill 1988). Thus the mass murder of mental patients by psychiatrists not only preceded the attempted genocide of Jews, it provided the scientific rationale, the staff and the equipment. One of the shamefully tiny number of papers on the killings published in psychiatric journals over the subsequent sixty years states: 'These programmes formed the template for the extension into concentration camps and the "Final Solution" which killed six million Jews' (Dudley and Gale 2002: 586).

Psychiatry has barely begun to even acknowledge the facts. It was 25 years before anyone wrote a book on the subject (Wertham 1966) and 45 years before the publication of the only book about it ever written by a psychiatrist (Lifton 1986). This is not including the report (published as a book) by the psychiatrist who was Head of the German Medical Commission to Military Tribunal No. 1 at the Nuremberg trials (Mitscherlich 1948). It includes the following statement: 'The granting of "dying-aid" in the case of incurable mental patients and malformed or idiot children may be considered to be still within the legitimate sphere of medical discussion' (p. 117). Mitscherlich became a prominent psychoanalyst in Germany, until his death in 1982.

Almost all the psychiatrists involved in the killing escaped censure or punishment by the Allies (Dudley and Gale 2002; Muller-Hill 1988; Wertham 1966). They returned to their careers. For example, Professor Heyde, the psychiatrist who had suggested carbon monoxide, practised from 1950 to 1959 in Flensberg, West Germany. His identity was known to psychiatrists and the legal establishment there (Muller-Hill 1988).

Classic is the judgment of a Frankfurt court about a psychiatrist who not only killed many patients – adults and children – personally, but also watched their death agonies though the peep window of the gas chambers. 'We deal', said the court, 'with a certain weakness which does not as yet deserve moral condemnation'.

(Wertham 1966: 189)

Of the first twelve presidents of the German Society for Psychiatry and Neurology after the War, three had been organizers of the 'euthanasia' programme. As late as 1985 German doctors published papers based on research using specimens acquired through Nazi murders (Dudley and Gale 2002).

Psychiatry beyond Germany has been equally unable to understand the significance of what was done in the name of its simplistic and unsubstantiated bio-genetic explanations of unusual behaviour. The profession cannot claim ignorance. In 1941, the 'euthanasia' programme had been described in *Reader's Digest* (Dudley and Gale 2002). In the same year, at the annual meeting of the American Psychiatric Association, Dr Foster Kennedy presented a paper entitled 'The problem of social control of the congenital defective: education, sterilization, euthanasia'. He argued, about 5-year-old children, that 'It is a merciful and kindly thing to relieve that defective – often tortured and convulsed, grotesque and absurd, useless and foolish, and entirely undesirable – of the agony of living' (Kennedy 1942: 14). The *American Journal of Psychiatry* published the paper. After the War, Werner Villinger, who was deeply implicated in the killing of children, became Chair of Psychiatry at the University of Marburg. He was invited to, and attended, a White House conference on Children and Youth.

Many histories of psychiatry have omitted any mention of the facts (e.g. Alexander and Selesnick 1966; Roback 1961; Schneck 1960), with more recent histories devoting less than a page (Freeman 1999; Shorter 1997). Howells's (1975) *World History of Psychiatry* has a separate chapter for each country. All but one ends in the early 1970s. The chapter on Germany stops at 1936.

In the USA, the scientific journals *Eugenics Quarterly* and *Eugenics Review* continued, into the 1960s, to provide credibility to the ideas that had led directly to the deaths of over a quarter of a million and indirectly to the deaths of a further six million. From 1947 to 1956, the *American Journal of Psychiatry* published annual updates of 'Psychiatric Progress' on the issue of 'Heredity and Eugenics', all written by Franz Kallman (e.g. Kallman 1955).

Dr Kallman had argued, in Germany in the 1930s, that the relatives of schizophrenics, as well as schizophrenics themselves, should be sterilized. He promulgated his beliefs, after the War, in the USA. His bogus reports on the genetics of schizophrenia headed, for decades, the list of genetic studies of schizophrenia in British and American psychiatric and psychology textbooks. Unable to fulfil his dream of removing schizophrenic genes from the gene pool by sterilization, he advocated 'genetic counselling' (e.g. Kallman 1955). This practice, of discouraging reproduction by actively informing potential parents that any offspring would have a high probability of developing 'schizophrenia', is still with us. A contemporary American psychiatric textbook believes that genetic counselling has 'the potential for reducing or preventing the transmission of the illness' (Rieder *et al.* 1994: 70). The authors begin their summary of the relevant research with: 'the pioneering work of Rudin, Kallman, and others of the Berlin school' (p. 51). At the end of the twentieth century we are told 'Research and practice in psychiatric genetic counselling are only in the early stages of development' (Moldin and Gottesman 1997: 553).

One of the most thorough documentations of the horrors perpetrated by psychiatry in Germany concludes: 'We are not dealing here with defects in the character of a few individuals, but rather with defects in psychiatry and anthropology as a whole' (Muller-Hill 1988: 109). A recent paper published, to its credit, in the *Australian and New Zealand Journal of Psychiatry*, argues:

German psychiatry offered conducive conditions. From mid-19th century, a somatic approach dominated, the psychiatrist Griesinger asserting that 'mental disease is brain disease'. Emil Kraepelin's classification reflected therapeutic pessimism: For example, schizophrenia was organic, incurable and deteriorating . . . Psychotherapy was separated from psychiatry, and regarded as suspect.

(Dudley and Gale 2002: 588–9)

How unique were these conditions to 1930s Germany? The belief in bio-genetic theories of madness (and the eugenics movement) held sway throughout Europe and the USA. The German classifications of Kraepelin and Bleuler were eagerly adopted beyond Europe, along with their bio-genetic notions about causation. How much have these conditions of sixty years ago changed? Dudley and Gale themselves draw important parallels with how Australian psychiatry treats Aboriginal people today. The engine powering the machine is no longer the racism of the eugenicists, having been largely superseded by the profit-motive of the pharmaceutical industry. The belief in the bio-genetic ideology that fuelled the engine remains as strong as ever. The function of expert theories has remained constant: the camouflaging of socio-political realities behind a mask of scientific and caring endeavour.

A footnote cements our grasp of the awesome power of the *current* bio-genetic ideology and classification system to distort reality and to destroy human beings. Two-thirds of the people in Israel's mental hospitals are Holocaust survivors. It took a film maker, Shosh Sshlam, to reveal, in December 2001, with *Last Journey into Silence*, that many or most had been in hospital for fifty years, diagnosed as suffering from an illness called 'schizophrenia':

Decades of using antipsychotic drugs like haloperidol and thorazine hadn't worked. In the lobby of the survivors' wards, patients still shake uncontrollably and grind their jaws grotesquely from the side effects of such drugs. Barak [a psychiatrist leading a campaign for change] changed the diagnosis of schizophrenia attached to most of the 120 survivors in his ward to 'long-term post-traumatic psychosis'.

(Rees 2002: 41)

Former nurses say patients were routinely beaten and strapped to beds . . . They had been kept heavily drugged and often in solitary confinement for decades. Many had lost the power of speech. 'If they'd been treated right by Israel, about half of them could have lived normal lives' says Jeff Starrfield, Shaar Meashe's chief social worker. 'Now it's too late'.

(Rees 2002: 42)

The two paragraphs devoted to Nazi psychiatry in the recent *A Century of Psychiatry* (Peters 1999: 89), edited by prominent British biological psychiatrist Hugh Freeman, concludes: 'The facts are well known, but we still need an answer to the question – what theoretical or other ideas made so many psychiatrists who were not Nazis break their Hippocratic oath?' Perhaps we need look no further than the opening words of the same article: 'Nazi psychiatry was not different in all respects from classical psychiatry. A shared belief between them was that endogenous psychoses were somatic, with mainly genetic causes, and they also shared a therapeutic nihilism'.

To remember the past requires an active effort and remembering is a prerequisite of mourning. All psychiatrists and every student of psychiatry should make this effort . . . The 'scientific' psychiatrist does not console those in despair, he calls them depressed. He does not unravel the tangled thought-processes of the confused, he calls them schizophrenic . . . This attitude reduces the person to a subservient depersonalised object. Such a process formed the bond which held the psychiatrists, anthropologists and Hitler together.

(Muller-Hill 1988: 110)

REFERENCES

Alexander, F. and Selesnick, S. (1966). *The History of Psychiatric Thought and Practice from Prehistoric Times to the Present*. New York: Harper & Row.

Anonymous (1938). Sterilization Law in Finland. *Eugenical News* 23: 47–8.

Binding, K. and Hoche, A. (1920). *Release and Destruction of Lives Not Worth Living*. Leipzig: Meiner.

Bleuler, E. ([1911] 1950). *Dementia Praecox or the Group of Schizophrenias* (translated by J. Zinkin). New York: International Universities Press.

Bleuler, E. (1924). *Textbook of Psychiatry* (translated by A. Brill). New York: Macmillan.

Dudley, M. and Gale, F. (2002). Psychiatrists as a moral community? *Australian and New Zealand Journal of Psychiatry* 36: 585–94.

Freeman, H. (ed.) (1999). *A Century of Psychiatry*. London: Harcourt.

Friedlander, H. (1995). *The Origins of Nazi Genocide*. Chapel Hill, NC: University of North Carolina Press.

Gallagher, H. (1990). *By Trust Betrayed*. Arlington, VA: Vandermere.

Gosney, E. (1937). Twenty-eight years of eugenic sterilization in California. *Eugenical News* 22: 86–7.

Hansen, K. (1936). The Norwegian sterilization law of 1934 and its practical results. *Eugenical News* 21: 129–31.

Hansen, S. (1939). Eugenical sterilization in Denmark. *Eugenical News* 21: 10–13.

Howells, J. (ed.) (1975). *World History of Psychiatry*. New York: Brunner-Mazel.

Kallman, F. (1955). Review of psychiatric progress 1954: heredity and eugenics. *American Journal of Psychiatry* 111: 502–5.

Kennedy, F. (1942). The problem of social control of the congenital defective: education, sterilization, euthanasia. *American Journal of Psychiatry* 99: 13–16.

Koupernick, C. (2001). Eugenisme et psychiatrie. *Annales Medico-Psychologique* 159: 14–18.

Kraepelin, E. ([1913] 1919). Dementia praecox. In *Psychiatrica*, 8th edn (translated by E. Barclay). Melbourne, FL: Krieger.

Lifton, R. (1986). *The Nazi Doctors*. New York: Basic Books.

Mitscherlich, A. (1949). *Doctors of Infamy*. New York: Schuman.

Moldin, S. and Gottesman, I. (1997). Genes, experience, and chance in schizophrenia. *Schizophrenia Bulletin* 23: 547–61.

Muller-Hill, B. (1988). *Murderous Science* (translated by G. Fraser). Oxford: Oxford University Press.

Peters, U. (1999). German psychiatry. In H. Freeman (ed.) *A Century of Psychiatry*. London: Harcourt.

Rees, M. (2002). Surviving the past. *Time*, 14 January, pp. 40–2.

Rieder, R. *et al.* (1994). Genetics. In R. Hales *et al.* (eds) *Textbook of Psychiatry*, 2nd edn. Washington, DC: American Psychiatric Press.

Roback, A. (1961). *History of Psychology and Psychiatry*. New York: Philosophical Library.

Schneck, J. (1960). *History of Psychiatry*. Springfield, IL: Charles Thomas.

Shorter, E. (1997). *A History of Psychiatry*. New York: Wiley.

Wertham, F. (1966). *A Sign for Cain*. New York: Macmillan.

Chapter 5

Does 'schizophrenia' exist?

Reliability and validity

John Read

To say schizophrenia doesn't exist is not to say people don't sometimes have experiences that are unusual or difficult to understand, and sometimes suffer extreme emotional pain and confusion. The questions addressed here are quite different: Does 'schizophrenia' meet accepted scientific requirements for establishing that a concept exists? – 'reliability'; and Is 'schizophrenia' useful in terms of understanding anything? – 'validity' (Bentall 1990, 2003; Bentall *et al.* 1988; Boyle 1990; Pilgrim 2000).

RELIABILITY: CAN WE AGREE WHO IS 'SCHIZOPHRENIC'?

The first fifty years

Eighty years ago, the textbook *Mental Diseases* stated:

> They [psychiatric diagnoses] do not contribute anything of value whatever to our knowledge of symptomatology, diagnosis or treatment. Practically the only point on which the writers of our textbooks agree is that there is no fundamental principle upon which a satisfactory classification can be based.
>
> (May 1922: 246)

By 1938, Boisen, finding huge variations in the application of the 'schizophrenia' diagnosis, concluded: 'It is clear that the Kraepelinian system is inadequate'. Nevertheless, it was predicted, with depressing accuracy, that:

> There always will be many who will use the existing system of classification irrespective of whether or not it has any meaning, and even those who decry the orthodox classification will invoke it as an atheist when off guard invokes God.
>
> (Jellinek 1939: 161)

Psychologists developed tests to try to improve diagnostic procedures. By 1949, it was concluded:

> Using techniques which are not too precisely validated, if they are validated at all, to place patients in psychiatric categories, the inadequacy of which is admitted by all concerned, is a treadmill procedure guaranteed to keep us moving in circles . . . The psychiatric taxonomy which psychologists have been constrained to adopt is so inadequate, even for psychiatry, that no patching can fix it up.
>
> (Roe 1949: 38)

Roe added that 'columns of figures are involved and mathematical procedures have great anxiety-reducing potentials'. In the same year it was discovered that clinicians agreed with others' diagnoses in only between a third and a half of cases (Ash 1949). One of the largest reliability studies ever undertaken, using the test–retest approach, found that consistency for schizophrenia was only 37% (Hunt et al. 1953).

A 'frontal attack' in search of schizophrenia

Researchers were urged to unleash 'a frontal attack' (Kreitman 1961) to discover why, 50 years after the 'discovery' of schizophrenia, experts still couldn't agree who had it. Typical of the response is the work of a group of Philadelphia diagnostic experts (Ward et al. 1962). Having produced 53% agreement between pairs of clinicians for schizophrenia, they claimed that this slightly increased reliability was achieved by having minimized 'factors that would artificially lower' reliability (Beck et al. 1962). In fact, they had introduced quite unreal conditions explicitly designed to artificially increase agreement. There were several ways in which their study, and the others trying to prove the existence of 'schizophrenia', were biased:

1   *Non-independent observations.* In many studies, the two diagnosticians used the same information. Any two diagnoses in the real world are based on different questions, at different times, in different settings, resulting in widely differing information.
2   *Few categories.* In the real world, clinicians choose between hundreds of diagnoses. Many reliability studies used as few as six or three.
3   *Participants trained.* In the real world, psychiatrists do not meet to agree definitions with all other psychiatrists before making diagnoses.
4   *Blatant statistical bias.* If two clinicians typically use a category 60% of the time, they will agree, by chance alone, about 36% (0.6 × 0.6) of the time. For instance, if the appropriate statistic for removing this inflation, kappa (κ), had been used, the reliability for schizophrenia found by Beck et al. (1962) would have been 0.42 not 0.53 (Spitzer and Fleiss 1974).

Because of these biases, the reliabilities did approach an illusion of respectability. However, it was soon reported that the average reliability, using the correct statistical procedure, was still only 0.57. It was agreed that there 'appears to have been no essential change in diagnostic reliability over time,' that 'there are no diagnostic categories for which reliability is uniformly high' and, unsurprisingly, that reliability in 'routine clinical settings is even poorer' than that found in research studies (Spitzer and Fleiss 1974: 344).

A recent study found no statistically significant relationship between clinical diagnoses of schizophrenia and diagnoses based on *either* of two diagnostic processes used by researchers ($\kappa = 0.11$ and 0.13, respectively) (Whaley 2001). There has been massive variation between countries. When 134 US and 194 British psychiatrists were given a description of a patient, 69% of the US psychiatrists diagnosed 'schizophrenia', but only 2% of the British psychiatrists did so (Copeland *et al.* 1971). For decades 'schizophrenia' researchers on either side of the Atlantic were researching different groups of people.

Redefining schizophrenia

The 'frontal attack' had failed. However, another approach was available: redefinition. Following Kraepelin's repeated redefinitions of his own invention, Bleuler had further altered the definition (see Chapter 3). These redefinitions continued throughout the twentieth century, reflected in numerous official versions of schizophrenia, including the various editions of the *Diagnostic and Statistical Manual* (*DSM*). The first edition survived for 16 years (1952–1968) and the second edition for 12. Those responsible for the third undertook a massive research project to develop new definitions that might finally produce adequate reliability. By 1987, however, the American Psychiatric Association (APA) admitted:

> Despite extensive field testing of the DSM-III diagnostic criteria before their official adoption, experience with them since their publication had revealed, as expected, many instances in which the criteria were not entirely clear, were inconsistent across categories, or were even contradictory.
>
> (APA 1987: xvii)

This admission of the DSM-III's failures is not the introduction to a paper arguing that psychiatry must finally recognize the futility of further redefinitions and abandon terms like 'schizophrenia'. It is the introduction to a 560-page book entitled *Diagnostic and Statistical Manual*, 3rd edn, Revised.

In 1968, British psychologist Don Bannister had delineated 'The logical requirements of research into schizophrenia' and concluded that: 'Schizophrenia as a concept, is a semantic Titanic, doomed before it sails, a concept so diffuse as to be unusable in a scientific context' (p. 181).

> We diagnose one person as schizophrenic because he manifests characteristics A and B and diagnose a second person as schizophrenic because he manifests characteristics C, D and E. The two people are now firmly grouped in the same category while not specifically possessing any common characteristic . . . Disjunctive categories are logically too primitive for scientific use.
>
> (Bannister 1968: 181–2)

The category remains disjunctive today. To receive a diagnosis of schizophrenia using the latest set of redefinitions in the DSM-IV (APA 1994), you need two of five 'characteristic symptoms' – hallucinations, delusions, disorganized speech, grossly disorganized or catatonic behaviour, and negative symptoms. There are 15 ways (1 + 2 *vs* 3 + 4; 1 + 2 *vs* 3 + 5, etc.) in which two people can meet DSM-IV's criteria for schizophrenia without having anything in common.

Only one of these characteristic symptoms is required 'if delusions are bizarre'. When 50 senior USA psychiatrists were asked to differentiate bizarre and non-bizarre delusions, they produced inter-reliability kappas (see earlier) of only 0.38–0.43. The researchers concluded: 'The symptom of bizarre delusions does not have adequate reliability' (Mojtabi and Nicholson 1995).

No changes were made to the diagnostic criteria for 'schizophrenia' in the DSM-IV text revision (APA 2000: 312). So, at the beginning of the twenty-first century, the construct, as employed by clinicians and researchers all over the world, remains disjunctive and therefore scientifically meaningless.

Bannister (1968) had recommended that 'research into schizophrenia as such, should not be undertaken'. This recommendation has been made repeatedly (e.g. Bentall 2003; Bentall *et al.* 1988; Boyle 1990; Ross and Pam 1995). In 1996, US psychiatrist Howard James stated, again, that schizophrenia is 'an unscientific and unprovable nosological construct, which has outlived its usefulness in the lexicon of modern psychiatry' (p. 148). In 1992, researchers identified 16 systems of classifying schizophrenia. Of 248 patients, the number diagnosed schizophrenic by these systems ranged from 1 to 203. This study was 'designed to maximise reliability and agreement' (Herron *et al.* 1992). Furthermore, within each of these 16 systems there are different ways of gathering and interpreting information. One study used four different recognized methods of assigning patients to eight DSM-IV diagnoses indicative of psychosis (including schizophrenia). The agreement between pairs of systems ranged from 53 to 65% (McGorry *et al.* 1995).

The absurdity of all this was illustrated by a famous study in which 'normal' people, admitted to psychiatric hospitals after saying they heard the words 'empty' or 'thud', were diagnosed schizophrenic. Many of the patients, but none of the staff, recognized that the 'pseudo-patients' were 'normal'. A follow-up study, in which hospital staff were told that 'pseudo-patients' would be admitted, produced a 21% detection rate by staff. No 'pseudo-patients' had been admitted (Rosenhan 1975).

VALIDITY: IS 'SCHIZOPHRENIA' WHAT IT IS SUPPOSED TO BE?

It is agreed within the scientific community that without reliability, researching validity is meaningless. If nobody can agree on who has 'schizophrenia', then the supposed properties of 'schizophrenia' cannot be evaluated. The people one researcher studies will be different from those studied by others.

If reliability *had* been established, however, we would investigate whether the construct was related to things which the theory underpinning the construct says it is related to. In the case of the illness theory of schizophrenia, one would search, as Kraepelin and Bleuler had done, unsuccessfully, for: (1) a set of symptoms that occur together but not in other 'mental illnesses', (2) a predictable outcome, (3) a biological cause and (4) responsivity to medical treatments.

In 1961, prominent diagnostic researchers Zigler and Phillips acknowledged:

> The problem of validity lies at the heart of the confusion which surrounds psychiatric diagnosis . . . Class membership conveys little information beyond the gross symptomatology of the patient and contributes little to the solution of the pressing problems of aetiology, treatment procedures, prognosis, etc.
>
> (Zigler and Phillips 1961: 612)

A comprehensive review of the research in each of the four validity areas (symptoms, aetiology, prognosis and treatment) concluded that '"schizophrenia" is not a useful scientific category and that for all these years researchers have been pursuing a ghost within the body of psychiatry' (Bentall *et al.* 1988: 318).

Later, we will analyse the attempts to discover a biological cause (Chapters 6 and 7) and effective medical treatments (Chapters 8 and 9). First, we will consider the two other areas of validity: symptom specificity and outcome consistency.

Symptoms

There has never been any evidence that there is a set of 'schizophrenic' behaviours and experiences that occur together but do not occur in other psychiatric conditions. In 1952, Guertin used factor analysis to answer the question, 'Is there such a thing as schizophrenia?' He found 'no suggestion of a group factor that could be called "schizophrenia"'. In 1973, the World Health Organization (WHO) compared clusters of symptoms which occur together in real people with the groupings produced by diagnostic categories. They found that 'The clusters are defining different and more homogeneous groups than are the clinical diagnoses' and 'Patients diagnosed as schizophrenic are distributed in all clusters. No single "schizophrenic profile" was elicited' (p. 350).

'Schizophrenic' symptoms are frequently found in many other disorders, including bipolar disorder (Crow 1990). People with dissociative identity disorder have more schizophrenic symptoms than people diagnosed schizophrenic (Ellason and Ross 1995). Most people diagnosed schizophrenic have sufficient symptoms of other disorders to earn additional diagnoses. This 'co-morbidity' has been found in relation to depression, obsessive-compulsive disorder, panic disorder, personality disorders, substance abuse, post-traumatic stress disorder and anxiety disorders (Craig and Hwang 2000; Torgalsboen 1999a).

Prognosis

There is no evidence that people receiving the diagnosis share a common prognosis. Eugen Bleuler (1911) had acknowledged that 'it is impossible to describe all the variations which the course of schizophrenia may take'. Two findings characterize all long-term outcome studies: (1) there are massive variations in outcomes (2) many people labelled 'schizophrenic' recover.

Estimates of long-term recovery rates vary from 13% (Stephens et al. 1997) to 72% (Thara and Eaton 1996), with most falling between 30 and 55% (Bleuler 1972; Ciompi 1980, 1984; Harding et al. 1987; Harrison et al. 2001; McGlashan 1988; Torgalsboen 1999b). There is 'mounting evidence of rates in excess of 50%' (Kruger 2000).

A clear demonstration of outcome variability was provided by Manfred Bleuler (1972). From a 20 year study of hospitalized 'schizophrenics' at the Burgholzi Clinic (where his father Eugen had worked), he found the following stable outcomes: severe, 15%; moderate, 17%; mild, 38%; recovery, 30%. Swiss psychiatrist Luc Ciompi (1980) found similar variability in a 37 year study: severe, 20%, intermediate, 26%; minor, 22%; recovery, 30%.

In Vermont, Harding and colleagues (1987) studied 'the sickest group in the hospital'. They had been hospitalized for ten years at the outset of the study. In the 12 months preceding the follow-up assessment, an average of 32 years later, 82% had not been in hospital, 40% were employed (despite two-thirds being 55 or older) and 68% had few or no symptoms. In 2001, a WHO review of 18 cities reported an average recovery rate, after 15 or 25 years, of 48% (Harrison *et al.* 2001).

Ciompi concludes:

> There is no such thing as a specific course for schizophrenia. Doubtless, the potential for improvement of schizophrenia has for a long time been grossly under-estimated. What is called 'the course of schizo-phrenia' more closely resembles a life process open to a great variety of influences of all kinds than an illness with a given course.
>
> (Ciompi 1980: 420)

The idea of a consistent, and negative, outcome is finally, after a century of devastation to millions, being challenged by some significant forces within psychiatry. A 2001 review of the WHO International Study of Schizo-phrenia (ISoS) concludes:

> Because expectations can be so powerful a factor in recovery, patients, families and clinicians need to hear this . . . The ISoS joins others in relieving patients, carers and clinicians of the chronicity paradigm which dominated thinking throughout much of the 20th century.
>
> (Harrison *et al.* 2001: 513)

The diagnosis 'schizophrenia' has *no* predictive validity. If we want to know who is most likely to do well over time we must turn to psycho-social factors. Predictors of good outcome include work performance, academic achievement, social skills, economic conditions, family tolerance, and low family involvement with treatment decisions (Harrison *et al.* 2001; McGlashan 1988; Torgalsboen 1999b). Two of the most powerful predic-tors are being female and having a good 'pre-morbid adjustment', especially in terms of social relationships (Malmberg *et al.* 1998; Mueser *et al.* 1990).

There is one more example of inconsistent outcome and of psycho-social factors predicting outcome. It has been repeatedly demonstrated that outcomes in poorer countries (e.g. Nigeria and India) are far superior to those in wealthy industrialized societies (Bresnahan *et al.* 2003; Harrison *et al.* 2001).

Progress into a theoretical vacuum

The repeated redefinitions discussed earlier were not based on a solid theoretical framework, but rather on the hope of increasing the chances that experts can agree about what they are looking at. Typical of this reliability-at-any-cost approach was the abandonment, by the designers of DSM-III, of 'blunted or inappropriate affect', which had been a corner-stone of the construct since its invention (Spitzer *et al.* 1978).

The logical conclusion of atheoretical redefinitions is to find any behaviour about which clinicians can agree, regardless of whether it has anything to do with the original theory, and call it 'schizophrenic'. An example of this is the obsessive quest to find measurable differences, any differences, between 'schizophrenics' and 'normals'. Here are just a few examples of the endless, theoretically incoherent, list of variables researched:

- handwriting (Coron *et al.* 2000);
- blood type (Rinieris *et al.* 1982);
- season of birth (Meltzer 1987);
- signs of homosexuality among men (Chaudhury and Jyothi 1996; Mujtaba and Mujtaba 1985);
- hip circumference among women (Singer *et al.* 1976);
- ear shape, position of eyes, size of gap between toes, finger curvature, snout reflex and upper lip width (Lawrie *et al.* 2001);
- inadequate 'attractiveness' among women (Higdon 1982);
- ability to smell accurately (Striebel *et al.* 1999) (turned out to be the effects of anti-psychotic medication);
- ability of one's relatives to smell accurately (Kopala *et al.* 2001);
- inappropriate masturbation (Brooks and Waikar 2000);
- tattoos (Birmingham *et al.* 1999);
- head circumference (too big or small), soft and pliable ears, third toe longer than second toe (Schiffman *et al.* 2002);
- proximity of mother to cats during pregnancy (Torrey and Yolken 1995);
- reaction to body products (Dimond and Hirt 1974).

This is what results from ignoring the basic rules of science, including the need to abandon concepts when they are repeatedly shown not to exist. Psychiatry's reliability-at-any-price and any-variable-in-a-storm approach, however, maintains the illusion of being engaged in scientific research.

In 1973, the World Health Organization admitted that 'Kraepelin's attempt to create a concept of dementia praecox was unsuccessful as all later attempts in this direction have been', but offered an argument for carrying on regardless:

> The word schizophrenia has come into such widespread use that it is necessary to have a practical definition of it in order to keep public discussion of schizophrenia within reasonable limits . . . for the benefit

of non-professional contemporaries who enjoy talking about schizophrenia without knowing what it is.

(WHO 1973: 17)

Imagine a 'schizophrenic' claiming that the reason she keeps on about her delusion is not because she believes in it any more but because everyone else now believes in it and she wants to make sure they get the facts right.

DIAGNOSIS FOR SOCIAL CONTROL

Zigler and Phillips, having acknowledged that diagnoses like schizophrenia contribute nothing to our understanding of causes or treatments, pointed out the following:

> The present diagnostic system is quite useful when evaluated in terms of its administrative implications . . . Examples would include legal determination of insanity, declaration of incompetence, type of ward required for custodial care, census figures and statistical data upon which considerable planning is based, screening devices for the military services, etc.
>
> (Zigler and Phillips 1961: 615)

They seemed unaware of the implications of the fact that the only fields in which diagnoses have any validity are not medical but socio-political. If they had been writing today, they would have included health insurance – a powerful force behind the continuing use of unscientific diagnoses.

ALTERNATIVES

There *are* scientific and productive ways to understand 'madness'. They form the theoretical underpinning for much of what follows in this book and, hopefully, for clinical practice and research in the twenty-first century.

Reliable constructs

Categorizing is not the problem. Categorizing is an inevitable human propensity, wired into our brains, without which we couldn't survive. The task is to find measurable categories about which we can agree (reliable) and which are meaningful and useful (valid). This is not difficult.

The heterogeneity of the schizophrenia construct has been acknowledged for nearly a hundred years. Bleuler highlighted it by entitling his famous

1911 monograph *Dementia Praecox or the Group of Schizophrenias*. There have been many attempts to break the construct into smaller, more reliable, lumps. The latest official version of these rather crude dissections, in the DSM-IV, is: 'Paranoid', 'Disorganized', 'Catatonic', 'Undifferentiated' and 'Residual'.

The best way to break down the construct into subtypes is to see which symptoms actually occur together. The first such division was into 'positive' symptoms (additions to 'normal' experience, such as hallucinations and delusions) and 'negative' symptoms (deficits, such as blunted affect and social withdrawal) (Andreasen and Olson 1982). The positives were subsequently found to consist of 'psychotic' (delusions and hallucinations) and 'disorganization' (thought disorder, inappropriate affect and bizarre behaviour), producing, with negative symptoms, a three-factor model (Liddle 1987; see Chapter 14). Others have found five, six and seven factors (Nakaya *et al.* 1999; Peralta *et al.* 1997).

Beyond these valuable efforts to discover reliable groupings of behaviours and experiences, there is an increasing focus on specific behaviours and experiences, free from any diagnostic baggage. We will see later (Chapters 14, 16 and 20) how once we forget about the non-existent ghost of 'schizophrenia' and focus instead on definable and measurable constructs like hallucinations and delusions, significant progress is made in our ability to understand and to help. Constructs like hallucinations and delusions can themselves be broken down into clinically valuable and highly reliable dimensional variables such as duration, intensity, frequency, conviction, disruption and distress.

Dimensions

Besides using only reliable variables, a second important principle is thinking in terms of dimensions rather than discrete categories (McGorry *et al.* 1998). 'Normal' human behaviours, thoughts and feelings vary significantly over time and between differing social contexts. So do those considered 'abnormal' (Pilgrim 2000).

The DSM-IV devotes just three of its 886 pages to its only dimensional measure (pp. 32–4). The Global Assessment of Functioning Scale (GAF) records the clinician's judgement of overall level of functioning. Its inclusion is an advance, an acknowledgement that mental health is a matter of degree.

Dimensional measures of mental health are more reliable than diagnoses. When asked to assess 258 patients in terms of *degree* of psychopathology, clinicians reported high agreement (Rosenthal *et al.* 1975). It was concluded that 'independent judges may not agree regarding what a person has, but they show remarkable agreement in deciding how severe it is'. The DSM-IV's GAF (and its two trial dimensions measuring relational and social/

occupational functioning, pp. 758–60) have 'very high levels of interrater reliability' (Hilsenroth *et al*. 2000).

This dimensional approach is also helpful in showing how many of the 'normal' population have psychotic experiences (Johns and van Os 2001). A recent review of studies comparing dimensional and categorical representations of behaviours considered indicative of schizophrenia concludes that the dimensional approach 'appeared to be more useful in terms of yielding information on patients' needs and outcome' (van Os and Verdoux 2003). Combining the specific/measurable and the dimensional approaches produces descriptions of us as real individuals engaging in certain behaviours, thoughts or feelings to various extents at various times, depending largely on what is happening around us.

REFERENCES

American Psychiatric Association (1987). *Diagnostic and Statistical Manual*, 3rd edn, revised. Washington, DC: APA.

American Psychiatric Association (1994). *Diagnostic and Statistical Manual*, 4th edn. Washington, DC: APA.

American Psychiatric Association (2000). *Diagnostic and Statistical Manual*, text revision. Washington, DC: APA.

Andreasen, N. and Olsen, S. (1982). Negative *v* positive schizophrenia. *Archives of General Psychiatry* 39: 789–94.

Ash, P. (1949). The reliability of psychiatric diagnoses. *Journal of Abnormal and Social Psychology* 4: 272–7.

Bannister, D. (1968). The logical requirements of research into schizophrenia. *British Journal of Psychiatry* 114: 181–8.

Beck, A. *et al*. (1962). Reliability of psychiatric diagnoses. *American Journal of Psychiatry* 119: 351–7.

Bentall, R. (ed.) (1990). *Reconstructing Schizophrenia*. London: Routledge.

Bentall, R. (2003). *Madness Explained: Psychosis and Human Nature*. London: Penguin.

Bentall, R. *et al*. (1988) Abandoning the concept of 'schizophrenia'. *British Journal of Clinical Psychology* 27: 303–24.

Birmingham, L. *et al*. (1999). The psychiatric implications of visible tattoos in an adult male prison population. *Journal of Forensic Psychiatry* 10: 687–95.

Bleuler, E. ([1911] 1950). *Dementia Praecox or the Group of Schizophrenias* (translated by J.J. Zinkin). New York: International Universities Press.

Bleuler, M. ([1972] 1978). *The Schizophrenia Disorders* (translated by S. Clemens). New Haven, CT: Yale University Press.

Boisen, A. (1938). Types of dementia praecox. *Psychiatry* 1: 233–6.

Boyle, M. (1990). *Schizophrenia: A Scientific Delusion?* London: Routledge.

Bresnahan, M. *et al*. (2003). Geographical variation in incidence, course and outcome of schizophrenia. In R. Murray *et al*. (eds) *The Epidemiology of Schizophrenia*. Cambridge: Cambridge University Press.

Brooks, J. and Waikar, M. (2000). Inappropriate masturbation and schizophrenia. *Journal of Clinical Psychiatry* 61: 451.

Chaudhury, S. and Jyothi, S. (1996). Relationship between homosexuality and paranoid schizophrenia. *Journal of Projective Psychology and Mental Health* 3: 147–52.

Ciompi, L. (1980). The natural history of schizophrenia in the long term. *British Journal of Psychiatry* 136: 413–20.

Ciompi, L. (1984). Is there really a schizophrenia? *British Journal of Psychiatry* 145: 636–40.

Copeland, J. *et al.* (1971). Differences in usage of diagnostic labels amongst psychiatrists in the British Isles. *British Journal of Psychiatry* 118: 629–40.

Coron, A. *et al.* (2000). Writing impairment in schizophrenia. *Brain and Cognition* 43: 121–4.

Craig, T. and Hwang, M. (2000). Comorbidity in schizophrenia. *Psychiatric Annals* 30: 76–8.

Crow, T. (1990). The continuum of psychosis and its genetic origins. *British Journal of Psychiatry* 156: 788–97.

Dimond, R. and Hirt, M. (1974). Investigation of the generalizability of attitudes toward body products as a function of psychopathology and long-term hospitalisation. *Journal of Clinical Psychology* 30: 251–2.

Ellason, J. and Ross, C. (1995). Positive and negative symptoms in dissociative disorder and schizophrenia. *Journal of Nervous and Mental Disease* 183: 263–41.

Guertin, W. (1952). An inverted factor-analytic study of schizophrenics. *Journal of Consulting Psychology* 16: 371–5.

Harding, C. *et al.* (1987). The Vermont longitudinal study of persons with severe mental illness. *American Journal of Psychiatry* 144: 718–26.

Harrison, G. *et al.* (2001). Recovery from psychotic illness. *British Journal of Psychiatry* 178: 506–17.

Herron, W. *et al.* (1992). A comparison of 16 systems to diagnose schizophrenia. *Journal of Clinical Psychology* 48: 711–21.

Higdon, J. (1982). Role of power, sex, and inadequate attractiveness in paranoid women. *Psychological Report* 50: 399–402.

Hilsenroth, M. *et al.* (2000). Reliability and validity of DSM-IV Axis V. *American Journal of Psychiatry* 157: 1858–63.

Hunt, W. *et al.* (1953). Theoretical and practical analysis of the diagnostic process. In P. Hoch and J. Zubin (eds) *Current Problems in Psychiatric Diagnosis*. New York: Grune & Stratton.

James, H. (1996). Requiem for 'schizophrenia'. *Integrative Physiological Behavioral Sciences* 31: 148–54.

Jellinek, E. (1939). Some principles of psychiatric classification. *Psychiatry* 2: 161–5.

Johns, L. and van Os, J. (2001). The continuity of psychotic experiences in the general population. *Clinical Psychology Review* 21: 1125–41.

Kopala, K.-M. *et al.* (2001). Impaired olfactory identification in relatives of patients with familial schizophrenia. *American Journal of Psychiatry* 158: 1286–90.

Kreitman, N. (1961). The reliability of psychiatric diagnosis. *Journal of Mental Science* 107: 876–86.

Kruger, A. (2000). Schizophrenia: recovery and hope. *Psychiatric Rehabilitation Journal* 24: 29–37.

Lawrie, S. *et al.* (2001). Neurodevelopmental indices and the development of psychotic symptoms in subjects at high risk of schizophrenia. *British Journal of Psychiatry* 178: 524–30.

Liddle, P. (1987). The symptoms of chronic schizophrenia. *British Journal of Psychiatry* 151: 145–51.

Malmberg, A. *et al.* (1998). Premorbid adjustment and personality in people with schizophrenia. *British Journal of Psychiatry* 172: 308–13.

May, J. (1922) *Mental Diseases.* Boston, MA: Gorham.

McGlashan, T. (1988). A selective review of recent North American long-term follow-up studies of schizophrenia. *Schizophrenia Bulletin* 14: 515–42.

McGorry, P. *et al.* (1995). Spurious precision: procedural validity of diagnostic assessment in psychotic disorders. *American Journal of Psychiatry* 152: 220–3.

McGorry, P. (1998). The dimensional structure of first episode psychosis. *Psychological Medicine* 28: 935–47.

Meltzer, H. (1987). Biological studies in schizophrenia. *Schizophrenia Bulletin* 13: 77–111.

Mojtabi, R. and Nicholson, R. (1995). Interrater reliability of ratings of delusions and bizarre delusions. *American Journal of Psychiatry* 152: 1804–8.

Mueser, K. *et al.* (1990). Social competence in schizophrenia. *Journal of Psychiatric Research* 24: 51–63.

Mujtaba, B. and Mujtaba, V. (1985). Homosexuality and paranoid schizophrenia: a study through Rorshach ink blots. *Journal of Personality and Clinical Studies* 1: 27–9.

Nakaya, M. *et al.* (1999). Latent structures underlying schizophrenic symptoms. *Schizophrenia Research* 39: 39–50.

Peralta, V. *et al.* (1997). Factor structure of symptoms of functional psychoses. *Biological Psychiatry* 42: 806–15.

Pilgrim, D. (2000) Psychiatric diagnosis: more questions than answers. *Psychologist* 13: 302–5.

Rinieris, P. *et al.* (1982). Subtypes of schizophrenia and ABO blood types. *Neuropsychobiology* 8: 57–9.

Roe, A. (1949). Integration of personality theory and clinical practice. *American Psychologist* 44: 36–41.

Rosenhan, D. (1975). On being sane in insane places. *Science* 179: 250–8.

Rosenthal, D. *et al.* (1975). Assessing degree of psychopathology from diagnostic statements. *Canadian Psychiatric Association Journal* 1975: 35–45.

Ross, C. and Pam, R. (1995). *Pseudoscience in Biological Psychiatry.* New York: Wiley.

Schiffman, J. *et al.* (2002). Minor physical anomalies and schizophrenia spectrum disorders. *American Journal of Psychiatry* 159: 238–43.

Singer, K. *et al.* (1976). Physique, personality and mental illness in Southern Chinese women. *British Journal of Psychiatry* 129: 243–7.

Spitzer, R. and Fleiss, J. (1974). A re-analysis of the reliability of psychiatric diagnoses. *British Journal of Psychiatry* 125: 341–7.

Spitzer, R. *et al.* (1978). Research diagnostic criteria. *Archives of General Psychiatry* 35: 773–85.

Stephens, J. *et al.* (1997). Long-term follow-up of patients hospitalised for schizophrenia. *Journal of Nervous and Mental Disorders* 185: 715–21.

Striebel, K.-M. *et al.* (1999). Olfactory identification and psychosis. *Biological Psychiatry* 45: 1419–25.

Thara, R. and Eaton, W. (1996). Outcome of schizophrenia: the Madras longitudinal study. *Australian and New Zealand Journal of Psychiatry* 30: 516–22.

Torgalsboen, A. (1999a). Comorbidity in schizophrenia. *Scandinavian Journal of Psychology* 40: 147–52.

Torgalsboen, A. (1999b). Full recovery from schizophrenia. *Psychiatry Research* 88: 143–52.

Torrey, E. and Yolken, R. (1995). Could schizophrenia be a viral zoonosis transmitted from house cats? *Schizophrenia Bulletin* 21: 167–77.

van Os, J. and Verdoux, H. (2003). Diagnosis and classification of schizophrenia: categories versus dimensions, distributions versus disease. In R. Murray *et al.* (eds) *The Epidemiology of Schizophrenia.* Cambridge: Cambridge University Press.

Ward, C. *et al.* (1962). The psychiatric nomenclature. *Archives of General Psychiatry* 7: 198–205.

Whaley, A. (2001). Cultural mistrust and the clinical diagnosis of paranoid schizophrenia in African American patients. *Journal of Psychopathology and Behavioral Assessment* 23: 93–100.

World Health Organization (1973). *The International Pilot Study of Schizophrenia,* Vol. 1. Geneva: WHO.

Zigler, E. and Phillips, L. (1961). Psychiatric diagnosis: a critique. *Journal of Social and Abnormal Psychology* 63: 607–18.

Chapter 6

Biological psychiatry's lost cause

John Read

We have seen that there is no relationship between 'schizophrenia' and two of the variables – symptomatology and outcome – to which it must be shown to be related if it is a scientifically valid construct (see Chapter 5). In this chapter and the next, we consider the evidence pertaining to the third of those variables, aetiology, before discussing the fourth, treatment (Chapters 8 and 9).

Three 'facts' are repeated in literature reviews, textbooks and 'educational' pamphlets funded by drug companies to show that 'schizophrenia' is a biologically based illness:

1   'Schizophrenia' is equally frequent in all countries.
2   The brains of 'schizophrenics' are abnormal.
3   There is a genetic predisposition to 'schizophrenia' (see Chapter 7).

THE UNIFORM FREQUENCY MYTH

The first of the three 'proofs' that schizophrenia is a medical illness is that it exists in the same proportion everywhere in the world. This is supposed to demonstrate that cultural or environmental factors are irrelevant and the cause must therefore be of the kind associated with medical illnesses. In fact, many medical illnesses show huge variations between populations and locations. Diabetes is roughly 30 times more common in some parts of the world than others. Multiple sclerosis varies by around fifty-fold (Torrey 1987). As a 1987 review of prevalence studies points out, 'If schizophrenia has no such differences it would be a unique disease and that fact alone would be one of its most significant aspects' (Torrey 1987: 599).

Nevertheless, the notion survives and is still used to justify the illness model. It survives, moreover, despite the 'facts' on which it is based being untrue. Early reviews of prevalence studies in different countries found the difference between lowest and highest was ten-fold (Jablensky and Sartorius 1975). A 1987 review of over 70 studies found that the highest rate (17 per

1000 in part of Sweden) was 55 times greater than the lowest rate (0.3 per 1000 among Amish people in the USA). There was even a complete absence of schizophrenia among 3000 Kwaio adults in Melanasia. Even after removing some of the lower rates, the reviewer still concluded that a 'ten-fold range of prevalence for schizophrenia is supported by this [*sic*] data' (Torrey 1987: 605). In addition, it must be noted that 'Incidence rates of schizophrenia vary widely within the same country, between urban and rural populations and between sociocultural majority and minority populations' (van Os and McGuffin 2003: 291; see also Chapter 13).

One possible explanation for the high variability is based on the different rates of recovery around the world. A study using 'incidence' rates (the number of people who become 'schizophrenic' in a certain period) might find two countries with roughly similar rates. If one of these countries has a higher recovery rate, a study using 'prevalence' rate (the number of people with 'schizophrenia' over a given period of time) will find different rates. The study most frequently cited in support of the equal frequency notion used incidence rates and thereby bypassed the effects of different outcomes (Sartorius *et al.* 1986). Differences in 'schizophrenia' rates of 'only' two- or three-fold resulted, rather than the ten- or 55-fold differences found by prevalence studies. However, to use different recovery rates to explain away the differences in 'schizophrenia' rates throughout the world involves denying a rather important fact. The 'illness' is supposed to have a consistent outcome.

Furthermore, there is a clear pattern to these variations in outcome, with 'developing' countries having much higher recovery rates than industrialized countries (see Chapter 5). It might be tempting for biological psychiatrists to use yet another variable, treatment, to explain away the differences in prevalence and outcome. This, however, is a dangerous argument for them. It wouldn't say much for the effectiveness of the drugs or electric shocks used in 'developed' countries. But that's another story (Chapters 8–10).

There is no scientific basis to the claim that the same amounts of an illness called 'schizophrenia' can be found in all populations. A recent review of the most rigorous studies to date found a 13-fold difference between highest (Puerto Rico) and lowest (Hong Kong) lifetime prevalence rates and a 55-fold difference between highest (USA) and lowest (Canada) one-year incidence rates, confirming that there is 'real variation in the distribution of schizophrenia around the world' (Goldner *et al.* 2002: 833). The claim was a ridiculous one in the first place when used as evidence of a medical illness.

An obvious explanation for these very large differences is that 'schizophrenia' is a label used to account for a range of different types of unacceptable or distressing behaviours. This would help explain not only differences in rates of 'schizophrenia' throughout the world, but differences (conveniently ignored by adherents of the uniform frequency notion) between ethnic and socio-economic groups within the same country (see Chapter 13).

A DISEASE OF THE BRAIN?

A more sensible way to prove that 'schizophrenia' is a medical illness is to show that 'schizophrenic' brains are different from 'normal' brains. However, there are three important issues that must be ignored if one is to draw any conclusions about causation from brain research. The first is the issue of reliability. If one set of researchers is using a different definition of 'schizophrenia' to another set, then any differences discovered are meaningless. Many studies of the brains of 'schizophrenics' do not even state which definition they are using or how the diagnosis was reached.

Secondly, if 'schizophrenic' brains are different from 'normal' brains, does that mean we have found the cause of the 'symptoms'? When we are grieving the loss of someone we loved, our brains act differently from usual. Is our sadness caused by the brain's slower functioning or by our loss? Childhood trauma can cause enduring changes in the structure and functioning of the human brain (see Chapter 16). This basic flaw in the logic of those who claim to have found the cause of schizophrenia in the brain has been raised repeatedly. For example:

> Biological psychiatry looks for pathological changes, and most authors uncritically assume that such changes as they find are necessarily primary. There is no reason to believe this . . . For the brain, since mental function has a physical substrate, the initiating event may well be the subject's own mental state.
>
> (Mclaren 2000: 131)

Richard Bentall (2003) locates the origin of this faulty logic in the more fundamental flaw of dualism, 'which holds that the mind and brain are different kinds of substances, the former nonmaterial and the latter physical'. He reminds us:

> Because our brains are affected by our experiences, peculiarities in the size of its anatomical components, in neuroactivations when we perform particular tasks, or in the biochemical transactions between neurones, can often be just as readily attributed to the impact of the environment as to causative biological factors such as early brain damage, viruses or endogenous neurotoxins.
>
> (Bentall 2003: 174)

The third issue ignored in this quest for brain differences is the fact that one of the things that can change the brains of 'schizophrenics' is something they really do have in common – the treatment they receive.

Kraepelin and Bleuler, the inventors of schizophrenia, admitted that they could find no evidence of a biological cause (see Chapter 3). They handed on the 'to be discovered later' argument and left it at that. A century later, have we yet discovered the cause? The cynical answer is: 'Yes, it has being discovered approximately every four or five years ever since'. I have space to summarize a few of the major brain-based 'discoveries' in vogue today. I begin, however, with just one of the countless theories that have briefly been believed but then discarded. In the 1960s, it was discovered that the urine of 'schizophrenics' contained more DMPEA, a substance related to tannine, than 'normal' urine. The finding was replicated several times. Theories were developed to link the finding to brain functioning and, thereby, to the cause of schizophrenia. Then it was discovered to be a result of psychiatric drugs and the amount of tea and coffee drunk in mental hospitals (Rose *et al.* 1984).

Biochemistry

Dopamine is a neurotransmitter. Neurotransmitters are chemicals which are released at the synapse, the point where two nerve cells meet, transmitting an impulse from one cell to receptors in the next cell. The receptors are sensitive to specific neurotransmitters. The popular dopamine theory of schizophrenia claims that in the 'schizophrenic' brain, those groups of nerve cells which communicate using dopamine are over-active.

The theory is based on indirect evidence from the effects on the brain of two types of chemical. The first type is the 'neuroleptics', or 'major tranquillizers', the drugs used for the last 50 years to treat schizophrenia (see Chapter 9). When first used in the 1950s, little was known about their effects on the brain. It was discovered later that one of the effects was to 'block' the dopamine system. Biological psychiatry jumped to the conclusion that if these drugs cure 'schizophrenia' and they also block the dopamine system, then the cause of 'schizophrenia' must be over-activity of the dopamine system. This is as logical as saying that headaches are caused by a lack of aspirin in the body (Jackson 1986). Biological psychiatry often relies on backward circular logic.

The other indirect evidence is from researchers who claimed to be either creating schizophrenia, or making it worse, with amphetamine or L-DOPA, which increase dopamine activity. It has since been demonstrated, however, that the experiences induced by these substances are qualitatively quite different from those experienced by 'schizophrenics' (Bentall 2003).

The dopamine theory was developed without any evidence that the dopamine systems of 'schizophrenics' are over-active. Later, some postmortems on 'schizophrenics' did report signs of increased dopamine concentrations. By then, however, it had been discovered that the drugs used to treat 'schizophrenia' not only cause a blockade of the dopamine system, but also initiate an attempt to compensate for the blockade. This important point was explained by Solomon Snyder, Professor of Psychiatry and Pharmacology at Johns Hopkins University:

> Something within the neurons recognises this sudden absence of neurotransmitter molecules at their appropriate receptor site and one way or another transmits a message back to the dopamine neurons saying something like the following: 'We don't have enough dopamine. Please send us some more!' Where upon the dopamine neuron in question proceeds to fire at a more rapid rate.
>
> (Snyder 1974: 241)

So over-activity in the dopamine system is caused by the drugs that are supposedly treating the illness, which is supposed to be caused by over-activity in the dopamine system. It is essential, therefore, that studies trying to show that 'schizophrenia' is caused by an over-active dopamine system use participants who have not received neuroleptic drugs. A 1982 review pointed out that most of the 'schizophrenics' in the post-mortem studies showing increased dopamine concentrations had received neuroleptics shortly before death, and that in drug-free 'schizophrenics' dopamine concentrations were normal. It was concluded that 'these findings do not support the presence of elevated DA [dopamine] turnover in the brains of schizophrenics' (Haracz 1982: 440). A later review reported that 'no consistent differences between drug-free schizophrenics and normals have been found in terms of dopamine levels' (Jackson 1986: 129).

An alternative approach to proving the dopamine theory is to measure the concentration of a dopamine metabolite (HVA) in the spinal fluid. This is an indirect and unreliable approach but does allow the use of live subjects and thereby makes it possible to withhold neuroleptics for a period of time before examining the fluid. Again, no differences were found (Haracz 1982).

Yet another approach focuses not on concentrations of dopamine but on the dopamine receptors. Heightened sensitivity or increased numbers of dopamine receptors would support the theory of an over-active dopamine system. By 1982, one laboratory had found no differences, but four had (Haracz 1982). It had also been discovered, however, that neuroleptic drugs cause super-sensitivity in dopamine receptors. Having pointed out that the four studies in question 'included only a small number of patients who were drug-free for one month or more before death', Haracz concluded that more work is needed to determine whether the results of the four studies were 'secondary to a drug effect or to the schizophrenic disease process' (p. 446).

One of the four research teams that had found receptor abnormalities published a subsequent paper in which they pointed out that in two of their studies the increase observed in the drug-free patients was smaller than in the patients who received medication (Mackay *et al.* 1982). Their new paper found no increased receptor sensitivity in those individuals who had not received neuroleptic drugs for a month before death. They also found that sensitivity was reduced to normal by washing out any remaining neuroleptic drug from the receptors. They concluded that 'the results suggest that these increases may be entirely explained by long-term neuroleptic medication' (p. 995).

The poor reliability of the construct whose cause is being sought, the flawed logic in assuming that any differences found would mean something about aetiology, and the role of 'anti-psychotic' medication in producing the differences that have been found, all failed to deter biological psychiatry. The computerized database MEDLINE (entering 'dopamine' and 'schizophrenia') shows 205 studies from 1981 to 1990, and 481 from 1991 to 2000.

The many recent studies have sought differences in the various types of dopamine receptors (DA_1, DA_2, etc.) and have had access to sophisticated neuroimaging technology, such as positive emission tomography and single photon emission computerized tomography. At the beginning of the twenty-first century, four reviews of the research regarding the dopamine theory provide a measure of how far we have progressed after a hundred years of brain research with ever more sophisticated technology. One review acknowledges that 'few studies have provided convincing evidence of altered dopaminergic activity' (Copolov and Crook 2000: 110), and reports that 11 of the 13 studies using the new neuroimaging techniques found no significant differences in dopamine receptor density. A second review concludes: 'While postmortem and imaging studies have identified numerous alterations in brain structure and function in schizophrenia, the fundamental nature of the pathological process associated with this illness remains poorly understood' (Laruelle 2000: 372). A third concludes that 'findings on dopamine and other neurotransmitters, as well as enzymes involved in the synthesis and degradation of neurotransmitters, have been inconsistent' (Dean 2000: 561). Finally, 'In spite of decades of extensive research, the causes and exact sites of the presumed dopamine-mediated hyperactivity remain elusive' (Gainetdinov *et al.* 2001: 527). Nevertheless, the dopamine theory remains intact and very popular. Without it there would be no way to justify the use of the drugs. Without the drugs, however, there may be no differences to support the theory.

Other neurotransmitters have been investigated. Some of these more recent theories have been used to justify the introduction of a new range of 'antipsychotic' drugs – the 'atypicals' (see Chapter 9). As noted by one of the recent reviews, however, these studies have been no more productive than those involving dopamine (Dean 2000). Serotonin, for instance, is another neurotransmitter that is 'blocked' by neuroleptic medication and is therefore another suspect in the search for the cause. Several studies, however, have found no evidence of serotonin abnormalities in 'schizophrenics' (Dean 2000). Such abnormalities as have been identified are not specific to schizophrenia. Similarly, the newer biochemical theories remain unsubstantiated (Gainetdinov *et al.* 2001).

Brain anatomy

Another popular notion is that 'schizophrenics' have larger spaces within their brains than 'normals'. The enlargement of these fluid-filled gaps, or ventricles, is related to a reduction in brain tissue. A review of relevant studies (Reveley 1985) revealed that the percentage of schizophrenics who have enlarged ventricles ranges from 6 to 60, adding that one study which had used methods 'far more sophisticated than the usual' (Jernigan *et al.* 1982) found no differences between schizophrenics and controls. A recent analysis of over 90 computerized tomography studies revealed 'a substantial overlap (approximately 60 percent) between the schizophrenic population and the control population' (Copolov and Crook 2000: 109). Even if we were to accept that a certain percentage of people labelled 'schizophrenic' have enlarged ventricles, what would this prove? Because they are found in many other disorders, such as depression and alcoholism (Coplov and Crook 2000), they do not constitute a specific cause of schizophrenia.

All we really know is that somewhere between 6 and 60 per cent of people labelled 'schizophrenic' have suffered one or more of the factors that cause enlarged ventricles. The finding that when one identical twin has 'schizophrenia' and the other doesn't the one with 'schizophrenia' has larger ventricles, has raised 'the possibility that presently unidentified environmental factors result in increased ventricular volume' (Copolov and Crook 2000: 109). Early trauma is important in this regard (see Chapter 16).

One of the many factors which can cause brain damage, including ventricular enlargement, is, once again, antipsychotic medication. This possibility had been consistently avoided by all but one of the 60 studies reviewed by Reveley in 1985. The other (Lyon *et al.* 1981) had found that as the dose of neuroleptics increased, the density of brain tissue decreased.

A recent review notes that despite 'extensive efforts to discover macro- or microscopic lesions in the brain' there has been 'a failure to identify such lesions' (Dean 2000: 560). Another reviewer identifies 'eight ways in which statements that refer to schizophrenia as a brain disease misrepresent research findings' (Siebert 1999). Siebert's paper is entitled 'Brain disease hypothesis for schizophrenia disconfirmed by all evidence'.

VIRUS

Space does not permit a discussion of all the other theories that claim to demonstrate that 'schizophrenia' is a medical disease. The fact that they are so many and varied is itself informative. One theory cannot be omitted, not only because it gained considerable credibility in the 1980s but because it is so bizarre. In support of his notion that 'schizophrenia' is caused by some kind of virus, prominent British psychiatrist Timothy Crow (1984) points to findings that non-identical twins are more likely to both be 'schizophrenic' than are ordinary brothers and sisters, despite sharing genes to the same extent. Similarly, same-sexed siblings are more likely to both be 'schizophrenic' than opposite-sexed siblings. These findings represent strong support for environmental factors, since twins are more likely to be treated more similarly than non-twins and same-sex siblings more similarly than opposite-sex siblings. Crow, however, cites these findings as support for his viral 'contagion hypothesis', because 'twins may be in closer contact than siblings' and 'same-sex pairs of relatives are in closer physical proximity'. 'What matters is proximity to an individual who already has the disease' (Crow 1984: 246).

Crow cites a finding (Kasanetz 1979) that 'first episodes of psychosis occur more frequently in individuals who live in apartment blocks where there is already a (unrelated) patient with schizophrenia'. This line of research is itself quite infectious. British researchers investigated whether nurses who work with 'schizophrenics' are more likely to catch the illness (Cooper *et al.* 1987). They are not.

Crow accepts that of 'all direct investigation of the viral hypothesis, none has provided strong evidence to the presence of an infectious agent'. In keeping with biological psychiatry's commitment to the creed that if results are consistently negative keep researching anyway, Crow argues: 'That schizophrenia should be due to an infectious agent is not widely entertained, but the paucity of alternative theories requires that it be considered' (p. 244). This was at least an admission that psychiatry has failed to provide evidence to support any of the other theories of 'schizophrenia' being an illness.

REFERENCES

Bentall, R. (2003). *Explaining Madness: Human Nature and Psychosis*. London: Penguin.

Cooper, S. *et al.* (1987). Can psychiatric nurses 'catch' schizophrenia? *British Journal of Psychiatry* 151: 546–8.

Copolov, D. and Crook, J. (2000). Biological markers and schizophrenia. *Australian and New Zealand Journal of Psychiatry* 34 (suppl.): S108–12.

Crow, T. (1984). A re-evaluation of the viral hypothesis. *British Journal of Psychiatry* 145: 243–53.

Dean, B. (2000). Signal transmission, rather than reception, is the underlying neurochemical abnormality in schizophrenia. *Australian and New Zealand Journal of Psychiatry* 34: 560–9.

Gainetdinov, R. *et al.* (2001). Genetic animal models: focus on schizophrenia. *Trends in Neurosciences* 24: 527–32.

Goldner, E. *et al.* (2002). Prevalence and incidence studies of schizophrenic disorders. *Canadian Journal of Psychiatry* 47: 833–43.

Haracz, J. (1982). The dopamine hypothesis. *Schizophrenia Bulletin* 8: 438–69.

Jablensky, A. and Sartorius, N. (1975). Culture and schizophrenia. *Psychological Medicine* 5: 113–24.

Jackson, H. (1986). Is there a schizotoxin? In N. Eisenberg and D. Glasgow (eds) *Current Issues in Clinical Psychology*. Aldershot: Gower.

Jernigan, T. *et al.* (1982). Computed tomography in schizophrenic and normal volunteers. *Archives of General Psychiatry* 39: 765–70.

Kasanetz, E. (1979). Tecnica per investigare il ruolo di fattori ambientale sulla genesi della schizofrenia. *Rivista di Psicologia Analitica* 10: 193–202.

Laruelle, M. (2000). The role of endogenous sensitisation in the pathophysiology of schizophrenia. *Brain Research Reviews* 31: 371–84.

Lyon, K. *et al.* (1981). Effects of long term neuroleptic use on brain density. *Psychiatry Research* 5: 33–7.

Mackay, A. *et al.* (1982). Increased brain dopamine and dopamine receptors in schizophrenia. *Archives of General Psychiatry* 39: 991–7.

Mclaren, N. (2000). Signal transmission, schizophrenia and the limits to biological psychiatry. *Australian and New Zealand Journal of Psychiatry* 35: 130–1.

Reveley, M. (1985). CT scans in schizophrenia. *British Journal of Psychiatry* 146: 367–71.

Rose, S. *et al.* (1984). *Not In Our Genes*. London: Penguin.

Sartorius, N. *et al.* (1986). Early manifestations and first-contact incidence of schizophrenia in different cultures. *Psychological Medicine* 16: 909–28.

Siebert, A. (1999). Brain disease hypothesis for schizophrenia disconfirmed by all evidence. *Ethical Human Sciences and Services* 1: 179–89.

Snyder, S. (1974). *Madness and the Brain*. New York: McGraw-Hill.

Torrey, E. (1987). Prevalence studies in schizophrenia. *British Journal of Psychiatry* 150: 598–608.

van Os, J. and McGuffin, P. (2003). Can the social environment cause schizophrenia? *British Journal of Psychiatry* 182: 191–2.

Chapter 7

Schizophrenia and heredity
Why the emperor has no genes

Jay Joseph

In 1990, psychologist Richard Marshall asked whether the genetic basis of schizophrenia is best understood as an axiom or a hypothesis. The position of mainstream psychiatry and psychology, as seen in countless books, articles, and textbook chapters, is that it is axiomatic. This position is based on the acceptance of the results of schizophrenia family, twin and adoption studies. Concurrently, the ongoing search for 'schizophrenia genes' is contingent upon the acceptance of these studies. The purpose of this review is to show that, contrary to prevailing opinions, the available evidence provides little support for a genetic basis or predisposition for schizophrenia. The fruitless search for genes (Bassett *et al.* 2001) is best understood by the failure to critically re-examine the literature upon which it is based, rather than the difficulty of finding schizophrenia genes.

FAMILY STUDIES

Family studies locate persons affected with a particular trait or condition and determine whether their biological relatives are similarly affected more often than members of the general population or a control group. If a condition is found to cluster or 'run' in families, it is said to be familial. Many people view the terms 'familial' and 'genetic' as being synonymous. They are not. Although the familiality of schizophrenia was once seen as positive proof that schizophrenia is a genetic disorder, most investigators now realize that conditions or behaviours can run in families for reasons such as exposure to common rearing patterns, and other aspects of the physical and social environment. For this reason, psychiatric genetics has turned to twin and adoption studies

TWIN STUDIES

The logic of the twin method seems straightforward: If reared-together monozygotic (identical) twins, who share 100% of the same genes, are

Table 7.1   Results of schizophrenia twin studies published before mid-2001

Study	Country	Monozygotic twins			Same-sex dizygotic twins		
		N	C	%	N	C	%
Classical studies							
Luxenburger (1928)[a]	Germany	17	10	59	13	0	0
Rosanoff et al. (1934)	USA	41	25	61	53	7	13
Essen-Möller (1941, 1970)[b]	Sweden	7	2	29	24	2	8
Kallmann (1946)	USA	174	120	69	296	34	11
Slater (1953)	UK	41	28	68	61	11	18
Inouye (1961)	Japan	55	20	36	17	1	6
Contemporary studies							
Tienari (1963, 1975)	Finland	20	3	15	42	3	7
Gottesman and Shields (1966b)	UK	24	10	42	33	3	9
Kringlen (1967)[c]	Norway	45	12	27	69	3	4
NAS-NRC (1970/1983)[d]	USA	164	30	18	268	9	3
Fischer (1973)[e]	Denmark	25	9	36	45	8	18
Koskenvuo et al. (1984)[f]	Finland	73	8	11	225	4	2
Onstad et al. (1991)	Norway	24	8	33	28	1	4
Franzek and Beckmann (1998)[g]	Germany	9	6	67	12	2	17
Cannon et al. (1998)[h]	Finland	—	—	—	—	—	—
Pooled rates		719	291	40.4	1186	88	7.4
Classical studies		335	205	61.1	464	55	11.9
Contemporary studies		384	86	22.4	722	33	4.6

Note: Concordance rates based on the authors' narrow or 'strict' definition of schizophrenia; age-correction factors not included. Unless otherwise noted, when two dates are stated the first indicates the year results were first published and the second indicates the final report, whose figures are reported here. N = number of twin pairs studied, C = number concordant.

[a]   Based on figures found in Gottesman and Shields (1966a); hospitalized co-twins only.
[b]   Identical twin figures from Essen-Möller (1970). Fraternal twin figures were not reported in this paper. Fraternal twin concordance rate based on 1941 definite cases among co-twins, as reported in Gottesman and Shields (1966a: 28).
[c]   Based on a strict diagnosis of schizophrenia; hospitalized and registered cases.
[d]   National Academy of Sciences/National Research Council. Original report by Hoffer and Pollin (1970); final report by Kendler and Robinette (1983).
[e]   Final report of an expanded sample originally collected by Harvald and Haugue (1965).
[f]   The study of Koskenvuo et al. (1984) is rarely mentioned in textbooks or reviews.
[g]   Concordance rates based on DSM-III-R schizophrenia in a twin having the same condition.
[h]   Cannon et al. (1998) reported probandwise concordance rates of 46% (identical) and 9% (same-sex fraternal). The pairwise equivalents of these figures are not listed here because the number of pairs in each group was not reported by Cannon et al.

significantly more concordant for schizophrenia than reared-together same-sex dizygotic (fraternal) twins, who share on average only 50% of the same genes, then the genetic position is confirmed. Table 7.1 lists all schizophrenia twin studies before mid-2001.

As shown in Table 7.1, the pooled pairwise concordance rates for schizophrenia are 40.4% monozygotic and 7.4% dizygotic. Schizophrenia twin studies are often divided into the 'classical' studies published before 1962 and the more methodologically sound 'contemporary' studies published after this date (Gottesman 1991; Neale and Oltmanns 1980). We can see that the older, more methodologically suspect classical studies, using non-blind diagnoses and potentially biased resident hospital samples (e.g. Kallmann 1946; Rosanoff et al. 1934; Slater 1953), reported higher rates than the more recent studies based on registers or consecutive hospital admissions. In these more recent studies, beginning with Tienari (1963, 1975), the pooled pairwise concordance rate falls to 22.4% monozygotic and 4.6% dizygotic. Identical twin concordance is 18% or less in three of the contemporary studies, as well as in two studies with large monozygotic samples. Nevertheless, twin researchers argue that the modern studies support the genetic position on the basis of a monozygotic concordance rate four to five times higher than the same-sex dizygotic rate (Torrey 1992; Walker et al. 1991).

The equal environment assumption

There are several methodological problems with the schizophrenia twin studies. These include: (1) lack of an adequate and consistent definition of schizophrenia; (2) non-blinded diagnoses, often made by investigators strongly devoted to the genetic position; (3) diagnoses made on the basis of sketchy information; (4) inadequate or biased methods of zygosity determination (that is, whether twins are monozygotic or dizygotic); (5) unnecessary age-correction formulas; (6) non-representative sample populations; and (7) lack of adequate descriptions of methods.

Although these are important problems, there is little doubt that monozygotic twins are more concordant than dizygotic twins for schizophrenia and most psychological traits. This leads to a major problem. The twin method is based on a crucial theoretical assumption, which holds that the environments of monozygotic and dizygotic twins are about the same. However, this 'equal environment assumption' has little basis in the evidence. Monozygotic twins' more similar social and physical environments contribute to monozygotic–dizygotic concordance rate differences (Joseph 1998, 2003). Because it is widely understood that monozygotic twins are treated more similarly, encounter more similar environments, and experience greater 'identity confusion' (Jackson 1960) than dizygotic twins, there is no reason to accept that monozygotic–dizygotic comparisons measure anything more than the *environmental* differences distinguishing the two types of twins.

Rather than accepting this obvious conclusion, twin researchers subtly redefined the equal environment assumption by adding the following provision: Although monozygotic twins were acknowledged to experience much more similar environments than dizygotic twins, critics must demonstrate that monozygotic and dizygotic twins' environments differ 'in respects which can be shown to be of etiological significance for schizophrenia' (Gottesman and Shields 1972: 25). This new definition, generally referred to as the 'trait-relevant equal environment assumption', has been promoted by many contemporary twin researchers. However, what these investigators fail to understand is that *the trait-relevant equal environment assumption has transformed the twin method into nothing more that a special type of family study.* This is because the comparison groups in both family studies and the twin method (in family studies, the general population or a control group; in the twin method, dizygotic twins) are acknowledged to experience different environments than the experimental groups (in family studies, the families of people diagnosed with schizophrenia; in the twin method, monozygotic twins). Why, then, do twin researchers retain the trait-relevant requirement for the twin method but *not* for family studies? Virtually every argument made by twin researchers in defence of drawing genetic inferences from monozygotic–dizygotic comparisons could also be made in defence of drawing genetic inferences from family studies. Yet, strangely, these investigators arbitrarily uphold the validity of the equal environment assumption and the twin method in the same breath as they admit that family studies are confounded by environmental factors.

Additional evidence against the equal environment assumption in the schizophrenia twin studies can be found elsewhere (see Jackson 1960; Joseph 1998, 2001b, 2003; Pam *et al.* 1996; Rose *et al.* 1984). The crucial point is that genetic inferences drawn from monozygotic–dizygotic comparisons are dependent upon an unsupported and counterintuitive theoretical assumption. Therefore, the twin method is confounded by environmental factors and cannot tell us anything about possible genetic influences on schizophrenia.

Other twin studies

Two other types of twin studies should be mentioned. The first type (Fischer 1971, 1973; Gottesman and Bertelsen 1989; Kringlen and Cramer 1989) studied rates of schizophrenia among the offspring of *discordant* monozygotic twins. (The genetic position predicts that the rate of schizophrenia should be the same among the offspring of monozygotic twins diagnosed with schizophrenia, as among the offspring of their 'well' monozygotic co-twins.) However, these studies were seriously flawed, and no valid conclusions about the role of genetic factors can be drawn from them (Joseph 2003; Torrey 1990).

The second method consists of single-case reports of concordant monozygotic twins whom the researchers regard as having been reared apart (in many cases, this is a very questionable claim; Joseph 2001c, 2002, 2003). Because the number of such pairs is small and because of the inherent bias in these types of reports, contemporary twin researchers do not place much value in them. As Gottesman (1982) concluded, 'After a quarter century of experience with twins reared together and twins reared apart, it is my conviction that twins reared apart are a wonderful source of hypothesis generation, but not a useful source for hypothesis testing' (p. 351).

ADOPTION STUDIES

Adoption studies have played a crucial role in establishing schizophrenia as a genetic disorder. Moreover, the early studies performed in Oregon and Denmark helped pave the way for the acceptance of an important role for genetic factors in shaping human psychological and behavioural differences in general. For Gottesman and Shields (1976), the early adoption studies of schizophrenia were 'the straw that broke the environmentalist's back' (p. 364).

There have been six major schizophrenia adoption studies. In the first, Heston (1966) compared the rate of schizophrenia among 47 adopted-away offspring of women diagnosed with schizophrenia who were confined to Oregon state mental hospitals, with a control group of 50 adoptees of non-diagnosed mothers. In the second, Rosenthal and colleagues (1968, 1971) studied the adopted-away offspring of parents diagnosed with schizo-phrenia, 'schizophrenia spectrum disorders' or manic depression. In the third, and using a different design, Kety and colleagues (1968) began with the records of adoptees from the greater Copenhagen area, identified those diagnosed with a schizophrenia spectrum disorder, and recorded diagnoses among their adoptive and biological relatives. In a follow-up (Kety et al. 1975), the investigators interviewed and re-diagnosed many of the 1968 relatives. The study was then extended to the rest of Denmark and the final results were published in 1994 (Kety et al. 1994).

The fourth major schizophrenia adoption study was the Danish–American 'cross-fostering' study of Wender and colleagues (1974). They studied the adopted-away children of non-schizophrenic biological parents, who were raised by an adoptive parent eventually diagnosed with schizo-phrenia. According to the investigators, the purpose of the study was to 'explore the hypothesis that rearing by or with schizophrenic parents will produce schizophrenic psychopathology among persons who carry a normal genetic load' (Wender et al. 1974: 122). This 'crossfostered' group was compared with the adopted-away children of normal biological parents (who were reared by normal adoptive parents), and with a group of adopted-away offspring of schizophrenic biological parents reared by normal adoptive parents.

The final study was performed by Tienari and colleagues (1987, 2000) in Finland. In contrast to the earlier investigations, Tienari and colleagues studied adoptees' family environments as well their genetic background. The Finnish study is by far the most methodologically sound and comprehensive schizophrenia adoption study.

The following results are taken from a 2000 publication by Tienari and colleagues. Of the 164 index adoptees, whose biological mothers were diagnosed with DSM-III-R schizophrenia or paranoid psychosis, 11 (6.7%) received a DSM-III-R schizophrenia diagnosis, whereas there were 4 (2.0%) such diagnoses among the 197 control adoptees. Tienari and colleagues created a 'narrow spectrum' of supposedly related disorders, which included 'schizoaffective disorder', 'schizophreniform disorder' and 'schizotypal personality disorder'. They also made diagnoses for a 'broad spectrum', which included the above diagnoses plus 'paranoid personality disorder', 'schizoid personality disorder', 'delusional disorder', 'bipolar psychosis' and 'depressive psychosis'. The index 'narrow' and 'broad' spectrum rates were statistically significant versus the control group rates.

The investigators concluded, 'The genetic liability to "typical" DSM-III-R schizophrenia is decisively confirmed. Additionally, the liability also extends to a broad spectrum of other psychotic and non-psychotic disorders' (Tienari *et al.* 2000: 433). If we limit the comparison to mothers and offspring diagnosed with DSM-III-R schizophrenia, however, the study produces different results. According to unpublished results graciously provided by Tienari, DSM-III-R schizophrenia was diagnosed in 7 of 137 adoptees (5.1%) whose biological mothers were also diagnosed with DSM-III-R schizophrenia, compared with 3 of 192 (1.6%) control DSM-III-R schizophrenia diagnoses (P. Tienari, personal communication). Therefore, the index–control DSM-III-R schizophrenia difference is not statistically significant (7/137 compared with 3/192, $p = 0.065$, Fisher's exact test, one-tailed). In another paper emanating from this study, Wahlberg and associates (2000) compared the scores of a subsample of index and control adoptees on the Thought Disorder Index (TDI). The results showed no significant differences between index and control adoptee TDI scores, and that both groups' scores were about the same as those of normal individuals. On the basis of other comparisons, however, Wahlberg and colleagues concluded that genetic factors influence some components of thought disorder.

Tienari and associates concluded that both genes *and* adoptive family rearing environment are 'predictor variables' for schizophrenia. The investigators found that index adoptees who grew up in seriously disturbed adoptive families are diagnosed with schizophrenia more often than control adoptees reared in seriously disturbed families. Thus,

the results were consistent with the hypothesis that healthy rearing families have possibly protected the vulnerable children, whereas in disturbed rearing families the vulnerable children have been more sensitive to dysfunctional rearing.

(Tienari *et al.* 1994: 23)

The correlation between adoptive family disturbance and index adoptee schizophrenia cases was so great that, at least through 1987, Tienari could report that 'all adoptees who had been diagnosed either as schizophrenic or paranoid had been reared in seriously disturbed adoptive families' (Tienari *et al.* 1987: 482).

Methodological problems

In all schizophrenia adoption studies, the investigators concluded that they found evidence to support important genetic influences on schizophrenia, while Tienari and colleagues added a finding that disturbed family environments also contributed to the condition. However, these studies have been the subject of several critical analyses questioning the investigators' methods and conclusions (Benjamin 1976; Boyle 1990; Breggin 1991; Cassou *et al.* 1980; Cohen and Cohen 1986; Gottesman and Shields 1976; Joseph 1999a, b, 2000a, 2001a, 2003; Rose *et al.* 1984; Lidz 1976; Lidz and Blatt 1983; Lidz *et al.* 1981; Pam 1995). These authors' criticisms of the schizophrenia adoption studies include the following:

- Most of these studies would not have found statistically significant differences without greatly expanding the definition of schizophrenia to include non-psychotic 'schizophrenia spectrum disorders'. The 1968 study of Kety *et al.* found *no* cases of chronic schizophrenia among the 65 identified first-degree biological relatives of adoptees diagnosed with a spectrum disorder. Rosenthal *et al.* (1971) found that only one of the 76 adopted-away biological offspring of parents diagnosed with a spectrum disorder had received a hospital diagnosis of schizophrenia.
- There was a failure to adequately define schizophrenia and schizophrenia spectrum disorders.
- In the 1971 study of Rosenthal *et al.*, manic depression was included in the schizophrenia spectrum in spite of the investigators' insistence elsewhere that this condition is genetically unrelated to schizophrenia (see Kety *et al.* 1976; Rosenthal 1971).
- In the interview studies of Kety *et al.*, there were inconsistencies in the way that dead or unavailable relatives were counted and diagnosed.
- There was a failure to provide case history information on adoptees or relatives and, apart from Tienari, to study important environmental variables.
- In the studies of Kety *et al.*, the 'procedure of counting up all the possible relatives of each index case and pooling them as if they were

independent samples . . . would allow some families to disproportionately affect the results' (Benjamin 1976: 1130). Thus, the investigators'
decision to emphasize the spectrum rate among individual *relatives*, as
opposed to individual *families*, violated the assumption of independent
observations underlying their statistical comparisons.

- First- and second-degree relatives were counted with equal weighting in
  the studies of Kety *et al.*
- In the Denmark and Oregon studies, the genetic bias of the investigators
  influenced the way that relatives were counted, the way schizophrenia
  was defined, the types of comparisons made and the conclusions that
  were reached.
- Many late-separated adoptees were included in the samples.
- In the studies of Kety *et al.*, many of the 'interviews' never took place
  and were simply fabricated by the investigators (Kendler and
  Gruenberg 1984; Rose *et al.* 1984). In the raw data they were called
  'pseudo-interviews' by Kety *et al.*, but no mention of them appeared in
  any of the Danish–American investigators' publications. Of the
  interviews that were conducted, a five-minute doorstep conversation
  was deemed sufficient to diagnose someone with schizophrenia (Paikin
  et al. 1974).
- Problems with Wender and colleagues' (1974) cross-fostering study
  include: (1) use of global mental health ratings in place of diagnosing
  schizophrenia; (2) *post-hoc* comparisons to support the genetic position;
  (3) failure to find statistically significant differences between important
  comparison groups; (4) failure to consider alternative explanations of
  results; and (5) the mean age of the cross-fostered adoptees at the time
  their adoptive parents were diagnosed with a spectrum disorder was 12
  years (based on a subsample reported by Van Dyke *et al.* 1975). By the
  1980s, Wender himself admitted that, in his 1974 study, 'the question of
  what would happen if children born of normal parents were placed in
  the homes of typical schizophrenics cannot be answered' (Wender and
  Klein 1981: 175).
- Failure to pay serious attention to the likelihood that the selective
  placement of adoptees biased the results of the studies.

Table 7.2 summarizes the presence or absence of important methodological
problems in each study.

Selective placement: the problem that won't go away

Like the twin method, adoption studies have their own crucial theoretical
assumptions. The most crucial is the assumed absence of selective placement, meaning that both index and control adoptees had equal chances
of being placed into the range of available adoptive homes. In the

Table 7.2 Important methodological problems of the schizophrenia adoption studies

Study	Country	Significant chronic schizophrenia first-degree bio relative rate vs controls?[a]	Significant chronic schizophrenia first-degree bio family rate vs controls?[b]	Used late separated adoptees?	Probable selective placement bias?	Blind diagnoses?[c]	Adequate definition of schizophrenia?	Used a schizophrenia spectrum?	Studied adoptive family-rearing environments?	Adequate case history information provided?	Used fabricated interviews to make diagnoses?	Counted first- and second-degree relatives equally?
Heston (1966)	USA (Oregon)	Yes	N/A	No	Yes	No[c]	No	No	No	No	No	N/A
Kety et al. (1968)	Denmark	No	No	N/A	Yes	Yes	No	Yes	No	No	N/A	Yes
Kety et al. (1975)	Denmark	No	No	N/A	Yes	Yes	No	Yes	No	No	Yes[e]	Yes
Kety et al. (1994)	Denmark	Yes	No	N/A	Yes	Yes	No	Yes	No	No	?	Yes
Rosenthal et al. (1968, 1971)	Denmark	No	N/A	Yes	Yes	Yes	No	Yes	No	No	No	N/A
Wender et al. (1974)	Denmark	No	N/A	Yes	Yes	Yes	No	Yes	No	No	No	N/A
Tienari et al. (1987, 2000)	Finland	No	N/A	Yes	Yes	Yes	Yes[d]	Yes	Yes	No	No	N/A

a Using the traditional one-tailed 0.05 level of statistical significance utilized by all schizophrenia adoption researchers. Based on a comparison between: (1) the first-degree biological relatives of chronic schizophrenia index adoptees vs the first-degree biological relatives of control adoptees (Kety); (2) the chronic schizophrenia rate among the adopted-away biological offspring of people diagnosed with chronic schizophrenia vs the biological offspring of controls (Heston, Rosenthal, Tienari); or (3) the chronic schizophrenia rate of crossfostered adoptees vs controls (Wender).

b Based on a comparison between the biological families of index adoptees diagnosed with chronic schizophrenia, with at least one first-degree biological relative diagnosed with chronic schizophrenia vs the biological families of controls with at least one first-degree biological relative diagnosed with chronic schizophrenia.

c Although two of the three raters made diagnoses while unaware of the adoptees' group status, the third rater, Heston, was not blind to their status.

d Although the validity of the DSM-III-R criteria (used by Tienari) is questionable, this is the only study to use clear and accepted diagnostic guidelines.

e For documentation of Kety and colleagues' use of fabricated 'pseudo-interviews', see Rose et al. (1984: 224) and Kendler and Gruenberg (1984: 556). It is not clear whether Kety et al. used pseudo-interviews in the 1994 study.

schizophrenia adoption studies, the likelihood that the adoptees' biological background influenced adoption placements is a major potentially invalidating factor.

The adoptees under study were placed in the early-to-middle part of the twentieth century in Denmark, the United States (Oregon) and Finland. However, all three regions had laws which permitted the compulsory eugenic sterilization of people diagnosed with schizophrenia and other 'mental disorders'.

Denmark

In 1929, Denmark became the first European nation to pass a eugenics-inspired sterilization law, and a more comprehensive statute was passed in 1935 (Hansen 1996). These laws were in force until well after the last studied Danish adoptees were placed (placements were made between 1924 and 1947). An investigator with intimate knowledge of the Danish adoption process wrote, 'Every weekend (at least in the 1930s), Danish people who wished to adopt would visit the orphanages and pick children' (Mednick 1996: 134). There were many more available children than there were available adoptive parents (Mednick et al. 1987). The Danish adoption agencies clearly stated that a potential adoptee's genetic family background was checked to determine suitability (or desirability) for adoption (Mednick and Hutchings 1977). One can conclude that the most qualified potential adoptive parents, who were usually informed of 'deviance' in the adoptee's family background (Mednick and Hutchings 1977), would not have selected children with a biological family history of mental disorders.

Oregon

Similar conditions existed in Oregon (Joseph 1999b, 2003), where the adoptees under study were placed between 1915 and 1945. Although unknown or unmentioned by Heston and most subsequent reviewers, in 1917 Oregon passed a law creating a State Board of Eugenics, whose duty was to authorize the compulsory sterilization of 'all feeble-minded, insane, epileptic, habitual criminals, moral degenerates and sexual perverts', because they might produce 'inferior' offspring (Olson 1920: 1487).

An additional law passed in 1919 stipulated that the mere fact that a person had been admitted to a mental hospital constituted 'prima facie evidence that procreation by any such person would produce children with an inherited tendency to feeble-mindedness, insanity, epilepsy, criminality or degeneracy' (Olson 1920: 3176). Given that all of Heston's index adoptees were born to women hospitalized with schizophrenia, it is extremely unlikely that these children were placed into the same types of adoptive homes as the 'untainted' control adoptees (and many were placed in foundling homes for several months or years). As twin researcher Einar Kringlen asked in relation to Heston's study, 'Because the adoptive parents evidently received information about the child's biological parents, one might wonder who would adopt such a child' (Kringlen 1987: 132–3).

Finland

Finland also had a long history of eugenics-inspired legislation aimed at curbing the reproduction of 'hereditarily tainted' people. In 1935, the Finnish Parliament passed the Sterilization Act, which allowed the compulsory sterilization and castration of 'idiots,' 'imbeciles' and the 'insane', which included people diagnosed with schizophrenia and manic-depression (Hemminki et al. 1997; Hietala 1996).

In 1950, Finland passed the Castration Act, which permitted the compulsory castration of criminals, the mentally retarded and the 'permanently mentally ill'. It was not until 1970 that compulsory sterilization was legally abolished in Finland (Hietala 1996).

Because they began with diagnosed adoptees (as opposed to diagnosed biological parents), the studies of Kety et al. might appear less vulnerable to selective placement bias. However, in 8 of 33 index adoptive (rearing) families, a parent had been admitted to a Danish psychiatric facility, which was true for none of the 34 control adoptive families (Rose et al. 1984). This finding suggests that index adoptees were placed into more psychologically harmful adoptive homes than the control adoptees. Thus, the higher rate of spectrum diagnoses among index than control biological relatives might reflect little more than the agencies' placement of children with 'tainted' biological relatives into more psychologically harmful adoptive homes.

Thus, the crucial assumption that selective placement (on the basis of an adoptee's perceived genetic heritage) did not occur in the Danish, Finnish and Oregon adoption processes cannot be sustained. Like family and twin studies, the investigators were unable to control for environmental factors confounding the results of their studies. When we consider these studies' other serious methodological problems, there is little reason to accept their authors' conclusions about the role of genetics in schizophrenia.

THE FUTILE SEARCH FOR SCHIZOPHRENIA GENES

The search for 'schizophrenia genes' has been underway for many years. The most common methods in molecular genetic research are linkage and association studies. In a linkage study, investigators look for genetic markers linked with the putative disease gene among consanguineous family members. Linkage studies are designed to identify areas of the chromosome where relevant genes might be located, but they are unable to identify actual genes. Association studies compare the frequency of genetic markers among unrelated affected individuals and a control group.

The past few years have seen the publication of several studies claiming to have found a marker for a schizophrenia gene. Invariably, these studies fail attempts at replication. For example, Sherrington and colleagues' claim to have identified a marker in their 1988 *Nature* publication was accompanied by an article in the same issue by Kennedy *et al.*, who failed to replicate the findings. Nevertheless, it is widely believed that genes or genetic markers for schizophrenia and other psychiatric conditions have been found, when it is simply not the case.

In 1999, Williams and colleagues published a genome-wide schizophrenia linkage study that looked at 196 sibling pairs diagnosed with DSM-IV schizophrenia. While the investigators found some evidence 'suggestive' of linkage, 'none approached the genome-wide significance of 0.05'. Williams *et al.* concluded, 'Our results suggest that common genes of major effect . . . are unlikely to exist for schizophrenia' (p. 1729). In 2001, a study was published by Meyer and colleagues, who claimed to have found a significant association between a marker and catatonic schizophrenia. However, it is unlikely that these results will be replicated.

To date, molecular genetic studies have failed to find genes for schizophrenia. Most leaders of the field now believe that many genes are involved (the polygenic theory), and have abandoned the single-gene approach (Moldin and Gottesman 1997; Portin and Alanen 1997). In 2000, psychiatric geneticists Tsuang and Faraone wrote, 'We can now conclusively reject the idea that there is one gene of major effect that causes schizophrenia'. They recommended that future researchers should design studies 'to detect the many genes of small effect that each increase susceptibility to the disorder' (p. 1).

Although the failure to find schizophrenia genes does not prove that such genes do not exist, the belief that twin and adoption studies have already established the genetic basis of schizophrenia is erroneous. It is ironic that, instead of confirming the results of schizophrenia twin and adoption studies, the failure to find schizophrenia genes may well lead researchers to take a second look at these greatly flawed and environmentally confounded twin and adoption studies. Schizophrenia genetic researcher Lynn DeLisi has acknowledged that 'psychiatric genetics appears to be at a crossroads or crisis', as investigators continue to look for the 'elusive gene or genes' for schizophrenia (DeLisi 2000: 190). The 'crisis' facing psychiatric genetics is that investigators are looking for genes that probably do not exist.

Instead, psychiatric geneticists should undertake their own critical reanalysis of the original twin and adoption studies, which inspired the search for genes in the first place. In doing so, they will discover the reason that their search has turned up nothing. But suppose that they do eventually find something. One could still argue that, like phenylketonuria (PKU) and farsightedness, society's emphasis should be placed on environmental interventions. And researchers on all sides of the issue agree that environmental triggers are necessary to be diagnosed with schizophrenia.

CONCLUSION

That the genetic basis of schizophrenia is a virtual proven fact in psychiatry speaks volumes about the discipline's failure to critically analyse the methods and assumptions of its own research. In countless textbooks in psychiatry, psychology and related fields, we find the same uncritical acceptance of the conclusions of twin and adoption researchers. Few textbooks present an accurate presentation of the evidence supporting the genetic position, and only a tiny handful attempt any kind of critical analysis (Joseph 2000b; Leo and Joseph 2002).

Moreover, genetic theories are very useful to the social and political elites' desire to locate the causes of psychological distress within people's bodies and minds, as opposed to their social environments. The widespread uncritical acceptance of the conclusions of schizophrenia twin and adoption researchers is an appalling development in the history of scientific research. It can be understood much more by psychiatry's interest in maintaining itself as a viable profession than on the basis of a careful review of the methods, assumptions and conclusions of the original studies.

REFERENCES

Bassett, A. *et al.* (2001). Genetic insights into the neurodevelopmental hypothesis of schizophrenia. *Schizophrenia Bulletin* 27: 417–30.

Benjamin, L. (1976). A reconsideration of the Kety and associates study of genetic factors in the transmission of schizophrenia. *American Journal of Psychiatry* 133: 1129–33.

Boyle, M. (1990). *Schizophrenia: A Scientific Delusion?* New York: Routledge.

Breggin, P. (1991). *Toxic Psychiatry.* New York: St Martin's Press.

Cannon, T. *et al.* (1998). The genetic epidemiology of schizophrenia in a Finnish twin cohort. *Archives of General Psychiatry* 55: 67–74.

Cassou, B. *et al.* (1980). Génétique et schizophrénie: réévaluation d'un consensus. *Psychiatrie de l'Enfant* 23: 87–201.

Cohen, D. and Cohen, H. (1986). Biological theories, drug treatments, and schizophrenia: a critical assessment. *Journal of Mind and Behaviour* 7: 11–36.

DeLisi, L. (2000). Critical overview of current approaches to genetic mechanisms in schizophrenia research. *Brain Research Review* 31: 187–92.

Essen-Möller, E. (1941). Psychiatrische Untersuchungen an einer Serie von Zwillingen. *Acta Psychiatrica et Neurologica* (suppl. 23).

Essen-Möller, E. (1970). Twenty-one psychiatric cases and their MZ cotwins. *Acta Geneticae Medicae et Gemellologiae* 19: 315–17.

Fischer, M. (1971). Psychoses in the offspring of schizophrenic monozygotic twins and their normal co-twins. *British Journal of Psychiatry* 118: 43–51.

Fischer, M. (1973). *Genetic and Environmental Factors in Schizophrenia.* Copenhagen: Munksgaard.

Franzek, E. and Beckmann, H. (1998). Different genetic background of schizophrenia spectrum diagnoses. *American Journal of Psychiatry* 155: 76–83.

Gottesman, I. (1982). Identical twins reared apart: a reanalysis [book review]. *American Journal of Psychology* 95: 350–2.

Gottesman, I. (1991). *Schizophrenia Genesis.* New York: W.H. Freeman.

Gottesman, I. and Bertelsen, A. (1989). Confirming unexpressed genotypes for schizophrenia. *Archives of General Psychiatry* 46: 867–72.

Gottesman, I. and Shields, J. (1966a). Contributions of twin studies to perspectives on schizophrenia. In B. Maher (ed.) *Progress in Experimental Personality Research*, Vol. 3. New York: Academic Press.

Gottesman, I. and Shields, J. (1966b). Schizophrenia in twins. *British Journal of Psychiatry* 112: 809–18.

Gottesman, I. and Shields, J. (1972). *Schizophrenia and Genetics.* New York: Academic Press.

Gottesman, I. and Shields, J. (1976). A critical review of recent adoption, twin, and family studies of schizophrenia. *Schizophrenia Bulletin* 2: 360–401.

Hansen, B. (1996). Something rotten in the state of Denmark. In G. Broberg and N. Roll-Hansen (eds) *Eugenics and the Welfare State: Sterilization Policy in Denmark, Sweden, Norway, and Finland.* East Lansing, MI: Michigan State University.

Harvald, B. and Haugue, M. (1965). Hereditary factors elucidated by twin studies. In J. Neel *et al.* (eds) *Genetics and the Epidemiology of Chronic Diseases.* Publication #1163. Washington, DC: Public Health Service.

Hemminki, E. *et al.* (1997). Sterilization in Finland. *Social Science and Medicine* 45: 1875–84.

Heston, L. (1966). Psychiatric disorders in foster home reared children of schizophrenic mothers. *British Journal of Psychiatry* 112: 819–25.

Hietala, M. (1996) From race hygiene to sterilization: the eugenics movement in Finland. In G. Broberg and N. Roll-Hansen (eds) *Eugenics and the Welfare State. Sterilization Policy in Denmark, Sweden, Norway and Finland.* East Lansing, MI: Michigan State University.

Hoffer, A. and Pollin, W. (1970). Schizophrenia in the NAS-NRC panel of 15,909 veteran twin pairs. *Archives of General Psychiatry* 23: 469–77.

Inouye, E. (1961). Similarity and dissimilarity of schizophrenia in twins. In *Proceedings of the Third World Congress of Psychiatry*, Vol. 1. Toronto: University of Toronto Press.

Jackson, D. (1960). A critique of the literature on the genetics of schizophrenia. In D. Jackson (ed.) *The Etiology of Schizophrenia.* New York: Basic Books.

Joseph, J. (1998). The equal environment assumption of the classical twin method: a critical analysis. *Journal of Mind and Behaviour* 19: 325–58.

Joseph, J. (1999a). A critique of the Finnish Adoptive Family Study of Schizophrenia. *Journal of Mind and Behaviour* 20: 133–54.

Joseph, J. (1999b). The genetic theory of schizophrenia: a critical overview. *Ethical Human Sciences and Services* 1: 119–45.

Joseph, J. (2000a). A critique of the spectrum concept as used in the Danish–American schizophrenia adoption studies. *Ethical Human Sciences and Services* 2: 135–60.

Joseph, J. (2000b). Inaccuracy and bias in textbooks reporting psychiatric research: the case of the schizophrenia adoption studies. *Politics and the Life Sciences* 19: 89–99.

Joseph, J. (2001a). The Danish–American Adoptees' Family studies of Kety and associates: do they provide evidence in support of the genetic basis of schizophrenia? *Genetic, Social and General Psychology Monographs* 127: 241–78.

Joseph, J. (2001b). Don Jackson's 'A critique of the literature on the genetics of schizophrenia' – a reappraisal after 40 years. *Genetic, Social and General Psychology Monographs* 127: 27–57.

Joseph, J. (2001c). Separated twins and the genetics of personality differences: a critique. *American Journal of Psychology* 114: 1–30.

Joseph, J. (2002). Twin studies in psychiatry and psychology: science or pseudoscience? *Psychiatric Quarterly* 73: 71–82.

Joseph, J. (2003). *The Gene Illusion: Genetic Research in Psychiatry and Psychology Under the Microscope.* Ross-on-Wye: PCCS Books.

Kallmann, F. (1946). The genetic theory of schizophrenia. *American Journal of Psychiatry*, 103: 309–22.

Kendler, K. and Gruenberg, A. (1984). An independent analysis of the Danish adoption study of schizophrenia. *Archives of General Psychiatry* 41: 555–64.

Kendler, K. and Robinette, C. (1983). Schizophrenia in the National Academy of Sciences, National Research Council Twin Registry. *American Journal of Psychiatry* 140: 1551–63.

Kennedy, J. *et al.* (1988). Evidence against linkage of schizophrenia to markers on chromosome 5 in a northern Swedish pedigree. *Nature* 336: 167–70.

Kety, S. *et al.* (1968). The types and prevalence of mental illness in the biological and adoptive families of adopted schizophrenics. In D. Rosenthal and S. Kety (eds) *The Transmission of Schizophrenia.* New York: Pergamon.

Kety, S. *et al.* (1975). Mental illness in the biological and adoptive families of adopted individuals who have become schizophrenic. In R. Fieve *et al.* (eds) *Genetic Research in Psychiatry.* Baltimore, MD: Johns Hopkins University Press.

Kety, S. *et al.* (1976). Studies based on a total sample of adopted individuals and their relatives. *Schizophrenia Bulletin* 2: 413–27.

Kety, S. *et al.* (1994). Mental illness in the biological and adoptive relatives of schizophrenic adoptees: replication of the Copenhagen study to the rest of Denmark. *Archives of General Psychiatry* 51: 442–55.

Koskenvuo, M. *et al.* (1984). Psychiatric hospitalization in twins. *Acta Geneticae Medicae Gemellologiae* 33: 321–32.

Kringlen, E. (1967). *Heredity and Environment in the Functional Psychoses.* Oslo: Universitetsforlaget.

Kringlen, E. (1987). Contributions of genetic studies on schizophrenia. In H. Häfner and W. Gattaz (eds) *Search for the Causes of Schizophrenia.* New York: Springer.

Kringlen, E. and Cramer, G. (1989). Offspring of monozygotic twins discordant for schizophrenia. *Archives of General Psychiatry* 46: 873–7.

Leo, J. and Joseph, J. (2002). Schizophrenia: medical students are taught it's all in the genes, but are they hearing the whole story? *Ethical Human Sciences and Services* 4: 17–30.

Lidz, T. (1976). Commentary on a critical review of recent adoption, twin, and family studies of schizophrenia. *Schizophrenia Bulletin* 2: 402–12.

Lidz, T. and Blatt, S. (1983). Critique of the Danish–American studies of the biological and adoptive relatives of adoptees who became schizophrenic. *American Journal of Psychiatry* 140: 426–35.

Lidz, T. *et al.* (1981). Critique of the Danish–American studies of the adopted-away offspring of schizophrenic parents. *American Journal of Psychiatry* 138: 1063–8.

Luxenburger, H. (1928). Vorläufiger Bericht über psychiatrische Serienuntersuchungen an Zwillingen. *Zeitschrift für die Gesamte Neurologie und Psychiatrie* 116: 297–347.

Marshall, R. (1990). The genetics of schizophrenia: axiom or hypothesis? In R. Bentall (ed.) *Reconstructing Schizophrenia*. London: Routledge.

Mednick, S. (1996). General discussion III. In G. Bock and J. Goode (eds) *Genetics of Criminal and Antisocial Behavior*. New York: Wiley.

Mednick, S. and Hutchings, B. (1977). Some considerations in the interpretation of the Danish adoption studies in relation to asocial behavior. In S. Mednick and K. Christiansen (eds) *Biosocial Bases of Criminal Behavior*. New York: Gardner.

Mednick, S. *et al.* (1987). Genetic factors in the etiology of criminal behavior. In S. Mednick *et al.* (eds) *The Causes of Crime*. Cambridge: Cambridge University Press.

Meyer, J. *et al.* (2001). A missense mutation in a novel gene encoding a putative cation channel is associated with catatonic schizophrenia in a large pedigree. *Molecular Psychiatry* 6: 302–6.

Moldin, S. and Gottesman, I. (1997). At issue: genes, experience, and chance in schizophrenia – positioning for the 21st century. *Schizophrenia Bulletin* 23: 547–61.

Neale, J. and Oltmanns, T. (1980). *Schizophrenia*. New York: Wiley.

Olson, C. (ed.) (1920). *Oregon Laws*, Vol. 2. San Francisco, CA: Bancroft-Whitney.

Onstad, S. *et al.* (1991). Twin concordance for DSM-III-R schizophrenia. *Acta Psychiatrica Scandinavica* 83: 395–401.

Paikin, H. *et al.* (1974). Characteristics of people who refused to participate in a social and psychopathological study. In S. Mednick *et al.* (eds) *Genetics, Environment and Psychopathology*. New York: Elsevier.

Pam, A. (1995). Biological psychiatry: science or pseudoscience? In C. Ross and A. Pam (eds) *Pseudoscience in Biological Psychiatry: Blaming the Body*. New York: Wiley.

Pam, A. *et al.* (1996). The 'equal environment assumption' in MZ–DZ comparisons. *Acta Geneticae Medicae et Gemellologiae* 45: 349–60.

Portin, P. and Alanen, Y. (1997). A critical review of genetic studies of schizophrenia. *Acta Psychiatrica Scandinavica* 95: 73–80.

Rosanoff, A. *et al.* (1934). The etiology of so-called schizophrenic psychoses. *American Journal of Psychiatry* 91: 247–86.

Rose, S., Lewontin, R. and Kamin, L. (1984). *Not in Our Genes*. New York: Pantheon.

Rosenthal, D. (1971). *Genetics of Psychopathology*. New York: McGraw-Hill.

Rosenthal, D. *et al.* (1968). Schizophrenics' offspring reared in adoptive homes. In D. Rosenthal and S. Kety (eds) *The Transmission of Schizophrenia.* New York: Pergamon Press.

Rosenthal, D. (1971). The adopted-away offspring of schizophrenics. *American Journal of Psychiatry* 128: 307–11.

Sherrington, R. *et al.* (1988). Localization of a susceptibility locus for schizophrenia on chromosome 5. *Nature* 336: 164–7.

Slater, E. (1953). *Psychotic and Neurotic Illnesses in Twins.* Medical Research Council Special Report Series No. 278. London: HMSO.

Tienari, P. (1963). *Psychiatric Illnesses in Identical Twins.* Copenhagen: Munksgaard.

Tienari, P. (1975). Schizophrenia in Finnish male twins. *British Journal of Psychiatry* (special publication No. 10): 29–35.

Tienari, P. *et al.* (1987). Genetic and psychosocial factors in schizophrenia: the Finnish adoptive family study. *Schizophrenia Bulletin* 13: 477–84.

Tienari, P. (1994). The Finnish adoptive family study of schizophrenia. *British Journal of Psychiatry* 164 (suppl. 23): 20–6.

Tienari, P. (2000). Finish Adoptive Family Study: sample selection and adoptee DSM-III-R diagnoses. *Acta Psychiatrica Scandinavica* 101: 433–43.

Torrey, E. (1990). Offspring of twins with schizophrenia. *Archives of General Psychiatry* 47: 976–7.

Torrey, E. (1992). Are we overestimating the genetic contribution to schizophrenia? *Schizophrenia Bulletin* 18: 159–70.

Tsuang, M. and Faraone, S. (2000). The frustrating search for schizophrenia genes. *American Journal of Medical Genetics* 97: 1–3.

Van Dyke, J. *et al.* (1975). Schizophrenia: effects of inheritance and rearing on reaction time. *Canadian Journal of Behavioural Science* 7: 223–36.

Wahlberg, K. *et al.* (2000). Thought Disorder Index of Finnish adoptees and communication deviance of their adoptive parents. *Psychological Medicine* 30: 127–36.

Walker, E. *et al.* (1991). Twin studies of psychopathology: why do concordance rates vary? *Schizophrenia Research* 5: 211–21.

Wender, P. and Klein, D. (1981). *Mind, Mood, and Medicine.* New York: Farrar, Straus, & Giroux.

Wender, P. *et al.* (1974). Crossfostering: a research strategy for clarifying the role of genetic and experiential factors in the etiology of schizophrenia. *Archives of General Psychiatry* 30: 121–8.

Williams, N. *et al.* (1999). A two-stage genome scan for schizophrenia susceptibility genes in 196 affected sibling pairs. *Human Molecular Genetics* 8: 1729–39.

Chapter 8

Electroconvulsive therapy

John Read

Electroconvulsive therapy (ECT) involves passing sufficient electricity through a human brain to cause a grand mal seizure. Although nowadays used most often for depression, ECT was invented to treat 'schizophrenia'. In 2001, the American Psychiatric Association (APA) stated: 'schizophrenia and related conditions (schizophreniform and schizoaffective disorders) constitute the second most common diagnostic indications for ECT' (p. 16).

Gender and age have as much to do with who gets ECT as do diagnoses. Women make up about 66% of ECT recipients in New Zealand (NZHIS 2002), 68% in England (Department of Health 1999), 72% in the USA (McCall and Dickerson 2001) and 76% in Finland (Huuhka *et al.* 2000). These surveys found that 41–49% of ECT recipients are 65 or older, with an average age of 61.

THE FIRST ECT

The first use of electricity to cause a convulsion was undertaken in Italy by Ugo Cerletti in 1938. His obituary in the *American Journal of Psychiatry* placed his invention in the historical context of 'attempts carried out in all possible ways, from the most cruel to the most bizarre, to cause a major shake-up in the psychic economy of mental patients' and lists 'surprise baths, sudden showers, rotating machines, intimidation systems and blood-letting' as methods of shocking madness out of mental patients (Mora 1964: 201).

The idea that schizophrenia could be cured by inducing grand mal epileptic seizures 'developed following reports that dementia praecox was rare in patients with severe epilepsy and that posttraumatic seizures in patients with dementia praecox ameliorated the psychotic condition' (Fink and Sackeim 1996: 28). Some doctors treated epilepsy with injections of the blood of schizophrenics (Kalinowsky 1986). Others sought ways to cause epilepsy in schizophrenics. In the 1930s, Hungarian psychiatrist Ladislas Meduna injected Metrazol into patients for this purpose. He was chastised by medical colleagues, not for causing epilepsy or because of the 'terrors induced by each injection' (Fink 2001: 2), but because he claimed to have found a treatment for 'schizophrenia'. Meduna reports: 'Professor Schaffer called me a swindler, a humbug, a cheat . . . How dare I claim that I cured schizophrenia, an endogenous, hereditary disease' (Fink 1984: 1036).

In 1930s Rome, Cerletti began experiments with electrical inductions of seizures, using electrodes in the mouth and rectum of dogs. Many died (Kalinowsky 1986). The idea of bypassing the heart by placing the electrodes on the head came from an unlikely source:

> I went to the slaughter house . . . The hogs were clamped at the temples with big metallic tongs which were hooked up to an electric current (125 volts) . . . They fell unconscious, stiffened, then after a few seconds they were shaken by convulsions in the same way as our experimental dogs . . . I felt we could venture to experiment on man.
>
> As soon as the current was introduced, the patient reacted with a jolt, and his body muscles stiffened; then he fell back on the bed without loss of consciousness . . . It was proposed that we should allow the patient to have some rest, and repeat the experiment the next day. All at once, the patient, who evidently had been following our conversation, said clearly and solemnly, without his usual gibberish: 'Not another one! Its deadly!'
>
> (Impastato 1960: 1113–14)

DOES ECT WORK?

The first ten years

In the 1930s and 1940s, psychiatrists who didn't accept the pessimistic genetic theories were, understandably, excited to discover an apparently effective treatment. American psychiatrist John Friedberg, points out, however, that during these early years there were no studies comparing recipients and non-recipients of ECT, and that 'the influence of ECT was on the minds of the psychiatrists, producing optimism and earlier discharges' (Friedberg 1976: 31). The first studies found lower recovery rates for ECT recipients than for non-recipients (Karagulla 1950) or no difference (Scherer 1951).

However, these studies were not conducted properly by modern standards. Because of frequent fractures of the spine and jaw, a disguisable placebo was not possible. In the early 1950s, muscle relaxants and general anaesthesia were introduced. It was now possible that this new 'modified ECT' could be properly evaluated with control groups rendered unconscious by general anaesthesia but not given ECT ('simulated-ECT').

Comparisons with simulated-ECT

The first comparison with a simulated-ECT group, in which neither psychiatrists nor patients knew who received ECT, found no difference in outcome between the two groups (Miller *et al.* 1953). This was replicated, for both depression and schizophrenia (Brill *et al.* 1959). ECT outcome research then went into recession.

The 1970s saw campaigns by aggrieved ECT recipients and their families leading to legislation curbing its use in several states in the USA. In 1982, the people of Berkeley, California, voted to ban its use entirely. These campaigns prompted renewed research efforts to disprove the protestors' claims about inefficacy and brain damage. In their eagerness to prove the campaigners wrong, some researchers abandoned even the most minimal of scientific standards. For example, a study in the *British Journal of Psychiatry* (Shukla 1981) claimed that the proportions showing at least 'moderate improvement' were: depression 100%, schizophrenia 97.6%. The description of how improvement was measured was: 'A record was kept of progress'. A large-scale survey for the British Royal College of Psychiatrists (RCP) simply gathered psychiatrists' opinions about improvement (Pippard and Ellam 1981: 87). Despite the heavily biasing influence of asking the prescribing psychiatrists about their perceptions of the patients' opinions, the number of patients reporting 'worse' was five times greater than that reported by psychiatrists.

Four studies between 1978 and 1982, with depressed patients, did include simulated-ECT control groups. Three claimed to have shown differences between real and simulated-ECT. Subsequent reports, including those of the APA (2001) and the government-funded UK ECT Review Group (2003), continue to make that claim about the studies, but don't mention that two of the three studies had invalidated their work, in terms of any lasting benefits, by giving real ECT to the control group after the first (Freeman *et al.* 1978) or third week (West 1981). The third was the famous Northwick Park study (Johnstone *et al.* 1980). A prominent ECT advocate described it as 'the most thoroughly designed and extensive trial of ECT's efficacy ever to be conducted in this country', but conceded that the 'modest' difference found was 'restricted to patients with delusions' and was 'short-lived' (Kendell 1981). The fourth study (Lambourn and Gill 1978) found no significant differences, even in the short-term.

The fact that there had been so few properly designed studies involving 'simulated-ECT' control groups has been justified in terms of 'ethical difficulties' withholding a treatment known to be effective and imposing on a control group 'a treatment which involves repeatedly rendering the person unconscious' (Kendell 1981: 265). Nowadays most ECT researchers ignore the need for control groups (e.g. Brodarty *et al.* 2000; Hirose *et al.* 2001; Huukha *et al.* 2000), including the recent study by the National Institute of Mental Health (O'Connor *et al.* 2001).

The UK ECT Review Group (2003) found that only 73 of 624 studies (12%) met their standards for inclusion in their review of efficacy, adding: 'The quality of reporting', of the 12%, 'was poor' (p. 800). One of the researchers in a recent New Zealand study publicly claimed that the study confirmed previous findings 'that 80% of patients respond favourably – a real response, not a result of placebo' (Plunkett 2001). The principal investigator later acknowledged that there was no placebo control group. The justification, as usual, was 'Simulated ECT has not been used in clinical ECT research for several years. It is considered unethical' (P. Melding, personal correspondence, 2002). The *assumption* that ECT is effective is used to justify not evaluating whether it *is* effective.

ECT and schizophrenia

With the advent of 'anti-psychotic' medications in the 1950s, interest in shocking 'schizophrenics' waned. By 1976, a reviewer concluded that 'ECT in schizophrenia had little to offer' (Clare 1976). Even the APA (2001) report acknowledges that none of five pre-1980 studies comparing ECT with simulated-ECT found any differences, even in the short term. It does claim that three later studies demonstrated 'a substantial advantage' for ECT. In all three studies, however, both groups were receiving anti-psychotic medication and the advantage was only short term. An example of the 'substantial advantage' is the Leicester ECT Trial (Brandon *et al.* 1985). Both the ECT and the simulated-ECT groups improved on all four measures used. The real ECT group showed faster improvement on two of the four scales. 'Global psychopathology' did not differ at all.

The APA (2001) lists 19 studies showing that ECT produces results no different from, or worse than, antipsychotic medication. The report fails to mention other post-1980 ECT versus simulated-ECT studies that failed to demonstrate even temporary benefits. A recent Indian study comparing ECT with simulated-ECT, with 36 'schizophrenics', found no differences in symptom reduction, even in the short term (Sarita *et al.* 1998).

It should be noted, as further evidence of particularly poor efficacy with this group, that 'schizophrenics' have repeatedly been shown to receive longer courses of treatments in efforts to get a result (e.g. Fink and Sackeim 1996). Given that the seizure threshold increases after each individual shock (by an average of 269% within one course (Chanpattana *et al.* 2000)), 'schizophrenics' are exposed not only to more frequent ECTs but to particularly dangerous dosages of electricity.

The advocates of ECT continue to argue that it is effective with schizophrenia (Fink and Sackeim 1996). In his ECT textbook, Richard Abrams (Professor of Psychiatry at the Chicago Medical School and President of Somatics Inc., a manufacturer of ECT machines) acknowledges that ECT is usually ineffective for the symptoms of schizophrenia, but recommends that 'every such patient deserves one full trial of ECT (preferably earlier rather than later) to insure that no treatment will be overlooked that has a chance, however slim, of halting the otherwise relentless progression of this devastating illness' (Abrams 1997a: 32).

Follow-up studies

Electroconvulsive therapy cannot be said to be effective, however, unless these immediate benefits (real or imagined) last for some period of time beyond the treatment. No studies of ECT for depression have found that the supposed short-term benefits of ECT last longer than 8 weeks.

The Northwick Park study (Johnstone *et al.* 1980), for example, found that the differences between real and simulated-ECT disappeared 4 weeks after treatment ended. The same lack of evidence of any lasting benefit is true for schizophrenia. Of the three 1980s studies which the APA Task Force (2001) claimed showed a 'substantial advantage' for ECT over simulated-ECT, any such advantage disappeared after 8 (Abraham and Kulhara 1987) or 4 weeks (Brandon *et al.* 1985; Taylor and Fleminger 1980).

Taylor and Fleminger (1980) found that during treatment there was equal improvement in both groups but that ECT reduced general psychopathology faster than simulated-ECT for the first 4 weeks. Psychiatrists perceived this difference; nurses and relatives did not. After 4 weeks the ECT group gradually deteriorated while the simulated-ECT group continued to improve, a pattern that was continuing 16 weeks after treatment.

Brandon *et al.* (1985) found that 8 weeks after treatment ECT recipients had deteriorated on three of the four measures. Meanwhile, the simulated-ECT group continued to improve on all four measures, overtaking the real ECT group on all four within 6 weeks. Abraham and Kulhara (1987) also found that the 'advantage was totally lost with the passage of time'. The UK ECT Review Group found only one study (Johnstone *et al.* 1980) that had followed up for 6 months. It found a slight advantage for the simulated-ECT group.

DOES ECT PREVENT SUICIDE?

An argument often used in support of ECT is that it prevents suicide. One study (Avery and Winokur 1976) often cited as evidence of this recorded all deaths for 3 years post-discharge. It found that 4.3% of ECT recipients and 8.0% of non-ECT recipients had died. There were, however, four suicides among the 257 who had received ECT (1.6%) and four among the 262 who had not (1.5%).

Many studies have found no difference in suicide rates between ECT and non-ECT patients (e.g. Milstein *et al.* 1986; Weeks *et al.* 1980). A US study of 1076 inpatients (Black *et al.* 1989) found no significant differences in suicide rates over 2 years between depressed people who received ECT (2.2%), those who received anti-depressant medication (2.6%) and those who received neither (1.9%).

Shortly before killing himself, soon after ECT, Ernest Hemingway asked: 'What is the sense of ruining my head and erasing my memory, which is my capital, and putting me out of business? It was a brilliant cure, but we lost the patient' (Hotchner 1967: 308).

DOES ECT CAUSE MEMORY DYSFUNCTION?

Retrograde amnesia

Retrograde amnesia is the inability to remember past events. Three facts are generally accepted: (1) retrograde amnesia occurs to some extent in almost all ECT recipients; (2) memory of events closest to the treatment are most affected; and (3) some improvement occurs over time, with distant memories returning before recent ones (APA 2001: 71). Even the APA Task Force (2001) report acknowledges: 'In some patients the recovery from retrograde amnesia will be incomplete, and evidence has shown that ECT can result in persistent or permanent memory loss'. The UK ECT Review Group (2003), however, describes memory deficits as 'temporary' (p. 806).

In 1950, Janis collected personal memories, from childhood to the present, from 30 people, 19 of whom later received ECT. Four weeks after ECT, all 19 suffered 'profound, extensive recall failures' that 'occurred so infrequently among the 11 patients in the control group as to be almost negligible'. Most of the gaps were for the period of 6 months before ECT, but in some cases the memory loss was for events more than 10 years previously. Surprisingly, retrograde amnesia was scarcely researched again until the 1970s protests compelled ECT proponents to try and prove ECT is safe.

One study established that immediately after ECT, memory gaps had been caused for a period spanning 25 years, which reduced to a 3-year span 7 months after ECT (Squire *et al.* 1981). Three years after ECT, memory for events during the 6 months immediately before treatment remained lost (Squire and Slater 1983). Recipients of ECT sometimes are unable to recognize events from their lives when reminded about them. For control patients, reminding led to 100% recall. For ECT recipients, reminding was effective 71% of the time (Squire *et al.* 1981).

A 1980 study (ironically designed to try and invalidate 'complaints' of memory loss) unintentionally produced the longest follow-up. Recipients of

ECT performed worse than non-recipients not only on ability to recall famous personalities from the 1960s, but also on personal memories from early childhood. The average time since the last ECT was 8.4 years (Freeman *et al.* 1980). Memory gaps after 3 years might, possibly, be open to slight further filling in over time. After 8 years the term 'permanent' seems reasonable.

The percentage for whom memory gaps are permanent remains unknown. It would appear that ECT researchers don't want to know.

Anterograde amnesia

Almost everyone receiving ECT suffers, as a result, anterograde amnesia, the inability to retain new information. For most this ability gradually returns over a period of a few weeks. The APA Task Force (2001) report cites 11 studies demonstrating anterograde amnesia in the first few weeks after ECT, concluding that during this time 'returning to work, making important financial or personal decisions, or driving may need to be restricted' (p. 70). The report claims that 'no study has documented anterograde amnesia effects of ECT for more than a few weeks'. Studies showing that anterograde amnesia persists for 2 months (Squire and Slater 1983) and 3 months (Halliday *et al.* 1968), not cited by the report, are possibly considered consistent with 'a few weeks'. Two other studies are not. One found that ECT recipients were significantly impaired, an average of 8.4 years after treatment, on retention of new information, such as repeating a spoken paragraph of text (Freeman *et al.* 1980). The other found that ECT recipients scored worse than a non-ECT control group on two short-term memory tests used to assess brain damage, *at both 10 and 15 years after ECT*. These findings 'suggest that ECT causes irreversible brain damage' (Goldman *et al.* 1972).

'Subjective' memory loss

Proponents of ECT, including the Chair of the APA's review panel Richard Weiner, respond by describing all this memory loss as 'subjective' (Coleman *et al.* 1996; Prudic *et al.* 2000; Weiner 1984; Weiner *et al.* 1986). It is further suggested that memory 'complaints' are found only in those who fail to respond to ECT, and that the memory loss is part of the unimproved illness (e.g. Weiner 1984).

This hypothesis that memory loss is 'subjective', found only in those who continue to be ill after ECT, has been tested empirically. McElhiney *et al.* (1995) identified five previous studies showing no significant relationship between anterograde or retrograde amnesia and clinical change after ECT. Their own study found that retrograde amnesia was related to the ECT and not to mood state before or after ECT. A recent study, which acknowledged that 'the memory loss for events immediately preceding, during and after the treatment course can be permanent' (Neylan *et al.* 2001: 331), found 'no significant correlation between the change in Hamilton depression rating and the change in any of the 12 cognitive measures' (p. 333). Memory loss is not just a 'subjective' experience on the part of 'ill' people.

BRAIN DAMAGE

Further evidence that the adverse effects of ECT are not imaginary is provided by many studies documenting brain damage (Breggin 1979, 1984, 1997; Frank 1978; Friedberg 1976, 1977; Morgan 1991; Sterling 2000). A recent review acknowledges that 'both anterograde and retrograde memory impairment are common' and documents the various forms of neuro-biological dysfunction underlying the subtypes of ECT-induced memory dysfunction (Rami-Gonzalez *et al.* 2001). Furthermore, the cognitive dysfunction is greater for those receiving more frequent (three a week *vs* two a week) or higher doses of electricity (UK ECT Review Group 2003).

In the 1940s, it had been accepted that ECT worked because it *does* cause brain damage and memory deficits. In 1941, Walter Freeman, who imported ECT from Europe to the USA, wrote: 'The greater the damage, the more likely the remission of psychotic symptoms . . . Maybe it will be shown that a mentally ill patient can think more clearly and more constructively with less brain in actual operation' (p. 83). The paper was entitled 'Brain damaging therapeutics'. Another US psychiatrist explained:

> There have to be organic changes or organic disturbances in the physiology of the brain for the cure to take place. I think the disturbance in memory is probably an integral part of the recovery process. I think that it may be true that these people have for the time being at any rate more intelligence than they can handle and that the reduction in intelligence is an important factor in the curative process . . . Some of the very best cures that one gets are in those individuals whom one reduces almost to amentia.
>
> (Myerson 1942: 39)

In the 1940s and 1950s, autopsies consistently provided evidence of brain damage, including necrosis (cell death). A review in the *Lancet* described ECT-induced haemorrhages and concluded that 'all parts of the brain are vulnerable – the cerebral hemispheres, the cerebellum, third ventrical and hypothalamus' (Alpers 1946). A review of the first 20 years of autopsies concluded: 'damage to the brain, sometimes reversible but often irreversible, occurred in the course of electric shock treatments' (Allen 1959).

In 1974, Karl Pribram, head of Stanford University's Neuropsychology Institute, wrote: 'I'd rather have a small lobotomy than a series of electroconvulsive shock . . . I just know what the brain looks like after a series of shock – and it's not very pleasant to look at' (p. 10).

It has also been found that CT scans reveal increased frontal lobe atrophy among both depressed (Calloway *et al.* 1981; UK ECT Review Group 2003) and schizophrenic (Weinberger *et al.* 1979) ECT recipients. Some ECT proponents rationalize the dangers of ECT by arguing that antipsychotic drugs (see Chapter 9) are even more dangerous:

> ECT may have gained in popularity . . . because of the increasing recognition of long-lasting and sometimes irreversible impairments in brain function induced by neuroleptic drugs. (In this instance the evidence of brain damage is not subtle, but is grossly obvious even to the casual observer!)
>
> (Small and Small 1984: 34)

ECT-RELATED DEATHS

Psychiatric textbooks and official reports claim that the risk of death from ECT is inconsequential. One example is the report of the APA (2001). Note, first, who the profession of psychiatry selected to assess the safety of ECT. Six of the eight Task Force members were Directors of ECT services. The group included the incoming and outgoing presidents of the Association for Convulsive Therapy as well as the editor of the *Journal of ECT*. Three were financially involved with companies manufacturing ECT machines.

The APA Task (2001) Force Report devotes just one of its 245 pages to deaths, which it calls 'General Issues'. It claims: 'Published estimates from large and diverse patient series over several decades report up to 4 deaths per 100,000 treatments'. This is not true. A 1977 report by the British Royal College of Psychiatrists had cited studies ranging from 4 to 9 per 100,000 treatments. The APA report further claims that the death rate 'appears to have decreased in recent years' and states, without citing any research, that 'A reasonable current estimate' is '1 per 10,000 patients or 1 per 80,000 treatments' (the average course per patient involves eight ECT treatments).

The Task Force report repeats the claim, made for decades, that the ECT death rate is about the same as that associated with general anaesthesia for minor surgery (Abrams 1997b). This conveniently ignores the fact that even if this were true for an individual ECT treatment, the risk to each ECT recipient is eight times (the average number of ECTs in a course of treatment) greater than that of minor surgery. In 1957, Impastato reported 254 deaths caused by ECT and calculated a death rate of one per 1000 patients overall and a death rate in people over 60 years old (today's modal ECT recipient) of one in 200, fifty times higher than the APA's claim.

As with the other adverse effects of ECT, it is often suggested that this unfortunate side-effect only occurred in the 'bad old days' before the introduction of modified ECT. However, in 1978 Leonard Frank reviewed 28 articles in which psychiatrists had spontaneously self-reported ECT-related deaths. Of 130,216 ECT recipients, there were 90 ECT-related deaths, one death per 1447 people. This is seven times higher than the APA's claim.

A 1980 survey asked British psychiatrists to report ECT-related deaths (Pippard and Ellam 1981). Excluding any deaths that occurred more than 72 hours after treatment there were four deaths in 2594 patients. This is one per 648.5 people, 15 times higher than the APA figure. Of the additional six that died within a few weeks of ECT, two were from heart attacks and one from a stroke, two of the most common causes of death from ECT (Impastato 1957; Kendell 1981). Inclusion of these three deaths produces a mortality rate of one death per 371 ECT recipients. This is roughly consistent with an earlier Norwegian survey in which three of 893 women (one in 298) died as a result of ECT (Strensrud 1958). (In critiquing this finding, Kendell (1981) states that all three had pre-existing brain disease. Imagine explaining that to the relatives.) Of nearly 1700 Texas ECT recipients, eight died within 2 weeks, a rate of one in 212 (Breggin 1997).

All of these findings, all far higher than the rate claimed by official sources today, had relied predominantly on the reporting of deaths by those responsible for giving the ECT. A more objective measure was inadvertently provided by a study of patients' attitudes (Freeman and Kendell 1980). The researchers wanted to interview 183 people an average of one year after ECT. However, 22 (12%) were either dead or missing. Twelve (7%) were definitely dead, four of whom had killed themselves. Since it is impossible to determine whether the suicides were partly the result of depression following loss of memory, I shall omit them from the mortality rate. Counting only the two deaths which occurred *during* ECT, the mortality rate was 1 per 91.5 patients. This finding, more than a hundred times higher than the APA's latest estimate (1 per 10,000 patients), is not mentioned by the APA report or, to my knowledge, any other report or review. The UK ECT Review Group doesn't mention *any* of the studies that show higher death rates than the APA claim.

An unclear picture emerges from long-term follow-up studies examining all causes of death. As noted, Avery and Winokur (1976) found a lower death rate (e.g. from cancer) in ECT recipients. However, a study of 372 ECT recipients found that 18 (5%) died within 2 years of treatment. This was significantly greater than the 8.2 (2%) deaths expected in the general population when matching for age and gender. It was also slightly greater than the 22 deaths in the 704 equally depressed patients (3%) who didn't get

ECT (Black *et al.* 1989). A recent Australian study (Brodarty *et al.* 2000) found a death rate among ECT recipients of 21% over 2 years in the age group (65–74 years) most likely to receive ECT.

Advocates of ECT continue to make misleading claims about mortality rates. Abrams (1997a) has even asserted that 'the death rate reported for ECT is an order of magnitude smaller than the spontaneous death rate in the general population' (p. 125). Such claims ignore all the findings cited above.

CONCLUSION

To acknowledge the true risk of death or the real extent of brain damage is virtually impossible for those who prescribe ECT. It would expose them to moral condemnation and serious legal and financial consequences. They need to believe the treatment is safe and effective.

It can safely be concluded that every case of ECT causes loss of memories covering the time surrounding the treatment. For some the loss is persistent and covers a greater time span. For a few the damage to memory is severe and permanent. Besides the frightening nature of the 'treatment', ECT recipients also experience 'a complex range of emotional responses including feelings of humiliation, increased compliance, failure, worthlessness, betrayal, lack of confidence and degradation, and a sense of having been abused and assaulted' (Johnstone 1999: 76). Those exposed to these risks, and to the slight but significant risk of death, receive little or no benefit, even in the short term. There is no evidence at all that the treatment has any benefit for anyone lasting beyond a few days. Electroconvulsive therapy does not prevent suicide and for a small number may precipitate it. The short-term benefit that is gained by some simply does not warrant the risks involved. In other branches of medicine, a treatment with this overwhelming imbalance between risk and benefit would be considered unethical and would, if the profession involved refused to regulate itself, be rendered illegal. This will come.

There has been, internationally, a steady decline in the use of ECT. The Finnish rate among inpatients, for instance, once as high as 14%, has remained steady at 2% since 1964 (Huuhka *et al.* 2000). In the USA, where the anti-ECT campaigns were particularly effective, the number of inpatients given ECT fell by 46% between 1975 and 1980 to a low of 33,384 (Thompson and Blaine 1987). However, US usage increased between 1980 and 1986, entirely due to targeting of the elderly (Thompson *et al.* 1994). Advocates and opponents alike estimate that about 100,000 US citizens are currently given ECT every year (Breggin 1997; Fink 2000). Europe did not follow the USA's reborn enthusiasm. In England, the rates have been falling steadily since the late 1970s. The number of individual administrations of ECT in

England was 159,600 in 1980; by 1989 it had fallen to 109,707. In 1999, there were 16,482 in 3 months, representing an annual total of 65,928 (Department of Health 1989, 1999). In two decades, ECT use in England had fallen by 59%. If the average annual reduction of about 4700 is sustained, ECT will disappear in England in 2013.

No doubt the overwhelming majority of that dwindling number of psychiatrists who continue to use ECT do so with the best of intentions. They believe ECT is a medical procedure treating an illness. Nevertheless, the research evidence indicates that ECT is a contemporary example of the continuation of the process, seen in our historical review (Chapter 2), of simplistic theories being used to portray punitive and damaging treatments as being beneficial to 'mad' people. It is hopefully only a matter of time before ECT will be looked back on as yet another futile and misguided attempt to shock and bully distressed people back to 'sanity'. The research suggests that the sooner this happens the better.

The way to accelerate this process has been mapped out for us by the most famous of all ECT enthusiasts. Max Fink (2001: 11) reminds us, with unconcealed disgust, that it was only when the professional bodies of psychotherapists, psychologists, psychoanalysts, nurses, social workers and clergy 'took public positions to restrict the availability of ECT' and 'lay groups, many led by former patients' demanded that 'ECT and lobotomy be outlawed', that ECT has been curbed in the past.

EXAMPLES OF PERSONAL ACCOUNTS OF, AND RESEARCH BY, ECT RECIPIENTS

Frame, J. (1961). *Faces In The Water*. New York: Avon.

Frank, L. (1976). The Frank Papers. In J. Friedberg (ed.) *Shock Treatment is Not Good For Your Brain*. San Francisco, CA: Glide.

Frank, L. (1990). Electroshock: death, brain damage, memory loss and brainwashing. *Journal of Mind and Behaviour* 11: 489–512.

Gotkin, J. (1977). *Too Much Anger, Too Many Tears*. New York: Quadrangle.

Johnstone, L. (1999). Adverse psychological effects of ECT (interviews with 20 ECT recipients). *Journal of Mental Health* 8: 69–85.

MIND (2001). *Shock Treatment: A Survey of People's Experiences of ECT*. London: MIND.

Plath, S. (1972). *The Bell Jar*. New York: Bantam.

Wallcraft, J. (1993). Women and ECT, *Spare Rib*, October.

REFERENCES

Abraham, K. and Kulhara, P. (1987). The efficacy of ECT in the treatment of schizophrenia. *British Journal of Psychiatry* 15: 152–5.

Abrams, R. (1997a). *ECT*, 3rd edn. Oxford: Oxford University Press.

Abrams, R. (1997b). The mortality rate with ECT. *Convulsive Therapy* 13: 125–7.

Allen, I. (1959). Cerebral lesions from ECT. *New Zealand Medical Journal* 58: 369–77.

Alpers, B. (1946). The brain changes associated with electrical shock treatment: a critical review. *Lancet* 66: 363–9.

American Psychiatric Association (2001). *The Practice of ECT: A Task Force Report*, 2nd edn. Washington, DC: APA.

Avery, D. and Winokur, G. (1976). Mortality in depressed patients treated with ECT and antidepressants. *Archives of General Psychiatry* 33: 1029–37.

Black, D. *et al.* (1989). Does treatment influence mortality in depressives? *Annals of Clinical Psychiatry* 1: 165–73.

Brandon, S. *et al.* (1985). Leicester ECT trial. *British Journal of Psychiatry* 146: 177–83.

Breggin, P. (1979). *Electroshock: Its Brain-disabling Effects*. New York: Springer.

Breggin, P. (1984). Electroshock therapy and brain damage: the acute organic brain syndrome as treatment. *Behavioral and Brain Sciences* 7: 24–5.

Breggin, P. (1997). *Brain-disabling Treatments in Psychiatry*. New York: Springer.

Brill, N. *et al.* (1959). Relative effectiveness of various components of ECT. *Archives of Neurology and Psychiatry* 81: 627–35.

Brodarty, H. *et al.* (2000). A prospective follow-up study of ECT outcome in older depressed patients. *Journal of Affective Disorders* 60: 101–11.

Calloway, S. *et al.* (1981). ECT and cerebral atrophy. *Acta Psychiatric Scandinavica* 64: 442–5.

Chanpattana, W. *et al.* (2000). Seizure threshold rise during ECT in schizophrenic patients. *Psychiatry Research* 96: 31–40.

Clare, A. (1976). *Psychiatry in Dissent*. London: Tavistock.

Coleman, E. *et al.* (1996). Subjective memory complaints before and after ECT. *Biological Psychiatry* 39: 346–56.

Department of Health (1989). *ECT: England – Financial Year 1988/1989*. London: Government Statistical Service.

Department of Health (1999). *ECT: Survey Covering the Period from January 1999 to March 1999, England*. Statistical Bulletin 1999/22. London: Government Statistical Service.

Fink, M. (1984). Meduna and the origins of ECT. *American Journal of Psychiatry* 141: 1034–41.

Fink, M. (2000). Electroshock revisited. *American Scientist* 88: 162–7.

Fink, M. (2001). Convulsive therapy: a review of the first 55 years. *Journal of Affective Disorders* 63: 1–15.

Fink, M. and Sackeim, H. (1996). Convulsive therapy in schizophrenia? *Schizophrenia Bulletin* 22: 27–39.

Frank, L. (1978). *The History of Shock Treatment*. San Franciso, CA: Frank.

Freeman, C. and Kendell, R. (1980). E.C.T: patients' experiences and attitudes. *British Journal of Psychiatry* 137: 8–16.

Freeman, C. *et al.* (1978). Double-blind controlled trial of ECT and simulated ECT in depressive illness. *Lancet* ii: 738–40.

Freeman, C. *et al.* (1980). ECT: patients who complain. *British Journal of Psychiatry* 137: 17–25.

Freeman, W. (1941). Brain-damaging therapeutics. *Diseases of the Nervous System* 2: 83.

Friedberg, J. (1976). *Shock Treatment is Not Good for Your Brain*. San Francisco, CA: Glide.

Friedberg, J. (1977). Shock treatment, brain damage, and memory loss: a neurological perspective. *American Journal of Psychiatry* 134: 1010–4.

Goldman, H. *et al.* (1972). Long-term effects of ECT upon memory and perceptual motor performance. *Journal of Clinical Psychology* 28: 32–4.

Halliday, A. *et al.* (1968). A comparison of the effects on depression of bilateral and unilateral ECT to the dominant and non-dominant hemispheres. *British Journal of Psychiatry* 114: 997–1012.

Hirose, S. *et al.* (2001). Effectiveness of ECT combined with risperidone against aggression in schizophrenia. *Journal of ECT* 17: 22–6.

Hotchner, A. (1967). *Papa Hemingway*. New York: Bantam.

Huuhka, M. *et al.* (2000). Historical perspective on ECT in Pitkaniemi Hospital. *Psychiatrica Fennica* 31: 55–64.

Impastato, D. (1957). Prevention of fatalities in ECT. *Diseases of the Nervous System* 18: 34–75.

Impastato, D. (1960). The story of the first ECT. *American Journal of Psychiatry* 116: 1113–14.

Janis, I. (1950). Psychological effects of ECT. *Journal of Nervous and Mental Disease* 111: 359–97.

Johnstone, E. *et al.* (1980). The Northwick Park ECT trial. *Lancet* ii: 1317–20.

Johnstone, L. (1999). Adverse psychological effects of ECT. *Journal of Mental Health* 8: 69–85.

Kalinowsky, L. (1986). History of convulsive therapy. *Annals of New York Academy of Sciences* 462: 5–11.

Karagulla, S. (1950). Evaluation of ECT as compared with conservative methods of treatment in depressive states. *Journal of Mental Science* 96: 1060–91.

Kendell, R. (1981). The present state of ECT. *British Journal of Psychiatry* 139: 265–93.

Lambourn, J. and Gill, D. (1978). A controlled comparison of simulated and real ECT. *British Journal of Psychiatry* 133: 514–19.

McCall, W. and Dickerson, L. (2001). The outcome of 369 ECT consultations. *Journal of ECT* 17: 50–2.

McElhiney, M. *et al.* (1995). Autobiographical memory and mood: effects of ECT. *Neuropsychology* 9: 101–17.

Miller, D. *et al.* (1953). A comparison between unidirectional current non-convulsive electrical stimulation, standard alternating current electroshock and pentothal in chronic schizophrenia. *American Journal of Psychiatry* 109: 617–21.

Milstein, V. *et al.* (1986). Does ECT prevent suicide? *Convulsive Therapy* 2: 3–6.

Mora, G. (1964). Ugo Cerletti. *American Journal of Psychiatry* 20: 620–2.

Morgan, R. (ed.) (1991). *Electroshock: The Case Against*. Toronto: IPI.

Myerson, A. (1942). Fatalities following ECT. *Transactions of the American Neurological Association* 68: 39.

New Zealand Health Information Service (2002). *Public Hospital Discharges for Psychiatric Somatotherapy (ECT) 1995–2000*. Wellington: Ministry of Health.

Neylan, T. *et al.* (2001). Cortisol levels predict cognitive impairment induced by ECT. *Biological Psychiatry* 50: 331–6.

O'Connor, M. *et al.* (2001). The influence of age on the response of major depression to ECT. *American Journal of Geriatric Psychiatry* 9: 382–90.

Pippard, J. and Ellam, L. (1981). *ECT in Great Britain*. London: Gaskell.

Plunkett, F. (2001). *The New Zealand Herald*, 20 November, p. A13.

Pribram, K. (1974). Lobotomy to physics to Freud. *American Psychological Association Monitor* 5: 9–10.

Prudic, J. *et al.* (2000). Subjective memory complaints. *Journal of ECT* 16: 121–32.

Rami-Gonzalez, L. *et al.* (2001). Subtypes of memory dysfunction associated with ECT. *Journal of ECT* 17: 129–35.

Royal College of Psychiatrists (1977). Memorandum on the use of ECT. *British Journal of Psychiatry* 131: 261–72.

Sarita, E. *et al.* (1998). Efficacy of combined ECT after two weeks of neuroleptics in schizophrenia. *NIMHANS Journal*, October, pp. 243–51.

Scherer, I. (1951). Prognoses and psychological scores in ECT, psychosurgery and spontaneous remission. *American Journal of Psychiatry* 107: 926–31.

Shukla, G. (1981). ECT in a rural teaching general hospital in India. *British Journal of Psychiatry* 139: 569–71.

Small, J. and Small, I. (1984). Current issues in ECT practice and research. *Behavioral and Brain Sciences* 7: 33–4.

Squire, L. and Slater, P. (1983). ECT and complaints of memory dysfunction. *British Journal of Psychiatry* 142: 1–8.

Squire, L. *et al.* (1981). Retrograde amnesia following ECT. *Archives of General Psychiatry* 38: 89–95.

Sterling, P. (2000). ECT damage is easy to find if you look for it. *Nature* 403: 242.

Strensrud, P. (1958). Cerebral complications following 24,562 convulsion treatments in 893 patients. *Acta Psychiatrica et Neurologica Scandinavica* 33: 115–26.

Taylor, P. and Fleminger, J. (1980). ECT for schizophrenia. *Lancet* i: 380–2.

Thompson, J. and Blaine, J. (1987). Use of ECT in the United States in 1975 and 1980. *American Journal of Psychiatry* 144: 557–62.

Thompson, J. *et al.* (1994). Use of ECT in the U.S. in 1975, 1980 and 1986. *American Journal of Psychiatry* 151: 1657–61.

UK ECT Review Group (Carney, S. *et al.*) (2003). Efficacy and safety of ECT in depressive disorders. *Lancet* 361: 799–808.

Weeks, D. *et al.* (1980). ECT: enduring cognitive effects? *British Journal of Psychiatry* 137: 26–37.

Weinberger, D. *et al.* (1979). Lateral ventricular enlargement in chronic schizophrenia. *Archives of General Psychiatry* 36: 735–9.

Weiner, R. (1984). Does ECT cause brain damage? *Behavioral and Brain Sciences* 7: 1–53.

Weiner, R. *et al.* (1986). Effects of stimulus parameters on cognitive side effects. *Annals of the New York Academy of Sciences* 462: 315–25.

West, E. (1981). ECT in depression. *British Medical Journal* 282: 355–7.

Chapter 9

Antipsychotic medication: myths and facts

Colin A. Ross and John Read

Psychiatry is littered with anecdote, folklore and superstition posing as scientific knowledge. Whether the subject be the safety and efficacy of electroconvulsive therapy, the genetic basis of schizophrenia or the scientific facts about antipsychotic medication, careful analysis reduces the sound, scientific knowledge in psychiatry to a very small fund of information. What *is* proven scientifically has limited generalizability beyond small, narrowly defined populations of the kind used in drug trials. In this chapter, we summarize the research showing that the prevailing beliefs about antipsychotic, or neuropletic, drugs are more myth than fact.

MYTH ONE: ANTIPSYCHOTIC DRUGS ARE PRESCRIBED TO ONLY A RELATIVELY SMALL NUMBER OF PEOPLE, NEARLY ALL OF WHOM ARE PSYCHOTIC

The second half of the twentieth century saw millions of people medicated for a growing list of problems, from feeling sad to sexual/relationship difficulties (see Chapter 10). 'Pharmaceutical companies sponsor diseases and promote them to prescribers and consumers . . . The social construction of illness is being replaced with the corporate construction of disease' (Moynihan *et al.* 2002).

The antipsychotics have been aptly called 'major tranquillizers'. They were developed for use in surgery to slow the pulse and other bodily functions. Within a year of the first use of chlorpromazine (brand names Largactil or Thorazine) for schizophrenia in the early 1950s, 2 million Americans were receiving it (Johnstone 2000). By the end of 1970, less than 20 years after the introduction of antipsychotics, about 250 million people worldwide had taken them (Jeste and Wyatt 1979). In 1987, there were 2.3 million prescriptions of antipsychotics in England (Department of Health 1988); in 2001, there were 5.7 million (Department of Health 2003).

The use of antipsychotic drugs is still expanding. In 2000, worldwide sales were US$6 billion, a 22% increase on 1999. In 2001, sales in North

America increased by 26% (IMS 2003). In New Zealand, expenditure on antipsychotics, which had been steady at about NZ$4 million for several years, jumped to 9.8 million in 1999 and to 23.1 million in 2000 (Pharmac 2002). In the year ending March 2001, there were approximately 43 million prescriptions of antipsychotics in France, Germany, Italy, Spain, the UK and USA (IMS 2003).

Older people

Much of the increase has resulted from the drug companies' targeting of old people and youth. Between 1992 and 1998, there was a 25% increase in antipsychotic prescriptions for 'the elderly and the financially disadvantaged' in Ontario (Dewa *et al.* 2002). A Scottish study found that a quarter of nursing home residents were taking antipsychotics, often for wandering and 'uncooperation' (McGrath and Jackson 1996). The newer 'atypical' anti-psychotics are promoted as a treatment for dementia, including Alzheimer's disease (Dewa *et al.* 2002), and 'geriatric conditions' such as 'aggression' (Glick *et al.* 2001).

Children and adolescents

A survey of nearly 900,000 American children and adolescents showed that from 1987 to 1996 the number receiving neuroleptics doubled. By 1996, one in every 172 youths (under 20) eligible for Medicaid (i.e. from poor families) were on neuroleptics (in contrast to one in a thousand from wealthier families with private health insurance) (Zito *et al.* 2003). Between 1996 and 2000, the number of Medicaid-eligible under 20-year-olds on anti-psychotic drugs increased 2.6-fold, up to one in 50. The largest increases were among 5- to 9-year-olds (4.5-fold increase) and 10- to 14-year-olds (2.7-fold increase) (Patel *et al.* 2002).

The drugs are now used for 'conduct and disruptive behavior disorders in children with subaverage IQs' (Snyder *et al.* 2002). Some early intervention psychosis programmes have raised ethical alarm bells about 'preventative' prescribing of antipsychotics to adolescents considered 'at risk' or suffering from what are considered the early 'prodromal' signs of schizophrenia (Bentall and Morrison 2002; Gosden 1999; McGorry *et al.* 2001).

> Drug company sponsored 'education' campaigns are urging GPs, school counsellors and parents to be alert to the signs of 'early psychosis' in schoolchildren and to start them on 'preventative' doses of neuroleptics, despite the fact that the so called 'symptoms', such as belief in telepathy and clairvoyance, are widely found in normal high school students.
>
> (Johnstone 2000: 183)

Prominent British cognitive psychologists have commented:

> The use of these drugs in the prevention of psychosis will increase the market for antipsychotics dramatically and is sure to be encouraged by the pharmaceutical industry. In contrast we believe that prescribing antipsychotic medication in this way is unethical . . . We have no real objection to preventative psychopharmacology between consenting adults. However, consent implies that potential participants be fully informed about the likely costs and benefits of treatment. They should be told, for example, that they may be receiving the treatment unnecessarily and that the side effects of treatment will very likely include weight gain and impotence, and less likely lead to their sudden demise.
>
> (Bentall and Morrison 2002: 354–5)

'Off-label' usage and co-morbidity

Besides increased use on older people and youngsters (with and without psychosis), these drugs are used on 'people with learning difficulties, whose mental functioning may be further impaired as a result' (Johnstone 2000: 183) and in prisons. In 2001, olanzapine was the most commonly prescribed drug in the US 'miscellaneous' category – 69% of which is prescribed in prisons (IMS 2003). Antipsychotics are used for an ever-expanding range of problems, from Huntington's disease (Bonelli *et al.* 2002) to gambling (Grant *et al.* 2002). Under 30% of 'atypical antipsychotics' are used for schizophrenia (Glick *et al.* 2001).

These 'off-label' usages are not approved by the Federal Drug Administration (FDA) or its equivalents because they are not supported by scientific data. Market approval is obtained from the FDA based on studies of narrowly defined clinical populations.

In real-world clinical practice, most people prescribed neuroleptics on a prolonged basis have extensive co-morbidity, including depression, substance abuse, eating disorders, personality disorders, obsessive-compulsive disorder, post-traumatic stress disorder and dissociative disorders (Ross 2000). Most if not all of these individuals are excluded from drug trials, so we have little scientific data on the effectiveness of the drugs as used in the real world.

MYTH TWO: ANTIPSYCHOTIC DRUGS MADE COMMUNITY CARE POSSIBLE

For drug companies and biological psychiatry, the assertion that community care became possible because of the neuroleptics is supposed proof of effectiveness. There is little evidence to support this assertion and much to refute it (Scull 1984; Warner 1985).

In countries where hospital usage declined after 1954, when Largactil was introduced, the decline had begun earlier and is explicable by other, usually economic, factors (Brenner 1973; Scull 1984). In England and Wales, the number of inpatients per 1 million of the population had peaked around 1930 and had been declining gradually but steadily before 1954. In Spain, hospitalization increased after the arrival of neuroleptics (1.08 per million in 1960, 1.80 per million in 1970, 2.39 per million in 1975). Other countries increased their psychiatric beds during the period when neuroleptics were supposedly reducing the use of hospitals: Belgium by 38% (1951–60); Czechoslovakia by 27% (1953–63); Finland by 115% (1951–75); East Germany by 21% (1962–74); West Germany by 10% (1953–63); Italy by 28% (1954–61); Norway by 53% (1951–62); Sweden by 15% (1952–62). In France, where chlorpromazine was first synthesized, inpatient numbers only began to fall after 1970, 16 years later (Sedgwick 1982: 198–201).

Furthermore, reductions in psychiatric beds do not constitute evidence of a reduction in hospital-based treatment. In England, the number of resident inpatients fell from 107,977 to 60,280 between 1970 and 1986. During this period, the number of admissions to psychiatric hospitals rose from 172,931 (3.74 per 1000 population) to 197,251 (4.17 per 1000).

One might argue, nevertheless, that it was the medications (rather than cost cutting) that at least made it possible for people to have stretches of time outside hospital. It is true that the average length of hospital stay in England (for people under 25) fell from 17 to 5½ weeks between 1954 and 1964. However, in the two decades before major tranquillizers (1934–54), the length of stay had fallen from 82 to 17 weeks, a rate three times greater than in the decade after the introduction of major tranquillizers.

It is also claimed that the new drugs increased schizophrenia recovery rates. Warner (1985) reviewed 68 studies and concluded that the drugs had little effect on long-term outcome.

Despite all this, the assertion that drugs made community care possible is still promulgated as fact. It is now being made about the new 'atypical' antipsychotics (Dewa *et al.* 2002), introduced decades after community care began.

MYTH THREE: ANTIPSYCHOTIC MEDICATIONS ARE MORE EFFECTIVE THAN PLACEBO

Conventional antipsychotics

Much of the evidence for the efficacy of the 'conventional' antipsychotics, used before (and since) the introduction of the 'atypical' antipsychotics in the early 1990s, concerns relapse. These studies compare the relapse rates of people on the drugs with the relapse rates of people whose drugs are replaced with placebos.

A review of 29 such studies, totalling 3519 people, found a difference in relapse rates in every study (Davis *et al.* 1980). These findings are used to argue that antipsychotic drugs are 'one of the most effective forms of therapy in psychiatry' (p. 70). However, when the numbers from the 29 studies are totalled, we see that relapse occurred in 55% of the people whose drugs were replaced with placebos and in 19% of those remaining on the drugs. A crude comparison involves subtracting the 45% benefiting from placebo from the 81% benefiting from the drugs. The drugs benefited only 36% of patients. The largest study, by far, found a difference of only 26%.

However, 45% of the 81% for whom the drugs were effective would have benefited from placebo. Therefore, the effectiveness of the drug component of the drug–placebo combination is actually 45% [81 − (81 × 0.45)]. So only 45% can genuinely be said to benefit from the chemical component of the drug–placebo combination, while 45% benefit from placebo alone.

Furthermore, these studies are not proper drug versus drug-free comparisons. They are drug versus acute-drug-withdrawal-state comparisons. Under the placebo condition of sudden, complete withdrawal, the previously blocked dopamine system is flooded. The heightened sensitivity and increased numbers of dopamine receptors (both of which occur in response to the drug-induced blockade of the dopamine system) result in a total overwhelming of the dopamine system. Neither this nor the inability to plan additional support during withdrawal (hard enough when done gradually and with support) are conducive to mental health. A proportion of the relapses in the placebo group are, therefore, explicable by the withdrawal effects of the drugs.

One of the studies showing a difference in relapse rates between drugged and un-drugged 'schizophrenics' (Vaughn and Leff 1976) found that the drugs did make a difference for those living with hostility and criticism, and who were unable to get out of the house very much: 53% on drugs relapsed compared with 92% on placebos. For those living in more supportive home environments, relapse rates were much lower and the drugs made no difference: 12% on drugs and 15% on placebos relapsed. Are these drugs treating an illness or are they numbing response to hostility?

Atypical antipsychotics

In the 1990s, the new 'atypical' antipsychotics, risperidone (Risperdal), olanzapine (Zyprexa), sertindole (Serdolect) and quetiapine (Seroquel) 'raised major expectations of improved outcomes for individuals with schizophrenia' (Leucht *et al.* 1999: 51). By 1999, a meta-analysis of studies revealed that the difference in efficacy between these drugs and placebo is only 'moderate'. Two of the four new drugs are only 'slightly more effective' than the conventional antipsychotics and these differences are so 'modest' that 'it is questionable whether the superiorities of risperidone and olanzapine are clinically relevant' (p. 63). The other two, sertindole and quetiapine, are no more effective than conventional antipsychotics. It had been claimed that the new atypical antipsychotics are particularly effective with the negative symptoms of schizophrenia. Two are only 'slightly more effective' than conventional antipsychotics, one equally effective and one slightly less effective (Leucht *et al.* 1999).

It is revealing to look at an example of the studies comparing atypical antipsychotics to placebo. Arvantis and Miller (1997) describe a study in which 361 'schizophrenics' from 26 centres participated in a randomized, prospective, double-blind trial of Seroquel versus placebo. Data from this study are summarized in Kasper and Muller-Spahn (2000). They describe the percentage of responders, defined as those with a 40% or greater reduction in Brief Psychiatric Rating Scale (BPRS) scores, and construct a convincing bar graph which does indeed show a difference between placebo (5.9%) and Seroquel (29.2%). The fact remains, however, that less than a third of participants responded to the medication.

Participants on 150 mg of Seroquel, the most effective dose, experienced an average BPRS score reduction of 8.67, whereas the participants receiving placebo experienced an average increase of 1.71. This too looks impressive on a bar graph. However, the average scores for those on Seroquel actually fell only from 47.2 to 38.3. Not only does this represent a reduction of less than 20% in symptoms, the level reached (38.3) remains within the severe psychosis range.

An even more misleading bar graph appears to provide evidence that Seroquel is as effective as olanzapine (Zyprexa). Kasper and Muller-Spahn (2000) compare the data of Arvantis and Miller (1997) with those in a study of Zyprexa (Beasley *et al.* 1996). Kasper and Muller-Spahn fail to comment that the response rate to placebo in the Zyprexa study was higher than the response rate to any dosage of Seroquel in the Seroquel study. Thus in some groups of schizophrenics, placebo works better than Zyprexa does in other groups

MYTH FOUR: THE THERAPEUTIC EFFECTS OUTWEIGH THE ADVERSE EFFECTS

The conventional antipsychotics have many severe side-effects. These include anticholinergic side-effects such as dry mouth, tachycardia, weight gain, constipation, urinary retention and delirium, all of which one of us (C.A.R.) treated repeatedly throughout the 1980s. The other major group of side-effects caused by the conventional antipsychotics is extrapyramidal symptoms. These include akathisia, tremor, rigidity, dystonia, oculogyric crisis and tardive dyskinesia.

Tardive dyskinesia

Tardive dyskinesia involves uncontrollable movements of the tongue, lips, face, hands and feet. The average prevalence of tardive dyskinesia among people on antipsychotic drugs is 30 per cent (Llorca *et al.* 2002). Among people over 45 years, 26% develop tardive dyskinesia after just 1 year on the drugs and 60% after 3 years (Jeste *et al.* 1995), with 23% developing *severe* tardive dyskinesia within 3 years (Caligiuri *et al.* 1997).

> Severe tardive dyskinesia represents a serious and potentially disabling movement disorder. Severe oral dyskinesia may result in dental and denture problems that can progress to ulceration and infection of the mouth, as well as muffled or unintelligible speech. Severe orofacial TD [tardive dyskinesia] can impair eating and swallowing, which in turn could produce significant health problems. Gait disturbances due to limb dyskinesia may leave patients vulnerable to falls, and injuries. Severe TD may impair mobility and often impacts on an individual's likelihood of returning to work. Psychosocially, ambulatory patients with obvious TD may experience shame, guilt, anxiety and depression.
> (Caligiuri *et al.* 1997: 148)

The pharmaceutical industry has admitted that tardive dyskinesia is irreversible in 75% of cases (Hill 1986). The drugs are significantly more likely to cause tardive dyskinesia in women and older people, two groups prescribed the drugs at particularly high rates (Llorca *et al.* 2002; Robinson 2002). Black Americans are more likely than white Americans to develop tardive dyskinesia (Glazer *et al.* 1994).

Tardive dyskinesia occurs because of the dopaminergic overactivity that develops in response to the blockade of the dopamine system by the antipsychotic drugs. This overactivity 'results in an imbalance between the dopamine and acetylcholine . . . which manifests itself in the symptoms of tardive dyskinesia' (Berger and Roxroth 1980: 105). The anti-cholinergic drugs (e.g. Cogentin) prescribed to counteract the extrapyramidal side-effects (tremors and rigidity) of the antipsychotics can further upset the balance between the dopaminergic and cholinergic systems and thereby exacerbate tardive dyskinesia (Gerlach *et al.* 1974) or even contribute to its development (Klawans *et al.* 1974).

The antipsychotic drugs mask the symptoms of tardive dyskinesia in up to 40% of people on them, so that they only discover the tardive dyskinesia if they manage to get off the drugs (Crane and Smith 1980). This renders the drugs that cause the brain damage the best, or only, treatment for the symptoms of the brain damage (Hill 1986). It also means that most estimates of the prevalence of tardive dyskinesia are underestimates.

The response of psychiatry to tardive dyskinesia has been shameful (Hill 1986). They were described as 'among the safest drugs available in medicine' (Baldessarini and Lipinski 1976: 48). The first book on the subject, published a quarter of a century after the introduction of the drugs, notes in its preface that 'The majority of psychiatrists either ignored the existence of the problem or made futile attempts to prove that these motor abnormalities were clinically unrelated to drug therapy' (Fann et al. 1980).

By the early 1980s, Roche still claimed that only between 3 and 6 per cent of people on antipsychotics develop tardive dyskinesia and, therefore, only 5–10 million of the 150 million people Roche estimated were on the drugs at the time had tardive dyskinesia (Hill 1986). A conservative estimate based on the research available at the time was 33 million tardive dyskinesia cases worldwide, for 21 million of whom the brain damage was irreversible (Hill 1986). A 1992 estimate, based on everyone who had ever received the drugs to that date, was 86 million tardive dyskinesia cases, 57 million of which were irreversible (Hill 1992).

By 1983, tardive dyskinesia had, justifiably, been described as 'one of the worst medically-induced disasters in history' (Breggin 1983). Recently, a large out-of-court settlement was won by an American tardive dyskinesia sufferer on the basis of Article 3 of the Human Rights Act 1988, which states that 'no one shall be subjected to inhuman or degrading treatment or punishment' (Chari et al. 2002).

Neuroleptic malignant syndrome

The most extreme side-effect is neuroleptic malignant syndrome. This is characterized by muscle rigidity, fever, autonomic nervous system instability and reduced consciousness. It occurs in between 0.02 and 1.9% of individuals treated with neuroleptics (Jeste and Naimark 1997). Of those who develop the condition, between 4 and 25% die.

If we assume that 0.5% of the population is treated with neuroleptics, these figures can be entered into a simple equation. The risk of death from NMS could be as high as $(0.005 \times 0.019 \times 0.25 = 0.000026)$, which is roughly one per 40,000 people. This means that as many as 7500 people among those currently alive in the USA will die of NMS. The low end of the death-rate estimate is $(0.005 \times 0.0002 \times 0.04 = 0.00000004)$, which yields approximately 12 deaths in the USA. Given that one of us (C.A.R.) saw two deaths from NMS in one hospital over a period of 9 years, the low end of the estimated death toll is unlikely to be accurate.

The new 'safer' atypical antipsychotics

> Although the new atypical drugs have been marketed as being more effective and having a kinder side-effect profile than traditional drugs, these claims are largely drug company hype. When compared to an appropriately low dose of a traditional compound the only real advantage of the atypicals is in a reduced risk of extra-pyramidal symptoms.
>
> (Bentall and Morrison 2002: 354)

Nowadays, the long ignored or minimized 'side-effects' of the conventional antipsychotics, including tardive dyskinesia, are enthusiastically publicized by drug companies to sell their 'atypical' antipsychotics. There does appear to be some basis to the claim that the atypical antipsychotics have fewer adverse-effects than the conventional antipsychotics, especially in the important area of tardive dyskinesia.

One of the first of the new wave of antipsychotic drugs was clozapine, marketed as especially useful in 'treatment-resistant' patients. (This term masks the fact that the drugs didn't work by locating the problem in the 'patient'.) It was also marketed as safer than the conventional antipsychotics. It was soon revealed, however, that it can cause agranulocytosis, a reduction in white blood cells leading to a decreased ability to combat infections (Kane and Marder 1993) and, therefore, death from infectious complications (Alvir et al. 1993). The risk is higher in two of the groups at whom the drugs are targeted, women and older people (Alvir et al. 1993). One study found that only 10% of people on these drugs knew about this danger (Angermeyer et al. 2001).

It is claimed repeatedly that the newer atypical antipsychotics have a lower risk of extrapyramidal adverse effects than conventional antipsychotics. For instance, Jeste et al. (1999) found tardive dyskinesia rates, after 9 months, of 30% for conventional antipsychotics but only 5% for atypical antipsychotics. However, many of these comparisons have been made, conveniently, with the 'high-potency' drug haloperidol, a particularly nasty drug in terms of extrapyramidal effects (Leucht et al. 1999). In fact, comparisons between atypical antipsychotics and 'low-potency' conventional antipsychotics (e.g. thioridazine) find no differences in extrapyramidal effects (Schillevoort et al. 2001). A recent review of the tardive dyskinesia research concluded that the atypical antipsychotics are 'promising' but that 'further long-term studies and observations are still necessary before reaching any conclusion' (Llorca et al. 2002).

The atypical antipsychotics, unlike the conventional antipsychotics, however, produce an increased risk of glucose intolerance and diabetes, especially in men (Hedenmalm et al. 2002). Atypical antipsychotics are also more likely than conventional antipsychotics to cause obesity, which, besides the social stigma involved, can lead to hypertension, cardiovascular disease, hyperlipidaemia and, again, diabetes (Allison *et al.* 1999; Russell and Mackell 2001). These adverse effects, combined with drug-induced sexual dysfunction and 'neuroleptic dysphoria', are largely why about half of the people prescribed antipsychotics today 'do not fully comply with treatment' (Perkins 2002). A British study found that the sexual dysfunction and weight gain 'are more troubling than the extra-pyramidal effects that the atypical compounds are designed to avoid' (Day *et al.* 1997).

The increasing use of cognitive-behavioural therapy with individuals ('compliance therapy'), or so-called 'psycho-education' with families (see Chapters 17 and 23), as an antidote to the high frequency with which people stop taking these drugs, seems to us to be as unprofessional and unethical as if we were to use our therapeutic techniques and professional power to persuade people to throw their drugs away, which, of course, we would never do.

Sudden death from cardiac arrest has been found most often with the conventional antipsychotics, particularly thioridazine (Reilly *et al.* 2002), for years one of the most commonly prescribed antipsychotics. However, 'all currently available antipsychotics have electrophysiological properties that should increase the risk of sudden cardiac death' (Ray and Meador 2002: 484) and there are case reports of sudden death for most of these. Sertindole, one of the atypical antipsychotics, has already been withdrawn from sale due to 'cardiac arrhythmias and sudden cardiac death' (World Health Organization 1998).

Simple lists of side-effects cannot convey the intensity of the torment caused by neuroleptic medications. In 4 years of residency and 6 years of general adult inpatient experience from 1981 to 1991, the clinical analysis by one the authors (C.A.R.) was that the cost–benefit of neuroleptic medications was negative. This was especially the case because of the common, extreme polypharmacy practised in psychiatry. In our experience, most patients with chronic, complex psychoses have received numerous different neuroleptics, antidepressants, anticholinergics and anxiolytics. It is not uncommon to find chronic psychotic patients on four to eight different psychotropic medications.

We are not ideologically opposed to psychotropic medications. One of us (C.A.R.) prescribes them and has participated in drug company-sponsored trials of anxiolytics, antipsychotics and antidepressants. Our point is that, although some individuals may experience a net benefit, an objective overall cost–benefit analysis would likely be negative or at best neutral if side-effects, drug–drug interactions, deaths, effects of concurrently prescribed anticholinergics and psychosocial consequences were weighed accurately. The psychosocial consequences of neuroleptics include stigmatization (from adverse effects such as obesity, shaking and slowed thinking, and just from being on the drugs), induction of a passive attitude towards one's disorder, dependency on government programmes for medication, and difficulty driving vehicles or finding employment.

Being given medication reinforces the view that there is something medically wrong with you. The idea that one's difficulties may be related to one's life history or current circumstances tends to get lost once one adopts the medical message that accompanies the pills. It is not, therefore, only the sedation and impaired intellectual functioning that prevents one thinking about the psychological and social causes of psychosis and finding solutions to them. Being prescribed neuroleptics reduces the motivation to even try to engage in such thinking or action.

If the cost–benefit of neuroleptic medication is indeed negative, then more funds should be invested in trials of psychosocial interventions for psychosis. Surely, the placebo response observed so consistently in the literature on psychopharmacology could be amplified by carefully designed psychosocial treatment packages.

REFERENCES

Allison, D. *et al.* (1999). Antipsychotic-induced weight gain: a comprehensive research synthesis. *American Journal of Psychiatry* 156: 1686–96.

Alvir, J. *et al.* (1993). Clozapine-induced agranulocytosis. *New England Journal of Medicine* 329: 162–7.

Angermeyer, M. *et al.* (2001). Patients' and relatives' assessment of clozapine treatment. *Psychological Medicine* 31: 509–17.

Arvantis, L. and Miller, B. (1997). Multiple fixed doses of 'Seroquel' (quetiapine) in patients with acute exacerbation of schizophrenia. *Biological Psychiatry* 42: 233–46.

Baldessarini, R. and Lipinski, J. (1976). Toxicity and side effects of antipsychotic, antimanic and antidepressant medication. *Psychiatric Annals* 6: 484–93.

Beasley, C. *et al.* (1996). Olanzapine versus placebo and haloperidol. *Neuropsychopharmacology* 14: 111–23.

Bentall, R. and Morrison, A. (2002). More harm than good: the case against using anti-psychotic drugs to prevent severe mental illness. *Journal of Mental Health* 11: 351–6.

Berger, P. and Roxroth, K. (1980). Tardive dyskinesia: clinical, biological and pharmacological perspectives. *Schizophrenia Bulletin* 6: 102–16.

Bonelli, R. *et al.* (2002). Olanzapine for Huntington's disease. *Clinical Neuropharmacology* 25: 263–5.

Breggin, P. (1983). *Psychiatric Drugs: Hazards to the Brain*. New York: Springer.

Brenner, N. (1973). *Mental Illness and the Economy*. Cambridge, MA: Harvard University Press.

Caligiuri, M. *et al.* (1997). Incidence and risk factors for severe tardive dyskinesia in older patients. *British Journal of Psychiatry* 171: 148–53.

Chari, S. *et al.* (2002). Quetiapine in tardive dyskinesia. *International Journal of Psychiatry in Clinical Practice* 6: 175–7.

Crane, G. and Smith, J. (1980). The prevalence of tardive dyskinesia. In W. Fann *et al.* (eds) *Tardive Dyskinesia: Research and Treatment*. New York: Spectrum.

Davis, J. *et al.* (1980). Important issues in the drug treatment of schizophrenia. *Schizophrenia Bulletin* 6: 70–87.

Day, J. *et al.* (1997). Discordant views of neuroleptic side effects: a potential source of conflict between patients and professionals. *Acta Psychiatrica Scandinavica* 97: 93–7.

Department of Health (1988). *Health and Personal Services Statistics for England*. London: Department of Health.

Department of Health (2003). http://www.doh.gov.uk/prescriptionstatistics/index. htm

Dewa, C. *et al.* (2002). How much are atypical antipsychotic agents being used, and do they reach the populations that need them? *Clinical Therapeutics* 24: 1466–76.

Fann, W. *et al.* (eds) (1980). *Tardive Dyskinesia*. New York: Spectrum.

Gerlach, J. *et al.* (1974). Dopaminergic hypersensitivity and cholinergic hypofunction in the pathophysiology of tardive dyskinesia. *Psychopharmacologia* 34: 21–35.

Glazer, W. *et al.* (1994). Race and tardive dyskinesia among outpatients at a CMHC. *Hospital and Community Psychiatry* 45: 38–42.

Glick, I. *et al.* (2001). Treatment with atypical antipsychotics. *Journal of Psychiatric Research* 35: 187–91.

Gosden, R. (1999). Prepsychotic treatment for schizophrenia: preventive medicine, social control, or drug marketing strategy. *Ethical Human Sciences and Services* 1: 165–77.

Grant, J. *et al.* (2002). Advances in the pharmacological treatment of pathological gambling. *Journal of Gambling Studies* 19: 85–109.

Hedenmalm, K. *et al.* (2002). Glucose intolerance with atypical antipsychotics. *Drug Safety* 25: 1107–16.

Hill, D. (1986). Tardive dyskinesia: a worldwide epidemic of irreversible brain damage. In N. Eisenberg and D. Glasgow (eds) *Current Issues in Clinical Psychology*. Aldershot: Gower.

Hill, D. (1992). Major tranquillizers: a good buy? *Clinical Psychology Forum* 49: 20–2.

IMS (2003). http://secure.imshealth.com

Jeste, D. and Naimark, D. (1997). Medication-induced movement disorders. In A. Tasman *et al.* (eds) *Psychiatry*. Philadelphia, PA: W.B. Saunders.

Jeste, D. and Wyatt, R. (1979). In search of treatment for tardive dyskinesia. *Schizophrenia Bulletin* 5: 251–93.

Jeste, D. *et al.* (1995). Risk of tardive dyskinesia in older patients. *Archives of General Psychiatry* 52: 756–65.

Jeste, D. *et al.* (1999). Lower incidence of tardive dyskinesia with risperidone compared with haloperidol in older patients. *Journal of the American Geriatrics Society* 47: 716–19.

Johnstone, L. (2000). *Users and Abusers of Psychiatry*, 2nd edn. London: Routledge.

Kane, J. and Marder, S. (1993). Psychopharmacological treatment of schizophrenia. *Schizophrenia Bulletin* 19: 287–302.

Kasper, S. and Muller-Spahn (2000). Review of quetiapine and its clinical applications in schizophrenia. *Expert Opinions in Pharmacotherapy* 1: 783–801.

Klawans, H. *et al.* (1974). Neuroleptic induced tardive dyskinesia in non-psychotic patients. *Archives of Neurology* 30: 338–9.

Leucht, S. *et al.* (1999). Efficacy and extrapyramidal side-effects of the new antipsychotics olanzapine, quetiapine, risperidole, and sertindole compared to conventional antipsychotics and placebo. *Schizophrenia Bulletin* 35: 51–68.

Llorca, P. *et al.* (2002). Tardive dyskinesia and antipsychotics. *European Psychiatry* 17: 129–38.

McGorry, P. *et al.* (2001). Ethics and early intervention in psychosis. *Schizophrenia Research* 51: 17–29.

McGrath, A. and Jackson, G. (1996). Survey of neuroleptic prescribing in residents of nursing homes in Glasgow. *British Medical Journal* 312: 611–12.

Moynihan, R. *et al.* (2002). Selling sickness: the pharmaceutical industry and disease mongering. *British Medical Journal* 324: 886–90.

Patel, N. *et al.* (2002). Trends in antipsychotic use in a Texas Medicaid population of children and adolescents. *Journal of Child and Adolescent Psychopharmacology* 12: 221–9.

Perkins, D. (2002). Predictors of noncompliance in patients with schizophrenia. *Journal of Clinical Psychiatry* 63: 1121–8.

Pharmac (New Zealand Pharmaceutical Management Agency) (2002). http://www.pharmac.govt.nz/stats/index.html

Ray, W. and Meador, K. (2002). Antipsychotics and sudden death. *British Journal of Psychiatry* 180: 483–4.

Reilly, J. *et al.* (2002). Thioridazine and sudden unexplained death in psychiatric in-patients. *British Journal of Psychiatry* 180: 515–22.

Ross, C. (2000). *The Trauma Model: A Solution to the Problem of Comorbidity in Psychiatry*. Richardson, TX: Manitou Communications.

Russell, J. and Mackell, J. (2001). Bodyweight gain associated with atypical anti-psychotics. *CNS Drugs* 15: 537–51.

Schillevoort, I. *et al.* (2001). Antipsychotic-induced extrapyramidal syndromes. *European Journal of Clinical Pharmacology* 57: 327–31.

Scull, A. (1984). *Decarceration: Community Treatment and the Deviant*. Cambridge: Polity Press.

Sedgwick, P. (1982). *Psycho Politics*. London: Pluto.

Snyder, R. *et al.* (2002). Effects of risperidone on conduct and disruptive behavior disorders in children with subaverage IQs. *Journal of the American Academy of Child and Adolescent Psychiatry* 41: 1026–36.

Vaughn, C. and Leff, J. (1976). The influence of family and social factors on the course of psychiatric illness. *British Journal of Psychiatry* 129: 127–37.

Warner, R. (1985). *Recovery from Schizophrenia*. London: Routledge.

World Health Organization (1998). www.who.int/medicines/library/qsm/drug alert78.htm

Zito, J. *et al.* (2003). Psychotropic practice patterns for youth. *Archives of Pediatric and Adolescent Medicine* 157: 17–25.

Chapter 10

Drug companies and schizophrenia
Unbridled capitalism meets madness

Loren R. Mosher, Richard Gosden and Sharon Beder

The major thrust of this book is an examination of the psycho-social origins of, and approaches to dealing with, the problem labelled as 'schizophrenia'. However, it needs also to provide a historical context and examine critically how the current complete domination of schizophrenia's 'treatment' by the neuroleptic drugs (we'll use this term and antipsychotic interchangeably) came to be. Not only do they dictate practice, but they also buttress the biomedical theorizing that dominates thinking about the problem.

Chlorpromazine (Thorazine), the first neuroleptic, arrived on the scene in the early 1950s. It received Food and Drug Administration (FDA) approval in 1955. By 1958 it was in almost universal use in American mental hospitals for the treatment of 'schizophrenia' and 'related conditions'. Such rapid adoption of a new treatment was unheard of in psychiatry. How did this occur? In 1956, Smith Klein and French, Thorazine's manufacturer, assembled its American drug 'detailers' (salespersons) to instruct them to behave as 'assault troops' (Johnson 1990) in their efforts to convince psychiatrists to use their new 'magic bullet'. This was the first massive public relations foray by a pharmaceutical company into a previously small market – institutional psychiatry. In its first year on the market, the drug made US$75 million for Smith Klein and French (Healy 2002a). The rest, as they say, is history. Thorazine and it successors, despite their adverse effects, are widely viewed as the only 'real' treatment for 'schizophrenia'. The basic elements of this aggressive sales campaign, refined and expanded (detailed below), would be used time and again to sell new drugs to the psychiatric market. The introduction of chlorpromazine was such a defining moment in American psychiatry that it has, over the years, generated a number of unsupportable beliefs about what these drugs actually did. While these are so firmly held they may warrant an attribution of being 'delusions', Mosher and Burti (1994) have charitably divided the beliefs into 'proven' and 'mythological' (see Table 10.1).

Against, this background, the current context of the influence of the pharmaceutical industry (capitalism) and psychopharmacology on psychiatry and 'schizophrenia' (madness) in particular can be examined.

Table 10.1   Neuroleptic drugs: proven and mythological effects

Proven effects
1   Reduce the 'positive' (externally expressed) symptoms of 'schizophrenia'
2   Shorten, overall, hospital stays
3   Usually reduce readmission rates
4   Produce serious, often permanent, iatrogenic diseases like tardive dyskinesia
5   Revitalized interest in 'schizophrenia'
6   Produce enormous corporate profits

Mythological effects
1   Responsible for depopulation of psychiatric hospitals – 'deinstitutionalization'
2   Improve long-term recovery rates for 'schizophrenia'
3   Enhance learning of new coping skills
4   Address the aetiology of 'schizophrenia'
5   Readmission rates would be nearly zero if drug compliance were assured

Modified from Mosher and Burti (1994: 52).

SOME FACTS, FIGURES AND OPINIONS

It is abundantly clear to any thoughtful observer of the psychiatric scene that drug company influence is pervasive and expanding. A few facts are illustrative. Between 1993 and 2001, prescription drug spending tripled in the USA, rising from US$50 billion to US$150 billion or more (Szegely-Marzak 2001). For the third consecutive year (2001) prescription drug prices rose in double digits (17%), in contrast to overall inflation, which remained in the 2–3% range (Public Citizen 2001). In 2000, psychotropic drug sales in the USA totalled US$23 billion and are expected to rise to US$42 billion by 2005. Of the US$23 billion, over US$10 billion was spent on antidepressants. Between 1990 and 2000, spending on antidepressant drugs rose 800% (Tanouye 2001), due principally to the introduction of the selective serotonin reuptake inhibitors (SSRIs). Over the same period, the availability of the new 'atypical' antipsychotic drugs caused spending on neuroleptics to rise 600%, to US$4 billion in 2001 (Moukheiber 2001). The successful selling of atypical antipsychotics – the reason for this 600% rise – to replace the older, no longer patented, neuroleptics, will be the major focus of this chapter. One indication of the success of the selling of the 'atypicals' is the increase in use of antipsychotic drugs in youth (under 18) in the last decade. In 1992, 50,000 outpatients received them; by 2002, the figure had reached 530,000 (Thomas 2002).

The large pharmaceutical companies averaged 30–40% of revenues spent on marketing and administration, 15–20% profit and 12–15% on research and development. In the USA, they paid an average of 16% of revenues in taxes, whereas all other industries averaged 27% (Angell and Relman 2001). They have 625 paid lobbyists in Washington, DC, one per congressperson (Public Citizen 2001)! They spent nearly US$2.7 billion on direct-to-consumer (TV and non-medical magazine) advertising in 2001. Until 1997, direct-to-consumer advertising had been forbidden, and still is in the rest of the Western industrialized world (except New Zealand, where it is currently under review). Roughly a third of the American Psychiatric Association's (APA) budget is derived from various drug sources (*Psychiatric News*, 15 August 1997, p. 4). American Psychiatric Association meetings are dominated by drug company sponsored exhibits and symposia providing attendees with a variety of enticements: music, food, drink, disc players, and so on.

Drug companies provide substantial support to nearly all of the mental health advocacy organizations like the National Alliance for the Mentally Ill (NAMI), the National Mental Health Association (NMHA), the National Alliance for Research on Schizophrenia and Affective Disorders (NARSAD), National Depressive Disorder Screening Day, the Anxiety Disorders Association, and so on (O'Harrow 2000). The only groups Big Pharma doesn't support are the true consumer advocacy organizations like the Support Coalition International (SCI), the National Empowerment Center (NEC) and the National Association for Rights Protection and Advocacy (NARPA).

Perhaps the industry's most successful marketing tool is direct personal contact with doctors by their 'detailers', recently reframed as 'sales representatives'. These representatives are portrayed as 'conduits of information'. Actually, they supply physicians with well-sanitized information, promotional materials and samples of their company's latest products. In 2001, there were, industry-wide, 83,000 such persons, twice the number in 1996. These 'conduits of information' cost about US$8 billion a year and their samples an equivalent amount (Angell and Relman 2001).

The drug industry supports clinical trial research at universities to the extent that it is doubtful that many departments of psychiatry could survive without it. The pharmaceutical industry owns the data from clinical trials it supports, decides which studies are published, chooses authors, ghost writes articles and revises them to present the best possible interpretation of the data (Angell 2000).

John LeCarre (2001), in 'In Place of Nations', an essay in *The Nation*, said the following about the pharmaceutical industry from the perspective of a non-scientist:

> BIG PHARMA (the multinational pharmaceutical world), as it is known, offered everything: the hopes and dreams we have of it; its vast, partly realized potential for good; and it's pitch-dark underside, sustained by huge wealth, pathological secrecy, corruption and greed. And of all these crimes of unbridled capitalism, it seemed to me, as I began to cast round for a story to illustrate this argument in my most recent novel, that the pharmaceutical industry offered me the most

eloquent example. But Big Pharma is also engaged in the deliberate seduction of the medical profession, country by country, worldwide. It is spending a fortune on influencing, hiring and purchasing academic judgment to a point where, in a few years' time, if Big Pharma continues unchecked on its present happy path, unbought medical opinion will be hard to find. And consider what happens to supposedly impartial academic medical research when giant pharmaceutical companies donate whole biotech buildings and endow professorships at universities and teaching hospitals where their products are tested and developed. There has been a steady flow of alarming cases in recent years where inconvenient scientific findings have been suppressed or rewritten, and those responsible for them hounded off their campuses with their professional and personal reputations systematically trashed by the machinations of public relations agencies in the pay of the pharmas.

(LeCarre 2001: 11)

In 'Is academic medicine for sale?' (2000), the editor of the *New England Journal of Medicine*, Marcia Angell, catalogued from her professional point of view the many ways that drug money flowed to academic doctors:

The ties between clinical researchers and industry include not only grant support, but also a host of other financial arrangements. Researchers also serve as consultants to companies whose products they are studying, join advisory boards and speakers' bureaus, enter into patent and royalty arrangements, agree to be the listed authors of articles ghostwritten by interested companies, promote drugs and devices at company sponsored symposiums and allow themselves to be plied with expensive gifts and trips to luxurious settings. Many also have equity interest in the companies.

(Angell 2000: 1517)

In 2002, the *British Medical Journal* published an article entitled 'Selling sickness: the pharmaceutical industry and disease mongering' (Moynihan *et al.* 2002). The authors argued that 'Pharmaceutical companies are actively involved in sponsoring the definition of diseases and promoting them to both prescribers and consumers. The social construction of illness is being replaced by the corporate construction of disease' (p. 886). They concluded that 'A publicly funded and independently run programme of "de-medicalisation", based on respect for human dignity, rather than shareholder value or professional hubris, is overdue' (p. 890). Psychiatrists Joanna Moncrieff and Phil Thomas (2002) replied:

The influence of the pharmaceutical industry is particularly pernicious in psychiatry where the possibilities for colonizing ever more aspects of human life are potentially limitless. Psychiatry is an area of controversy, where different paradigms and approaches to treatment are hotly contested. The financial muscle of the pharmaceutical industry has helped to tip the scales in favour of a predominantly biological view of psychiatric disorder. This has submerged alternative therapeutic approaches, despite the fact that user-led research indicates that service users find a wide variety of non-medical approaches valuable in coping with emotional distress.

A PRIMER FOR UNDERSTANDING 'BIG PHARMA'S' MARKET TACTICS

The strategies, tactics and techniques used by the industry to market its products are legion. We present them in outline form to give readers a basic understanding.

The approval process

The American process will be described, but it is roughly similar in all Western European countries. For a new drug, two studies must be submitted to the FDA that indicate the drug is better than placebo and is without serious adverse effects for condition X. The drug need not be more effective than ones already available for condition X. Data from 'failed studies' – those showing no significant differences between drug and placebo – are not supplied to the FDA. If approved, the drug can be marketed for condition X. The companies can later apply, by submitting new studies or new analyses from old studies, for the drug's indications to be extended to new conditions or new populations (e.g. youth, the elderly). This opens a new market. The 'new indications' technique has proved to be highly successful with the SSRIs, first approved only for depression but now approved for obsessive compulsive disorder, post-traumatic stress disorder and various anxiety disorders.

Of great importance is the fact that once a drug is on the market, an individual doctor can legally prescribe it for 'off label' (unapproved) indications. Because doctors are often given a variety of drug company 'perks', beginning while in training, they are 'open' to listening to the detailers and may in fact be rewarded with more goodies if they prescribe enough (the companies track prescribing practices) of a new 'silver bullet' (Wazana 2000).

Sales campaigns

- 'Carpet bombing' of doctors' offices with visits from sales representatives who distribute promotional materials and samples.
- Sponsorship of nationwide symposia keynoted by 'thought leaders' in the field who are on the company's payroll. This includes organizing 'educational' forums for government, academia and the public.
- Publication of selected (most positive) studies of the drug authored by high-profile investigators to lend extra credibility. Up to 50% of these may be 'ghost authored' (Healy 2002b).
- Endorsements by various organizations with paid alliances with the drug company – NAMI, NMHA, etc. A remarkable example of this type of activity is that of the Global Alliance Mental Illness Advocacy Network. It was started based on the results of a 1998 survey, funded mostly by Bristol Meyers, showing that most people didn't like taking psychiatric drugs, primarily because of their adverse effects. There was therefore a 'need' to undertake a 'worldwide' campaign to 'encourage' more people to seek psychiatric treatment. Like other organizations, it promotes Big Pharma's agenda.
- Generation of 'media hype' via celebrity endorsements, articles placed by public relations agencies and direct-to-consumer advertising. The latter is a relatively new technique that has proven highly successful.
- Expanding the prescriber base. The company focuses its detailers' efforts on getting primary care doctors comfortable with prescribing their new 'safe, effective and well-tolerated' drug that has ordinarily been the province of a particular specialty group. This has been an extraordinarily successful technique with both the SSRI antidepressants (i.e. 60% or more of SSRI prescriptions are written by non-psychiatrists) and the 'atypical' antipsychotic drugs.
- Large market formulary makers are lobbied to convince them the drug should be included in the formularies so it will be paid for by programmes like the relevant National Health Care agency or Medicaid, managed care companies, insurers and the military in the USA.
- Substantial political campaign contributions are made, and legislators and government regulatory bodies are lobbied to be sure pharmaceutical company interests are protected and advanced.
- Persons less suspect than drug corporation executives (prominent academicians and scientists) are paid to represent them in taking the lead to counter criticisms. If this fails, critics are systematically discredited, demonized or harassed by colleagues employed in some capacity by the company (Healy 2002b,c). Funding will be withdrawn from journals or other outlets that publish material unfavourable to the pharmaceutical company's interests (Healy 2002b,c). Investigators have

even been sued by the company that paid for the research when negative results were published (Bodenheimer and Collins 2001).

- If sued because of a drug's adverse effect(s), companies prefer to settle out of court and 'seal' the case to avoid harmful publicity and to insure the parties can't reveal the details of the settlement.
- As patents begin to run out, the companies engage in a number of strategies to keep generic versions of the drug off the market. They buy off the potential generic drug makers, tie them up in long court proceedings, produce a new form of the drug (e.g. long acting) and threaten groups working to enhance the availability of generic drugs.

For example, the *New York Times* published a report (Peterson and Abelson 2002) entitled 'Companies Reduce Roles in Lobby Group for Generics'. In summary, it reported that two members of a lobbying coalition for generic drugs (Business for Affordable Medicine) had left the group or reduced their roles after drug companies, Eli Lilly and Wyeth, threatened to end contracts with Georgia Pacific Paper and Verizon Communications, who had been supporting the lobbying.

CONFLICT OF INTEREST: IS THE FOX WATCHING THE CHICKEN COOP?

A special problem is that it has become nearly impossible for the American drug regulatory agency, the FDA, to convene advisory groups that do not contain members with conflicts of interest in the discussion of drugs under consideration. *USA Today* (2000) analysed the financial conflicts at 159 FDA advisory committee meetings between 1 January 1998 and 30 June 2000. They found that at 92% of the meetings, at least one member had a financial conflict of interest. At 55% of the meetings, half or more of the FDA advisors had conflicts of interest. Conflicts of interest were most frequent at the 57 meetings when broader issues were discussed; 92% of members had conflicts. At the 102 meetings dealing with the fate of a specific drug, 33% of the experts had a financial conflict. In addition, about half of the FDA's budget is derived from drug company fees. Is the fox watching the chicken coop?

A CURRENT EXAMPLE: SELLING THE ATYPICAL ANTIPSYCHOTIC DRUGS

Good drug/bad drug

Although the drug companies made handsome profits early on from their neuroleptic drugs, their sales of this class of drugs stopped growing when the indications for their use were fairly clearly confined to psychosis because of their dangers. Also, the increasing number of 'me-too' antipsychotic drugs (17 by 1980) split the profit pie into many modest size pieces. Finally, by the mid-1980s, the patent lives of nearly all of these agents had run out and cheaper generic versions had become available. This meant that spending on these agents was basically flat, at about US$400 million a year, from 1980 until the approval of clozapine in 1990, the first of the so-called atypical antipsychotics. However, it was not until risperidone's (Risperdal) approval in 1994 that this new class of drugs became a realistic alternative to the older ones. Clozapine is a complicated and dangerous drug to administer, with limited indications; hence it was approached with caution. Three additional atypical agents were not far behind risperidone in the FDA approval process: olanzapine (Zyprexa), quietapine (Seroquel) and ziprasidone (Geodon). So, the task of Big Pharma was to have its new, patented, far more expensive drugs replace the older ones. With four to choose from, they had to be concerned about market share and market penetration.

Not unexpectedly, the older drugs – made by the very same pharmaceutical companies – were suddenly portrayed as not very good, especially when compared with the new ones. It was as if the deficiencies and toxicities of the older agents (e.g. chlorpromazine, haloperidol, fluphenazine, etc.) had been suddenly discovered. They were ineffective in 30–40% of cases, had very high rates of unpleasant side-effects and caused, over the longer term, the now 'terrible' iatrogenic diseases of tardive dyskinesia, tardive dementia and neuroleptic-induced deficiency syndrome (Healy 2002a). Before the pricey new patented drugs arrived, these problems were never sufficient to warrant questioning their use. Suddenly they became intolerable. All stops were pulled out as Big Pharma used its tried and true public relations methods, perfected with the selling of the SSRIs to replace the older tricyclic antidepressants.

However, in introducing the new drugs the pharmaceutical companies were confronted by two difficult public relations problems: first, the new drugs are many times more expensive than the older drugs and, second, according to critics, they are no more effective or safer than the drugs they have replaced (Breggin and Cohen 1999; Geddes *et al.* 2000; see also Chapter 9). In its final letter of approval to Janssen, the FDA made explicit its conclusions about the relative merits of risperidone and haloperidol. Robert Temple, director of the FDA's Office of Drug Evaluation, told Janssen:

> We would consider any advertisement or promotion labeling for RISPERDAL false, misleading, or lacking fair balance under section 502 (a) and 502 (n) of the ACT if there is presentation of data that conveys the impression that risperidone is superior to haloperidol or

any other marketed antipsychotic drug product with regard to safety or effectiveness.

(Whitaker 2002: 277)

Geddes *et al.* (2000) reviewed the results of 52 studies involving 12,649 patients and concluded, 'there is no clear evidence that atypical antipsychotics are more effective or are better tolerated than conventional antipsychotics'.

Setting the agenda

The companies wanted to maximize profits in what appeared to be a potentially critical environment and a tight market. They decided the best approach would be to find ways to expand the size of the market. Hitherto the market for schizophrenia drugs had been restricted by diagnostic conventions on the one hand and civil liberties protections on the other. Until recently, diagnostic conventions generally limited the recognition of schizophrenia and, therefore, the application of neuroleptic drug treatment, to persons with active clinical symptoms indicative of psychosis. The drug company agenda setters determined to expand the market by breaking this convention and promoting the concept of an additional pre-psychotic phase of schizophrenia that requires preventive treatment with their new drugs. To expand the market further, they also participated in campaigns to weaken civil liberties protections and thereby increase the number of people who could be treated involuntarily. Finally, as they did to promote the SSRIs, they expanded the prescriber base to primary care physicians, gerontologists and paediatricians. This was accomplished by sending sales representatives to these physicians' offices to promote the 'safety, effectiveness and well tolerated' mantra, this time about the atypical antipsychotics compared with the 'problematic' older neuroleptics. So, the impression was left that these newer agents would be safe to use in youth, non-psychotic persons and the elderly. The previously noted ten-fold increase in use of antipsychotic drugs in the 18 and under population in the last decade is stark testimony to the success of this effort.

The overall solution was the development of a two-part public relations campaign. The first part involves harnessing support groups for relatives of people suffering from schizophrenia as the driving force for an advocacy coalition (see NAMI's contribution to the media hype below). This has been achieved by carefully focused funding of these organizations (Gosden 2001). Once they were made dependent on drug company 'sponsorship', they could then be used as public relations front-groups to assist with planting stories in the media about the efficacy and safety of the new drugs. They also supported claims that schizophrenia has supposedly been scientifically proven to be a brain disease requiring urgent drug treatment at the earliest signs. A ready example of this practice can found at Schizophrenia.com (2001a), which purports to be 'A Not-for-Profit Information, Support and Education Center' representing consumers. However, Schizophrenia.com acknowledges on its web site that it is funded by Janssen Pharmaceuticals (Schizophrenia.com 2001b). The slant on schizophrenia promoted by drug company funded organizations like Schizophrenia.com is intended to impact on governments as expressions of public interest advocacy and to position the new drugs as preferred methods of treatment by government mental health services.

Media hype

Another part of their strategy involved a media hype by 'experts'. Risperidone, the *Washington Post* reported (16 February 1993), 'represents a glimmer of hope for a disease that until recently had been considered hopeless'. George Simpson, a prominent psychopharmacologist (and long-term drug company 'consultant', 'advisor', 'investigator') at the Medical College of Pennsylvania, told the *Post*, 'The data is very convincing. It is a new hope, and at this moment it appears, like clozapine, to be different from all existing drugs'. The *New York Times* (15 January 1992), quoting Richard Meibach, Janssen's clinical research director (no conflict of interest here for sure), reported that 'no major side effects' had appeared in *any* of the 2000-plus patients who had been in the clinical trials.

Olanzapine, the *Wall Street Journal* (10 April 1996) announced, has 'substantial advantages' over other current therapies. 'Zyprexa is a wonderful drug for psychotic patients', said John Zajecka, at Rush Medical College in Chicago. Stanford University psychiatrist Alan Schatzberg, meanwhile, confessed to the *New York Times* (14 April 1998) 'It's a potential breakthrough of tremendous magnitude' (Whitaker 2002: 260). Endorsements for specific drugs like these, from academic psychiatrists, usually indicate drug company sponsorship.

Or as the *Los Angeles Times* (30 January 1998) put it: 'It used to be that schizophrenics were given no hope of improving. But now, thanks to new drugs and *commitment*, they're moving back into society like never before' (Whitaker 2002: 259). Laurie Flynn, then Executive Director of NAMI, put an exclamation point on it all: 'These new drugs truly are a breakthrough. They mean we should finally be able to keep people out of the hospital, and it means that the long-term disability of schizophrenia can come to an end' (Whitaker 2002: 261).

NAMI put it together into its full mythic glory. In 1999, it copyrighted *Breakthroughs in Antipsychotic Medications* (Weiden *et al.* 1999). Inside the front cover were framed colour photos of the new wonder pills. The NAMI authors wrote:

Conventional antipsychotics all do about the same job in the brain. They all correct brain chemistry by working on the dopamine systems in the brain . . . the newer medications seem to do a better job of balancing all of the brain chemicals, including dopamine and serotonin . . . just give the new medication plenty of time to do a good job!

(Weiden *et al.* 1999, in Whitaker 2002: 283)

These glowing endorsements should be contrasted with the views of the FDA, Breggin and Cohen (1999) and Geddes *et al.* (2000) noted above, and with Chapter 9.

A question of ethics

One aspect of the campaign involves funding selected psychiatric researchers to promote the doubtful belief that schizophrenia must be detected and treated in a pre-psychotic stage to avoid brain deterioration (Gosden 2001). This argument has the potential to vastly expand the market for schizophrenia drugs and has already led to the development in Australia of government-sponsored preventive treatment programmes for schizophrenia that utilize the new drugs. Treating 'at risk' adolescents with these very powerful agents raises serious ethical issues that the drug companies fail to attend to in any meaningful way. The risk of serious adverse effects, treating large numbers of 'false-positive' youth with these powerful drugs, the potential for stigmatization and the creation of self-fulfilling prophecies are given scant consideration in this 'damn the torpedoes, full speed ahead' endeavour. A project studying 'pre-psychotic at risk' youth at Yale University has already been criticized for its failure to provide an accurate informed consent document. Mysteriously, it did not mention the possible consequences of treatment with olanzapine! Most recently, the Institute of Psychiatry at the Maudsley Hospital in London has approved a controversial protocol to treat 'at risk' youngsters with an atypical psychotic drug (McKie 2002).

Let the force be with you

A key element of the public relations strategy involves funding from the drug company Eli Lilly being channelled through both the World Psychiatric Association (Rosen *et al.* 2000) and NAMI (Oaks 2000; Silverstein 1999) to mount an anti-stigma campaign. The thrust of the anti-stigma campaign is to advocate for the elimination of discrimination against people diagnosed with schizophrenia, *so long as they are taking medication*, by force if necessary.

Meanwhile, in what appears to be a coordinated strategy, the Treatment Advocacy Center (TAC), which was originally established as a branch of

NAMI, has been feeding a very different, but complementary, line to the media and the public about the dangers of untreated schizophrenia. This line involves associating untreated schizophrenia with news stories about violent behaviour (Torrey and Zdanowicz 1999) and promoting wild hyperbole about the murderous intentions of untreated schizophrenics: 'Violent episodes by individuals with untreated schizophrenia and bipolar disorder have risen dramatically, now accounting for an estimated 1,000 homicides annually in the United States' (TAC 2001). This approach is intended to send an agenda-setting spin in the opposite direction by scaring the public and impacting on governments as a law and order imperative. The policy intention of this counter-spin is to weaken civil liberties protections in mental health laws to increase the number of people eligible for involuntary treatment.

Involuntary treatment is an essential part of the market for schizophrenia drugs. Without involuntary treatment, there would be a smaller market because many people diagnosed with schizophrenia initially have to be force-treated with neuroleptic drugs. A central objective of this hyper-stigmatizing, law and order part of the campaign is the introduction of community treatment orders, or outpatients' commitment. Outpatients' commitment involves a court order that allows the forced treatment of people living in their own homes. Until the introduction of outpatients' commitment, people could only be force-treated in hospital. This limited the number of involuntary patients at any one time to the number of beds available. However, considering the doubtful nature of diagnostic methods used for identifying schizophrenia, outpatient commitment promises to provide an open-ended expansion of the market for the new schizophrenia drugs. Outpatients' commitment is already well established in most states of Australia and is being progressively introduced, state by state, in the USA.

By the numbers

In the mid-1990s, as several of the new schizophrenia drugs were passing through their final stages of approval, and these public relations campaigns were gaining momentum, one analyst of the pharmaceutical market argued that the US$1 billion a year American market for schizophrenia drugs could be expanded to US$4.5 billion a year. Annual sales of Eli Lilly's drug Zyprexa alone were projected 'at $1 billion after five years on the market'. But the analyst argued that the market expansion depended on the removal of two barriers. The first barrier was that currently only half of the 2.5 million Americans with schizophrenic symptoms were then receiving treatment. The implication was that ways would have to be found to ensure treatment reached this other half. The second barrier was that a cheap generic drug was then dominating the market (Reuters Information Service 1996).

As things have turned out, this analyst underestimated the potential for a public relations driven expansion of the market for schizophrenia drugs. A *Wall Street Journal* report in May 2001 describes the market for schizophrenia drugs as a 'fast-growing, $5 billion-a-year market' in which Eli Lilly's Zyprexa has already gained a US$2.35 billion share and is 'on course to surpass $2.5 billion this year' (Hensley and Burton 2001). Using a sales figure of US$4 billion for atypical antipsychotic drugs in the USA in 2001, the *profit* realized by Big Pharma is about US$740 million! In addition, the atypicals had achieved a market penetration of nearly 90% in the USA. In Europe, probably because of national health care systems, their penetration has been around 40% (Nina Schoder, personal communication, April 2002). So, Big Pharma succeeded in every respect: high profitability and full market penetration for the 'atypicals'. Their patents will probably have expired before we really know their serious adverse effects.

POLICY IMPLICATIONS

Public policy analysts often dissect the strategies and techniques of vested interests like Big Pharma using agenda-setting theory. Cobb *et al.* (1976) propose three models of agenda building: an outside-initiative model where citizens' groups gain broad public support and get an issue onto the formal agenda; a second model where the issues are initiatives that come from government and may need to be placed on the public agenda for successful implementation; and an inside-access model where the policy proposals come from policy communities with easy access to government, usually with support from particular interest groups, but little public involvement.

It is clear that the types of campaigns that have been run by public relations consultants to set the mental health agenda for the pharmaceutical industry utilize all three of these models. They run coordinated campaigns that involve funding consumer advocacy groups to simulate outside-initiatives; they plant stories in the media that are designed to gain public acceptance of policies that are already on the government agenda; and they use the insider-access model when they utilize pharmaceutical industry lobbying organizations to gain easy access to government. This access is facilitated by the millions of dollars pharmaceutical companies and associations donate to politicians and political parties (Mintz 2000; Public Citizen 2000).

The use of sophisticated public relations techniques for setting political agendas has become a standard practice in most advanced democracies. The consequences are slowly becoming apparent. The system of representative democracy is being reshaped into a new kind of 'managed corporatocracy' in which public opinion and government policy are custom-made products that can be shaped, packaged and sold by skilled public relations experts. This example of a successful campaign to sell a very expensive product – the atypical antipsychotic drugs – is chilling testimony to the power of Big Pharma to have its way with us.

The cynical way in which this shaping, packaging and selling has been carried out in terms of mental health policy making over the last two decades should serve as a warning to anyone who believes that the public good should come before corporate profits. Policies tailored to this commercial purpose are not necessarily beneficial either for patients or society at large

The acute vulnerability of mental patients to exploitation, and the existence of mental health laws that provide for involuntary detention and treatment of certain classes of mentally disordered people, creates conditions that require vigilant protection of civil liberties and human rights. To do so in the face of the power of a US$150 billion a year industry (in the USA) that has only the 'bottom line' to guide its activities is a formidable, and perhaps impossible, task without assertive governmental regulatory intervention. Given the current American political climate, it appears that such intervention is unlikely in the foreseeable future.

However, Big Pharma's power may be curbed by legal actions against the industry for failure to adequately disclose potential adverse drug effects and against doctors for overuse and misuse (failure to adequately monitor) psychotropics. Professional associations (like the American Psychiatric Association) could implement strict disclosure rules about conflicts of interest that should at least highlight the extent to which they exist among its members.

Individual policy makers, managers and professionals working in the mental health field, and psychiatrists in particular, have an ethical and professional responsibility to consider the extent to which they, and their professions, are influenced by drug company money and propaganda and, having considered, to act. Refusing to take drug company money would be a start. If that proves difficult, you will at least have learned just how dependent your department, journal or professional organization has become. We have to start somewhere to gain control again.

REFERENCES

Angell, M. (2000). Is academic medicine for sale? *New England Journal of Medicine* 342(20: 1516–18.

Angell, M. and Relman, A. (2001). Prescription for profit. *Washington Post*, 20 June.

Bodenheimer, T. and Collins, R. (2001). The ethical dilemmas of drugs, money, medicine. *Seattle Times*, 15 March.

Breggin, P. and Cohen, D. (1999). *Your Drug May Be Your Problem*. Reading, MA: Perseus.

Cobb, R. *et al.* (1976). Agenda building as a comparative political process. *American Political Science Review* 70: 126–38.

Geddes, J. *et al.* (2000). Atypical antipsychotics in the treatment of schizophrenia. *British Medical Journal* 321: 1371–6.

Gosden, R. (2001). *Punishing the Patient: How Psychiatrists Misunderstand and Mistreat Schizophrenia*. Melbourne: Scribe.

Healy, D. (2002a). *The Creation of Psychopharmacology*. Cambridge, MA: Harvard University.

Healy, D. (2002b). 'The Current Status of the Antidepressants', Lecture, Institute of Psychiatry, 13 February 2002.

Healy, D. (2002c). Conflicting interests in Toronto: anatomy of a controversy at the interface of academia and industry. *Perspectives in Biology and Medicine* 45: 250–63.

Hensley, S. and Burton, T. (2001). Pfizer, Eli Lilly battle for share of growing schizophrenia market. *Wall Street Journal*, 8 May.

Johnson, A. (1990). *Out of Bedlam: The Truth About Deinstitutionalization*. New York: Basic Books.

LeCarre, J. (2001). In place of nations. *The Nation*, 9 April, p. 11.

McKie, R. (2002). Row over mental illness drug trial. *The Guardian*, 25 August.

Mintz, J. (2000). Drug firms, unions funnel millions to parties. *Washington Post*, 26 October, p. A26.

Moncrieff, J. and Thomas, P. (2002). Psychiatry should reduce commercial sponsorship. Letter to *British Medical Journal* website (www.bmj-com/cgi/eletters/324/7342/886#21632).

Mosher, L. and Burti, L. (1994). *Community Mental Health: A Practical Guide*. New York: Norton.

Moukheiber, Z. (2001). Health. *Forbes Magazine*, 14 May, pp. 267–8.

Moynihan, R. *et al.* (2002) Selling sickness: the pharmaceutical industry and disease mongering. *British Medical Journal* 324: 886–90.

Oaks, D. (2000). NAMI: the story behind the story. *Dendron* 43: 14–15.

O'Harrow, R., Jr. (2000). Grass roots seeded by drugmaker. *Washington Post*, 12 September (www.fdncenter.org/pnd/20000912/003633.html).

Peterson, M. and Abelson, R. (2002). Two companies reduce roles in lobby group for generics. *New York Times*, 4 September, C1.

Public Citizen (2000). Addicting Congress: drug companies' campaign cash & lobbying expenses (www.citizen.org/congress/reform/addicting2.htm).

Public Citizen (2001). The other drug war: Big Pharma's 625 Washington lobbyists. *Public Citizen Congress Watch Report*, 23 July.

Reuters Information Service (1996). Drugmakers look for home-runs with schizophrenia drugs (www.somerset.nando.net/newsroom/ntn/health/032496/health3_14068.html).

Rosen, A. *et al.* (2000). Combating psychiatric stigma: an overview of contemporary initiatives. *Australasian Psychiatry* 8: 19–26.

Schizophrenia.com (2001a). Legitimating brain disease: the case against 'mental illness'. Originally published in the *Journal of the California AMI*. Posted on web site by D. Jaffe of the Alliance for the Mentally Ill/Friends and Advocates of the Mentally Ill in NYC (www.schizophrenia.com/family/Braindisease.html).

Schizophrenia.com (2001b). A not-for-profit information, support and education center (www.schizophrenia.com/).

Silverstein, K. (1999). Prozac.org: an influential mental health nonprofit organisation finds its 'grassroots' watered by pharmaceutical millions. *Mother Jones*, November/December (www.motherjones.com/mother_jones/ND99/nami.html).

Szegely-Marzak, M. (2001). The career of a celebrity pill. *US News*, 8 August (www.usnews.com/usnewsissue/010806/ideas/prozac.html).

Tanouye, E. (2001). Marketplace. *Wall Street Journal*, 13 June (data from IMS Health Inc.).

Thomas, K. (2002). Surge in drugs given to kids draws concern. *USA Today*, 22 July.

Torrey, E. and Zdanowicz, M. (1999). How freedom punishes the severely mentally ill. *USA Today*, 7 June, p. 27A.

Treatment Advocacy Center (2001). Violence: unfortunate and all too often tragic side-effect of untreated severe mental illness (www.psychlaws.org/General Resources/Fact4.htm).

USA Today (2000). FDA conflicts of interest. *USA Today*, 25 September.

Wazana, A. (2000). Physicians and the pharmaceutical industry: is a gift ever just a gift? *Journal of the American Medical Association* 283: 373–80.

Weiden, P. *et al.* (1999). *Breakthroughs in Antipsychotic Medications*. New York: Norton.

Whitaker, R. (2002). *Mad in America: Bad Science, Bad Medicine and the Enduring Mistreatment of the Mentally Ill*. Cambridge, MA: Perseus.

Part II

Social and psychological approaches to understanding madness

Chapter 11

Public opinion

Bad things happen and can drive you crazy

John Read and Nick Haslam

Studies consistently find that while members of the public understand that many factors influence our mental health, they place much more emphasis on adverse life events than on biology or genetics. Nevertheless, biological psychiatry, aided by the pharmaceutical industry, insists on trying to 'educate' the public that they are wrong. It does so despite research showing that bio-genetic explanations fuel fear and prejudice.

THE PUBLIC'S REJECTION OF BIO-GENETIC CAUSAL THEORIES

United States

By 1961, the US Joint Commission on Mental Illness and Health had concluded:

> The principle of sameness as applied to the mentally sick versus the physically sick has become a cardinal tenet of mental health education . . . Psychiatry has tried diligently to make society see the mentally ill in its way and has railed at the public's antipathy or indifference.
>
> (JCMIH 1961: 59)

A decade later, a research review confirmed that the public rejected the idea that 'mental illness is just like any other illness' (Sarbin and Mancuso 1970). University students more frequently endorsed psycho-social causes than bio-genetic ones (Hill and Bale 1981). Wahl (1987) surveyed three 'lay groups' – police, community and students. The two most frequently cited causes of schizophrenia were 'environmental stress' and 'major unpleasant emotional experiences'. All three groups cited 'poor parenting, bad upbringing' more often than mental health professionals. A recent survey of US citizens found that 91% cited 'Stressful circumstances' as a cause of schizophrenia, compared with 'Chemical imbalance' (85%) and 'Genetic or inherited' (67%) (Link *et al.* 1999).

England

Rogers and Pilgrim (1997) found, in relation to mental health in general, that 'Life events, family problems and economic hardship were mentioned frequently, with genetic and biological causes noted much less frequently' (p. 29). When Londoners were asked more specifically about schizophrenia: 'Overall subjects seemed to prefer environmental explanations referring to social stressors and family conflicts – e.g. "being mercilessly persecuted by family and friends" and "having come from backgrounds that promote stress"' (Furnham and Rees 1988: 218). Another London study found that the most endorsed causal model of schizophrenia was 'Unusual or traumatic experiences or the failure to negotiate some critical stage of emotional development', followed by 'Social, economic, and family pressures'. 'It seems that lay people have not been converted to the medical view and prefer psychosocial explanations' (Furnham and Bower 1992: 207). 'Subjects agreed that schizophrenic behaviour had some meaning and was neither random nor simply a symptom of an illness' (p. 206).

Ireland

A rural survey found that for a vignette portraying the positive symptoms of schizophrenia, the most commonly cited causes were stressful life events. Only 11% cited bio-genetic causes. For negative symptoms, the most frequently cited cause was childhood problems such as 'lack of adequate parental love' (Barry and Greene 1992). Only 5% cited bio-genetic causes.

New Zealand

Two studies replicated a finding in the USA (Hill and Bale 1981) that students endorse 'interactional' items of the Mental Health Locus of Origin scale more frequently than 'endogenous' items (Read and Harre 2001; Read and Law 1999). In both studies the item most strongly endorsed was 'The mental illness of some people is caused by abuse or neglect in childhood'.

Australia

A survey of over 2000 Australians found that for schizophrenia, the most likely cause (94%) was 'Day-to-day-problems such as stress, family arguments, difficulties at work or financial difficulties'. 'Problems from childhood such as being badly treated or abused, losing one or both parents when young or coming from a broken home' was rated as a likely cause by 88.5%. 'The recent death of a close friend or relative' and 'Traumatic events' were both rated as a likely cause by 85%. Furthermore, 72% believed that the unemployed are more likely to have schizophrenia. Only 59% endorsed 'inherited or genetic' (Jorm et al. 1997).

Canada

There is one exception to these consistent findings of preference for psycho-social explanations for schizophrenia. The findings of an Alberta survey were: brain chemistry, 64%; genetics, 29%; stress, 12%; trauma, 6%. Thompson et al. (2002) acknowledge that their methodology differed from studies in other countries in that they used just the word 'Schizophrenia' rather than a vignette showing behaviours indicative of schizophrenia. We shall see later that this diagnostic labelling significantly increases belief in bio-genetic causation, as well as prejudice.

Germany

The most common causes of schizophrenia cited in a survey of over 2000 Germans were: isolation, 73%; unemployment, 72%; stress in partnership or family, 64%. Disorder of the brain was cited by 49% and heredity by 45% (Angermeyer and Matschinger 1996a). This preference for psycho-social over bio-genetic causes has been replicated, with both western and eastern Germans (Angermeyer and Matschinger 1999).

Germans (Angermeyer and Klussman 1988; Holzinger et al. 2002) and Britons (Pistrang and Barker 1992) who are themselves labelled 'schizophrenic' hold particularly strong psycho-social beliefs. However, relatives (belonging to organizations for the families of 'schizophrenics') believe in brain disorder and heredity more strongly than psycho-social factors (Angermeyer and Matschinger 1996a). The researchers attribute this to 'greater exposure to the knowledge of psychiatric experts and their having to deal with their own feelings of guilt'.

Turkey

The possibility that the German relatives' beliefs are shaped by exposure to the bio-genetic ideology of 'Western' psychiatry is supported by a study of relatives of 'schizophrenics' in Turkey, where there are only 0.6 psychiatrists per 100,000 people. They cited stressful events (50%) and family conflicts (40%) more often than biological/genetic factors (23%) (Karanci 1995).

India

Similarly, of 254 relatives in India, 55% identified psycho-social stressors (at work and in the family), whereas only 15% cited heredity and 14% brain disorder (Srinivasan and Thara 2001).

THE PUBLIC'S REJECTION OF MEDICAL TREATMENTS

The public also strongly prefers psycho-social solutions over medical interventions for schizophrenia. This has been demonstrated in Australia (Jorm *et al.* 1997), Austria (Katschnig *et al.* 1993), Canada (Thompson *et al.* 2002), England (Furnham and Bower 1992) and Germany (Angermeyer and Matschinger 1994). The reasons for rejecting antipsychotic drugs are that they 'have more risks than benefits', 'lack efficacy because they do not deal with the roots of the problem' and 'are prescribed for the wrong reasons (e.g. to avoid talking about problems, to make people believe things are better than they are, as a straight jacket)' (Jorm *et al.* 2000: 404). These studies found that psychiatric hospitals are seen as even more unhelpful than medication.

Psychotherapy is seen as even more helpful for schizophrenia than for depression in both Germany and Australia. In Australia, the public is more likely than mental health professionals not only to recommend a counsellor but to endorse: help from friends, becoming physically active, self-help books, relaxation and yoga (Jorm *et al.* 1997). In Canada, 90% or more endorse work/recreation opportunities, involvement of family/friends and group homes. Only 49% endorse drug treatment and 42% (only 18% of relatives) endorse psychiatric hospitals (Thompson *et al.* 2002). When Austrians are asked what they would do if a relative became psychotic, the most common response is 'talk to them' (Jorm *et al.* 2000).

'MENTAL HEALTH LITERACY'

Prominent destigmatization researchers in the USA (Wahl 1987, 1999) and Australia (Jorm *et al.* 1997, 1999, 2000) believe, along with many biological psychiatrists and the drug companies, that they must simply redouble their efforts to 'educate' the public to think more like themselves. One of the first research papers (Thompson *et al.* 2002) emanating from the current World Psychiatric Association campaign to improve attitudes about schizophrenia (Sartorius 2002) portrays as 'sophisticated' and 'knowledgeable' the belief that schizophrenia is a 'debilitating disease', caused predominantly by biochemical imbalance. The study was funded by drug company Eli Lilly.

The term 'mental health literacy' (Jorm 2000) has been coined to describe level of agreement with bio-genetic ideology, and to bemoan the public's supposed ignorance. 'What is most surprising is that psychological interventions are seen by the public as highly effective for psychotic disorders (p. 397). 'If the public's mental health literacy is not improved, this may hinder public acceptance of evidence-based mental health care' (p. 396), meaning drugs.

PREJUDICE AND DISCRIMINATION

Prejudice against people diagnosed as having schizophrenia and other 'mental illnesses' has been well documented (Sayce 2000). Findings are remarkably consistent over place and time, with dangerousness and unpredictability at the core of the stereotype (Green et al. 1987; Nunnally 1961; Read and Harre 2001; Thompson et al. 2002). Discrimination in the workplace or when seeking housing, loans or insurance, and rejection by friends and families, are commonplace (Page and Day 1990; Read and Baker 1996; Rogers et al. 1993). Children learn early to be prejudiced against 'schizophrenics' (Orleman 2002).

The perception of dangerousness continues despite evidence that the relationship between being a psychiatric patient and being violent (to others) is non-existent or grossly exaggerated (Monahan 1992; Mullen 1997). Contrary to the popular notion of the violent 'schizophrenic', people with this diagnosis are about ten times more likely to be the victim of a violent crime than to commit one (Brekke et al. 2001). The belief that 'schizophrenics' are particularly unsafe around children is also a myth (Oates 1997).

Although there is good reason for mental health professionals to hold the media partly responsible (Allen and Nairn 1997; Angermeyer and Schulze 2001) for perpetuating prejudice, the fundamental cause may be closer to home. Health professionals have worse attitudes towards the 'mentally ill' than the public (Jorm et al. 1999). Many mental health professionals prefer not to work with the severely disturbed (Mirabi et al. 1985) or have negative attitudes towards the more severely psychotic (Heresco-Levy et al. 1999). One survey of mental health service users and their families found that 'The overwhelming belief was that they experience more stigma and discrimination from mental health professionals than from any other sector of society' (Walter 1998: 70).

DESTIGMATIZATION PROGRAMMES

This prejudice and discrimination, from the public and professionals, has a powerful effect on people already experiencing problems in their lives (Link et al. 2001; Sayce 2000). Efforts to reduce this additional burden are too often driven by ideology rather than research and have, therefore, been conceptually ill-founded and ineffective. They may even be maintaining or worsening the problem.

For decades our efforts have been predominantly based on the belief that the best approach is to 'educate' the public to adopt the dominant biological paradigm, to improve 'mental health literacy'. Destigmatization programmes, enthusiastically funded by the drug industry, have sought to persuade the public that people with emotional or psychological difficulties are 'ill' in the same sense as people with medical conditions. That such efforts have failed is evident from research, spanning four decades, of consistently negative attitudes, including studies of specific populations showing no improvement over time (Green *et al.* 1987; Huxley 1993). Some reviewers suggest attitudes are actually worsening (Crisp 1999; Sayce 2000).

THE RELATIONSHIP OF CAUSAL BELIEFS TO ATTITUDES

Numerous studies have shown that rather than biological and genetic causal beliefs being related to positive attitudes, the opposite is the case. Having documented that the public tolerates more unusual behaviour than psychiatrists, Sarbin and Mancuso (1970) showed that on the rare occasions that the public does employ the 'illness' metaphor, they tend to reject the person concerned and 'relegate them to a childlike, non-person role'. Golding *et al.* (1975) confirmed that people espousing medical explanations are reluctant to befriend 'mental patients'. A Chinese study found that as 'knowledge' based on the traditional mental illness perspective increased, attitudes became more negative (Chou and Mak 1998).

In 1980, the US National Institute of Mental Health reported that being treated by medical professionals or modalities, or in medical settings, is more stigmatizing than alternative approaches. Furthermore, the specific effects of medical treatments, such as drooling, tardive dyskinesia and obesity, are also stigmatizing (Chaplin 2000; Sartorius 2002). Mehta and Farina (1997) reported several studies showing that 'the disease view engenders a less favorable estimation of the mentally disordered than the psychosocial view'. Their own research found that participants in a learning task increased electric shocks faster if they understood their partner's mental health problems in disease terms than if they believed they were a result of childhood events.

Two New Zealand studies found that young adults with bio-genetic causal beliefs experience 'mental patients' as more dangerous and unpredictable, and are less likely to interact with them, than those with psychosocial causal beliefs (Read and Law 1999; Read and Harre 2001). Presenting information about psycho-social causes, and critiquing biological theories, significantly improved attitudes (Read and Law 1999). A successful German destigmatization project for teenage school students, *Crazy? So what! – It's Normal to be Different*, chose not to use the mental health literacy approach of just presenting standard information about 'mental illnesses'. Instead, the students met a young person diagnosed 'schizophrenic' and focused on similarities rather than differences. This included the understanding that 'events in life' ('e.g. poverty, illness,

disability, violence, drugs, loneliness') are, for *everyone*, important determinants of our well-being (Schulze *et al.* 2003).

Another New Zealand study found that viewing a video of a person
describing their psychotic experiences followed by a bio-genetic explanation
significantly increased perceptions of dangerousness and unpredictability. A
video that explained the same behaviours in terms of life events, including
childhood trauma, led to a slight improvement in attitudes (Walker and
Read 2002).

Those espousing the 'mental illness is an illness like any other' approach
to destigmatization bemoan the public's inability or unwillingness to
recognize and name 'mental illnesses' like 'schizophrenia' (Jorm *et al.* 1997,
Wahl 1987, 1999). The act of labelling behaviours 'schizophrenic' does
indeed increase belief in bio-genetic causes (Jorm *et al.* 1997). However, this
diagnostic labelling also increases the perceived seriousness of the person's
difficulties (Cormack and Furnham 1998), adversely effects evaluations of
the person's social skills (Benson 2002), produces a more pessimistic view
about recovery (Angermeyer and Matschinger 1996b) and leads to rejection
(Sarbin and Mancuso 1970). Awareness of the damage done by a diagnosis
of 'schizophrenia' has even led to the suggestion that the diagnosis be kept
more secret (Sartorius 2002).

The relationship between bio-genetic causal beliefs and negative attitudes
also exists among professionals and 'patients'. Mental health staff with a
biological perspective assess patients as more disturbed (Langer and
Abelson 1974) and are less inclined to involve patients in planning services
(Kent and Read 1998). Presenting a psychosocial explanation to clients
induces more efforts to change than a disease explanation, with the latter
group more often using alcohol to relieve their distress (Fisher and Farina
1979). Birchwood *et al.* (1993) found that 'patients who accepted their
diagnosis reported a lower perceived control over illness' and that depression in psychotic patients is 'linked to patients' perception of controllability
of their illness and absorption of cultural stereotypes of mental illness'
(p. 387).

People who experience psychotic 'symptoms' have a wide and complex
range of understandings of those experiences (see Chapter 12). For
instance, one recent study of British voice-hearers (including users and non-
users of mental health services) found that the two factors accounting for
most variance were *positive spiritual* and *personal relevance* (Jones *et al.*
2003). Voice-hearers adopting the positive spiritual perspective 'condemned
a biomedical framework'. Those espousing the personal relevance perspective (all of whom 'reported difficult childhoods with elements of sexual,
emotional, or physical abuse, and related this to their voice hearing') 'did
not adhere to a biomedical model, treatment model or spiritual model of
understanding voices' (p. 199). Even the 10% that adopted a *mental illness*
perspective 'endorsed all psychological perspectives that referred to the role

of stress and problematic life events' (p. 204). One of these individuals reported a relatively common experience within the mental health system, which parallels campaigns to persuade the public that they suffer from mental health illiteracy:

> Denise elaborated on how she believed that she had been psychic since she was young and therefore originally believed that her voices were from spiritual sources. She described how her psychiatrist had persuaded her against this belief and told her that this belief was part of her 'illness'.
>
> Jones *et al*. 2003: 204)

Organizations of 'psychiatric patients' have long railed against the effects of a 'medical model' perspective, accusing it of ignoring the multiplicity and complexity of their own explanations of their experiences, decreasing their self-esteem, ignoring the importance of their life events, increasing stigma and minimizing their capacity for recovery (Campbell 1992; O'Hagan 1992). 'Psychiatric patients' tend to have more positive attitudes than the general population (Segal *et al*. 1991; Walker and Read 2002) and, as we have seen, are particularly likely to reject medical model explanations. (When 'patients' *don't* accept that they have an illness, this is viewed as 'lack of insight' and evidence that they are still 'sick'. This is precisely the opposite of its original psychodynamic meaning – the ability to relate current difficulties to past life events.)

Hill and Bale (1981) showed that individuals with medical causal beliefs accept a passive role with mental health professionals. They concluded:

> Not only has the attempt to have the public view deviant behaviour as symptomatic of illness failed, but the premise that such a view would increase public acceptance of persons engaging in such behavior seems to have been a dubious one to begin with . . . The notion that psychological problems are similar to physical ailments creates the image of some phenomenon over which afflicted individuals have no control and thereby renders their behavior apparently unpredictable. Such a viewpoint makes the 'mentally ill' seem just as alien to today's 'normal' populace as the witches seemed to fifteenth century Europeans.
>
> (Hill and Bale 1981: 289–90)

HOW DOES THE MEDICAL MODEL PRODUCE SUCH NEGATIVE ATTITUDES?

A belief in categories that are discrete, immutable and invariably rooted in a biological abnormality reflect the medical model's essentialist view of mental disorders as 'natural kinds' (Haslam 2000). Viewing mental disorders in this essentialist fashion (Haslam and Ernst 2002) is associated with prejudice along multiple pathways (Haslam *et al.* 2002). Believing in immutability may promote pessimism and avoidance. Believing in a biological essence promotes the view that the disorder represents uncontrollable, untamed nature. Believing in discreteness promotes the view that sufferers are categorically different, rather than sharing in our common humanity. These essentialist beliefs form a toxic ensemble.

A recent discussion of the origins and functions of stigmatization covered evolution, economics, politics and self-interest (Haghighat 2000). Mehta and Farina (1997) suggest that viewing distressed people as sick, while discouraging blame, produces a patronizing attitude in which they 'like children, must be treated firmly. They must be shown how to do things and where they have erred. Hence the harsher treatment'. They add that believing in 'biochemical aberrations' renders them 'almost another species', an explanation reminiscent of Hill and Bale's conclusion two decades earlier.

Another factor may be our need to deny our own fear of 'going crazy' and to project our 'madness' onto others. Causal beliefs that not only create the impression of a categorically separate group (thereby denying the dimensionality of emotional distress) but also exaggerate the difference between the two groups by proposing genetic aberrations, are likely to fuel the reciprocal processes of distancing, fear, projection and scapegoating. When the suggested differences imply brain functioning so grossly abnormal that a person is denied responsibility for their actions, then our fear is further fuelled by the belief that the person could at any moment totally lose control. This may be accompanied by the belief that this unpredictability, which may express itself violently, needs to be severely – even harshly – controlled. This hypothesis draws support from the finding that the less we hold 'mental patients' responsible for their behaviour the more harshly we treat them, and the less aware we are of the harshness of that treatment (Mehta and Farina 1997).

PSYCHO-SOCIAL SOLUTIONS TO FEAR AND PREJUDICE

Factors that reduce perceived differences are likely to break this circle of fear, projection, distancing and rejection. Two such factors that have been demonstrated to be related to more positive attitudes are: (1) establishing contact (directly or through the media) with users of mental health services and, (2) in so doing, portraying their difficulties in terms of their life histories and circumstances rather than portraying them as suffering from illnesses (Angermeyer and Matschinger 1996c; Huxley 1993; Penn and

James 1998; Read and Law 1999; Read and Harre 2001; Schulze *et al.* 2003). Future destigmatization programmes must choose between approaches that have been demonstrated to be effective and those that have been repeatedly shown to increase fear and prejudice.

REFERENCES

Allen, R. and Nairn, R. (1997). Media depictions of mental illness. *Australian and New Zealand Journal of Psychiatry* 31: 375–81.

Angermeyer, M. and Klusmann, D. (1988). The causes of functional psychoses as seen by patients and their relatives. *European Archives of Neurological and Psychiatric Sciences* 238: 47–54.

Angermeyer, M. and Matschinger, H. (1994). Lay beliefs about schizophrenic disorder. *Acta Psychiatrica Scandinavica* 89 (suppl. 382): 39–43.

Angermeyer, M. and Matschinger, H. (1996a). Relatives' beliefs about the causes of schizophrenia. *Acta Psychiatrica Scandinavica* 93: 199–204.

Angermeyer, M. and Matschinger, H. (1996b). The effects of labelling on the lay theory regarding schizophrenic disorders. *Social Psychiatry and Psychiatric Epidemiology* 31: 316–20.

Angermeyer, M. and Matschinger, H. (1996c). The effect of personal experience with mental illness on the attitude towards individuals suffering from mental disorders. *Social Psychiatry and Psychiatric Epidemiology* 31: 321–6.

Angermeyer, M. and Matschinger, H. (1999). Lay beliefs about mental disorders: a comparison between the western and eastern parts of Germany. *Social Psychiatry and Psychiatric Epidemiology* 34: 275–81.

Angermeyer, M. and Schulze, B. (2001). Reinforcing stereotypes. *International Journal of Law and Psychiatry* 24: 469–86.

Barry, M. and Greene, S. (1992). Implicit models of mental disorder. *Irish Journal of Psychology* 13: 141–60.

Benson, R. (2002). The influence of bias against the schizophrenia diagnostic label in social skills assessment. Unpublished doctoral dissertation, Illinois Institute of Technology.

Birchwood, M. *et al.* (1993). Depression, demoralisation and control over psychotic illness. *Psychological Medicine* 23: 387–95.

Brekke, J. *et al.* (2001). Risks for individuals with schizophrenia who are living in the community. *Psychiatric Services* 52: 1358–66.

Campbell, P. (1992). A survivor's view of community psychiatry. *Journal of Mental Health* 1: 117–22.

Chaplin, R. (2000). Psychiatrists can cause stigma too. *British Journal of Psychiatry* 177: 467.

Chou, K. and Mak, K. (1998). Attitudes to mental patients among Hong Kong Chinese. *International Journal of Social Psychiatry* 44: 215–24.

Cormack, S. and Furnham, A. (1998). Psychiatric labelling, sex role stereotypes and beliefs about the mentally ill. *International Journal of Social Psychiatry* 44: 235–47.

Crisp, A. (1999). The stigmatisation of sufferers with mental disorders. *British Journal of General Practice* 49: 3–4.

Fisher, J. and Farina, A. (1979). Consequences of beliefs about the nature of mental disorders. *Journal of Abnormal Psychology* 88: 320–7.

Furnham, A. and Bower, P. (1992). A comparison of academic and lay theories of schizophrenia. *British Journal of Psychiatry* 62: 201–10.

Furnham, A. and Rees, J. (1988). Lay theories of schizophrenia. *International Journal of Psychiatry* 34: 212–20.

Golding, S. *et al.* (1975). The Behavioural Expectations Scale. *Journal of Consulting and Clinical Psychology* 43: 109.

Green, D. *et al.* (1987). Community attitudes to mental illness in New Zealand twenty-two years on. *Social Science and Medicine* 24: 417–22.

Haghighat, R. (2000). A unitary theory of stigmatisation. *British Journal of Psychiatry* 178: 207–15.

Haslam, N. (2000). Psychiatric categories as natural kinds. *Social Research* 67: 1031–58.

Haslam, N. and Ernst, D. (2002). Essentialist beliefs about mental disorders. *Journal of Social and Clinical Psychology* 21: 682–711.

Haslam, N. *et al.* (2002). Are essentialist beliefs associated with prejudice? *British Journal of Social Psychology* 41: 87–100.

Heresco-Levy, U. *et al.* (1999). Treatment-resistant schizophrenia and staff rejection. *Schizophrenia Bulletin* 25: 457–65.

Hill, D. and Bale, R. (1981). Measuring beliefs about where psychological distress originates and who is responsible for its alleviation. In H. Lefcourt (ed.) *Research with the Locus of Control Construct*, Vol. 2, New York: Academic Press.

Holzinger, A. *et al.* (2002). Subjective illness theory and antipsychotic medication compliance by patients with schizophrenia. *Journal of Nervous Mental Disease* 190: 597–603.

Huxley, P. (1993). Location and stigma. *Journal of Mental Health* 2: 73–80.

Joint Commission on Mental Illness and Health (1961). *Action for Mental Health.* New York: Basic Books.

Jones, S. *et al.* (2003). A Q-methodological study of hearing voices: a preliminary exploration of voice hearers' understanding of their experiences. *Psychology and Psychotherapy: Theory, Research and Practice* 76: 189–209.

Jorm, A. (2000). Mental health literacy. *British Journal of Psychiatry* 177: 396–401.

Jorm, A. *et al.* (1997). Public beliefs about causes and risk factors for depression and schizophrenia. *Social Psychiatry and Psychiatric Epidemiology* 32: 143–8.

Jorm, A. *et al.* (1999). Attitudes towards people with a mental disorder. *Australian and New Zealand Journal of Psychiatry* 33: 77–83.

Jorm, A. *et al.* (2000). Public knowledge of and attitudes to mental disorders. In G. Andrews and S. Henderson (eds) *Unmet Needs in Psychiatry*. Cambridge: Cambridge University Press.

Karanci, A. (1995). Caregivers of Turkish schizophrenic patients. *Social Psychiatry and Psychiatric Epidemiology* 30: 261–8.

Katschnig, H. *et al.* (1993). *Nicht nur eine minderwertige Gesundheit – eine Untersuchung über die Einstellung der österreichischen Bevölkerung zu psychisch Kranken und zur Psychiatrie.* Vienna: Abschlussbericht und den FWF.

Kent, H. and Read, J. (1998). Measuring consumer participation in mental health services. *International Journal of Psychiatry* 44: 295–310.

Langer, E. and Abelson, R. (1974). A patient by any other name. *Journal of Consulting and Clinical Psychology* 42: 4–9.

Link, B. *et al.* (1999). Public conceptions of mental illness. *American Journal of Public Health* 89: 1328–33.

Link, B. *et al.* (2001). Stigma as a barrier to recovery. *Psychiatric Services* 52: 1621–6.

Mehta, S. and Farina, A. (1997). Is being 'sick' really better? *Journal of Social and Clinical Psychology* 16: 405–19.

Mirabi, M. *et al.* (1985). Professional attitudes toward the chronic mentally ill. *Hospital and Community Psychiatry* 36: 404–5.

Monahan, J. (1992). Mental disorder and violent behaviour: perceptions and evidence. *American Psychologist* 47: 511–21.

Mullen, P. (1997). A reassessment of the link between mental disorder and violent behaviour, and its implications for clinical practice. *Australian and New Zealand Journal of Psychiatry* 31: 3–11.

National Institute of Mental Health (1980). *Attitudes Towards the Mentally Ill.* Washington, DC: Department of Health and Human Services.

Nunnally, J. (1961). *Popular Conceptions of Mental Health.* New York: Holt, Rinehart & Winston.

Oates, M. (1997). Patients as parents. *British Journal of Psychiatry* 170 (suppl. 32): 22–7.

O'Hagan, M. (1992). On being 'Not Quite Human'. In D. Patten (ed.) *Public Attitudes to Mental Illness.* Wellington, NZ: Department of Health.

Orleman, E. (2002). Peer discrimination and children's conceptions of mental illness. Unpublished doctoral dissertation, St. John's University, New York.

Page, S. and Day, D. (1990). Acceptance of the 'mentally ill' in Canadian society. *Canadian Journal of Community Mental Health* 9: 51–60.

Penn, D. and James, M. (1998). The stigma of mental illness. *Psychiatric Quarterly* 69: 235–47.

Pistrang, N. and Barker, C. (1992). Clients' beliefs about psychological problems. *Counselling Psychology Quarterly* 5: 325–35.

Read, J. and Baker, S. (1996). *Not Just Sticks and Stones: A Survey of the Stigma, Taboos and Discrimination Experienced by People with Mental Health Problems.* London: MIND.

Read, J. and Harre, N. (2001). The role of biological and genetic causal beliefs in the stigmatisation of 'mental patients'. *Journal of Mental Health* 10: 223–35.

Read, J. and Law, A. (1999). The relationship of causal beliefs and contact with users of mental health services to attitudes to the 'mentally ill'. *International Journal of Psychiatry* 45: 216–29.

Rogers, A. and Pilgrim, D. (1997). The contribution of lay knowledge to the understanding and promotion of mental health. *Journal of Mental Health* 6: 23–36.

Rogers, A. *et al.* (1993). *Issues in Mental Health: Experiencing Psychiatry, Users' Views of Services.* London: Macmillan.

Sarbin, T. and Mancuso, J. (1970). Failure of a moral enterprise. *Journal of Consulting and Clinical Psychology* 35: 159–73.

Sartorius, N. (2002). Iatrogenic stigma of mental illness: begins with behaviour and attitudes of medical professionals, especially psychiatrists. *British Medical Journal* 324: 1470–1.

Sayce, L. (2000). *From Psychiatric Patient to Citizen*. New York: St Martin's Press.

Schulze, B. *et al.* (2003). Crazy? So what! Effects of a school project on students' attitudes towards people with schizophrenia. *Acta Psychiatrica Scandinavica* 107: 142–50.

Segal, S. *et al.* (1991). Attitudes of sheltered care residents toward others with mental illness. *Hospital and Community Psychiatry* 42: 1138–43.

Srinivasan, T. and Thara, R. (2001). Beliefs about causation of schizophrenia. *Social Psychiatry and Psychiatric Epidemiology* 36: 134–40.

Thompson, A. *et al.* (2002). Attitudes about schizophrenia from the pilot site of the WPA worldwide campaign against the stigma of schizophrenia. *Social Psychiatry and Psychiatric Epidemiology* 37: 475–82.

Wahl, O. (1987). Public versus professional conceptions of schizophrenia. *Journal of Community Psychology* 15: 285–91.

Wahl, O. (1999). Mental health consumers' experience of stigma. *Schizophrenia Bulletin* 25: 467–78.

Walker, I. and Read, J. (2002). The differential effectiveness of psycho-social and bio-genetic causal explanations in reducing negative attitudes towards 'mental illness'. *Psychiatry* 65: 313–25.

Walter, G. (1998). The attitude of health professionals towards carers and individuals with mental illness. *Australian Psychiatry* 6: 70–2.

Chapter 12

Listening to the voices we hear

Clients' understandings of psychotic experiences

Jim Geekie

INTRODUCTION

Schizophrenia is the lynchpin of models of mental illness. Regardless of what we as individuals make of this term, it would be difficult to dispute that it is *the* central concept around which Western notions and practices of mental health care revolve. Rather than (or as well as) viewing schizophrenia as the 'lost cause' of psychiatry, we could view it as the 'Holy Grail' of mental health workers, including, but not limited to, psychiatrists. The term schizophrenia also has a broader significance in Western culture, beyond the field of mental health. The common everyday translation of the term is, I propose, roughly equivalent to 'madness' or 'insanity'. Thus, we could view our search for the Holy Grail of schizophrenia in broader terms as reflecting the efforts of our culture to come to grips with 'madness'.

I will discuss this search for the Grail, focusing not on what has been found (or, more accurately, not found) but on certain aspects of the nature of the search itself. In particular, my interest here is in who it is that has been deemed able to contribute to this search and who has been excluded. I will argue that the very people who have, by definition, the closest relationship with experiences considered indicative of schizophrenia – clients of mental health services who happen to have that diagnosis – have been largely excluded from the search. I will locate this discussion within the context of power relationships, drawing on the work of Foucault. I will then discuss how mental health workers may contribute to remedying this situation, by paying greater attention to the sense clients make of 'schizophrenic experiences'. As part of this discussion, I will outline my research looking at clients' understandings of their psychotic experiences.

SCHIZOPHRENIA AS AN ESSENTIALLY CONTESTED CONCEPT

Even the most superficial glance at the schizophrenia literature reveals considerable controversy. As outlined earlier in this book (see Chapters 3,

5–7) and elsewhere (Pilgrim 1990), this disagreement is as old as the concept itself. Disagreements about schizophrenia relate to some of the most fundamental aspects of the concept, such as whether it exists outside the minds of those who use the term, whether it should be viewed as a medical or social problem and how best to assist those who may be troubled with schizophrenia (Bentall 1990; Boyle 1993). For example, in an extensive review of factors influencing prognosis for those diagnosed schizophrenic, Warner (1985) questions the received wisdom that the introduction of antipsychotic medications led to improved outcomes (see Chapter 8). Whether one accepts such arguments, it is impossible to dispute that they illustrate considerable disagreement in this field.

What, then, are we to make of this controversy, given that is seems to permeate the concept? Should we view it as an unfortunate, but temporary, stage in the development of our investigations into schizophrenia? On what ground might we make such a claim, given that the term has been imbued with controversy since its inception, and, as books such as this demonstrate, the controversy shows no signs of abating? It appears, rather, to make more sense to see the controversy as being *integral* to the concept itself.

One possible response to this situation would be to view 'schizophrenia' as what the philosopher Gallie (1955–56) referred to as an 'essentially contested concept'. In keeping with Wittgenstein's (1958) notion that meaning is determined by usage, Gallie (1955–56) suggests that there are some concepts 'which are essentially contested, concepts the proper use of which inevitably involves endless disputes about their proper use on the part of their users' (p. 169).

We could view schizophrenia as such an 'essentially contested concept', thus implying that the disagreement surrounding the term is not incidental, accidental or temporary, but is an *essential* aspect of the concept itself. And like the search for the Holy Grail, efforts to resolve this debate are doomed to failure, as this debate constitutes the primary meaning of the term.

MARGINALIZATION OF THE CLIENT'S VOICE

Whether the notion of schizophrenia as an 'essentially contested concept' is accepted, the more general point that schizophrenia literature is characterized by disagreement is undeniable. This leads us now to consider *who* it is that has a voice in this debate. A whole range of professionals and academics have made significant contributions to the vast literature. This is perhaps not too surprising given the amount of health care resources dedicated to providing treatment to those diagnosed schizophrenic (Knapp 1997). However, what is surprising is the almost total absence of the voices of those who have most direct experience of schizophrenia – the person diagnosed as 'schizophrenic'. An important qualification needs to be made at this point. I am not suggesting that those who have this diagnosis have not expressed their thoughts about the nature of this experience. One could argue that they do so at each and every meeting with a clinician. Furthermore, there is an extensive literature where those who experience mental health problems (including schizophrenia) have expressed their thoughts and feelings on the experience (Fahy and Lysaght 1999; Kaplan 1964; Ruocchio 1991). I argue that those voices, both in the professional literature and in clinical settings, have been marginalized and that this has been to the detriment of clients' interests, clinical practice and research efforts directed at investigating the nature of the experience. This neglect of the clients' understandings of their own experience is reflected in the conclusion of a review article: 'research dealing with patients' own attributions for their illness has been virtually non-existent' (Molvaer *et al.* 1992).

One manifestation, and consequence, of this marginalization is the paucity of terms available to us to refer to the multitude of ways in which people with a diagnosis of schizophrenia relate to their experience. The term which first comes to mind in this regard is 'insight'. Unfortunately, as the term is now used, it usually refers to whether the client agrees with the clinician's position (e.g. that the client is suffering from an 'illness') rather than being truly concerned with the client's understanding (Amador and Kronengold 1998; Kirmayer and Corin 1998).

Rare exceptions in this area are the related concepts of 'sealing over' and 'integration' as ways of conceptualizing clients' recovery styles following a psychotic episode (McGlashan *et al.* 1975). 'Sealing over' is the tendency to dismiss the experience as having little personal relevance, whereas 'integration' reflects a curiosity about the experience and its personal significance. Drayton *et al.* (1998) found that those who 'seal over' are more likely than 'integrators' to become depressed. Such research supports the notion that there are sound clinical grounds for attending to clients' responses to their psychotic experiences. Other variables such as distress (Romme and Escher 1989) and coping strategies (Carr 1988) have also been found to be associated with the sense the client makes of psychotic experiences. There is also a strong moral case to be made for attending to how the individual thinks about her or his experience. Shotter (1981) argues that 'authoring' one's own experience is a basic human right: 'In a moral world, no one but the person in question has the status, the authority, under normal conditions, to decide what his experience means to him'.

POWER AND KNOWLEDGE

How, then, are we to account for the 'paucity of research concerned with the individual's psychological adaptation to psychosis'? (Drayton *et al.* 1998). In examining the relationship between power, knowledge and social practice, Foucault (1980) proposes that those with power act in such a way as to legitimize their own knowledge (and hence practice), while simultaneously discrediting other knowledges, which may challenge their dominant knowledge. Foucault refers to the knowledge of those who are subject to the particular social practice or institution (such as prisons, mental health services, etc.) as 'subjugated knowledge' and proposes that simply giving voice to such knowledge is one way of challenging the hegemony. 'It is through the re-appearance of this knowledge, of these local popular knowledges, these disqualified knowledges, that criticism performs its work' (Foucault 1980: 82).

The knowledge that people with a diagnosis of schizophrenia have about their own experience (and hence about 'schizophrenia') is an example of 'subjugated knowledge', marginalized because it challenges the dominant discourses of professionals. This marginalization occurs in both research literature and in the face-to-face clinical encounters between client and clinician.

I want to make clear that I am *not* claiming that the knowledge that people diagnosed schizophrenic have is necessarily superior to, or more accurate than, the professional, 'scientific' knowledge. Rather, I propose only that it is a legitimate form of knowledge and, as such, has an important contribution to make. Incorporating this knowledge within the debate will not magically lead to a resolution of all controversy. However, I believe that the debate will be richer if clients' voices are included rather than excluded, and that these voices will enhance understandings of 'schizophrenia' and efforts to provide effective support to people with that diagnosis.

A STUDY OF THE EXPLANATORY MODELS OF PEOPLE WHO EXPERIENCE PSYCHOSIS

How, then, might we, in both research and clinical settings, attend more to the voices of those with this diagnosis? I will outline one way in which this might be achieved, by describing a research project looking at how people make sense of their 'psychotic' experiences.

As a clinical psychologist working in a first episode psychosis service, my primary role is to offer psychological support/therapy to the clients of this service. The exact nature of the work varies from client to client, but I have found that whatever the focus of therapy, the client's 'explanatory model' (Kleinman 1980) of his or her 'psychotic' experience is always of importance, and sometimes the main focus. The research I describe here is an investigation into clients' explanatory models for their psychotic experiences, as expressed in their psychotherapy with me.

This research is qualitative, using recordings of therapy sessions (with participants having given consent, of course) as the basic raw data upon which analysis is made. Only clients who are already engaged with me in psychological work are invited to participate in the research, and then only when the client's understanding of his or her own psychotic experiences has already become a significant part of our work together. It is made clear to potential participants that their ongoing therapeutic work with me is not influenced by whether or not they participate in the research. To date, 13 clients (9 males, 4 females; 10 European, 2 Maori, 1 Pacific Islander; age range 19–35 years) have agreed to participate in the research. The findings are based on analyses of transcriptions of 51 sessions with those participants.

The research methodology is based on grounded theory (Charmaz 1990; Glaser and Strauss 1967), an explicit methodology for analysing qualitative data, which specifies procedures aimed to ensure that the analysis is based on, or 'grounded' in, the data. This involves the researcher systematically coding and then categorizing the data with a view to establishing theoretical constructs that provide an explanation for the data.

The findings reported here are based on a provisional analysis of data collected to date. Indeed, because of the nature and richness of the data, it may be impossible ever to claim to have reached a definitive analysis that would not be open to subsequent revision.

General findings

Participants in the study were very welcoming of the opportunity to discuss their experience in some depth and to explore the possible meanings of this experience. This is consistent with my clinical experience. Of course, no universal statements can be made about this being something that all clients of first episode psychosis services will accept or benefit from. Using McGlashan and colleagues' (1975) terminology, we might expect that 'integrators' are more likely to benefit from such discussions than those who 'seal over' (although these tendencies are probably not independent of the kind of help the client is offered). However, for some clients at least, the opportunity to talk in depth about what their experience means to them is important, and as such should be offered as a routine part of clinical services.

A second general finding is that there is a great variety of ways in which clients understand their psychotic experiences. These differences are manifest in both style and content. Stylistically, participants varied from adopting concrete, literal terms to using more poetic, metaphorical idioms for expressing understandings of their experiences. At times, participants' uses of metaphor conveyed a depth of meaning largely absent from typical textbook descriptions of psychotic phenomena. For example, one participant described his thought processes while psychotic as follows: 'It's kind of like going out to the mail box, and it's full of mail, but I feel I can't sort out the junk mail from the mail I want to read'. In terms of content, there was even greater variety in participants' notions about their psychotic experiences. It is worth pointing out that this variety existed not only between participants, but also for individual participants, some of whom had more than one possible explanation for their experiences.

Specific findings

The framework I have developed for conceptualizing the range of ways clients spoke about their psychotic experiences is illustrated in Figure 12.1. As can be seen, I have developed three broad categories, each containing sub-categories. 'The nature of the psychotic experience' and 'The personal meaning of the experience' relate to the psychotic experience itself, whereas 'Narrating experience' relates to the more general issue of the telling of one's story or, in Shotter's (1981) terms, 'authoring'. I will discuss these three broad categories, providing examples to illustrate.

The nature of the psychotic experience

This category covers participants' thoughts about the causes of psychotic experience, as well as attempts to explain what is happening when they have a psychotic experience. I have found it helpful to distinguish between participants' thoughts about *why* they have psychotic experiences (*causes*) and ideas about what processes might be involved when they have a psychotic experience (*explanations*). These two domains are closely related, overlapping at times, and as both pertain primarily to the nature of the experience, I have found it useful to categorize them together.

Because of constraints of space, I will not be able to discuss in depth participants' explanations for how psychotic experiences arise, but I will give a few illustrations. One participant, who spoke of the causes of his psychotic experiences as including constitutional shyness and difficult experiences as a child, explained his tendency to manic thinking (which included 'delusional' ideas) as follows:

> I suppose maybe that was my attempt to crush my inferior feelings. Maybe I thought if I just push myself enough to be overly confident then I wouldn't get those feelings, because I was thinking that when I was in the manic state.

Another participant saw impoverished communication at home when growing up as having caused his tendency to have psychotic thoughts and suggested the process involved consisted of him filling in gaps where verbal information was missing:

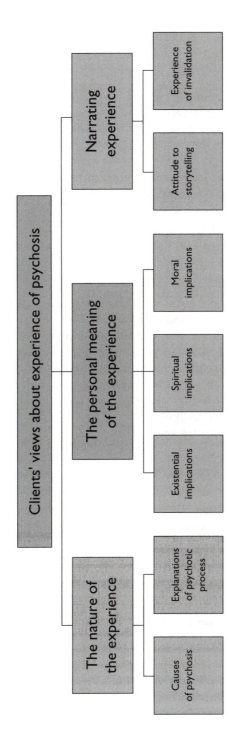

Figure 12.1   General categorization of clients' views of experience of psychosis.

It happened especially when there was very little verbal communication. When there was verbal communication, it was great, just like normal chatting. But, because I had nothing to say, I took in the world non-verbally, body language and that sort of thing, that's all I had. And, because it could be many things, as it's not quite concrete, I would interpret it in a certain way.

Causes of psychotic experiences

Possible causes of psychosis were of great interest to participants. A wide range of factors was considered. Participants did not appear troubled by multi-factorial accounts of psychotic experiences, even when these contained apparent contradictions. Although most had no difficulty in expressing and exploring ideas about possible causes of psychosis, there were times when participants said quite simply that they had no idea why they had psychotic experiences. This was sometimes associated with distress, as with K, who stated, 'I can't figure it out. But, I mean, I think about it, about why it's happening, but I just don't know and that makes me feel bad'. Or with curiosity, as with M, who explained 'I don't understand much, but I am curious about it'. Statements such as the above were relatively rare, with participants (including the two who made the comments above) mostly having fairly well formed but flexible ideas about causality.

Although participants' notions of causality were, indeed, varied, it was possible to classify these into psychological, social/interpersonal and biological accounts. Within each of the three main classes of causality, I have made further sub-categorizations. Figure 12.2 illustrates the range of factors contained within each of the three main classes of causation.

Psychological causes

Psychological causes include accounts where an internal psychological process of some sort was implicated in the genesis of psychosis. There was considerable variety in the range of psychological factors considered by participants as possible causes of psychosis.

Emotional explanations covered an array of specific emotions, including guilt, anxiety, fear and uncertainty, as well as the more general notion of overwhelming emotional arousal (with the specific emotion considered of less import). Within 'aspects of self', further sub-categorizations include low self-esteem, a tendency to introspection, being 'out of balance' with the self and conflict between different aspects of the self. 'Information processing' factors implicated by participants included those relating to cognitive overactivity ('too many thoughts'), information processing styles (such as tending to see connections between events) and the questioning of fundamental beliefs.

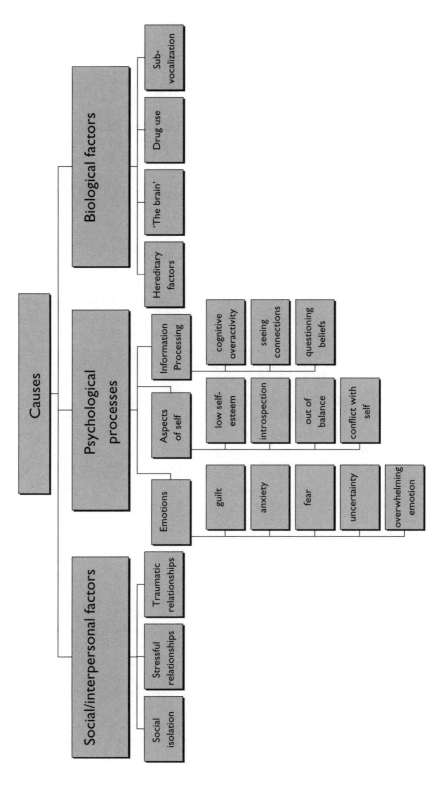

Figure 12.2   The wide range of variables viewed by participants as possible causes of their psychotic experiences.

The notion of psychosis having been caused by the questioning of one's own beliefs is illustrated by A, who believed he had become psychotic because:

> I questioned too many things all at once and without having an answer drew assumptions. It was just like cutting out my own foundation, and I didn't have much to stand on in the end, so I made myself vulnerable. I think we all have values in our life and if we take those away or we shatter them, we can be very vulnerable to the circumstances around us. I think that is what I did.

Social/interpersonal causes

This class of causal explanation for psychotic experiences included boredom, social isolation, stressful relationships and traumatic experiences. 'Traumatic experiences' refers largely to experiences from childhood, including abuse, as well as events such as teasing at school and parental divorce. A very clear and persuasive argument for the causal role of abuse was provided by B, a 30-year-old white female, who stated:

> When I think of the way my father used to behave around me and that, well, I think to myself 'it's no bloody wonder I've got a mind like that'. When my father exposed himself in front of me and things like that, it's no wonder I've got this shit going on inside of me.

The same participant went on to explain *how* the abuse played a causal role: 'I can see what's happening is the lack of boundaries, and that was the cause of all this in the first place'.

Biological causes

Participants suggested a range of biological factors which they considered causal, including hereditary factors, the brain, use of illicit drugs and one participant who attributed his hallucinations to sensations in the 'voice box', an idea which has a striking resemblance to Frith's (1992) notion of sub-vocalization, of which the participant had no prior knowledge. Examples of quotes from participants who saw the use of drugs as implicated in the onset of psychosis include D, who argued 'I think it's because I started taking the drugs and it just changed my state and everything'. An example of an hereditary explanation was given by one woman who saw her psychosis as caused by 'having been born with something not right that I inherited'.

The personal meaning of the experience

The kinds of themes which emerge in this area include *existential*, *spiritual* and *moral* aspects or implications of the experience as seen by the participants, who found themselves faced with some profound questions about the nature of life and the nature of self. These questions, and the kinds of answers participants came up with, were clearly influenced by the recent experience of psychosis. For example, one participant found herself repeatedly wondering whether the content of her psychotic experiences means that she is a 'bad' person. Similarly, questions about the nature of one's relationship with God were also commonly provoked by the psychotic experience. Issues such as the above were clearly of great concern to participants; this is an area where the professional literature on psychosis is particularly deficient.

Narrating experience

In addition to expressing thoughts about the nature and personal meaning of psychotic experiences, participants also spoke about their experiences of telling their story to others, clearly seeing this as an important aspect of their psychotic episode.

Comments on story telling could be fitted into two sub-categories: *attitude to story telling* and the *experience of invalidation*. Some clients spoke passionately about the importance of telling their story. S explained 'I've *got* to tell this story, got to summarize it' and proceeded to spend a number of sessions going over his story in great detail, with great enthusiasm and with apparent benefit. F expressed eagerness to explore her story because 'I want to find out what has happened and why it has happened to me'. And, finally, M asked to talk in greater depth about his experience because 'I just hope that I will be able to make sense of the whole lot'. Thus, participants made clear pronouncements that they see making sense of their experience, including sharing it with someone else, as of considerable importance to them. Furthermore, they viewed being actively involved in this sense making as a vital part of this process (as opposed to being told what their experience meant). The importance of active participation was expressed succinctly by one participant who commented on the contents of a psycho-educational brochure explaining the nature of psychosis: 'That is very interesting and it makes good sense, but I want to make my *own* sense of it'.

The importance of being author of one's own experience relates closely to the second sub-category within *narrating experience*. *Invalidation* refers to comments on the experience of feeling that their attempts to narrate experience have been undermined, undervalued or overlooked. This feeling was noted in connection both with making sense of psychosis and, at times, with the feeling that, as a consequence of having been psychotic, one's viewpoint on other issues was also invalidated. For example, M, whose spiritual interpretation of her experience had been dismissed by associates in her church, complained, with an obvious sense of loss, 'I had a lot of very profound experiences, but they have all been put down to "No, it's all in your own mind, you're talking to yourself"'. She later went on to say that she felt that her viewpoint on other, unrelated matters was also dismissed by friends: 'All my close friends, including a very close friend, have written me off. They don't even bother with me now. It's like they see me as a lost cause, as cracked'.

CONCLUSIONS AND CLINICAL IMPLICATIONS

I hope I have demonstrated that clients of a first episode psychosis service have much to contribute to the understanding of psychosis. Participants in my research, and others that I have worked with clinically, welcome the opportunity to discuss their experience in depth and to develop an understanding of the experience that is personally meaningful to them. As the examples above indicate, clients can do this with considerable sophistication, providing accounts that cover both aetiology and process, shedding light on the experience which is often lacking from the professional literature.

Given that a psychotic episode can sometimes be an overwhelming experience, it is not surprising that clients are eager to make sense of it. Clients' explanatory models may not always correspond to professional understandings of psychosis and it may, therefore, be necessary for some form of discussion and negotiation to take place if a shared understanding between clinician and client is to be established. (If this does not occur, therapeutic work will be more difficult, if not impossible.) It is important to recognize that clients want to be active participants in this process rather than passive recipients of the clinician's model. Clinicians who insist on 'telling' clients what their experience is or means run the risk of further engendering a sense of invalidation in the client, at the same time as missing out on an opportunity to learn something.

Following a first episode of psychosis, clients are no doubt in the process of building up their understanding of the experience, and it is at this point that clinicians may be able to contribute most to the client's efforts to develop a useful explanatory model. This contribution may involve challenges to some of the client's notions about the experience. It will need some sensitivity on the part of the clinician to be able to do this without leaving the client feeling invalidated. I am not arguing that we should abandon our professional notion and explanations for psychotic experience. However, if we remind ourselves that there is not one but many professional perspectives on psychosis, and if we resist the temptation to adopt wholeheartedly one or other of these perspectives, this may make it easier for us to work with clients whose views do not correspond with our own. It is, of course, important that we provide clients with whatever information we may have that relates to their experience. But, we should also be cognizant of the importance for the client to be actively participating in the authoring of their own experience.

A recent report on psychotic experiences by the British Psychological Society (2000) recommends that 'Service users should be acknowledged as experts on their own experiences'. Such an acknowledgement would, I believe, have important implications for research and clinical practice. I hope the research findings presented here show that this is both possible and desirable. Acknowledging service users as experts need not be viewed as undermining the expertise that clinicians and researchers bring to the subject. Rather, recognizing that there are multiple perspectives (or multiple 'knowledges') on schizophrenia may enhance the quality and usefulness of the debate, illuminate the nature of the experience and lead to improved clinical services, even if it brings us no closer to finding the Holy Grail.

REFERENCES

Amador, X. and Kronengold, H. (1998). The descriptions and meaning of insight in psychosis. In X. Amador and A. David (eds) *Insight and Psychosis*. Oxford: Oxford University Press.

Bentall, R. (ed.) (1990). *Reconstructing Schizophrenia*. London: Routledge.

Boyle, M. (1993). *Schizophrenia: A Scientific Delusion?* London: Routledge.

British Psychological Society (2000). *Recent Advances in Understanding Mental Illness and Psychotic Experiences*. Leicester: BPS.

Carr, V. (1988). Patients' techniques for coping with schizophrenia. *British Journal of Medical Psychology* 61: 339–52.

Charmaz, K. (1990). 'Discovering' chronic illness: using grounded theory. *Social Science and Medicine* 30: 1161–72.

Drayton, M. *et al.* (1998). Early attachment experience and recovery from psychosis. *British Journal of Clinical Psychology* 37: 269–84.

Fahy, M. and Lysaght, V. (eds) (1999). *The Sun Will Shine Again: Stories of Survival and Optimism in the Face of Mental Illness*. Wellington, NZ: Schizophrenia Fellowship.

Foucault, M. (1980). *Power/Knowledge: Selected Interviews and Other Writings*. New York: Pantheon.

Frith, C. (1992). *The Cognitive Neuropsychology of Schizophrenia*. Hove: Lawrence Erlbaum.

Gallie, W. (1955–56). Essentially contested concepts. *Proceedings of the Aristotelian Society* LVI: 167–98.

Glaser, B. and Strauss, A. (1967). *The Discovery of Grounded Theory*. New York: Aldine.

Kaplan, B. (ed.) (1964). *The Inner World of Mental Illness.* New York: Harper & Row.

Kirmayer, L. and Corin, E. (1998). Inside knowledge: cultural constructions of insight in psychosis. In X. Amador and A. David (eds) *Insight and Psychosis.* Oxford: Oxford University Press.

Kleinman, A. (1980). *Patients and Healers in the Context of Culture.* Stanford, CA: University of California Press.

Knapp, M. (1997). Costs of schizophrenia. *British Journal of Psychiatry* 171: 509–18.

McGlashan, T. *et al.* (1975). Integration and sealing over. *Archives of General Psychiatry* 32: 1269–72.

Molvaer, J. *et al.* (1992). Psychotic patients' attributions for mental illness. *British Journal of Clinical Psychology* 31: 210–12.

Pilgrim, D. (1990). Competing histories of madness. In R. Bentall (ed.) *Reconstructing Schizophrenia.* London: Routledge.

Romme, M. and Escher, A. (1989). Hearing voices. *Schizophrenia Bulletin* 15: 209–16.

Ruocchio, P. (1991). The first person account. *Schizophrenia Bulletin* 17: 357–9.

Shotter, J. (1981). Vico, moral worlds, accountability and personhood. In P. Heelas and A. Lock (eds) *Indigenous Psychologies of Self.* London: Academic Press.

Warner, R. (1985). *Recovery from Schizophrenia.* London: Routledge.

Wittgenstein, L. (1958). *Philosophical Investigations.* New York: Macmillan.

Chapter 13

Poverty, ethnicity and gender

John Read

One of the many issues minimized by overemphasis of bio-genetic factors is the role of belonging to a disempowered group. In response to overwhelming evidence that poverty and racism are causative factors for psychosis, biological psychiatry oscillates between ignoring the evidence and distorting it in ways that leaves the primacy of bio-genetic causal theories intact. The issue of gender is more complex.

This chapter does not cover all groups that experience discrimination or disadvantage. For example, homosexuality was only removed from the DSM's list of mental disorders in 1974. Lesbians and gay men, like poor people, ethnic minorities and women, have a higher prevalence of mental health problems (Gilman *et al.* 2001). There is evidence that they, too, are often badly let down by mental health services (Bradford *et al.* 1994; Golding 1997; Nystrom 1997). For instance, recent New Zealand research (Semp, in press) suggests that one significant problem is clinicians' difficulties talking about same-sex sexuality with clients, producing a silence (similar to the silence on other psycho-social issues) that is often interpreted, by clients, as 'don't talk about it, homosexuality is not okay'.

Clearly, being poor, a member of an 'ethnic minority' or a colonized people, being female in a patriarchal society, or lesbian or gay in a homophobic society, can have psychological consequences. One common thread is relative lack of power, and the concomitant lack of access to the physical and social resources necessary to establish and maintain emotional well-being (see Chapter 18).

POVERTY

The facts

Mental hospitals have always been filled predominantly with poor people. In seventeenth-century France, for example, the people confined in the Hôpital General were 'the poor of Paris' (see Chapter 2). In 1939, Faris and

Dunham found that the deprived central areas of Chicago had higher psychiatric admission rates than the wealthier suburbs. Contrary to the notion that milder mental health problems but not schizophrenia are socially caused, the difference was particularly high for 'schizophrenia'. People in the poorest areas of Chicago were seven times more likely to be diagnosed 'schizophrenic' than those in the richest parts. This relationship between poverty and 'schizophrenia' was soon replicated in nine other cities throughout the USA (Clark 1949). During the 1950s, the same relationship was found in Norway, Bristol, Liverpool and London (Kohn 1976).

The famous New Haven study (Hollingshead and Redlich 1958) measured class directly on the basis of education and occupation rather than location. The poorest class (V: 'unskilled, manual') was three times more likely than the wealthiest two classes (I and II: 'business, professional and managerial') to be treated for psychiatric problems. The diagnosis having the strongest relationship with class was 'schizophrenia'. The poorest people were eight times more likely to be diagnosed 'schizophrenic' than the wealthiest.

By 1976, a review concluded:

> There have been more than 50 studies of the relationship between social class and rates of schizophrenia. Almost without exception, these studies have shown that schizophrenia occurs most frequently at the lowest social class levels of urban society. The evidence comes from research in Canada, Denmark, Finland, Great Britain, Norway, Sweden, Taiwan, and the United States – an unusually large number of countries and cultures for establishing the generality of any relationship in social science.
>
> (Kohn 1976: 177)

A New York study of first admissions found that class V were 12 times more likely to be hospitalized than class I. Furthermore:

> The variable related to the most other variables in this population and hence important for understanding many processes involved in the functioning of these patients is membership in class V. None of the clinical variables such as a particular symptom dimension or even level of social functioning relates to as many other variables . . . This is in striking contrast to the low level of attention often paid to social class in psychiatric practice and research.
>
> (Strauss *et al.* 1978: 620)

The following year a Tennessee study of 10,000 first admissions again confirmed that the diagnosis most strongly related to socio-economic status was 'schizophrenia' (Rushing and Ortega 1979). The relationship between schizophrenia and poverty was described as 'one of the most consistent findings in the field of psychiatric epidemiology' (Eaton 1980).

In the subsequent 20 years, the proportion of studies of schizophrenia investigating socio-economic status has declined from a meagre 0.6% (1971–80) to 0.2% (1991–2000). During the 1990s, there were 43 times more schizophrenia studies focusing on genetics, biochemistry or neuropsychology than on socio-economic status (Read et al. 2001). The dwindling number of studies continue, with some exceptions (see Bresnahan and Susser 2003), to confirm the earlier findings, in Bristol (Ineichen et al. 1984), Nottingham (Giggs and Cooper 1987), London (Castle et al. 1993), Wales (Koppel and McGuffin 1999), Finland (Aro et al. 1995), New Zealand (Kydd et al. 1991), Canada (Goldner et al. 2003) and Nigeria (Iheuze et al. 1984). More often than not the strongest relationship between class and psychiatric admission is for 'schizophrenia'. Specific 'symptoms', such as hallucinations and delusions, are also more common among people who grew up in relative poverty (Brown et al. 2000).

Furthermore, psychiatric admission rates increase during economic declines (Brenner 1973). This relationship is, yet again, particularly strong for 'psychoses' in general and 'schizophrenia' in particular. Three studies confirmed Brenner's findings (Warner 1985).

A British study found that deprived children are four times more likely to develop 'non-schizophrenic psychotic illness' but eight times more likely to grow-up to be 'schizophrenic' than non-deprived children (Harrison et al. 2001). Even among children with no family history of psychosis, the deprived children were seven times more likely to develop schizophrenia, confirming that you do not need a genetic predisposition to develop schizophrenia (see Chapter 7).

Although researchers of 'childhood-onset schizophrenia' often ignore what happens in children's lives (Read et al. 2001), in one study 89% came from classes IV and V (Green et al. 1992).

Urbanicity

Nowadays, researchers tend to focus on the politically more neutral issue of urban living rather than class. Not only is being diagnosed 'schizophrenic' related to living in urban areas (Peen and Decker 1997), but the greater the numbers of years lived in urban areas *before becoming schizophrenic*, the greater the risk of becoming schizophrenic (Pedersen and Mortensen 2001). As is the case for poverty, the relationship is even stronger for schizophrenia than for other psychotic diagnoses (Lewis et al. 1992; Marcelis et al. 1998; Mortensen et al. 1999). Furthermore, a general population study had shown that urban birth and upbringing is associated with psychosis-like experiences as well as with psychotic disorder (van Os et al. 2001).

Two studies confirm the influence of psycho-social factors in the absence of the supposed genetic predisposition to 'schizophrenia'. The relationship between urban living and schizophrenia remains after controlling for family history of psychiatric disorder in general (Lewis *et al.* 1992), or of schizophrenia specifically (Mortensen *et al.* 1999). The 'attributable risk' from urban birth was four times greater than that from having a mother with 'schizophrenia'.

The explanations

A neutral observer might conclude that schizophrenia, like other expressions of human distress, is caused – at least partially – by growing up with the disadvantages and stresses associated with poverty. The observer might assume that professionals who work with extremely distressed people would prioritize assistance with income, housing and employment, and would advocate social and political change designed to alleviate poverty, thereby helping to prevent 'schizophrenia' in the next generation. Sadly, the most common response, when not ignoring the findings altogether, has been to try to avoid the obvious 'social causation' explanation by interpreting the facts in any way that leaves intact the dominance of bio-genetic ideology.

Madness causes poverty: 'social drift', 'social selection' and 'social residue'

A popular strategy is to argue that 'schizophrenia' afflicts all classes equally but those at the top of the economic pyramid dribble down to the bottom as a result of their illness. This is the 'social drift' theory. Of course, there *are* social and economic consequences to being extremely distressed, alienated or disoriented. There are additional consequences to having one's response to adversity explained in terms of having a 'mental illness' (see Chapter 11). However, to use the consequences of one's distress to dismiss or minimize the social causes of the distress is scientifically nonsensical and unhelpful.

Because of the paucity of evidence to support the 'social drift' notion, psychiatry has fallen back on weaker variations of the same theme. 'Social selection' theory (Eaton 1980) suggested that although 'schizophrenics' have not actually drifted downwards themselves, their impoverished circumstances are still a result, rather than a cause, of their 'illness', because they are of a lower social status than their parents, or, weaker still, because they have not climbed up the pyramid as far as they should have – the 'social residue' theory.

The New Haven study tested the 'social drift' theory by investigating whether 'class V patients had drifted to the slums in the course of their lives' and whether 'schizophrenics' were socially downward mobile. No evidence of such 'social drift' was found. The study also rejected the weaker social selection theory because 91% of the 'schizophrenics' were in the same social class as their parents – rather than a lower class as predicted (Hollingshead and Redlich 1958). An earlier 25-year study had also failed to find evidence of social drift and concluded that 'The excess of psychoses from the poorer area is a product of the life conditions entailed in the lower socio-economic strata of the society' (La Pousse et al. 1956). A Canadian study reported measurements of class and psychiatric disorder taken 10 years apart and found 'that socio-economic status was more likely to have causal priority over psychiatric disorder than the reverse' (Lee 1976). This longitudinal approach was repeated in Illinois and Michigan, using multiple points in time. In both states, the results 'favour a social causation inter-pretation' (Wheaton 1978).

Beyond predicting who becomes 'schizophrenic' in the first place, low 'social class of origin' (at birth or during childhood), which 'cannot be caused by schizophrenia', also predicts negative outcome among people with severe psychosis (Samele et al. 2001). Similarly, the relationship between urban life and schizophrenia has been shown not to be a conse-quence of social drift or social residue (Dauncey et al. 1993), but rather a consequence of growing up in the city (Lewis et al. 1992; Marcelis et al. 1998). Recent reviewers cite the following causal factors: stressful life-events, social isolation, overcrowding, overstimulation, crime levels, poverty and pollution (Sharpley et al. 2001).

Poor people don't face more stress, they just can't deal with it

Another strategy is to argue that it is not the disadvantages accompanying poverty that are responsible, and to claim instead that poor people are oversensitive to stress and can't deal with it. Some psychiatrists even argue that poverty doesn't involve exposure to disproportionate amounts of stressors. The researchers who found ten-fold differences in schizophrenia between the poorest and wealthiest parts of Nottingham (Giggs and Cooper 1987) saw 'no clues' about causes: 'There was no particular suggestion of unusually high rates of stressful events' (p. 633). Others have claimed 'there is little evidence that lower-status individuals suffer from more situationally induced stress' (Rushing and Ortega 1979: 1192).

We are told that 'at any given level of stress, people of lower social class position are more likely to become mentally disturbed than are people of higher social class position'. From this it is concluded that the 'relationship of class to schizophrenia is not attributable to the amount of stress that people endure. There must also be important class differences in how effectively people deal with stress'. In particular, the poor have inadequate 'conceptions of social reality' characterized by 'fearfulness and distress, and by a fatalistic belief that he is at the mercy of forces beyond his control and often beyond his understanding' (Kohn 1976: 179). Paranoia, it seems, is sometimes a heightened state of awareness! The point, though, is that if poor people do have limited ways to deal with stress, this is just another consequence of being poor.

It was seriously proposed that no further research be undertaken on the topic and that researchers 'look for class-constant stresses, not stressors that are more frequent in the lower class, such as events related to the economy' (Eaton 1980). This blatantly ideological recommendation has not gone unheeded. Recent reviewers note that 'Societal influences have rarely been addressed in recent reviews of schizophrenia' (Bresnahan and Susser 2003: 8). These particular reviewers argue that 'socioeconomic status has at most a modest effect on risk of schizophrenia' and that 'no clear findings have emerged' (p. 5). Other reviewers, however, concur with my own reading of the research – that is, that 'both social causation and social selection processes' have been clearly demonstrated (Mohler and Earls 2002).

Controlling for 'mediating variables'

Another way to minimize the relationship between poverty and madness is to find other variables that are related to both and argue that without these factors the relationship disappears. This is proper scientific process when trying to understand the relationship between two things; but not if the variables controlled for are themselves aspects of either of the two things in question.

Typical is a study (Goodman et al. 1983) often cited to support claims that class is unrelated to schizophrenia. Despite finding, again, that poorer people are significantly more likely to be hospitalized for 'schizophrenia', the researchers concluded that 'socio-economic class had no effect on the distribution of schizophrenia'. They did so by highlighting the fact that the poor areas included 'skid-row populations living in single-room-occupancy housing' and lots of 'non-white' people (the latter being 4.5 times more likely to be hospitalized for 'schizophrenia') and, therefore, the 'estimate of schizophrenia in the lowest socio-economic groups may be inflated'.

Biased diagnoses/self-fulfilling prophecy

There is another reason, besides direct social causation, why so many poor people are diagnosed 'schizophrenic'. By 1977, there were nine studies showing that more severe diagnoses are applied to poorer people than wealthier people with the same symptoms (Abramowitz and Docecki 1977). A tenth study found that psychiatrists assigning severe diagnoses on the basis of class genuinely believed they were basing diagnoses on 'patient behaviour' rather than 'occupation and education'. Thus there was 'intellectual denial of social status effects and a subconscious utilization of status information' (Lebedun and Collins 1976: 206). Continuing denial is evidenced by the lack of research into diagnostic biases since the 1970s. Nevertheless, commentators continue to note that:

> A number of studies have found that severer diagnoses are given to working- than to middle-class patients, regardless of symptoms; that the former are seen as having a poorer prognosis; and that professionals are less interested in treating them.
>
> (Johnstone 2000: 238)

Treatment

Class bias also operates in treatment selection. Hollingshead and Redlich (1958) found that 57% of class V 'schizophrenics', but 24% of class I and II 'schizophrenics', received nothing more than 'custodial care'. Class V 'patients' were more likely to receive physical treatments such as electro-convulsive treatment (ECT), drugs and lobotomy. In the same population, 10 years later, the poor were more likely to be hospitalized, were kept in hospital longer and received fewer treatments associated with discharge (Myers and Bean 1968). A 1977 review confirmed that working-class people were more likely to be treated with drugs than with psychotherapy (Abramowitz and Docecki 1977). Little has changed. A recent survey of nearly 900,000 American children and adolescents showed that youths whose families are eligible for Medicaid (i.e. from poor families) are 5.8 times more likely to be on antipsychotic drugs than those from families with private health insurance (Zito et al. 2003).

> Working class patients are, like black and ethnic minority patients, more likely to be prescribed physical treatments such as drugs and ECT, to spend longer periods in hospital regardless of diagnosis, and to be readmitted, and, correspondingly less likely to be referred for the more 'attractive' treatments such as psychotherapy or group therapy.
>
> (Johnstone 2000: 238)

Poverty remains the 'strongest and most consistent predictor' of compulsory admission (Bindman et al. 2002).

The circle of oppression

Psychiatry presents itself as a helping profession based on medical science. Yet the proven facts that those it claims to help are predominantly working class is responded to by mental gymnastics designed to prove that the poor do not really experience more stress and if they do it has nothing to do with their 'mental illness'. This is scientifically and morally indefensible.

There appears to be a circle of oppression operating, in which biological psychiatry plays a crucial role. Of course the poor in any society are subjected to more sources of stress than the wealthy. In many societies poverty extends to hunger and homelessness. Even those with enough to eat and somewhere to live are more likely to experience powerlessness, isolation, lack of self-respect, physical ill-health, and so on. They are also many times more likely to suffer neglect, violence and sexual abuse as children (van der Kolk *et al.* 2001), and child abuse – contrary to current psychiatric ideology – is strongly related to the development of psychosis later in life (see Chapter 16).

Having entered the system they are more likely, regardless of their behaviour, to be hospitalized and labelled 'schizophrenic'. This is likely to further lower their self-esteem and motivation, and to frighten and distance loved ones. They will find it even harder to find employment, since employers share the prejudices of the labellers (see Chapter 11). They are less likely to be able to understand the real origins of their distress, since this has all been explained away by their being 'schizophrenic'. They will, as a result, be even more powerless to change the circumstances that cause them to enter the psychiatric system in the first place. And then there are the effects of the 'treatments' themselves (see Chapters 8 and 9).

It is sad enough that we all suffer an economic system that forces us to compete for basic needs such as housing, food, health care and education; a system that perpetuates poverty and powerlessness in many so that a few may be wealthy and powerful. It is profoundly depressing that when the poor and powerless crack under the strain, experts step in to explain that there is something wrong with their brains, and condemn them with their labels, drugs and electricity to even greater depths of powerlessness, hopelessness and loneliness. When this happens the individual is called a 'chronic schizophrenic'.

RACE

The facts

'Ethnic minorities' (whether immigrants or colonized indigenous peoples) are significantly more likely to be diagnosed 'schizophrenic' than members of the dominant culture. This has been demonstrated in Australia (Bruxner *et al.* 1997), Belgium (Charalabaki *et al.* 1995), Denmark (Mortensen *et al.* 1997), Germany (Haasen *et al.* 1998), Greenland (Mortensen *et al.* 1999), Israel (Al-Krenawi and Ophir 2001), the Netherlands (Schrier *et al.* 2001), New Zealand (Sachdev 1997), Sweden (Zolkowska *et al.* 2001), the UK and the USA. These rates are only partially explained by higher overall admission rates. In New Zealand, for instance, Maori inpatients are twice as likely to be diagnosed 'schizophrenic' than European inpatients (Te Puni Kokiri 1993).

By 1974, 24 of 25 US studies had found higher rates of admission for 'schizophrenia' among foreign-born individuals compared with the 'native' population (Rosenthal 1974). In a 1983 survey of New York inpatients, the prevalence of 'schizophrenia' among non-Whites was 3.5 times higher than that among White patients, but only 1.4 times as great for affective disorders (Goodman *et al.* 1983). A Tennessee study found that African Americans constituted 16% of the population, 30% of psychiatric inpatients and 48% of patients diagnosed 'schizophrenic' (Lawson *et al.* 1994). Black Americans admitted for the first time for psychosis are seven times more likely to be diagnosed 'schizophrenic' than Whites (Strakowski *et al.* 1993). A study of 26,400 Los Angeles patients found that Black and Asian patients received psychotic diagnoses, including schizophrenia, at higher rates than Whites. Ethnicity was even more related to diagnosis than socio-economic status (Flaskerud and Hu 1992).

In Britain, incidence rates for schizophrenia are 3.6 times higher among all ethnic minority groups combined than among Whites (King *et al.* 1994). Afro-Caribbeans have been found to be nine (Thomas *et al.* 1993) and twelve times (Harrison *et al.* 1988) more likely to be diagnosed schizophrenic than White people.

The explanations

This time the 'social drift' theory is unavailable. Biological psychiatry cannot claim that the 'illness' occurs at the same rate in all ethnic groups, but white English people become Irish or African as a result. A range of other approaches have been deployed to deflect attention away from the relationship between racism and being driven, or labelled, 'psychotic'.

No explanation – no problem

Many psychiatrists and researchers prefer not to deal with the issue at all. Only one in six research studies about schizophrenia even bothers to report the racial composition of the sample and only one in 36 actually analyse data by race (Lewine and Caudle 1999). Perhaps the attitudes underlying this avoidance are exemplified in a recent New Zealand survey of psychiatrists:

> I don't have to think of my client in terms of their culture. All people are the same.

Do you really think psychiatrists need to have an understanding of spirituality – give me a break.

The way I work with patients does not depend on the colour of their skin or their ethnicity.

(Johnstone and Read 2000: 141)

Migration

The predominant research focus for the past two decades has been migration. The tendency has been not to focus on the racism of the country to which people migrate, but to determine whether the immigrants are particularly prone to schizophrenia – the 'selective migration' theory (Cochrane and Bal 1987). The individualized version of this theory argues that people who migrate are predisposed to, or already have, schizophrenia. The collective version attempts to pathologize entire nations or cultures by arguing that there are higher rates in the countries from which people had emigrated (conveniently forgetting that one of the central proofs that 'schizophrenia' is a biologically based illness is that it occurs in all countries at the same rate; see Chapter 6). It is now acknowledged that there is no evidence to support either of these notions (Boydell and Murray 2003; McKenzie and Murray 1999).

The idea of 'migratory stress' has also been deployed. Again the focus was not on the racism experienced on arrival but the general stresses of moving. This idea, too, has since been largely abandoned. It is several years after arriving that the incidence of schizophrenia increases, and rates are even higher in 'second-generation' descendants of immigrants than in those who migrated (Bhugra et al. 1997; Harrison et al. 1988). The specific stressors associated with the migration process are unrelated to schizophrenia (Zolkowska et al. 2001). A large British community survey showed that hallucinations are more common in non-migrants than in migrants (South Asia) or are equally common (Caribbean) (Johns et al. 2002).

Paranoid 'perceptions' of racism

Other explanations focus on supposedly faulty perceptions of members of ethnic minorities. Harrison et al. (1988) suggest that Afro-Caribbeans in Nottingham, whom they found to be twelve times more likely to have 'schizophrenia', live in 'a culture which they may perceive as discriminatory and even hostile'. The key word is 'perceive'. British researchers have recently argued (despite finding higher levels of financial hardships) that it is not increased exposure to adverse life events that differentiates Afro-Caribbeans from other patients so much as their greater likelihood to attribute adverse events to discrimination (Gilvarry et al. 1999).

Where could these perceptions and attributions possibly originate? In their discussion of perceptions and experiences of discrimination, Harrison and his colleagues (1988) write: 'It is possible that individuals genetically or constitutionally vulnerable to schizophrenia on account of selection factors in their parents are especially sensitive to these forms of social stress' (p. 654). So, we are asked to believe, people genetically predisposed to be mad are also genetically predisposed to perceive racism or be disturbed by it.

Genetic inferiority

Indeed, higher rates of a supposedly genetically based 'illness' in certain ethnic groups should, logically, lead to theories of greater genetic predisposition in those groups. Perhaps it is because of the horrors perpetrated by psychiatrists in the name of genetic racial theories just 60 years ago (see Chapter 4) that most psychiatrists stay away from publicly enunciating the logical conclusion.

Nevertheless, some *have* argued that 'genetic as well as social factors have contributed' (Harrison *et al.* 1988: 654). Others even claim to have found a relationship between a particular gene and schizophrenia in African Americans that was absent in their White counterparts (Nimgaonkar *et al.* 1992). Like other claims about specific genes (see Chapter 7), this has not been replicated.

A recent survey, responded to by 692 New Zealand psychologists and psychiatrists, asked 'Why do you think Maori are over-represented in psychiatric institutions?' Most identified issues related to colonization, loss of land and language, and poverty. However, 18.5% of the male psychiatrists (but no female psychiatrists and only one psychologist – a male) stated that it was because Maori are biologically or genetically more predisposed to mental illness than Europeans. Examples included: 'Genetic loading'; 'Maori are biologically predetermined to mental illness, especially psychosis'; 'Maori are biologically more vulnerable'; 'Genetically Maori as a culture seem predisposed to mental illness'; 'Minority races/cultures are more predisposed to mental illness than Europeans' (Johnstone and Read 2000: 142). Most (61%) of the New Zealand-born male psychiatrists with 10 or more years clinical experience expressed this belief. Some elaborated:

> Stop sending me crap studies like this, about pointless, meaningless, cultural rubbish.

> Maoris are always going on about the importance of land etc. etc. So why did they bloody well give it away?

> Your study is a waste of time. Why do people like you single out the Maoris for topics of research – what makes them so special?
>
> (Johnstone and Read 2000: 141–2)

Medication is the answer – but they just don't take their pills – if cannabis was prescribed I'd bet they'd bloody take that.

(Johnstone and Read 2000: 290)

One male psychiatrist wrote to the *Australian and New Zealand Journal of Psychiatry* (which had demonstrated considerable integrity in publishing our findings) characterizing our research as 'repression of new thought through fear and intimidation'. By calling the attitudes 'racist', we had apparently 'chosen to pursue a political agenda and replaced objectivity with name calling' (Kuten 2001). Our response included:

Dr Kuten tries to draw a parallel between biological illnesses with proven genetic predisposition and the (totally unsubstantiated) notion that a 'minority' race is genetically more predisposed than members of a dominant culture to behaviours, thoughts and feelings which that dominant culture deems indicative of 'mental illness' . . . How can anyone from a culture that believes that 'voices' are often important messages from ancestors possibly be understood, let alone helped, by someone who believes that the only contribution from their ancestors is illness-inducing chromosomes?

(Johnstone and Read 2001: 854)

It would appear that the attitudes and genetic racial theories that culminated in the murder of a quarter of a million patients (see Chapter 4) are still with us. However, as our Mental Health Commissioner said about the research, 'It is good to see the attitudes of younger psychiatrists have shifted'. A senior male psychiatrist commented to a newspaper that there was 'no excuse for the racist comments, and social issues were far more likely to affect Maori mental health' (Johnstone and Read 2001).

Misdiagnosis based on cultural differences

Some have attempted to protect the medical model by arguing that some unfortunate but innocent diagnostic mistakes have been made. The huge number of errors required to sustain this argument would constitute further evidence of the lack of reliability of the 'schizophrenia' diagnosis itself (see Chapter 5), particularly when applied by a dominant culture to other cultures.

The dilemma for psychiatry is how to argue that ethnic minorities have been so massively misdiagnosed while demonstrating that there is no racist bias involved. The predominant explanation, in Britain, is that the mistakes are the result of Black people having something that looks like 'schizophrenia' but isn't. Studies have indeed suggested that Afro-Caribbean 'schizophrenics' have a shorter 'illness' with a better outcome (McKenzie *et al.* 1995) and are more likely to have experienced a stressful event shortly before admission (Littlewood and Lipsedge 1981). This has led to the proposition that what is often mistaken for 'schizophrenia' among Afro-Caribbeans is actually an 'acute psychotic reaction' or a 'psychogenic psychosis' – that is, madness brought on as a psychological reaction to unpleasant life events (Lewis *et al.* 1990).

This approach to explaining high rates of psychosis among Afro-Caribbeans involves, therefore, admitting that social events can cause the types of behaviour which psychiatrists call 'psychosis'. This is what is so adamantly denied by the medical model. Nevertheless, this psychiatric anathema is deployed when it comes to explaining why so many Black people go, or are labelled, 'mad'.

In *Aliens and Alienists*, Littlewood and Lipsedge (1982) pointed out that symptoms of schizophrenia are intelligible in terms of the patient's life situation and culture. Rack states:

> When we are dealing with an Asian or Afro-Caribbean subject who appears to be suffering from acute schizophrenia, we should pay full attention to psychological and environmental factors. The conflicts and traumas mentioned by the relatives may be genuine causes, not merely trigger factors.
>
> (Rack 1982: 125)

I agree with this view and believe it holds generally rather than just for ethnic minorities.

Another explanation for all these diagnostic errors is that professionals don't understand what is normal and abnormal in other cultures. This is probably true. This approach, however, suspends another basic tenet of the medical model: that 'schizophrenia' is a bio-genetic illness and has nothing to do with breaking cultural norms (see Chapter 6). What is being suggested is that what is considered 'insane' for White people may be 'normal' for Black people. This can come dangerously close to suggesting that 'Black culture' is not just difficult to understand but actually breeds 'mental illness'. The collective version of the selective migration theory blamed the cultures of the countries of origin for the high rates of 'schizophrenia'. While psychiatry has spent two decades trashing theories about the role of the family in the aetiology of psychosis (see Chapter 17), we are told, by one of the founders of the 'transcultural psychiatry' movement, that 'my Northern Ireland data led me to favour a child-rearing hypothesis with regard to schizophrenia' (Murphy 1986).

All this attention on 'diagnostic errors' may have more to do with avoiding issues of societal or psychiatric racism than with doing anything to improve the situation. Psychiatrists from dominant cultures around the world have not responded to the findings by abandoning, or even amending, their lists of symptoms and illnesses when assessing members of other cultures. In New Zealand, only 1% of psychiatrists and 13% of psychologists agree that 'European diagnostic systems should not be used with Maori' (Johnstone and Read 2000).

Social causation: racism can help drive you crazy

The few researchers who have either tested the competing bio-genetic and psycho-social explanatory theories, or reviewed the relevant research, tend to reach the conclusion that it is an interaction of racism and poverty that causes the high rates of schizophrenia in ethnic minorities. The dilemma this poses for psychiatry has been summarized by Kwame McKenzie and Robin Murray of the Institute of Psychiatry in London:

> Establishing the role of such social factors would not only raise possibilities of prevention within the Afro-Caribbean community but could also provide an important pointer towards a possible causal role, rather than a precipitating role, for social factors in psychosis, a role that is currently discounted by much orthodox psychiatric research.
>
> (McKenzie and Murray 1999: 57)

One reviewer found that the various attempts to explain high rates of schizophrenia among British Afro-Caribbeans by locating the pathology in the biology or culture of this group are unsubstantiated and that the higher rates are entirely explicable by the 'sociodemographic factors prevalent in this community', such as poverty (Sashidharan 1993). This is confirmed by the finding that although the parents of Afro-Caribbeans diagnosed 'schizo-phrenic' have the same rate of 'schizophrenia' as the parents of White 'schizophrenics', their siblings are nine times more likely to be diagnosed 'schizophrenic' than the siblings of White 'schizophrenics'. The researchers conclude that 'the increased frequency of the disorder is due to environ-mental factors that are most common in the Afro-Caribbean community' (Sugarman and Craufurd 1994).

Of these environmental factors, those most consistently linking ethnicity to schizophrenia are financial disadvantage, unemployment, social isolation and racist discrimination (Gilvarry et al. 1999; Hutchinson et al. 1999; Mallett et al. 2002; Sproston and Nazroo 2002). A study showing that Afro-Caribbean child and adolescent 'psychiatric patients' were more likely than their white counterparts to be diagnosed psychotic also found that they experienced more socio-economic disadvantage, but less family dys-function (Goodman and Richards 1995). Another study, of adult psychotic patients, found that the only one of seven socio-demographic factors that differentiated Afro-Caribbeans from Whites was unemployment (Bhugra et al. 1997).

The role of racist discrimination and social isolation in causing 'schizophrenia' is illustrated by the fact that admission rates are lower in areas where there is 'clustering' of an ethnic minority group (Boydell *et al.* 2001). 'Social causation, in the form of reduced exposure to direct prejudice and increased social support, is a likely cause of the effect' (Halpern and Nazroo 2000: 34).

Actual racism plays a greater role in psychosis than perceived racism. Members of ethnic minorities who believed that British employers were racist were 1.6 times more likely to be experiencing psychotic symptoms than their counterparts. However, those who had experienced racist verbal abuse in the past year were 2.9 times more likely than others to be experiencing psychotic symptoms. Those who had suffered a racist physical attack were 4.8 times more likely to have such symptoms. The relationship between racism and psychosis was stronger than the relationship between racism and depression and the relationship between unemployment and psychosis (Karlsen and Nazroo 2002). Karlsen and Nazroo concluded: 'We can no longer use assumptions about the biological and cultural basis of ethnic inequalities either to limit the search for the underlying mechanisms producing them or to justify our inaction in reducing them' (p. 630).

Two studies adopted the approach, recommended elsewhere (see Chapters 5, 14, 16 and 20), of studying definable constructs like hallucinations and delusions rather than the heterogeneous construct of 'schizophrenia'. Suhail and Cochrane (2002) found that among people diagnosed 'schizophrenic', the type and content of delusions and hallucinations of Pakistanis living in Britain was more similar to British Whites than to Pakistanis in Pakistan. They concluded: 'Although cultural factors are important in phenomenology of delusions and hallucinations, immediate environment and life experiences seem to be of greater importance' (p. 137).

Janssen *et al.* (2003) recorded the experiences of discrimination in 4067 Dutch people who had shown no signs of psychosis and, 3 years later, the frequency of delusions and hallucinations. Those who had reported discrimination in two or more domains (skin colour/ethnicity, gender, age, etc.) were three times more likely to be experiencing psychotic hallucinations than those who had reported no discrimination, and five times more likely to be experiencing psychotic delusions.

Racist diagnoses in a racist society

As was the case with class, estimating the relative contributions of the 'social causation' and 'biased labelling' explanations is somewhat academic. They are part of the same process, at different points in a circle of racism. The high rates of 'schizophrenia' cannot be explained entirely in terms of the stresses of poverty and discrimination. Some reviewers who accept the social causation hypothesis dismiss the misdiagnosis hypothesis

(McKenzie and Murray 1999; Sharpley *et al.* 2001). However, there is evidence that biased diagnoses may be an even stronger determinant of who ends up being called 'schizophrenic' than the fact that racism can drive some people mad.

Compared with the three-, nine- or twelve-fold differences in rates of diagnosed 'schizophrenia' among British Afro-Caribbeans in clinical settings, a large community survey found that they are only twice as likely to experience psychosis (Sproston and Nazroo 2002). Further evidence of the extent of diagnostic bias is found in studies comparing diagnoses made with and without knowledge of the participant's race (Goodman *et al.* 1983), studies showing that when structured diagnostic protocols are used fewer ethnic minority members are diagnosed than is the case in real-life clinical settings (Whaley 2001), studies showing that Black patients are more likely to be diagnosed 'schizophrenic' than their White counterparts in the absence of any differences in symptom presentation or co-morbid diagnoses (Strakowski *et al.* 1993, 1995) and, finally, studies showing that ethnic minorities are diagnosed 'schizophrenic' on the basis of fewer symptoms than the number required for White patients (Mellor 1970; Teggin *et al.* 1985).

One study, which found that race was even more strongly related to being diagnosed 'schizophrenic' than class, traced this finding to diagnosticians' 'expectation that black people were more likely to be schizophrenic' (Watkins *et al.* 1975). This is a circular process that feeds on itself, becoming a self-fulfilling prophecy. The bias can occur both at the level of what constitutes a symptom (e.g. hallucinations being more readily perceived by psychiatrists in African Americans than in other patients) as well as at the level of deciding that a given symptom is indicative of schizophrenia (Trierweiler *et al.* 2000).

Psychiatrists have even invented new illnesses for ethnic minorities, starting with the nineteenth-century 'Drapetomania', which made slaves run away (Cartwright 1851). British examples include 'Caribbean psychosis' and 'cannabis psychosis'. In one study male Afro-Caribbean inpatients were 95 times more likely than White male patients to be diagnosed 'cannabis psychosis' (McGovern and Cope 1987). A survey of British psychiatrists found that 57% thought cannabis psychosis was more common among Afro-Caribbeans. Of these, 95% believed they smoke more cannabis and 21% thought they are more susceptible to cannabis psychosis (Littlewood 1989). Recent studies have shown these ideas to be myths (Boydell and Murray 2003; McKenzie and Murray 1999).

I have seen colleagues struggle hard to avoid the biases described above, by finding ways to avoid a 'schizophrenia' diagnosis. Unpublished data from a study of 200 outpatients (Read *et al.* 2003) show that 43% of Maori patients were given no diagnosis compared with 13% of non-Maori patients. Similarly, 17% of Pacific Islanders but only 1% of Europeans were diagnosed 'psychosis not otherwise specified'.

Treatment

Beyond being more likely to receive the stigmatizing label of 'schizophrenia' (see Chapter 11), ethnic minority groups are sometimes 'treated' differently. Immigrants, colonized indigenous peoples and other ethnic minority groups are more likely, compared with their representation in the general population or in 'clinical samples' of inpatients or psychotic patients, to be forcibly admitted to – and detained in – hospital, to have the police involved in their admission, to be admitted to secure/forensic/special hospitals and to public rather than private hospitals, to receive antipsychotic drugs or electroconvulsive therapy, and to not be offered psychotherapy. One or more of these examples of discrimination has been documented in Australia (Bruxner *et al.* 1997), Belgium (Charalabaki *et al.* 1995), Germany (Haasen *et al.* 1998), Israel (Al-Krenawi and Ophir 2001), New Zealand (Sachdev 1989), the UK (Commander *et al.* 1999; McKenzie *et al.* 1995; Rwegellera 1980) and the USA (Feinstein and Holloway 2002).

Data from a study of 200 New Zealand outpatients (Read *et al.* 2003) shows that non-European men (mostly Maori and Pacific Islanders) were three times more likely to have been treated under the Mental Health Act than European men. A study in Birmingham, England found that Caribbean men between 16 and 29 years of age were 11 times more likely than white men of the same age to be hospitalized against their will (McGovern and Cope 1987).

Even after controlling for other variables such as class, diagnosis, gender and age, the probability of compulsory admission, or being given medication or electroconvulsive therapy is still related to ethnicity (Rwegellera 1980; Singh *et al.* 1998). Admission to psychiatric hospital may be even more ineffective for some groups than it is in general. In New Zealand, Maoris are far more likely to be readmitted, particularly if diagnosed 'schizophrenic' (Te Puni Kokiri 1993: 17).

Some countries have laws barring entry to foreigners with diagnoses like 'schizophrenia' and/or allowing for 'repatriation'.

Conclusion

Psychiatrists who themselves are members of ethnic minorities are often in the forefront of efforts to address the issues raised here (e.g. Bhugra and Bahl 1999; Sashidharan 1993). Black psychiatrists in Britain reached the following conclusions:

> The evidence points to the conclusion that racism does lead to mental illness; firstly, by fermenting and maintaining social deprivation and so impairing chances of attaining mental health . . . Even if the medical model carries with it a kernel of truth, it cannot be generalised to all

cases of mental illness most of which are entirely the result of the social environment that we live in.

(Burke 1986: 147, 154)

The diagnosis may cover up and legitimise the social extrusion of black people from society by psychiatrising their problems – just as the legal system does so by criminalising them. Strategies to deal with the over-diagnosis of schizophrenia must confront the question of racist (mis)perceptions of black people . . . The freeing of the profession of psychiatry and its institutional counterpart from its present subservience to general forces in society is a necessary first step.

(Fernando 1988: 176)

GENDER

The relationship between gender and 'schizophrenia' requires a different sort of analysis. Depending on the diagnostic criteria employed, some researchers find more men than women 'have schizophrenia' while others find equal proportions (Seeman and Fitzgerald 2000). More importantly, there are some clear differences between men given the diagnosis and women given the diagnosis. These differences are so pronounced that they have been summarized in terms of men having 'typical schizophrenia' and women 'atypical schizophrenia' (Lewine 1981).

The differences

Age of onset

The best known gender difference is that men have an earlier onset (Angermeyer and Kuhn 1988). Kraepelin actually characterized the illness he invented (see Chapter 3) as a disorder of young men. The peak period of onset for men is 18–25 years old, but for women it is 25–30 years (Castle 2000; Goldstein and Lewine 2000; Salem and Kring 1998). This difference is 'specific to schizophrenia, not an artefact of admission practices, and similar across cultures' (Goldstein and Lewine 2000: 112). Sub-clinical psychotic experiences have recently also been shown to occur more frequently in 17- to 21-year-old males than in females of this age group, with similar rates between the sexes in the 22–28 year age range (Spawen *et al.* 2003).

However, gender differences in rates of new cases of schizophrenia change dramatically over the lifespan. Childhood-onset schizophrenia is between two and three times more common in boys than girls. This difference lessens (Goldstein and Lewine 2000) or disappears (Orr and Castle

2003) in early adolescence and then the male preponderance reappears again in late adolescence and continues through the twenties (Orr and Castle 2003). In the thirties, rates are roughly the same. However women over 40 are nearly twice as likely as men to be diagnosed 'schizophrenic' for the first time. The difference increases to four-fold after age 60 years (Castle 2000).

Behaviours, thoughts and feelings

Male and female 'schizophrenics' tend to have different experiences and behaviours. To preserve the impression that there is an illness at work, and that it is the *same* illness, the differences are called variations in 'disease expression' (Seeman and Fitzgerald 2000). In schizophrenia research, 'The most replicated findings of sex differences in symptomatology have been negative symptoms in men and affective symptoms in women' (Goldstein and Lewine 2000: 115). The preponderance of negative symptoms in men was recently confirmed in a general population study of over 7000 people (Maric *et al.* 2003).

The women are not only more depressed but are more emotionally expressive in other ways, including being more angry and explosive. Men have more cognitive deficits than women. Some studies find positive symptoms, overall, distributed equally, while others find a higher overall rate in women (Lewine 1981; Ragland *et al.* 1999). Women experience more auditory hallucinations, paranoia and persecutory delusions, while men have more grandiose delusions and ideas of reference (believing that events are related to oneself). Women's delusions focus more often on spiritual issues and interpersonal wrongs (Goldstein *et al.* 1990; Goldstein and Lewine 2000; Salem and Kring 1998). Men are far more likely to be experiencing symptoms associated with abuse of drugs or alcohol (Seeman and Fitzgerald 2000).

Thus men tend to be emotionally and socially closed down, have problems thinking clearly, try to medicate themselves and sometimes believe themselves to be extremely important. Meanwhile, women tend to have very strong feelings, to dislike themselves and to be frightened that others will hurt them.

Triggers and 'pre-morbid functioning'

There are also gender issues before the 'illness' onset. Young girls who later become 'schizophrenic' are more shy and sensitive than other girls, while 'pre-schizophrenic' boys 'act out' more than other boys, often to the point of aggression. This difference appears to reverse itself as the children enter adolescence. 'Pre-schizophrenic' male youth, compared with their female counterparts, are more socially isolated and withdrawn and perform less adequately in all social and occupational functions (Salem and Kring 1998). During late adolescence, the best predictors of 'schizophrenia' for hetero-sexual males are in the interpersonal domain, including having fewer than two friends, not having a girlfriend and feeling sensitive (Malmberg *et al.* 1998).

Course and outcome

Apart from being in better shape than men before the 'illness', women also fare better than men after being diagnosed 'schizophrenic'. Women's 'symptoms' remit more quickly and they have fewer and shorter hospital-izations (Angermeyer *et al.* 1989). Men respond even less well than women to antipsychotic drugs (Salem and Kring 1998).

Brain functioning

Men diagnosed 'schizophrenic' have more structural brain abnormalities, particularly enlarged ventricles and a reduction in hippocampus volume, than their female counterparts (Salem and Kring 1998).

The explanations

Biology

As was the case for poverty and ethnicity, the predominant response of biological psychiatry to all these gender differences is to ignore them. 'The examination of gender differences in schizophrenia and other chronic mental illnesses has not kept pace with the literature on depression' (Sparks 2002: 306). Only about 1% of the 450-page text *The Epidemiology of Schizophrenia* (Murray *et al.* 2003) deals with gender.

The few researchers who do deal with gender differences take the pre-dictable stance of considering only biological factors as possible causes. In the recent book *Women and Schizophrenia* any psychosocial factors that might explain gender differences are portrayed, by terms like 'artefacts due to psycho-social differences' or 'social confounding factors', as getting in the way of understanding the real, biological causes (Castle 2000: 24, 28). The book makes no reference to gender roles, power differences, relative poverty or violence. The single paragraph dealing with sexual abuse locates the problem, in classic 'victim-blaming' fashion, entirely within the abused woman, with explanations such as 'poor judgment, poor impulse control' and 'the relative passivity and isolation that accompany schizophrenia' (Seeman and Fitzgerald 2000: 96).

Having made a transparently ideological decision to dismiss the possibility of psycho-social factors having any causal role, *Women and Schizophrenia* unsurprisingly concurs with psychiatry's favourite explanation for all gender differences: hormones and reproductive functions. The hypotheses are not unreasonable. The singular focus on these issues does, however, perpetuate the difficulty psychiatry appears to have seeing anything other than hormones and reproductive functions whenever it comes to women. The tradition is a long-standing one, reaching back to the male priest-physicians of Ancient Greece (see Chapter 2) and maintained by male psychiatrists of the nineteenth century and beyond, including such revered 'fathers' of modern psychiatry as Henry Maudsley and Thomas Clouston (Showalter 1985).

I shall offer just a few examples of the type of possible explanations for the gender differences that come into view once bio-genetic blinkers are removed. None are intended as singular explanations for any of the gender differences, because none will apply to all women or all men diagnosed 'schizophrenic'. They are offered in the hope that they may help some of the individual men and women, and those wanting to understand and assist them, to reflect on what has gone on in their lives and to consider new ways of responding to the issues in the future.

Gender roles – exaggerated role as causal factor or diagnostic punishment for role reversal?

Most of the gender differences in the symptoms of people diagnosed 'schizophrenic' can be found in the general population (Lewine 1981), leading to the conclusion that 'Sex differences in schizophrenic symptomatology may represent an exaggerated reflection of the small but consistent sex differences that are seen in the normal population' (Raine 1992). In two clinical populations of young men, an extreme masculine role (particularly 'restrictive emotionality') was correlated with psychosis (Good *et al.* 1996). So, one possible explanation for the gender differences in 'symptoms' is that severely disturbed men and women are falling back on an exaggerated version of their learned gender role in an attempt to find solid ground. Alternatively, perhaps adopting an extreme version of the traditional masculine or feminine social roles contributes to the development of psychological disturbance. Both could be true, with the two interacting in a downward reciprocal spiral towards either intense helplessness, despair and paranoia or to total emotional shutdown and social withdrawal into a secret fantasy world in which one believes oneself to be very important.

However, others propose the opposite. In *Women and Madness*, Chesler (1972) suggested that women and men who do *not* conform to traditional gender roles are particularly likely to be diagnosed 'schizophrenic'. She cites studies showing that female 'schizophrenics' are more dominant and aggressive than either male 'schizophrenics' or 'normal' women. Meanwhile, 'schizophrenic' men had been shown to be more passive than 'normal males'. Clear examples of broken gender roles were among Kraepelin's original symptom list (see Chapter 3). Subsequent research has provided additional support, with 'schizophrenics' (male and female) more often showing a 'confused gender role' or choosing opposite gender roles than either 'normals' or other psychiatric patients (LaTorre and Piper 1979).

Two interpretations are possible here. One is that 'inappropriate' gender roles are causal factors in mental health problems and require treatment (La Torre and Piper 1979). Chesler, however, is adamant that women and men are being diagnostically punished for rejecting restrictive societal norms.

There is certainly evidence that men and women are treated differently diagnostically (Davison and Abramowitz 1980). The most famous study in this field is that of Broverman *et al.* (1970). American clinicians considered behaviours they deemed mentally healthy in men to be the same as those they deemed mentally health for adults in general. Different behaviours were deemed mentally healthy for women. Therefore, women were perceived as less mentally healthy according to a general standard of adult mental health. Studies have found more severe diagnostic evaluations are made of 'physically unattractive' women (Cash *et al.* 1975) and, among 'non-liberal' clinicians, women with 'left' political values, especially if they act on them (Abramowitz *et al.* 1973). As is the case for most psycho-social issues in mental health, research into diagnostic bias in relation to gender waned after the 1970s. The studies that *have* been conducted continue to find bias (Beckwith 1993). Diagnostic bias, and the disproportionate use of drugs and electroconvulsive therapy on women, are discussed by Ussher (1991), Russell (1995), Busfield (1996) and Williams (1999).

The differing hypotheses, that extreme gender roles, or rejection of gender roles, are related to being diagnosed 'schizophrenic', are not contradictory. One will apply to some women diagnosed 'schizophrenic' and the other will apply to other women. For some neither will be relevant.

> Definitions of 'mental illness' may themselves be influenced by sex-role expectations, with women being seen as 'mad' if they either display too much traditional 'feminine' behaviour, or conversely deviate too far from traditional 'feminine' norms.
>
> (Johnstone 2000: 118)

A true case of damned if you do and damned if you don't, especially when we remember that there is no escape from diagnostic bias in adopting a 'normal' amount of femininity. Just being female increases your chances of mental health staff perceiving you as abnormal (Broverman *et al.* 1970).

The stressors of adolescence and early adulthood

One of the defining characteristics of Bleuler and Kraepelin's illness was that it is something that develops early in life. 'Praecox' in dementia praecox means 'early' (see Chapter 3). Because of the simplistic bio-genetic ideology that spawned the construct little attention is given to wondering what might be going on in late adolescence and early adulthood that could cause young people to go mad. One of the rare exceptions was Bleuler's son, Manfred (1978). He was not alone in pointing out that:

> Tasks such as leaving home, establishing independence quarters, obtaining a job, and competing with others seem to be especially associated with schizophrenia in men, whereas childbirth and family conflict are associated with schizophrenia in women.
>
> (Lewine 1981: 441)

In 'Why does schizophrenia develop at late adolescence?', Harrop and Trower (2001) highlight the blocking of the normal adolescent tasks of separating from and de-idealizing parents and establishing peer relationships. They contrast the clinical utility of this focus with labelling developmental difficulties 'schizophrenic'. They also put the hormonal theories about gender differences into perspective by documenting that age of puberty and hormonal levels are themselves strongly influenced by the social environment.

One finding that can help us here is that those women who, like most men, have an earlier onset are similar to men (Gureje and Bamidele 1998). Both men and women with earlier onset have a poorer 'pre-morbid' social functioning. So if we want to know why men go mad earlier than women we must ask: Why do young men in general perform worse than young women in the social domain? The possibility that the interpersonal and emotional limitations of the male gender role are implicated here is supported by the finding that the stronger the masculine role, the more likely young men are to be interpersonally sensitive, paranoid and psychotic (Good et al. 1996). Understanding the contribution of intergenerational patterns of disturbed child–parent attachment to the development of psychosis is also important (Diamond and Doane 1994). The implications for prevention of madness in young men are obvious, but seldom mentioned.

It is possible that another component of traditional masculinity, high expectations for autonomy and independence (Angermeyer and Kuhn 1988), may expose young men to more stressors outside home at an earlier age. Pressure to take the initiative in sexual interactions may be an additional burden. Not having a girlfriend is very common for young heterosexual men who later become psychotic (Harrop and Trower 2001; Malmberg et al. 1998).

In addition, the finding that at first signs of 'mental illness' more men than women are still living at home (Hafner *et al.* 1998) suggests that a significant proportion of the men may be 'blocked' at the first of the two stages (separation from parents) identified by Harrop and Trower (2001). Men and women are equally damaged by living with highly critical or overinvolved parents, but men are more likely than women to be living in such a situation (Bebbington and Kuipers 1995). Men living at home are exposed to more criticism than their female counterparts, perhaps because – again – of gender role expectations regarding autonomy and independence. Parents show less tolerance and greater rejection and criticism of 'schizophrenic' sons than of 'schizophrenic' daughters even when their 'illness severity' is the same (Goldstein and Kreisman 1988; Haas *et al.* 1990). This is important in relation to the earlier hospitalization of males (Lewine 1981).

> . . . regardless of the severity of the illness, the parents will be more protective and tolerant of daughters than of sons, while sons will more often be sent to hospital for care. The implicit assumption here is that sons are expected to function in a self-sufficient manner, an expectation that does not exist in the same way for daughters.
>
> (Goldstein and Kreisman 1988: 862)

This greater tolerance of 'madness' in women, which also exists in society in general (Angermeyer *et al.* 1989), may be partly explicable in terms of lower expectations emanating from the belief that women are naturally and inevitably less mentally healthy, more 'emotionally disturbed', than men (Broverman *et al.* 1970; Showalter 1985).

The importance of gender roles in the earlier hospitalization of men becomes clearer in the light of findings that fathers of 'schizophrenics' are less tolerant of cross-gender behaviour, including depression, passivity and dependence, in sons than in daughters (Goldstein and Kreisman 1988; Schwoon and Angermeyer 1980).

'Schizophrenics' have childhoods too

Many researchers conclude that men are more prone to a 'poor-prognosis, neurodevelopmental subtype of schizophrenia, for which early environmental brain insults play an important etiological role' (Salem and Kring 1998: 795). However, the only brain insults ever mentioned are *medical* complications, usually around pregnancy and birth. Such complications are more common in men and are related to early onset of 'schizophrenia' in both men and women. This may indeed be a partial explanation for the greater neurocognitive deficits in men and for men having an earlier onset of 'schizophrenia'.

All other possible sources of brain insult are ignored or dismissed with comments revealing ignorance, such as 'there is no empirical evidence to suggest that exposure to interpersonal aggression is important in the etiology or course of schizophrenia' (Salem and Kring 1998: 803). Child abuse is, in fact, found in the majority of adult psychiatric inpatients and is strongly related not only to the symptoms of schizophrenia but to earlier onset of psychotic symptoms and earlier admission to hospital (see Chapter 16). This ignored body of research may shed light on both the earlier onset in men and gender differences in symptoms.

For example, one inpatient study found that while only 9% of non-abused men were first admitted before age 18 years, this was the case for 44% of those sexually abused as boys ($P < 0.05$) and 60% of those who had been physically abused ($P < 0.01$). Although the differences for the abused and non-abused women were in the same direction, they were not statistically significant (Read 1998).

Why might child abuse in men be related to an earlier onset and worse outcome than in women? It has been suggested that: 'The greater vulnerability of the male brain to environmental insults is presumed to underlie the sex differences in severity, age of onset and other aspects of schizophrenia' (Harrison 1995: 6). Traumatic brain injury is significantly correlated with 'schizophrenia' (Malaspina et al. 2001). It seems that the male pathway to greater cognitive deficits, more negative symptoms and earlier onset of 'schizophrenia' includes, for some men, structural brain damage (Sachdev et al. 2001) resulting from the kind of physical trauma to the head to which boys are exposed at higher rates than girls (Boney-McCoy and Finkelhor 1995). Even without brain injury, 'increased stress especially in the form of competition and aggression', leads to earlier breakdown in men (Lewine 1981).

An alternative hypothesis is that because men are less likely to disclose child abuse (physical or sexual), to be asked about abuse (Holmes et al. 1997; Read and Fraser 1998) or have abuse disclosures properly responded to (Agar and Read 2002), they are less likely to receive help that might prevent deterioration into psychosis.

The effects of psychological trauma, such as sexual abuse, on the developing brain of the child are remarkably similar to the brain dysfunction and structural abnormalities found in many adult 'schizophrenics' (Read et al. 2001). The preponderance of negative symptoms in males and positive symptoms in women might be partially explained by the differential response of boys and girls to trauma. Boys tend to react to psychological trauma with hyperarousal, while girls typically respond with dissociation (Perry 1994; Read et al. 2001). Both the dissociative response to trauma (Perry et al. 1995) and the positive symptoms of schizophrenia (Andreasen and Olsen 1982) are primarily dopamine-mediated. Meanwhile, the hyperarousal trauma response and negative symptoms, more common in males, are more related to structural brain changes such as cerebral atrophy and ventricular enlargement. Ventricular enlargement is more common in male 'schizophrenics' and is correlated with negative symptoms (Andreasen *et al.* 1990a,b). It is plausible, then, that the typically male hyperarousal response to childhood trauma leads to more profound disturbance, mediated by cerebral atrophy and marked more by negative symptoms, both of which are more common in men. One study has even found that the correlation between negative symptoms and early onset is true for men but not for women (Gureje and Bamidele 1998). This hypothesis would also explain why men respond less to antipsychotic medication aimed at biochemical imbalance, since their brain disturbance is, either as a result of traumatic brain injury or because of the atrophy resulting from their hyperarousal response to psychological trauma, more often of a structural nature rather than biochemically mediated.

Women tend to be poorer than men

All the issues discussed in the section on poverty are more likely to relate to women. Similarly, ethnic minority women have more than one set of adverse psycho-social dynamics to contend with and may well get the worst deal of anyone from our current mental health system (Sparks 2002).

HOPE

Within psychiatry there are those who see the problems and understand what must be overcome to move things forward. The last words go to two members of the Institute of Psychiatry in London:

> The interaction of social and biological processes may explain behaviour at an individual level, but greater credence must also be given to an understanding of social dynamics, in particular how power relationships within a society can give rise to psychosocial pathology. Until psychiatry recognizes its responsibility in this way and abandons some of its outdated assumptions it will continue to be seen as a perpetrator of social abuse rather than an instrument of care and rehabilitation for those who already feel excluded by the society in which they live.
>
> (Hutchinson and Hickling 1999: 165)

ACKNOWLEDGEMENTS

I am very grateful to Vanessa Beavan, Angus Maxwell, David Semp and Melissa Taitimu for their invaluable assistance in gathering some of the material discussed in this chapter.

REFERENCES

Abramowitz, C. and Docecki, P. (1977). The politics of clinical judgement: what nonliberal examiners infer about women who do not stifle themselves. *Psychological Bulletin* 84: 460–76.

Abramowitz, S. *et al.* (1973). The politics of clinical judgement. *Journal of Consulting and Clinical Psychology* 41: 383–91.

Agar, K. and Read, J. (2002). What happens when people disclose sexual or physical abuse to staff at a community mental health centre? *International Journal of Mental Health Nursing* 11: 70–9.

Al-Krenawi, A. and Ophir, M. (2001). Ethnic and gender differences in mental health utilization. *International Journal of Social Psychiatry* 47: 42–54.

Andreasen, N. and Olsen, S. (1982). Negative *v* positive schizophrenia. *Archives of General Psychiatry* 39: 789–94.

Andreasen, N. *et al.* (1990a). Ventricular enlargement in schizophrenia evaluated with computed tomographic scanning. *Archives of General Psychiatry* 47: 1008–15.

Andreasen, N. *et al.* (1990b). Magnetic imaging resonance of the brain in schizophrenia. *Archives of General Psychiatry* 47: 35–44.

Angermeyer, M. and Kuhn, L. (1988). Gender differences in age at onset of schizophrenia. *European Archives of Neurological and Psychiatric Sciences* 237: 351–64.

Angermeyer, M. *et al.* (1989). Gender differences in schizophrenia. *Psychological Medicine* 19: 365–82.

Aro, S. *et al.* (1995). Educational level and hospital use in mental disorders. *Acta Psychiatrica Scandinavica* 91: 305–12.

Bebbington, P. and Kuipers, E. (1995). Predicting relapse in schizophrenia. *International Journal of Mental Health* 24: 7–22.

Beckwith, J. (1993). Gender stereotypes and mental health revisited. *Social Behaviour and Personality* 21: 85–8.

Bhugra, D. and Bahl, V. (eds) (1999). *Ethnicity: An Agenda for Mental Health*. London: Gaskell.

Bhugra, D. *et al.* (1997). Incidence and outcome of schizophrenia in whites, Afro-Caribbeans and Asians in London. *Psychological Medicine* 27: 791–8.

Bindman, J. *et al.* (2002). Poverty, social services, and compulsory psychiatric admission in England. *Social Psychiatry and Psychiatric Epidemiology* 37: 341–5.

Bleuler, M. (1978). *The Schizophrenic Disorders* (translated by S. Clemens). New Haven, CT: Yale University Press.

Boney-McCoy, S. and Finkelhor, D. (1995). Psychosocial sequelae of violent victimization in a national youth sample. *Journal of Consulting and Clinical Psychology* 63: 726–36.

Boydell, J. and Murray, R. (2003). Urbanization, migration and risk of schizophrenia. In R. Murray *et al.* (eds) *The Epidemiology of Schizophrenia*. Cambridge: Cambridge University Press.

Boydell, J. *et al.* (2001). The incidence of schizophrenia in ethnic minorities is highest in London neighbourhoods which are mainly white. *British Medical Journal* 323: 1336–8.

Bradford, J. *et al.* (1994). National Lesbian Health Care Survey: implications for mental health care. *Journal of Consulting and Clinical Psychology* 62: 228–42.

Brenner, M. (1973). *Mental Illness and the Economy*. Cambridge, MA: Harvard University Press.

Bresnahan, M. and Susser, E. (2003). Investigating socioenvironmental influences in schizophrenia. In R. Murray *et al.* (eds) *The Epidemiology of Schizophrenia*. Cambridge: Cambridge University Press.

Broverman, I. *et al.* (1970). Sex-role stereotypes and clinical judgments of mental health. *Journal of Consulting and Clinical Psychology* 34: 1–7.

Brown, A. *et al.* (2000). Social class of origin and cardinal symptoms of schizophrenic disorders over the early illness course. *Social Psychiatry and Psychiatric Epidemiology* 35: 53–60.

Bruxner, G. *et al.* (1997). Aspects of psychiatric admissions of migrants to hospitals in Perth. *Australian and New Zealand Journal of Psychiatry* 31: 532–42.

Burke, A. (1986). Racism, prejudice and mental illness. In J. Cox (ed.) *Transcultural Psychiatry*. London: Croom Helm.

Busfield, J. (1996). *Men, Women and Madness*. London: Macmillan.

Cartwright, A. ([1851] 1981). Report on the diseases and physical peculiarities of the negro race. In A. Caplan *et al.* (eds) *Concepts of Health and Disease*. Boston, MA: Addison-Wesley

Cash, T. *et al.* (1975). When counsellors are heard but not seen. *Journal of Counselling Psychology* 22: 273–9.

Castle, D. (2000). Women and schizophrenia: an epidemiological perspective. In D. Castle *et al.* (eds) *Women and Schizophrenia*. Cambridge: Cambridge University Press.

Castle, D. *et al.* (1993). Does social deprivation in gestation and early life predispose to later schizophrenia? *Social Psychiatry and Psychiatric Epidemiology* 28: 1–4.

Castle, D. *et al.* (eds) (2000). *Women and Schizophrenia*. Cambridge: Cambridge University Press.

Charalabaki, E. *et al.* (1995). Immigration and psychopathology. *European Psychiatry* 10: 237–44.

Chesler, P. (1972). *Women and Madness*. New York: Avon.

Clark, R. (1949). Psychosis, income and occupational prestige. *American Journal of Sociology* 54: 433–40.

Cochrane, R. and Bal, S. (1987). Migration and schizophrenia. *Social Psychiatry* 22: 181–91.

Commander, M. *et al.* (1999). Mental health care for Asian, black and white patients with non-affective psychoses. *Social Psychiatry and Psychiatric Epidemiology* 34: 484–91.

Dauncey, K. *et al.* (1993). Schizophrenia in Nottingham. *British Journal of Psychiatry* 163: 613–19.

Davison, C. and Abramowitz, S. (1980). Sex bias in clinical judgement. *Psychology of Women Quarterly* 4: 377–95.

Diamond, D. and Doane, J. (1994). Disturbed attachment and negative affective style. *British Journal of Psychiatry* 164: 770–81.

Eaton, W. (1980). A formal theory of selection for schizophrenia. *American Journal of Sociology* 86: 149–58.

Faris, R. and Dunham, H. (1939). *Mental Disorders in Urban Areas.* Chicago, IL: University of Chicago Press.

Feinstein, A. and Holloway, F. (2002). Evaluating the use of a psychiatric intensive care unit. *International Journal of Social Psychiatry* 48: 38–46.

Fernando, S. (1988). *Race and Culture in Psychiatry.* London: Croom Helm.

Flaskerud, J. and Hu, L. (1992). Relationship of ethnicity to psychiatric diagnosis. *Journal of Nervous and Mental Disease* 180: 296–303.

Giggs, J. and Cooper, J. (1987). Ecological structure and the distribution of schizophrenia and affective psychoses in Nottingham. *British Journal of Psychiatry* 151: 627–33.

Gilman, S. *et al.* (2001). Risk of psychiatric disorders among individuals reporting same-sex sexual partners in the national comorbidity survey. *American Journal of Public Health* 91: 933–9.

Gilvarry, C. *et al.* (1999). Life events, ethnicity and perceptions of discrimination in patients with severe mental illness. *Social Psychiatry and Psychiatric Epidemiology* 34: 600–8.

Golding, J. (1997). *WithOut Prejudice: Mind Lesbian, Gay and Bisexual Mental Heatlh Awareness Research.* London: MIND.

Goldner, E. *et al.* (2003). Using administrative data to analyze the prevalence and distribution of schizophrenic disorders. *Psychiatric Services* 54: 1017–21.

Goldstein, J. and Kreisman, D. (1988). Gender, family environment and schizophrenia. *Psychological Medicine* 18: 861–72.

Goldstein, J. and Lewine, R. (2000). Overview of sex differences in schizophrenia. In D. Castle *et al.* (eds) *Women and Schizophrenia.* Cambridge: Cambridge University Press.

Goldstein, J. *et al.* (1990). The role of gender in identifying subtypes of schizophrenia. *Schizophrenia Bulletin* 16: 263–75.

Good, G. *et al.* (1996). The relation between masculine role conflict and psychological distress in male university counselling center clients. *Journal of Counselling and Development* 75: 44–9.

Goodman, A. *et al.* (1983). The relationship between socioeconomic class and prevalence of schizophrenia, alcoholism and affective disorders treated by inpatient care. *American Journal of Psychiatry* 140: 166–70.

Goodman, R. and Richards, H. (1995). Child and adolescent psychiatric presentations of second generation Afro-Caribbeans in Britain. *British Journal of Psychiatry* 167: 362–9.

Green, W. *et al.* (1992). Schizophrenia with childhood onset. *Journal of the American Academy of Child and Adolescent Psychiatry* 31: 968–76.

Gureje, O. and Bamidele, R. (1998). Gender and schizophrenia. *Australian and New Zealand Journal of Psychiatry* 32: 415–23.

Haas, G. *et al.* (1990). Gender and schizophrenia outcome. *Schizophrenia Bulletin* 16: 277–92.

Haasen, C. *et al.* (1998). Impact of ethnicity on the prevalence of psychiatric disorders among migrants in Germany. *Ethnicity and Health* 3: 159–65.

Hafner, H. *et al.* (1998). Causes and consequences of the gender difference in age of onset of schizophrenia. *Schizophrenia Bulletin* 24: 99–113.

Halpern, D. and Nazroo, J. (2000). The ethnic density effect. *International Journal of Social Psychiatry* 46: 34–46.

Harrison, G. *et al.* (1988). A prospective study of severe mental disorder in Afro-Caribbean patients. *Psychological Medicine* 18: 643–57.

Harrison, G. *et al.* (2001). Association between schizophrenia and social inequality at birth. *Brtish Journal of Psychiatry* 179: 346–50.

Harrison, P. (1995). On the neuropathology of schizophrenia and its dementia. *Neurodegeneration* 4: 1–12.

Harrop, C. and Trower, P. (2001). Why does schizophrenia develop at late adolescence? *Clinical Psychology Review* 21: 241–66.

Hollingshead, A. and Redlich, F. (1958). *Social Class and Mental Illness.* New York: Wiley.

Holmes, R. *et al.* (1997). See no evil, hear no evil, speak no evil. *Clinical Psychology Review* 17: 69–88.

Hutchinson, G. and Hickling, F. (1999). Problems in society, problems in psychiatry. *International Review of Psychiatry* 11: 162–7.

Hutchinson, G. *et al.* (1999). Are the increased rates of psychosis reported for the population of Caribbean origin in Britain an urban effect? *International Review of Psychiatry* 11: 122–8.

Iheuze, I. *et al.* (1984). A psychosocial study of schizophrenic patients treated at a Nigerian psychiatric hospital. *Acta Psychiatrica Scandinavica* 70: 310–15.

Ineichen, I. *et al.* (1984). Psychiatric hospital admissions in Bristol. *British Journal of Psychiatry* 145: 600–11.

Janssen, I. *et al.* (2003). Discrimination and delusional ideation. *British Journal of Psychiatry* 182: 71–6.

Johns, L. *et al.* (2002). Occurrence of hallucinatory experiences in a community sample and ethnic variations. *British Journal of Psychiatry* 180: 174–8.

Johnstone, K. and Read, J. (2000). Psychiatrists' recommendations for improving bicultural training and Maori mental health services. *Australian and New Zealand Journal of Psychiatry* 34: 135–45.

Johnstone, K. and Read, J. (2001). Correspondence. *Australian and New Zealand Journal of Psychiatry* 35: 854–5.

Johnstone, L. (2000). *Users and Abusers of Psychiatry*, 2nd edn. London: Brunner-Routlege.

Karlsen, S. and Nazroo, J. (2002). Relation between racial discrimination, social class and health among ethnic minority groups. *American Journal of Public Health* 92: 624–31.

King, M. *et al.* (1994). Incidence of psychotic illness in London: Comparison of ethnic groups. *British Medical Journal* 309: 1115–19.

Kohn, M. (1976). The interaction of social class and other factors in the etiology of schizophrenia. *American Journal of Psychiatry* 133: 177–80.

Koppel, S. and McGuffin, P. (1999). Socio-economic factors that predict psychiatric admission at a local level. *Psychological Medicine* 29: 1235–41.

Kuten, J. (2001). Correspondence. *Australian and New Zealand Journal of Psychiatry* 35: 852–3.

Kydd, R. *et al.* (1991). Mental health needs in Auckland 1982–6. *New Zealand Medical Journal* 104: 255–7.

La Pousse, R. *et al.* (1956). The drift hypothesis and socio-economic differentials in schizophrenia. *American Journal of Public Health* 46: 978–86.

LaTorre, R. and Piper, W. (1979) Gender identity and gender role in schizophrenia. *Journal of Abnormal Psychology* 88: 68–72.

Lawson, W. *et al.* (1994). Ethnicity as a factor in inpatient and outpatient admission and diagnosis. *Hospital and Community Psychiatry* 45: 72–4.

Lebedun, M. and Collins, J. (1976). Effects of status indicators on psychiatrists' judgements of psychiatric impairments. *Social Science Research* 60: 199–210.

Lee, R. (1976). The causal priority between socio-economic status and psychiatric disorder. *International Journal of Social Psychiatry* 22: 1–8.

Lewine, R. (1981). Sex differences in schizophrenia. *Psychological Bulletin* 90: 432–44.

Lewine, R. and Caudle, J. (1999). At issue: race in the 'Decade of the Brain'. *Schizophrenia Bulletin* 25: 1–5.

Lewis, G. *et al.* (1990). Are British psychiatrists racist? *British Journal of Psychiatry* 157: 410–15.

Lewis, G. *et al.* (1992). Schizophrenia and city life. *Lancet* 340: 137–40.

Littlewood, R. (1989). Community-initiated research: a study of psychiatrists' conceptualisations of 'cannabis psychosis'. *Psychiatric Bulletin* 13: 486–8.

Littlewood, R. and Lipsedge, M. (1981). Acute psychotic reactions in Caribbean-born patients. *Psychological Medicine* 11: 301–18.

Littlewood, R. and Lipsedge, M. (1982). *Aliens and Alienists: Ethnic Minorities and Psychiatry*. London: Penguin.

Malaspina, D. *et al.* (2001). Traumatic brain injury and schizophrenia in members of schizophrenia and bipolar disorder pedigrees. *American Journal of Psychiatry* 158: 440–6.

Mallett, R. *et al.* (2002). Social environment, ethnicity and schizophrenia. *Social Psychiatry and Psychiatric Epidemiology* 37: 329–35.

Malmberg, A. *et al.* (1998). Premorbid adjustment and personality in people with schizophrenia. *British Journal of Psychiatry* 172: 308–13.

Marcelis, M. *et al.* (1998). Urbanization and psychosis. *Psychological Medicine* 28: 871–9.

Maric, N. *et al.* (2003). Sex differences in symptoms of psychosis in a non-selected, general population study. *Schizophrenia Bulletin* 63: 89–95.

McGovern, D. and Cope, R. (1987). The compulsory detention of males of different ethnic groups. *British Journal of Psychiatry* 150: 505–12.

McKenzie, K. and Murray, R. (1999). Risk factors for psychosis. In D. Bhugra and V. Bahl (eds) *Ethnicity: An Agenda for Mental Health*. London: Gaskell.

McKenzie, K. *et al.* (1995). Psychosis with good prognosis in Afro-Caribbean people living in the U.K. *British Medical Journal* 311: 1325–8.

Mellor, C. (1970). First rank symptoms of schizophrenia. *British Journal of Psychiatry* 117: 15–23.

Mohler, B. and Earls, F. (2002). Social selection and social causation as determinants of psychiatric disorders. In E. Waring and D. Weisburd (eds) *Crime and Social Organization*. New Brunswick, NJ: Transaction Books.

Mortensen, P. *et al.* (1997). Increased rates of schizophrenia among immigrants. *Psychological Medicine* 27: 813–20.

Mortensen, P. *et al.* (1999). Effects of family history and place and season of birth on the risk of schizophrenia. *New England Journal of Medicine* 340: 603–8.

Murphy, H. (1986). The mental health impact of British cultural traditions. In J. Cox (ed.) *Transcultural Psychiatry*. London: Croom Helm.

Murray, R. *et al.* (eds) (2003). *The Epidemiology of Schizophrenia*. Cambridge: Cambridge University Press.

Myers, J. and Bean, L. (1968). *A Decade Later: A Follow-up of Social Class and Mental Illness*. New York: Wiley.

Nimgaonkar, V. *et al.* (1992). A negative association of schizophrenia with an allele of the HLA DQB1 gene among Afro-Americans. *Schizophrenia Research* 8: 199–209.

Nystrom, N. (1997). Oppression by mental health providers: a report by gay men and lesbians about their treatment. Unpublished doctoral dissertation, University of Washington, Seattle, WA.

Orr, K. and Castle, D. (2003). Schizophrenia at the extremes of life. In R. Murray *et al.* (eds) *The Epidemiology of Schizophrenia*. Cambridge: Cambridge University Press.

Pedersen, C. and Mortensen, P. (2001). Urbanization and schizophrenia. *Schizophrenia Research* (suppl. 41): 65–6.

Peen, J. and Dekker, J. (1997). Admission rates for schizophrenia in the Netherlands. *Acta Psychiatrica Scandinavica* 96: 301–5.

Perry, B. (1994). Neurobiological sequelae of childhood trauma. In M. Murberg (ed.) *Catecholamines in Post-traumatic Stress Disorder*. Arlington, VA: American Psychiatric Press.

Perry, B. *et al.* (1995). Childhood trauma, the neurobiology of adaptation, and 'use-dependent' development of the brain. *Infant Mental Health Journal* 16: 271–91.

Rack, P. (1982). *Race, Culture and Mental Illness*. London: Tavistock.

Ragland, D. *et al.* (1999). Neuropsychological laterality indices of schizophrenia: interactions with gender. *Schizophrenia Bulletin* 25: 79–89.

Raine, A. (1992). Sex differences in schizotypal personality in the general population. *Journal of Abnormal Psychology* 101: 361–4.

Read, J. (1998). Child abuse and severity of disturbance among adult inpatients. *Child Abuse and Neglect* 22: 359–68.

Read, J. and Fraser, A. (1998). Abuse histories of psychiatric inpatients. *Psychiatric Services* 49: 355–9.

Read, J. *et al.* (2001). The contribution of early traumatic events to schizophrenia in some patients. *Psychiatry* 64: 319–45.

Read, J. *et al.* (2003). Sexual and physical abuse during childhood and adulthood as predictors of hallucinations, delusions and thought disorder. *Psychology and Psychotherapy: Theory, Resarch and Practice* 76: 11–22.

Rosenthal, D. (1974). Migration, heredity and schizophrenia. *Psychiatry* 37: 321–9.

Rushing, W. and Ortega, S. (1979). Socioeconomic status and mental disorder. *American Journal of Sociology* 84: 1175–200.

Russell, D. (1995). *Women, Madness and Society*. New York: Polity.

Rwegellera, G. (1980). Differential use of psychiatric services by West Indians, West Africans and English in London. *British Journal of Psychiatry* 137: 428–32.

Sachdev, P. (1989). Psychiatric illness in the New Zealand Maori. *Australian and New Zealand Journal of Psychiatry* 23: 529–41.

Sachdev, P. (1997). The Maori of New Zealand. In I. Al-Issa and M. Tousignant (eds) *Ethnicity, Immigration, and Psychopathology*. New York: Plenum Press.

Sachdev, P. *et al.* (2001). Schizophrenia-like psychoses following traumatic brain injury. *Psychological Medicine* 31: 231–9.

Salem, J. and Kring, A. (1998). The role of gender differences in the reduction of etiologic heterogeneity in schizophrenia. *Clinical Psychology Review* 18: 795–819.

Samele, C. *et al.* (2001). Does socio-economic status predict course and outcome in patients with psychosis? *Social Psychiatry and Psychiatric Epidemiology* 36: 573–81.

Sashidharan, S. (1993). Afro-Caribbeans and schizophrenia. *International Review of Psychiatry* 5: 129–43.

Schrier, A. *et al.* (2001). Point prevalence of schizophrenia in immigrant groups in Rotterdam. *European Psychiatry* 16: 162–6.

Schwoon, D. and Angermeyer, M. (1980). Congruence of personality assessments within families with a schizophrenic son. *British Journal of Medical Psychology* 53: 255–65.

Seeman, M. and Fitzgerald, P. (2000). Women and schizophrenia: clinical aspects. In D. Castle *et al.* (eds) *Women and Schizophrenia*. Cambridge: Cambridge University Press.

Semp, D. (in press). Queer on the inside: interviews with lesbian and gay staff of public mental health services in Aotearoa/New Zealand. In D. Riggs and G. Walker (eds) *Out in the Antipodes: Australian and New Zealand Perspectives on Gay and Lesbian Psychology*. Frenchs Forest, NSW: Pearson Education Australia.

Sharpley, M. *et al.* (2001). Understanding the excess of psychosis among the African-Caribbean population in England. *British Journal of Psychiatry* 178(suppl.40): s60–s68.

Showalter, E. (1985). *The Female Malady: Women, Madness and English Culture 1830–1980*. London: Virago.

Singh, S. *et al.* (1998). Perceived ethnicity and the risk of compulsory admission. *Psychiatric Epidemiology* 33: 39–44.

Sparks, E. (2002). Depression and schizophrenia in women. In M. Ballou and L. Brown (eds) *Rethinking Mental Health and Disorder: Feminist Perspectives*. New York: Guilford Press.

Spawen, J. *et al.* (2003). Sex differences in psychosis: normal or pathological? *Schizophrenia Research* 62: 45–9.

Sproston, K. and Nazroo, J. (2002). *Ethnic Minority Psychiatric Illness Rates in the Community*. London: National Centre for Social Research.

Strakowski, S. *et al.* (1993). The effect of race and comorbidity on clinical diagnosis in patients with psychosis. *Journal of Clinical Psychiatry* 54: 96–102.

Strakowski, S. *et al.* (1995). The effects of race on diagnosis and disposition from a psychiatric emergency service. *Journal of Clinical Psychiatry* 56: 101–7.

Strauss, J. *et al.* (1978). Patterns of disorder in first admission psychiatric patients. *Journal of Nervous and Mental Disease* 166: 611–23.

Sugarman, P. and Craufurd, D. (1994). Schizophrenia in the Afro-Caribbean community. *British Journal of Psychiatry* 164: 474–80.

Suhail, K. and Cochrane, R. (2002). Effect of culture and environment on the phenomenology of delusions and hallucinations. *International Journal of Social Psychiatry* 48: 126–38.

Teggin, A. *et al.* (1985). A comparison of Catego class 'S' schizophrenia in three ethnic groups. *British Journal of Psychiatry* 147: 683–7.

Te Puni Kokiri (1993). *Nga ia o te oranga hinengaro Maori*. Wellington, NZ: Ministry of Maori Development.

Thomas, C. *et al.* (1993). Psychiatric morbidity and compulsory admission among UK born Europeans, Afro-Caribbeans and Asians in central Manchester. *British Journal of Psychiatry* 163: 91–9.

Trierweiler, S. *et al.* (2000). Clinical attributions associated with the diagnosis of schizophrenia in African American and non-African American patients. *Journal of Consulting and Clinical Psychology* 68: 171–5.

Ussher, J. (1991). *Women's Madness: Misogyny or Mental Illness?* Amherst, MA: University of Massachusetts Press.

van der Kolk, B. *et al.* (2001). Child abuse in America. In K. Franey *et al.* (eds) *The Cost of Child Maltreatment*. San Diego, CA: Family Violence and Sexual Assault Institute.

van Os, J. *et al.* (2001). Prevalence of psychotic disorder and community level of psychotic symptoms: an urban–rural comparison. *Archives of General Psychiatry* 58: 663–8.

Warner, R. (1985). *Recovery from Schizophrenia*. London: Routledge.

Watkins, B. *et al.* (1975). Differential diagnosis imbalance as a race-related phenomena. *Journal of Clinical Psychiatry* 31: 267–8.

Whaley, A. (2001). Cultural mistrust and the clinical diagnosis of paranoid schizophrenia in African American patients. *Journal of Psychopathology and Behavioural Assessment* 23: 93–100.

Wheaton, B. (1978). The sociogenesis of psychological disorder. *American Sociological Review* 43: 383–403.

Williams, J. (1999). Social inequalities and mental health. In C. Newnes *et al.* (eds) *This is Madness*. Ross-on-Wye: PCCS Books.

Zito, J. *et al.* (2003). Psychotropic practice patterns for youth. *Archives of Pediatric Adolescent Medicine* 157: 17–25.

Zolkowska, K. *et al.* (2001). Increased rates of psychosis among immigrants to Sweden. *Psychological Medicine* 31: 669–78.

Chapter 14

Abandoning the concept of schizophrenia

The cognitive psychology of hallucinations and delusions

Richard P. Bentall

MOVING BEYOND THE DIAGNOSIS OF SCHIZOPHRENIA

Many thousands of pages of journal space have been devoted to scientific investigations designed to reveal how schizophrenia patients differ from other people, in the hope of finding differences that are of aetiological significance (Sarbin and Mancuso 1980). It is difficult to believe that a dispassionate observer, surveying the results of these efforts, would believe that the field has much to be proud of. Like their predecessors in past decades, schizophrenia patients today continue to suffer impoverished, socially marginalized existences, and their needs are poorly served by services that are designed more to contain dangerous behaviour than to help people in psychological distress (Laurence 2003). Meanwhile, progress in understanding the causes of the disorder has been painfully slow, with just about every variable known to affect human behaviour being implicated at one time or another, but with few findings surviving the test of replication (Bentall 2003; Bentall *et al.* 1988). In this chapter, I argue that our confusion about what schizophrenia is, and how schizophrenia patients should be helped, reflects the incoherence of the concept itself. There is an alternative to this incoherence.

A wide range of evidence suggests that our current system of diagnostic classification has led psychiatry down a path that is no more scientific than astrology. Like star signs, psychiatric diagnoses are widely believed to tell us something specific about ourselves, to explain our behaviour and personality, and to predict what will happen to us in the future. Like star signs, diagnoses fail on all of these counts, and peddle meaningless generalizations ('schizophrenia is the result of an interaction between genes and the environment') or extravagant but unsubstantiated claims ('schizophrenia is a disease of the dopamine system') as if they are scientific truths.

The evidence that schizophrenia is not a reliable construct has been documented earlier in this book (see Chapter 5). The historical origins of this problem (Chapter 3), and the continuing adherence to Kraepelin's flawed approach to madness, have been discussed elsewhere (Bentall 2003). This lack of reliability renders the word useless for either clinical communication or research. Even if the reliability problem were one day solved, there would be no guarantee that the resulting diagnoses would be scientifically valid or clinically useful. If a disease is operationally defined in terms of an arbitrary but unrelated set of criteria, a meaningless diagnosis can be assigned to patients with a high degree of reliability. This would be the case if, for example, we defined 'Bentall's Disease' in terms of such easily defined symptoms as hair colour, the number of summer colds experienced in the last 5 years and the number of Pink Floyd albums owned.

There is considerable evidence (Bentall 2003) that the diagnosis of schizophrenia has failed to demonstrate validity in the key areas of symptomatology and outcome (see Chapter 5), aetiology (Chapters 6 and 7) and response to treatment (Chapter 9). When factor analysis is used to assess the extent to which the symptoms of schizophrenia patients cluster together, the most common finding is that schizophrenia symptoms fall into three independent clusters: positive symptoms (hallucinations and delusions), negative symptoms and symptoms of cognitive disorganization (Andreasen et al. 1995; Liddle 1987). Similar factors emerge from factor analyses of the symptoms experienced by patients with non-schizophrenia diagnoses, for example psychotic depression and bipolar disorder (Maziade et al. 1995; Toomey et al. 1998). Furthermore, scores on these three dimensions of psychopathology appear to be better predictors of outcome than Kraepelinian diagnoses (van Os et al. 1999).

An early challenge to the assumption that there is a clear dividing line between psychotic illness and 'normal' functioning came from personality theorists (Chapman and Chapman 1980; Chapman et al. 1994; Claridge 1990), who argued that psychosis existed at the end of a continuum of functioning, and who elicited reports of psychotic-like experiences from otherwise 'normal' individuals. When factor-analytic studies were carried out on measures of 'schizotypal traits', it was found that these, too, seemed to reflect the same three dimensions of individual differences identified by some schizophrenia researchers: positive schizotypy (hallucinatory experiences and eccentric beliefs), negative schizotypy (introversion and subjective anhedonia) and subjective cognitive disorganization (Bentall et al. 1989; Claridge et al. 1996; Reynolds et al. 2000).

Analysing data for 18,000 people, Tien (1991) estimated that between 11 and 13% of the population experienced hallucinations at some time in their lives. In a survey of over 7000 Dutch citizens, van Os et al. (2000) estimated that, when abnormal experiences secondary to drug-taking or physical illness were excluded, 1.7% had experienced clinically significant hallucinations but a further 6.2% had experienced hallucinations that were judged not clinically relevant because they were not distressing. In the Dutch study, 3.3% of the sample reported 'true' delusions and 8.7% had delusions that were not clinically relevant. Overall, the evidence suggests that people experiencing psychotic symptoms without seeking treatment outnumber those who do seek treatment by about ten to one.

When someone is said to suffer from 'schizophrenia', it is often assumed that this somehow explains their difficulties. However, even if the concept of schizophrenia was coterminus with a specific set of neurological signs, this alone would not tell us why patients with the diagnosis hear voices scolding them or telling them what to do, hold elaborate conspiracy theories, or emit an apparently meaningless word salad when trying to talk to others.

This objection leads us to an alternative approach to the Kraepelinian paradigm, which an increasing number of psychological researchers have begun to pursue over the past two decades. This strategy involves trying to explain the specific experiences and behaviours of patients (what psychiatrists call 'symptoms' but which might more neutrally be labelled 'complaints'). I will illustrate this strategy be describing some recent findings about the psychological processes responsible for one of the three clusters of complaints, hallucinations and delusions.

HALLUCINATIONS

Auditory hallucinations, such as voices issuing commands or commenting on the individual's actions, are one of the most common complaints reported by people with a diagnosis of schizophrenia. Early psychological theories suggested that they might be the result of conditioning processes, some kind of intrusion of unconscious material into consciousness (perhaps because of some kind of dysfunction of mechanisms regulating wakefulness and sleeping), or abnormal mental imagery, but each of these theories was inadequate (Slade and Bentall 1988).

More recent theories have been informed by four crucial observations. First, the tendency to experience hallucinations appears to vary with culture. A variety of studies (Al-Issa 1995), including large-scale cross-cultural investigations (Jablensky *et al*. 1992), find that visual hallucinations are more commonly experienced in the developing than the developed world. Moreover, in some cultures, hallucinatory experiences are positively valued and encouraged (Bourguignon 1970). Second, hallucinatory experiences are affected by ongoing environmental stimulation; individuals with a disposition towards auditory hallucinations are especially likely to experience them during periods of reduced sensory stimulation or when stimulation is unpatterned (Gallagher *et al*. 1994; Margo *et al*. 1981). Third, it has long been known that auditory hallucinations are associated with activations of the speech musculature (a phenomenon known as *subvocalization*) (Gould 1950; Inouye and Shimizu 1970; McGuigan 1966).

Brain-imaging techniques show that they also coincide with activation of the left frontal areas of the brain involved in speech production (McGuire *et al.* 1993). Fourth, when individuals experiencing auditory hallucinations engage in verbal tasks such as reading, naming objects or humming, this temporarily suppresses their voices (Erickson and Gustafson 1968; Gallagher *et al.* 1995; Margo *et al.* 1981).

These findings all point to a close relationship between auditory hallucinations and inner speech (roughly, verbal thinking), the process by which we talk covertly to ourselves. This develops during early childhood (Vygotsky 1962), and in ordinary people is accompanied by subvocalization (McGuigan 1978). The various theories that try to account for this relationship (Bentall 1990; Frith 1992; Hoffman 1986) all amount to the proposition that people hear hallucinated voices when they misattribute their own inner speech to a source that is external or alien to themselves. Hallucinations in other modalities can presumably be explained in the same way. Visual hallucinations, for example, may be the result of failing to discriminate between mental imagery and visual perceptions.

This theory has stimulated a series of attempts to investigate the ability of hallucinating persons to discriminate between their own verbal thoughts and other stimuli (a process known as source monitoring), beginning with the work of Heilbrun (1980). Many of these studies used complex experimental designs (Bentall *et al.* 1991; Bentall and Slade 1985; Brebion *et al.* 2000; Morrison and Haddock 1997; Rankin and O'Carrol 1995). A recent procedure (Johns and McGuire 1999; Johns *et al.* 2001) is relatively simple. Participants were asked to speak into a microphone and their speech was immediately played back to them through earphones after being distorted electronically. They were then asked whether the speech they heard was theirs or someone else's. Hallucinating patients were much more likely than non-hallucinating patients or ordinary people to say that their voice belonged to someone else, especially if what was being said was derogatory.

The discovery that auditory hallucinations arise when individuals mistake their own inner speech for speech from elsewhere helps to explain the increased tendency to hear voices when exposed to unpatterned stimulation (e.g. when standing in a noisy crowd). This presumably reflects the fact that judging the source of a stimulus is more difficult in these circumstances. However, it is less easy to explain why hallucinating patients are more prone to make these errors than other people.

One possible explanation is that there is some kind of malfunction in the neuropsychological mechanisms responsible for judging the source of a stimulus (Szechtman *et al.* 1998). Even if this hypothesis is supported by future research, much more work will be required before it will be possible to say why these circuits function differently in some people compared with others.

Another approach (not incompatible with physiological research) is to look at how various factors affect the source monitoring judgements of hallucinating patients and other people. When making these kinds of judgements hallucinating patients are excessively influenced by contextual information or suggestions (Haddock *et al.* 1995). For example, when blindfolded in a quiet room, hallucinating patients, and also ordinary people who report hallucinatory experiences, are more likely than others to respond to suggestions to hear a tune such as 'Jingle Bells' (Mintz and Alpert 1972; Young *et al.* 1987). This is consistent with the clinical observation that patients' beliefs about their voices influence how likely they are to persist.

Many patients with a diagnosis of schizophrenia attribute omniscience and omnipotence to their voices, and carefully challenging these beliefs often has a therapeutic affect (Chadwick and Birchwood 1994). Interestingly, in a Dutch study, Honig *et al.* (1998) found that people who heard voices but who had avoided psychiatric services and a diagnosis of schizophrenia were much less likely to hold these kinds of beliefs than psychiatric patients.

Morrison (2001) has drawn a parallel between auditory hallucinations and the intrusive thoughts of obsessional patients, which are similarly experienced as unbidden and uncontrollable. Morrison points to research that shows that obsessional thoughts are maintained by dysfunctional attempts to control them, which, in turn, reflect catastrophizing 'meta-cognitive' beliefs such as the belief that having less than perfect control over one's mental processes is bad, or the belief that thinking of doing something bad is morally equivalent to performing the act itself (Salkovskis 1985). Morrison and Baker (2000) have shown that hallucinating patients hold meta-cognitive beliefs that are similar to those held by obsessional patients.

DELUSIONS

Until recently, delusions have been almost entirely neglected by psychologists (Oltmanns and Maher 1988). Most psychiatric researchers accepted that they are 'empty speech acts, whose informational content refers to neither world or self' (Berrios 1991). This assumption flies in the face of the clinical observation that patients' abnormal beliefs are nearly always about their position in the social universe (Bentall 1994) or core existential concerns (Musalek *et al.* 1989). Surveys of psychiatric patients have shown that the most common type of delusional belief is persecutory (paranoid), followed closely by extreme negative beliefs about the self, and grandiose beliefs of unusual powers, special identity or secret wealth (Garety and Hemsley 1987; Jorgensen and Jensen 1994). This finding seems to have some cross-cultural validity (Stompe *et al.* 1999).

The psychological theories of delusions that have emerged in recent years have all pointed to the same processes that influence the acquisition of ordinary beliefs and attitudes. One of the earliest was put forward by Maher (1974), who suggested that reasoning might be normal in deluded patients, and that their apparently irrational beliefs might reflect attempts to explain anomalous experiences. For example, someone experiencing the slow onset of deafness might notice that people were speaking more quietly in her presence, and might thereby conclude that bad things were being said about her. However, early studies that showed an apparent association between the onset of deafness and paranoid beliefs (e.g. Cooper and Curry 1976) were not replicated in later investigations (e.g. Watt 1985).

Better evidence of an association between perceptual abnormalities and abnormal beliefs exists for a rare delusion first described by Capgras and Reboul-Lachaux (1923). Capgras patients (as they are known) believe that someone, usually a loved one, has been replaced by some kind of impostor or doppelganger. Although traditionally explained in terms of the patient's emotional ambivalence towards the person thought to have been substituted (Enoch and Trethowan 1979), the condition has been studied by neuropsychologists researching the processes involved in recognizing faces. Ellis and Young (1990) suggested that a psychoanalytic explanation is precluded by the observation that Capgras patients are never confused about the identities of voices (e.g. when talking over the telephone), by the fact that the delusion sometimes concerns individuals who are only casual acquaintances and by the fact that many patients have brain damage. They suggest instead that it results from a dysfunction of those neural circuits responsible for generating the feeling of familiarity when we see someone we know. As a consequence, the Capgras patient recognizes others in an intellectual way ('Its my wife Margaret, who I've lived with for 18 years') but not emotionally, and the delusion arises in an attempt to explain this experience. Consistent with this account, it has recently been shown that Capgras patients do not produce the mild physiological reaction that ordinary people demonstrate when shown a familiar face (Ellis *et al.* 2000).

Hemsley and Garety (1986) suggested that people might develop abnormal beliefs as a consequence of being unable to weigh up evidence that either favoured or disfavoured their theories. In an influential series of studies, they set out to measure probabilistic reasoning in deluded patients (Garety *et al.* 1991; Huq *et al.* 1988). Participants were shown two jars, in each of which there were beads of two colours. In one jar, one colour predominated and the beads in the other jar were of the opposite ratio. They were then shown a sequence of beads apparently drawn from one of the two jars, and were told to ask for beads until they felt able to decide which jar they were being taken from. Deluded patients, in comparison with others, 'jumped to conclusions', guessing more quickly. This has been replicated with different tasks (John and Dodgson 1994) and with non-patients who score highly on a measure of delusional beliefs (Linney *et al.* 1998).

Problems remain in explaining how the reasoning biases observed in these experiments contribute to the actual beliefs of patients. They do not explain the highly social nature of most delusions, although, interestingly, the jumping to conclusions bias appears stronger when patients are tested with materials that are emotionally salient (Dudley *et al.* 1997; Young and Bentall 1997). A greater difficulty is that, in some of the experiments, when the sequence of beads was carefully chosen to suggest first one hypothesis and then the alternative, deluded patients changed their minds more quickly than controls (Garety *et al.* 1991). This seems inconsistent with the conventional view that delusions are beliefs that are resistant to counter-evidence, and highlights the need not only to identify cognitive abnormalities associated with different kinds of psychotic experience, but to show how those abnormalities actually lead to the experiences in question.

A third line of research on delusions has addressed the question of belief content directly. Most people generate a causal explanation for an event (an 'attribution') in every few hundred words of speech (Zullow *et al.* 1988). It is reasonable to hypothesize that an abnormal belief might result from some kind of bias or abnormality in the way that such explanations are generated. Interestingly, ordinary people are neither rational nor fair-minded in the way we do this. We typically show a 'self-serving bias' towards making an internal (self-blaming) attribution for a positive event, and an external attribution (one which implicates either circumstantial factors or the actions of others) for negative events. This bias is especially evident when we feel threatened (Campbell and Sedikides 1999). Although the cognitive processes involved in generating attributions are not completely understood, it appears that situational explanations for events require considerable cognitive effort, so that, when making external attributions, most people tend to account for events in terms of the actions of other people when their cognitive resources are taxed (Gilbert *et al.* 1988). Depressed people, in contrast, tend to make relatively internal attributions for negative events and relatively external attributions for positive events (Abramson *et al.* 1978). Well people with this tendency are at high risk of becoming depressed in the future (Alloy *et al.* 1999).

When patients with paranoid delusions are asked to make attributions for hypothetical events, they tend to make relatively external attributions for negative events and internal attributions for positive events (Fear *et al.* 1996; Kaney and Bentall 1989); in other words, they have an exaggerated self-serving bias. This finding has also been reported in Canada (Candido and Romney 1990) and South Korea (Lee and Won 1998). It has also been demonstrated using other types of measures, for example by seeing how patients explain their successes and failures on a 'rigged' computer game

(Kristev *et al.* 1999). When external attributions have been specifically coded according to whether they implicate the intentions and actions of other people or implicate circumstantial factors, those made by paranoid patients have been found to be mostly other-blaming (Kinderman and Bentall 1997).

This all leads to the rather simple idea that each of the main types of attribution has a different implication for our mental health. In the face of a negative event, an internal attribution ('I lost my job because I'm stupid') will make us feel more depressed; an external-situational attribution ('I lost my job because of the terrible state of the world economy') will make us feel not quite so bad; and an external-personal attribution ('I lost my job because my boss hates me'), while preserving self-esteem to some extent, will feed a paranoid world-view.

The idea that in the face of adversity repeated resort to external-personal attributions will lead to paranoia makes obvious sense, and is consistent with some of the less exotic psychoanalytic attempts to account for this kind of delusion (Colby 1977). However, some researchers have objected to the idea that paranoid delusions are defensive on the grounds that self-esteem is generally low in paranoid patients (Garety and Freeman 1999).

Making a prediction about self-esteem on the basis of a defensive model is a complex task, as the defence may be more or less successful. Research on self-esteem in paranoid patients has been inconsistent, some investigators reporting high self-esteem (Candido and Romney 1990; Lyon *et al.* 1994) and others reporting low self-esteem in both deluded patients in general (Bowins and Shugar 1998) and paranoid patients in particular (Freeman *et al.* 1998). However, when immediate shifts in beliefs about the self and others following different kinds of attributions are measured in ordinary people, the changes are as predicted by the theory: internal attributions for negative events result in increasingly negative beliefs about the self, external-personal attributions result in an increase in negative beliefs about others, whereas external-situational attributions result in self-esteem being maintained (Kinderman and Bentall 2000).

These observations suggest that self-esteem might be highly labile in paranoid patients. This prediction has not been tested, but it is interesting that ordinary people with highly fluctuating self-esteem tend to make external-personal attributions for negative events (Kernis 1993). (For a detailed discussion of some of these issues, see Bentall *et al.* 2001.)

Whether or not paranoid delusions can be said to be defensive, it is likely that other factors are involved. One possibility is that people with persecutory delusions generate attributions in a different way than other people. An implication of research with ordinary people (Gilbert *et al.* 1988) is that attributions for negative events that are generated rapidly, when mental resources are scarce (either because of distraction or cognitive disablement), are likely to be external-personal and hence paranoid in nature. Reduced cognitive functioning is commonly observed during psychotic episodes (Nuechterlein and Subotnik 1998). Another possible factor is the range of information that patients draw on when making attributions. There is evidence that paranoid patients selectively attend to and recall threat-related information (Bentall *et al.* 1995; Kaney *et al.* 1992), so perhaps it should not be surprising that their attributions tend to implicate the actions of others. These observations suggest that, in future, it will be fruitful to examine both the neurobiological processes responsible for attributional judgements, and also developmental and environmental influences on these processes.

EXPLANATIONS AND CAUSES

I hope that this brief summary of what is known about hallucinations and delusions is sufficient to convince the reader that research on specific complaints constitutes a viable alternative to the Kraepelinian paradigm. Positive symptoms have been most extensively investigated in this way, but there has also been a considerable amount of work on psychotic speech disorder and, in recent years, an emerging research literature on specific negative symptoms such as anhedonia. If this programme of research is successful, after the full range of psychotic complaints has been explained in this way, there will be no ghostly 'schizophrenia' left behind also requiring an explanation.

It has been argued that the complaint-orientated approach does not reveal the aetiology of severe mental illness (Mojtabai and Rieder 1998). This objection is only true in as much as research on individual complaints has so far focused on cognitive processes that are immediate precursors of the complaints, and in as much as researchers have yet to examine bio-logical and environmental influences on those processes. In fact, recent research by developmental psychologists has begun to tease out environ-mental factors that influence the development of both source-monitoring skills (Fernyhough and Russell 1997) and attributional processes (Durkin 1995). Moreover, there is evidence that specific complaints are associated with specific environmental influences – for example, that thought disorder is associated with exposure to care-givers who communicate incoherently (Singer and Wynne 1965; Wahlberg *et al.* 1997), that paranoid symptoms tend to emerge after exposure to victimization (Mirowsky and Ross 1983) and discrimination (Bhurgra *et al.* 1999), and that hallucinations are associated with a history of childhood traumas such as sexual abuse (Hammersley *et al.* 2003; Read *et al.* 2003; Ross *et al.* 1994). Attempts are already underway to develop models which integrate what we know about the cognitive processes involved with these complaints and the adverse life events that so often seem to precede those processes and complaints (e.g.

Barker-Collo and Read 2003). Although there is not sufficient space to fully sketch out the claim (for a detailed account see Bentall 2003), I believe that complaint-orientated research is leading to a much richer understanding of the aetiology of psychotic experiences than has been possible within the framework of the Kraepelinian paradigm. It therefore offers us a better chance of being able to develop more effective ways (see Chapter 20) of helping people deal with their complaints.

REFERENCES

Abramson, L. *et al.* (1978). Learned helplessness in humans. *Journal of Abnormal Psychology* 78: 40–74.

Al-Issa, I. (1995). The illusion of reality or the reality of an illusion: hallucinations and culture. *British Journal of Psychiatry* 166: 368–73.

Alloy, L., *et al.* (1999). Depressogenic cognitive styles. *Behaviour Research and Therapy* 37: 503–31.

Andreasen, N. *et al.* (1995). Positive and negative symptoms. In S. Hirsch and D. Weinberger (eds) *Schizophrenia*. Oxford: Blackwell.

Barker-Collo, S. and Read, J. (2003). Models of response to childhood sexual abuse. *Trauma Violence and Abuse* 4: 95–111.

Bentall, R. (1990). The illusion of reality: A review and integration of psychological research on hallucinations. *Psychological Bulletin* 107: 82–95.

Bentall, R. (1994). Cognitive biases and abnormal beliefs: towards a model of persecutory delusions. In A. David and J. Cutting (eds) *The Neuropsychology of Schizophrenia*. London: Lawrence Erlbaum.

Bentall, R. (2003). *Madness Explained: Psychosis and Human Nature*. London: Penguin.

Bentall, R. and Slade, P. (1985). Reliability of a measure of disposition towards hallucinations. *Personality and Individual Differences* 6: 527–9.

Bentall, R. *et al.* (1988). Abandoning the concept of schizophrenia. *British Journal of Clinical Psychology*, 27: 303–24.

Bentall, R. *et al.* (1989). The multidimensional nature of schizotypal traits. *British Journal of Clinical Psychology* 28: 363–75.

Bentall, R. *et al.* (1991). Reality monitoring and psychotic hallucinations. *British Journal of Clinical Psychology* 30: 213–22.

Bentall, R. *et al.* (1995). Persecutory delusions and recall of threat-related, depression-related and neutral words. *Cognitive Therapy and Research*, 19: 331–43.

Bentall, R. *et al.* (2001). Persecutory delusions: a review and theoretical integration. *Clinical Psychology Review* 21: 1143–92.

Berrios, G. (1991). Delusions as 'wrong beliefs'. *British Journal of Psychiatry* 159(suppl. 14): 6–13.

Bhurgra, D. *et al.* (1999). Schizophrenia and Afro-Caribbeans. *International Review of Psychiatry* 11: 145–52.

Bourguignon, E. (1970). Hallucinations and trance. In W. Keup (ed.) *Origins and Mechanisms of Hallucinations*. New York: Plenum Press.

Bowins, B. and Shugar, G. (1998). Delusions and self-esteem. *Canadian Journal of Psychiatry* 43: 154–8.

Brebion, G. *et al.* (2000). Positive symptomatology and source monitoring failure in schizophrenia. *Psychiatry Research* 95: 119–31.

Campbell, W. and Sedikides, C. (1999). Self-threat magnifies the self-serving bias: a meta-analytic integration. *Review of General Psychology* 3: 23–43.

Candido, C. and Romney, D. (1990). Attributional style in paranoid vs depressed patients. *British Journal of Medical Psychology* 63: 355–63.

Capgras, J. and Reboul-Lachaux, J. ([1923] 1994). L'illusion des 'sosies' dans un delire systematise chronique. *History of Psychiatry* 5: 117–30.

Chadwick, P. and Birchwood, M. (1994). The omnipotence of voices: a cognitive approach to auditory hallucinations. *British Journal of Psychiatry* 164: 190–201.

Chapman, L. and Chapman, J. (1980). Scales for rating psychotic and psychotic-like experiences as continua. *Schizophrenia Bulletin* 6: 477–89.

Chapman, L. *et al.* (1994). Putatively psychosis-prone subjects 10 years later. *Journal of Abnormal Psychology* 103: 171–83.

Claridge, G. *et al.* (1996). The factor structure of 'schizotypal' traits. *British Journal of Clinical Psychology* 35: 103–15.

Claridge, G. (1990). Can a disease model of schizophrenia survive? In R. Bentall (ed.) *Reconstructing Schizophrenia*. London: Routledge.

Colby, K. (1977). Appraisal of four psychological theories of paranoid phenomena. *Journal of Abnormal Psychology* 86: 54–9.

Cooper, A. and Curry, A. (1976). The pathology of deafness in the paranoid and affective psychoses of later life. *Journal of Psychosomatic Medicine* 20: 97–105.

Dudley, R. *et al.* (1997). The effect of self-referent material on the reasoning of people with delusions. *British Journal of Clinical Psychology* 36: 575–84.

Durkin, K. (1995). *Developmental Social Psychology*. Oxford: Blackwell.

Ellis, H. and Young, A. (1990). Accounting for delusional misidentifications. *British Journal of Psychiatry* 157: 239–48.

Ellis, H. *et al.* (2000). Automatic without autonomic responses to familiar faces. *Cognitive Neuropsychiatry* 5: 255–69.

Enoch, M. and Trethowan, W. (1979). *Uncommon Psychiatric Syndromes*, 2nd edn. Bristol: Wright.

Erickson, G. and Gustafson, G. (1968). Controlling auditory hallucinations. *Hospital and Community Psychiatry* 19: 327–9.

Fear, C. *et al.* (1996). Cognitive processes in delusional disorder. *British Journal of Psychiatry* 168: 61–7.

Fernyhough, C. and Russell, J. (1997). Distinguishing one's own voice from those of others. *International Journal of Behaviour and Development* 20: 651–65.

Freeman, D. *et al.* (1998). The London–East Anglia randomized controlled trial of cognitive-behaviour therapy for psychosis. *British Journal of Clinical Psychology* 37: 415–30.

Frith, C. (1992). *The Cognitive Neuropsychology of Schizophrenia*. Hillsdale, NJ: Lawrence Erlbaum.

Gallagher, A. *et al.* (1994). The effects of varying auditory input on schizophrenic hallucinations. *British Journal of Medical Psychology* 67: 67–76.

Gallagher, A. *et al.* (1995). The effects of varying information content and speaking aloud on auditory hallucinations. *British Journal of Medical Psychology* 68: 143–55.

Garety, P. and Freeman, D. (1999). Cognitive approaches to delusions. *British Journal of Clinical Psychology* 38: 113–54.

Garety, P. and Hemsley, D. (1987). The characteristics of delusional experience. *European Archives of Neurological and Psychiatric Sciences* 236: 294–8.

Garety, P. *et al.* (1991). Reasoning in deluded schizophrenic and paranoid patients. *Journal of Nervous and Mental Disease* 179, 194–201.

Gilbert, D. *et al.* (1988). On cognitive busyness: when person perceivers meet persons perceived. *Journal of Personality and Social Psychology* 54: 733–40.

Gould, L. (1950). Verbal hallucinations and automatic speech. *American Journal of Psychiatry* 107: 110–19.

Haddock, G. *et al.* (1995). Auditory hallucinations and the verbal transformation effect. *Personality and Individual Differences* 19: 301–6.

Hammersley, P. *et al.* (2003). Childhood trauma and hallucinations in bipolar affective disorder. *British Journal of Psychiatry* 182: 543–7.

Heilbrun, A. (1980). Impaired recognition of self-expressed thought in patients with auditory hallucinations. *Journal of Abnormal Psychology* 89: 728–36.

Hemsley, D. and Garety, P. (1986). The formation and maintenance of delusions. *British Journal of Psychiatry*, 149: 51–6.

Hoffman, R. (1986). Verbal hallucinations and language production processes in schizophrenia. *Behavioral and Brain Sciences* 9: 503–48.

Honig, A. *et al.* (1998). Auditory hallucinations: a comparison between patients and nonpatients. *Journal of Nervous and Mental Disease* 186: 646–51.

Huq, S. *et al.* (1988). Probabilistic judgements in deluded and nondeluded subjects. *Quarterly Journal of Experimental Psychology* 40A: 801–12.

Inouye, T. and Shimizu, A. (1970). The electromyographic study of verbal hallucination. *Journal of Nervous and Mental Disease* 151: 415–22.

Jablensky, A. *et al.* (1992). Schizophrenia: manifestations, incidence and course in different cultures. *Psychological Medicine* (suppl. 20): 1–97.

John, C. and Dodgson, G. (1994). Inductive reasoning in delusional thought. *Journal of Mental Health* 3: 31–49.

Johns, L. and McGuire, P. (1999). Verbal self-monitoring and auditory hallucinations in schizophrenia. *Lancet* 353: 469–70.

Johns, L. *et al.* (2001). Verbal self-monitoring and auditory hallucinations in people with schizophrenia. *Psychological Medicine* 31: 705–15.

Jorgensen, P. and Jensen, J. (1994). Delusional beliefs in first admitters. *Psychopathology* 27: 100–12.

Kaney, S. and Bentall, R. (1989). Persecutory delusions and attributional style. *British Journal of Medical Psychology* 62: 191–8.

Kaney, S. *et al.* (1992). Persecutory delusions and the recall of threatening and non-threatening propositions. *British Journal of Clinical Psychology* 31: 85–7.

Kernis, M. (1993). The role of stability and level of self-esteem in psychological functioning. In R. Baumeister (ed.) *Self-Esteem: The Puzzle of Low Self-Regard.* New York: Plenum Press.

Kinderman, P. and Bentall, R. (1997). Causal attributions in paranoia. *Journal of Abnormal Psychology* 106: 341–5.

Kinderman, P. and Bentall, R. (2000). Self-discrepancies and causal attributions. *British Journal of Clinical Psychology* 39: 255–73.

Kristev, H. *et al.* (1999). An investigation of attributional style in first-episode psychosis. *British Journal of Clinical Psychology*, 88: 181–94.

Laurence, J. (2003). *Pure Madness: How Fear Drives the Mental Health System.* London: Routledge.

Lee, H. and Won, H. (1998). The self-concepts, the other-concepts, and attributional style in paranoia and depression. *Korean Journal of Clinical Psychology* 17: 105–25.

Liddle, P. (1987). The symptoms of chronic schizophrenia. *British Journal of Psychiatry* 151: 145–51.

Linney, Y. *et al.* (1998). Reasoning biases in delusion-prone individuals. *British Journal of Clinical Psychology* 37: 247–70.

Lyon, H. *et al.* (1994). The defensive function of persecutory delusions. *British Journal of Psychiatry*, 164: 637–46.

Maher, B. (1974). Delusional thinking and perceptual disorder. *Journal of Individual Psychology* 30: 98–113.

Margo, A. *et al.* (1981). The effects of varying auditory input on schizophrenic hallucinations. *British Journal of Psychiatry* 139: 122–7.

Maziade, M. *et al.* (1995). Negative, psychoticism, and disorganized dimensions in patients with familial schizophrenia or bipolar disorder. *American Journal of Psychiatry* 152: 1458–63.

McGuigan, F. (1966). Covert oral behavior and auditory hallucinations. *Psychophysiology* 3: 73–80.

McGuigan, F. (1978). *Cognitive Psychophysiology: Principles of Covert Behavior.* Englewood Cliffs, NJ: Prentice-Hall.

McGuire, P. *et al.* (1993). Increased blood flow in Broca's area during auditory hallucinations. *Lancet* 342: 703–6.

Mintz, S. and Alpert, M. (1972). Imagery vividness, reality testing and schizophrenic hallucinations. *Journal of Abnormal and Social Psychology* 19: 310–16.

Mirowsky, J. and Ross, C. (1983). Paranoia and the structure of powerlessness. *American Sociological Review* 48: 228–39.

Mojtabai, R. and Rieder, R. (1998). Limitations of the symptom-orientated approach to psychiatric research. *British Journal of Psychiatry* 173: 198–202.

Morrison, A. (2001). The interpretation of intrusions in psychosis. *Behavioral and Cognitive Psychotherapy* 29: 257–76.

Morrison, A. and Baker, C. (2000). Intrusive thoughts and auditory hallucinations. *Behaviour Research and Therapy* 38: 1097–1106.

Morrison, A. and Haddock, G. (1997). Cognitive factors in source monitoring and auditory hallucinations. *Psychological Medicine* 27: 669–79.

Musalek, M. *et al.* (1989). Delusional theme, sex and age. *Psychopathology* 22: 260–7.

Nuechterlein, K. and Subotnik, K. (1998). The cognitive origins of schizophrenia and prospects for intervention. In T. Wykes *et al.* (eds) *Outcome and Innovation in Psychological Treatment of Schizophrenia.* Chichester: Wiley.

Oltmanns, T. and Maher, B. (eds) (1988). *Delusional Beliefs.* New York: Wiley.

Rankin, P. and O'Carrol, P. (1995). Reality monitoring and signal detection in individuals prone to hallucinations. *British Journal of Clinical Psychology* 34: 517–28.

Read, J. *et al.* (2003). Sexual and physical abuse during childhood and adulthood as predictors of hallucinations, delusions and thought disorder. *Psychology and Psychotherapy: Theory, Research and Practice* 76: 1–22.

Reynolds, C. *et al.* (2000). Three-factor model of schizotypal personality. *Schizophrenia Bulletin* 26: 603–18.

Ross, C. *et al.* (1994). Childhood abuse and the positive symptoms of schizophrenia. *Hospital and Community Psychiatry* 42: 489–91.

Salkovskis, P. (1985). Obsessional-compulsive problems. *Behaviour Research and Therapy* 23: 571–83.

Sarbin, T. and Mancuso, J. (1980). *Schizophrenia: Diagnosis or Moral Verdict?* Oxford: Pergamon Press.

Singer, M. and Wynne, L. (1965). Thought disorder and family relations of schizophrenics. *Archives of General Psychiatry* 12: 201–12.

Slade, P. and Bentall, R. (1988). *Sensory Deception: A Scientific Analysis of Hallucination.* London: Croom-Helm.

Stompe, T. *et al.* (1999). Comparisons of delusions among schizophrenics in Austria and Pakistan. *Psychopathology* 32: 225–34.

Szechtman, H. *et al.* (1998). Where the imaginal appears real: a positron emission tomography study of auditory hallucinations. *Proceedings of the National Academy of Sciences, USA* 95: 1956–60.

Tien, A. (1991). Distribution of hallucinations in the population. *Social Psychiatry and Psychiatric Epidemiology* 26: 287–92.

Toomey, R. *et al.* (1998). Negative, positive and disorganized symptom dimensions in schizophrenia, major depression and bipolar disorder. *Journal of Nervous and Mental Disease* 186: 470–6.

van Os, J. *et al.* (1999). A comparison of the utility of dimensional and categorical representations of psychosis. *Psychological Medicine* 29: 595–606.

van Os, J. *et al.* (2000). Strauss (1969) revisited: a psychosis continuum in the normal population? *Schizophrenia Research* 45: 11–20.

Vygotsky, L. (1962). *Thought and Language.* Cambridge, MA: MIT Press.

Wahlberg, K.-E. (1997). Gene–environment interaction in vulnerability to schizophrenia: findings from the Finnish Family Study of Schizophrenia. *American Journal of Psychiatry* 154: 355–62.

Watt, J. (1985). Hearing and premorbid personality in paranoid states. *American Journal of Psychiatry* 142: 1453–5.

Young, H. and Bentall, R. (1997). Probabilistic reasoning in deluded, depressed and normal subjects. *Psychological Medicine* 27: 455–65.

Young, H. *et al.* (1987). The role of brief instructions and suggestibility in the elicitation of hallucinations in normal and psychiatric subjects. *Journal of Nervous and Mental Disease* 175: 41–8.

Zullow, H. *et al.* (1988). Pessimistic explanatory style in the historical record. *American Psychologist* 43: 673–82.

Chapter 15

Psychodynamic psychotherapy of schizophrenia

Its history and development

Ann-Louise Silver, Brian Koehler and Bertram Karon

> The various modes of actually being with another person are more important than any method.
>
> (Benedetti 1987: 164)

As psychoanalysts who work with people diagnosed 'schizophrenic', our contribution to understanding causation comes in the form of trying to understand the meaning of psychosis in the context of the lives of individual human beings. It is only in the uniqueness of the history of each individual, and in the meanings that each person assigns to that history and to their 'symptoms', that any true cause can be discovered.

Although people diagnosed schizophrenic are very different from each other, their symptoms very often represent manifestations of, or defences against, chronic terror (Karon and VandenBos 1981). Any human being can develop such symptoms under enough stress, and every patient's life, as subjectively experienced, would drive anyone psychotic. (Conscious and unconscious meanings determine severity of stress.) Probably something, large or small, happens early in life which changes existing fantasies, which then change how later experiences are met, which again change the fantasy structures, and so forth. When experience, as given meaning by conscious and unconscious fantasies, is literally unbearable, when one seems on the brink of annihilation, blatant psychosis results.

The seemingly meaningless utterances and acts of schizophrenic patients, observed through a psychoanalytic lens, often have obvious meanings, drawing us to discover the rest.

MIND AND EMOTION

The contemporary emphasis on the brain and its molecular functioning obscures the significant role of affect regulation, relationships, subjectivity and culture in the inception and course of schizophrenia. Which more fundamentally explains anxiety: a molecular biological analysis involving the limbic-hypothalamic-pituitary-adrenal axis and such neurochemicals as gaba and dopamine, or subjective awareness of danger? Have we forgotten that evolutionary forces designed the brain to mediate meaning and encode the vital interactions between self and world?

Some outstanding exceptions to modern reductionistic and dehumanizing approaches include: Strauss's work (1994, 1997) integrating person and disorder, Alanen's (1997 a,b) caveat that human biology includes inter-actionality between persons, and Ciompi's (1988) theory of affect logic, which restores the vital role of anxiety in cognition and illness. Eisenberg (1986) cautions against adherence to either a mindless or a brainless psychiatry. Bolton and Hill (1996) remind us to plumb the depths of meaning before falling back on non-intentional (e.g. physico-chemical) factors as explanatory. Intentionality (beliefs, fears, values, goals) pervades biological systems down to the level of DNA. Neuroscience and neural plasticity research offer confirmatory evidence. Hopper and Wanderling (2000), in reviewing the World Health Organization's International Study of Schizophrenia (ISoS), delineate far better outcomes in schizophrenia in the developing nations, with their more cohesive communities and lack of modern pharmaceuticals.

Attachment theorists explore transgenerational transmission of trauma (Abraham and Torok 1994; Ainsworth et al. 1978). Jaffe and colleagues (2001) demonstrate that cognitive development is inseparable from social interaction and adaptation. Fonagy (1997) stresses the role of attachment in treating psychosis: experiencing security is the overriding goal of the attachment system. Ordinary family life is permeated with guilt, magnified for families of patients. Misunderstandings, splitting (not having integrated views of others or oneself) and paranoid projective processes pervade the issue of parental impact on children who later become psychotic.

Attachment assists in regulating emotion, overriding extremes of affect. Individual psychotherapy maximizes this potential. Separation can be particularly terrifying for people with depressed or traumatized parents. These parents may have absorbed trauma from their own parents and so on. Suomi (1997) demonstrates that early experiences sculpt neurodevelopment in non-human primates (with whom we share 98–99% of our genome), and that the most dramatic manifestations of early experience occur in the context of stress or challenge. Tustin (1990) describes the universality of autistic defences (areas of deadness or severe schizoid defences) and urges us to respect these encapsulated pockets which ward off self-fragmentation. We are all somewhat estranged from ourselves.

THE RISE AND FALL OF MORAL TREATMENT

Even before psychoanalysis and psychopharmacology, 'moral treatment' (which meant psychological treatment) in the 1800s achieved a 70%

discharge rate for first admissions, improved or recovered (Alexander and Selesnick 1966; Bockoven 1972). In these same hospitals by 1900, after moral treatment was abandoned for 'more scientific' somatic treatments, discharge rates dropped to 20–30%.

'Moral treatment' always includes:

1   Striving to understand the patient as an individual.
2   Developing a full and accurate history.
3   Encouraging work and socializing.
4   Never humiliating patients.
5   Using physical force only to prevent patients from harming self or others, never as punishment.

'Moral treatment' demonstrated superiority to somatic treatments, and yet was abandoned, while psychiatry congratulated itself on becoming scientific. It ignored the fact that helpable patients no longer recovered. Often when somatic treatments failed, patients were called incurable. History repeats itself as Whitaker's (2002) *Mad in America* and McGovern's (1985) *Masters of Madness* document.

EARLY PSYCHOANALYTIC WORK

Freud thought that schizophrenics and other psychotics could not be analysed, believing they could not form a transference. However, he told his younger colleague, Richard Sterba, that schizophrenic patients scared him (B. Karon, personal communication). Nonetheless, in *On Psychotherapy*, Freud (1905) expressed hope that future modifications in psychoanalytic technique would make psychoanalytic therapy for psychosis possible, maintaining this guarded hopefulness to the end (Freud 1940).

Eugen Bleuler was awed, finding that applying Freud's ideas when treating schizophrenia at the Burghölzli Clinic discharges tripled (Federn 1943a,b). By 1907, Carl Jung, working with Bleuler, published *Psychology of Dementia Praecox*. Fifty years later, Jung (1960) reiterated that schizophrenia can be completely cured psychodynamically.

In Europe, Ferenczi, the charismatic founder of psychoanalysis in Hungary, launched the interpersonalist branch of psychoanalysis that prizes countertransference feelings as our most powerful clinical tool (Dupont 1988; Grossman and Grossman 1965; Silver 1993). Unlike Freud, he liked working with psychotic patients. Even analysts disagreeing with his theories, such as Richard Sterba, quipped, 'If you even had a sick horse, it would get better if it saw Ferenczi' (B. Karon, personal communication).

Karl Abraham (1916) described the oral dynamics in a case of simple schizophrenia. Waelder (1925) emphasized the narcissistic transference in schizophrenia. Bychowski (1954) discussed analytic working-through and systematic correction of schizophrenic ego regression.

Federn (1934) cautioned against adverse environmental influences, increased regression, premature uncovering and negative transference, and against withholding the (positive) countertransference. He felt that using the analytic couch increased schizophrenic symptoms. He reported good results with modified psychoanalytic therapy with a five-year follow-up: 'One wins the normal transference of the psychotic by sincerity, kindness, and understanding' (Federn 1943b: 251).

In Britain, Melanie Klein, a student of Abraham and Ferenczi, developed her theory of internalized object relations and early oral dynamics, and included work with psychotics (Klein 1930, 1948, 1975), focusing on conflicts over hostile and sadistic fantasies. Kleinian analysts such as Bion (1957), Rosenfeld (1965) and Segal (1973) routinely treated borderline and psychotic individuals, interpreting positive and negative transference phenomena, encouraging free association on the couch and, most importantly, interpreting manifest and latent anxieties and transference psychosis (psychotic symptoms arising in therapy based unconsciously on the patient's past feelings and experiences).

Kleinian analysts understand schizophrenic phenomenology as a defence against overwhelming annihilation and persecutory anxieties. They interpret unconscious material at the level of greatest anxiety, to develop awareness of the links between fantasy and reality (Jackson 2001; Jackson and Williams 1994; Steiner 1993). Winnicott (1965) emphasized maturational processes in infancy and early childhood. He related environmental deficiencies and abnormalities to the development of schizophrenia.

In Scotland, Fairbairn (1954) and Guntrip (1969) developed object relations theory, stressing the universal human need for a good object (person). We all feel compelled to preserve the fantasy of the parent's goodness, even if the cost is maintaining the badness of the self, thus sacrificing possibilities of finding good objects in other people (including therapists). Fearing that one's love will destroy the object (schizoid anxiety) is more debilitating than fearing that one's anger will destroy the object (depressive anxiety). Guntrip added the fear of never finding one's way back to a human relationship, as well as the dread of being merged into oblivion. Today, we refer to Fairbairn, Guntrip and Winnicott as the 'independents', as distinguished from Kleinian and ego-analytic theorists in England. Boyer and Giovacchini (1967) have integrated insights from British object-relations with American ego-psychology. So, too, have Searles (1963), Volkan (1976) and Kernberg (1986).

UNITED STATES CONTRIBUTIONS

Adolf Meyer, the first head of psychiatry at Johns Hopkins University, pioneered US psychoanalysis. Even before the 1909 Clark University

Lectures (by Freud, Jung and Meyer), he and his hospital-based colleagues had published detailed and vibrant psychodynamic case presentations (Silver 2002). At the Binghamton State Hospital in upstate New York in the late 1800s, William Alanson White and Smith Ely Jelliffe applied Freudian discoveries, later co-editing the first US psychoanalytic journal, the *Psychoanalytic Review*. White became superintendent of the federal mental hospital, St Elizabeths, in Washington, DC. White's (1907) text, *Outlines of Psychiatry*, set the standard for decades.

St Elizabeths became a national centre for the psychodynamic treatment of severe mental illness (Noble and Burnham 1969). White hired Harry Stack Sullivan in 1921 (Perry 1982). Sullivan later launched his famous unit at the Sheppard and Enoch Pratt Hospital. He met Clara Thompson, later the head of the William A. White Institute in New York. At Sullivan's suggestion, she underwent a personal analysis with Ferenczi in Budapest. She had earlier realized the clinical power of psychoanalysis through a discussion group, meeting at her home. The patients under discussion made such progress that the group named itself The Miracle Club.

In 1935, Fromm-Reichmann escaped Nazi Germany and came to Washington, DC. Fromm-Reichmann and Sullivan formed an immediate team, calling for analytically oriented treatments (Bullard 1959; Hornstein 2000; Perry 1982; Silver 1989, 1993, 2002). Fromm-Reichmann's work, best portrayed in *I Never Promised You a Rose Garden* (Greenberg 1964), took place within a hospital that analysed itself (Stanton and Schwartz 1954). Sullivan's and Fromm-Reichmann's many students shaped practices world-wide. The most prolific and influential, Harold Searles, set an unrivalled standard for brutally honest self-awareness.

CLINICIANS OF PSYCHOSIS

Especially with patients others consider incurable, a very good outcome often results (Benedetti and Furlan 1993; Boyer and Giovacchini 1967; Karon and VandenBos 1981; Robbins 1993). Patients respond to insight and to internalizing a tolerant, kind, confused and stubborn therapist, one who is there to help, can tolerate negative affect as well as not under-standing, and who doesn't quit. We match our stubbornness against their stubborn symptoms. We need confidence in our unique subjectivities, our most powerful healing instruments. Thus, we argue against guidelines for treatment emphasizing medications and superficial re-shaping of behaviour. A rich array of theory and technique has evolved, providing security for clinicians. Most effective therapists, however, are more concerned with helpfulness than theoretical consistency.

Psychodynamic approaches form a romantic heroic quest, clinician and patient joining forces to quell terror and create a secure place for creativity.

Shared understanding of psychotic experience inspires hope. A strengthening mutual trust provides the glue to repair the shattered ego. Our 'schizophrenic' patients form inherently analysable transference reactions. Limitations in therapy may lie in the therapist's capacity to, as the Kleinians say, 'take the transference' (Mitrani 2001).

This relational transition from I-it to I-Thou (Buber 1958) marks the essence of spirituality. Psychotherapy of psychosis becomes a form of prayer: striving to bring order out of chaos, helping patients recover confidence in their humanness, seeking something of a resurrection, returning the patient to emotional life from a position of deadness. We all could become psychotic; all have entered its territory (Winnicott 1974) and those suffering psychosis can recover.

Some unifying principles emerge (Fromm-Reichmann 1950):

1   Primary process in dreams, psychosis and creativity all have metaphoric significance. Insight converts raw anxiety into sublimated cohesive work.
2   A psychotic person's emotional responses to the analyst and the analyst's countertransference each provide clues to understanding and thus containing anxieties.
3   Life events, both traumas and sources of security, contribute to each person's unique attempts to adapt to an always unknowable future.
4   Developing respect for each patient's stubbornly fixed defences is therapeutic.

We all are more simply uniquely human than otherwise (Sullivan 1953, 1962). As humans, we can say how we think and feel; we know the inevitability of our death. We all strive to make our lives meaningful. Clinicians must not diagnose, predict deterioration and then urge compliance to prescriptions of impersonal treatment. We reject Kraepelin's pronouncements and the pessimism still conveyed today in the DSM-IV (APA 1994). Kraepelin's original cohort of deteriorating schizophrenic patients probably included many with not-yet-delineated viral influenza encephalitis lethargica (Whitaker 2002).

We find no commonalities in backgrounds or adult life adjustments among clinicians of psychosis. Few work exclusively with psychotic patients. All see mental health and illness on a continuum. Many could dominate the lecture hall. Sitting calmly in the presence of enormous chaos lends the clinician an aura of superhuman implacability (Farber 1966). In 'An autobiographical study', Freud (1925) states: 'Since the analysts have never relaxed their efforts to come to an understanding of the psychoses . . . they have managed now in this phase and now in that, to get a glimpse beyond the wall'. Rosenfeld, Searles and Benedetti have done so. They provide valuable guidance for clinical work.

Herbert Rosenfeld (1910–1986)

Rosenfeld (1987), like Segal and Bion (Koehler 1994), applied Kleinian theory to treating psychoses. Rosenfeld emphasizes that during the acute state schizophrenic patients put themselves so completely into objects (other people whom they love and/or hate) that there is very little of the self left outside the other person. This interferes with ego functions, most importantly the capacity to experience relations with others. The impulse to intrude into the analyst with positive and negative aspects of the self, and the defences against this primitive object relationship, form the typical transference manifestations (positive and negative relationships with the analyst based on early relationships with others). Rosenfeld's interpretations emphasize the patient's manifest and latent anxieties, since psychotic symptomatology attaches itself to the transference, resulting in a transference-psychosis.

The psychotic patient communicates anxieties and desires predominately non-verbally; so the analyst must be open and receptive, and recognize the value of verbal interpretations. A precise interpretation, offered sensitively, lets a psychotic patient feel held together by the analyst's words. Patients rarely experience correct interpretations as rejections provided that the analyst's attitude and behaviour convey acceptance and understanding. Inevitably, such work activates the analyst's own psychotic anxieties, most frequently the dread the patient will drive one mad. The analyst must avoid the extremes of over-involvement and entanglement or an emotionless detachment and objectification (Rosenfeld 1987).

Patients also respond to interpretations as reflections of the analyst's state of mind, in particular his or her capacity to retain quietness while focusing on the patient's conscious and unconscious anxieties. Severely traumatized patients compulsively repeat past traumatic interactions and situations within the treatment, projecting these terrifying experiences into the analyst. The violence of the patient's projections diminishes gradually if the analyst correctly interprets the patient's anxieties and the patient's need to share these experiences (Rosenfeld 1987).

Harold F. Searles (1918–   )

Searles, like Semrad (1969), Robbins (1993), Garfield (1995) and others, understands schizophrenic experience as a defence against intense emotions. The most basic problem in schizophrenia is the patient's failure to develop a human identity. The phase of therapy Searles terms therapeutic symbiosis, a state of emotional oneness between patient and therapist, is crucial for all patients, schizophrenic or otherwise. Here, a process of mutual re-individuation and re-humanization occurs once each person can accept his or her feeling of having non-human features, and lets these come into play in the transference (Searles 1965, 1979).

Patients' symptoms develop sadomasochistic transference meanings and come to represent a kind of mother–infant dependency between patient and therapist. The patient's illness gradually serves as a security blanket for the patient, personifying both the early mother and the patient's own rudimentary ego. The illness takes on this meaning for analyst as transference deepens. Therefore, the eventual resolution of patients' symptoms causes both satisfaction and loss.

Psychosomatic symptoms especially have transference meanings as the patient unconsciously identifies the analyst with some part-aspects of significant others:

> Thus, for example, when the patient complains . . . of his excruciating headache, or bellyache, or whatever, the analyst soon finds reason to surmise that this is an unconscious transference reference to himself, but that the patient is not yet able to experience the contempt and rage toward him, as well as the body-image degree of dependent symbiosis with him, which is crystallized in the symptom in question
>
> (Searles 1979: 519–20)

> Innate among man's most powerful strivings toward his fellow men . . . is an essentially psychotherapeutic striving . . . The patient is ill because, and to the degree that, his own psychotherapeutic strivings have been subjected to such vicissitudes that they have been rendered inordinately intense, frustrated of fulfillment or even acknowledgment, and admixed therefore with unduly intense components of hate, envy, and competitiveness . . . In transference terms, the patient's illness is expressive of his unconscious attempt to cure the doctor . . . The more ill the patient, the greater the need that the analyst acknowledge the patient as having become a therapist to 'his officially designated therapist'.
>
> (Searles 1979: 380–1)

Gaetano Benedetti (1920–)

Benedetti joined the staff at the Zurich University Clinic Burghölzli in Switzerland in 1947 (two years before Searles came to Chestnut Lodge). There, Eugen Bleuler had created the term 'schizophrenia' and worked closely with Jung, as well as Freud. As the psychopharmacologic era began, Benedetti emphasized psychodynamics, working closely with Gustav Bally, Medard Boss, Marguerite Sechehaye and Christian Müller. Benedetti and Müller founded the International Symposium for the Psychotherapy of Schizophrenia in 1956. This evolved into the currently thriving International Society for the Psychological Treatments of the Schizophrenias and Other Psychoses (www.isps.org).

In psychosis, interpretation 'meets a nothingness into whose vacuum the therapist may feel himself being dragged. From this springs up fear of, and social aggression towards, psychotics' (Benedetti 1987: 187). Therapists must provide the schizophrenic patient's ego 'with that amount of narcissism [self-love] it needs to integrate and understand itself' (Benedetti 1990: 11).

When we partially identify with patients' suffering, we encourage them to 'dare to seek out the places in our unconscious where human existence comes into contact with death . . . I came to the conclusion that the symbiosis of the patients with the world is a basic symptom of their suffering' (Benedetti and Peciccia 1998: 170). Patients react to the danger of fusion by autistic retreat. However, this withdrawal does not provide a sense of safety or protection, since the patient feels alone in his isolated world pursued by projected negative introjects.

Schizophrenia's core psychological deficits are two incompatible nuclei of the self, which are both non-self, with respect to each other. One is characterized by excessive symbiotic needs, the other by excessive needs for separation which take on autistic connotations. 'The two nuclei of the self, symbiotic and autistic, fragment each other every time separative needs or symbiotic needs are both contemporaneously present and therefore intensely felt because they are not integrated' (Peciccia and Benedetti 1998: 119–20). This model incorporates the primary dialectic between autonomy and interdependency, identified by many as key determinants in personality development and psychopathology (Blatt and Ford 1994; Bullard 1959).

Karon's research contributions

Most paranoid delusions are (1) transferences to the world at large, (2) defences against the fear of pseudo-homosexuality (Freud 1911), (3) family-unique meanings of concepts (Lidz 1973), or (4) attempts to make organized sense out of one's self and world, despite unusual experiences (Karon 1989). Hallucinations are waking dreams, similar to night dreams, but with stronger motivation. Catatonic stupor is a terror response that has evolved to cope with predators (Ratner et al. 1981). A series of thematic apperception test (TAT) studies consistently indicated that most (but not all) parents of schizophrenics tend to have unconscious defences that make it harder for their children to cope (Karon and Widener 1994; Meyer and Karon 1967).

Karon's outcome research compared and blindly evaluated chronic (but not medicated) inner-city schizophrenic patients randomly assigned to one of three groups: (1) an average of 70 sessions of psychoanalytic therapy without medication, (2) combined psychoanalytic therapy and medication, or (3) medication and support. Psychoanalytic therapy with continued medication is better than medication alone, but not as helpful as psychoanalytic therapy without medication or with initial medication withdrawn as the patient can tolerate it. While there are greater improvements in symptoms, work, affect, relations with spouses and children, discharge and less rehospitalization, the most striking advantage of psychoanalytic therapy compared with medication is the greater improvement in thought disorder – that is, the ability to think rationally when you want to (Karon and VandenBos 1981).

WHAT MAKES A THERAPIST?

In the 1980s, a group of women psychiatrists at Chestnut Lodge formed a study group, *What's a nice girl like you doing in a place like this?* Knowing each other only as colleagues, we introduced ourselves. Without exception, we focused disproportionately on our mothers' stories, each diagnosing them as depressed, one suicidally and another psychotically so.

One recounted her mother's insomnia, rages and conviction that neighbours were plotting against them. She claimed to hear them through the party wall. The future therapist listened and heard nothing. She studied her father's copies of Freud on paranoia. Her mother was house-bound, afraid to take college courses even though she had been first in her high school class. Working with psychotic patients gave this now-grown daughter, finally, some authority. At home, there was no nursing staff. At the Lodge, she had the necessary support.

Perhaps this displaced vindication appeals to many clinicians of psychosis. The other person has our madness for us, and our efforts are supported by our institutions. There is a high incidence of childhood traumas in the lives of schizophrenic patients (Read *et al.* 2001). Did the parents of strong therapists suffer similarly? Fromm-Reichmann (1989) spoke for us: 'If you want to know something for my epitaph, you could say I had a lot of fun, but a different sort of fun from other people. It was a special kind of fun' (p. 481).

REFERENCES

Abraham, K. ([1916] 1927). The first pregenital stage of the libido. In *Selected Papers on Psycho-analysis 9*. New York: Brunner/Mazel.

Abraham, N. and Torok, M. (1994). *The Shell and the Kernel: Renewals of Psychoanalysis* (translated by N. Rand). Chicago, IL: University of Chicago Press.

Ainsworth, M. *et al* (1978). *Patterns of Attachment*. Hillsdale, NJ: Lawrence Erlbaum.

Alanen, Y. (1997a). Vulnerability to schizophrenia and psychotherapeutic treatment of schizophrenic patients. *Psychiatry* 60: 142–57.

Alanen, Y. (1997b). *Schizophrenia: Its Origins and Need-Adapted Treatment.* London: Karnac.

Alexander, F. and Selesnick, S. (1966). *The History of Psychiatry.* New York: Harper & Row.

American Psychiatric Association (1994). *Diagnostic and Statistical Manual of Mental Disorders*, 4th edn. Washington, DC: APA.

Benedetti, G. (1987). *Psychotherapy of Schizophrenia.* New York: New York University Press.

Benedetti, G. (1990). Depression, psychosis, schizophrenia. In P. Borri and R. Quartesan (eds) *USA–Europe Joint Meeting on Therapies and Psychotherapy of Schizophrenia.* Perugia, Italy: ARP.

Benedetti, G. and Furlan, P. (eds) (1993). *The Psychotherapy of Schizophrenia.* Seattle, WA: Hogrefe & Huber.

Benedetti, G. and Peciccia, M. (1998). The ego structure and the self-identity of the schizophrenic human and the task of psychoanalysis. *International Forum of Psychoanalysis* 7: 169–75.

Bion, W. ([1957] 1967). Differentiation of the psychotic from the nonpsychotic personalities. In *Second Thoughts.* New York: Aronson.

Blatt, S. and Ford, R. (1994). *Therapeutic Change: An Object Relations Perspective.* New York: Plenum Press.

Bockoven, J. (1972). *Moral Treatment in Community Mental Health.* New York: Springer.

Bolton, D. and Hill, J. (1996). *Mind, Meaning, and Mental Disorder.* Oxford: Oxford University Press.

Boyer, L. and Giovacchini, P. (1967). *Psychoanalytic Treatment of Schizophrenic and Characterological Disorders.* New York: Science House.

Buber, M. (1958). *I and Thou.* New York: Scribner.

Bullard, D. Sr. (ed.) (1959). *Psychoanalysis and Psychotherapy: Selected Writings of Frieda Fromm-Reichmann.* Chicago, IL: University of Chicago Press.

Bychowski, G. (1954). On the handling of some schizophrenic defence mechanisms and reaction patterns. *International Journal of Psychoanalysis* 35: 147–53.

Ciompi, L. (1988). *The Psyche and Schizophrenia: The Bond between Affect and Logic.* Cambridge, MA: Harvard University Press.

Dupont, J. (ed.) (1988). *The Clinical Diary of Sandor Ferenczi* (translated by M. Balint and N. Jackson). Cambridge, MA: Harvard University Press.

Eisenberg, L. (1986). Mindlessness and brainlessness in psychiatry. *British Journal of Psychiatry* 148: 497–508.

Fairbairn, R. (1954). *An Object-Relations Theory of Personality.* New York: Basic Books.

Farber, L. (1966). Schizophrenia and the mad psychotherapist. In *The Ways of the Will.* New York: Basic Books.

Federn, P. (1934). The analysis of psychotics. *International Journal of Psychoanalysis* 15: 209–14.

Federn, P. (1943a). Psychoanalysis of psychoses I. *Psychiatric Quarterly* 17: 3–19.

Federn, P. (1943b). Psychoanalysis of psychoses II. *Psychiatric Quarterly* 17: 246–57.

Fonagy, P. (1997). Discussion of W. Fenton's 'An overview of contemporary research pointers'. Paper presented to the *12th International Symposium for the Psychotherapy of Schizophrenia*, London.

Freud, S. (1905). On psychotherapy. *Standard Edition* 7: 255–68.

Freud, S. (1911). Psychoanalytic notes on an autobiographical account of paranoia (dementia paranoids). *Standard Edition* 12: 1–84.

Freud, S. (1925). An autobiographical study. *Standard Edition* 20: 7–74.

Freud, S. (1940). Outline of psychoanalysis. *Standard Edition* 23: 139–301.

Fromm-Reichmann, F. (1950). *Principles of Intensive Psychotherapy*. Chicago, IL: University of Chicago Press.

Fromm-Reichmann, F. (1989). Reminiscences of Europe. In A.-L. Silver (ed.) *Psychoanalysis and Psychosis*. Madison, CT: International Universities Press.

Garfield, D. (1995). *Unbearable Affect: A Guide to the Psychotherapy of Psychosis*. New York: Wiley.

Greenberg, J. (1964). *I Never Promised You a Rose Garden*. New York: Holt, Rinehart & Winston.

Grossman, C. and Grossman, S. (1965). *The Wild Analyst: The Life and Work of George Groddeck*. New York: Braziller.

Guntrip, H. (1969). *Schizoid Phenomena, Object Relations, and the Self*. New York: International Universities Press.

Hopper, K. and Wanderling, J. (2000). Developed versus developing country distinction in schizophrenia. *Schizophrenia Bulletin* 26: 835–46.

Hornstein, G. (2000). *To Redeem One Person is to Redeem the World: The Life of Frieda Fromm-Reichmann*. New York: Free Press.

Jackson, M. (2001). *Weathering the Storms: Psychotherapy for Psychosis*. London: Karnac.

Jackson, M. and Williams, P. (1994). *Unimaginable Storms: A Search for Meaning in Psychosis*. London: Karnac.

Jaffe, J. *et al.* (2001). *Rhythms of Dialogue in Infancy*. Boston, MA: Blackwell.

Jung, C. ([1907] 1960). Schizophrenia. In *The Psychology of Dementia Praecox*. Princeton, J: Princeton University Press.

Karon, B. (1989). On the formation of delusions. *Psychoanalytic Psychology* 6: 169–85.

Karon, B. and VandenBos, G. (1981). *Psychotherapy of Schizophrenia: The Treatment of Choice*. Northvale, NJ: Jason Aronson.

Karon, B. and Widener, A. (1994). Is there really a schizophrenogenic parent? *Psychoanalytic Psychology* 11: 47–61.

Kernberg, O. (1986). Identification and its vicissitudes as observed in psychosis. *International Journal of Psychoanalysis* 67: 147–59.

Klein, M. (1930). The psychotherapy of the psychoses. *British Journal of Medical Psychology* 10: 242–4.

Klein, M. (1948). *Contributions to Psychoanalysis 1931–1945*. London: Hogarth.

Klein, M. (1975). *Envy and Gratitude*. New York: Free Press.

Koehler, B. (1994). Kleinian contributions to the understanding and treatment of psychotic patients. Paper presented to the *11th International Symposium for the Psychotherapy of Schizophrenia*, Washington, DC.

Lidz, T. (1973). *The Origin and Treatment of Schizophrenic Disorders*. New York: Basic Books.

McGovern, C. (1985). *Masters of Madness*. Hanover, NH: University of New England.

Meyer, R. and Karon, B. (1967). The schizophrenogenic mother concept and the TAT. *Psychiatry* 30: 173–9.

Mitrani, J. (2001). 'Taking the transference': some technical implications in three papers by Bion. *International Journal of Psychoanalysis* 82: 1085–104.

Noble, D. and Burnham, D. ([1969] 1989). A history of The Washington Psychoanalytic Institute and Society. In A.-L. Silver (ed) *Psychoanalysis and Psychosis*. Madison, CT: International Universities Press.

Peciccia, M. and Benedetti, G. (1998). The integration of sensorial channels through progressive mirror drawing in the psychotherapy of schizophrenic patients with disturbance in verbal language. *Journal of the American Academy of Psychoanalysis* 26: 109–22.

Perry, H. (1982). *Psychiatrist of America: The Life of Harry Stack Sullivan*. Cambridge, MA: Harvard University Press.

Ratner, S. *et al.* (1981). The adaptive significance of the catatonic stupor in humans and animals from an evolutionary perspective. *Academic Psychology Bulletin* 3: 273–9.

Read, J. *et al.* (2001). The contribution of early traumatic events to schizophrenia in some patients. *Psychiatry* 64: 19–45.

Robbins, M. (1993). *Experiences of Schizophrenia*. New York: Guilford Press.

Rosenfeld, H. (1965). *Psychotic States*. New York: International Universities Press.

Rosenfeld, H. (1987). *Impasse and Interpretation*. London: Tavistock.

Searles, H. (1963). Transference psychosis in the psychotherapy of chronic schizophrenia. *International Journal of Psychoanalysis* 44: 249–81.

Searles, H. (1965). *Collected Papers on Schizophrenia and Related Subjects*. New York: International Universities Press.

Searles, H. (1979). *Countertransference and Related Subjects*. New York: International Universities Press.

Segal, H. (1973). *Introduction to the Work of Melanie Klein*. New York: Basic Books.

Semrad, E. (1969). *Teaching Psychotherapy of Psychotic Patients*. New York: Grune & Stratton.

Silver A.-L. (ed.) (1989). *Psychoanalysis and Psychosis*. Madison, CT: International Universities Press.

Silver, A.-L. (1993). Countertransference, Ferenczi, and Washington, DC. *Journal of the American Academy of Psychoanalysis* 21: 637–54.

Silver, A.-L. (2002). Psychoanalysis and psychosis: players and history in the United States. *Psychoanalysis and History* 4: 45–66.

Stanton, A. and Schwartz, M. (1954). *The Mental Hospital*. New York: Basic Books.

Steiner, J. (1993). *Psychic Retreats*. London: Routledge.

Strauss, J. (1994). Is biological psychiatry building on an adequate base? In N. Andreasen (ed.) *Schizophrenia: From Mind to Molecule*. Washington, DC: American Psychiatric Press.

Strauss, J. (1997). Processes of healing and the nature of schizophrenia. In H. Brenner *et al.* (eds) *Towards a Comprehensive Therapy for Schizophrenia*. Seattle, WA: Hogrefe & Huber.

Sullivan, H. (1953). *The Interpersonal Theory of Psychiatry*. New York: Norton.

Sullivan, H. (1962). *Schizophrenia as a Human Process*. New York: Norton.

Suomi, S. (1997). Long-term effects of different early rearing experiences on social, emotional, and physiological development in nonhuman primates. In M. Keshavan and R. Murray (eds) *Neurodevelopment and Adult Psychopathology*. Cambridge: Cambridge University Press.

Tustin, F. (1990). *The Protective Shell in Children and Adults*. London: Karnac.

Volkan, V. (1976). *Primitive Internalized Object Relations: Clinical Studies of Schizophrenic, Borderline, and Narcissistic Patients*. New York: International Universities Press.

Waelder, R. (1925). The psychoses: their mechanisms and accessibility to influence. *International Journal of Psychoanalysis* 6: 254–81.

Whitaker, R. (2002). *Mad in America*. New York: Perseus.

White, W. (1907). *Outlines of Psychiatry*. Washington, DC: Nervous and Mental Disease Publishers.

Winnicott, D. (1965). *The Maturational Process and the Facilitating Environment*. New York: International Universities Press.

Winnicott, D. (1974). Fear of breakdown. *International Review of Psychoanalysis* 1: 103–7.

Chapter 16

Childhood trauma, loss and stress

John Read, Lisa Goodman, Anthony P. Morrison, Colin A. Ross and Volkmar Aderhold

Child abuse has been shown to have a causal role in depression, anxiety disorders, post-traumatic stress disorder, eating disorders, substance abuse, sexual dysfunction, personality disorders and dissociative disorders (Boney-McCoy and Finkelhor 1996; Kendler *et al.* 2000). The more severe the abuse, the greater is the probability of these problems in adulthood (Mullen *et al.* 1993). Yet it is often assumed that child abuse is less related to the more severe psychiatric disorders, such as psychosis in general and schizophrenia in particular. We will demonstrate, however, that the relationship between childhood trauma and the symptoms of schizophrenia is as strong, or stronger, than the relationships between childhood trauma and less severe disorders.

This should be unsurprising. Child abuse is related to severity of psychological disturbance however you measure it. Psychiatric patients subjected to child sexual abuse or child physical abuse have earlier first admissions and longer and more frequent hospitalizations, spend longer in seclusion, receive more medication, are more likely to self-mutilate, and have higher global symptom severity (Beck and van der Kolk 1987; Briere *et al.* 1997; Goff *et al.* 1991a; Lipschitz *et al.* 1999a; Pettigrew and Burcham 1997; Read *et al.* 2001a; Rose *et al.* 1991; Sansonnet-Hayden *et al.* 1987). Psychiatric patients who have suffered child physical or sexual abuse try to kill themselves more often than non-abused psychiatric patients (Briere *et al.* 1997; Lanktree *et al.* 1991; Lipschitz *et al.* 1999a; Read 1998; Read *et al.* 2001a).

CHILD ABUSE, NEGLECT AND PARENTAL LOSS AMONG PSYCHIATRIC PATIENTS

Childhood sexual and physical abuse

Tables 16.1 and 16.2 report studies of female and male psychiatric inpatients, and outpatients where 50% or more had a diagnosis of psychosis. Because reviews of medical files underestimate abuse rates (Read 1997), only

Table 16.1   Prevalence of child abuse among female psychiatric inpatients and among outpatients of whom at least half were diagnosed psychotic

		n	Child sexual abuse	Incest	Child physical abuse	Sexual or physical abuse	Sexual and physical abuse
Friedman and Harrison (1984)	SC	20	60				
Bryer et al. (1987)		66	44	23	38	59	23
Jacobson and Richardson (1987)		50	22		44	56	10
Sansonnet-Hayden et al. (1987)	AD	29	38		23		
Craine et al. (1988)		105	51	42	35	61	26
Goodwin et al. (1988)		40	50				
Hart et al. (1989)	AD	16	75		69	81	62
Chu and Dill (1990)		98	36		51	63	23
Jacobson and Herald (1990)		50	54				
Shearer et al. (1990)		40	40		25		
Goff et al. (1991a)	PS	21				48	
Lanktree et al. (1991)	CH	18	50	44			
Margo and McLees (1991)		38	58		66	76	47
Rose et al. (1991)	OP	39	50	41	38		
Carlin and Ward (1992)		149	51				
Lobel (1992)		50	60				
Ito et al. (1993)	CH	51				73	
Muenzenmaier et al. (1993)	OP	78	45	22	51	64	32
Mullen et al. (1993)	EX	27	85				
Greenfield et al. (1994)	PS	19	42		42	53	32
Ross et al. (1994)	SC	25	32		32	48	16
Swett and Halpert (1994)		88	61	40	57	76	50
Trojan (1994)	PS	48	25				
Darves-Bornoz et al. (1995)	PS	89	34	18			
Goodman et al. (1995)	OP	99	65		87	92	60
Cohen et al. (1996)	AD	73	51		52	68	34
Davies-Netzley et al. (1996)	OP	120	56	26	59	77	38
Miller and Finnerty (1996)	SC	44	36				
Wurr and Partridge (1996)		63	52	17			
Briere et al. (1997)	OP	93	53		42		
Mueser et al. (1998)	OP	153	52		33		
Goodman et al. (1999)	PS	29	78[a]				
Lipschitz et al. (1999a,b)	AD	38	77		47	90	34
Lipschitz et al. (2000)	AD	57	39		30	65	
Fehon et al. (2001)	AD	71	55		51		
Goodman et al. (2001)	OP	321	49		54	67	36
Friedman et al. (2002)	SC	9	78				
Holowka et al. (2003)	SC	7	57		17	57	17
Offen et al. (2003)	PS	7	71				
Resnick et al. (2003)	SC	30	47				
Weighted average			50%	29%	48%	69%	35%
			1199	193	831	944	437
			2396	666	1723	1370	1241

Abbreviations: SC = all diagnosed schizophrenic, PS = all diagnosed psychotic, OP = outpatients with at least 50% diagnosed psychotic, AD = adolescent inpatients, CH = child inpatients.

[a]   Midpoint of two measures.

Table 16.2 Prevalence of child abuse among male psychiatric inpatients and among outpatients of whom at least half were diagnosed psychotic

		n	Child sexual abuse	Incest	Child physical abuse	Sexual or physical abuse	Sexual and physical abuse
Jacobson and Richardson (1987)		50	16		54	58	12
Sansonnet-Hayden et al. (1987)	AD	25	24		52		
Metcalfe et al. (1990)	OP	100	34[a]				
Jacobson and Herald (1990)		50	26				
Goff et al. (1991a)	PS	40				42	
Lanktree et al (1991)	CH	17	12				
Rose et al. (1991)	OP	50	22	9	38		
Ito et al. (1993)	AD	53				34	
Greenfield et al. (1994)	PS	19	16		47	53	11
Palmer et al. (1994)	OP	100		6			
Ross et al. (1994)	SC	56	30		23	43	11
Trojan (1994)	PS	48	27				
Cohen et al. (1996)	AD	32	34		47	62	19
Wurr and Partridge (1996)		57	39	7			
Mueser et al. (1998)	OP	122	36		38		
Goodman et al. (1999)	OP	21	45[a]				
Lipschitz et al. (1999a,b)	AD	33	33		45	66	12
Lipschitz et al. (2000)	AD	38	16		55	71	
Fehon et al. (2001)	AD	59	12		68		
Goodman et al. (2001)	OP	461	29		58	65	22
Lysaker et al. (2001a)	SC	52	35				
Friedman et al. (2002)	SC	13	0				
Holowka et al. (2003)	SC	19	47		21	53	16
Offen et al. (2003)	PS	19	26				
Resnick et al. (2003)	SC	17	18				
Weighted average			28%	7%	51%	60%	19%
			386	14	489	477	128
			1356	207	964	801	670

Abbreviations: SC = all diagnosed schizophrenic, PS = all diagnosed psychotic, OP = outpatients with at least 50% diagnosed psychotic, AD = adolescent inpatients, CH = child inpatients.

[a] Midpoint of two measures.

studies where people were actually asked about abuse are included. Studies of inpatient alcohol services (Windle *et al.* 1995) and military inpatient units with low proportions of psychotic patients (Brown and Anderson 1991) were excluded. A mixed gender (predominantly male) outpatient study could not be included because the child sexual abuse and child physical abuse rates were not analysed by gender. This study, which included abuse since childhood, found that 55% of the women and 24% of the men had been either sexually or physically abused at some point in their lives (with higher rates of adulthood abuse than childhood abuse) (Coverdale & Turbott 2000). Also excluded were two studies of inpatient units serving populations with particularly high rates of child abuse. The rates of child sexual abuse were 87% in a unit for post-traumatic stress disorder (Kirby *et al*. 1993) and 92% in a unit treating dissociative identity disorder (Ellason *et al*. 1996).

Much of the variation is caused by the use of different definitions of abuse. For example, the lowest rate of female child sexual abuse (22%) included only genital contact (Jacobson and Richardson 1987), whereas most studies included non-genital contact (e.g. repeated fondling of breasts) and some included non-contact abuse (e.g. being forced to watch adults masturbate).

Many studies provided details of the abuse. For instance, in a study of child and adolescent inpatients (Lipschitz *et al*. 1999b), the sexual abuse began on average at 8 years of age and lasted on average 2.1 years. Most of the sexual abuse was intrafamilial and involved penetration or oral sex. The physical abuse started on average at 4.4 years of age, lasted an average of 6.4 years and involved physical injury in most cases (Lipschitz *et al*. 1999a).

Thus most (about two-thirds) women psychiatric patients and more than half of male psychiatric patients (about 60%) have suffered either child sexual or physical abuse. It has been calculated that both women and men in psychiatric hospitals are at least twice as likely as women and men in general to have suffered child abuse (Jacobson and Herald 1990; Palmer *et al*. 1994). This estimate may be conservative because people tend to underreport abuse while in hospital (Dill *et al*. 1991; Read 1997). When researchers surveyed female inpatients after they returned to the community, 85% disclosed child sexual abuse (Mullen *et al*. 1993).

Three other inpatient studies confirm high abuse rates among psychiatric inpatients. They were not included in the tables because the question was 'Have you ever been sexually [or physically] abused?' This produces significantly lower response rates than using questions which do not require a judgement about whether the actions constituted 'abuse', such as 'Were you pressured into doing more sexually than you wanted to do or were too young to understand?' (Swett and Halpert 1994). Nevertheless, they allow comparisons with a large general population study that used the same questions and categories (Kessler *et al*. 1995). While child physical abuse was reported by 3% of men in general, the rate among male psychiatric inpatients was 30% (Cloitre *et al*. 2001; Switzer *et al*. 1999). Five per cent of women in general reported child physical abuse, compared with 34% (Cloitre *et al*. 1996) and 42% (Switzer *et al*. 1999) among female inpatients. 'Sexual molestation' among women in general was 12%, but among female psychiatric patients it was 51% (Switzer *et al*. 1999). For men, the molestation figures were 3% in the general population and 18% among psychiatric patients.

The majority of the physical abuse is perpetrated by family members, predominantly fathers (Carmen *et al*. 1984; Greenfield *et al*. 1994; Livingston 1987; Swett and Halpert 1994).

Incest

The weighted average incest rate among female patients was 29%. Three studies, excluded from Table 16.1 because they did not involve direct questioning of all patients, reported incest rates of 26% (Cole 1988) to 35% (Beck and van der Kolk 1987; Kohan *et al.* 1987). These findings can be compared with community surveys reporting incest rates of 13 and 17% (Bushnell *et al.* 1992; Russell *et al.* 1988).

Thirteen clinical studies provide data from which the proportion of the sexual abuse of girls that was incestuous can be calculated (Bryer *et al.* 1987; Cole 1988; Craine *et al.* 1988; Darves-Bornoz *et al.* 1995; Davies-Neltzey *et al.* 1996; Kohan *et al.* 1987; Lanktree *et al.* 1991; Livingston 1987; Muenzenmaier *et al.* 1993; Read *et al.* 2003; Rose *et al.* 1991; Swett and Halpert 1994; Wurr and Partridge 1996). The proportions range from 33 to 89%, with a weighted average of 62%. This can be compared with two community surveys that found the proportion of child sexual abuse of girls committed by family members to be 29% (Russell 1983; Wyatt 1985).

Table 16.2 shows a weighted average of 7% for incest among men. Two other studies found rates of 3% (Cole 1988) and 12% (Kohan *et al.* 1987). Among male patients, the proportion of child sexual abuse perpetrated by relatives ranges from 18 to 89% (Cole 1988; Kohan *et al.* 1987; Palmer *et al.* 1994; Read *et al.* 2003; Rose *et al.* 1991; Swett *et al.* 1990; Wurr and Partridge 1996). The weighted average is 62%.

Psychological abuse and neglect

Adult inpatient studies report rates of childhood neglect ranging from 22 to 62% (Heads *et al.* 1997; Muenzenmaier *et al.* 1993; Saxe *et al.* 1993). In a study of adult outpatient 'schizophrenics', 35% had suffered emotional abuse as children, 42% physical neglect and 73% emotional neglect (Holowka *et al.* 2003). A study of adolescent inpatients found that 52% had experienced emotional abuse, 61% physical neglect and 31% emotional neglect (Lipshitz *et al.* 1999a). Two studies allow comparison with a community survey using identical methods. Two per cent of women in general reported being 'seriously neglected as a child' (Kessler *et al.* 1995), compared with 4% (Neria *et al.* 2002) and 36% (Switzer *et al.* 1999) of women psychiatric patients. The figures for men are: 3% in the general population and 8% and 35% among psychiatric patients, respectively. In a community survey, women emotionally abused as children were five times more likely than other women to have had a psychiatric admission (Mullen *et al.* 1996).

Parental loss

In 1939, it was found that 38% of 'dementia praecox' patients had lost a parent in childhood, compared with 17% of 'manic-depressives' (Pollock *et al.* 1939). In 1949, Ruth and Theodore Lidz found a similar rate of child-hood parental loss (40%) among 'schizophrenic' patients, compared with 20% among psychotically depressed patients. A 1966 review reported that eight of 13 studies had found that 'schizophrenics' have higher rates of parental death in childhood than comparison groups (Granville-Grossman 1966).

Manfred Bleuler's (1978) remarkable book *The Schizophrenic Disorders* includes five of his own studies, totalling 932 people diagnosed 'schizo-phrenic'. These produced a combined rate of parental loss before the age of 15 years of 31%, significantly greater than among the general population. While Ragan and McGlashan (1986) found no differences in parental loss between eight diagnostic categories, a recent outpatient study found that loss of mother during childhood was significantly higher (55%) in 'schizo-phrenics' than for other diagnoses (23%) (Friedman *et al.* 2002). Bereave-ment, in general, was related to predisposition to auditory hallucinations in young adults (Morrison and Petersen, 2003).

CHILD ABUSE AND 'SCHIZOPHRENIA'

Child abuse and research measures of psychosis and schizophrenia

The Psychoticism scale of the Symptom Checklist 90-Revised is often more related to child abuse than the other nine clinical scales (Bryer *et al.* 1987; Ellason and Ross 1997; Lundberg-Love *et al.* 1992; Swett *et al.* 1990). The Schizophrenia scale of the Minnesota Multiphasic Personality Inventory (MMPI) has been found to be significantly elevated in adults who suffered child physical abuse (Cairns 1998), child sexual abuse (Hunter 1991; Tsai *et al.* 1979) and incest (Scott and Stone 1986). Medical patients who had suffered child sexual abuse scored significantly higher on the Schizophrenia and Paranoia scales but not on the Depression scale (Belkin *et al.* 1994).

Child abuse and clinical diagnoses of psychosis and schizophrenia

Some studies find that diagnoses of psychosis and schizophrenia are no more or less related to child abuse than other diagnoses (Cohen *et al.* 1996; Davies-Neltzey *et al.* 1996; Friedman *et al.* 2002; Neria *et al.* 2002; Ritsher *et al.* 1997; Wurr and Partridge 1996). Others find that child abuse and neglect are more strongly related to diagnoses of schizophrenia and other forms of psychosis than to diagnoses indicating less severe disturbance. In a 30 year study of over 500 child guidance clinic attenders, 35% of those who later became 'schizophrenic' had been removed from home because of neglect, a rate double that of any other diagnosis (Robins 1966). Among over 1000 people, those who at age 3 years had mother–child interactions characterized by 'harshness towards the child; no effort to help the child' were, at age 26, significantly more likely than others to be diagnosed with 'schizophreniform disorder', but not mania, anxiety or depression (Cannon *et al.* 2002).

Among children admitted to a psychiatric hospital, 77% of those who had been sexually abused were diagnosed psychotic, compared with 10% of those not abused (Livingston 1987). From a study of 93 women attending a psychiatric emergency room, it can be calculated that child sexual abuse was more common in psychosis (70%) and depression (74%) than in anxiety (27%) and mania (43%) (Briere *et al.* 1997). In a mixed gender sample of adult outpatients diagnosed 'schizophrenic', 85% had suffered some form of childhood abuse or neglect (73% emotional neglect, 50% sexual abuse) (Holowka *et al.* 2003). Among 139 female outpatients, 78% of those diagnosed 'schizophrenic' had suffered child sexual abuse. The percentages for other diagnoses were: panic disorder, 26%; anxiety disorders, 30%; major depressive disorder, 42% (Friedman *et al.* 2002).

Of 5362 children, those whose mothers had poor parenting skills when they were aged 4 years (presumably indicative of neglect of children's needs and not abuse) were significantly more likely to be schizophrenic as adults (Jones *et al.* 1994). Adults diagnosed 'schizophrenic' are significantly more likely than the general population to have run away from home as children (Malmberg *et al.* 1998), to have attended child guidance centres (Ambelas 1992) and to have been placed in children's homes (Cannon *et al.* 2001).

A chart review found that 52% of female inpatients diagnosed schizophrenic had suffered 'parental violence' (Heads *et al.* 1997). In a study of 426 inpatients diagnosed psychotic, the child physical abuse rate for the women was 29% (Neria *et al.* 2002), compared with 5% in the general population using identical methods (Kessler *et al.* 1995). The rates for men were 17% among inpatients diagnosed psychotic and 3% in the general population. In one study, traumatic brain injury was significantly related to diagnosed 'schizophrenia'. The researchers did not report what proportion of the injuries were inflicted intentionally (Malaspina *et al.* 2001).

Child abuse and the symptoms of schizophrenia

In a study of 'chronically mentally ill women', those who had been abused or neglected as children experienced more psychotic symptoms than other patients (Muenzenmaier *et al.* 1993). The same is found in the general population (Berenbaum 1999; Janssen *et al.* in press; Ross and Joshi 1990; Startup 1999). In another community survey, 46% of people with three or more schizophrenic symptoms had suffered child physical or sexual abuse, compared with 8% of those with none (Ross and Joshi 1990).

The five DSM-IV 'characteristic symptoms' of schizophrenia are hallucinations, delusions, disorganized thinking ('thought disorder'), grossly disorganized or catatonic behaviour, and negative symptoms (APA 1994: 285). An inpatient study found one or more of these symptoms in 75% of those who had suffered child physical abuse, in 76% of those who had suffered child sexual abuse and in 100% of those subjected to incest (Read and Argyle 1999). Usually, two of the five symptoms are required for a diagnosis of schizophrenia. A study of 200 adult outpatients found that 35% of those abused as children had two or more symptoms, compared with 19% of the non-abused patients (Read *et al.* 2003).

Within an inpatient sample of 'schizophrenics', those who had suffered child sexual or physical abuse had significantly more 'positive' symptoms of schizophrenia, but slightly fewer 'negative' symptoms, than those not abused. The symptoms that were significantly related to abuse were, in order of the strength of the relationship: voices commenting, ideas of reference, thought insertion, paranoid ideation, reading others' minds and visual hallucinations (Ross *et al.* 1994).

Hallucinations

As noted, 'schizophrenics' exposed to child sexual or physical abuse are more likely than other 'schizophrenics' to experience voices commenting and visual hallucinations (Ross *et al.* 1994). Voices commenting are considered so indicative of 'schizophrenia' that it is by itself sufficient to warrant the diagnosis (APA 1994). An inpatient study found hallucinations of some form in 53% of those subjected to child sexual abuse, 58% of those subjected to child physical abuse and 71% of those who suffered both forms of abuse (Read and Argyle 1999).

An outpatient study found hallucinations in 19% of the non-abused patients but 47% of those subjected to child physical abuse, 55% of those subjected to child sexual abuse and 71% of those subjected to both forms of abuse (Read *et al.* 2003). The figures for 'command hallucinations' to harm self or others were: non-abused, 2%; child physical abuse, 18%; child sexual abuse, 15%; both forms of abuse, 29%. The figures for voices commenting were: non-abused, 5%; child physical abuse, 21%; child sexual abuse, 27%; both forms of abuse, 36%. A study of adult bipolar affective disorder patients found that those subjected to child physical abuse were no more likely than other patients to experience hallucinations (or delusions). Those subjected to child sexual abuse were no more likely to have visual hallucinations but were twice as likely to have auditory hallucinations and six times as likely to hear voices commenting (Hammersley *et al.* 2003).

The finding that abused adult inpatients are more likely to hallucinate has been replicated with adolescent and child inpatients (Famularo *et al.* 1992; Sansonnet-Hayden *et al.* 1987). Hallucinations are especially common in incest survivors (Ellenson 1985; Ensink 1992; Heins *et al.* 1990; Read and Argyle 1999).

Among non-patients (average age 21), predisposition to auditory, but not visual, hallucinations was significantly higher in those who reported multiple trauma. Emotional abuse (strongly) and physical assault (to a lesser extent) were related to predisposition to auditory hallucinations. Bullying was related to predisposition to visual hallucinations (Morrison and Petersen 2003).

One outpatient study found tactile hallucinations *only* in those who had suffered child sexual or physical abuse. The figures for olfactory hallucinations were: non-abused, 1%; child physical abuse, 9%; child sexual abuse, 10%, both forms of abuse, 21% (Read *et al.* 2003). No such differences were found in bipolar affective disorder patients (Hammersley *et al.* 2003).

Table 16.3 summarizes the evidence that child abuse is strongly related to psychotic hallucinations. Table 16.4 suggests this is the case for both visual and auditory hallucinations, especially voices commenting. The relationship is also demonstrated by the 'dose-effect', with the more severe forms of abuse – incest and being subjected to both child sexual and physical abuse – being related to particularly high rates of hallucinations. Thus the severity of the abuse (e.g. age at onset, degree of violence, duration and intrafamilial abuse) may partly determine which abused people develop psychotic symptoms. In a study of 100 incest survivors, a cumulative trauma-score (involving multiple types of abuse and multiple abusers) was significantly higher in those who later experienced auditory or visual hallucinations (Ensink 1992).

Delusions

The study of 200 outpatients (Read *et al.* 2003) produced weaker support for a relationship between child abuse and delusions. Although 40% of the child sexual abuse patients experienced some form of delusion, compared with 27% of the non-abused, this was not statistically significant. Furthermore, the study did not replicate the relationships (Ross *et al.* 1994) between child abuse and ideas of reference or mind reading. It did, however, provide some support for their finding of a relationship between child abuse and paranoid ideation. Paranoid delusions were present for 40% of the outpatients who had experienced child sexual abuse, compared with 23% of the non-abused patients.

Studies that found a significant relationship between child abuse and hallucinations in adolescent inpatients (Sansonnet-Hayden *et al.* 1987), child inpatients (Famularo *et al.* 1992) and in adults diagnosed with bipolar affective disorder (Hammersley *et al.* 2003) found no relationship with delusions. However, an outpatient study found paranoid delusions in 36% of incest survivors but in none of the non-familial cases of child sexual abuse (Read *et al.* 2003).

If child abuse is related to delusions, and no such conclusion can yet be drawn, the relationship seems to be with persecutory or paranoid, not

Table 16.3 Relationships between child abuse and the DSM characteristic symptoms of schizophrenia

	Hallucinations	Delusions	Thought disorder	Negative symptoms
Child abuse (CSA or CPA)				
Bryer et al. (1987)		0	+[e]	
Goff et al. (1991a)	0		0	(−)
Famularo et al. (1992)	+	0	0	0
Ross et al. (1994)	++	++		(−)
Read and Argyle (1999)	(+)	(+)	(+)	
Read et al. (2003)	++	(+)	(+)	0
Resnick et al. (2003)[f]	+	+		(−)
Janssen et al. (in press)[g]	++	++		
Physical abuse				
Goff et al. (1991b)		(+)[c]		
Read and Argyle (1999)	(+)	0	0	
Read et al. (2003)	++	(+)	0	0
Hammersley et al. (2003)	0	0	0	
Sexual abuse				
Bryer et al. (1987)		0	+[e]	
Sansonnet-Hayden et al. (1987)	++	0		
Goff et al. (1991b)		+[c]		
Ensink (1992)	(+)			
Read and Argyle (1999)	(+)	0	(+)	
Lysaker et al. (2001a)			0	
Read et al. (2003)	++	(+)	(+)	0
Hammersley et al. (2003)	++	0	0	
Incest				
Beck and van der Kolk (1987)		(+)[d]		
Bryer et al. (1987)[a]		0	0[e]	
Ellenson (1985)	(+)			
Heins et al. (1990)	(+)			
Read and Argyle (1999)[a]	++	0	0	
Read et al. (2003)[a]	(+)	(+)	0	0
CSA + CPA				
Bryer et al. (1987)[b]		0	(+)[e]	
Read and Argyle (1999)[b]	(+)	0	0	
Read et al. (2003)[b]	(+)	0	(−)	0

+ = *P* < .05, ++ = *P* < .01; (+) and (−) = non-significant trend, or high rates with no control group; 0 = no difference; blank cells mean the relationship was not examined in that study.

[a] Comparison of incest and non-familial sexual abuse. [b] Comparison of those subjected to both child sexual and physical abuse versus those subjected to one form of abuse only. [c] Delusions of possession. [d] Sexual delusions. [e] 'Psychotic thinking'. [f] Measure of positive symptoms in general. [g] A combined measure including other forms of trauma and abuse.

Table 16.4 Relationships between child abuse and the sub-types of hallucinations and delusions

	Hallucinations						Delusions		
	Auditory	Voices commenting	Command	Visual	Olfactory	Tactile	Paranoid	Grandiose	Thought insertion
Child abuse (CSA or CPA)									
Bryer et al. (1987)	(+)[c]						(+)[f]		
Goff et al. (1991a)	+			(+)					
Famularo et al. (1992)		++		+			+		
Ross et al. (1994)	++								++
Read and Argyle (1999)	(+)	++							
Read et al. (2003)	++	++	++	++	(+)	++	(+)	0	0
Physical abuse									
Goff et al. (1991a)	0			0					
Read and Argyle (1999)	(+)								
Read et al. (2003)	++	++	++	++	+	++	0	0	0
Hammersley et al. (2003)	0	0		0	0	0	0	0	0
Sexual abuse									
Goff et al. (1991a)	(+)[c]			(+)					
Metcalfe et al. (1990)	(+)[d]						(+)[d]		
Ensink (1992)	(+)			(+)					
Read and Argyle (1999)	(+)								
Read et al. (2003)	++	++	++	++	++	++	(+)	0	(+)
Hammersley et al. (2003)	++	++		0	0	0	0	0	0

continues overleaf

Table 16.4 (Continued)

	Hallucinations						Delusions		
	Auditory	Voices commenting	Command	Visual	Olfactory	Tactile	Paranoid	Grandiose	Thought insertion
Incest									
Bryer et al. (1987)[a]	(+)						0		
Ellenson (1985)	(+)	(+)[e]	(+)	(+)					
Heins et al. (1990)	++								
Read and Argyle (1999)[a]	(+)								
Read et al. (2003)[a]	(+)	(+)			(+)	(+)	(+)		(+)
CSA + CPA									
Bryer et al. (1987)[b]	(+)						+[f]		
Read and Argyle (1999)[b]	(+)	+	+	+	++	0	0		
Read et al. (2003)[b]						0	0	(−)	0

+ = P < .05, ++ = P < .01; (+) and (−) = non-significant trend, or high rates with no control group; 0 = no difference; blank cells mean the relationship was not examined in that study.

[a] Comparison of incest and non-familial sexual abuse. [b] Comparison of those subjected to both child sexual and physical abuse versus those subjected to one form of abuse only. [c] Voices inside head. [d] Diagnosis of 'schizophrenia: paranoid type' (see text). [e] Persecutory voices. [f] 'Paranoid ideology'.

grandiose, delusions. Even this more specific relationship may exist only for more severe cases, such as incest or multiple forms of abuse.

Thought disorder

Table 16.3 suggests that child abuse is not related to thought disorder.

Catatonia

There seems to be no research examining the relationship between trauma and 'grossly disorganized or catatonic behaviour'. In his original 1874 conception of catatonia, Kahlbaum stated that it was usually precipitated by 'very severe physical or mental stress . . . [such as] a very terrifying experience' (p. 4). Some commentators still see catatonia as an extreme fear response (Moskowitz, in press; Perkins 1982).

Negative symptoms

Studies of adult (Lysaker 2001a; Read et al. 2003; Resnick et al. 2003) and child (Famularo et al. 1992) inpatients have found no differences in rates of negative symptoms between abused and non-abused individuals. Two adult inpatient studies found slightly fewer such symptoms in abused patients (Goff et al. 1991a; Ross et al. 1994).

Child abuse and the content of schizophrenic symptoms

Ensink (1992) found that the content of hallucinations of survivors of child sexual abuse contain both 'flash-back elements and more symbolic representations' of traumatic experiences (p. 126). Her many examples include visual hallucinations, for example 'I saw sperm in my food and in my drinks' (p. 124). In maltreated 5–10-year-olds, 'the content of the reported visual and/ or auditory hallucinations or illusions tended to be strongly reminiscent of concrete details of episodes of traumatic victimization' (Famularo et al. 1992: 866). High rates of sexual delusions have been found in psychotic incest survivors (Beck and van der Kolk 1987) but not in those exposed to child sexual abuse in general or to child physical abuse (Goff et al. 1991a). Examples of the delusions of incest survivors include: 'One believed that her body was covered with ejaculate and another that she had had sexual relations with public figures' (Beck and van der Kolk 1987: 1475).

Heins et al. (1990) documented more examples. A man who had been raped several times by an uncle at age 7 years heard voices telling him he was 'sleazy' and should kill himself. A woman who had been sexually assaulted by her father from a very young age and raped as a teenager had the delusion that 'people were watching her as they thought she was a sexual pervert and auditory hallucinations accusing her of doing "dirty sexy things"'. Another woman, whose father had raped her monthly from age 8 and who was raped several times by a cousin at age 11, heard voices calling her a 'slut' and a 'whore.'

Read and Argyle (1999) found that the content of just over half of the 'schizophrenic symptoms' of abused adult inpatients were obviously related to the abuse. A woman who had been sexually abused by her father from age 5 heard 'male voices outside her head and screaming children's voices inside her head'. In another example, involving command hallucinations to commit suicide, the patient identified the voice as the perpetrator of the child abuse. A man who had been sexually abused from age 4 believed his body was asymmetrical and that women only wanted sex with him because of the thrill of being with a freak.

More examples emerged from a New Zealand outpatient study (Read *et al.* 2003). One person, sexually abused at age 8–9 years, had auditory hallucinations in the form of the 'voice of the abuser'. Another's chart read: 'Sexual abuse: Abused from an early age . . . Raped several times by strangers and violent partners'. This person believes 'was being tortured by people getting into body, for example "the Devil" and "the Beast"' and 'had bleeding secondary to inserting a bathroom hose into self, stating wanting to wash self as "people are trying to put aliens into my body"'. Another, whose chart records child sexual and physical abuse and multiple rapes, believes that 'has never been a child but is an old man who had his penis gouged out and had silicone injected into chest and hips'. Another, whose chart documents child sexual abuse also documents 'olfactory hallucinations (smells sperm)'. Another, who suffered 'ongoing sexual abuse by relative who is a violent person' hears 'the voice of the relative telling to jump from the bridge and kill self. Has already tried to commit suicide several times'.

Nearly 100 years ago, psychoanalyst Karl Abraham (1907) noted that a woman who was sexually abused as a child and then again by her husband 'saw the devil, bearing her husband's features and carrying a spear, with which he thrust at her' (p. 17). In the New Zealand study, reference to evil or the Devil was more common in the child sexual abuse group (15%) and in the group who had been sexually abused as children and then again as adults (29%), than in the non-abused group (3%) (Read *et al.* 2003). A recent British study has found that that child sexual abuse is related to a tendency to regard auditory hallucinations as more malevolent, particularly among those for whom the abuse occurred at an early age (Offen *et al.* 2003).

CAUSAL OR COINCIDENTAL?

Most studies demonstrating the relationship between childhood trauma and the diagnosis or symptoms of schizophrenia are correlational and therefore do not prove that the relationship is a causal one. It is indeed possible that it is not so much (or not only) the child abuse itself but other co-existing factors, such as poverty, violence between parents, parental substance abuse and parental mental health problems, that predict which children will later develop psychosis. However, the relationships between child abuse and many psychiatric disorders in adulthood remain after controlling for these potentially mediating variables (Boney-McCoy and Finkelhor 1996; Kendler *et al.* 2000; Pettigrew and Burcham 1997). After controlling for other childhood disruptions and disadvantages, women whose child sexual abuse involved intercourse were 12 times more likely than non-abused females to have had psychiatric admissions (Mullen *et al.* 1993).

Two such studies have examined psychosis and schizophrenia, one using a clinical sample and one examining the general population. Among women attending a psychiatric emergency room, 53% of those who had suffered child sexual abuse had 'nonmanic psychotic disorders (e.g. schizophrenia, psychosis not otherwise specified)' compared with 25% of those who were not victims of sexual abuse. After controlling for 'the potential effects of demographic variables, most of which also predict victimization and/or psychiatric outcome', child sexual abuse was still strongly related to psychotic disorders ($P = 0.001$), had a weaker relationship with depression ($P = 0.035$) and was unrelated to manic or anxiety disorders (Briere *et al.* 1997).

The general population study controlled for a broader range of potential confounders of the relationship between child abuse and psychosis, including drug use, unemployment, urbanicity, neuroticism and other non-psychotic diagnoses, age, sex, educational level and ethnicity (Janssen *et al.*, in press). It was, moreover, a prospective study, measuring the development of psychotic symptoms over a 2-year period in a sample of 4045 people with no previous lifetime psychotic or psychotic-like symptoms. After adjustment for all confounding variables, child abuse (emotional, physical, psychological or sexual) before age 16 was significantly related to all three measures of psychosis employed in the study. For example, those subjected to child abuse were 7.3 times more likely than those not exposed to child abuse to develop the most severe measure of psychosis used in the study (i.e. in need of mental health care because of psychotic symptoms). Furthermore, there was a dose–response relationship for all three psychoses outcomes, indicating that the risk of developing the psychosis outcomes increased with increased frequency of reported childhood abuse. Those reporting the highest frequency of abuse were 30 times more likely than those not abused to develop psychotic symptoms requiring mental health care.

RE-TRAUMATIZATION

Besides the severity or frequency of the abuse, another determinant of which child abuse survivors end up psychotic is whether the individual encounters further traumas later in life. Most psychiatric patients, both males and females, suffer serious physical assaults as adults, and the majority of the women suffer sexual assaults (Goodman *et al.* 1995, 1999, 2001; Jacobson and Richardson 1987; Mueser *et al.* 1998; Switzer *et al.* 1999), with about a third being raped (Briere *et al.* 1997; Cloitre *et al.* 2001; Craine *et al.* 1988; Miller and Finnerty 1996; Neria *et al.* 2002; Switzer *et al.* 1999). About a quarter of male patients are sexually assaulted as adults (Goodman *et al.* 1999, 2001; Mueser *et al.* 1998) and between 3 and 17% are raped (Cloitre *et al.* 2001; Neria *et al.* 2002; Switzer *et al.* 1999).

One study found that in the year before being admitted to hospital, 63% of patients had suffered physical violence by their partners and 46% of those who lived at home had been assaulted by family members, predominantly parents (Cascardi *et al.* 1996). Assaults come from outside the family too, including mental health staff (Davidson and McNamara 1999; Ritsher *et al.* 1997).

Unsurprisingly, this violence is associated with more severe disturbance. A study of 409 female inpatients found that sexual assault was significantly related to a diagnosis of schizophrenia, but not to mania, depression, substance abuse or borderline personality disorder (Cloitre *et al.* 1996). Among female psychiatric patients, physical assault (by non-partners) was significantly related to only one diagnostic group: 'nonmanic psychotic disorders (e.g. schizophrenia, psychosis not otherwise specified)'. Overall, 37% had been raped, but this was the case for 51% of those with a diagnosis of 'nonmanic psychotic disorder' (Briere *et al.* 1997).

People who have been abused as children are more likely to be abused as adults (Cloitre *et al.* 1996; Muenzenmaier *et al.* 1993). If, as a result of early trauma, one is already hypersensitive to threat, then it can be devastating when that threat becomes reality. We saw earlier that childhood abuse is related to hallucinations and, less strongly, to delusions. When the ability of child abuse and adulthood abuse to predict these symptoms were analysed in relation to each other (by logistic regression), only voices commenting and tactile hallucinations were predicted by child abuse if no adult abuse followed. However, both hallucinations and delusions are predicted by child abuse if that child abuse *is* followed by abuse in adulthood. Even thought disorder and grandiose delusions are predicted by child and adult abuse together (Read *et al.* 2003).

In 1907, Abraham had noted several cases of dementia praecox in which 'the illness followed upon trauma' and others 'in which a subsequent experience similar to the traumatic one was the precipitating factor' (p. 17). A Dutch study of people diagnosed with schizophrenia or dissociative disorder (85% of whom suffered child abuse or neglect) found an external trigger for hallucinations in 70% of cases. 'In most patients, the onset of auditory hallucinations was preceded by either a traumatic event or an event that activated the memory of earlier trauma' (Honig *et al.* 1998: 646).

The retriggering can result from any trauma, including hospitalization, or even the experience of the psychotic symptoms themselves (Frame and Morrison 2001; McGorry *et al.* 1991; Morrison *et al.*, in press; Shaw *et al.* 2001). However, it is hard to separate the effects of the symptoms from the effects of previous traumas when the symptoms are trauma-based.

The powerful role of combined childhood and adulthood victimization is not, of course, unique to behaviours labelled 'schizophrenic' (Cheasty *et al.* 2002). That is our point. The symptoms of the supposedly biologically based illness 'schizophrenia' originate in adverse life events in the same way as other mental health problems. The relative roles of the severity of the original abuse, re-traumatization in adulthood, and a whole range of other factors (e.g. support at the time of the abuse, attributions about blame, etc.) in determining who ends up psychotic, depressed or relatively well can now be researched using complex path analysis procedures (Barker-Collo and Read 2003).

Of more immediate importance is that clinicians shed themselves of the notion that the symptoms of schizophrenia are less trauma-based than other mental health problems.

UNANSWERED QUESTIONS AND NEXT STEPS

Many questions, some theoretical and some with urgent practical implications, emerge from the research we have reviewed.

Positive symptoms

1 Is child abuse really more predictive of hallucinations than it is of delusions and thought disorder?
2 Is child abuse really more related to some subtypes (e.g. voices commenting, paranoid delusions, tactile hallucinations) than to others?
3 What is the relationship between child abuse and catatonia?
4 What is the relationship of neglect and psychological abuse to the symptoms of 'schizophrenia'?
5 Will longitudinal studies, and studies controlling for other adverse circumstances in childhood, confirm that the relationships between child abuse and some of the symptoms of schizophrenia are causal?
6 Is it only severe abuse (e.g. early age, intrafamilial, multiple instances and perpetrators) that is predictive of these symptoms?
7 Will the findings about the role of later assaults retriggering the effects of childhood abuse be replicated?

Negative symptoms

8 Were Ross and his colleagues (1994) correct to suggest 'There may be at least two pathways to positive symptoms of schizophrenia? One may be primarily endogenously driven and accompanied by predominantly negative symptoms. The other may be primarily driven by childhood psychosocial trauma and accompanied by fewer negative symptoms' (p. 491).

9 What does it mean that negative symptoms are similar to the post-traumatic stress disorder symptoms of emotional numbing and avoidance of trauma-related stimuli (Stampfer 1990)?

Rediagnosis when abuse is identified

10 Is a hallucination less 'psychotic' or less 'schizophrenic' just because it is an abuse flashback (Ensink 1992)?

11 Will the recent trend towards redefining hallucinations, once trauma is identified, as 'pseudo-hallucinations', 'dissociative hallucinations', 'psychotic-like hallucinations', etc. (e.g. Bryer et al. 1987; Chu and Dill 1990; Heins et al. 1990), and the subsequent changing of diagnoses from 'schizophrenic' to post-traumatic stress disorder or dissociative disorder, etc. (Read 1997), prove to be justified?

12 Will future studies confirm that voices heard by survivors of child sexual abuse are experienced only inside the head, except if substance abuse is also present (Heins et al. 1990), or that they are heard both inside and outside the head with or without substance abuse (Ensink 1992; Honig et al. 1998; Read and Argyle 1999)?

13 Which should be prioritized: the advantages to abused patients of not being called 'schizophrenic' and thereby being more likely to receive trauma-related therapy, or the theoretical point that this rediagnosing perpetuates a circular logic that abuse can't cause 'schizophrenia' (Read 1997)?

A 'post-traumatic dissociative psychosis'?

14 Rather than separating abuse sequelae into discrete categories (post-traumatic stress disorder, dissociative disorders, schizophrenia, borderline personality disorder, etc.), is it more productive to view the abuse-related symptoms of these 'disorders' as related components of a long-term process beginning with adaptive responses to early aversive events and evolving into a range of interacting maladaptive disturbances in multiple personal and interpersonal domains (Ensink 1992; Morrison et al., in press; Mueser et al. 2002; Putnam and Trickett 1997; Read et al. 2001b; Read and Ross 2003; Resnick et al. 2003; Ross and Joshi 1990)?

15 Given that the *DSM* states that in post-traumatic stress disorder the re-experiencing of the trauma includes 'hallucinations and dissociative flashback episodes', what does it mean that between 46% and 67% of acutely psychotic people also have post-traumatic stress disorder (Frame and Morrison 2001; McGorry *et al.* 1991; Shaw *et al.* 2002), and that combat veterans with this disorder have more schizophrenic symptoms – particularly hallucinations and paranoia – than those without it (Butler *et al.* 1996; Sautter *et al.* 1999)?

16 What does it mean that there is massive overlap between dissociative symptoms and the positive symptoms of schizophrenia (Ellason *et al.* 1996; Ensink 1992; Greenfield *et al.* 1994; Nurcombe *et al.* 1996; Offen *et al.* 2003; Read and Ross 2003; Ross and Joshi 1990), that inpatients with dissociative disorders have four times as many schizophrenic symptoms as other inpatients (Tutkun *et al.* 1998), that a group of 30 people with dissociative identity disorder all had positive symptoms of schizophrenia (Kluft 1987), and that more positive symptoms occur in dissociative identity disorder than in schizophrenia (Ellason and Ross 1995)?

17 Do the strategies that people adopt to cope with trauma (such as dissociation and hypervigilance) confer vulnerability to psychosis (Morrison *et al.*, in press; Morrison and Petersen 2003)?

Integration of trauma research with psychological paradigms

Self-trauma model

18 Is the self-trauma model (Briere 2002) helpful in our efforts to understand the relationship between the symptoms of post-traumatic stress disorder, dissociative disorders and psychosis? This model, usually applied to post-traumatic stress disorder, dissociative disorders and borderline personality disorder, understands that fragmented abuse memories and flashbacks are attempts to integrate the trauma, while avoidance and numbing strategies (such as dissociation and substance abuse) are attempts to regulate the affect triggered in this process.

Psychodynamic model

19 Are some trauma-based hallucinations flashbacks that are projected into the present external world as a defence against re-experiencing the pain in the past (Read *et al.* 2003)?

20 Are some delusions attempts to explain these trauma-based hallucinations in a way that, however distorted and dysfunctional, serves a defensive function of not having to remember the original reality-based trauma?

Cognitive model

21   Can research into the psychological processes underlying paranoid delusions (Bentall 2003; Bentall *et al.* 2001; Freeman *et al.* 2002; Garety *et al.* 2001; see also Chapters 14 and 20), with its focus on our need to develop causal explanations (even inaccurate ones) rather than tolerate the anxiety of not knowing, and its emphasis on external attributions for negative events as a defence against depression, help us understand trauma-based delusions? Might cognitive models also help us understand the psychological processes by which trauma is linked to hallucinations (Birchwood *et al.* 2000; Garety *et al.* 2001; Morrison *et al.*, in press; Morrison and Petersen 2003)?

The 'traumagenic neurodevelopmental' model

22   What does it mean that the heightened sensitivity to stressors found in 'schizophrenia' consists, for many patients, of long-lasting neurodevelopmental changes to the brain caused by trauma in the early years of life? The evidence for this is that all the structural and functional differences between the brains of 'schizophrenics'and 'normal' adults are the same differences found between young children who have been traumatized and those who have not. These include: overactivity of the hypothalamic–adrenal–pituitary axis; dopamine, serotonin and norepinephrine abnormalities; and structural differences such as hippocampal damage, cerebral atrophy, ventricular enlargements and reversed cerebral asymmetry. The same differences are found between children with and without childhood-onset schizophrenia (Read *et al.* 2001b).

23   Can the traumagenic neurodevelopmental model also explain some of the cognitive impairments associated with schizophrenia, which are also found in abused children (Lysaker *et al.* 2001b; Read *et al.* 2001b), such as deficits in verbal functioning (Heinrichs and Zakzanis 1998) and intellectual decline during childhood (Kremen *et al.* 1998)?

24   What does it mean that many of the effects of trauma on the developing brain, which are so similar to the dysfunctions found in the brains of adult and childhood 'schizophrenics', are also found in other trauma-based symptom clusters including post-traumatic stress disorder and dissociative disorders (Ito *et al.* 1993; Sapolsky 2000)?

Gender differences

25   Can research on the effects of trauma on the developing brains of children (Perry *et al.* 1995) shed some light on why men experience more negative symptoms and have earlier onset of 'schizophrenia' than women (see Chapter 13)?

Assessment, formulation and treatment planning

26 Why does most sexual or physical abuse cases (typically more than 70%) remain unidentified by mental health staff, in both child (Lanktree *et al.* 1991) and adult psychiatric services (Agar *et al.* 2002; Briere and Zaidi 1989; Cascardi *et al.* 1996; Craine *et al.* 1988; Goodwin *et al.* 1988; Jacobson and Richardson 1987; Lipschitz *et al.* 1996; Lothian and Read 2002; McGregor 2003; Read and Fraser 1998a; Rose *et al.* 1991; Wurr and Partridge 1996)?

27 Is the identification of psychological abuse and neglect any better (Thompson and Kaplan 1999)?

28 Why is the response of mental health services when abuse is disclosed so often inadequate (McGregor 2003; Nelson and Phillips 2001), specifically in terms of offering information, support or treatment, or considering reporting to legal or protection agencies (Agar and Read 2002; Eilenberg *et al.* 1996; Read and Fraser 1998b; Trojan 1994)?

29 Why are people diagnosed psychotic or schizophrenic asked about abuse even less often than other patients (Read and Fraser 1998a; Young *et al.* 2001), and less likely to receive an adequate response when they do disclose abuse (Agar and Read 2002; Read and Fraser 1998b)?

30 Why are staff with a strong bio-genetic orientation less likely than their colleagues to ask people diagnosed schizophrenic about abuse (Young *et al.* 2001), and why are psychiatrists less likely than other staff to respond adequately to disclosures of abuse by their clients (Agar and Read 2002)?

31 What kind of assessments, policies and training programmes will remedy the poor inquiry and response rates in general, and for psychotic people in particular (Briere 1999; Cavanagh *et al.* in press; Read 2000; Read, forthcoming; Young *et al.* 2001)?

Treatment

32 What are the implications for establishing therapeutic relationships of findings that people who hear voices (Jones *et al.* 2003) and users of mental health services (Lothian and Read 2002) often relate their psychotic experiences to child abuse, but that mental health staff appear less willing to make that connection (Lothian and Read 2002)?

33 What treatments are helpful for people who experience psychosis and have suffered child abuse (Goodman *et al.* 1997; Harris and Landis 1997; Nelson and Phillips 2001; Read and Ross 2003; Rosenberg *et al.* 2001)?

34 Will trauma models for abuse survivors in general (Briere 2002; Courtois 1991; Herman 1992) suffice, or (Read and Ross 2003) do we

need to integrate the psycho-social treatments shown, elsewhere in this book, to be effective with hallucinations and delusions?

35 How valuable is a group approach (Heins *et al.* 1990; Herder and Redner 1991; Talbot *et al.* 1998)?

Economics

36 How much money would be saved by providing timely, appropriate help for child abuse survivors (psychotic or otherwise) in the mental health system (Franey *et al.* 2001; Newmann *et al.* 1998)?

Prevention

37 What are the implications for the prevention of psychosis (see Chapter 18)?

The authors do not agree on the answers to all these questions. Many of them are unanswerable because of a lack of research. We do agree about the urgent need for researchers, clinicians, and managers and funders of mental health agencies to address these questions. They have been ignored long enough.

REFERENCES

Abraham, K. ([1907] 1955). On the significance of sexual trauma in childhood for the symptomatolgy of dementia praecox. In K. Abraham and H. Abraham (eds) *Clinical Papers and Essays on Psychoanalysis.* New York: Brunner-Mazel.

Agar, K. and Read, J. (2002). What happens when people disclose sexual or physical abuse to staff at a community mental health centre? *International Journal of Mental Health Nursing* 11: 70–9.

Agar, K. *et al.* (2002). Identification of abuse histories in a community mental health centre. *Journal of Mental Health* 11: 533–43.

Ambelas, A. (1992). Preschizophrenics: adding to the evidence, sharpening the focus. *British Journal of Psychiatry* 31: 401–44.

American Psychiatric Association (1994). *Diagnostic and Statistical Manual of Mental Disorders,* 4th edn. Washington, DC: APA.

Barker-Collo, S. and Read, J. (2003). Models of response to childhood sexual abuse. *Trauma, Violence and Abuse* 4: 95–111.

Beck, J. and van der Kolk, B. (1987). Reports of childhood incest and current behavior of chronically hospitalized psychotic women. *American Journal of Psychiatry* 144: 1474–6.

Belkin, D. *et al.* (1994). Psychopathology and history of sexual abuse. *Journal of Interpersonal Violence* 9: 535–47.

Bentall, R. (2003). On the paranoid world view. In R. Bentall, *Madness Explained: Psychosis and Human Nature*. London: Penguin.

Bentall, R. *et al.* (2001). Persecutory delusions: a review and theoretical integration. *Clinical Psychology Review* 21: 1143–92.

Berenbaum, H. (1999). Peculiarity and reported child maltreatment. *Psychiatry* 62: 21–35.

Birchwood, M. *et al.* (2000). The power and omnipotence of voices: subordination and entrapment by voices and significant others. *Psychological Medicine* 30: 337–44.

Bleuler, M. (1978). *The Schizophrenic Disorders* (translated by S. Clemens). New Haven, CT: Yale University Press.

Boney-McCoy, S. and Finkelhor, D. (1996). Is youth victimization related to trauma symptoms and depression after controlling for prior symptoms and family relationships? *Journal of Consulting and Clinical Psychology* 64: 1406–16.

Briere, J. (1999). Psychological trauma and the psychiatric emergency room. *New Directions in Mental Health Services* 82: 43–51.

Briere, J. (2002). Treating adult survivors of severe childhood abuse and neglect. In J. Myers *et al.* (eds) *ASPAC Handbook on Child Maltreatment*, 2nd edn. Newbury Park, CA: Sage.

Briere, J. and Zaidi, L. (1989). Sexual abuse histories and sequelae in female psychiatric emergency room patients. *American Journal of Psychiatry* 146: 1602–6.

Briere, J. *et al.* (1997). Lifetime victimization history, demographics, and clinical status in female psychiatric emergency room patients. *Journal of Nervous and Mental Disease* 185: 95–101.

Brown, G. and Anderson, B. (1991). Psychiatric morbidity in adult inpatients with childhood histories of sexual and physical abuse. *American Journal of Psychiatry* 148: 55–61.

Bryer, J. *et al.* (1987). Childhood sexual and physical abuse as factors in psychiatric illness. *American Journal of Psychiatry* 144: 1426–30.

Bushnell, J. *et al.* (1992). Long-term effects of intrafamilial sexual abuse in childhood. *Acta Psychiatrica Scandinavica* 85: 136–42.

Butler, R. *et al.* (1996). Positive symptoms of psychosis in PTSD. *Biological Psychiatry* 39: 839–44.

Cairns, S. (1998). MMPI-2 and Rorschach assessments of adults physically abused as children. Unpublished doctoral dissertation, University of Manitoba.

Cannon, M. *et al.* (2001). Predictors of later schizophrenia and affective psychoses among attendees at a child psychiatry department. *British Journal of Psychiatry* 178: 420–6.

Cannon, M. *et al.* (2002). Evidence for early-childhood, pan-developmental impairment specific to schizophreniform disorder. *Archives of General Psychiatry* 59: 449–56.

Carlin, A. and Ward, N. (1992). Subtypes of psychiatric inpatient women who have been sexually assaulted. *Journal of Nervous and Mental Disease* 180: 392–7.

Carmen, E. *et al.* (1984) Victims of violence and psychiatric illness. *American Journal of Psychiatry* 141: 378–83.

Cascardi, M. *et al.* (1996) Physical aggression against psychiatric inpatients by family members and partners. *Psychiatric Services* 47: 531–3.

Cavanagh, M. *et al.* (in press). Sexual abuse inquiry and response: A New Zealand training programme. *New Zealand Journal of Psychology.*

Cheasty, M. *et al.* (2002). Child sexual abuse: A predictor of persistent depression in adult rape and sexual assault victims. *Journal of Mental Health* 11: 79–84.

Chu, J. and Dill, D. (1990). Dissociative symptoms in relation to childhood physical and sexual abuse. *American Journal of Psychiatry* 147: 887–92.

Cloitre, M. *et al.* (1996). Childhood abuse and subsequent sexual assault among female inpatients. *Journal of Traumatic Stress* 9: 473–82.

Cloitre, M. *et al.* (2001). Consequences of childhood abuse among psychiatric inpatients. *Journal of Traumatic Stress* 14: 47–60.

Cohen, Y. *et al.* (1996). Physical and sexual abuse and their relation to psychiatric disorder and suicidal behavior among adolescents who are psychiatrically hospitalised. *Journal of Child Psychology and Psychiatry and Allied Disciplines* 37: 989–93.

Cole, C. (1988). Routine comprehensive inquiry for abuse. *Clinical Social Work Journal* 16: 33–42.

Courtois, C. (1991). Theory, sequencing, and strategy in treating adult survivors. In J. Briere (ed.) *Treating Victims of Child Sexual Abuse.* New York: Jossey-Bass.

Coverdale, J. and Turbott, S. (2000). Sexual and physical abuse of chronically ill psychiatric outpatients with a matched sample of medical outpatients. *Journal of Nervous and Mental Disease* 188: 440–5.

Craine, L. *et al.* (1988). Prevalence of a history of sexual abuse among female psychiatric patients in a state hospital system. *Hospital and Community Psychiatry* 39: 300–4.

Darves-Bornoz, J.-M. *et al.* (1995). Sexual victimization in women with schizophrenia and bipolar disorder. *Social Psychiatry and Psychiatric Epidemiology* 30: 78–84.

Davidson, J. and McNamara, L. (1999). Systems that silence. In J. Breckenridge and L. Laing (eds) *Innovative Responses to Sexual and Domestic Violence.* Sydney: Allen and Unwin.

Davies-Netzley, S. *et al.* (1996). Childhood abuse as a precursor to homelessness for homeless women with severe mental illness. *Violence and Victims* 11: 129–42.

Dill, D. *et al.* (1991). The reliability of abuse history report. *Comprehensive Psychiatry* 32: 166–9.

Eilenberg, J. *et al.* (1996). Quality and use of trauma histories obtained from psychiatric outpatients through mandated inquiry. *Psychiatric Services* 47: 165–9.

Ellason, J. and Ross, C. (1995). Positive and negative symptoms in dissociative disorder and schizophrenia. *Journal of Nervous and Mental Disease* 183: 236–41.

Ellason, J. and Ross, C. (1997). Childhood trauma and psychiatric symptoms. *Psychological Reports* 80: 447–50.

Ellason, J. *et al.* (1996). Lifetime Axis I and II comorbidity and childhood trauma history in dissociative identity disorder. *Psychiatry* 59: 255–66.

Ellenson, G. (1985). Detecting a history of incest. *Social Casework*, November, pp. 525–32.

Ensink, B. (1992). *Confusing Realities.* Amsterdam: Vu University Press.

Famularo, R. *et al.* (1992). Psychiatric diagnoses of maltreated children. *Journal of the American Academy of Child and Adolescent Psychiatry* 31: 863–7.

Fehon, D. *et al.* (2001). Gender differences in violence exposure and violence risk among adolescent inpatients. *Journal of Nervous and Mental Disease* 189: 532–40.

Frame, L. and Morrison, A. (2001). Causes of PTSD in psychotic patients. *Archives of General Psychiatry* 58: 305–6.

Franey, K. *et al.* (eds) (2001). *The Cost of Child Maltreatment*. San Diego, CA: Family Violence Sexual Assault Institute.

Freeman, D. *et al.* (2002). A cognitive model of persecutory delusions. *British Journal of Clinical Psychology* 41: 331–47.

Friedman, S. and Harrison, G. (1984). Sexual histories, attitudes and behavior of schizophrenic and normal women. *Archives of Sexual Behaviour* 13: 555–67.

Friedman, S. *et al.* (2002). The incidence and influence of early traumatic life events in patients with panic disorder. *Anxiety Disorders* 16: 259–72.

Garety, P. *et al.* (2001). A cognitive model of the positive symptoms of psychosis. *Psychological Medicine* 31: 189–95.

Goff, D. and Brotman, A. (1991a). Self-reports of childhood abuse in chronically psychotic patients. *Psychiatry Research* 37: 73–80.

Goff, D. *et al.* (1991b). The delusion of possession in chronically psychotic patients. *Journal of Nervous and Mental Disease* 179: 567–71.

Goodman, L. *et al.* (1995). Physical and sexual assault prevalence among episodically homeless women with serious mental illness. *American Journal of Orthopsychiatry* 65: 468–78.

Goodman, L. *et al.* (1997). Physical and sexual assault history in women with serious mental illness. *Schizophrenia Bulletin* 23: 685–6.

Goodman, L. *et al.* (1999). Reliability of reports of violent victimization and PTSD among men and women with serious mental illness. *Journal of Traumatic Stress* 12: 587–99.

Goodman, L. *et al.* (2001). Recent victimization in women and men with severe mental illness. *Journal of Traumatic Stress* 14: 615–32.

Goodwin, J. *et al.* (1988). Reporting by adult psychiatric patients of childhood sexual abuse. *American Journal of Psychiatry* 145: 1183.

Granville-Grossman, K. (1966). Early bereavement and schizophrenia. *British Journal of Psychiatry* 112: 1027–39.

Greenfield, S. *et al.* (1994). Childhood abuse in first-episode psychosis. *British Journal of Psychiatry* 164: 831–4.

Hammersley, P. *et al.* (2003). Childhood traumas and hallucinations in bipolar affective disorder. *British Journal of Psychiatry* 182: 543–7.

Harris, M. and Landis, C. (1997). *Sexual Abuse in the Lives of Women Diagnosed with Serious Mental Illness*. London: Harwood.

Hart, L. *et al.* (1989). Effects of sexual and physical abuse. *Child Psychiatry and Human Development* 20: 49–57.

Heads, T. *et al.* (1997). Childhood experiences of patients with schizophrenia and a history of violence. *Criminal Behaviour and Mental Health* 7: 117–30.

Heinrichs, R. and Zakzanis, K. (1998). Neurocognitive deficit in schizophrenia. *Neuropsychology* 12: 426–45.

Heins, T. *et al.* (1990). Persisting hallucinations following childhood sexual abuse. *Australian and New Zealand Journal of Psychiatry* 24: 561–5.

Herder, D. and Redner, L. (1991). The treatment of childhood sexual abuse in chronically mentally ill adults. *Health Social Work* 16: 50–7.

Herman, J. (1992). *Trauma and Recovery*. New York: Basic Books.

Holowka, D. *et al.* (2003). Childhood abuse and dissociative symptoms in adult schizophrenia. *Schizophrenia Research* 60: 87–90.

Honig, A. *et al.* (1998). Auditory hallucinations. *Journal of Nervous and Mental Disease* 186: 646–51.

Hunter, J. (1991). A comparison of psychosocial maladjustment of adult males and females sexually molested as children. *Journal of Interpersonal Violence* 6: 205–17.

Ito, Y. *et al.* (1993). Increased prevalence of electrophysiological abnormalities in children with psychological, physical, and sexual abuse. *Journal of Neuropsychiatry* 5: 401–8.

Jacobson, A. and Herald, C. (1990). The relevance of childhood sexual abuse to adult psychiatric inpatient care. *Hospital and Community Psychiatry* 41: 154–8.

Jacobson, A. and Richardson, B. (1987). Assault experiences of 100 psychiatric inpatients. *American Journal of Psychiatry* 144: 908–13.

Janssen, I. *et al.* (in press). Childhood abuse as a risk factor for psychotic experiences. *Acta Psychiatrica Scandinavica*.

Jones, P. *et al.* (1994). Child developmental risk factors for adult schizophrenia in the British 1946 birth cohort. *Lancet* 344: 1398–402.

Jones, S. *et al.* (2003). A Q-methodological study of hearing voices: a preliminary exploration of voice hearers' understanding of their experiences. *Psychology and Psychotherapy: Research and Practice* 76: 189–209.

Kahlbaum, K. ([1874] 1973). *Catatonia*. Baltimore, MD: Johns Hopkins University Press.

Kendler, K. *et al.* (2000). Childhood sexual abuse and adult psychiatric and substance use disorders in women. *Archives of General Psychiatry* 57: 953–9.

Kessler, R. *et al.* (1995). Posttraumatic stress disorder in the national comorbidity survey. *Archives of General Psychiatry* 52: 1048–60.

Kirby, J. *et al.* (1993). Correlates of dissociative symptomatology in patients with physical and sexual abuse histories. *Comprehensive Psychiatry* 34: 258–63.

Kluft, R. (1987). First-rank symptoms as a diagnostic clue to multiple personality disorder. *American Journal of Psychiatry* 144: 293–8.

Kohan, M. *et al.* (1987). Hospitalized children with history of sexual abuse. *American Journal of Orthopsychiatry* 57: 258–64.

Kremen, W. *et al.* (1998). IQ decline during childhood and adult psychotic symptoms in a community sample. *American Journal of Psychiatry* 155: 672–7.

Lanktree, C. *et al.* (1991). Incidence and impact of sexual abuse in a child outpatient sample. *Child Abuse and Neglect* 15: 447–53.

Lidz, R. and Lidz, T. (1949). The family environment of schizophrenic patients. *American Journal of Psychiatry* 106: 332–45.

Lipschitz, D. *et al.* (1996). Prevalence and characteristics of physical and sexual abuse among psychiatric outpatients. *Psychiatric Services* 47: 189–91.

Lipschitz, D. (1999a). Perceived abuse and neglect as risk factors for suicidal behavior in adolescent inpatients. *Journal of Nervous and Mental Disease* 187: 32–9.

Lipschitz, D. (1999b). PTSD in hospitalized adolescents. *Journal of American Academy of Child and Adolescent Psychiatry* 38: 385–93.

Lipschitz, D. (2000). Gender differences in the associations between posttraumatic stress symptoms and problematic substance use in psychiatric inpatient adolescents. *Journal of Nervous and Mental Disease* 188: 349–56.

Livingston, R. (1987). Sexually and physically abused children. *Journal of the American Academy of Child and Adolescent Psychiatry* 26: 413–15.

Lobel, C. (1992). Relationship between childhood sexual abuse and borderline personality disorder in women psychiatric inpatients. *Journal of Child Sexual Abuse* 1: 63–80.

Lothian, J. and Read, J. (2002). Asking about abuse during mental health assessments: clients' views and experiences. *New Zealand Journal of Psychology* 31: 98–103.

Lundberg-Love, P. *et al.* (1992). The long-term consequences of childhood incestuous victimization upon adult women's psychological symptomatology. *Journal of Child Sexual Abuse* 1: 81–102.

Lysaker, P. *et al.* (2001a). Childhood sexual trauma and psychosocial functioning in adults with schizophrenia. *Psychiatric Services* 52: 1485–8.

Lysaker, P. *et al.* (2001b). Neurocognitive and symptom correlates of self-reported childhood sexual abuse in schizophrenia spectrum disorders. *Annals of Clinical Psychiatry* 13: 89–92.

Malaspina, D. *et al.* (2001). Traumatic brain injury and schizophrenia in members of schizophrenic and bipolar disorder pedigrees. *American Journal of Psychiatry* 158: 440–6.

Malmberg, A. *et al.* (1998). Premorbid adjustment and personality in people with schizophrenia. *British Journal of Psychiatry* 172: 308–13.

Margo, G. and McLees, E. (1991). Further evidence of the significance of a childhood abuse history in psychiatric inpatients. *Comprehensive Psychiatry* 32: 62–6.

McGorry, P. *et al.* (1991). PTSD following recent-onset psychosis. *Journal of Nervous and Mental Disease* 179: 253–8.

McGregor, K. (2003). Therapy – a two-way process: women survivors of child sexual abuse describe their therapy experiences. Unpublished doctoral dissertation, University of Auckland.

Metcalfe, M. *et al.* (1990). Childhood sexual experiences reported by male psychiatric inpatients. *Psychological Medicine* 20: 25–9.

Miller, L. and Finnerty, M. (1996). Sexuality, pregnancy, and childrearing among women with schizophrenia-spectrum disorders. *Psychiatric Services* 47: 502–6.

Morrison, A. and Petersen, T. (2003). Trauma and metacognition as predictors of predisposition to hallucinations. *Behavioral and Cognitive Psychotherapy* 31: 235–46.

Morrison, A. *et al.* (in press). Relationships between trauma and psychosis: a review and integration. *British Journal of Clinical Psychology*.

Moskowitz, A. (in press). 'Scared stiff': catatonia as an evolutionary-based fear response. *Psychological Review*.

Muenzenmaier, K. *et al.* (1993). Childhood abuse and neglect among women outpatients with chronic mental illness. *Hospital and Community Psychiatry* 44: 666–70.

Mueser, K. *et al.* (1998). Trauma and PTSD in severe mental illness. *Journal of Consulting and Clinical Psychology* 66: 493–9.

Mueser, K. *et al.* (2002). Trauma, PTSD, and the course of severe mental illness: an interactive model. *Psychiatric Research* 53: 123–43.

Mullen, P. *et al.* (1993). Childhood sexual abuse and mental health in adult life. *British Journal of Psychiatry* 163: 721–32.

Mullen, P. *et al.* (1996). The long-term impact of the physical, emotional, and sexual abuse of children. *Child Abuse and Neglect* 20: 7–21.

Nelson, S. and Phillips, A. (2001). *Beyond Trauma: Mental Health Care Needs of Women Who Have Survived Childhood Sexual Abuse.* Edinburgh: Edinburgh Association for Mental Health.

Neria, Y. *et al.* (2002). Trauma exposure and PTSD in psychosis. *Journal of Consulting and Clinical Psychology* 70: 246–51.

Newmann, J. *et al.* (1998). Abuse histories, severe mental illness, and the cost of care. In B. Levin *et al.* (eds) *Women's Mental Health Services.* Thousand Oaks, CA: Sage.

Nurcombe, B. *et al.* (1996). Dissociative hallucinosis and allied conditions. In F. Volkmar (ed.) *Psychoses and Pervasive Developmental Disorders in Childhood and Adolescence.* Washington, DC: American Psychiatric Press.

Offen *et al.* (2003). Is reported childhood sexual abuse associated with psychopathological characteristics of patients who experience auditory hallucinations? *Child Abuse & Neglect* 27: 919–27.

Palmer, R. *et al.* (1994). Childhood sexual experiences with adults. *British Journal of Psychiatry* 165: 675–9.

Perkins, R. (1982). Catatonia: the ultimate response to fear? *Australian and New Zealand Journal of Psychiatry* 16: 282–7.

Perry, B. *et al.* (1995). Childhood trauma, the neurobiology of adaptation, and 'use-dependent' development of the brain. *Infant Mental Health Journal* 16: 271–91.

Pettigrew, J. and Burcham, J. (1997). Effects of childhood sexual abuse in adult female psychiatric patients. *Australian and New Zealand Journal of Psychiatry* 31: 208–13.

Pollock, H. *et al.* (1939). *Hereditary and Environmental Factors in the Causation of Manic-Depressive Psychoses and Dementia Praecox.* Ithaca, NY: State Hospital Press.

Putnam, F. and Trickett, P. (1997). Psychobiological effects of sexual abuse. In R. Yehuda and A. McFarlane (eds) Psychobiology of PTSD. *Annals of the New York Academy of Sciences* 821: 150–9.

Ragan, P. and McGlashan, T. (1986). Childhood parental death and adult psychopathology. *American Journal of Psychiatry* 143: 153–7.

Read, J. (1997). Child abuse and psychosis. *Professional Psychology: Research and Practice* 28: 448–56.

Read, J. (1998). Child abuse and severity of disturbance among adult psychiatric inpatients. *Child Abuse and Neglect* 22: 359–68.

Read, J. (2000). The role of psychologists in the assessment of psychosis. In H. Love and W. Whittaker (eds) *Practice Issues for Clinical and Applied Psychologists in New Zealand,* 2nd edn. Wellington: New Zealand Psychological Society.

Read, J. (forthcoming). Breaking the silence: Learning why, when and how to ask about trauma. In W. Larkin and A. Morrison (eds) *Understanding Trauma and Psychosis: New Horizons for Theory and Therapy.* Hove: Brunner-Routledge.

Read, J. and Argyle, N. (1999). Hallucinations, delusions, and thought disorder among adult psychiatric inpatients with a history of child abuse. *Psychiatric Services* 50: 1467–72.

Read, J. and Fraser, A. (1998a). Abuse histories of psychiatric inpatients. *Psychiatric Services* 49: 355–9.

Read, J. and Fraser, A. (1998b). Staff response to abuse histories of psychiatric inpatients. *Australian and New Zealand Journal of Psychiatry* 32: 206–13.

Read, J. and Ross, C. (2003). Psychological trauma and psychosis. *Journal of the American Academy of Psychoanalysis and Dynamic Psychiatry* 31: 247–68.

Read, J. *et al.* (2001a). Assessing suicidality in adults. *Professional Psychology: Research and Practice* 32: 367–72.

Read, J. *et al.* (2001b). The contribution of early traumatic events to schizophrenia in some patients. *Psychiatry* 64: 319–45.

Read, J. *et al.* (2003). Sexual and physical abuse during childhood and adulthood as predictors of hallucinations, delusions and thought disorder. *Psychology and Psychotherapy: Theory, Research and Practice* 76: 11–22.

Resnick, S. *et al.* (2003). Trauma and PTSD in people with schizophrenia. *Journal of Abnormal Psychology* 112: 415–23.

Ritsher, J. *et al.* (1997). A survey on issues in the lives of women with severe mental illness. *Psychiatric Services* 48: 1273–82.

Robins, L. (1966). *Deviant Children Grown Up*. London: Williams & Wilkins.

Rose, S. *et al.* (1991). Undetected abuse among intensive case management clients. *Hospital and Community Psychiatry* 42: 499–503.

Rosenberg, S. *et al.* (2001). Developing effective treatments for posttraumatic disorders among people with severe mental illness. *Psychiatric Services* 52: 1453–61.

Ross, C. and Joshi, S. (1992). Schneiderian symptoms and childhood trauma in the general population. *Comprehensive Psychiatry* 33: 269–73.

Ross, C. *et al.* (1994). Childhood abuse and positive symptoms of schizophrenia. *Hospital and Community Psychiatry* 45: 489–91.

Russell, D. (1983). The incidence and prevalence of intrafamilial and extrafamilial sexual abuse of female children. *Child Abuse and Neglect* 7: 133–46.

Russell, D. *et al.* (1988). The long-term effects of incestuous abuse. In G. Wyatt and G. Powell (eds) *Lasting Effects of Child Sexual Abuse*. London: Sage.

Sansonnet-Hayden, H. *et al.* (1987). Sexual abuse and psychopathology in hospitalized adolescents. *Journal of the American Academy of Child Adolescent Psychiatry* 26: 753–7.

Sapolsky, R. (2000). Glucocorticoids and hippocampal atrophy in neuropsychiatric disorders. *Archives of General Psychiatry* 57: 925–35.

Sautter, F. *et al.* (1999). PTSD and comorbid psychotic disorder. *Journal of Traumatic Stress* 12: 73–88.

Saxe, G. *et al.* (1993). Dissociative disorders in psychiatric inpatients. *American Journal of Psychiatry* 150: 1037–42.

Scott, R. and Stone, D. (1986). MMPI profile constellations in incest families. *Journal of Consulting and Clinical Psychology* 54: 364–8.

Shaw, K. *et al.* (2001). The aetiology of postpsychotic PTSD following a psychotic episode. *Journal of Traumatic Stress* 15: 39–47.

Shearer, S. *et al.* (1990). Frequency and correlates of childhood sexual and physical abuse histories in adult female borderline inpatients. *American Journal of Psychiatry* 147: 214–16.

Stampfer, H. (1990). Negative symptoms: a cumulative trauma stress disorder? *Australian and New Zealand Journal of Psychiatry* 24: 1–12.

Startup, M. (1999). Schizotypy, dissociative experiences and childhood abuse. *British Journal of Clinical Psychology* 38: 333–44.

Swett, C. and Halpert, M. (1994). High rates of alcohol problems and history of physical and sexual abuse among women inpatients. *American Journal of Drug and Alcohol Abuse* 20: 263–73.

Swett, C. *et al.* (1990). Sexual and physical abuse histories and psychiatric symptoms among male psychiatric outpatients. *American Journal of Psychiatry* 147: 632–36.

Switzer, G. *et al.* (1999). PTSD and service utilization among urban mental health centre clients. *Journal of Traumatic Stress* 12: 25–39.

Talbot, N. *et al.* (1998). Women's safety in recovery: group therapy for patients with a history of childhood sexual abuse. *Psychiatric Services* 49: 213–17.

Thompson, A. and Kaplan, C. (1999). Emotionally abused children presenting to child psychiatry clinics. *Child Abuse and Neglect* 23: 191–6.

Trojan, O. (1994). Sexual experiences of psychotic patients. *International Journal of Adolescent Mental Health* 7: 209–17.

Tsai, M. *et al.* (1979). Childhood molestation. *Journal of Abnormal Psychology* 88: 407–17.

Tuktun, H. *et al.* (1998). Frequency of dissociative disorders among psychiatric inpatients in a Turkish university clinic. *American Journal of Psychiatry* 155: 800–5.

Windle, M. *et al.* (1995). Physical and sexual abuse and associated mental disorders among alcoholic inpatients. *American Journal of Psychiatry* 152: 1322–8.

Wurr, J. and Partridge, I. (1996). The prevalence of a history of childhood sexual abuse in an acute adult inpatient population. *Child Abuse and Neglect* 20: 867–72.

Wyatt, G. (1985). The sexual abuse of Afro-American and white-American women in childhood. *Child Abuse and Neglect* 9: 507–19.

Young, M. *et al.* (2001). Evaluating and overcoming barriers to taking abuse histories. *Professional Psychology: Research and Practice* 32: 407–14.

Chapter 17

Unhappy families

John Read, Fred Seymour and Loren R. Mosher

Our question is: are the experiences and behaviour that psychiatrists take as symptoms and signs of schizophrenia more socially intelligible than has come to be supposed?

(Laing and Esterson 1970: 12)

If we look at some experience and behaviour without reference to family interactions, they may appear comparatively socially senseless, but if we look at the same experience and behaviour in their original family context they are liable to make more sense.

(Laing and Esterson 1970: 26)

HONESTY

Few people doubt that our emotional well-being as adults has a lot to do with how we were raised as children. However, the possible role of families in the causation of 'schizophrenia' has become a taboo subject. Although relatives are told that changing their behaviour can help prevent relapse, they are also informed that they couldn't possibly have had anything to do with the development of the 'illness' in the first place. The research, however, paints a different picture.

When something goes badly wrong for our sons or daughters, for most of us our first reaction is to wonder what *we* might have done wrong. What is often needed is an honest discussion based on our own circumstances and feelings, not a pre-packaged answer designed to sweep all those circumstances and all our feelings under the carpet. It is unhelpful, therefore, to try and convince families that they couldn't possibly have contributed to the problem. Many families do not believe this, even after receiving 'educational' programmes specifically designed to get them to adopt this illness model (see Chapter 23). Many families see through the contradictory message, 'It's not in any way your fault but we want you to change your behaviour so it doesn't happen again'. It can be frightening to people to imply that the possibility that they might have played a role in bringing about the problem is so awful that it must never be talked about.

Although every family will be different, the research discussed here is vitally important in helping families consider what might have gone wrong in their own family and, most importantly, what might usefully be tried to make things better for all concerned. Before summarizing the research showing that many families are indeed part of the picture when it comes to understanding the causes of 'schizophrenia', we must discuss how such an obvious, common-sense approach became such a taboo subject.

FEAR OF 'FAMILY-BLAMING'

A common reason for excluding family research as admissible evidence in the search for causal factors is that relationships between relatives and professionals are important (which is true) and that these relationships will inevitably be damaged if we discuss whether families might have contributed to the problems of the 'patient' (which is not true). Research investigating this possibility is often denigrated as 'family-blaming' (Johnstone 1999).

What is missing from the 'family-blaming' notion is discussion of what the word 'blame' actually means. This complex issue is reduced, by proponents of a narrow biological model, to the idea that if any family factors are identified, then the parents would be morally responsible and, therefore, bad parents. However, our struggles as parents are best understood not from some simplistic moral notion of 'badness', but in terms of multiple factors including stressors on the whole family (such as poverty), conflicts within the parental relationship, isolation, lack of education about parenting skills, and intergenerational cycles of unhelpful parenting.

Furthermore, for the past three decades the dominant model used to explain extreme distress and confusion in family members has been an illness paradigm (see Chapters 3–7). More specifically, the 'vulnerability-stress' model of schizophrenia has assumed that psycho-social stressors, such as unhelpful parenting styles, only have a causal role to the extent that they trigger off, exacerbate or accelerate the expression of an underlying genetic vulnerability. Those who reject the possibility that family factors might have a more direct causal role presume, wrongly, that the vulnerability must be biological or genetic in origin. It is this narrow version of the vulnerability-stress model that psychiatry's 'psycho-educational' programmes try to sell to parents (see Chapter 23). However, the originators of the vulnerability-stress model of schizophrenia stated that there is 'acquired vulnerability' which can be 'due to the influence of trauma, specific diseases, perinatal complications, family experiences, adolescent peer interactions, and other life events that either enhance or inhibit the development of subsequent disorder' (Zubin and Spring 1977: 109).

FAMILY INTERACTIONS AND RELAPSE

The largest body of research relating family issues to schizophrenia for the last 30 years has focused on the relationship between 'expressed emotion' and relapse. The term expressed emotion is a euphemism, designed to create an impression of neutrality. What it measures is far from neutral. Expressed emotion has three components: the *hostility* component measures global criticisms and rejection; the *criticism* component measures negative comments about what the 'patient' does, thinks or feels; and the *emotional over-involvement* component measures over-protectiveness, intrusiveness, emotional display, excessive praise, self-sacrifice and preoccupation (Vaughn and Leff 1976).

By 1992, a review reported on 23 studies (in 12 countries) of expressed emotion (EE) and relapse over 9 or 12 months. Twenty of these 23 studies found higher relapse rates in high EE than in low EE families. The median relapse rate was 21% in low EE and 48% in high EE families. In four studies with a follow-up period of 2 years, post-discharge the median relapse rates were 27% for low EE and 66% for high EE families (Kavanagh 1992). Two studies have found similar differences at 5 years and one at 8 years (Weardon *et al.* 2000). As the number of hours per week spent with high EE families increases, so does the relapse rate (Kavanagh 1992; Vaughn and Leff 1976).

Three other sources of evidence confirm these findings that, after someone has gone crazy, being on the receiving end of hostile criticism is not good for one's mental health: (1) the effectiveness of treatment programmes targeted at parental expressed emotion; (2) cultural variations; and (3) the effects of high expressed emotion in mental health professionals.

Programmes to decrease parental criticism, hostility and emotional over-involvement reduce relapse rates. A review of six studies calculated that while normal treatment (primarily medication) led to a 24-month relapse rate of 71%, the EE-targeted interventions led to a rate of just 33% (Kavanagh 1992).

There is great variation in the rates of high EE families between industrialized and developing countries. In Kavanagh's 1992 review, 718 of the 1325 families (54%) were high in expressed emotion. However, among rural Indian families of 'schizophrenics', only 8% were high in expressed emotion (Wig *et al.* 1987). This might help explain the much higher recovery rates found in developing countries (Castillo *et al.* 2003; see Chapter 5).

Several studies have found high expressed emotion in some mental health staff. Critical attitudes in staff are related to poor outcomes for both symptoms and quality of life (Snyder *et al.* 1994; Tattan and Tarrier 2000).

FAMILY INTERACTIONS BEFORE ONSET

The UCLA Family Project

Expressed emotion

Expressed emotion cannot be considered causative unless it precedes the 'illness'. This possibility has received far less attention than the role of families in relapse. When not ignored altogether, it is usually couched in terms of family factors merely hastening the timing of, or 'precipitating', the first episode rather than helping to cause the disorder itself.

Compelling evidence that expressed emotion precedes, and is predictive of, 'schizophrenia' comes from the UCLA Family Project, a 15-year prospective study (Doane *et al.* 1981; Goldstein 1987). The researchers noted that: 'It is sometimes implied that current interest in the family's role in the course of schizophrenia has little bearing on etiological issues', adding, however, that they find it difficult 'to view family life as so discontinuous across the life-span that those attributes of the family environment related to the onset of schizophrenia do not overlap with those associated with differential course after an initial episode' (Goldstein and Doane 1982: 693). Their thinking is consistent with earlier findings by the pioneers of research into the role of stressful events, including expressed emotion, in both relapse *and* onset. Birley and Brown (1970) had found that in the 3 weeks before admission, most 'schizophrenics' had experienced significant life events that were beyond their control. Leff and Vaughn (1980) found that episodes of schizophrenia (but not depression) are *predicted* by living in high EE families.

The importance of the UCLA Family Project lies in its power to address the 'chicken–egg' question that plagues all retrospective studies of people already diagnosed 'schizophrenic'. The parents of 64 troubled adolescents, none of whom had current or previous symptoms of psychosis, were tested for expressed emotion. Fifteen years later, the diagnoses for the adolescents (now adults) whose parents had both been rated low expressed emotion were: broad-spectrum schizophrenia, 6%; narrow-spectrum schizophrenia, 0%; definite diagnoses of schizophrenia, 0%. Where one parent had been high in expressed emotion, the results were: broad-spectrum, 37.5%; narrow-spectrum, 12.5%; definite schizophrenia, 0%. Where both parents had been high in expressed emotion, the rates were: broad-spectrum, 73%; narrow-spectrum, 45%; definite schizophrenia, 36% (Goldstein 1987). It has since been found that the parents of children with schizophrenia-spectrum disorders 'were more likely to direct harsh criticism toward the child than were parents of depressed children or parents of normal controls' (Hamilton *et al.* 1999).

Affective style

The UCLA Family Project also measured 'affective style' and 'communication deviance'. Affective Style (AS) has three sub-categories: personal criticism (e.g. 'You have an ugly, arrogant attitude'), guilt induction ('Most of our fights are because of you') and intrusiveness ('I know damn well that you agree with me though you refuse to admit it') (Diamond and Doane 1994). Intrusiveness here implies imagined knowledge of the other's thoughts or feelings, which is different from the emotional over-involvement component of expressed emotion.

After 15 years, the adolescents (now adults) from 'negative AS' families were twice as likely to have a diagnosable mental disorder as those from 'benign AS' families. The difference was even greater for schizophrenia. Of those from benign AS families, 4% had schizophrenic spectrum diagnoses, compared with 56% of those from negative AS families. None from the benign AS families but 16% from the negative AS families had a definite diagnosis of schizophrenia (Goldstein 1987).

Communication deviance

While expressed emotion and affective style are concerned with the emotional content of attitudes and behaviours, communication deviance (CD) measures the tendency to speak in a way that makes shared meaning difficult or impossible by failing to establish a shared focus. Communication deviance does not seem to be related to expressed emotion or affective style (Nugter *et al.* 1997a). As is the case with expressed emotion and affective style, parental communication deviance is related to probability of relapse (Velligan *et al.* 1996).

The UCLA study rated parental communication deviance as high, intermediate or low. At the 15 year follow-up, the figures for the broader schizophrenia spectrum diagnoses were: low CD, 9%; intermediate CD, 26%; high CD, 50%. For the narrower definition of the spectrum, the findings were: low CD, 0%; intermediate CD, 11%; high CD, 20%. None from the low CD group but 11% of the intermediate and 10% of the high CD group had definite diagnoses of schizophrenia. When siblings were included, 70% of high CD families had an offspring with a broad-spectrum diagnosis and 15% had a definite schizophrenia diagnosis (Goldstein 1987).

A powerful interaction between communication deviance and affective style emerged. After 15 years, none of the sons and daughters of families rated as benign on affective style and low on communication deviance had any diagnosable mental disorders. All of the offspring of families rated as negative for affective style and high on communication deviance had at least one such diagnosis, and 89% of these were broad-spectrum schizophrenia diagnoses, with 33% receiving narrow-spectrum diagnoses and 22%

having definite diagnoses of schizophrenia. Doane and colleagues spelt out the various scenarios:

> Parents with High CD may be experienced by their adolescent as a chronic source of vague and confusing messages. If, in this setting, the adolescent also experiences critical, intrusive, or guilt-inducing affect from his parents, he would have little recourse through communication with them for exploring, clarifying or correcting his feelings of unworthiness, rejection, or isolation. A second adolescent would have parents poorly focussed in their communication but providing compensatory emotional support. A third teenager, one whose parents were hostile but clear thinking, would at least have the avenue of functional communication as a means of understanding and adapting to their negative posture.
>
> (Doane *et al.* 1981: 685)

The early studies

Goldstein and Doane were not the first to study the communication of families of 'schizophrenics'. In 1956, Gregory Bateson, Don Jackson, Jay Haley and John Weakland (the 'MRI Group') published 'Toward a theory of schizophrenia'. Unenthusiastic about either biological psychiatry or intrapsychic psychology, they focused on social context. Their aim was to understand the unusual behaviour of 'schizophrenics' in terms of communication patterns learned within their families, and thereby develop an effective model of family therapy. They described the 'Double-Bind' situation whereby conflicting messages render an effective response, or clarification, impossible (Bateson *et al.* 1956). Their case studies are complex, thoughtful and convincing (e.g. Haley 1959).

They were not at all in the business of blaming parents: 'The group prefers an emphasis on circular systems of interpersonal relations to a more conventional emphasis upon the behavior of individuals alone or single sequences in the interaction' (Bateson *et al.* 1962: 157). They were also among the first to focus on intergenerational cycles of family difficulties.

In 1949, Ruth and Theodore Lidz had already found that most parental relationships (61%) in a sample of families of 'schizophrenics' were 'marked by strife', including 42% that were either 'seriously incompatible' or had led to separation or divorce. Child-rearing patterns were rated 'bizarre or extremely faulty according to conventional standards' in 41% of the families. In 23%, at least one parent had rejected the patient 'to an extreme degree'. In 48%, at least one parent was 'either psychotic or chronically and seriously neurotic or psychopathic'. Only 11% of the patients had experienced none of the above and had therefore 'come from reasonably stable homes in which they had been raised by two stable and compatible parents according to fairly acceptable principles of child rearing' (p. 343).

The many subsequent studies of Theodore Lidz and his Yale colleagues, including Stephen Fleck and Alice Cornelison, focused more on the relationships between the parents than on interactions with the children (Lidz 1990; Lidz et al. 1986). They identified two predominant patterns of parental relationships. The 'schismatic' relationship was characterized by differences, competition and hostility. In the 'skewed' relationship, 'an apparent harmony or pseudomutuality was maintained because the aberrant ideas and ways of childrearing of one parent were not countered by the passive spouse' (Lidz 1969). Far from blaming parents the focus was, again, on the intergenerational spiral of damaging interpersonal patterns.

By 1969, Lidz concluded that the serious problems found in virtually all the families studied 'had started prior to the birth of the patient and were continuing when the patient became overtly psychotic'. Reviewing his own studies, those of the MRI Group, the work of Alanen (1960) in Finland, Delay et al. (1957) in France and a group of Maryland researchers (to whom we turn next), he found that 'they reveal essentially the same difficulties'.

The first to use the term 'communication deviance' were Lyman Wynne and Margaret Singer. In their research at Bethesda in Maryland, for the National Institute of Mental Health, they identified 'pseudo-mutuality' as a valuable concept for understanding schizophrenia (Wynne et al. 1958). Pseudo-mutuality is one attempt to solve the essential human conflict between needing to be related to others and needing one's own identity. This 'absorption in fitting together at the expense of the differentiation of the identities of the persons in the relation', they hypothesize, 'contributes significantly to the family experience of people who later, if other factors are also present, develop acute schizophrenic episodes'. Wynne and Singer stressed that pseudo-mutuality occurred to varying extents in most families but if the available roles for family members were rigid and few, and were all based on the need to preserve the illusion of sameness between family members, individuation could sometimes only be achieved by withdrawal into the isolated and distorted world of madness.

Like the other research groups working in this area, they presented convincing case studies. Their first empirical demonstration that parents of 'schizophrenics' score significantly higher than 'normal' controls on measures of communication deviance (Wynne and Singer 1963) was replicated repeatedly over the next 40 years. For instance, Wild et al. (1965) found that in 58% of the families of 'schizophrenics', both parents were high in communication deviance compared to 12% in a control group. There was evidence that having one parent who communicates satisfactorily is a protective factor.

By 1984, the Wynne and Singer group, apart from having conducted five studies of their own demonstrating high communication deviance (CD) in the families of 'schizophrenics', could point to five independent reviews of the relevant research concluding that 'parental CD is an aspect of family interaction that has consistently been found to characterize families of schizophrenics' (Sass *et al.* 1984). By 1992, at least 12 studies had found higher communication deviance among the parents of schizophrenia patients than among the parents of other patients or normal individuals (Miklowitz and Stackman 1992). A recent study found high communication deviance in 73% of a sample of families of 'schizophrenics (Nugter *et al.* 1997b). Norwegian studies have even linked specific subtypes of parental communication deviance to the same subtypes in their offspring (Rund and Bakar 1986).

The UCLA study had shown that parental communication deviance precedes and predicts the onset of schizophrenia. Parental communication deviance is also related to 'pre-schizophrenic' behaviours in young children (Velligan *et al.* 1988). In one inpatient sample, 84% of children with 'schizophrenia-spectrum' diagnoses were living in families with high communication deviance, compared with 52% of depressed children (Asarnow *et al.* 1988).

WHAT CAUSES WHAT? WHO NEEDS WHAT?

It is clear from the research reviewed above that negative feelings and intrusiveness (expressed emotion, affective style) and poor communication (communication deviance) within families are not just related to the exacerbation of 'symptoms', but are present well before the first signs of the 'illness'. But are the 'symptoms' caused by the parents' behaviour? Isn't it possible that the parents' behaviour is a reaction to the difficult behaviour of the children or adolescents who later become 'schizophrenic'?

One approach to addressing this question is the investigation of the stability of expressed emotion, affective style and communication deviance in family members. If these behaviours are stable over time, their causative role in the problems of the offspring is more plausible. Whereas 'on the other hand, when parental CD turns out to be an unstable, state-dependent characteristic of parents, the assumption that parental CD reflects a reaction to the disturbance of the offspring would be supported' (Nugter *et al.* 1997b).

It turns out that communication deviance is indeed a stable and enduring trait (Doane and Mintz 1987; Velligan *et al.* 1988), even in the face of a treatment programme specifically designed to reduce it (Nugter *et al.* 1997b). The Finnish Adoptive Family Study, led by Pekka Tienari and including Lyman Wynne, found communicative deviance to be 'a traitlike feature, stabilizing after adolescence, as with certain personality traits' (Wahlberg *et al.* 2001). They also found that the communication deviance of the adopting parents during the adoptees' adolescence *predicted* thought disorder, 11 years later, in both adoptees who did and did not have a 'schizophrenic' parent (Wahlberg *et al.* 2000).

In contrast to the trait-like stability of communication deviance, several studies have shown that expressed emotion and affective style are, for some parents, quite variable over time, and can be reduced by targeted programmes (Kavanagh 1992; Miklowitz 1994). This is consistent with the hypothesis that parental criticism and hostility might be explained partly in terms of parents reacting to the annoying symptoms of their ill offspring.

However, parents high in expressed emotion do have other personality traits that are stable, including intolerance, lack of empathy and inflexibility (Hooley and Hiller 2001). Goldstein *et al.* (1992) found that 100% of those parents whose high expressed emotion was stable over time had themselves experienced a major psychiatric disorder. (Communication deviance was unrelated to parental psychiatric disorder.) The percentage of the relatives of 'schizophrenics' who have a 'psychiatric disorder' at the time of onset of their offsprings' 'psychiatric disorder' ranges from 57% to 79% in studies from Norway (Bentsen *et al.* 1997), England (Barrowclough and Parle 1997) and Australia (Winefield and Harvey 1993), with relatives high in expressed emotion consistently having more disorders than relatives low in expressed emotion.

There is strong evidence that high expressed emotion (EE) is, in many cases, not a reaction to the offsprings' behaviour. A recent review cites four studies showing that 'EE does not appear to be correlated with any obvious clinical or demographic characteristics of patients' (Hooley and Hiller 2001). Another review found seven studies showing that the relationship between expressed emotion and relapse 'is not explained by patient characteristics such as severity of symptoms or premorbid adjustment' (Kavanagh 1992: 610). Another reviewer concludes that the relationship between expressed emotion and relapse is 'independent of patient symptom severity, history of illness or medication regime' (Miklowitz 1994). These findings have been replicated with mental health staff (Tattan and Tarrier 2000). Similarly, the contribution of expressed emotion to relapse is independent of any specific patient variables (Kavanagh 1992). Even after the 'patient' improves, expressed emotion remains high for many parents, especially those with a history of psychiatric problems themselves (Goldstein *et al.* 1992). Negative affective style has even been found to increase despite the offspring's improvement (Doane *et al.* 1986).

The search for a generalizable answer to the question 'what causes what' really should have been called off 40 years ago. In 1962, George Brown, whose work had inspired the expressed emotion approach to schizophrenia research, found, unsurprisingly, that there were different answers in different families:

In about one-third of the interviews it seemed that the past or current behavior of the patient was a sufficient cause of the 'high emotional involvement' . . . In roughly another third the 'high emotional involvement' was clearly due to unusual behavior of the relative, and could be independent of the severity of the illness of the patient . . . The remaining families could be included in neither group . . . it is possible that an interaction between the behavior of the patient and that of the relative was responsible for the 'high emotion'.

(Brown *et al.* 1962: 56)

Of course, there is reciprocal interaction between parents and their sons and daughters. The interactions will often have been going on for years. However, some 'interactional' models tend to consider only interactions after the onset of schizophrenia and still insist on calling the behaviours of some family members 'reactions' and the behaviour of other family members 'symptoms' (e.g. Kavanagh 1992). So there is still a danger of replacing a simplistic unidirectional *causal* model blaming parents with an equally simplistic unidirectional *reactive* model blaming the sons and daughters. There is little room in such a model for the possibility that the disturbing behaviour of the sons and daughters might be a reaction to years of parental criticism and hostility, perhaps from an early age. Kavanagh is far from alone in encouraging us to avoid the 'temptation to label people', meaning the labelling of parents as being high in expressed emotion, while being comfortable with the equally pejorative labelling of another set of family members as 'schizophrenic', 'patients', 'ill', and so on. This is unhelpful to both sets of relatives. It merely switches responsibility for the origins of the families' problems from one family member to another while pretending that no blaming is going on at all.

Others have developed more genuinely interactional models (Hahlweg *et al.* 1989; Wichstrom and Holte 1992). Miklowitz (1994) presents findings that the offspring frequently 'countercriticize' their parents, thereby reciprocating the high expressed emotion or negative affective style behaviours, and coins the term 'long chains of negative reciprocity'. Weardon *et al.* (2000) prefer 'complex circular relationship' to describe an interactional pattern of prolonged and escalating mutual negativity.

BEHIND THE ARGUMENTS

Sensitive sons and daughters

Other researchers have taken the valuable step of getting behind what family members do and say by studying the perceptions they have of one another. It turns out that the patients' experience of their parents' attitudes and feelings towards them is an even more powerful predictor of negative outcomes than the actual parental attitudes and feelings (Lebell *et al.* 1993; Scott *et al.* 1993; Tompson *et al.* 1995). 'Parents in the relapse group were not in touch with how the patient saw them, whereas the patients were sensitively aware of how they were seen' (Scott *et al.* 1993). These findings invite the explanation that the 'patients' were paranoid. However, in one study only the views of the 'patients' who relapsed turned out to be accurate (Scott *et al.* 1993).

Troubled parents

Equally important are the perceptions of the other family members. For example, one study found that: 'The more a relative perceives his or her own life to be unpredictable, and thus exposed to uncontrollable dangers, the greater the likelihood that he or she will overprotect the patient' (Bentsen *et al.* 1997: 562). Relatives who were emotionally over-involved were more prone to feeling guilty in general, while critical and hostile relatives have low 'hostility-guilt', meaning they have weak internal inhibitors against being aggressive to others. These researchers stressed the need to work with relatives' guilt feelings, whether deficient or excessive. This is virtually taboo for expressed emotion-based family interventions that dogmatically adhere to the 'It's not your fault because it's an illness' line.

A study of particular value when ascertaining who needs what kind of help found that critical relatives experienced their offspring's behaviour as more upsetting and felt less able to cope with or control it than did other relatives. When all the patient variables and all the relative variables were analysed, the extent to which the relatives perceived the offsprings' symptoms as upsetting, but *not* the actual severity of those symptoms, predicted whether the relatives were rated as a psychiatric 'case' (Barrowclough and Parle 1997). Compared with parents low in expressed emotion, parents high in expressed emotion more often explain their offspring's difficulties in 'illness' terms (Barrowclough *et al.* 1994), and estimate that the difficulties have gone on for longer before admission to hospital (Mintz *et al.* 1989).

Thus some relatives are less critical, hostile, intrusive and overprotective than others, and these relatives tend to be more flexible, tolerant and empathic and to have fewer 'psychiatric disorders'. This group is slower to believe an 'illness' has started in a distressed relative than relatives who are more critical, hostile, intrusive, overprotective, inflexible, non-empathic, intolerant and often have their own mental health problems. This second group's use of hostility and criticism has been described as a futile attempt to reduce their anxiety by deploying 'an intense interpersonal social control coping response' (Greenley 1986).

In these circumstances, the most disturbed relatives are the most critical of, and hostile to, their sons and daughters. Their own poor mental health is sustained by their tendency to experience unusual behaviours as upsetting and, therefore, to be more easily distressed than other relatives by their offspring's behaviour. In many families, it seems, there is more than one person who will need help before the family as a whole can 'get better'.

MOVING BEYOND BLAME

What these studies show is that a truly interactional approach must address not only the reciprocal and circular pattern of behaviours between family members, but also the perceptions of those behaviours by the other people involved. All families have misunderstandings and misperceptions. It is not sufficient to merely adopt the typical expressed emotion approach of trying to get relatives to behave differently (which, ironically, is a truly 'family-blaming' stance) but the behaviours and interpersonal perceptions of *all* family members must be on the agenda for discussion. This might appear complex. That's because families *are* complex. Working with families demands something more sophisticated than inaccurate, unhelpful statements about whose fault it is or isn't – as used in many 'psycho-educational' programmes. It requires us to get off the soapbox of promulgating a particular model and doing some genuine family work (see Chapter 23).

Instead of relying on pre-packaged 'psycho-education' programmes, we would be more effective and helpful to parents if we focused on acknowledging, normalizing and discussing the inevitable confusion and ambivalence about causes. This might be more helpful than trying to suppress or deny the feelings of relatives by forcing them to accept either a simplistic illness-blaming model that says it's *not at all* their fault, or an equally simplistic family-blaming model that says it's *all* their fault. Everyone would learn more and produce better outcomes if we listened to relatives' thoughts and feelings and offered support rather than insisting on 'educating' them to think like biological psychiatrists.

Helping families is hard using a manual based on studies that have measured just one or two 'variables' from the complicated, ongoing, circular, reciprocal and dynamic processes occurring in all families. Just as the world of a very distressed or disorientated individual is neither described nor understood by the word 'schizophrenic', the efforts of a parent or family to do their best cannot be encapsulated by terms like 'high expressed emotion'. Both are equally simplistic and do more damage than good to the people concerned. Both convey permanence where there is variation over time and circumstances. Both convey categories where there are dimensions. Both convey something within the person that is somehow separate from the world in which they are doing their best to cope, where there is really a myriad of forces operating on the families and on all the individual family members, in the present and from the past.

In 1994, Karon and Widener described a series of studies in which they and others measured 'the degree to which the parent, when there is a potential conflict between the needs of the child and the needs of the parent, unconsciously acts in terms of the parent's needs without regard to the potentially conflicting needs of the child'. The parents of 'schizophrenics' did this more often than the parents of 'normal' people. Far from blaming anyone, however, the researchers point out: 'This is not a conscious choice by the parent: the parent is typically unaware of the potential conflict'. They add that parenting problems 'are better understood as symptoms or coping devices developed in order to come to terms with the parent's own childhood' (pp. 52, 53). This issue of intergenerational cycles of parenting difficulties (Diamond and Doane 1994) is of crucial importance if we are ever to develop effective prevention programmes to reduce the amount of suffering that is going on in so many families (see Chapter 18).

Bertram and Widener share our view of the function of biological psychiatry's approach to families:

> To cause – even inadvertently – such terrible suffering in someone you love seems unbelievable and insulting. One of the reasons for emphasizing heredity and disturbed physiology is to avoid the guilt engendered by focussing on the possible mistakes of the parents. But all parents make mistakes. No one knows how to be a perfect parent . . . Parents generally believe that they have a great deal to do with how their children turn out; when children do not turn out well, parents have to cope with the question, 'What did I do?' Because our knowledge is so inexact, the answers are apt to be wrong. A parent guided by a wrong theory makes the situation worse rather than better.
>
> (Karon and Widener 1994: 47–8)

Families used to be largely ignored by mental health professionals. We have now succeeded in making more contact with them. But we still often make no real contact with what has been going on in the family. Until we are ready to ask parents and other relatives how they are dealing with the 'What did I do?' question, and to listen properly without making silly claims that we know the answer, we will remain less helpful than we ought to be. Propagating our own pet theory is no substitute for responding to the different fears, worries, anger and guilt experienced by different families, and by different family members within each family.

Most families will benefit more from some help to understand what has happened in their own unique situation, than they will from being told to stop thinking, or feeling, about it because 'It's an illness'. New understandings can bring new solutions, for all members of a family.

REFERENCES

Alanen, Y. (1960). Some thoughts on schizophrenia and ego development in the light of family investigations. *Archives of General Psychiatry* 3: 650–6.

Asarnow, J. *et al.* (1988). Parental communication deviance in childhood onset schizophrenia spectrum and depressive disorders. *Journal of Child Psychology and Psychiatry and Allied Disciplines* 29: 825–38.

Barrowclough, C. and Parle, M. (1997). Appraisal, psychological adjustment and EE in relatives of patients suffering from schizophrenia. *British Journal of Psychiatry* 171: 26–30.

Barrowclough, C. *et al.* (1994). Attributions, expressed emotions, and patient relapse: an attributional model of relatives' response to schizophrenic illness. *Behaviour Therapy* 25: 67–88.

Bateson, G. *et al.* (1956). Toward a theory of schizophrenia. *Behavioral Science* 1: 251–64.

Bateson, G. *et al.* (1962). A note on the Double Bind. *Family Process* 2: 154–61.

Bentsen, H. *et al.* (1997). Relatives' locus of control and EE in schizophrenia and related psychoses. *British Journal of Clinical Psychology* 36: 555–67.

Birley, J. and Brown, G. (1970). Crises and life changes preceding the onset of relapse of acute schizophrenia. *British Journal of Psychiatry* 116: 327–33.

Brown, G. *et al.* (1962). Influence of family life on the course of schizophrenic illness. *British Journal of Preventative Social Medicine* 16: 55–68.

Castillo, R. (2003). Trance, functional psychosis and culture. *Psychiatry: Interpersonal and Biological Processes* 66: 9–21.

Delay, J. *et al.* (1957). Le milieu familial des schizophrenes. *Encephale* 49: 1–21.

Diamond, D. and Doane, J. (1994). Disturbed attachment and negative affective style: an intergenerational spiral. *British Journal of Psychiatry* 164: 770–81.

Doane, J. and Mintz, J. (1987). Communication deviance in adolescence and adulthood: a longitudinal study. *Psychiatry: Journal for the Study of Interpersonal Processes* 50: 5–13.

Doane, J. *et al.* (1981). Parental communication deviance and affective style: predictors of subsequent schizophrenia spectrum disorders in vulnerable adolescents. *Archives of General Psychiatry* 38: 679–85.

Doane, J. *et al.* (1986). Parental affective style and the treatment of schizophrenia. *Archives of General Psychiatry* 42: 34–42.

Goldstein, M. (1987). The UCLA High-Risk Project. *Schizophrenia Bulletin* 13: 505–14.

Goldstein, M. and Doane, J. (1982). Family factors in the onset, course, and treatment of schizophrenic spectrum disorders. *Journal of Nervous and Mental Disease* 170: 692–700.

Goldstein, M. *et al.* (1992). Family interaction versus individual psychopathology. *British Journal of Psychiatry* 161(suppl. 18): 97–102.

Greenley, J. (1986). Social control and expressed emotion. *Journal of Nervous and Mental Disease* 174: 24–30.

Hahlweg, K. *et al.* (1989). EE and patient–relative interaction in families of recent onset schizophrenics. *Journal of Consulting and Clinical Psychology* 57: 11–18.

Haley, J. (1959). The family of the schizophrenic. *Journal of Nervous and Mental Disease* 129: 357–74.

Hamilton, E. *et al.* (1999). Family interaction styles of children with depressive disorders, schizophrenia-spectrum disorders, and normal controls. *Family Process* 38: 463–76.

Hooley, J. and Hiller, J. (2001). Family relationships and major mental disorder. In B. Saranson and S. Duck (eds) *Personal Relationships*. Chichester: Wiley.

Johnstone, L. (1999). Do families cause 'schizophrenia'? Revisiting a taboo subject. In C. Newnes *et al.* (eds) *This is Madness*. Ross-on-Wye: PCCS Books.

Karon, B. and Widener, A. (1994). Is there really a schizophrenogenic parent? *Psychoanalytic Psychology* 11: 47–61.

Kavanagh, D. (1992). Recent developments in EE and schizophrenia. *British Journal of Psychiatry* 160: 601–20.

Laing, R. and Esterson, A. (1970). *Sanity, Madness and the Family*, 2nd edn. New York: Basic Books.

Lebell, M. *et al.* (1993). Patients' perceptions of family emotional climate and outcome in schizophrenia. *British Journal of Psychiatry* 162: 751–4.

Leff, J. and Vaughn, C. (1980). The interaction of life events and relatives' EE in schizophrenia and depressive neurosis. *British Journal of Psychiatry* 136: 146–53.

Lidz, R. and Lidz, T. (1949). The family environment of schizophrenic patients. *American Journal of Psychiatry* 106: 332–45.

Lidz, T. (1969). The influence of family studies on the treatment of schizophrenia. *Psychiatry* 32: 237–51.

Lidz, T. (1990). *The Origin and Treatment of Schizophrenic Disorders*. Madison, CT: International Universities Press.

Lidz, T. *et al.* (1986). *Schizophrenia and the Family*, 2nd edn. New York: International Universities Press.

Miklowitz, D. (1994). Family risk indicators in schizophrenia. *Schizophrenia Bulletin* 20: 137–49.

Miklowitz, D. and Stackman, D. (1992). Communication deviance in families of schizophrenic and other psychiatric patients. *Progress in Experimental Personality and Psychopathology Research* 15: 1–46.

Mintz, L. *et al.* (1989). The initial onset of schizophrenia and family expressed emotion. *British Journal of Psychiatry* 154: 212–17.

Nugter, M. *et al.* (1997a). The relationships between EE, affective style and communication deviance in recent-onset schizophrenia. *Acta Psychiatrica Scandinavica* 96: 445–51.

Nugter, M. *et al.* (1997b). Parental communication deviance. *Acta Psychiatrica Scandinavica* 95: 199–204.

Rund, B. and Bakar, R. (1986). Schizophrenic patients and their parents. *Acta Psychiatrica Scandinavica* 74: 396–408.

Sass, L. *et al.* (1984). Parental communication deviance and forms of thinking in male schizophrenic offspring. *Journal of Nervous and Mental Disease* 172: 513–20.

Scott, R. *et al.* (1993). The importance of the role of the patient in the outcome of schizophrenia. *British Journal of Psychiatry* 163: 62–8.

Snyder, K. *et al.* (1994). EE by residential care operators and residents' symptoms and quality of life. *Hospital and Community Psychiatry* 45: 1141–3.

Tattan, T. and Tarrier, N. (2000). The EE of case managers of the seriously mentally ill. *Psychological Medicine* 30: 195–204.

Tompson, M. *et al.* (1995). Schizophrenic patients' perceptions of their relatives' attitudes. *Psychiatry Research* 57: 155–67.

Vaughn, C. and Leff, J. (1976). The influence of family and social factors on the course of psychiatric illness. *British Journal of Psychiatry* 129: 125–37.

Velligan, D. *et al.* (1988). Parental communication deviance. *Psychiatry Research* 26: 313–25.

Velligan, D. *et al.* (1996). The relationship between parental communication deviance and relapse in schizophrenic patients in the 1-year period after hospital discharge. *Journal of Nervous and Mental Disease* 184: 490–6.

Wahlberg, K. *et al.* (2000). Thought disorder index of Finnish adoptees and communication deviance of their adoptive parents. *Psychological Medicine* 30: 127–36.

Wahlberg, K. *et al.* (2001). Long-term stability of communication deviance. *Journal of Abnormal Psychology* 110: 443–8.

Weardon, A. *et al.* (2000). A review of EE research in health care. *Clinical Psychology Review* 20: 633–66.

Wichstrom, L. and Holte, A. (1992). Reciprocated self-disqualification among parents of schizophrenics. *Acta Psychiatrica Scandinavica* 86: 201–6.

Wig, N. *et al.* (1987). EE and schizophrenia in North India. *British Journal of Psychiatry* 151: 156–73.

Wild, C. *et al.* (1965). Measuring disordered styles of thinking. *Archives of General Psychiatry* 13: 471–6.

Winefield, H. and Harvey, E. (1993). Determinants of psychological disturbance in relatives of people with chronic schizophrenia. *Schizophrenia Bulletin* 19: 619–25.

Wynne, L. and Singer, M. (1963). Thought disorder and family relations of schizophrenics. *Archives of General Psychiatry* 9: 191–212.

Wynne, L. *et al.* (1958). Pseudo-mutuality in the family relations of schizophrenics. *Psychiatry* 21: 205–20.

Zubin, J. and Spring, B. (1997). Vulnerability: a new view of schizophrenia. *Journal of Abnormal Psychology* 86: 103–26.

Part III

Evidence-based psycho-social interventions

Chapter 18

Preventing 'schizophrenia'

Creating the conditions for saner societies

Emma Davies and Jim Burdett

The dominant bio-genetic model of mental health argues that psycho-social factors have little or nothing to do with causing what mental health professionals call 'schizophrenia' (see Chapters 3, 6 and 7). It is, therefore, widely assumed that little or nothing can be done to prevent children developing into adults who experience frightening hallucinations and delusions.

Research into the social aetiology of 'schizophrenia', buried under bio-genetic ideologies for several decades, has recently begun to again receive the attention it deserves (see Chapters 13, 16 and 17). Boyle (in press) has argued that such attention is essential to confront the dominant ideological position that apparently bizarre experiences and behaviours cannot be caused by anything other than disorders of the brain. The accumulating evidence indicates that the social factors (Boyle, in press; see also Chapters 13 and 16) and psychological mechanisms (Bentall 2003; see also Chapters 14 and 20) that lead to other mental health problems are similar to those likely to lead to the behaviours and experiences described as schizophrenic.

Although it is important to understand and analyse these behaviours and experiences, prevention initiatives that address the underlying social factors are likely to have a more long-term impact (Albee 1996; Boyle, in press; Joffe 1996). What lays the foundation for the prevention of what is called 'schizophrenia' will also help prevent post-traumatic stress disorder, depression, suicidality and other expressions of emotional pain. The only differences are likely to be in terms of greater multiplicity of severe problems associated with trauma, neglect, family dysfunction (see Chapters 16 and 17) and poverty (see Chapter 13), leading to greater severity of mental health problems.

In this chapter, therefore, we will not be advocating for specialized programmes to prevent 'schizophrenia'. Instead, using George Albee's 1985 model of prevention, we focus on decreasing stress and exploitation of children while enhancing coping skills, self-esteem and support networks of children and their primary carers. In essence, we endeavour to outline some pathways to creating the conditions for mental health.

Can we change our world to create fewer traumatic memories to carry into the next generations – fewer traumatic events to shape our children who will create our future social structures? How can we heal the scars of individual and group trauma that haunt us today? Can we ever make racism, misogyny, maltreatment of children – distant memories? There are solutions. These conditions are not the inevitable legacy of our past . . . The challenge of our generation is to understand the dynamics and realities of our human living groups in a way that can result in group insight – which, inevitably, will lead to the understanding that we must change our institutionalized ignorance and maltreatment of children.

(Perry 1999: 35)

WHAT IS PREVENTION?

Preventing madness in this context is not about the identification of individuals 'at risk' and offering treatment. While some of these recent developments may well be worthwhile (Wahlberg and Wynne 2001; see also Chapter 21), we wish to discuss a broader approach to prevention.

Preventing madness is about laying the foundations for building a more emotionally healthy and just society that values children, and where parents and other primary carers of children are better supported. This requires a shift in thinking by policy makers and practitioners, from prioritizing the treatment of distressed and dysfunctional adults (the 'hospital at the bottom of the cliff' approach) to ensuring an equal emphasis on enhancing children's resilience and potential (Daro and Donnelly 2002; Kinard 1998; Masten et al. 1990; Wolfe 1999). We need to overcome the structural barriers to promoting mental health (e.g. Tomison 1997) so that more lives are experienced as worth living. For most people, a life worth living is a life that has meaning. Contrary to popular opinion, meaning is not *discovered*. It is not something lying around on life's road waiting to be tripped over. One *makes* meaning. The importance that any element of one's life has is ultimately dependent on the value one gives to it, whether it be one's favourite article of clothing, best friend, cultural identity, spirituality or life itself.

Prevention of mental illness is about creating the preconditions necessary for a life worth living; the essential one being having sufficient autonomy to determine one's own life. Autonomy is having the will, information and freedom to make choices, and the power to act on them; in effect, the wherewithal to make meaning. There are two main strands to achieving this. The first is building the capacity for autonomy in individuals. In some cultures, there is equal emphasis on the autonomy of the family group. The second is ensuring that the social, political and economic environment is fertile ground for the promotion and exercise of autonomy. Both strands require equal focus on interrelatedness with others, without which autonomy is meaningless.

Albee's (1985) model illustrates these two strands and how they interact, offering insights into the systematic development of a prevention system:

$$\text{incidence of emotional illness} = \frac{\text{organic factors} + \text{stress} + \text{exploitation}}{\text{coping skills} + \text{self-esteem} + \text{support groups}}$$

To reduce the incidence of madness, we must increase the size of the denominator and decrease the size of the numerator. This requires reducing our exposure to stressful or traumatic events and increasing our capacity to participate fully in the world by creating a more just society. At the same time, it involves increasing our ability to cope with trauma and inequity, by learning better coping skills, enhancing our self-esteem, and developing better formal and informal social support systems.

Neurobiological and longitudinal research published since this model highlights the importance of focusing particular attention on the early years of life (Shonkoff and Phillips 2000). Developments in neurobiology in the 1990s indicate that early childhood experiences of neglect, stress and trauma, which often emanate from within the immediate caregiving environment, can lead to compromised brain development (Perry 1997, 1999; Perry and Pollard 1998; Shonkoff and Phillips 2000). Brain changes found in severely traumatized children are the same as those found in people with 'schizophrenia' (Read *et al.* 2001) or post-traumatic stress disorder (Putnam and Trickett 1997). These insights help to diffuse the long-standing nature–nurture debate. The structures and functions of the brain are affected by the environment and vice versa, particularly in early critical periods of brain development. Although we still have a lot to learn about these critical periods and the specifics of the interactions, the fact that children's immediate social environment affects brain development is unequivocal (Shonkoff and Phillips 2000).

DECREASING ORGANIC FACTORS

While organic factors contribute to emotional illness, they are arguably less relevant to prevention initiatives. The dangers of using organic factors to identify which people to nurture are evident by examining the history of the Eugenics Movement. If we have learnt anything from the horrors of Nazi Germany, it is the danger of combining simplistic scientific theories with the political power of the State (see Chapter 4). Perinatal and birth complications receive attention in the medical literature on 'schizophrenia'.

Of course we should do all we can to prevent these. This is another example of how addressing issues relevant to everybody will likely decrease the incidence of 'schizophrenia'.

DECREASING STRESS AND EXPLOITATION

Decreasing stress and exploitation covers a multitude of issues, many of which have been covered in this book (see Chapters 13, 16 and 17). Policies and programmes that focus on a reduction of poverty, and child abuse and neglect, will contribute to reducing stress and exploitation. To do this, we need to create and resource more just social structures and processes. Issues like child abuse, poverty and equitable social structures are considered irrelevant by biological psychiatrists. They are wrong.

Child abuse

It was encouraging to see the World Federation of Mental Health choose violence against children and adolescents as its focus for Mental Health Week 2002. There is substantial research evidence that child abuse and neglect are associated with various manifestations of emotional pain in adolescence and adulthood, including post-traumatic stress disorder, depression and suicide, substance abuse and eating disorders (Kendall-Tackett 2002). We also now know that traumatic events, particularly physical and sexual abuse of young children by family members, can precipitate psychotic symptoms (see Chapter 16), especially if the trauma is re-triggered by further abuse later in life (Read et al. 2003).

Poverty

Poverty is a risk factor for both child abuse (Bethea 1999; Duncan and Brooks-Gunn 1997; Pelton 1994; van der Kolk et al. 2001) and psychosis (see also Chapter 16). Higher rates of child abuse and neglect are associated with poverty via stress, inadequate income to meet children's needs for food and adequate shelter, and inadequate income to meet the needs of parents for space away from children through alternative care arrangements. Poverty signals low social status and rejection and can be socially isolating. These factors are conducive to neither positive parenting nor mental health. While in most OECD countries the absolute standards of living of the poor are higher than they were 30 years ago, the differences between rich and poor children within many nations have in fact increased. Poverty within nations matters because those with the lowest incomes are effectively excluded from mainstream society (UNICEF 2000).

Creating more just social structures

It is tempting to dismiss as unrealistic the creation of more just social structures and processes in which poverty and marginalization of social groups (on the basis of, for example, race, class or sexual orientation) is reduced (Krupinski and Burrows 1998). Giving up, however, ensures the perpetuation of our current unnecessarily high levels of human distress and despair.

Prevention programmes aimed at individuals and families are unlikely to create the change required to seriously reduce the numbers of people that ultimately go mad. There is wisdom in putting as much effort into changing the social structures that keep groups of people powerless as into initiatives that help people to cope better with the status quo (Albee 1985, 1996). To do the latter without the former is to develop a prevention system that has the potential to exploit the very people it is trying to help (Rappaport 1992), by encouraging them to merely adjust to, rather than challenge, a situation which has caused and is maintaining their distress. The term 'adjustment disorder' is revealing when seen from this perspective. One of the goals of a just society is, and will always be, individual freedom to participate fully in that society (Sen 1999).

Social and emotional justice is partly about equitable distribution of resources to diminish poverty. This can be implemented through a range of state measures, including direct financial assistance to the poorest, universal child benefit packages (including paid parental leave), quality preventative as well as rehabilitative health care, and emotionally and cognitively competent schools and pre-schools. Inequality can also be offset by a well-coordinated spectrum of accessible community services to facilitate the development of emotionally literate and interpersonally functional children and adults.

Most importantly, society must exist within a moral framework that places value on social and economic equity. The competition, individualism and materialism that are the lingering heritage of the New Right policies of the 1980s and early 1990s must be replaced with a collective commitment to building systems that serve people rather than the reverse.

STRENGTHENING COPING SKILLS, SELF-ESTEEM AND SUPPORT NETWORKS

It is perhaps rather obvious to state that we adults are largely products of our own child-rearing environments. The mass of evidence from neurobiological and longitudinal research indicates that we are most likely to maximize our impact on coping skills, self-esteem and support networks within communities when we focus on the needs and rights of children and those who care for them.

There is a plethora of programmes and services that aim to do just that. The detail is beyond the scope of this chapter. Suffice it to say that research has shown positive effects from investing in early intervention programmes (Karoly *et al.* 1998; Olds and Kitzman 1993). There is also some evidence for the efficacy of other types of programmes, for example those that teach children interpersonal cognitive skills (Shure 1997), social awareness and social problem-solving skills (Bruene-Butler *et al.* 1997).

There is increased awareness in OECD countries of the need to back these programmes with substantive public policy for children that aims to raise children's status in society and increase their primary carers' access to non-stigmatizing services that can assist them with their parenting. It is often said that parenting is the hardest job of all, a job for which many of us receive no training or support and, therefore, for which we are often ill-equipped. In the words of neurobiologist Professor Bruce Perry, Director of Alberta's child mental health services:

> We need to change our childrearing practices. We need to change the malignant and destructive view that children are the property of their parents. Human beings evolved not as individuals, but as communities. Despite Western conceptualizations, the smallest functional biological unit of humankind is not the individual – it is the clan. No individual, no simple parent–child dyad, no nuclear family could survive alone. We survived and evolved as clans – interdependent socially, emotionally and biologically. Children belong to the community; they are entrusted to parents. American society, and its communities, have failed parents and children alike. We have not provided parents with the information and resources to optimize their children's potential and, when parents fail, we act too late and with impotence to protect and care for maltreated children.
>
> (Perry 1997: 44)

This stands in stark contrast to encouraging parents to identify 'problem' 8-year-olds and to get them to a psychiatrist who will come up with a label – 'attention deficit hyperactivity disorder' (ADHD), 'conduct-disorder', 'childhood-onset schizophrenia', and so on. This usually leads to prescription of a drug, some of which have serious adverse effects on the child's development. For instance, studies have shown, for 30 years, that the stimulants used to 'treat' millions of children for difficulties concentrating or sitting still (ADHD) stunt their physical growth (Poulton and Cowell 2003; Safer and Allen 1973).

Most countries, with the exception of the USA and Somalia, have signed the United Nations Convention on the Rights of the Child (UNCROC).

This document offers a framework for signatory nations to raise the status of children. UNCROC's comprehensive series of 54 articles includes those on children's rights to live free from violence, to appropriate health care, to freedom of expression, to access to appropriate information and to universal quality education. Greater implementation of this Convention is likely to ultimately impact on the numbers of people that go mad. It is perhaps interesting that the only country in the world with a democratically elected government that has not signed UNCROC is the USA, a country in which some States are still mandated to kill some youth offenders and where rates of child physical abuse are high. The USA also has one of the most medicalized models of mental health in the world (Whitaker 2002).

Early intervention programmes

There is strong evidence that early intervention programmes targeted at pregnant women and high-risk families with very young children have positive effects. These include the High Scope Perry Preschool Program (Weikart and Schweinhart 1997) and Families and Schools Together (FAST) (McDonald et al. 1997). Randomized controlled trials have indicated that well-resourced, intensive and long-term prenatal and early childhood home-visiting programmes can be effective in reducing the incidence of abuse and neglect and promoting positive outcomes for children (Olds and Kitzman 1993). However, the combination of case management and parenting education delivered through home visits is not sufficient to overcome the effects of poverty and inadequate parenting (Chaffin et al. 2001; Goodson et al. 2000; Nelson et al. 2001).

The elements outlined in Table 18.1 characterize the Sure Start Initiative in England that has yet to be evaluated (Davies et al. 2002) and the Better Beginnings, Better Futures programme that has been implemented in eight disadvantaged communities in Ontario, Canada (including one First Nations community) (OMCSS 1989). Five of these were directed at families with pre-school children and three at families with school-age children. Significant outcome gains were reported in a number of sites, including reductions in behavioural/emotional problems and improvements in the quality of parent–child interaction, particularly in the pre-school sites.

Ending corporal punishment

Research has clearly demonstrated the negative effects of corporal punishment on children's emotional health (Straus 2000, 2001). In New Zealand, as in the USA and UK, more than 50% of parents report hitting their children more than once a week (Ritchie 2002). In these countries, it is still legal to hit children in their homes, which is inconsistent with the United Nations Convention on the Rights of the Child. While legislative reform

Table 18.1   Elements of successful prevention programmes with children and families

- Based on an ecological model – programmes that address the whole child and the family and their connectedness to the community
- Long-term and intensive, starting at birth or before
- Flexible and responsive to local needs
- Owned by local communities – partly facilitated by involvement of local parents in design and delivery.
- High-quality management and administration plus well-trained, well-supervised and well-paid staff
- Integrated – linked with other programmes and community activities, including the development of common goals, objectives and collaboration
- Based on research and evaluation
- Non-stigmatizing enrolment strategies

Note: List developed from Davies *et al.* (2002), Nelson *et al.* (2001) and OMCSS (1989).

cannot change this parental behaviour, it can lay one of the foundations for this change to occur (Durrant 1999). Since 1979, when Sweden banned corporal punishment, another 14 OECD countries, mainly in Europe, have changed their legislation to set a standard of no physical punishment of children.

Reforming education

To promote emotionally healthy children and adults, quality education needs to focus as much attention on nurturing learning through a 'community of inquiry' process, prevention of violence and emotional literacy (including conflict resolution skills) as it currently does, in Anglo-Saxon countries, on promoting academic excellence. Reform of our education system is a key factor in moving towards a child-friendly society. Currently, some of our schools are models of institutional repression, ironically manifesting the same limiting institutionalism that we are trying, with some success, to move away from in our mental health services. As with mental health services, the best intentions of individual staff members cannot overcome the fact that schools are often controlling and confining institutions.

The starting point of our education system should be the most basic of human questions, 'How am I to live?' This is particularly important in an increasingly diverse and rapidly changing society. There may have been halcyon days gone by when all that was required of schools was to instruct children in a single, simple moral code, ensure literacy and numeracy, and provide lots of facts for memorizing. 'This is how you will live' forestalled the need to ask the question. Regardless of whether such an approach ever met children's needs, it is certainly no longer the case.

The task of schools should be to engender a spirit of inquiry, to build on children's inevitable curiosity and natural love of learning to prepare them to find personal answers to a universal question. This is not difficult. Children are natural philosophers, innate 'lovers of learning'. Using a process of collective philosophical inquiry (Lipman 1985), we can offer children opportunities to both explore that which is of immediate importance to them and learn the skills of philosophy (Lipman 1985; Splitter and Sharp 1995).

If we are ever to create a society that nurtures people rather than driving some of them mad, it is most likely to be both developed and sustained by students leaving our schools not as automatons that can conform and obey, but as practical philosophers who have the tools to make meaning and live well.

CONCLUSION

> Psychologists must join with persons who reject racism, sexism, colonialism, and exploitation and must find ways to redistribute social power and to increase social justice. Primary prevention research inevitably will make clear the relationship between social pathology and psychopathology and then will work to change social and political structures in the interests of social justice. It is as simple and as difficult as that!
>
> (Albee 1996: 1131)

Many mental health professionals see more human pain in a week than most of us see in a lifetime. Paradoxically, these societally ordained witnesses seem paralysed into silence about the source of the pain flowing over them. To ask a human being to sit day after day with often frightened and sometimes frightening survivors of the worst that life can throw at people, *and* to find the energy and hope to simultaneously try to plug the source, seems unfair.

On the other hand, an exclusive focus on the distressed individual may be stopping us from focusing on what we mean by mental health, healthy families, healthy communities and just societies. If we focus more of our debate here, we might learn more about how to enhance their development.

The focus of this chapter has been to go beyond merely stopping something happening – that is, preventing people from becoming mentally ill. While it is commendable that we are seeking to move from sending ambulances to the bottom of the cliff to building fences at the top, we need to go further and challenge the factors underlying the trauma that is endemic in our present society. Merely attempting to prevent things going wrong is too passive, too disengaged, essentially lacking commitment to being involved in one another, and thus ultimately sterile. If prevention means no more than structural elimination of risk, then we are living in a society that has failed to recognize that lives experienced as worth living need a social context of vibrant interconnectness and interdependence. Loving relationships, nurturing families, caring friends, economic equity, enfranchisement in the local and wider community, all are hallmarks of mental health. Seen in this light, prevention is not a matter of stopping something, it is a matter of building a society that is a fertile ground for humans to flourish.

REFERENCES

Albee, G. (1985). The argument for primary prevention. *Journal of Primary Prevention* 5: 213–19.

Albee, G. (1996). Revolutions and counter-revolutions in prevention. *American Psychologist* 51: 1130–3.

Bentall, R. (2003). *Madness Explained: Psychosis and Human Nature*. London: Penguin.

Bethea, L. (1999). Primary prevention of child abuse. *American Family Physician*, March, pp. 1–11.

Boyle, M. (in press). Preventing a non-existent illness? Some issues in the prevention of 'schizophrenia'. *Journal of Primary Prevention*.

Bruene-Butler, L. *et al.* (1997). The improving social awareness–social problem solving project. In G. Albee and T. Gullotta (eds) *Primary Prevention Works: Issues in Children's and Families' Lives*, Vol. 6. Thousand Oaks, CA: Sage.

Chaffin, M. *et al.* (2001). Family preservation and family support programs. *Child Abuse and Neglect* 25: 1269–89.

Daro, D. and Donnelly, A. (2002). Charting the waves of prevention: two steps forward, one step back. *Child Abuse and Neglect* 26: 731–42.

Davies, E. *et al.* (2002). From rhetoric to action: a case for a comprehensive community-based initiative to improve developmental outcomes for disadvantaged children. *Social Policy Journal of New Zealand* 19: 28–47.

Duncan, G. and Brooks-Gunn, K. (1997). *Consequences of Growing Up Poor*. New York: Russell-Sage.

Durrant, J. (1999). Evaluating the success of Sweden's corporal punishment ban. *Child Abuse and Neglect* 23: 435–8.

Goodson, B. *et al.* (2000). Effectiveness of a comprehensive, five-year family support program for low-income children and their families. *Early Childhood Research Quarterly* 5: 5–39.

Joffe, J. (1996). Searching for the causes of the causes. *Journal of Primary Prevention* 17: 201–7.

Karoly, L. *et al.* (1998). *Investing in Our Children*. Santa Monica, CA: Rand.

Kendall-Tackett, K. (2002). The health effects of childhood abuse. *Child Abuse and Neglect* 26: 715–30.

Kinard, M. (1998). Methodological issues in assessing resilience in maltreated children. *Child Abuse and Neglect* 22: 669–80.

Krupinski, J. and Burrows, G. (1998). Mental health promotion. *International Sociology Association Paper* 98S34903.

Lipman, M. (1985). *Thinking, Children and Education*. Dubuque, IA: Kendal/Hunt.

Masten, A. *et al.* (1990). Resilience and development: contributions from the study of children who overcome adversity. *Development and Psychopathology* 2: 425–44.

McDonald, L. *et al.* (1997). Families and Schools Together. *Families and Society* 15: 140–53.

Nelson, G. *et al.* (2001). A review and analysis of programs to promote family wellness and prevent the maltreatment of preschool and elementary school aged children. In I. Prilleltensky *et al.* (eds) *Promoting Family Wellness and Preventing Child Maltreatment: Fundamentals for Thinking and Action.* Toronto: University of Toronto Press.

Olds, D. and Kitzman, H. (1993). Review of research on home visiting for pregnant women and parents of young children. *The Future of Children* 3: 53–92.

OMCSS (1989). Better beginnings, better futures: primary prevention of emotional and behavioural problems in children (http//:bbbf.queens.ca/pub.html).

Pelton, L. (1994). The role of material factors in child abuse and neglect. In G. Melton and F. Barry (eds) *Protecting Children from Abuse and Neglect.* New York: Guilford Press.

Perry, B. (1997). Incubated in terror: neurodevelopmental factors in the 'cycle of violence'. In J. Osofsky (ed.) *Children in a Violent Society.* New York: Guilford Press.

Perry, B. (1999). Memories of fear. In J. Goodwin and R. Attias (eds) *Splintered Reflections.* Washington, DC: Basic Books.

Perry, B. and Pollard, B. (1998). Homeostasis, stress, trauma, and adaptation: a neurodevelopmental view of childhood trauma. *Child and Adolescent Psychiatric Clinics of North America* 7: 33–51.

Poulton, A. and Cowell, C. (2003). Slowing growth in height and weight on stimulants. *Journal of Paediatrics and Child Health* 39: 180–5.

Putnam, F. and Trickett, P. (1997). Psychobiological effects of sexual abuse. In R. Yehuda and A. McFarlane (eds) Psychobiology of PTSD. *Annals of the New York Academy of Sciences* 821: 150–9.

Rappaport, J. (1992). The dilemma of primary prevention in mental health services: rationalize the *status quo* or bite the hand that feeds you. *Journal of Community and Applied Social Psychology* 2: 95–9.

Read, J. *et al.* (2001). The contribution of early traumatic events to schizophrenia in some patients: a traumagenic neurodevelopmental model. *Psychiatry* 64: 319–45.

Read, J. *et al.* (2003). Sexual and physical abuse during childhood and adulthood as predictors of hallucinations, delusions and thought disorder. *Psychology and Psychotherapy: Theory, Research and Practice* 76: 1–22.

Ritchie, J. (2002). Parents: discipline, punishment and child abuse. *Bulletin of the New Zealand Psychological Society* 100: 30–3.

Safer, D. and Allen, R. (1973). Factors influencing the suppressant effects of two stimulant drugs on the growth of hyperactive children. *Pediatrics* 51: 660–7.

Sen, A. (1999). *Development as Freedom.* Oxford: Oxford University Press.

Shonkoff, J. and Phillips, D. (2000). *From Neurons to Neighbourhoods: The Science of Early Development.* Washington, DC: National Academy Press.

Shure, M. (1997). Interpersonal cognitive problem solving: primary prevention of early high-risk behaviors in the pre-school and primary years. In G. Albee and T.

Gullotta (eds) *Primary Prevention Works: Issues in Children's and Families' Lives*, Vol. 6. Thousand Oaks, CA: Sage.

Splitter, L. and Sharp, A. (1995). *Teaching for Better Thinking*. Camberwell: ACER.

Straus, M. (2000). Corporal punishment and primary prevention of child abuse. *Child Abuse and Neglect* 24: 1109–14.

Straus, M. (2001). *Beating the Devil Out of Them*. New York: Lexington.

Tomison, A. (1997). *Overcoming Structural Barriers to the Prevention of Child Abuse and Neglect*. Melbourne, VIC: Australian Institute of Family Studies.

UNICEF (2000). *League Table of Child Poverty in Rich Nations* (Innocenti Report Card Issue No. 1 June). Florence: UN Children's Fund.

van der Kolk, B. *et al.* (2001). Child abuse in America: prevalence, costs, consequences and intervention. In K. Franey *et al.* (eds) *The Cost of Child Maltreatment: Who Pays?* San Diego, CA: Family Violence and Sexual Assault Institute.

Wahlberg, K. and Wynne, L. (2001). Possibilities for prevention of schizophrenia. *International Journal of Mental Health* 30: 91–103.

Weikart, D. and Schweinhart, L. (1997). High/Scope Perry Preschool Program. In G. Albee and T. Gullotta (eds) *Primary Prevention Works: Issues in Children's and Families' Lives*, Vol. 6. Thousand Oaks, CA: Sage.

Whitaker, R. (2002). *Mad in America*. Cambridge, MA: Perseus.

Wolfe, D. (1999). *Child Abuse: Implications for Child Development and Psychopathology*, Vol. 10. New York: Sage.

Chapter 19

User-run services

Judi Chamberlin

One of the outgrowths of the consumer/survivor[1] movement[2] has been the development of projects and programmes run by service users themselves. These take many forms, including support groups, drop-in centres, advocacy programmes, housing programmes, warm lines,[3] skill teaching services and others. In all cases, these programmes adhere to certain basic principles:

- They are run and managed by people who have themselves received mental health services.
- They are based on a model of peer support rather than professional expertise.
- They value one-to-one contact as the primary mode of delivering service.
- They strive to minimize hierarchy and to value the contributions of every participant.

When consumers/survivors come together, they often identify critical needs that are largely unmet in traditional mental health programming. This occurs whether the participants have a broad critical analysis of the mental health service delivery system, or whether they are accepting of its basic tenets. Although critics of the consumer/survivor movement often label it 'anti-psychiatry', this is a broad over-simplification. In fact, there is

---

[1] In the USA, consumer/survivor is the preferred usage for a person who receives or has received mental health services. In general, 'consumer' describes an individual who accepts the medical model of mental illness, and 'survivor' describes someone who takes a more critical stance. Other terms that may be used include 'client', 'user' and 'ex-user'.

[2] In broad terms, the movement consists of local, regional, national and international groups and organizations run and controlled by consumer/survivors, and networks of such organizations.

[3] As distinct from hot lines, warm lines are telephone services that people can call when they are not in crisis, but feeling lonely and in need of human connection.

a wide range of opinion within the movement on many questions, including the value of psychiatric treatment and the validity of the medical model of mental illness. However, even those consumers/survivors who adhere closely to traditional psychiatric theories are critical of many features of the mental health system, particularly the lack of respect people encounter within the system and the inability of people to get many of their self-defined needs met.

In general, mental health services for people who have been identified as long-term clients are focused on maintenance and medication. There are limited opportunities, in most cases, for access to ongoing emotional support, educational programmes (especially those focused on higher education), long-term housing in integrated settings or, in general, routes out of the mental health system. Many people end up living in mental health housing, attending dead-end day programmes, surviving on meagre public benefits and, in general, leading lives that are emotionally impoverished.

Many user-run services originate when consumers/survivors come together and begin to articulate their unmet needs. Often, people tell stories about how they have tried to make the system meet their needs; for example, gathering in the waiting room of a programme to socialize with their peers, only to be told that this is an 'inappropriate' use of the facility. Consumers/survivors often express much frustration that when they express the wish to lead more independent lives, to complete their educations or to have satisfying careers, they are told they are being 'unrealistic', 'grandiose' or 'non-compliant'. It becomes clear that to get the help they want, they will have to do it themselves.

This is, for example, the way the Mental Patients' Association (MPA) started in Vancouver, Canada:

> In early 1971 a group of ex-patients in Vancouver, British Columbia, called a public meeting to discuss dissatisfaction with the psychiatric system. The organizers had been patients together in a psychiatric day hospital, a supposedly progressive arrangement that treats patients during the day and permits them to go home evenings and weekends. This group of patients, however, did not find the setup supportive, since they discovered that crises frequently arose precisely during the times when staff was unavailable (evenings and weekends), and it was against the rules for patients to see one another or talk on the phone outside the institution. One Monday morning the patients arrived on the ward and learned that over the weekend one of their number had committed suicide. Many strong emotions were expressed, and one immediate result was the clandestine circulation of a patients' phone list.
>
> As time went on, some of the patients discovered that they were relying on these 'illegal' phone calls far more than on the therapy they were receiving during the day hospital hours, and they began to talk

among themselves about the kinds of 'help' that were truly useful. By this time all of them had been discharged from the hospital, and they felt that their informal network was the one form of real support they had. They decided to try to find more people who had similar feelings about psychiatric treatment and to discuss with this larger group what could be done.

(Chamberlin 2001: 86)

MPA's experience is typical. The group identified a problem, the lack of ongoing peer support, and the fact that the structure of the professionally run programme overtly discouraged such support. They came up with a solution, the development of the phone list and the utilization of it by members for support. They recognized that this support was extremely helpful to the members. They decided to develop a more permanent solution and, as a result of the public meeting, started their first drop-in centre. Starting out with one small volunteer drop-in centre, the organization grew. They wrote grant applications, hired staff and enlarged the programme to include cooperative housing. MPA became incorporated and over several years became an established service providing agency that utilized a self-help model to serve hundreds of members. MPA differed from many of the groups established later, in that it was open to people who had never been service users, which meant, in practice, that many of the paid positions were filled by people who had never used psychiatric services.

Another example is the Ruby Rogers Advocacy and Drop-In Center (RRC) in Somerville, Massachusetts, which this author helped to start in 1985. RRC developed from an older consumer/survivor organization, the Mental Patients' Liberation Front (MPLF), which was founded in Boston in 1971. MPLF was a political action group that organized meetings and demonstrations aimed at bringing about radical change in the mental health system. MPLF (1973) published a handbook, *Your Rights as a Mental Patient in Massachusetts*, which provided legal and practical information for people who wanted to challenge decisions made about their care, particularly involving involuntary commitment and forced medication, and distributed the booklet directly to patients in hospitals and programmes. MPLF was also instrumental in a court case, *Rogers v. Commissioner*, which established a limited right to refuse medication in Massachusetts.

Many MPLF members wanted more companionship and support than a weekly business meeting and committee work could provide. This led to the decision to seek funding from the Massachusetts Department of Mental Health (DMH) to establish RRC. The decision to seek DMH funding was controversial. Some members objected to the idea of the agency of which they were so critical also being a funder, but, in the end, the grant application was submitted and accepted. RRC was operated as a totally peer-run programme. Like MPA, programmatic decisions were made by members through business meetings open to all; unlike MPA, however, participation was limited to those who themselves had psychiatric histories. This enabled a number of members to have their first paid employment in many years.

The basic philosophy of MPA, RRC and many similar programmes is that people who have been labelled as mentally ill have the capability to help themselves and one another. In the traditional mental health system, there is a strong division between professionals and clients. Professionals are there to give help, clients to receive it, and these roles are seen as immutable. In self-help programmes, on the other hand, roles are fluid. People may come into the group seeking help, or may come because they see themselves as wanting to help others, but it is common and expected that members will fulfil both roles at different times. One of the most important things that happens to people within self-help groups is that they get to experience themselves filling a different role. A person who has been seen – and has always seen him or herself – as needy and dependent responds dramatically when he or she has the opportunity to help another member. Often, a person's entire self-image begins to change when he or she experiences another member's appreciation for some piece of advice or support. The learned helplessness instilled by the mental health system is challenged by such experiences.

It is often stressed to members of self-help groups that they need to value each person's perceptions and experiences. Whether in a formal support group setting, or in the more informal membership interaction which is the heart of the self-help experience, words of comfort and empathy often have dramatic results. Knowing that another person has had similar experiences, and that they have overcome them, provides valuable insights. Labelling and diagnostic terminology is discouraged, although many people, because of years of experience in the mental health system, have learned to use labels to describe their behaviour and the behaviour of others. Members are encouraged to use common sense terminology instead; for example, 'I'm feeling bad today' rather than 'I am having a crisis'. This is one of many ways in which members are encouraged to see their thoughts, feelings and actions, and those of their peers, as normal reactions to real-life stresses, rather than as mysterious 'symptoms' over which they have no control.

Often subgroups form in which people who have had similar experiences, such as hearing voices or engaging in self-harming behaviours, come together to discuss the meaning such experiences have and coping strategies for dealing with them. It is common for participants to report that they received more practical help in such groups than they ever found within the mental health system, and that their behaviour changed in positive ways.

One of the key differences between self-help programmes and traditional mental health services is the voluntary nature of self-help. The mental health system is built on coercion. Even when services are offered in an ostensibly voluntary manner, coercion is never far from the surface. Often programmes are linked in such a way that clients cannot get a service they want (such as housing or job training) without getting one they don't want (such as forced medication). Most community mental health programmes which are, themselves, non-coercive are linked into the overall system, so that coercive interventions are easily obtainable when programme staff decides that a member 'needs' such interventions. A participant in a day programme, for example, may be transported to an emergency room and involuntarily committed because a staff member is alarmed about something the person has said or done. Ostensibly, voluntary community programmes, in addition, often play a powerful role in enforcing compliance with prescribed medication, even when the individual supposedly has freedom of choice about whether or not to use medication.

In self-help programmes, on the other hand, members are free to engage in whatever degree of contact and participation they choose. There is no single right way to utilize a self-help programme. One member may attend on a daily basis, another only when he or she is feeling particularly troubled or needy. This flexibility allows people to tailor the service to meet their self-defined needs, rather than having to fit into a programme or structure designed by others.

Self-help groups are structured with the minimal number of rules. Often, groups start with the idea that no rules are necessary. This is a common reaction when people try to structure something which they intend to be totally different from the coercive mental health system of which they are critical. In time, however, most groups realize that a few basic rules are necessary; the same rules that govern civil behaviour generally. This author has seen posters in many client-run programmes, in many countries, which list the rules that the group has arrived at cooperatively. Although independently arrived at, these rules are remarkably similar. They usually include prohibitions against stealing, weapons, violence, illegal drugs and verbal harassment of others. Usually a process is put into place to deal with violations of the rules, in which every attempt is made to deal with the rule-breaker in a caring and respectful manner.

Another important feature of these groups is that they take a pragmatic stance about such questions as the nature (or existence) of 'mental illness', or the utility of psychiatric medication, with members holding various positions. Although critics frequently accuse self-help groups of condemning psychiatric treatment or medication, many members may also be seeing mental health professionals and using psychiatric drugs. These are seen as matters of individual choice. Members who have questions about their rights within the psychiatric system often find that self-help groups are good sources of information which they are unable to get in other places. Because people may find out for the first time that they have a right to refuse psychiatric drugs, or that they have choices about programming, some mental health professionals may find this threatening, but it is hardly the mythical 'anti-psychiatry' of which groups are frequently accused.

Of course, not all mental health professionals are critical of self-help groups, and they are becoming more widely accepted by the mainstream. Psychiatrists Loren Mosher and Lorenzo Burti, for example, state that:

> We believe that the development of a strong consumer mutual help group should be a high priority of every community mental health program. It is the most direct and clear statement of a program's commitment to the principle of preservation and enhancement of power. The nature of the relationship of the client-run program to the local community mental health system must be allowed to change over time and will vary between locales. What is most critical is that the mental health system *not* attempt to control it or take it over. The system's role should be to provide as much material support and *consultative* expertise as needed to get the program (as defined by users) up and running. After that, the community mental health system should make itself available as needed, with 'needed' being defined by the users' group. The client-run program can be completely outside the mental health system and serve, for example, a watchdog function for it. Or it can be at the boundary of the community mental health program by providing a way for clients to make the transition out of the mental health system via the peer support and advocacy offered in a drop-in center.
>
> (Mosher and Burti 1989: 101–2)

In the USA, the National Association of State Mental Health Program Directors and the federal Center for Mental Health Services are among the mainstream groups that have expressed support for self-help services and the involvement of service users in policy making. Self-help groups of one sort or another exist in virtually every US state, with some states having wide-ranging networks of local groups, while in others there may be just scattered individual groups.

Consumer/survivor groups have also sprung up in the virtual world of the Internet. Numerous websites are run by psychiatric survivors and mental health consumers, including sites where people can get information about the mental health system, specific treatment modalities, consumer/survivor activism, and how to find like-minded people in their local areas. In addition, there are numerous mailing lists and listservs where people can post messages and receive replies, as well as sites where they can engage in real-time interaction with peers. The Internet is particularly helpful for people who live in isolated areas without access to others who share their concerns (see list of websites below).

Although self-help groups have proliferated dramatically over the last 10 years, they still form a tiny and precarious part of the overall range of services available to people diagnosed with mental illness. Funding is often tenuous and may be withdrawn at any time. Most people involved with the mental health system are still unaware of their existence. Many people who are dissatisfied with the services they are receiving, and are actively looking for alternatives, still have difficulty in learning about the existence of the consumer/survivor movement. This shows how far this movement still has to go to become a truly viable alternative to the traditional system.

REFERENCES

Chamberlin, J. (2001). *On Our Own: Patient-Controlled Alternatives to the Mental Health System.* Lawrence, MA: National Empowerment Center.

Mental Patients' Liberation Front (1973). *Your Rights as a Mental Patient in Massachusetts.* Boston, MA: MPLA.

Mosher, L. and Burti, L. (1989). *Community Mental Health: Principles and Practice.* New York: Norton.

FURTHER READING

Campbell, P. (1999). The service user/survivor movement. In C. Newnes *et al.* (eds) *This is Madness.* Ross-on-Wye: PCCS Books.

Coleman, R. (1999). Hearing voices and the politics of oppression. In C. Newnes *et al.* (eds) *This is Madness.* Ross-on-Wye: PCCS Books.

Lawson, M. (1991) A recipient's view. In S. Ramon (ed.) *Beyond Community Care.* London: MIND.

Lindow, V. (1999). Survivor controlled alternatives to psychiatric services. In C. Newnes *et al.* (eds) *This is Madness.* Ross-on-Wye: PCCS Books.

Lindow, V. (2001). Survivor research. In C. Newnes *et al.* (eds) *This is Madness Too.* Ross-on-Wye: PCCS Books.

O'Hagan, M. (1992). On being 'not quite human'. In D. Patten (ed.) *Public Attitudes to Mental Illness.* Wellington, NZ: Department of Health.

Pilgrim, D. and Hitchman, L. (1999). User involvement in mental health service development. In C. Newnes *et al.* (eds) *This is Madness.* Ross-on-Wye: PCCS Books.

Wallcraft, J. (1998). *Healing Minds.* London: Mental Health Foundation.

WEBSITES

1 www.mindfreedom.org: Support Coalition International (SCI), in Eugene, Oregon, publishes *MindFreedom Journal* (formerly Dendron), which expresses the views of people opposed to biological psychiatry and forced treatment.

2 www.madnation.cc: 'People Working Together for Social Justice and Human Rights in Mental Health'.

3 www.antipsychiatry.org: Articles, comments on news stories, and photographs of demonstrations and actions by psychiatric survivor organizations. In several languages.

4 www.narpa.org: The National Association for Rights Protection and Advocacy is a US organization that holds an annual rights conference, publishes a newsletter, and conducts public policy efforts to promote choice and freedom for people labelled with psychiatric disabilities.

5 www.enusp.org: The European Network of (Ex-)Users and Survivors of Psychiatry. In numerous languages.

6 www.ect.org: Run by a survivor of electroconvulsive therapy (ECT). Information about ECT from a critical viewpoint. Promotes informed consent and full information about the dangers of ECT.

7 www.power2u.org: The National Empowerment Center is a US survivor-run organization promoting recovery and self-help.

8 www.peoplewho.org: A web-based organization for 'people who experience mood swings, fear, voices, and visions'.

Chapter 20

Cognitive therapy for people with psychosis

Anthony P. Morrison

INTRODUCTION

Over the last decade or so, the cognitive model originally outlined by Beck (1976) has been applied to the understanding and treatment of psychosis. This model suggests that the way we interpret events has consequences for how we feel and behave, and that such interpretations are often maintained by unhelpful thinking biases and behavioural responses. Beck's cognitive model also suggests that these interpretations are influenced by our core beliefs, which are formed as a result of life experience. There have been several recent attempts to develop cognitive models of psychosis and psychotic symptoms or experiences (Bentall *et al.* 2001; Chadwick and Birchwood 1994; Garety *et al.* 2001; Morrison 1998a, 2001, 2002). Many of these models suggest that it is the way that people interpret psychotic phenomena that accounts for distress and disability, rather than the psychotic experiences themselves.

Cognitive therapy (CT) for psychosis is based on the same principles that were outlined for standard cognitive therapy for emotional disorders (Beck 1976; Beck *et al.* 1979). Cognitive therapy is also time-limited, based on a cognitive model of the disorder in question and on idiosyncratic case formulations derived from the model.

There is an increasing body of evidence regarding the efficacy of cognitive therapy for psychosis. Several randomized controlled trials have shown cognitive behavioural approaches to the treatment of psychosis to be superior to both routine care or treatment-as-usual (Kuipers *et al.* 1997, 1998; Tarrier *et al.* 1998), in addition to demonstrating benefits in comparison with befriending or supportive psychotherapy (Sensky *et al.* 2000; Tarrier *et al.* 1998). Recent meta-analyses have concluded that cognitive behavioural treatment of psychosis is effective and should be delivered routinely as part of the treatment package that is offered to people with a diagnosis of schizophrenia (Gould *et al.* 2001).

The primary aims of CT for psychosis are to reduce the distress experienced by people with psychosis and to improve their quality of life. The purpose of CT is not necessarily to reduce the frequency of psychotic symptoms, but rather to help patients to achieve the specific goals that they have set in relation to the problems that they have identified. CT for panic disorder does not aim to eliminate body sensations; instead, it aims to help people generate less upsetting appraisals of these experiences. CT for psychosis works similarly, focusing on generating less distressing explanations for psychotic experiences, rather than attempting to eliminate these experiences. Indeed, CT should recognize that psychotic experiences may well serve a function for the person.

The process of CT for psychosis begins with assessment and the identification of problems and goals. It then involves the development of a cognitive behavioural formulation that is used to guide selection of treatment strategies. These strategies are implemented and evaluated, and the outcomes of interventions are used as data with which to modify the formulation, if indicated. The process ends with relapse prevention in an attempt to consolidate and maintain treatment gains.

ASSESSMENT

Assessment of a person with psychosis is very similar to a cognitive behavioural assessment of a non-psychotic patient. After setting the scene, explaining confidentiality and the practicalities of therapy, it is often helpful to begin with an analysis of a recent problematic incident. The aim of this is to generate information that will be useful in understanding the development and maintenance of problems and in suggesting change strategies.

Problem maintenance

It is common to begin with an assessment of problem maintenance. This can be done by examining a recent incident in terms of events, thoughts, feelings and behaviours, and collaboratively searching for meaningful links between these factors. For example, Chadwick and Birchwood (1994) recommend viewing auditory hallucinations as an antecedent event within this kind of framework. This kind of analysis of a recent time when someone was distressed by his or her voices is likely to provide information about how people interpret their voices and how this makes them feel. If they believe that the voice belongs to the Devil, who is trying to make them do bad things, this is likely to make them feel scared, angry or hopeless (depending on their belief system), whereas if they interpret the voice as being a sign that they are special, or as a dead friend who is advising them, then they may feel happier about the experience. The interpretation of the voice, combined with the emotional response, is likely to determine what the person does in relation to the voices. This framework is also applicable to delusional beliefs, as illustrated below:

Event   → Interpretation   → Feeling → Behaviour

See man in suit → They're following me → scared → evasive action
                   They're going to hurt me   paranoid   avoid going out

The main purpose of an assessment is to generate information that can be used to develop a formulation. The cognitive model of psychosis should therefore guide the process of assessment. Questions should be asked to identify problematic events or intrusions, the subsequent interpretation of these, and emotional, behavioural, cognitive and physiological responses. Specific factors to focus on include culturally unacceptable interpretations, selective attention, control strategies, positive beliefs about psychotic phenomena, imagery in relation to psychotic phenomena and metacognitive beliefs (thoughts about thoughts and thought processes). It is also important to examine environmental factors that may be involved in the maintenance of the problem, such as the kind of neighbourhood a person lives in, their housing, (un)employment and financial circumstances.

Problem history and development

It is important to assess early experiences that may have contributed to the development of current difficulties. Life events in childhood contribute to the development of core beliefs and dysfunctional assumptions or rules that guide behaviour and the selection of information-processing strategies (Beck 1976; Wells and Matthews 1994). Particular events that are worth assessing include childhood sexual and physical abuse, emotional abuse and neglect, social isolation and bullying. This is especially important in patients with psychosis, given the high prevalence of such experiences in this population (Mueser et al. 1998; Read 1997). Similar experiences in adulthood should also be examined (Read et al. 2003). A general assessment of family life, cultural and spiritual upbringing, school experiences and friendships should also be performed.

The influence of life experiences on the development of self and social knowledge should be considered. Assessment should include an analysis of a client's core beliefs. These are unconditional statements about themselves, the world and other people (for example, 'I am bad', 'Other people cannot be trusted' and 'The world is dangerous'). The conditional beliefs or rules that people adopt to compensate for these core beliefs should also be assessed. These often occur in the form of 'If . . . then . . .' statements; for example, 'If I am perfect, then I will be lovable'. The compensatory strategies that are the behavioural expressions of these rules should also be identified (such as striving for perfection or subjugating personal needs).

Procedural beliefs, which guide the selection of information-processing strategies, should also be assessed (Wells and Matthews 1994). Procedural beliefs that are particularly relevant to people with psychosis include beliefs about the utility of paranoia and suspiciousness (e.g. 'Staying on your toes keeps you safe') or beliefs about unusual perceptual experiences (such as 'Having odd experiences can make life more interesting' or 'Hearing voices can help me cope').

PROBLEM AND GOAL LIST

The development of a shared list of problems and goals, which can then be collaboratively prioritized, is a central part of CT and is invaluable in engaging patients (whether they are psychotic or not). Problems should start out quite general and be phrased in a more specific manner after additional information is gained. The goals set in relation to the problems should then be made as SMART as possible. This means making the goals Specific, Measurable, Achievable, Realistic and Time-limited. Here are some examples:

- *Problem*: hearing distressing voices that interfere with relationships.
  Goal: within 6 weeks, to reduce distress from 70 to 40%, or to reduce frequency from about 6 hours per day to 4 hours per day, or to increase belief that 'I can have a conversation despite my voices' from 0 to 25%.
- *Problem*: feeling paranoid in social situations.
  Goal: within 4 weeks, to reduce belief that 'Other people are trying to harm me' from 90 to 50%, or to reduce anxiety when in social situations from a weekly average of 85% to a weekly average of 50%.
- *Problem*: uncertainty about the link between childhood abuse and my current difficulties.
  Goal: within 1 week, to find out more about traumatic life events and the development of unusual experiences, and to increase belief that 'I know what research says about childhood trauma and hearing voices' from 10 to 80%.
- *Problem*: having no close friends to confide in.
  Goal: within 4 weeks, to find one person that I would feel comfortable telling some personal details to.

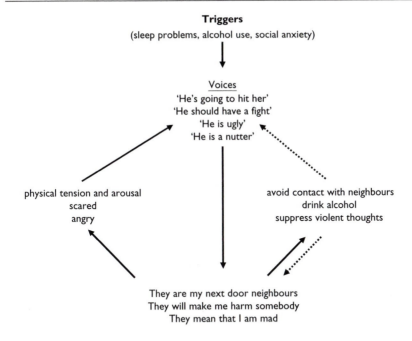

Figure 20.1   A formulation of the maintenance of voices.

FORMULATIONS

Once assessment has been conducted and problems and goals agreed upon, the next step is the development of a shared formulation. There are several levels at which a person's difficulties can be formulated. Basic formulations can be easily constructed summarizing recent incidents in the format of event–thought–feeling–behaviour cycles, as mentioned earlier. More detailed maintenance formulations that focus on specific symptoms can also be useful. For example, a recent model of the maintenance of auditory hallucinations has suggested that safety behaviours (strategies designed to avoid feared outcomes in relation to voices) can prevent disconfirmation of the interpretation and also increase the frequency of voices (Morrison 1998a). It also emphasizes the role of affect and physiology in the maintenance cycle, and incorporates normalizing triggers such as sleep deprivation, drug use, stressful life events and biochemical changes. This model can be easily translated into a case conceptualization if a patient prioritizes voices on their problem list. An example of this type of formulation is given in Figure 20.1.

Another level of formulation is the development of an historical case conceptualization. This type of formulation incorporates early experiences

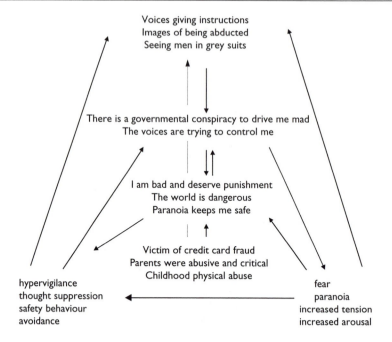

Voices giving instructions
Images of being abducted
Seeing men in grey suits

There is a governmental conspiracy to drive me mad
The voices are trying to control me

I am bad and deserve punishment
The world is dangerous
Paranoia keeps me safe

Victim of credit card fraud
Parents were abusive and critical
Childhood physical abuse

hypervigilance
thought suppression
safety behaviour
avoidance

fear
paranoia
increased tension
increased arousal

Figure 20.2   An idiosyncratic formulation of the cognitive model of psychosis.

and life events and the impact that these have had on core beliefs, procedural beliefs, dysfunctional assumptions and compensatory strategies, in addition to information regarding the current maintaining factors. A recent model of psychotic symptoms (Morrison 2001) has suggested that it is the cultural acceptability of interpretations that determines whether someone is viewed as psychotic or not, and that these interpretations are influenced by life experiences and beliefs. It also suggests that it is the initial interpretation of psychotic experiences, and the way in which people respond to such experiences, that determines whether or not the experience will cause distress and recur. This model of psychosis is also easily translated into an idiosyncratic case conceptualization that can explain the development and maintenance of psychosis (see Figure 20.2 for an example).

INTERVENTIONS

Once a case formulation has been collaboratively developed, strategies for change can be chosen on the basis of what is likely to achieve quick success or what will have the most significant effect on the person's quality of life.

Most change strategies can be described as verbal reattribution methods or behavioural reattribution methods.

Verbal reattribution

Advantages and disadvantages

It is important to consider the advantages and disadvantages of a particular belief or experience. This should be done before attempting to change a belief, even if the belief is distressing. Positive beliefs about psychotic experiences can be identified through this process. These can include the advantages of being paranoid, such as safety and excitement, or beliefs about the benefits of hearing voices. Such beliefs are important, as they have been shown to be associated with predisposition to psychosis (Morrison *et al.* 2000) and are implicated in the development and maintenance of psychotic experiences (Morrison *et al.* 2002a). Common positive beliefs about hallucinations include the benevolence of the voices (Chadwick and Birchwood 1994), and perceiving the voices as providing companionship or relaxation (Miller *et al.* 1993). The origins of psychotic experiences should also be explored within this context, as they may have been functional at some stage as coping or survival strategies. For example, paranoia is helpful if you are in a dangerous or abusive environment. Romme and Escher (1989) suggest that voices frequently evolve as a coping response to trauma. Some negative symptoms can also be conceptualized in a similar way (see below).

If significant advantages are identified, then these should be evaluated with regard to current utility, alternative potential sources of the benefits, and the relative weighting of advantages and disadvantages. It may be that work is required to provide an alternative way of achieving the benefits before the problematic aspects of the psychotic experience can be dealt with. For example, if someone has their self-esteem maintained by a belief that they are special and chosen by God (but is experiencing difficulties as a result of behaviour arising from this), then it is important to provide alternative sources of self-esteem. Similarly, if someone views the company that their voices provide as very significant, then it is important to help them develop social networks that will address this need. At times, it is necessary to recognize that the benefits of a psychotic experience outweigh the disadvantages, and that other ways of proving the advantages are not achievable or realistic. In such cases, the patient should be enabled to make their own decision and be supported as best as possible in relation to their environment (familial, social or psychiatric). Facilitating contact with support groups or interest groups with similar experiences or beliefs can be helpful.

Usually, however, it is possible to provide an alternative way of achieving the benefits, or the advantages are outweighed by the disadvantages. In

Table 20.1   Evidence for and against a belief

Evidence for 'The neighbours are going to attack me'	Evidence against 'The neighbours are going to attack me'
There are rowdy noises from next door	I have seen them three times this week and they haven't attacked me
I have been assaulted by other people in the past	I have never been assaulted by anyone from my street
They can read my mind	I have never seen the neighbours be violent to anyone
	I don't think they are going to attack me when I am drunk or when I am with other people

addition, many positive beliefs about psychosis are inaccurate. Also, survival strategies that have been helpful in the past may no longer be necessary if the environment has changed. If a decision is reached to proceed, then therapist and patient can continue to evaluate, and possibly change, the belief or reduce the frequency of, or distress associated with, an experience. Strategies that will facilitate this process are described below.

Evidential analysis

A standard procedure in CT is to examine the evidence for and against a particular thought or interpretation of events (Wells 1997, 2000). This process begins with the identification of a specific thought or belief to be considered, and some discussion of what can be construed as evidence (e.g. a feeling that something is true is unlikely to be viewed as evidence in a courtroom). Two columns can then be used to collate evidence for and against the particular belief (see Table 20.1). The evidence should be elicited Socratically, using questions such as 'What makes you think that this is true?' and 'Is there anything that is incompatible with your belief?' Consideration of modulating factors can also be helpful in generating evidence, as can questions specifically related to the content of the belief.

Generation of alternative explanations

Generating alternative explanations is another useful strategy to help reduce the distress associated with psychotic experiences. Delusional ideas and beliefs about voices are open to examination and it is important to help people to consider a wide variety of possible explanations for their experiences if they are distressed by their current explanation. Brainstorming exercises, and the consideration of what other people have suggested or would suggest, can facilitate this process. These alternative explanations should be rated for degree of belief or conviction on an ongoing basis, and recent problematic situations and moderators can be evaluated in relation to consistency with each explanation. This process can be applied to general beliefs or specific incidents. For example, one piece of evidence in the analysis above was the rowdy noises from next door. The person in this example should be encouraged to generate as many possible explanations for such an incident as possible. It can be helpful to include some highly unlikely alternatives, as humour can help develop the therapeutic relationship and lighten the tone in therapy. This process may yield a list such as:

The rowdy noises from next door are due to:
Conviction

Initial belief: The neighbours want to attack me	80%
The neighbours are having a party	25%
The neighbours are having an argument	50%
The neighbours are making noises to wind me up	50%
I am imagining the noises	10%
The noises are being beamed into the house from outer space	0%

Normalization

The use of normalizing information can combat the negative effects of stigma, reduce distress and provide information to facilitate the generation of alternatives. Such information can include facts about the prevalence of psychotic experiences and beliefs in the general population. For example, 5% of the population hear voices at any given time (Tien 1991), and up to 70% of the general population endorse beliefs that could be labelled as delusional (Verdoux *et al.* 1998). When providing such information, calculating the implications for the prevalence in your own country can increase the impact that results. For example, in the UK, approximately 3 million people will hear voices, many of whom will never have contact with psychiatric services. Such information can be liberating for someone who believed that they were the only person with such experiences, or that such experiences automatically meant they were mad.

Information about the links between life events and specific psychotic experiences can also be helpful in reducing distress and providing an alternative explanation for hallucinations and delusions. For example, there is evidence to suggest that auditory hallucinations are linked to experiences such as childhood trauma (Read 1997; Romme and Escher 1989), bereavement (Grimby 1993; Reese 1971) and drug abuse (Aggernaes 1972), and that psychotic experiences are related to urban living (van Os *et al.* 2001). A summary of the normalizing approach to psychosis is provided in Kingdon and Turkington's (1994) book, which can be helpful for patients to read.

Imagery

People with psychotic experiences often have recurrent images associated with them (Morrison *et al.* 2002b). For example, people who hear voices will frequently have an image of the perceived source of their voice (e.g. God, the Devil, their next-door neighbour or a celebrity) or an image that is associated with the content of the voices. Patients with persecutory ideas often have images of their persecutors or images that are associated with their feared outcomes (e.g. going mad or being assaulted or killed). Such images can be a useful way of accessing personal meaning and core beliefs, and can be modified to become less distressing or powerful (Hackmann 1997).

Core beliefs and content of voices

Core beliefs, such as 'I am bad' or 'Other people cannot be trusted', can be evaluated and changed using the techniques outlined above. They are also amenable to other strategies such as historical tests (searching for information from any time in the past that is inconsistent with the belief), the use of criteria continua (operationalizing factors such as badness, and rating self or others on the resulting continua) and positive data logs (Padesky 1994).

Trauma-based strategies

Given the high prevalence of trauma in patients with psychosis (Read 1997), it is likely that treatment strategies that have been developed for patients with post-traumatic stress disorder or dissociative disorders may be helpful. Such strategies include examining the idiosyncratic meaning of the trauma or the sequelae of the trauma and developing an explanatory narrative for the trauma to aid contextualization in memory (Ehlers and Clark 2000). In addition, strategies for dissociation, such as the use of grounding and distraction techniques, refocusing and cognitive restructuring, can be useful (Kennerley 1996).

Behavioural reattribution

The use of behavioural strategies within a cognitive framework can be an extremely effective way of achieving belief change and reducing distress (Chadwick and Lowe 1990). Behavioural experiments are a vital component of CT. It can be particularly important to address safety behaviours that are used to prevent feared outcomes (especially in relation to negative symptoms).

Behavioural experiments

Behavioural experiments are central to effective CT for psychosis. Beliefs about voices and delusional ideas are frequently translatable into testable hypotheses that can be collaboratively investigated by patient and therapist. Behavioural experiments should be designed very carefully to ensure a 'no-lose' outcome. Predictions should be stated in a concrete way, and the possible results should be reviewed in advance to ensure that the outcome is meaningful and will not be dismissed or accommodated within the problematic belief system. Examples of behavioural experiments include the use of activity scheduling to evaluate beliefs about the consequences of activity or the lack of pleasure (which can be helpful for negative symptoms) or exposure to feared situations in order to evaluate beliefs about voices or paranoid ideas.

An example illustrates the process. Jim, a 19-year-old man, was certain that his thoughts were being transmitted via telepathy. He cited evidence from several examples in which it appeared that people around him had made comments about the topic he was thinking about, or reacted in a way that suggested that they were aware of his thoughts. An experiment was devised in which he was asked to operationalize the kind of response that would occur if people were able to read thoughts of imminent personal attack. He decided that people would flee a building by the nearest exit. He then decided, after considerable time had been spent using verbal reattribution methods to allow experimentation to feel safe, that an appropriate test of this belief would be to try to broadcast thoughts that implicated him as a terrorist who was about to set off a bomb. He did this in several different buildings, and noticed no sudden rush for the exit (although he did notice a few people leaving, this had been discussed in advance, and it had been agreed that the majority of people would have to leave quickly to confirm his belief). This resulted in a sustained decrease in both conviction and distress associated with the beliefs.

Safety behaviours

Safety behaviours, first identified in relation to anxiety disorders, are behaviours adopted to prevent a feared outcome. They are problematic when they prevent disconfirmation of the catastrophic beliefs about the feared outcome. People with psychotic experiences frequently use safety behaviours (Morrison 1998b). Studies have demonstrated the presence of such behaviours in people with distressing auditory hallucinations and persecutory delusions (Freeman *et al.* 2001). Examples of such safety behaviours include avoidance of particular places, hypervigilance and selective attention, and idiosyncratic strategies to prevent psychosis-related fears. For example, if someone believes that their voices will make them go mad, then they will adopt behaviours designed to maintain mental well-being (e.g. thought suppression, monitoring for signs of impending madness, staying in the company of others or trying to relax), which prevent disconfirmation of this belief and may actually increase the frequency or intensity of the voices. If someone believes they are being persecuted, then they may develop strategies such as taking different routes to the shops, being hypervigilant for men in suits, suppressing signs of arousal or avoiding eye contact, which can be similarly problematic. Such safety behaviours can be manipulated to demonstrate their counter-productive effects, and are amenable to being dropped in behavioural experiments to evaluate the relevant beliefs.

Negative symptoms

Negative symptoms include apathy, withdrawal, flat or blunted affect, anhedonia and poverty of speech. Such symptoms are frequently assumed to be the result of a biological syndrome or deficit state. However, many of these experiences can be understood, from a CT perspective, as safety behaviours. Some patients report having developed flat affect as a deliberate survival or coping strategy to avoid the feared outcome of physical punishment or humiliation in childhood. Others report having developed a similar strategy to manage their contact with the psychiatric system, since strong expressions of emotion frequently lead to increases in medication or admission to hospital. Poverty of speech can develop for similar reasons, and inactivity is frequently adopted to avoid exacerbations in positive symptoms. Other possible causes of negative symptoms include over-medication, depression, anxiety and substance abuse.

ADJUSTMENT AND RECOVERY

Once people with psychosis have recovered from the distress associated with their psychotic experiences, there are many other factors that are potential targets for CT. Such difficulties should also be considered at the beginning of CT, as many people will prioritize problems that are traditionally viewed as 'co-morbid' as being more distressing than their experience of psychosis. For example, there is a significant literature that suggests that post-traumatic stress disorder is a common problem for people with psychosis (Mueser et al. 1998), which is unsurprising given the prevalence of traumatic life events in people with psychosis (Mueser et al. 1998; Read 1997). It is also worth considering that people with psychosis frequently develop post-traumatic stress disorder in response to their treatment experiences or the psychotic symptoms themselves (Frame and Morrison 2001; McGorry et al. 1991). Depression and hopelessness are also common responses to an episode of psychosis (Birchwood et al. 2000). Such problems are clearly appropriate targets for CT.

RELAPSE PREVENTION

Core beliefs and conditional assumptions, as well as positive beliefs about psychotic experiences, can be conceptualized as vulnerability factors for relapse. These can be addressed at this stage of therapy, providing that the patient consents to this, using the strategies outlined earlier. A more formal approach to relapse prevention has been described by Max Birchwood and colleagues (Birchwood 1996; Birchwood *et al.* 1989). This approach involves the identification and subsequent monitoring of early warning signs such as sleep difficulties, anxiety, depression, unusual thoughts, irritability and social withdrawal.

Monitoring systems, often involving case managers and relatives or friends, are then developed, and action plans are collaboratively generated. There is evidence to suggest that CT targeted at people exhibiting such signs is feasible (Gumley and Power 2000) and can reduce relapse rates by 50% (Gumley and Power 2001). It is also important to help people distinguish between a lapse and relapse, and to ensure that they do not overly catastrophize the emergence of early signs, as this could potentially fuel the development of a relapse (Gumley *et al.* 1999).

MONITORING OUTCOMES

The most useful method of monitoring outcomes is to develop idiosyncratic measures that are related to the SMART goals that have been set. These could include regular ratings of belief, distress, frequency, severity and impairment in relation to specific psychotic experiences or other problems, using methods such as Likert scales, visual analog scales or percentage ratings. It can also be useful to use standardized interview-based or self-report measures such as the PSYRATS (Haddock *et al.* 1999) to assess dimensions of hallucinations and delusions, and the Beck Depression Inventory (Beck *et al.* 1961) to monitor mood and risk of self-harm. There are other scales that can be used to monitor beliefs about voices or responses to voices (Chadwick *et al.* 2000; Morrison *et al.* 2002a). It is also important to monitor social and occupational outcomes. All measures should reflect user-defined outcomes.

SUMMARY AND FUTURE DIRECTIONS

Many studies have clearly shown CT for psychosis to be effective. However, there are several areas that are showing promise in the psychological treatment of psychosis that require further development and evaluation. The development of trauma-based interventions for people with psychosis is in its infancy (Morrison *et al.*, in press). The role of beliefs and safety behaviours in the development and maintenance of negative symptoms has yet to be empirically demonstrated, and the efficacy of treatment strategies based on such a conceptualization is largely unknown. The use of CT for people with psychosis should also be extended to specific populations such as those in forensic settings, first episode patients, acute psychiatric settings and with patients not taking antipsychotic medication. Another recent development is the use of CT for the prevention of psychosis in populations defined to be at high-risk of developing a psychotic disorder within the subsequent year. A recent randomized, controlled trial has demonstrated that people from such a high-risk population are significantly less likely to develop psychosis over a 12-month period if they receive cognitive therapy, without medication, in comparison with a monitoring control condition (Morrison *et al.* 2003), whether this is defined using a severity threshold of psychotic symptoms or DSM-IV diagnostic criteria. Future directions should also include a consideration of the possible side-effects of CT. Normalizing CT hopefully minimizes side-effects, but problems such as stigmatization, pathologizing the variety of human experience and increased short-term distress remain possibilities.

REFERENCES

Aggernaes, A. (1972). The difference between the experienced reality of hallucinations in young drug abusers and schizophrenic patients. *Acta Psychiatrica Scandinavica* 48: 287-99.

Beck, A. (1976). *Cognitive Therapy and the Emotional Disorders*. New York: International Universities Press.

Beck, A. *et al.* (1961). An inventory for measuring depression. *Archives of General Psychiatry* 41: 53–63.

Beck, A. *et al.* (1979). *Cognitive Therapy of Depression*. New York: Guilford Press.

Bentall, R. *et al.* (2001). Persecutory delusions. *Clinical Psychology Review* 22: 1–50.

Birchwood, M. (1996). Early intervention in psychotic relapse. In G. Haddock and P. Slade (eds) *Cognitive-Behavioural Interventions with Psychotic Disorders*. London: Routledge.

Birchwood, M. *et al.* (1989). Predicting relapse in schizophrenia. *Psychological Medicine* 19: 649–56.

Birchwood, M. *et al.* (2000). Cognitive approach to depression and suicidal thinking in psychosis. *British Journal of Psychiatry* 177: 516–21.

Chadwick, P. and Birchwood, M. (1994). The omnipotence of voices. *British Journal of Psychiatry* 164: 190–201.

Chadwick, P. and Lowe, C. (1990). The measurement and modification of delusional beliefs. *Journal of Consulting and Clinical Psychology* 58: 225–32.

Chadwick, P. *et al.* (2000). The revised Beliefs about Voices Questionnaire. *British Journal of Psychiatry* 177: 229–32.

Ehlers, A. and Clark, D. (2000). A cognitive model of posttraumatic stress disorder. *Behaviour Research and Therapy* 38: 319–45.

Frame, L. and Morrison, A. (2001). Causes of posttraumatic stress disorder in psychotic patients. *Archives of General Psychiatry* 58: 305–6.

Freeman, D. *et al.* (2001). Persecutory delusions. *Psychological Medicine* 31: 1293–1306.

Garety, P. *et al.* (2001). A cognitive model of the positive symptoms of psychosis. *Psychological Medicine* 31: 189–95.

Gould, R. *et al.* (2001). Cognitive therapy for psychosis in schizophrenia. *Schizophrenia Research* 48: 335–42.

Grimby, A. (1993). Bereavement among elderly people: grief reactions, post-bereavement hallucinations and quality of life. *Acta Psychiatrica Scandinavica* 87: 72–80.

Gumley, A. and Power, K. (2000). Is targeting cognitive therapy during early relapse in psychosis feasible? *Behavioral and Cognitive Psychotherapy* 28: 161–74.

Gumley, A. and Power, K. (2001). *The West of Scotland Early Intervention Trial* (Grant Number K/RED/18/13). Edinburgh: Chief Scientist Office, Scottish Executive.

Gumley, A. *et al.* (1999). An interacting cognitive subsystems model of relapse and the course of psychosis. *Clinical Psychology and Psychotherapy* 6: 261–78.

Hackmann, A. (1997). The transformation of meaning in cognitive therapy. In M. Power and C. Brewin (eds) *Transformation of Meaning in Psychological Therapies*. Chichester: Wiley.

Haddock, G. *et al.* (1999). Scales to measure dimensions of hallucinations and delusions. *Psychological Medicine* 29: 879–89.

Kennerley, H. (1996). Cognitive therapy for dissociative symptoms associated with trauma. *British Journal of Clinical Psychology* 35: 325–40.

Kingdon, D. and Turkington, D. (1994). *Cognitive-Behavioural Therapy of Schizophrenia*. Hove: Lawrence Erlbaum.

Kuipers, E. *et al.* (1997). The London–East Anglia randomised controlled trial of cognitive-behaviour therapy for psychosis I: Effects of the treatment phase. *British Journal of Psychiatry* 171: 319–27.

Kuipers, E. *et al.* (1998). The London–East Anglia randomised controlled trial of cognitive-behaviour therapy for psychoses III: Follow-up and economic considerations. *British Journal of Psychiatry* 173: 61–8.

McGorry, P. *et al.* (1991). Post-traumatic stress disorder following recent onset psychosis. *Journal of Nervous and Mental Disease* 179: 253–8.

Miller, L. *et al.* (1993). Patients' attitudes to hallucinations. *American Journal of Psychiatry* 150: 584–8.

Morrison, A. (1998a). A cognitive analysis of the maintenance of auditory hallucinations. *Behavioral and Cognitive Psychotherapy* 26: 289–302.

Morrison, A. (1998b). Cognitive behaviour therapy for psychotic symptoms in schizophrenia. In N. Tarrier *et al.* (eds) *Treating Complex Cases*. Chichester: Wiley.

Morrison, A. (2001). The interpretation of intrusions in psychosis. *Behavioral and Cognitive Psychotherapy* 29: 257–76.

Morrison, A. (2002). *A Casebook of Cognitive Therapy for Psychosis*. London: Routledge.

Morrison, A. *et al.* (2000). Cognitive factors in predisposition to auditory and visual hallucinations. *British Journal of Clinical Psychology* 39: 67–78.

Morrison, A. *et al.* (2002a). Cognitive and emotional factors as predictors of predisposition to hallucinations in non-patients. *British Journal of Clinical Psychology* 41: 259–70.

Morrison, A. *et al.* (2002b). Imagery and psychotic symptoms. *Behaviour Research and Therapy* 40: 1063–72.

Morrison, A. *et al.* (in press). Relationships between trauma and psychosis. *British Journal of Clinical Psychology*.

Morrison, A. *et al.* (2003). Cognitive therapy for people who are at high risk of developing psychosis: the results of a randomised control trial. Paper presented at the British Association of Behavioural and Cognitive Psychotherapy Annual Conference, July 16–19, York, UK.

Mueser, K. *et al.* (1998). Trauma and posttraumatic stress disorder in severe mental illness. *Journal of Consulting and Clinical Psychology* 66: 493–9.

Nothard, S. *et al.* (in prep.). Safety behaviours and auditory hallucinations.

Padesky, C. (1994). Schema change processes in cognitive therapy. *Clinical Psychology and Psychotherapy* 1: 267–78.

Read, J. (1997). Child abuse and psychosis. *Professional Psychology: Research and Practice* 28: 448–56.

Read, J. *et al.* (2003). Sexual and physical abuse during childhood and adulthood as predictors of hallucinations, delusions and thought disorder. *Psychology and Psychotherapy: Theory, Research and Practice* 16: 1–22.

Reese, W. (1971). The hallucinations of widowhood. *British Medical Journal* 210: 37–41.

Romme, M. and Escher, A. (1989). Hearing voices. *Schizophrenia Bulletin* 15: 209–16.

Sensky, T. *et al.* (2000). A randomized controlled trial of cognitive-behavioral therapy for persistent symptoms in schizophrenia resistant to medication. *Archives of General Psychiatry* 57: 165–72.

Tarrier, N. *et al.* (1998). A randomized controlled trial of intense cognitive behaviour therapy for chronic schizophrenia. *British Medical Journal* 317: 303–7.

Tien, A. (1991). Distribution of hallucinations in the population. *Social Psychiatry and Psychiatric Epidemiology* 26: 287–92.

van Os, J. *et al.* (2001). Prevalence of psychotic disorder and community level of psychotic symptoms. *Archives of General Psychiatry* 58: 663–8.

Verdoux, H. *et al.* (1998). A survey of delusional ideation in primary-care patients. *Psychological Medicine* 28: 127–34.

Wells, A. (1997). *Cognitive Therapy for Anxiety Disorders*. London: Wiley.

Wells, A. (2000). *Emotional Disorders and Metacognition: Innovative Cognitive Therapy*. New York: Wiley.

Wells, A. and Matthews, G. (1994). *Attention and Emotion*. London: Lawrence Erlbaum.

Chapter 21

Psychodynamic psychotherapy for schizophrenia

Empirical support

William H. Gottdiener

WHY WE CONDUCTED OUR META-ANALYTIC REVIEW

In 1990, Mueser and Berenbaum called for a moratorium on the use of psychoanalytically oriented treatments for schizophrenia. They claimed there was no good empirical evidence to support them. In 1998, The Schizophrenia Patient Outcome Research Team (PORT) were even more pointed in their critique of the literature and their clinical recommendation, arguing that some forms of psychodynamic therapy are harmful for people with schizophrenia. This, in conjunction with the fact that 'there is no evidence in support of the superiority of psychoanalytic therapy to other forms of therapy', led them to adopt a position 'strongly against the use of psychoanalytic therapy, even in combination with effective pharmaco-therapy' (Lehman and Steinwachs 1998: 7–8).

Misgivings about the efficacy of psychoanalytic treatments for schizophrenia have haunted psychoanalysis since Sigmund Freud voiced them 100 years ago (Freud 1904). Even with the Father's doubts, psychoanalytic treatments for schizophrenia have been used for nearly a century. To this day, their efficacy remains one of the most contentious issues in psychiatry in general and even within psychoanalysis. A large clinical literature has accrued. Most of this describes creative interventions that psychotherapists have developed to achieve positive results. Some of the more prominent psychotherapists and clinical researchers include psychoanalysts such as Arieti, Boyer, Giovacchini, Federn, Fromm-Reichmann, Lotterman, Karon, VandenBos, Robbins, Searles and Sullivan (see Chapter 15).

In contrast to the clinical literature, research on the efficacy of psycho-analytic psychotherapy for people diagnosed with schizophrenia has pro-duced contradictory findings. Two frequently cited studies exemplify these mixed results (Karon and VandenBos 1981; May 1968). Both were ran-domized controlled clinical trials comparing individual psychotherapy with and without antipsychotic medication to standard treatment in which medication was the primary intervention. May found that patients treated with supportive psychodynamic psychotherapy and conjoint antipsychotic medication, or those treated solely with medication, had significantly greater improvement rates than patients who received only supportive psychodynamic psychotherapy. In the Karon and VandenBos study, also conducted in the 1960s, the opposite was found. Psychotherapists treated two groups of patients with individual exploratory psychodynamic psychotherapy. One group did not receive medication and the other did, but only in small doses that were ended within the first few weeks of treatment. These two treatment groups were compared with a third group of patients who received standard hospital care, with antipsychotic medication as the primary treatment. Significantly more patients treated with individual psychotherapy (including those receiving a brief course of medication) improved than those patients who received medication only.

Since these two landmark studies, many others have been conducted. The results have been summarized in several reviews (Fenton 2000; Gomes-Schwartz 1984; Heinrichs and Carpenter 1981; Liberman 1994; Malmberg and Fenton 2001; Mosher and Keith 1980; Mueser and Berenbaum 1990; Scott and Dixon 1995; Smith *et al.* 1980). With the exception of Smith *et al.* (1980), most reviewers have concluded that little evidence exists to support the efficacy of psychodynamic psychotherapy.

Despite the contention that surrounds the topic, the treatment guidelines of the American Psychiatric Association (1997) recommend that supportive interventions are effective for schizophrenia when combined with antipsychotic medications, and that exploratory interventions (e.g. psychodynamic) might be useful for some patients.

To date, two reviews have employed meta-analysis to grapple with the problem (Gottdiener and Haslam 2002; Malmberg and Fenton 2001). Meta-analysis is the quantitative synthesis of similar empirical reports. Although meta-analysis is not without its limitations, it is the most useful way to resolve controversial findings across a body of literature and has advantages over qualitative literature reviews.

Malmberg and Fenton (2001) concluded that the methods of existing research were too poor to draw definitive conclusions for or against the efficacy of individual psychodynamic psychotherapy. Realizing that the issue had not been settled by previous efforts, my colleague Nick Haslam, from the University of Melbourne, and I conducted a meta-analysis on the efficacy of individual psychotherapy for people diagnosed with schizophrenia. In the rest of this chapter, I will show that when the empirical literature is examined broadly, the data support the efficacy of individual psychotherapy for people diagnosed with schizophrenia. To accomplish this goal, I compare the efficacy of psychodynamic psychotherapy with the efficacy of cognitive-behavioural and non-psychodynamic supportive therapies. This is necessary to appreciate the utility of psychoanalytic treatments in the context of those that are also widely practised.

To determine the efficacy of individual psychotherapy for people diagnosed with schizophrenia, we conducted a comprehensive meta-analytic review of all studies in which an effect size was calculable regardless of study design. This enabled us to determine the overall efficacy of individual psychotherapy for schizophrenia. It also enabled us to examine a number of potential moderator variables (for detailed methods and results, see Gottdiener and Haslam 2002).

HOW GOOD IS INDIVIDUAL PSYCHOTHERAPY FOR PEOPLE DIAGNOSED WITH SCHIZOPHRENIA?

To determine the efficacy of individual psychotherapy, and individual psychodynamic psychotherapy in particular, for people diagnosed with schizophrenia, we reviewed 37 studies published between 1954 and 1999. We calculated 232 effect sizes. These reports are based on the treatment of 2642 patients with a mean age of 31.1 years. Treatment lasted for an average of 20.2 months with a mean of 1.4 sessions per week.

To establish the overall efficacy of individual psychotherapy for people diagnosed with schizophrenia, we averaged all the effect sizes from all 37 studies. The results show that individual psychotherapy was associated with improvement in overall functioning. The results include the grand mean effect size, the corrected effect size (the grand mean effect size divided by the artefact attenuation factor) and improvement rates determined by the binomial effect size display (BESD). The grand mean effect size was $r = 0.31$ (95% CI $\pm$ 0.22 to 0.41). The corrected effect size was $r = 0.36$. The BESD results showed that improvement rate increased from 35 to 66%, which indicates that 66% of patients are better off after treatment compared with 35% without treatment. What does this mean? Rosenthal *et al.* (2000) write: 'r of .32 (or a r^2 of .10) will amount to a difference between rates of improvement of 34% and 66% if half the population received psychotherapy and half did not, and if half the population improved and half did not' (p. 17). In this meta-analysis, the BESD means that 66% of the population that received psychotherapy improved compared with only 35% of the population that did not receive psychotherapy.

The grand mean effect size shows the general efficacy of individual psychotherapy for people diagnosed with schizophrenia. Treatment efficacy was, however, moderated by several factors. We examined variables for which there was abundant information throughout the database. We present these below.

The effects of random assignment

Nineteen studies employed random assignment. The mean effect size for these studies was $r = 0.31$ (95% CI $\pm$ 0.17 to 0.43). Another 18 studies either did not employ random assignment or did not report if it was used. The mean effect size for these studies was $r = 0.34$ (95% CI ± 0.20 to 0.46). Thus, in this database there was essentially no difference in outcome between studies that employed random assignment and those that did not. This suggests that failure for primary studies to employ random assignment did not pose meaningful threats to the internal validity of this meta-analysis.

Source of data

Within-groups data examine change in one group over time, whereas between-groups data examine change in one group relative to another group over time. Because of this it has been questioned whether or not it is appropriate to combine within-groups and between-groups data. It has been stated that within-groups data tend to inflate effect sizes compared with between-groups data (Morris and DeShon 2002). The advantage to combining both types of data in one meta-analysis would be for the between-groups data to correct for effect size inflation that could be caused by within-groups data. Whether or not within-groups data inflate effect sizes is open to debate. Rather than inflating effect sizes, within-groups data have been thought to simply address different questions than between-groups data. Morris and DeShon (2002) suggest that it is appropriate to combine such data when effect size estimates are similar, or when between-groups and within-groups data are conceptually addressing the same fundamental issues. We present both forms of data combined and separately as follows. For between-groups data, the mean effect size was $r = 0.10$ (95% CI ± 0.02 to 0.18). For within-groups data, the mean effect size was $r = 0.58$ (95% CI ± 0.43 to 0.70).

The between-groups results suggest that individual psychotherapy provides a similar advantage to other treatments. The specific results of the between-groups comparisons are as follows: (a) individual psychotherapy alone compared with antipsychotic medication, $r = -0.01$ (95% CI ± -0.21 to 0.19); (b) individual psychotherapy plus antipsychotic medication compared with antipsychotic medication, $r = 0.19$ (95% CI ± 0.07 to 0.31); (c) individual psychotherapy plus medication compared with other psychosocial treatments plus medication, $r = 0.08$ (95% CI ± -0.16 to 0.31). Thus the only comparison showing a distinct advantage over another treatment was the comparison of individual psychotherapy plus antipsychotic medication compared with antipsychotic medication.

The within-groups data suggest that there is a dramatic change during treatment and that most patients are much better off than they were before treatment. The findings show that the efficacy of treatment between individual psychotherapy and alternative treatments (e.g. antipsychotic medication) was approximately equal. It is, therefore, plausible to think that a similar amount of change occurs from pre-test to post-test in patients treated with individual psychotherapy and with antipsychotic medication. Because of this we thought it justifiable to combine all of the effects irrespective of whether the data came from a within-groups or between-groups design. Although both types of data address different issues, they also address the same fundamental issue of whether individual psychotherapy is an effective treatment for schizophrenia.

Type of individual psychotherapy

We found similar effect sizes for each form of treatment. The grand mean effect size for psychodynamic psychotherapy was $r = 0.33$ (95% CI ± 0.21 to 0.44). The corrected effect size was $r = 0.39$. The BESD results showed that improvement rate increased from 34 to 67%. The grand mean effect size for cognitive-behavioural therapy was $r = 0.35$ (95% CI ± 0.08 to 0.58). The corrected effect size was $r = 0.41$. The BESD results showed that improvement rate increased from 33 to 68%. The grand mean effect size for non-psychodynamic supportive therapy was $r = 0.23$ (95% CI ± 0.00 to 0.44). The corrected effect size was $r = 0.27$. The BESD results showed that improvement rate increased from 38 to 62%.

These results contrast with some of the reviews mentioned above and show that all three treatments are beneficial. Furthermore, psychodynamic and cognitive-behavioural therapies produce similar therapeutic benefit, which is more than that produced by non-psychodynamic supportive therapies.

Use of conjoint medication

There is a long-standing controversy about the use of conjoint medication in the psychotherapy of people with schizophrenia. For many years, psychotherapists were reluctant to employ antipsychotic medication as an adjunct to psychotherapy because they thought it would disturb the therapeutic process. However, since at least the 1960s most therapists that treat people with schizophrenia have used antipsychotic medication in conjunction with psychotherapy. Many therapists think it indispensable. However, between 40 and 75% of patients do not take their medication (Perkins 1999) and there are many for whom medications fail to work (see Chapter 9).

When antipsychotic medication was used with individual psychotherapy, the mean effect size was $r = 0.31$ (95% CI ± 0.19 to 0.42). When antipsychotic medications were not administered with individual psychotherapy, the mean effect size was also $r = 0.31$ (95% CI ± 0.12 to 0.48). The corrected effect size and BESD results for psychotherapy with medication and without medication were the same. The corrected effect size was $r = 0.36$ and the BESD results showed that improvement rate increased from 35 to 66%.

Chronicity of the disorder

People diagnosed with acute schizophrenia have long been thought to have better prognoses than people diagnosed with chronic schizophrenia. For people with acute schizophrenia, the mean effect size was $r = 0.37$ (95% CI ± 0.10 to 0.59). The corrected effect size was $r = 0.44$. The BESD results showed that improvement rate increased from 32 to 69%. For people with chronic schizophrenia (with a somewhat arbitrary cut-off point of 2 years), the mean effect size was $r = 0.36$ (95% CI ± 0.21 to 0.49). The corrected effect size was $r = 0.42$. The BESD results showed that improvement rate increased from 32 to 68%.

Treatment context

Clinical lore suggests that treatment context has a strong influence on outcome. We could only examine this factor by looking at inpatients and outpatients. For inpatients, the mean effect size was $r = 0.29$ (95% CI ± 0.14 to 0.42). The corrected effect size was $r = 0.34$. The BESD results showed that improvement rate increased from 35 to 65%. For those that were treated in both inpatient and outpatient facilities during the study, the mean effect size was $r = 0.30$ (95% CI ± 0.03 to 0.53). The corrected effect size was $r = 0.35$. The BESD results showed that improvement rate increased from 35 to 65%. For outpatients, the mean effect size was $r = 0.37$ (95% CI ± 0.19 to 0.52). The corrected effect size was $r = 0.44$. The BESD results showed that improvement rate increased from 31 to 69%. The results show that outpatients improved at a higher rate than inpatients, which supports the prediction made based on clinical lore.

Diagnostic criteria

All of the participants in each treatment were diagnosed with schizophrenia, but reports vary according to the specificity of the diagnostic information provided. One study used DSM-II criteria, four used DSM-III, three used DSM-III-R (American Psychiatric Association 1968, 1980, 1987), two employed Research Diagnostic Criteria, four used multiple criteria including either DSM criteria or RDC criteria, another four used other diagnostic criteria, 10 used interviewer agreement, and nine did not report the method they used.

The diagnostic criteria for schizophrenia were broader before the DSM-III was published in 1980. Before then, people with schizoaffective disorder and schizophreniform disorder were often diagnosed with schizophrenia. People with these latter two disorders tend to have better prognoses than people diagnosed with schizophrenia. Given this, it might be expected that patients in pre-1980 studies might have improved more than those in later studies. However, the mean effect size for studies conducted after DSM-III was $r = 0.39$ (95% CI $\pm$ 0.19 to 0.56), whereas the mean effect size for studies conducted before its publication was $r = 0.28$ (95% CI $\pm$ 0.16 to 0.38).

Summary

The meta-analytic findings suggest that individual psychotherapy, with or without antipsychotic medication, is an effective treatment for schizophrenia. Individual psychotherapy without medication appears to have a roughly similar therapeutic efficacy to antipsychotic medication and each treatment seems to have a roughly similar incremental benefit when combined with the other. Studies that employed random assignment did not have larger effects than those that did not. Effect sizes from within-groups data were considerably larger than those from between-groups data. People diagnosed with acute and chronic schizophrenia obtained similar success rates. Outpatient treatment was associated with larger incremental benefit than inpatient treatment. Effect sizes were noticeably larger for studies published after the publication of DSM-III than before it.

DISCUSSION

Our findings indicate that individual psychotherapy is associated with improved functioning in most patients diagnosed with schizophrenia who receive it. All forms of individual psychotherapy (psychodynamic, cognitive-behavioural and non-psychodynamic supportive) were associated with an improvement in functioning, but the highest rates of improvement were associated with psychodynamic and cognitive-behavioural therapies.

The finding that the proportion of patients likely to improve without conjoint medication is similar to the proportion of patients likely to improve with a combination of individual psychotherapy and antipsychotic medication is contrary to many therapists' clinical expectations. The finding that individual psychotherapy can be effective without medication is not new (see Karon and VandenBos 1981; see also Chapter 15). It is important, however, because it suggests that individual psychotherapy alone might be a viable treatment option for some patients who do not improve from treatment with antipsychotic medications, for some patients who refuse to take medications, or for patients who are treated by therapists that choose to use little or no adjunctive medication.

The findings of our meta-analysis are consistent with those of the clinical literature, the findings of Smith *et al.* (1980) and Mojtabai *et al.* (1998), and the practice guidelines of the American Psychiatric Association (1997). They contradict, however, those of Malmberg and Fenton (2001) and

Cormac *et al.* (2002), most previous qualitative reviews of the literature, and the PORT guidelines (Lehman and Steinwachs 1998). The findings are especially contrary to suggestions that individual psychodynamic psychotherapy is contraindicated for people diagnosed with schizophrenia.

Limitations

There were a small number of studies to review. A larger sample of studies will enable more accurate estimates of effect sizes, and analysis of more moderator variables, such as estimation of changes in effect sizes over time during treatment and through several follow-up periods. The small number of studies also limited the amount of information available to conduct analyses of clinically important moderator variables such as therapist experience or training. It also limited the amount of information available to correct for attenuation due to study artefacts, such as the unreliability of the independent variable of individual psychotherapy.

Second, about half of the studies we reviewed did not assign participants randomly. The purpose of random assignment is to minimize potential threats to a study's internal validity. Observational or naturalistic designs are believed to be inferior to randomized controlled trials because they are thought to inflate effect size estimates. These long-held assumptions about randomized controlled trials have been challenged recently (Benson and Hartz 2000; Concato *et al.* 2000; Pawson and Tilley 1997; Shrout 1998). In two separate meta-analyses of medical treatments, no differences in effect sizes and confidence intervals were found to exist between randomized controlled trials and observational studies (Benson and Hartz 2000; Concato *et al.* 2000). Statistical techniques like structural equation modelling can also be used to help make strong causal inferences in observational and naturalistic studies (Shrout 1998). Random assignment is, therefore, not necessary to draw causal inferences or to obtain accurate estimates of population effect sizes. It might be the clearest way to do so, but not the only way.

See Gottdiener (2000) and Gottdiener and Haslam (2002) for discussion of other study limitations, including the possibility of having missed some unpublished data, and the focus on a generalized concept of outcome rather than analysing the effect sizes for different types of outcome measure or the amount of change occurring at different times in the therapy process.

Future directions

Additional studies would increase our understanding of the benefits of individual psychotherapy for people diagnosed with schizophrenia. They would allow reviewers to assess which therapeutic interventions benefit which patients and when. Several authors have pointed out that the goals of treatment, and the interventions used, will vary as a function of the type of schizophrenia being treated, the duration of the disorder, the personality of the patient and the context of treatment (Eissler 1951; Fenton 2000; McGlashan and Keats 1989). In addition, a number of therapists have developed psychotherapeutic approaches divided into stages that represent steps of progression that patients pass through as they recover (e.g. Arieti 1974; Pao 1979). The clinical literature also suggests that the most important issue in the use of individual psychotherapy for people diagnosed with schizophrenia is for therapists to maintain flexibility and to use supportive and insight-oriented interventions as needed (see Fenton 2000). Although none of the reports we reviewed reported outcomes specifically as a function of the type of interventions used, it is possible to infer from our review that both supportive and insight-oriented interventions are beneficial. Cognitive-behavioural and non-psychodynamic supportive therapies primarily consist of supportive interventions (see Hogarty *et al.* 1995; Kingdon and Turkington 1994; Morrison 2002; see also Chapter 20), but not exclusively. Some cognitive-behavioural treatments extensively use insight-oriented interventions (Perris 1989). Although psychodynamic therapies are generally thought to consist of insight-oriented interventions (Robbins 1993), they traditionally consist of supportive interventions in the early stages of treatment with severely disturbed patients, and for some patients supportive interventions will be the core of their treatment (Rockland 1989).

What would be most useful to draw from future research is to learn which patients could benefit from which types of interventions at which stage of treatment. It would also be useful to employ the Jacobson-Truax (Jacobson and Truax 1991) statistic to establish how much clinically meaningful change actually takes place for which patients under which conditions. And to understand the efficacy of psychodynamic psychotherapy for people diagnosed with schizophrenia, it would be useful to employ measures of psychodynamic constructs to determine in what ways and how much psychodynamic processes change due to treatment.

A final aspect that future research should address is the cost–benefit ratio of individual psychotherapy. One argument against using individual psychotherapy, even by those who believe in its efficacy, is that its expense prohibits its use on a large scale. Some also suggest that because individual psychotherapy does not appear to be considerably more efficacious than medication, it is simply not worth the added expense. There is some evidence, however, to suggest that the overall cost of treating severely mentally ill patients decreases significantly with the use of psychotherapy (Gabbard *et al.* 1997; Karon and VandenBos 1981) because they tend to use less inpatient treatment, they function at a higher level and their psychiatric problems become less likely to interfere with obtaining and maintaining employment than those not in psychotherapy (Gabbard *et al.* 1997; see also Chapter 23). The current meta-analytic review shows that dramatic improvement rates are associated with the use of individual psychotherapy, which suggests that over the course of a person's lifetime, the use of individual psychotherapy could actually help to reduce treatment costs. However, this is an issue that requires further study.

Related to the issue of cost-effectiveness are the costs due to the side-effects of, or adverse reactions to, antipsychotic medications. About 75% of patients diagnosed with schizophrenia stop taking their antipsychotic medication within 2 years, and problematic side-effects are the primary reason (Perkins 1999; see also Chapter 9). Antipsychotic medication is the primary treatment for schizophrenia, but if the compliance rate is so poor, then many people are foregoing treatment. It is plausible to speculate that the adverse effects of antipsychotic medications might contribute to the long-term high costs of treatment, lower capacity to be employed and diminished psychosocial functioning. This hypothesis also needs to be investigated empirically.

Final remarks

The findings of this meta-analysis clearly show that there is a positive relationship between the use of individual psychotherapy and improvement in overall functioning in people diagnosed with schizophrenia, when used with medication *and* without medication. Furthermore, all major forms of individual psychotherapy appear to be effective. Primarily because of limitations of the available data on this topic, a more fine-grained understanding of the role of individual psychotherapy in general and psychodynamic psychotherapy in particular for the treatment of schizophrenia remain to be elucidated by future primary research and by future meta-analyses.

Nevertheless, this review shows that the pessimism and scepticism that have long surrounded the utility of individual psychotherapy for people diagnosed with schizophrenia – especially that which has surrounded psychodynamic psychotherapy – is unwarranted. The denouncements by Mueser and Berenbaum (1990) and Lehman and Steinwachs (1998) are unconvincing in light of the evidence presented here. It should now be patently clear that there is strong empirical evidence that individual psychodynamic psychotherapy can play an integral and important role in the treatment of people diagnosed with schizophrenia. It is now time to learn more about how this and other treatments work, and how they can be made as effective and as available as possible.

ACKNOWLEDGEMENTS

Much of this chapter was adapted from Gottdiener and Haslam (2002). The opinions expressed in this chapter do not necessarily represent the official positions of National Development and Research Institutes, Inc.

REFERENCES

American Psychiatric Association (1968). *Diagnostic and Statistical Manual of Mental Disorders (DSM-II)*, 2nd edn. Washington, DC: APA.

American Psychiatric Association (1980). *Diagnostic and Statistical Manual of Mental Disorders (DSM-III)*, 3rd edn. Washington, DC: APA.

American Psychiatric Association (1987). *Diagnostic and Statistical Manual of Mental Disorders (DSM-III-R)*, 3rd edn revised. Washington, DC: APA.

American Psychiatric Association (1997). *Practice Guideline for the Treatment of Patients with Schizophrenia*, 1st edn. Washington, DC: APA.

Arieti, S. (1974). *Interpretation of Schizophrenia*. New York: Jason Aronson.

Benson, K. and Hartz, A.J. (2000). A comparison of observational studies and randomized, controlled trials. *New England Journal of Medicine* 342: 1878–86.

Concato, J. *et al.* (2000). Randomized, controlled trials, observational studies, and the hierarchy of research designs. *New England Journal of Medicine* 342: 1887–92.

Cormac, I. *et al.* (2002). Cognitive behaviour therapy for schizophrenia (Cochrane Review). *Cochrane Database of Systematic Reviews* (1) [Electronic database]. The Cochrane Library.

Eissler, K.R. (1951). Remarks on the psychoanalysis of schizophrenia. *International Journal of Psychoanalysis* 32: 139–56.

Fenton, W.S. (2000). Evolving perspectives on individual psychotherapy for schizophrenia. *Schizophrenia Bulletin* 26: 47–72.

Freud, S. (1904). *On Psychotherapy*, Vol. 7, pp. 255–68. London: Hogarth Press.

Gabbard, G. *et al.* (1997). The economic impact of psychotherapy: a review. *American Journal of Psychiatry* 154: 147–55.

Gomes-Schwartz, B. (1984). Individual psychotherapy of schizophrenia. In A. Bellack (ed.) *Schizophrenia: Treatment, Management and Rehabilitation*. New York: Grune & Stratton.

Gottdiener, W. (2000). The benefits of psychotherapy for schizophrenic patients: a meta-analytic review of the psychotherapy outcome literature. Unpublished doctoral dissertation, The New School University, TOWN.

Gottdiener, W. and Haslam, N. (2002). The benefits of individual psychotherapy for people diagnosed with schizophrenia: a meta-analytic review. *Ethnical Human Science and Services* 4: 163–87.

Heinrichs, D.W. and Carpenter, W.T. (1981). The efficacy of individual psychotherapy: a perspective and review emphasizing controlled outcome studies. In S. Arieti and H.K. Brodie (eds) *American Handbook of Psychiatry*, pp. 586–613. New York: Basic Books.

Hogarty, G.E. *et al.* (1995). Personal therapy: a disorder-relevant psychotherapy for schizophrenia. *Schizophrenia Bulletin* 21: 379–93.

Jacobson, N.S. and Truax, P. (1991). Clinical significance: a statistical approach to defining meaningful change in psychotherapy research. *Journal of Consulting and Clinical Psychology* 59: 12–19.

Karon, B.P. and VandenBos, G.R. (1981). *Psychotherapy of Schizophrenia: The Treatment of Choice*. Northvale, NJ: Jason Aronson.

Kingdon, D.G. and Turkington, D. (1994). *Cognitive-behavioral Therapy of Schizophrenia*. New York: Guilford Press.

Lehman, A.F. and Steinwachs, D.M. (1998). At issue: translating research into practice. The schizophrenia patient outcomes research team (PORT) treatment recommendations. *Schizophrenia Bulletin* 24: 1–10.

Liberman, R.P. (1994). Psychosocial treatments for schizophrenia. *Psychiatry* 57: 104–13.

Malmberg, L. and Fenton, M. (2001). Individual psychodynamic psychotherapy and psychoanalysis for schizophrenia and severe mental illness (Cochrane Review). *Cochrane Database of Systematic Reviews* (1) [Electronic database]. The Cochrane Library.

May, P.R.A. (1968). *Treatment of Schizophrenia: A Comparative Study of Five Treatment Methods.* New York: Science House.

McGlashan, T.H. and Keats, C.J. (1989). *Schizophrenia: Treatment Process and Outcome.* Washington, DC: American Psychiatric Press.

Mojtabai, R. *et al.* (1998). Role of psychosocial treatments in management of schizophrenia: a meta-analytic review of controlled outcome studies. *Schizophrenia Bulletin* 24: 569–87.

Morris, S.B. and DeShon, R.P. (2000). Combining effect size estimates in meta-analysis with repeated measures and independent-groups designs. *Psychological Methods* 7: 105–25.

Morrison, A. (2002). *A Casebook of Cognitive Therapy for Psychosis.* London: Routledge.

Mosher, L.R. and Keith, S.J. (1980). Psychosocial treatment: individual, group, family, and community support approaches. *Schizophrenia Bulletin* 6: 10–41.

Mueser, K. and Berenbaum, H. (1990). Psychodynamic treatment for schizophrenia: is there a future? *Psychological Medicine* 20: 253–62.

Pao, P.-N. (1979). *Schizophrenic Disorders: Theory and Treatment from a Psychodynamic Point of View.* New York: International Universities Press.

Pawson, R. and Tilley, N. (1997). *Realistic Evaluation.* London: Sage.

Perkins, D.O. (1999). Adherence to antipsychotic medications. *Journal of Clinical Psychiatry* 60(suppl.): 21–5.

Perris, C. (1989). *Cognitive Therapy with Schizophrenic Patients.* New York: Guilford Press.

Robbins, M. (1993). *Experiences of Schizophrenia.* New York: Guilford Press.

Rockland, L. (1989). *Supportive Therapy: A Psychodynamic Approach.* New York: Basic Books.

Rosenthal, R. *et al.* (2000). *Contrasts and Effect Sizes in Behavioral Research: A Correlational Approach.* Cambridge: Cambridge University Press.

Scott, J.E. and Dixon, L.B. (1995). Psychological interventions for schizophrenia. *Schizophrenia Bulletin* 21: 621–30.

Shrout, P. (1998). Causal modeling of epidemiological data on psychiatric disorders. *Social Psychiatry and Psychiatric Epidemiology* 33: 400–4.

Smith, M.L. *et al.* (1980). *The Benefits of Psychotherapy.* Baltimore, MD: Johns Hopkins University Press.

Chapter 22

The development of early intervention services

Jan Olav Johannessen

If we ask the question 'for how long is it decent to let a young person suffering from psychosis go undiagnosed and untreated in our society?', the answer would be obvious to most people.

There seems to be, among some clinicians and researchers, an underlying assumption that some psychotic disorders such as the schizophrenias are best compared with diseases such as Huntington's chorea or Creutzfeldt-Jakob's syndrome. They seem to think that there is no effective treatment, that the timing of the treatment is of no importance, and that both the ill person and the relatives are best off not knowing what is going on, until it is inevitable due to the manifestation of a chronic disorder with a certain downhill course. And there is the notion that if the person recovers, then it was not 'a real case of schizophrenia' after all. That this fundamentalist Kraepelanian view has been contradicted by well-performed outcome studies (Fenton 1997; see also Chapter 5) has had limited impact in some circles.

The next step in this logic is that these disorders must be of a biological origin, and hence that the only treatments must be those that work on a biochemical level, directly. People with psychosis do not benefit from talking to or relating to therapists, as the disorders are endogenous brain diseases with no connection to significant people or interpersonal relationships. The only acceptable reason for trying to form an alliance with the patient is that it improves medication compliance.

THE LOGIC OF EARLY INTERVENTION

People working with early intervention strategies rely on a different logic. The most fundamental difference is the belief that psychotic disorders are dynamic, psychobiosocial, reversible processes, where the psychotic breakdown is only one stage in the illness process, which can be prevented, delayed, modified and reversed.

The notion of psychotic disorders developing in stages is not new (Figure 22.1). Clinicians and researchers have held a corresponding view that the

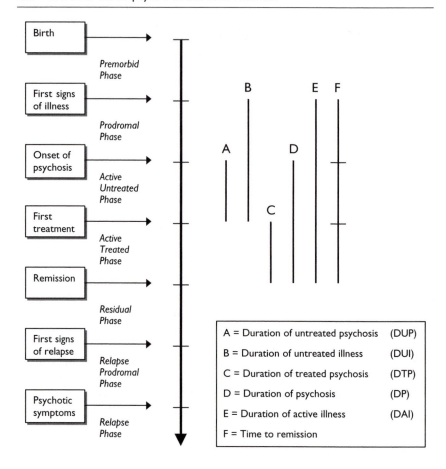

Figure 22.1   Early course of schizophrenia: phases and definitions (adapted from McGlashan and Johannessen 1996).

treatment of such disorders should be phase-specific and need-adapted. Both in the Anglo-American and the Scandinavian tradition, this has been a prevalent view for decades.

Sullivan pointed out in 1927 that 'the psychiatrist sees to many end-states and deals professionally with too few of the pre-psychotic', and that 'the great number of our patients have shown for years before the breakdown, clear signs of coming trouble'. Thus, like Cameron (1938) and Meares (1959), he indicates the possibility of intervening at an early stage of illness development, preventing a chronic course of schizophrenia. Docherty *et al.* (1978) have outlined the process of decompensation in a review article (see Table 22.1).

Table 22.1 Five stages of decompensation
(after Docherty et al. 1978)

0	Equilibrium
I	Overextension
II	Restricted consciousness
III	Disinhibition
IV	Psychotic disorganization
	1 Destructuring of the external world
	2 Destructuring of the self
	3 Total fragmentation
V	Psychotic resolution

There are three possible levels of prevention. Primary prevention involves efforts to reduce the incidence of a disorder. Secondary prevention will reduce the prevalence of the disorder. Tertiary prevention decreases the morbidity of the disorder – that is, improves the prognosis. In Figure 22.2, the different types of prevention are related to the different stages of psychosis development.

Regarding tertiary prevention, it has been shown that structured long-term treatment with psycho-social interventions involving family treatment, supportive psychotherapy, cognitive behaviour therapy and the monitoring of early symptoms of relapse can improve long-term outcome (Hogarty

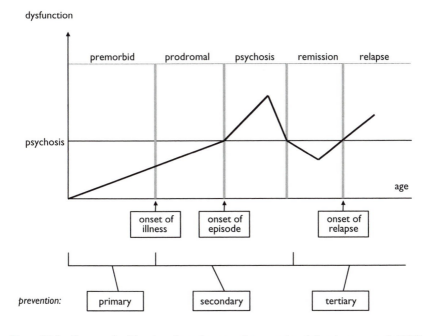

Figure 22.2 Stages of schizophrenia and types of prevention (after Larsen et al. 1998).

et al. 1986; Wyatt 1991; see also Chapters 20, 21, 23 and 25). Many practical models for the identification of the prodromal symptoms of relapse in schizophrenia, or 'relapse signature' (Birchwood 1992), have been developed.

It has been clearly demonstrated that relapse rates can be significantly reduced through a systematized mapping of early warning signs. Many family studies have shown a marked reduction in relapse rates (Leff 1994; see also Chapter 17). In principle, there is no difference between relapse prevention and the prevention of the first outbreak of psychosis. High expressed emotion is an expression of high basic stress in the milieu of the patient. Thus, the capacity to handle additional stress will be reduced. Stress reduction and easy access to mental health services upon early warning signs are important features of most psychoeducational family programmes. This is exactly what one wants to implement for patients that have not yet experienced their first psychotic breakdown, using early intervention programmes.

There are other strong indicators pointing to the importance of environmental factors. First, there is a large variance in the incidence of schizophrenia between different parts of the world, and also between those raised in a city versus those raised in rural areas (Buhgra *et al.* 1997; Mulvany *et al.* 2001; Schelin *et al.* 2000; see also Chapter 6). The high incidence of schizophrenia among second-generation immigrants in the UK, the Netherlands and other European countries points in the same direction (see Chapter 13). These functional psychotic disorders are the result of person–environment interaction and hence are possible to prevent (see Chapter 18).

Mrazek and Haggerty (1994) have developed another classification of preventive interventions. Their terms 'universal', 'selective' and 'indicated' preventive interventions reflect interventions focused on the whole population, asymptomatic subgroups and individuals at high risk for developing a specific disorder. Early intervention in first-episode psychosis reflects indicated prevention, and includes the possibility for primary prevention when applied in the prodromal phase.

INTERVENTION IN THE PRE-PSYCHOTIC PHASE (THE PRODROMAL PERIOD)

The term 'prodromal psychosis' is by definition a retrospective concept and as such, is of limited value. Furthermore, to talk about 'prodromal schizophrenia' in non-established cases raises difficult ethical questions. To my mind it is better to address a suspected case of a possible psychotic development in terms of the presenting symptom or symptoms. Hafner *et al.* (1999) showed that in approximately 80–90% of cases, the first symptom to appear is depression, with a mean duration of symptoms before psychosis of 5 years. Several studies have addressed efforts to prevent the conversion of suspected 'prodromal' cases into psychosis.

The Buckingham Study

A pioneering project was carried out by Falloon and colleagues (Falloon 1992) in Buckinghamshire, England, between 1984 and 1988. The mental health service systems were directly connected to the general practitioners (GPs) in the area (population 35,000). The GPs were trained in detecting early cases of psychosis, using the DSM-III-R prodromal signs. There was immediate access to the specialized services, located in the same buildings as the GPs. Comprehensive treatment, including assertive crisis treatment, carer-based stress management, cognitive-behavioural strategies, psycho-education and targeted minimal dose medication, were initiated within hours of referral. The treatment was tailored to the patient's individual needs. The expected annual incidence of schizophrenia was reduced ten-fold.

The study highlights the potential gains of early detection and intervention by focusing on the prodromal phase of psychosis. It suggests that deterioration may be less irreversible and resistant to intervention than has been expected. The main limitation of this study was the low number of patients. The strategy of prevention at the prodromal level is also problematic due to the non-specific nature of the symptoms, and the danger of falsely labelling persons that would actually never have developed psychosis.

The PACE Study

The Personal Assessment and Crisis Evaluation (PACE) clinic in Melbourne aims to identify individuals at high risk of becoming psychotic, and then to prevent the transition into psychosis. The rate of transition to psychosis in a pilot study was 41% at 12 months and more than 50% at 24 months. In a larger sample using the same criteria, transition to psychosis occurred in 35% of cases.

To identify possible prodromal cases, the Melbourne group developed a screening instrument called Comprehensive Assessment of At Risk Mental States (CAARMS) (Edwards and McGorry 2002). The basic characteristics of this and some other early intervention programmes are outlined in Table 22.2.

The Bonn Early Recognition Study

In the German tradition, early symptoms of schizophrenia have been called basic symptoms and are measured by the Bonn Scale for Assessment of Basic Symptoms (BSABS). In this tradition, greater emphasis is put on subjective experiences of the patients, before they develop psychosis.

Table 22.2   Early intervention programmes

	Buckingham	PACE	EPPIC	TIPS
1	Catchment area 35,000 population	No defined catchment area	Catchment area 800,000 population	Catchment area 400,000
2	Primary health care and psychiatric specialists located together	Services situated at health promotion centre for adolescents	Ordinary psychiatric services, community-oriented, ambulatory teams	Ordinary outpatient unit, detection team, community-oriented
3	Immediate access to treatment, home-based	No referral from primary care needed (i.e. direct access)	Direct access to services for users 7 days a week	Direct access to services for users 5 days a week
4	Comprehensive treatment focused on presenting problems	Psychosocial and medication-based treatment	Comprehensive treatment programmes	Comprehensive treatment programmes
5	Focus on prodromal/ early psychosis, preventing conversion into psychosis	Focus on prodromal period, preventing conversion into psychosis	Focus on early, first-episode, psychosis; reducing DUP	Focus on early, first-episode, psychosis; reducing DUP

Abbreviations: PACE = Personal Assessment and Crisis Evaluation clinic in Melbourne; EPPIC = Early Psychosis Prevention and Intervention Centre in Melbourne; TIPS = Treatment and Intervention in Psychosis project. DUP = duration of untreated psychosis.

In a study of 96 patients, 81% had at least one basic symptom at baseline (Klosterkötter *et al.* 2000). At 8-year follow-up, 58% of the patients had developed schizophrenia. Predictors of the transition to schizophrenia were the basic symptoms 'cognitive thought', 'perception' and 'mood disturbances'.

The PRIME Study

This study (Prevention through Risk Identification and Management) is a multi-centre study in America, originating at Yale Medical School. The screening instrument used is the Structured Interview for Prodromal States (SIPS) (McGlashan *et al.* 2001), which bears some similarity to CAARMS.

All patients receive a psycho-social intervention consisting of stress management and problem-solving skills training. The patients are then randomized to medication or non-medication. The conversion to psychosis rate as of January 2000 was 33% (New Haven site).

The TOPP Study

This project is situated at Rogaland Psychiatric Hospital in Norway and, in contrast to the other prodromal projects, covers a catchment area and thus does not have a selected sample. The acronym TOPP stands for early Treatment Of PrePsychosis and relates to the TIPS Project (early Treatment and Intervention in Psychosis), which is a first-episode psychosis study. Using the SIPS, a conversion rate of about 40% has been observed for the first 15 patients.

The DEEP Study

Detection of Early Psychosis (DEEP) is a Finnish project, also using the SIPS. A 3-year follow-up study to describe conversion into psychosis is being carried out. One group consists of first-degree relatives of discharged schizophrenic patients. Other groups are 'ordinary' help-seeking patients in the outpatient units, an unselected group of volunteers and controls. Data are not yet available.

INTERVENTION IN THE PSYCHOTIC PHASE AND DURATION OF UNTREATED PSYCHOSIS

Early intervention after the onset of psychosis means that treatment is given as soon as possible after the psychosis is present. The key concept here is duration of untreated psychosis (DUP), the time between the onset of first psychotic symptoms and first adequate treatment.

More than 10 studies have shown that the typical DUP average is 1–2 years (Johannessen et al. 2001a). In addition, the duration of untreated prodromal symptoms is between 1 and 5 years. This represents a major public health problem in itself. Even if one presumed that it made no difference to the long-term prognosis whether one intervenes early or late in the development of a schizophrenic disorder, it represents an additional and in most cases almost intolerable extra burden to be psychotic without receiving adequate help. People in active psychosis are vulnerable to initiating irrational, unpredictable and often permanently damaging behaviours, both to themselves and others (Lieberman and Fenton 2000).

The reasons for treatment delay include ignorance, denial, stigma, a lack of motivation, absence of information about early psychosis and a lack of access to appropriate interventions. Larsen et al. (1998) found that the treatment delay was correlated with social withdrawal and poor social functioning, and that young males have particularly long durations of untreated psychosis. Lincoln and McGorry (1999) found that lack of knowledge about mental illness and mental health services in the general community, the health delivery system and the educational system also contribute to delay.

Reducing the duration of untreated psychosis: health promotion aspects

Effective health promotion programmes must include multi-level strategies targeting individuals, families, neighbourhoods, schools, workplaces and communities. The community component includes modifying the organization of health services to emphasize prevention and supplementary training for health personnel. There seems to be a significant effect of education on attitudes and knowledge about mental illness, when the information strategies use multiple access points, for example media, health service personnel and schools (US Department of Health and Human Services 1994). It has been demonstrated that schoolteachers are capable of identifying individuals that later develop serious mental illness, when given adequate information about such disorders (Olin et al. 1998).

The TIPS Study

The early Treatment and Intervention in Psychosis (TIPS) project is a prospective clinical trial designed to examine whether it is possible within a sectorized catchment area to reduce the duration of untreated psychosis, and whether earlier treatment in first-episode psychosis can improve the course of the disorder. We have studied whether it is possible to establish an effective early detection system (ED) based on: (a) information programmes directed towards the general population, health professionals and schools (teachers and students), and (b) easy access to the services through a low threshold and ED-teams.

The study involves three sites: Rogaland county, Norway (370,000 inhabitants), Ullevål sector, Oslo, Norway (190,000) and Roskilde county, Denmark (100,000). First-episode non-affective psychotic patients are treated with the same psycho-social and medical protocol across all three sites.

The inclusion period was 1997–2000, with a 5-year follow-up period. An extensive education and information system has been carried out in Rogaland, while Ullevål and Roskilde are control sectors that rely on existing detection and referral systems for first-episode cases. Details are provided in Johannessen et al. (2001b) and Larsen et al. (2001).

The average duration of untreated psychosis in Rogaland was reduced from 114 to 26 weeks. The earlier detected patients were younger and had better premorbid adjustment, less severe psychosis, with more frequent drug abuse. (This latter characteristic probably reflects developments regarding drug abuse in the area.)

It thus appears that patients access the psychiatric services when the symptoms were less severe. The pattern of referral also changed significantly, with more that 50% of the referrals coming from family, schools and friends, as compared to pre-TIPS when all referrals came through the general practitioners.

It is still too early to draw final conclusions from the comparison between sites, but preliminary results indicate that the duration of untreated psychosis is significantly less in the ED-sector than in the non ED-sectors. The second major research question, whether this reduction in the duration of untreated psychosis will influence the long-term prognosis, remains to be answered.

The treatment programme

The basic requisite of treatment is continuity of care – that is, that the same therapist should stay with the patient for at least two years. Preliminary data indicate that 50% of the patients have only one therapist in these two years and 40% have two. Teams working with the patient also secure continuity of treatment. This team consists of the patient's individual psychotherapist and primary contact nurse. In some cases, the main focus will be individual psychotherapy, but this will not be the most relevant in all cases. The psychotherapist has the main responsibility for all aspects of the treatment.

This emphasis on continuity of care is based upon the psychological needs of patients experiencing a psychological disintegration. We believe that this disintegration, pathognomonic for psychosis, can be reduced by stable external structures and that the inherent anxiety and suffering requires time, stability and a stable human relationship to re-establish inner structure where structure has been dissolved. What the patients with psychosis need the least are new, unstable and/or broken relationships.

Active outreach psychotherapy

The supportive, active outreach psychotherapy guarantees a minimum of one psychotherapeutic contact per week with an experienced psychotherapist. The main focus of the therapy is supportive and psychodynamic. This dynamic understanding forms the basis for all treatment efforts and emphasizes the active interaction between the single biological individual and the psycho-social and physical environment. We aim to understand the psychological development of each individual, as well as factors contributing to the person's psychological breakdown, or psychosis, in this context. The psycho-social needs of the individual patient beyond the standardized treatment are identified and addressed.

The phase specificity of the treatment is fundamentally important when relating to psychotic patients. There is a strong Scandinavian tradition for 'needs-specific treatment', originating from Finland in the late 1970s. The Finnish psychoanalyst Veikko Tähkä (1979) introduced the concept 'psychotherapy as phase-specific treatment'. Alanen (1997) and others have developed this approach further.

> People suffering from schizophrenia should be met flexibly and individually in each case, on the basis of both an individual and interactional interpretation of the situation, and it is from these that the therapeutic needs should be defined. Patients' needs vary, sometimes from day to day, as must be reflected by the frequency of meetings between therapist and patient and the length of each session. The supportive elements will always be an important part of psychodynamically-oriented psychotherapy for this group of patients.
>
> (Alanen 1997: 144)

McGlashan and Keats (1989) underline the importance of a thorough evaluation of the different therapeutic steps when treating a person with psychosis, moving gradually from building a relation to a more active traditional psychotherapeutic phase, when the patient's psychological apparatus has been gradually re-established. In some cases, the therapist will, for long periods, work primarily at establishing contact and/or getting the patients to attend sessions. Other patients can be strongly motivated for psychological treatments and an insight-oriented process. The therapist has to be flexible and also offer practical help. A main focus will be helping the patient to develop internal coping strategies and to enhance the understanding of illness-related experiences and personal vulnerability factors. It is of the outmost importance not to overstretch the patient's psychological capacity, including his or her cognitive capacity, at any stage during the recovery process. Recent reports (Turkington 2001) demonstrate that cognitive-behavioural therapy applied in the acute phase may actually make the short-term prognosis worse. There will also be a focus on accepting loss in a way that avoids demoralization, preserves hope and encourages reintegration into society. Active outreach approaches are close to modern cognitive-behaviour treatment strategies (see Chapter 20), and imply an explicit responsibility to call the patient if he or she does not show up for appointments, or visit the patient at home if that's what is needed.

Psychoeducative family work

Few studies on family intervention have been carried out on first-episode samples. Most studies have been in relation to patients with a more chronic course of illness. We have modified the approach of McFarlane (Øxnevad *et al.* 2000) for first-episode patients and their families. In first-episode samples the patients will be different and the prognosis will vary. We do not explain psychosis, in the way that has been the tradition in most psycho-educational approaches (see Chapters 17 and 23), as a biological brain disease. We leave the question open and emphasize the psychological vulnerability that will vary from case to case, within the framework of a stress/vulnerability model. It is our experience that this is well understood and received by both patients and families.

The family work consists of three elements: single family meetings, multi-family groups and a workshop for the families. In the single-family meetings, the family meets with the therapist at least three times during the first weeks after the patient has been admitted. These meetings can be with or without the patient, depending on the patient's condition. A multi-family group consists of five or six families. The sessions last for 90 minutes and have a supportive, non-threatening atmosphere. They meet every second week and focus on problem solving, crisis management, communication training and education about psychiatric disorders. In the TIPS Project, about 50% of the 300 families have participated in the multi-family groups.

A one-day educational workshop is conducted for new participants, including family members, close friends, teachers and other people the patients want to include. The content of the workshop is as follows:

- information on psychiatric health services;
- information on psychosis;
- possible outcome/prognosis;
- stress/vulnerability model;
- experiences of being a relative;
- what relatives can do to help;
- treatment and coping.

Medication

The medication has been based on treatment with olanzapine as first choice, risperidone as second and perhenazine as third. The recommended dose of olanzapine has been 10 mg and that for risperidone 1–4 mg per day. Compliance with medication improved significantly when perphenazine was replaced by olanzapine as first choice after the first year.

The EPPIC Study

In Melbourne, Australia, the Early Psychosis Prevention and Intervention Centre (EPPIC) is established as a psychiatric service, including early detection and specialized treatment for early psychosis. The catchment area is the western metropolitan area of Melbourne with about 800,000 inhabitants. The model is outlined in Table 22.2.

The EPPIC model aims to reduce both primary and secondary morbidity in patients with early psychosis, through the dual strategy of identifying patients as early as possible after onset of illness and providing intensive phase-specific treatment for up to 18 months. The service has been evaluated by comparing a matched group of patients from 1989 to 1992 with patients included in the EPPIC programme in 1993 (Edwards and McGorry 2002). The EPPIC patients had a significantly better one-year outcome than the pre-EPPIC group, including better quality of life scores and fewer negative symptoms. The effect was strongest for patients with a duration of untreated psychosis of 1–6 months. The studies did not show that the EPPIC programme was able to reduce the duration of untreated psychosis significantly. The better one-year outcome in the EPPIC group is probably due to an improved and more comprehensive treatment.

The Birmingham Early Intervention Service (EIS)

The EIS in Birmingham, UK, is for people experiencing first-episode psychosis. It is part of the Northern Birmingham Mental Health National Service Trust, which also includes 24 hours psychiatric emergency and home treatment teams, primary care and liaison services, assertive outreach, and rehabilitation and recovery services. The core component of the EIS is an assertive outreach team, operating 7 days a week and staffed by 10 case managers with case loads of 15 patients. The treatment protocol includes the following elements:

- low-dose antipsychotic regimes;
- cognitive therapy for delusions and hallucinations;
- cognitive therapy aimed at improving adjustment and reducing co-morbidity;
- psycho-social intervention for problem drug and alcohol use;
- prevocational training.

Other studies and services for first-episode psychosis

Important projects are being carried out in Canada (London, Ontario and Calgary, Alberta). The OPUS (early detection and assertive community treatment of young persons with untreated psychosis) study in Denmark, the 'Parachute-project' in Sweden, the RAPP (recognition and prevention of psychological problems) project in New York, USA, and the FETZ (early detection and treatment for psychosis) study in Cologne, Germany, are also aimed at both primary and secondary prevention. There are also

Early Psychosis Intevention and First Episode Psychosis services in New Zealand. A comprehensive overview of early intervention programmes is given by Edwards and McGorry (2002) in their book *Implementing Early Intervention in Psychosis*.

CONCLUSION

For decades, patients with schizophrenia and other psychotic disorders have been treated without recognizing their individuality and individual needs. Psychosis is better described as a continuum than in categories (van Os *et al.* 2000; see Chapter 5). The growing understanding of psychosis as something that develops gradually, in phases or stages, and which is therefore possible to prevent, delay, modify and reverse, has serious implications for how we structure and deliver our services.

Our basic beliefs about these disorders strongly influence the way we meet and treat people with psychosis, both in terms of the content of the treatment and the way in which we provide available treatment modalities. In recent years in many western countries, the 'talking therapies' have often not been offered to the most serious ill. This reflects an underlying attitude that these patients will not profit from telling their story, and working through their experiences and subjective suffering. For those of us working with the early stages of illness development, and meeting people in the phase where they are 'losing their grip' – that is, going into a psychotic state of mind – we know that this simply is not true.

We meet people who suffer, who experience the deepest possible anxiety, the deepest despair and depression that any human being can experience. And we, being therapists, find that in this phase, before the psychosis and psychotic way of reasoning has tightened its grip, it is easier to talk, easier to relate and easier to re-establish a normal psychological pattern. We see that the social consequences are less devastating, the suffering person has better insight, the families and social network are better preserved.

Today we know that it is possible to reduce the duration of untreated illness for people suffering from a psychotic condition. We do not have conclusive evidence that reducing the duration of untreated psychosis improves the long-term prognosis, although most of us assume that it does, out of simple logic.

Many groups around the world have now established clinical programmes and research focusing on early psychosis. In many countries, including the UK, Australia, Norway, Denmark, Germany and Canada, there are government-supported development programmes for a national implementation of early intervention services. Hopefully, this will secure a place for the psychological treatments for these serious disorders in the future.

REFERENCES

Alanen, Y. (1997). Vulnerability to schizophrenia and psychotherapeutic treatment for schizophrenic patients. *Psychiatry* 60: 142–50.

Birchwood, M. (1992). Early intervention in schizophrenia. *British Journal of Psychiatry* 31: 257–78.

Buhgra, D. *et al.* (1997). Incidence and outcome of schizophrenia in whites, African-Caribbeans and Asians in London. *Psychological Medicine* 27: 791–8.

Cameron, D. (1938). Early schizophrenia. *American Journal of Psychiatry* 95: 567–78.

Docherty, J. *et al.* (1978) Stages of onset of schizophrenic psychosis. *American Journal of Psychiatry* 135: 420–6.

Edwards, J. and McGorry, P. (2002). *Implementing Early Intervention in Psychosis.* London: Dunitz.

Falloon, I. (1992). Early intervention for first episode of schizophrenia. *Psychiatry* 55: 4–14.

Fenton, W. (1997). Course and outcome in schizophrenia. *Current Opinion in Psychiatry* 10: 40–4.

Hafner, H. *et al.* (1999). Depression, negative symptoms, social stagnation and social decline in the early course of schizophrenia. *Acta Psychiatrica Scandinavica* 100: 105–8.

Hogarty, G. *et al.* (1986). Family education, social skills, training and maintenance chemotherapy in the after care of schizophrenia. *Archives of General Psychiatry* 43: 633–42.

Johannessen, J. *et al.* (2001a). Early detection strategies for untreated first-episode psychosis. *Schizophrenia Research* 51: 39–46.

Johannessen, J. *et al.* (2001b). The TIPS project. In T. Miller *et al.* (eds) *Early Intervention in Psychotic Disorders.* Dordrecht: Kluwer.

Klosterkötter, J. *et al.* (2000). The Cologne early recognition project. *European Psychiatry* 15: 14.

Larsen, T. *et al.* (1998). First episode schizophrenia with long duration of untreated psychosis. *British Journal of Psychiatry* 172: 45–52.

Larsen, T. *et al.* (2001). Shortened duration of untreated first episode of psychosis. *American Journal of Psychiatry* 158: 1917–19.

Leff, J. (1994). Stress reduction in the social environment of schizophrenic patients. *Acta Psychiatrica Scandinavica* 89: 16–24.

Lieberman, J. and Fenton, W. (2000). Delayed direction of psychosis: causes, consequences, and effects on public health. *American Journal of Psychiatry* 157: 1727–30.

Lincoln, C. and McGorry, P. (1999). Pathways to care in early psychosis: Clinical and consumer perspectives. In P. McGorry and H. Jackson (eds) *The Recognition and Management of Early Psychosis: A Preventive Approach.* Cambridge: Cambridge University Press.

McGlashan, T. *et al.* (2001). Instrument for the assessment of prodromal symptoms and states. In T. Miller *et al.* (eds) *Early Intervention in Psychotic Disorders.* Dordrecht: Kluwer.

McGlashan, T. and Johannessen, J. (1996). Early detection and intervention with schizophrenia: rationale. *Schizophrenia Bulletin* 22: 201–22.

McGlashan, T. and Keats, C. (1989). *Treatment Process and Outcome*. Washington, DC: American Psychiatric Press.

Meares, A. (1959). The diagnosis of prepsychotic schizophrenia. *Lancet* i: 55–9.

Mrazek, P. and Haggerty, R. (1994). *Reducing Risk for Mental Disorder*. Washington, DC: National Academy Press.

Mulvany, F. *et al.* (2001). Effect of social class at birth on risk and presentation of schizophrenia. *British Medical Journal* 323: 1398–1401.

Olin, S. *et al.* (1998). School teachers' ratings predictive of psychiatric outcome 25 years later. *British Journal of Psychiatry* 172: 7–13.

Øxnevad, A. *et al.* (2000). *Family Work with Psychosis: Towards a Common Goal*. Stavanger: The Foundation for Psychiatric Information.

Schelin, E. *et al.* (2000). Regional differences in schizoprenia incidence in Denmark. *Acta Psychiatrica Scandinavica* 101: 293–9.

Sullivan, H. ([1927] 1994). The onset of schizophrenia. *American Journal of Psychiatry* 151: 134–9.

Tähkä, V. (1979). Psychotherapy as phase-specific interaction. *Scandinavian Psychoanalytic Review* 2: 113–20.

Turkington, D. (2001). Brief CBT for first episode schizophrenia compared to treatment as usual. Paper presented to the *World Psychiatric Association, European Regional Meeting/The Royal College of Psychiatrists' Annual Meeting*, London, July.

US Department of Health and Human Services (1994). *Predictive Tobacco Use Among Young People: A Report of the Surgeon General*. Atlantic City, NJ: Center for Disease Control and Prevention.

van Os, J *et al.* (2000). A comparison of the utility of dimensional and categorical representations of psychosis. *European Psychiatry* 15: 286.

Wyatt, R. (1991). Neuroleptics and the natural course of schizophrenia. *Schizophrenia Bulletin* 17: 325–51.

Chapter 23

Family therapy and schizophrenia

Replacing ideology with openness

Volkmar Aderhold and Evelin Gottwalz

HISTORICAL OVERVIEW

In the last few decades, family therapy has become a well-established treatment for many mental health problems. Psychotherapy and family therapy for schizophrenia have traditionally been applied after the acute symptoms have subsided. Recently, however, approaches emphasizing early intervention and treatment involving the patient and the family (Alanen 1997; Krausz and Naber 2000; McGorry 2000; see Chapter 22) have successfully introduced a combination of different therapeutic approaches (Alanen 2000; Hogarty *et al.* 1995; Martindale *et al.* 2000; Reich and Riehl-Emde 2001).

Family treatment has always played an important role in the treatment of schizophrenic psychoses. In the 1930s and 1940s, Harry Stack Sullivan's (1953) interpersonal theory of schizophrenia was widely accepted in the USA. Sullivan was among the first to point out the interdependence between 'schizophrenics' and their families:

> The aetiology of a schizophrenic illness is to be sought in events that involve the individual. The significant events seem to me to lie wholly within one category, events relating the individual with other individuals more or less highly significant to him.
>
> (Sullivan 1962: 248)

In the 1950s and 1960s, researchers made important progress (see Chapter 17), including the double-bind model (Bateson *et al.* 1956), the first proof of unusual thought and communication patterns in the families of schizophrenic patients (Wynne and Singer 1963), and the description of disturbed interaction patterns in some families (Lidz *et al.* 1958).

The pioneers of family therapy worked with the families of very disturbed patients (Boszormenyi-Nagy and Framo 1965; Bowen 1960; Haley 1963; Minuchin 1967; Richter 1970; Satir 1964). Their methods quickly became popular. However, interest in family therapy faded because of the lack of well-designed evaluation studies, routine treatment with neuroleptics since the 1960s, and the development of genetic and neurobiological models of schizophrenia.

The situation changed again in the mid-1970s. When the big psychiatric institutions closed, many patients returned home to their families. This was often too great a burden on all concerned. It became evident that neuroleptic treatment cannot solve psycho-social problems. Moreover, many patients were not willing to take medication over long periods of time. Psychotic crises every one or two years became the rule, leading to the so-called 'revolving door' phenomenon of continual readmissions. When problems of living together were recognized as a major risk factor for relapse, it again became evident that families need to be included in treatment efforts.

'PSYCHOEDUCATIONAL' FAMILY TREATMENT

By the end of the 1970s, research on family treatment had developed the concept of the emotional family climate, with a particular focus on 'expressed emotion', with its two components of criticism/hostility and overinvolvement (see Chapter 17). At the same time, the idea that family factors could cause schizophrenia was abandoned (Hahlweg et al. 2000). Although it had become taboo to discuss the role of families in terms of causation, it was acceptable to talk about their role in helping to prevent relapse. Expressed emotion research proved that unfavourable attitudes and opinions of close relations with respect to the patient are related to a higher risk of relapse (Brown et al. 1972; Vaughn and Leff 1976). Therefore, family-oriented approaches began to try to improve the relational system within the family and to discover the family's own resources.

By the end of the 1970s, various 'psychoeducational' family treatment programmes for schizophrenia had been developed (Dixon et al. 2001; Goldstein and Miklowitz 1995). This was a new way of working with families. These programmes are mainly based on the vulnerabity–stress (Zubin and Spring 1977), or VSBK (Vulnerabilitäts–Stress–Bewältigungs–Kompetenz; vulnerability–stress–coping–competence), model. Ignoring Zubin and Spring's original view that 'family experiences' could contribute to the vulnerability, most proponents of the psychoeducational approach to families assumed a biological disposition due to hereditary transmission and possibly intrauterine and/or perinatal damage, causing a later vulnerability to stress via neuronal developmental processes, and (not necessarily) leading to the manifestation of schizophrenic symptoms only by additional current stressors (Johnstone 1993). Conditions within the family during childhood were now considered irrelevant.

Thus the vulnerability–stress and VSBK models became an explicit exoneration of the family of origin. Specific family dynamics are not considered as possible causal factors. Techniques of the 'traditional' (e.g. strategic or systemic) family therapies are therefore not applied. The treatment goal is not an understanding of how the family might have contributed to the problem and how that might be resolved, but rather prevention or delaying of the recurrence of a psychotic episode and the reduction of the subjective burden on family members. Therein lies an important contradiction. Families are told that they could not have played any role in the development of the problem, while simultaneously being asked to change their behaviour to help prevent the same problem from reoccurring.

Psychoeducational family programmes consist of two general ingredients:

- 'Education' about schizophrenia, from the predominantly disease model offered by the vulnerability–stress model.
- Active skills training in communication, problem solving, stress management and crisis intervention, primarily designed to reduce high expressed emotion.

The skills training ingredient is adapted from other behavioural and cognitive treatment programmes and is basically independent of the disease model taught in the educational component. Many studies have demonstrated that these family psychoeducation approaches can indeed prevent, delay or shorten relapses (Goldstein and Strachan 1986; Hogarty *et al.* 1986) by reducing high expressed emotion or the amount of contact between patient and parents (Falloon *et al.* 1982; Leff *et al.* 1982; see also Chapter 17).

It is often assumed that the educational component (which would be more accurately named 'bio-education' than 'psycho-education') is an important contributor to reduced relapse rates. It is believed that it lowers parents' hostility towards their sons and daughters, by encouraging the view that they have no control over their behaviour (Falloon *et al.* 1982; Leff *et al.* 1982; McGill *et al.* 1983). However, studies have shown that interventions that contain only the 'educational' component are not effective in reducing relapse rates. Relapse is actually prevented by teaching parents communication and stress management skills, actively discouraging criticism, intrusiveness and overprotection, and reducing the amount of contact between parents and patients (Kavanagh 1992; Tarrier *et al.* 1989).

There isn't even much evidence that families are convinced by efforts to persuade them that their offspring have a biologically based illness waiting to be 'triggered' by stressors. One study that assessed whether the relatives had retained the new 'knowledge' about the 'illness' found 'absolutely no change in the amount of knowledge between pretests and posttests' (Cozolino *et al.* 1988: 683). Another study assessed the impact of the educational component of the 'integrated mental health care' approach (Falloon *et al.* 1982). Before the 'education' 11% of the relatives had stated that the problems were caused by a disordered brain, whereas 32% stated this 3 months later. Thus only 21% had changed their minds, or their statements, as a result of the teaching. The number who stated a belief in genetic inheritance increased from 11 to 15%. Only 3% of the patients adopted an illness model, either before or after the attempt to 'educate' them (McGill *et al.* 1983).

The researchers nevertheless asserted: 'This knowledge enables them to become effective participants in aftercare'. In fact they had made no attempt to discover whether the new 'knowledge' (to the very limited extent that it existed) was related to attitude change, behaviour change or relapse. In 1987, Smith and Birchwood found that the amount of 'knowledge' gained from their educational intervention (which, like Falloon's, taught relatives to think in illness terms) was unrelated to relatives' stress or their fear of the 'patient'.

Our hypothesis that it is new skills, rather than a new ideology, that are helpful is supported by a survey of New Zealand mental health professionals one year after they had been trained in Falloon's 'integrated mental health care' model. The components the staff found most useful were teaching patients and relatives to identify early warning signs and to use problem-solving techniques (Allen and Read 1997).

Anecdotal evidence that diagnosing their offspring as having an illness can be unhelpful for relatives comes from a rare study asking parents about their experiences (Tuck *et al.* 1997). One of the strongest messages from the parents was about the distress caused by being told their offspring were ill. The researchers record that 'there was shock and grief associated with the chronic nature of the diagnosis and the relatively poor prognosis'.

The 'psychoeducation' approach to working with families, with its narrow focus on expressed emotion, excludes or minimizes other important family dynamics, including conflicts between autonomy and attachment. Furthermore, an ideologically driven and manualized approach can fail to adapt treatment to the needs of individual families. It forfeits the chance of an open dialogue that would recognize the specific problems of each family (Wynne 1994).

The ideology of biological reductionism permeating most 'psychoeducative' family programmes, with its intention of exonerating the family, means a loss of basic neutrality and openness for individual possibilities. Because psycho-social family causalities, transgenerative processes, circularities, and so on are unnecessarily equated to having to feel guilty, any aetiological relevance is denied. These issues have been made taboo topics of discussion (see Chapter 17).

These manualized treatment programmes do not adequately address, therefore, feelings, attributions of guilt and related emotions within the family. The two components of expressed emotion – criticism/hostility and overprotectiveness – can be understandable defences against feelings, especially guilt. Where this is the case, talking about it, rather than superficial statements bestowing an illusion of absolution, is required. An open and honest dialogue about the guilt question, which will be different for different families, seems to be a better approach. The focus should be on the acceptance of responsibility, grieving and forgiveness.

Real family work requires a setting where it is possible to ask questions and where a shared search for answers that make sense for all family members can occur (Wynne 1994). Therapists should not impose answers but should assist families to feel safe enough to search for their own.

PSYCHOANALYTIC FAMILY THERAPY

Psychoanalytical family treatment, sometimes with weekly sessions for 1–3 years, obviously requires high motivation to change on behalf of the family. The focus is on long-standing family conflicts. These may or may not be interpreted in terms of early interactions in childhood, depending on whether the family finds this helpful. Treatment may concentrate on autonomy–dependence conflicts if the patient is still strongly attached to the family (Schwarz 2000).

Similar to systemic family treatment (see below), an important goal is for diffuse and unclear communication within the family to become more transparent and clear. From an analytical point of view, this communication pattern can be seen as a resistance against anxiety-inducing changes in relationships. The anxiety may relate to the loss of stabilizing family constellations. The therapist becomes a mediator in a constructive dialogue between family members. 'It should be possible for all family members to converse freely on all topics, especially on those topics that had been avoided so far' (Boszormenyi-Nagy and Framo 1965; translation by authors). The reactions of transference and countertransference between family members, and with respect to the therapist, may be interpreted. Anxiety and shame released that way will have to be 'worked through', sometimes repeatedly. Reconciliation and mourning for what cannot be changed may also need to be discussed.

Work with several generations is sometimes possible. Grandparents can be particularly constructive in finding solutions (Sperling 1975). Schwarz (2000) points out that it can take at least 2–3 years for psychoanalytic treatment of schizophrenic patients to result in a reduction of acute psychotic relapses and an improvement in social relationships, emotional vitality, self-esteem and the development of a clear identity separate from that of others.

SYSTEMIC FAMILY TREATMENT

The conception of a systemic treatment of schizophrenic patients is based on suggestions from American researchers in the 1950s (e.g. Bateson *et al.* 1969; Lidz *et al.* 1958; Wynne *et al.* 1958). During the last four decades, systemic family treatment was further developed by three treatment and research centres: the Palo-Alto group (Bateson), the Milan group (Palazzoli) and the Heidelberg group (Stierlin, Retzer, Simon).

The double-bind hypothesis of Bateson *et al.* (1969) became particularly well known and entered everyday language. It led to new therapeutic opportunities to resolve paradoxes of communication. Starting from there, Palazzoli *et al.* (1975) developed specific intervention strategies that represented a 'counterparadox' to paradoxically disturbed communication. Based on Stierlin's (1975) work, the Heidelberg group also developed specific approaches to finding solutions, especially in cases of psychosis. However, the course can be set in very different ways depending on the assumptions and models that are used.

Important basic models of systemic family treatment are cybernetics, information and communication theory, mathematical theories and chaos theory (Retzer 2000). They are mostly concerned with formal organizational processes that determine the origin and change of structures. They are applied to the question of how a complex family system maintains its structure. Retzer and Simon (2001) consider schizophrenic symptoms to be a deviation from what is expected. In the case of positive symptoms such as delusions or hallucinations, patients behave in an unexpected way. In the case of negative symptoms, they do not behave in the expected way. Similar to the psychoanalytic approach, the emphasis lies on the crucial issues of autonomy and dependence, guilt and responsibility. A major problem of many families is the unclear position of the family members with respect to the boundaries between generations. It can also be helpful to talk about who is different, and in what ways, from the other members.

Systemic family therapy is primarily concerned with reversing the 'excommunication' – that is, the patient's exclusion from the 'tone-setting community' (Stierlin 1996). The therapist must take great care not to take on any family functions. This becomes possible by adopting a neutral position, supportive of all family members. The aim is to create space for new opportunities.

Symptoms, initially seen as entirely negative by all family members, are discussed in such a way as to discover the function they play in the family. In this way, they can come to be seen in a more positive light. This increases the chances of both self-regulation and tolerance.

The essential goal of this treatment is the softening of the hardened and incompatible positions of the individual family members. Helping families learn new ways to manage conflict between members is crucial.

COMBINING PSYCHOANALYTIC AND SYSTEMIC FAMILY THERAPY

Alanen's 'need-adapted treatment' (1997) offers a broad range of possibilities. During recent decades, a comprehensive psychotherapeutic treatment of first-episode patients, designed to meet the specific needs of the individual patient and family, has been developed at the Psychiatric University Hospital of Turku, Finland (see Chapter 24). Therapeutic meetings with the treatment team and the patient and family at the beginning of treatment proved to be therapeutically significant and important in determining the therapeutic requirements in each individual case. The success of this treatment model is demonstrated by the follow-up results (Alanen 2000).

Alanen and his co-workers found that individual psychotherapy was well suited for some patients, whereas others benefited from family treatment. These two kinds of treatment do not exclude each other but are instead complementary. The decision to use one of them or both should be taken case by case. In some cases, individual treatment is more successful if it is preceded by family treatment and/or prolonged treatment in a psychotherapeutic community.

Lehtinen (1994) distinguishes between different patient–family constellations:

1   Patients with psychotic reactions in acute stress situations. Early intervention and psychodynamic re-definition of the trigger situation led to remission with favourable prognosis after 2–5 family sessions.
2   Patients with somewhat less psycho-social integration, and a recognizable relation between their life situation and psychotic symptoms, where a re-definition remained insufficient and whose rather rigid families were more opposed to changes so that therapists lost their emotional access. In this situation, women were often able to develop in the longer term by using individual therapy. Men more often withdrew from treatment and developed psychotic symptoms.
3   If, at the beginning of treatment, patients had already been ill for many years and were socially isolated, a long-term rehabilitative treatment with concomitant psychoeducative family treatment has proved successful (Alanen 1997).

The therapeutic meeting

Since 1981, a special kind of family intervention has been developed mainly under the influence of Lehtinen in Turku, Finland. This intervention is still considered to be very innovative for the formation of relationships and the therapeutic work with families, for the individual structuring of treatment systems and for theoretical discussion.

Influenced by the Milan approach (Palazzoli), the ward staff started to meet all patients and their families at the beginning of the treatment. This step was part of the 'systemic revolution' (Lehtinen 2003) within the need-adapted treatment approach (Turku model) (Alanen 1997). This step was a shift from mainly assuming early developmental deficiencies to discovering that patients had quite understandable problems in their lives. Psychosis always seemed to be the result of a long development with several years of problems, increasing symptoms and difficulties and, finally, psychosis.

The whole family is supported from the beginning and becomes or remains motivated for further family-focused treatment. This first network meeting should provide enough common ground for the next meeting. These initial meetings should give patients and their families access to the knowledge and experience of the treatment staff and are mostly used for treatment planning and decision making. Only later do they focus more on psychotherapy.

These initial treatment meetings are part of the basic principle of the need-adapted approach that requires the patient's presence in a situation that concerns her or himself and her or his own treatment. They are held whenever needed. This can be daily to start with and less frequently later. They can be for making decisions about the treatment process, or they can be more therapeutically oriented with a specific focus. In some areas, like in Turku, the patient and family can be referred to specialized family therapists for more focused work on family dynamics while the treatment meetings with the psychosis team continue.

Open dialogue approach

Under the leadership of Seikkula and Aaltonen, therapy meetings or treatment meetings, based on the need-adapted treatment model (Alanen), were developed in Western Lapland (Finland). This treatment system was deeply influenced philosophically and epistemologically by social constructivism, which was introduced into family treatment by H. Anderson, H. Goolishian and T. Andersen. They describe the psyche as an essentially social phenomenon, and reality as something constructed through conversations. Thus it is essential that psychotherapy is an open dialogue because new understanding cannot be processed by a single consciousness but only through a process of interaction between people. The treatment meetings offer the best scene for this kind of dialogical interaction (Seikkula 1996).

No individual idea is considered more correct than any other. Meaning is created in social relations or later on in the inner dialogue between different voices which contain our life experiences. If many different views are given a voice, a greater potential for understanding and change is created. All voices must be heard, and the professionals must try to build bridges between the different voices. Therapists don't try to control the system but try to process a dialogue, generating new meanings that become part of the inner dialogues of each individual. Continuity is a crucial element of this process. The whole period of the treatment process can be anything between three meetings or many years.

The Turku Schizophrenia Project compared a cohort of first admission schizophrenia patients from 1976–77 (n = 56) with one from 1983–84 (n = 30). The treatment meeting approach had been implemented in the meantime. The study found significantly more persons with no psychotic symptoms (61 vs 38%) and more full-time employment (57 vs 30%) in the later cohort. The method was particularly successful in the acute crisis group (Alanen 1997; Alanen et $al.$ 2000). In a 4–8 year outcome study of 37 patients, none had a psychotic relapse, and 17 of the 37 cases never used neuroleptics (Alanen et $al.$ 2000).

In the multicentre API Project from 1992–93, the group receiving treatment based on the open dialogue family approach (43% of whom received no neuroleptics) were three times less likely to experience psychotic symptoms at 2-year follow-up than a control group (94% of whom received neuroleptics) (Alanen et $al.$ 2000). The efficacy of the open dialogue approach has also been demonstrated in Western Lapland, where the API approach also involved only limited use of neuroleptic medication (Seikkula et $al.$ 2003).

GLOBAL EFFICACY OF FAMILY TREATMENT

There are no controlled efficacy studies comparing psychoeducational approaches with systemic or other family therapy models, and there are as yet no data to support the superiority of any particular form of marital or family therapy over any other. Shadish et $al.$ (1995) concluded in their meta-analysis, 'that if all treatments were equally designed, implemented, measured, and reported, significant differences among orientations might not be found' (p. 350). However, for severe disorders, treatments that combined conventional family therapy sessions with other interventions were more efficacious than standard family therapy approaches alone. Family therapy or systemic therapy seem to potentiate other interventions for many disorders. Many of the positive changes do not last for significant periods of time (i.e. beyond 2 years) and there are preliminary data to suggest that longer-term treatments have more lasting effects. The economic savings of short-term treatments may be offset by high relapse rates and levels of service utilization (Pinsof and Wynne 1995). Hopefully, future research will discover the active components, for which types of patient or family, in the process of family therapy.

CONCLUSION

Psychotic disorders are heterogeneous and are determined by many factors that vary greatly from one individual to another. Therapeutic work with families must be conceived accordingly. The origin and development of psychotic disorders and their social systems must be seen as a complex and interactive process, involving reciprocal determinism between the widely divergent levels of a bio-psycho-social self/environment system. We also acknowledge the essential role that traumatic and over-exacting life events can play in the genesis of psychotic disorders (Read *et al.* 2001; see also Chapter 16). It is impossible to predict the course of psychological illness in a reliable way. The course is not set by the disorder alone, but is influenced by many factors, especially psycho-social ones.

Families with a member diagnosed 'schizophrenic' are clearly not all the same. Each has its own structural organization and communication patterns. Therefore, only tentative hypotheses and interactive explanations are possible or sincere in the therapeutic work with patients and their families. Our own position is that of experts with a certain knowledge concerning hypotheses that may or may not fit for a given family, and with a certain ability to initiate a constructive dialogue, with and within the families, on the origins of and solutions to the subjectively experienced problems.

We do not try to work through a ready-made treatment programme that would not be suited to the needs of the individual family. We first provide information about the various treatment components and options. We retain the greatest possible openness to all subjects that may arise. We are only mediators, if possible, and regulators, if necessary. We try to detect each family's individual access to problems (their phenomenology) and use it to activate their own specific resources. Because of our different training, we use a variety of methods, but only if they make sense to the family.

In the event of a true dialogue, new meanings are discovered in life events, relationships become clearer, with clearer boundaries and greater independence. Then we feel we are on the right path. Guilt or exculpation are obsolete opposites. The subtle handling of this question is part of the discussion and not – either as an exoneration or as an accusation – an expression of morals. It is not for us to judge.

Evaluation of any treatment system must assess its flexibility, especially its ability to adapt itself to the specific needs of different individuals and different families. As the system is in a continuous process of development, any treatment programme falls short of the optimal possibilities. This must be stated truthfully, to the reader of this chapter, and to the families with whom we work.

REFERENCES

Alanen, Y. (1997). *Schizophrenia: Its Origins and Need-Adapted Treatment*. London: Karnac.

Alanen, Y. (2000). Schizophrenie und Psychotherapie. *Psychotherapeut* 45: 214–22.

Alanen, Y. *et al.* (2000). The Finnish integrated model for early treatment of schizophrenia and related psychoses. In B. Martindale *et al.* (eds) *Psychosis: Psychological Approaches and their Effectiveness*. London: Gaskell.

Allen, R. and Read, J. (1997). Integrated Mental Health Care: Practitioners' perspectives. *Australian and New Zealand Journal of Psychiatry* 31: 496–503.

Bateson, G. *et al.* (1956). Toward a theory of schizophrenia. *Behavioral Science* 1: 251–64.

Bateson, G. *et al.* (1969). *Schizophrenie und Familie*. Frankfurt: Suhrkamp.

Boszormenyi-Nagy, I. and Framo, J. (eds) (1965). *Intensive Family Therapy*. New York: Harper & Row.

Bowen, M. (1960). A family concept of schizophrenia. In D. Jackson (ed.) *The Etiology of Schizophrenia*. New York: Basic Books.

Brown, G. *et al.* (1972). Influence of family life on the course of schizophrenic disorders. *British Journal of Psychiatry* 121: 241–58.

Cozolino, L. *et al.* (1988). The impact of education about schizophrenia on relatives varying in expressed emotion. *Schizophrenia Bulletin* 14: 675–87.

Dixon, L. *et al.* (2001). Evidence-based practices for services to families with psychiatric disabilities. *Psychiatric Services* 52: 903–10.

Falloon, I. *et al.* (1982). Family management in the prevention of exacerbations of schizophrenia. *New England Journal of Medicine* 306: 1437–40.

Goldstein, M. and Miklowitz, D. (1995). The effectiveness of psychoeducational family therapy in the treatment of schizophrenic disorders. *Journal of Marital and Family Therapy* 21: 361–76.

Goldstein, M. and Strachan, A. (1986). The impact of family intervention programs on family communication and the short term course of schizophrenia. In M. Goldstein *et al.* (eds) *Treatment of Schizophrenia: Family Assessment and Intervention*. Berlin: Springer.

Hahlweg, K. *et al.* (2000). Familienbetreuung als verhaltenstherapeutischer Ansatz zur Rückfallprophylaxe bei schizophrenen Patienten. In M. Krausz and D. Naber (eds) *Integrative Schizophrenietherapie*. Freiburg: Karger.

Haley, J. (1963). *Strategies of Psychotherapy*. New York: Grune & Stratton.

Hogarty, G. *et al.* (1986). Family education, social skills training, and maintenance chemotherapy in the aftercare of schizophrenia. *Archives of General Psychiatry* 43: 633–42.

Hogarty, G. *et al.* (1995). Personal therapy: a disorder-relevant psychotherapy for schizophrenia. *Schizophrenia Bulletin* 21: 379–93.

Johnstone, L. (1993). Family management in 'schizophrenia': its assumptions and contradictions. *Journal of Mental Health* 2: 255–69.

Kavanagh, D. (1992). Recent developments in expressed emotion and schizophrenia. *British Journal of Psychiatry* 160: 601–20.

Krausz, M. and Naber, D. (eds) (2000). *Integrative Schizophrenietherapie*. Freiburg: Karger.

Leff, J. *et al.* (1982). A controlled trial of social intervention in the families of schizophrenic patients. *British Journal of Psychiatry* 141: 121–34.

Lehtinen, K. (1994). Need-adapted treatment of schizophrenia: family interventions. *British Journal of Psychiatry* 164(suppl. 23): 89–96.

Lehtinen, K. (2003). Family therapy in the need-adapted approach. In V. Aderhold *et al.* (eds) *Psychotherapie der Psychosen. Integrative Behandlungsansätze aus Skandinavien*. Gießen: Psychosozial-Verlag.

Lidz, T. *et al.* (1958). *Schizophrenia and the Family*. New York: International Universities Press.

Martindale, B. *et al.* (eds) (2000). *Psychosis: Psychological Approaches and their Effectiveness*. London: Gaskell.

McGill, C. *et al.* (1983). Family educational intervention in the treatment of schizophrenia. *Hospital and Community Psychiatry* 34: 934–8.

McGorry, P. (2000). Psychotherapy and recovery in early psychosis. In B. Martindale *et al.* (eds) *Psychosis: Psychological Approaches and Their Effectiveness*. London: Gaskell.

Minuchin, S. (1967). *Families of the Slums*. New York: Basic Books.

Palazzoli, S. *et al.* (1975). *Paradoxon und Gegenparadoxon*. Stuttgart: Klett-Cotta.

Pinsof, W. and Wynne, L. (1995). The efficacy of marital and family therapy. *Journal of Marital and Family Therapy* 21: 585–613.

Read, J. *et al.* (2001). The contribution of early traumatic events to schizophrenia in some patients. *Psychiatry* 64: 319–45.

Reich, G. and Riehl-Emde, A. (2001). Familientherapie – Aktuelle Trends und Diskussionen. *Psychotherapeut* 46: 355–67.

Retzer, A. (2000). Systemische familientherapie. In H. Moller (ed.) *Therapie Psychiatrischer Erkrankungen*. Stuttgart: Thieme.

Retzer, A. and Simon, F. (2001). Grundlagen der systemischen Therapie bei schizophrenen Psychosen. In F. Schwarz and C. Maier (eds) *Psychotherapie der Psychosen*. Stuttgart: Thieme.

Richter, H. (1970). *Patient Familie*. Reinbek: Rowohlt.

Satir, V. (1964). *Conjoint Family Therapy*. Palo Alto, CA: Science and Behavior Books.

Schwarz, F. (2000). Empirische Studien zur psychoanalytischen. *Psychosentherapie Psychotherapie Forum* 8: 123–9.

Seikkula, J. (1996). Die Kopplung von Familie und Krankenhaus. Eine Untersuchung am Grenzsystem. In T. Keller and N. Greve (eds) *Systemische Praxis in der Psychiatrie*. Bonn: Psychiatrie Verlag.

Seikkula, J. *et al.* (2003). Open dialogue approach: principles and research results on first episode psychosis. In V. Aderhold *et al.* (eds) *Psychotherapie der Psychosen*. Gießen: Psychosozial-Verlag.

Shadish, W. *et al.* (1995). The efficacy and effectiveness of marital and family therapy. *Journal of Marital and Family Therapy* 21: 345–60.

Smith, J. and Birchwood, M. (1987). Specific and non-specific effects of educational intervention with families living with a schizophrenic relative. *British Journal of Psychiatry* 150: 645–52.

Sperling, E. (1975). Ehe- und Familienberatung als Über-Ich-Therapie. *Praxis des Psychotherapie* 20: 1–12.

Stierlin, H. (1975). *Von der Psychoanalyse zur Familientherapie*. Frankfurt: Suhrkamp.

Stierlin, H. (1996). Erfahrungen mit der systemischen Therapie bei Psychosen. In W. Böker and H. Brenner (eds) *Integrative Therapie der Schizophrenie*. Bern: Huber.

Sullivan, H. (1953). *The Interpersonal Theory of Psychiatry*. New York: Norton.

Sullivan, H. (1962). *Schizophrenia as a Human Process*. New York: Norton.

Tarrier, N. *et al.* (1989). The community management of schizophrenia. *British Journal of Psychiatry* 154: 625–8.

Tuck, I. *et al.* (1997). The experience of caring for an adult child with schizophrenia. *Archives of Psychiatric Nursing* 11: 118–25.

Vaughn, C. and Leff, J. (1976). The measurement of expressed emotion in the families of psychiatric patients. *British Journal of Social and Clinical Psychology* 15: 157–65.

Wynne, L. (1994). The rationale for consultation with the families of schizophrenic patients. *Acta Psychiatrica Scandinavica* 90(suppl. 384): 125–32.

Wynne, L. and Singer, M. (1963). Thought disorder and family relations of schizophrenia. *Archives of General Psychiatry* 9: 191–206.

Wynne, L. *et al.* (1958). Pseudomutuality in the family relations of schizophrenics. *Psychiatry* 21: 205–20.

Zubin, J. and Spring, B. (1977). Vulnerability – a new view of schizophrenia. *Journal of Abnormal Psychology* 86: 103–26.

Chapter 24

Non-hospital, non-drug intervention with first-episode psychosis

Loren R. Mosher

It can be safely stated that over the last four decades psycho-social approaches to 'schizophrenia' have been largely replaced or relegated to an adjunctive role by psychopharmacologic interventions. The current pharmacological domination of the treatment of 'schizophrenia' began with the introduction of chlorpromazine (Thorazine) in the early 1950s. As luck would have it, about the time the serious limitations of these neuroleptics were finally being acknowledged, the pharmaceutical industry introduced the so-called 'atypical' antipsychotic drugs. These drugs were touted as being as or more effective than the older ones but without their adverse iatrogenic consequences, such as tardive dyskinesia and neuroleptic-induced deficiency syndrome. Thus, new drugs like resperidone (Risperdal), olanzapine (Zyprexa) and others have largely replaced the older neuroleptics in the treatment of schizophrenia. As intended, these agents provided new sustenance for everyone's wish to find the magic bullet to 'cure' 'schizophrenia'. A less sanguine view of them is presented in Chapter 9.

As drug treatment became ever more dominant, it relegated the study and application of psycho-social methods to being 'add-ons' or adjunctive to the drugs. It is widely held today that persons labelled as having 'schizophrenia' will not recover without antipsychotic medication and will usually 'relapse' when it is discontinued. So, the issue is, have such persons recovered without these drugs?

Two lines of evidence will be presented: long-term follow-up studies and experiments utilizing a psycho-social treatment with a no or low-dosage drug regime compared with 'usual' treatment with neuroleptic drugs. Each of the experiments avoided the use of psychiatric hospitalization with its known adverse consequences, while treating newly identified psychotic persons 'deemed in need of hospitalization'. All considered their psycho-social methods as the essential ingredients (i.e. drugs, when used, were seen as adjunctive). These approaches used treatment 'packages' that provided multiple specially designed interventions. In this way, they can be seen as more holistic than usual in-office psycho-social interventions (see Chapters 15, 20 and 21).

WHAT DO WE KNOW ABOUT RECOVERY FROM SCHIZOPHRENIA?

We know, from pre-neuroleptic era long-term follow-up studies, that about two-thirds of persons hospitalized in enlightened settings made good social recoveries (Bleuler 1968; Ciompi 1980; Huber *et al.* 1980; see also Chapter 6).

We know that two-thirds or more (depending on the definition of recovery) of former 'back ward' Vermont State Hospital patients were doing well in the community 30 years after being discharged (Harding *et al.* 1987). Their key to success seems to have been well-organized individualized rehabilitation programmes. The vast majority had stopped taking neuroleptics.

We know from the World Health Organization's nine-country study of schizophrenia that at 5-year follow-up, 63% of patients from developing countries versus 39% of those from developed countries were doing well. The most parsimonious explanation for this finding is that 16% of developing country patients were maintained on neuroleptics, compared with 59% from developed countries (Whitaker 2002). It also appears that outcome for persons with this diagnosis is worse now than it was before neuroleptics dominated treatment (Hegarty *et al.* 1994).

We know that newly identified psychotic patients, treated with specialized psycho-social methods and minimal or no neuroleptic drugs, recover as well as drug-treated patients in the short run (Ciompi 1997a; Ciompi *et al.* 1992; Mosher and Menn 1978a,b; Mosher *et al.* 1995). At 2 years, patients treated in specialized psychosis programmes without drugs do better than those in similar programmes who receive neuroleptics (Bola and Mosher 2003; Lehtinen *et al.* 2000). Therefore, it appears justified to expect recovery for most persons with early-episode psychosis, if the proper conditions exist around them. These experiments will now be presented in greater detail.

THE SOTERIA PROJECT

This study was perhaps the most radical and innovative attempt to 'treat' 'schizophrenia' in the second half of the twentieth century. The words in quotation marks are there because the Soteria method denied the 'doing to' connotation of 'treatment' and it did not believe in the disease model of 'schizophrenia' – in fact, it specifically rejected it. At its core was the notion that psychosis should be dealt with face to face without the usual external impediments of theory, artificial institutions, professionally acquired belief systems and practices and without chemical alteration of consciousness by antipsychotic drugs. It focused on finding shared meaning and understanding of the subjective experience of 'schizophrenia' (actually 'personal or developmental crisis' was the operant term), including the experience of others involved in the interactional process. In doing so, the approach eschewed the medical (or any other) theoretical model. Its facility was a home in the community, rather than a hospital. It utilized non-professional staff specially selected and trained to relate to and understand madness without preconceptions, labels, categories, judgements or the need 'to do' anything to change, control, suppress or invalidate the experience of psychosis. Neuroleptics were not ordinarily used for at least the initial 6 weeks.

Many reports of the Soteria Project are available (e.g. Bola and Mosher 2002, 2003; Matthews *et al.* 1979; Mosher 1999; Mosher and Menn 1978a,b; Mosher *et al.* 1995; Wendt *et al.* 1983).

Background

Soteria was loosely fashioned after the Philadelphia Association's Kingsley Hall (1964–72) in London, combined with an existential/phenomenological-interpersonal psychotherapy orientation. The project incorporated ideas from: the era of moral treatment in American psychiatry (Bockhoven 1963); Sullivan's (1962) interpersonal theory and his specially designed milieu for persons with schizophrenia at Shepard-Pratt Hospital in the 1920s; and the notion that growth was possible from psychosis (Laing 1967; Menninger 1959).

Based on the author's Kingsley Hall experience, it was evident that when dealing with psychotic persons in an open community residential (non-medical) setting, some *contextual constraints* were required:

- do no harm;
- treat everyone, and expect to be treated, with dignity and respect;
- guarantee sanctuary, quiet, safety, support, protection, containment and interpersonal validation;
- ensure food and shelter;
- most importantly, the atmosphere must be imbued with hope – that recovery from psychosis is to be expected – without antipsychotic drugs.

Within this defined and predictable social environment, *interpersonal phenomenology* was practised. Its most basic tenet is 'being with' – an attentive but non-intrusive, gradual way of getting oneself 'into the other person's shoes' so that a *shared meaningfulness* of the subjective aspects of the psychotic experience can be established within a confiding relationship. This requires unconditional acceptance of the experience of others as valid and understandable within the historical context of each person's life, even when it cannot be consensually validated. The Soteria approach also included thoughtful attention to the caregiver's experience of situation (not unlike the psychoanalytic concept of 'transference'). However, for traditional phenomenology, this represented a new emphasis on the *interpersonal*, bringing the method more into step with modern concepts of systems and the requirements of interactive fields without sacrificing its basic open-minded, immediate, accepting, non-judgemental, non-categorizing, 'what you see is what you get' core principles.

Research methods

The Soteria Project used a quasi-experimental treatment comparison using consecutive admission, space-available treatment assignment in the first cohort (1971–76; $n = 79$), and an experimental design with random assignment in the second cohort (1976–79; $n = 100$). Data were collected for two years after admission. The participants were recruited from two county hospital psychiatric emergency screening facilities in the San Francisco Bay Area. All persons meeting the following criteria were asked to participate:

1   Initial diagnosis of schizophrenia by three independent clinicians (DSM-II; APA 1968) and judged in need of hospitalization.
2   No more than one previous hospitalization for 4 weeks or less with a diagnosis of schizophrenia.
3   Ages 15–32 years.
4   Not currently married.

These criteria were intended to produce a relatively poor prognosis group by the exclusion of individuals with the more favourable characteristics of an older age of onset or being married (Strauss and Carpenter 1978). Assessments were conducted by an independent research team trained and regularly reassessed to maintain good inter-rater reliability (κ of 0.80 or better). This team conducted diagnostic assessments before entry into Soteria or hospitalization and again at 72 hours (to exclude drug-induced psychoses).

The original Soteria House opened in 1971. A replication facility (Emanon) opened in 1974 in another suburban San Francisco Bay Area City. Despite (or perhaps because of) the publication of consistently positive results with the first cohort (1971–76) (Matthews *et al.* 1979; Mosher and Menn 1978a,b) the project ended in 1983. Due to administrative problems and lack of funding, data from 1976 to 1983 were not analysed until 1992.

Results

Admission characteristics

The experimental ($n = 82$) and control subjects ($n = 97$) were remarkably similar on 10 demographic, five psychopathology, seven prognostic and seven psycho-social pre-admission (independent) variables. Because of our selection criteria and the suburban location of the intake facilities, both Soteria-treated and control participants were young (mean age 21), mostly white (10% minority), relatively well educated (high school graduates) men and women raised in typical lower middle-class, blue-collar American suburban families.

Six-week outcomes: global psychopathology

Because measures of community adjustment are more or less irrelevant at 6 weeks after admission only changes on the 7-point Global Psychopathology Scale (1 = normal, 3 = mildly ill, 5 = markedly ill, 7 = among the most extremely ill) were reported (Mosher and Menn 1978b; Mosher *et al.* 1995). The results for the two groups were similar: *significant and comparable improvement* (experimental group admission mean = 5.2, control = 5.3). At 6 weeks, experimental mean = 3.5, control = 3.5. Improvement significant in both groups, $P = 0.01$).

This meant that Soteria-treated participants, only 24% of whom received any neuroleptic drug treatment during the initial 6 weeks (only 16% of the drug-treated experimental participants received 'substantial' drug treatment, i.e. > 7 days), improved as much and as quickly as the neuroleptic-treated controls. Hence, much to our surprise, the Soteria environment proved to be as powerful as antipsychotic drugs for acute symptom reduction.

Milieu assessments (Mosher 1992; Mosher et al. 1995; Wendt et al. 1983)

Systematic measures

Because the core of the Soteria programme was its social environment, systematic study and comparison of the milieu's characteristics with those of the general hospital psychiatric wards was particularly important. The Moos Ward Atmosphere Scale (WAS) and Community Oriented Program Environment Scale (COPES) were used (Moos 1974, 1975). This 100-item self-report true–false measure taps the participants' (clients and staff) perceptions of the environment. It yields scores on 10 variables: involvement, support, spontaneity, autonomy, practicality, personal problem orientation, tolerance of anger, order, programme clarity and staff control. The Soteria–hospital differences were significant on 8 of the 10 WAS/ COPES subscales, with Soteria's scores very much higher than the hospital's on the three 'psychotherapy' variables: involvement, support and spontaneity. Soteria scores were also significantly higher on personal problem orientation and programme clarity, and lower on practicality and staff control.

Clinical description

- *Milieu characteristics*: quiet, stable, predictable, consistent, clear and accepting.
- *Early milieu functions*: supportive relationships, control of stimulation, provision of respite or asylum, and personal validation.
- *Later functions*: structure, involvement, socialization, collaboration, negotiation and planning (Mosher and Burti 1994).

Staff characteristics

Soteria staff were characterized as psychologically strong, independent, mature, warm and empathic (Hirschfeld *et al.* 1977; Mosher *et al.* 1973, 1994). They shared these traits with the hospital staff. However, Soteria staff were significantly more intuitive, introverted, flexible and tolerant of altered states of consciousness than the hospital staff. It is this cluster of cognitive-attitudinal variables that appear to be highly relevant to the Soteria staff's work. Because they worked 24- or 48-hour shifts, staff were able to 'be with' residents (their term for clients/patients) for periods of time that staff of ordinary psychiatric facilities could not. Although the official staff to clients ratio at Soteria was 2:6, over time it became clear that the optimal ratio was about 50% disorganized and 50% more-or-less sane persons. This 1:1 ratio was usually made possible by use of volunteers and clients who were well into recovery from psychosis who developed close supportive relationships with other residents. In this context, it is important to remember that the average length of stay at Soteria House was about 5 months. For the most part, partial recovery took about 6–8 weeks. Hence, many clients were able to be 'helpers' during the latter parts of their stays.

Two-year outcomes (Bola and Mosher 2002, 2003)

Data analysis

Multivariate outcomes for individuals who completed the 2-year follow-up period (*n* = 129 completers, 68 experimental and 61 controls), comparing Soteria and hospital-treated groups as a whole, and then divided into schizophrenia and schizophreniform subgroups, are presented. Two-year outcomes for the 43% of the Soteria group that received no neuroleptics between 6 weeks and 2 years are also presented. Due to between-group differences on three important variables related to outcome, these variables were employed as statistical controls in all analyses. They were: a higher proportion of insidious onset participants in the Soteria group at 2-year follow-up; a shorter post-discharge follow-up period for the Soteria residents due to longer index stays; and a much higher rate of attrition in the hospital-treated group.

Eight outcome measures (representing five domains: rehospitalization, psychopathology, independent living, working and social functioning) were used. A composite outcome scale was created from these eight measures by converting each to standardized (z) scores, oriented with positive values for better outcomes and summing the measures. Missing values were set to the individual's mean score on available standardized measures. All statistical tests were two-tailed.

All DSM-II schizophrenia participants with symptoms evident for 6 months or longer (insidious onset) were re-diagnosed as having schizo-phrenia (71 of 169, 42%), because the addition of the 6-month length of symptom criterion was the primary change from DSM-II to DSM-III (APA 1980) and DSM-IV (APA 1994). Participants with an acute onset with symptoms evident for less than 6 months were re-diagnosed as having schizophreniform disorder (98 of 169, 58%).

'All completers' (n = 129)

Compared with individuals receiving usual treatment, Soteria residents had:

- +0.47 standard deviation better composite outcome ($t = 2.20$, $P = 0.03$);
- 20% higher probability of being in the lowest psychopathology catagories ($z = 2.7$, $P = 0.03$); and
- one less readmission ($z = -2.37$, $P = 0.02$).

DSM-III 'schizophrenia' individuals (n = 49)

- +0.81 standard deviation better composite outcome ($t = 2.42$, $P = 0.02$);
- 44% higher probability of no or little psychopathology ($z = -2.11$, $P = 0.04$);
- 48% higher probability of excellent or good improvement in psychopathology ($z = -2.68$, $P = 0.01$); and
- 40% higher probability of working ($z = 2.3$, $P = 0.02$).

Table 24.1   Soteria versus 'usual treatment' summary results

6 weeks
Significant and comparable reduction in psychopathology

2 years ('completers' corrected for attrition)
Composite outcomes:
All subjects: better overall outcomes, $P = 0.03$
DSM III 'schizophrenia' individuals: better overall outcome, $P = 0.02$
DSM III 'schizophreniform' individuals: no significant difference
'Drug-free responders': better outcome, + 0.82 standard deviation

Table 24.2   Essential characteristics of Soteria

 1   Small and home-like, sleeping no more than 10 persons including staff
 2   Two staff on duty, a man and a woman, working 24- to 48-hour shifts
 3   Ideologically uncommitted staff (to avoid failures of 'fit'), with positive expectations of recovery
 4   Peer/fraternal relationship orientation, to mute authority
 5   Preservation of personal power and, with it, maintenance of autonomy
 6   Open social system to allow easy access, departure and return if needed
 7   Everyone shares day-to-day running of the house to the extent they can
 8   Minimal role differentiation to encourage flexibility
 9   Minimal hierarchy to allow relatively structureless functioning
10   Integrated into the local community
11   Post-discharge continuity of relationships encouraged
12   No formal 'therapy'

DSM-III 'Schizophreniform' individuals (n = 80)

- +0.34 standard deviation better composite outcome ($t = 1.22$, not significant);
- 1.24 fewer readmissions ($z = -2.36$, $P = 0.02$).

'Drug-free responders' (n = 29)

- Of the experimentally treated individuals, 43% used no antipsychotic medications during the 2-year follow-up period and were designated 'drug-free responders'. At 2-year follow-up, this group was performing well above the overall group mean (at +0.82 standard deviation) on the composite outcome scale.

A SOTERIA REPLICATION: SOTERIA BERN

In 1984, Professor Luc Ciompi and collaborators established a replication of the original Soteria House. It remains open at the time of writing (2003), although now directed by Ciompi's successors. The research reported below covered the period 1984–91. Clinically, this project was able to replicate the original, with some exceptions. First, because of its association with the Department of Social Psychiatry at Bern University, and being paid for by the local health insurance system, it was required that nurses compose at least half its staff. This made the setting nearly as costly as hospitals. Second, it came to have a rather systematized four-phase scheme for recovery from psychosis. Basically, because of Ciompi's life-long commitment to the development of an explanatory theory for 'schizophrenia' (Ciompi 1994, 1997b), the Bern project did not entirely share the view embodied in the original Soteria Project's interpersonal phenomenology. Third, the majority of Soteria Bern's patients received low-dose neuroleptic medication during their index admissions (31 of 51, average daily dose of 172 mgs chlorpromazine equivalents, reported in 1992). These differences moved it more into the mainstream than the original Soteria study.

There was also a major difference in the research strategy. A random assignment study could not be implemented, so matched hospitalized control participants were drawn from nearby hospitals at the 2-year follow-up point. In the last Soteria Bern outcome analysis available in English, Professor Ciompi wrote:

The evaluative research was mainly done in two studies, the first one concerning immediate outcomes without a control group, and the second one comparing the outcomes of Soteria patients after two years with carefully matched controls coming from four different hospital settings in Switzerland and Germany. From these studies, the following findings are of particular interest: Firstly, by using a German version of the well known 'Ward Atmosphere Scale' (WAS) by Moos (1974), it was verified that the therapeutic atmosphere in Soteria differed significantly from the atmosphere in four traditional control institutions (Ciompi *et al.* 1993). Main differences concern greater emotional closeness and more warmth and spontaneity of patient–staff relations in Soteria and less hierarchy, order and control. [*L. M.: This replicates the Moos data from Soteria-California.*] Secondly, immediate results on the four 'axes' of psychopathology, housing situation, work situation, and global outcome were very good or good in about 2/3 of the first 56 treated cases. Statistically, women and less medicated patients had a significantly better outcome than men did, respectively, than patients receiving higher doses of neuroleptics (Ciompi *et al.* 1991). The main result of this first study is, therefore, the confirmation that actual psychotic patients with schizophrenic spectrum disorders (full schizophrenia in 39 out of 56 cases according to DSM III criteria, 14 schizophreniform psychoses, 3 unclear) can in fact be successfully treated in a Soteria like setting, as claimed by Mosher *et al.* (1978, 1995). Thirdly, our comparative study revealed no significant differences between Soteria patients and controls, two years after first admission, concerning the same four axes, and, in addition, the relapse rates. [*L. M.: These results are at variance with those of Soteria-California; see above and Bola and Mosher 2002.*] Significant differences existed, on the contrary, concerning daily and total doses of neuroleptic medication that were about 3–5 times lower in Soteria, and also concerning the average duration of institutional care which was 6 months in Soteria, versus 3 months in the control settings (Ciompi *et al.* 1993). [*L. M.: Average length of stay for original Soteria Project control participants was 42 days.*] Globally, our evaluation confirms that with much lower doses of neuroleptic medication and without higher costs, similar 2-year results can be obtained with the Soteria approach, as with traditional drug-centered hospital treatments. In addition, observations and follow-up information over up to 13 years suggest that many former Soteria patients have had a considerably better long-term evolution than usual.

(Ciompi 1997a: 641–4)

Comment

Although the Bern project found no substantial 2-year advantages for the Soteria group as a whole, it does appear that those participants who availed themselves of post-discharge individual or family psychotherapy – much like what is universally accessed in Scandinavia (see description of the Finnish API Project below) – had better outcomes. The Bern project showed that the original Soteria concept of using only non-professional staff was not necessary to achieve good short-term results, although they were more costly. In addition, Ciompi achieved similar results in a setting that was theory based, in contrast to Soteria California's atheoretical position. What must be emphasized is the fact that Soteria Bern and Soteria California were both able to achieve very good results during the acute phase of psychosis with interpersonal methods and no or low-dose neuroleptic drug treatment. In addition, the two social environments were similar (at least on the Moos Scale), giving credence to the notion that these caring, supportive, humane, protective, interpersonally focused non-hospital environments can reduce or eliminate the need for antipsychotic drug treatment during the most disorganized period of psychosis. This aspect of the Bern replication provides support for our contention that a properly organized social environment can virtually eliminate the need for the rapid introduction of drugs into the treatment of acute psychosis. The Finnish API Project provides further support for this assertion.

THE FINNISH COLLABORATIVE STUDY

The Finnish project has a long history of theoretical and practice innovation. This research is being conducted and integrated into a living, breathing treatment system, in contrast to special projects like Soteria-California and, to some extent, Soteria Bern. Beginning in 1967, Professor Yrjo Alanen and colleagues in Turku quietly developed, and modified over time, a primarily psycho-social approach to the care of first-time psychotic persons. It has come to be called the Finnish 'need-adapted' or 'integrated' system of care (Alanen 1997; Alanen *et al.* 2000; see also Chapter 23). The method evolved from a hospital-based psychotherapy focus to an outpatient- and in-home-oriented family crisis intervention system. The model is now the norm for the treatment of psychosis in Finland and has spawned projects based on it in other parts of Scandinavia (e.g. Cullberg *et al.* 2002). Its principles are:

1   Therapeutic activities are planned and carried out flexibly and individually to meet the real needs of the patient and family. This occurs in a context in which both the patient and significant others are present with the special psychosis team that collaboratively develops a shared understanding of the experiences, observations and hypotheses that emerge within the meetings.
2   Examination and treatment are dominated by a psychotherapeutic attitude – an attempt to understand what is going on with all parties involved.
3   Various therapeutic activities should complement, not compete with, each other. Teamwork is key.
4   Continuity of involvement by the same team should be maintained for as long as required.

In contrast to the original Soteria Project, this is a very professional system, with both psychotherapy and family therapy training provided to all staff. An increased emphasis on family treatment began in the mid-1980s (Lehtinen 1994). Although several studies indicated the model's progressively increasing effectiveness (Lehtinen 1993), the role of the antipsychotic drugs in the treatment was not addressed directly until the Acute Psychosis Integrated Treatment Project ('API') was begun in 1992 (Lehtinen *et al.* 1996). The original Turku model included routinely withholding antipsychotic drugs for the initial 3-week 'assessment' period for newly identified psychotic persons. This constituted an attempt to allow recovery facilitated by psycho-social methods. The usual DSM diagnostic labelling process was circumvented by using a family problem-oriented system of categorization in their treatment discussions.

The 'API' Project

Although intended to be a 10-year follow-up study, only 2-year outcome data have been published (Lehtinen *et al.* 2000). Five-year outcome data were presented by Dr Klaus Lehtinen in Madrid at the World Psychiatric Association (Lehtinen 2001) and will be summarized here.

Methods

The participants were consecutive first time patients with non-affective psychosis, collected from six study centres in the year 1992–93. Three centres used a no or low-dose neuroleptic drug strategy, while the others used neuroleptics as 'usual'. The no or low-dose centres used an initial 3-week neuroleptic-free period and introduced the drugs only when 'absolutely necessary'. Both groups were treated in centres utilizing the 'need-adapted model'.

Results

At 2 years, 67 experimental and 39 control patients were followed up. Overall, both groups were doing well, especially when compared with contemporary American community-based treatment: 69% had spent a month or less in the hospital over the 2 years. Just over 50% of the entire group had had no psychotic symptoms in the previous year and only 20% had five or more psychotic symptoms. Forty percent had Global Assessment Scale (GAS) scores of 7 or more and the group mean was 6. About 60% had retained their 'grip on life'. However, 22% were unemployed or on sick leave and an additional 31% were on disability pensions. That is, 47% were working, compared with American data that indicate only 15–20% of persons with schizophrenia are working 2 years post-admission.

Altogether, 43% of the experimental and 6% of the control participants had never received antipsychotic drugs during the 2 years. Baseline assessments of the experimental group were unable to identify those who would receive drugs versus those who would not. Those who received neuroleptics had worse outcomes. The no or low-dose experimental group had received less hospital treatment ($P = 0.01$), fewer had psychotic symptoms during the previous year ($P = 0.08$) and a higher proportion had GAS scores of 7 or more ($P = 0.01$). Also, *no* association between time since first psychiatric or psychotic symptoms and outcome was found (the currently popular 'duration of untreated psychosis' variable).

At the 5-year follow-up, 37% of experimental participants had still used no antipsychotic medications. Of the experimental participants, 88% had not been hospitalized between the 2- and 5-year follow-ups, compared with 68% of usual-care participants ($P = 0.01$). Grip on life scores were higher in the experimental group ($P = 0.03$); GAS and Brief Psychiatric Rating Scale scores were comparable across groups (Lehtinen 2001).

Comment

It is notable that, as in the Soteria experiment, a rich psycho-social programme enabled 43% of newly diagnosed persons with psychosis to remain neuroleptic-free for 2 years. The treatment approach in this research included organized follow-up care in a real-world system.

WHY DID THESE INTERVENTIONS WORK?

Three successful psycho-social approaches to first-time psychotic persons have been described. They differ in a number of ways: theoretical basis, level of professional experience and involvement, principal site of intervention, type of culture, and myriad other ways less easily defined. What are the common elements that may account for the effectiveness of them all? I would posit that they all succeeded by maximizing Frank's (1972) five non-specific factors common to all successful psychotherapy. In his massive review of studies of therapy, Frank found, to his amazement, that variables ordinarily thought to be predictive of outcome, such as therapist experience, duration of treatment, type of problem, patient characteristics, theory of the intervention, and so on, generally bore no relationship to client outcome. The five he did identify warrant discussion in light of the subject at hand: why these programmes 'worked'. They are:

1   The presence of what is perceived as a *healing context.*
2   The development of a *confiding relationship with a helper.*
3   The gradual evolution of a *plausible causal* explanation for the reason the problem at hand developed.
4   *The therapist's personal qualities generate positive expectations.*
5   The therapeutic process provides *opportunities for success experiences.*

Certainly, the two programmes that involved residential alternatives to hospitalization (Soteria California and Soteria Bern) came to be seen as healing contexts. In the Finnish project, it would appear that the residence or the 'team' came to be seen this way. Because relationships were so highly valued in all the programmes the development of confiding relationships was very *difficult to avoid.* In addition, in all three the context was structured in such a way as to remove common institutional barriers to the growth of such relationships. Each of these programmes placed high value on finding 'meaningfulness' in the psychosis as part of the recovery process. This is really only a synonym for a 'plausible causal explanation'. The programmes' positive expectation of recovery from psychosis was seemingly a critical element of the therapeutic 'culture'. What could be more positive than to expect recovery of persons experiencing the most severe, and putatively least curable, of personal crises, 'schizophrenia'? It is self-evident that being non-hospital based and thus 'normalizing' produces many opportunities for success experiences. While I do not believe Frank's formulation can account completely for why these psycho-social programmes 'work', it does provide a rather simple set of generic principles to apply in the evaluation of therapeutic programmes.

THE TAKE HOME MESSAGE

Clearly, it is easier to deal with an initial crisis than with persons who have learned the mental patient role and have antipsychotic drug treatment effects. This is the strategy of the two Soteria projects and the Scandinavian approaches (there are a number in addition to 'API'). These endeavours all seek to minimize medicalization and labelling, as they are seen as impediments to recovery. They have shown that early psychosis can be successfully 'treated' with a no or low-dose antipsychotic drug strategy. What this means is that persons in these studies will suffer few, if any, of the adverse effects of the major tranquillizers. Tardive dyskinesia, tardive dementia and neuroleptic-induced deficiency syndrome are serious iatrogenic diseases; avoiding them is a tremendous accomplishment. This is why attention to 'first break' persons is critical. It can prevent the continued accumulation of persons suffering from irreversible iatrogenically induced neurological diseases.

REFERENCES

Alanen, Y. (1997). *Schizophrenia: Its Origins and Need Adapted Treatment*. London: Karnac.

Alanen, Y. *et al.* (2000). The Finnish model for early treatment of schizophrenia and related psychoses. In B. Martindale *et al.* (eds) *Psychosis: Psychological Approaches and their Effectiveness*. London: Gaskell.

American Psychiatric Association (1968). *Diagnostic and Statistical Manual of Mental Disorders-II*. Washington, DC: APA.

American Psychiatric Association (1980). *Diagnostic and Statistical Manual of Mental Disorders-III*. Washington, DC: APA.

American Psychiatric Association (1994). *Diagnostic and Statistical Manual of Mental Disorders-IV*. Washington, DC: APA.

Bleuler, M. (1968). A 23 year follow-up study of 208 schizophrenics. In D. Rosenthal and S. Kety (eds) *The Transmission of Schizophrenia*. Oxford: Pergamon Press.

Bockhoven, J. (1963). *Moral Treatment in American Psychiatry.* New York: Springer.

Bola, J. and Mosher, L. (2002). Predicting drug-free treatment response in acute psychosis from the Soteria project. *Schizophrenia Bulletin* 28: 559–75.

Bola, J. and Mosher, L. (2003). Treatment of acute psychosis without neuroleptics: two-year outcomes from the Soteria project. *Journal of Nervous and Mental Disease* 191: 219–29.

Ciompi, L. (1980). Catamnestic long-term study of the life course and aging of schizophrenics. *Schizophrenia Bulletin* 6: 606–18.

Ciompi, L. (1994). Affect logic: an integrative model of the psyche and its relations to schizophrenia. *British Journal of Psychiatry* 164: 51–5.

Ciompi, L. (1997a). The Soteria concept: theoretical bases and practical 13-year experience with a milieu-therapeutic approach of acute schizophrenia. *Psychiatria et Neurologia Japanica* 9: 634–50.

Ciompi, L. (1997b). The concept of affect logic: an integrative psycho-socio-biological approach to understanding and treatment of schizophrenia. *Psychiatry* 60: 158–70.

Ciompi, L. *et al.* (1992). The pilot project 'Soteria Berne'. *British Journal of Psychiatry* 161(suppl. 18): 145–53.

Cullberg, J. *et al.* (2002). One year outcome in first episode psychosis patients in the Swedish Parachute Project. *Acta Psychiatrica Scandinavica* 106: 276–85.

Frank, J. (1972). *Persuasion and Healing.* Baltimore, MD: Johns Hopkins University Press.

Harding, C. *et al.* (1987). The Vermont longitudinal study of persons with severe mental illness. *American Journal of Psychiatry* 144: 718–26.

Hegarty, J. *et al.* (1994). One hundred years of schizophrenia: a meta-analysis of the outcome literature. *American Journal of Psychiatry* 151: 1409–16.

Hirschfeld, R. *et al.* (1977). Being with madness: personality characteristics of three treatment staffs. *Hospital and Community Psychiatry* 28: 267–73.

Huber, G. *et al.* (1980). Longitudinal studies of schizophrenic patients. *Schizophrenia Bulletin* 6: 592–605.

Laing, R. (1967). *The Politics of Experience.* New York: Ballantine.

Lehtinen, V. (1993). Need adapted treatment of schizophrenia: a 5 year followup from the Turku Project. *Acta Psychiatrica Scandinavica* 87: 96–101.

Lehtinen, V. (1994). Need adapted treatment of schizophrenia family interventions. *British Journal of Psychiatry* 164(suppl. 23): 79–92.

Lehtinen, V. (2001). Finnish needs-adapted project: 5-year outcomes. *Communication to the World Psychiatric Association International Congress*, Madrid, September.

Lehtinen, V. *et al.* (1996). Integrated treatment model for first contact patients with a schizophrenia type psychosis: the Finnish API Project. *Nordic Journal of Psychiatry* 50: 281–7.

Lehtinen, V. *et al.* (2000). Two-year outcome in first-episode schizophrenia treated according to an integrated model: is immediate neuroleptisation always needed? *European Psychiatry* 15: 312–20.

Matthews, S. *et al.* (1979). A non-neuroleptic treatment for schizophrenia: analysis of the two-year post-discharge risk of relapse. *Schizophrenia Bulletin* 5: 322–33.

Menninger, K. (1959). *Psychiatrist's World: The Selected Papers of Karl Menninger*. New York: Viking.

Moos, R. (1974). *Evaluating Treatment Environments: A Social Ecological Approach*. New York: Wiley.

Moos, R. (1975). *Evaluating Correctional and Community Settings*. New York: Wiley.

Mosher, L. (1992). The social environment treatment of psychosis: critical ingredients. In A. Webart and J. Cullberg (eds) *Psychotherapy of Schizophrenia*. Oslo: Scandinavian University Press.

Mosher, L. (1999). Soteria and other alternatives to acute hospitalization. *Journal of Nervous and Mental Disease* 187: 142–9.

Mosher, L. and Burti, L. (1994). *Community Mental Health: A Practical Guide*. New York: Norton.

Mosher, L. and Menn, A. (1978a). Community residential treatment for schizophrenia: two-year follow-up. *Hospital and Community Psychiatry* 29: 715–23.

Mosher, L. and Menn, A. (1978b). Enhancing psychosocial competence in schizophrenia: preliminary results of the Soteria Project. In W. Fann *et al.* (eds) *Phenomenology and Treatment of Schizophrenia*. New York: Spectrum.

Mosher, L. (1973). Characteristics of nonprofessionals serving as primary therapists for acute schizophrenics. *Hospital and Community Psychiatry* 24: 391–6.

Mosher, L. *et al.* (1994). Dabeisein: das manual zur praxis in der Soteria. *Psychosoziale Arbeitshilfen* 7. Berlin: Psychiatrie-Verlag.

Mosher, L. (1995). The treatment of acute psychosis without neuroleptics. *International Journal of Social Psychiatry* 41: 157–73.

Strauss, J. and Carpenter, W. (1978). The prognosis of schizophrenia: rationale for a multidimensional concept. *Schizophrenia Bulletin* 4: 56–67.

Sullivan, H. (1962). *Schizophrenia as a Human Process*. New York: Norton.

Wendt, R. *et al.* (1983). A comparison of two treatment environments for schizophrenia. In J. Gunderson *et al.* (eds) *The Principles and Practices of Milieu Therapy*. New York: Jason Aronson.

Whitaker, R. (2002). *Mad in America: Bad Science, Bad Medicine, and the Enduring Mistreatment of the Mentally Ill*. Cambridge, MA: Perseus.

Index

Understanding Autism

Parents, Doctors, and the History of a Disorder

Chloe Silverman

PRINCETON UNIVERSITY PRESS

Princeton and Oxford

Copyright © 2012 by Princeton University Press

Published by Princeton University Press, 41 William Street,
Princeton, New Jersey 08540

In the United Kingdom: Princeton University Press, 6 Oxford Street,
Woodstock, Oxfordshire OX20 1TW

press.princeton.edu

Cover Art: Jim Dine, *Blue Clamp*, 1981; painting; acrylic on canvas with English C-clamp,
84 1/4 in. x 96 1/2 in. x 5 in. (214 cm x 245.11 cm x 12.7 cm); Collection SFMOMA, Gift of
Harry W. and Mary Margaret Anderson; © Jim Dine / Artists Rights Society (ARS), New York

All Rights Reserved

Second printing, and first paperback printing, 2013
Paperback ISBN 978-0-691-15968-3

The Library of Congress has cataloged the cloth edition of this book as follows
Silverman, Chloe.
    Understanding autism : parents, doctors, and the history of a disorder / Chloe Silverman.
        p.   cm.
    Includes bibliographical references and index.
    1. Autism in children.   2. Parents of autistic children.   3. Autistic children—Family
relationships.   4. Autism in children—Treatment.   I. Title.
    RC553.A88S55 2012
    618.92'85882—dc23 2011013942

British Library Cataloging-in-Publication Data is available

This book has been composed in Minion Pro

Printed on acid-free paper. ∞

Printed in the United States of America

10 9 8 7 6 5 4 3 2

This book is dedicated to my parents,

Peter and Noele Silverman.

CONTENTS

ACKNOWLEDGMENTS

This project began with a chance meeting at an MIT workshop and an exhilarating introduction to the worlds of autism research, treatment, and advocacy. Without Martha Herbert's help and encouragement, I would never have been able to conduct this research or write this book. I hope that I have done justice to the generosity she showed in welcoming me into her life and work.

Susan Lindee, my mentor and chair of my dissertation committee, is an inspiration. She continues to teach me about what it means to be both a scholar and a good person, and her own work on emotional knowledge and biomedicine has informed every part of this project. The other members of my dissertation committee, Robert Kohler and Joe Dumit, provided invaluable input at key moments. A Jacob K. Javits Fellowship from the Department of Education supported my graduate work, and the first two years of work on this book were funded by a Mellon Foundation postdoctoral fellowship at Cornell University's Science & Technology Studies Department.

Writing this book depended on the passion, intellectual openness, and kindness of researchers, advocates, and parents who willingly shared their work. I am grateful in particular to everyone associated with ARI/Defeat Autism Now! conferences and to Jacquelyn Sanders. Researchers made time in their schedules to explain the technical details of their studies. Owners of laboratories walked me through their facilities. Physicians allowed me into their offices and homes. Librarians at the University of Chicago Special Collections and Yale University Manuscripts and Archives Collection offered guidance in navigating their collections. As this book makes clear, I am in awe of many of the parents that I met. Their devotion to their children and their intellectual creativity and resourcefulness animate this book.

I shared portions of this book at a number of institutions, workshops and conferences: the "Lively Politics" conference at UC Irvine in November 2004, the Hastings Center, the BIOS Centre at the London School of

Economics, a Society for Critical Exchange conference on "Autism and Representation" in October 2005, the Mellon Seminar and Science Studies Reading Group at Cornell, and the SUNY Center for Medical Humanities, Compassionate Care, and Bioethics. As a result of these workshops, an earlier version of one chapter was published as "Brains, Pedigrees and Promises: Lessons from the Politics of Autism Genetics," in *Biosocialities, Genetics and the Social Sciences: Making Biologies and Identities,* edited by Sahra Gibbon and Carlos Novas (Routledge, 2008), and another was published as "Desperate and Rational: Parents and Professionals in Autism Research," in *Lively Capital: Biotechnologies, Ethics and Governance in Global Markets,* edited by Kaushik Sunder Rajan (Duke University Press, 2012). I am grateful to Fred Appel, Benjamin Holmes, Serena Leigh Krombach, and Sarah David at Princeton University Press for their care and hard work in making this book.

A number of colleagues, friends, and students have taught me about the history and social studies of medicine and the life sciences, autism, and disability studies. These include Jesse Ballenger, Michael Bérubé, Sarah Birge, Paul Burnett, Alexandra Choby, Adele Clarke, Biella Coleman, Rich Doyle, Greg Eghigian, Noah Feinstein, Mike Fischer, Brendan Hart, Stephen Hilgartner, Sheila Jasanoff, Andrew Lakoff, Martine Lappe, Janet Lyon, Jonathan Marks, Aryn Martin, Pamela Moss, Esra Ozkan, Kris Peterson, Trevor Pinch, Rachel Prentice, Nikolas Rose, Erich Schienke, Jeanette Simmonds, Ilina Singh, Jennifer Singh, Olga Solomon, Susan Squier, Kaushik Sunder Rajan, and Audra Wolfe. Erik Olin Wright was a generous and encouraging reader at a critical moment. Other friends sustained me and kept my priorities straight: Ruth Ainsworth, Becky Charnas Grant, Jen Hsiung, Eric Jenson, Stephen Motika, Jeffrey Stutz, Bowie Snodgrass, John Thompson, and Kate Winchell.

My grandparents, Dot and Eliot Silverman, provided a home away from home. My Granddad did not get to see this book published, but his omnivorous intelluctal curiosity and belief in getting the story right are a constant inspiration.

Bob Vitalis, my most important reader, favorite working companion, and partner in all things, edited every page of this book. In the process, he taught me a lot about writing. More important, he makes every day sweeter and brighter.

This book focuses on the unique kinds of knowledge that parents possess, and the responsibilities—and pleasures—of parental love. I am not a parent yet, and I have had to rely on the accounts of others to understand parental love and labor. I do know a great deal about what it means to be a well-loved child, and I am forever grateful for that. This book is for my parents, Peter and Noele Silverman. Thank you.

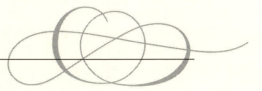

Understanding Autism

Love as an Analytic Tool

Women's work is of a particular kind—whether menial or requiring the sophisticated skills involved in child care, it always involves personal service. Perhaps to make the nature of this caring, intimate, emotionally demanding labor clear, we should use the ideologically loaded term "love." For without love, without close interpersonal relationships, human beings, and it would seem especially small human beings, cannot survive.[1]

Of course, love is never innocent, often disturbing, given to betrayal, occasionally aggressive, and regularly not reciprocated in the ways the lovers desire. Also love is relentlessly particular, specific, contingent, historically various, and resistant to anyone having the last word.[2]

If You Think My Hands Are Full . . . You Should See My Heart![3]

This is a book about love. It is a history of autism, one that pays particular attention to the importance of affect in biomedical research during the second half of the twentieth century and the first few years of the twenty-first. I explore the role of love as a social experience and technical discipline. I do this for several reasons. Passions are a key part of the production of knowledge and the identities of contemporary scientists and medical practitioners. Theories of affect, and love in particular, shape the discourses of developmental psychology, psychiatry, and, more recently, biology. Affect and its synonyms, including despair, anger, caring, and love, work as "good enough" analytic tools for interpreting contemporary biomedicine. Like the parents described as "good enough" by the child psychologist and autism researcher Bruno Bettelheim in one of his warmer portrayals, our analytical categories need only be up to the task of illuminating key themes and conflicts in the material. Love works pretty well. It also helps me think through the role of the social scientist and historian negotiating the thorny issues of trust, complicity, and participant observation.

Autism refers to a symptom, a disorder, and a syndrome.[4] The concept derived from the idea of negative social affect: "autistic isolation" in patients with psychiatric disorders. According to the current *Diagnostic and Statistical Manual of Mental Disorders* used by most psychiatrists and physicians in the United States, autism is a developmental disorder involving "qualitative impairments" in language, communication, and social relationships, alongside "restricted, repetitive and stereotyped patterns of behavior," with onset before the age of three. Any additional claim is contentious, but the standardized diagnosis obscures the complexity of the behavioral and physiological syndrome in any given individual. Autism is also commonly seen as a lifelong disorder. To focus on children is to ignore entire lifetimes of membership in families and communities. Nevertheless, this book is about childhood because those are the years when families have to wrestle with the ambiguities of the diagnosis, invest in therapies and treatments, and prepare to live with the impact of their choices on their child's future.

Understanding Autism traces the evolution of the diagnostic category of autism as people have understood it in different places and times, paying particular attention to how people have thought about autism in different ways depending on the type of work they performed. These practices included diagnostic interviews with parents, psychoanalytic milieu therapy, genetics research, and biomedical interventions. The first three chapters deal mostly with the past, the final three with the present. Because the focus is on practice, even the sections of the book that draw on archival sources read in parts like ethnography, as I describe social practices as symbolic systems and seek to illuminate how participants understood the meanings of their actions. However, unlike ethnography, my analysis depends on public statements. I focus on how people describe informal practices of nurturance and care—private activities—in journal articles, memoirs, conferences, and courtrooms.[5] I attend to the language they use to communicate insights about the affective content of practices to those outside their professional or social communities. When people work to explain those parts of biomedical care that are difficult to render in technical language, they talk about love.

Looking at autism in terms of the affective content of practices associated with it does three things. First, it illustrates the degree to which ways of representing autism depend on particular institutional and epistemological arrangements. Second, it shifts the focus from psychiatrists, epidemiologists, and geneticists to parents, counselors, diagnosticians, and lawyers, as they try to make sense of and apply systematic, authoritative knowledge in their daily lives and work. Third, and most important, in describing changes in autism over time and how expert knowledge works in practice, it highlights the centrality of love as a way of knowing about bodies, persons, and relationships in biomedicine.

I use "love" because it is the term used by the people and found in the texts that I have studied. Love is one of those terms in a conversation where expert discourses inform everyday language and where the quotidian in turn shapes biomedical knowledge. It might be more accurate at points to refer, ecumenically, to "affective commitments" or "emotional connections." I prefer the everyday term, even if it is occasionally necessary to point out the technical alternatives employed by particular actors. Freud called psychoanalysis a "cure through love," but contemporary social psychologists favor "empathy."[6] Needless to say, empathy also has a specific and localized technical meaning. Therapeutic practitioners might insist that their work involves "caring" and "help" while resisting "love" on the grounds that it does not involve a rational or intellectual component, a criticism that I will return to.

I focus less on love as an abstract concept than on the statements of participants in several domains of autism research when they talk about love as a form of labor. Love has been seen sometimes as a liability, a barrier to reliable knowledge, and sometimes as the source of specific, focused, and committed knowledge. It entered autism research as something that psychologists studied. Autism seemed to demonstrate what happened when people developed without giving or receiving affection. Love became for a while a behavior that might be encouraged or cultivated externally, before clinicians abandoned it for terms more in keeping with behavioral and cognitive models. Beyond the laboratories, however, love continues to function in normative claims about the practice of research. Parents and their allies say that emotional knowledge enables them to observe and attend to their children in the right way, guides them in medical decisions, and helps them make the right choices for the person whom they love. Those who are concerned about the actions and choices of parents say that it is love that blinds parents and incites acts of desperation. They also worry that the idea of love is used to rationalize and naturalize labor by making the hard work that parents do seem instinctive instead of intentional and sensible. There is truth in both sets of claims. These examples all show how the emotional work of science is made visible when parents and professionals interact.

People do not just talk about love in the world of research on developmental disorders like autism—they actively practice it, often because they are also parents. Clara Claiborne Park, whose daughter was diagnosed with autism in the 1960s, said that she had followed "the imperative that an eminent mathematician has given as a two-word definition of the scientific method: 'Try everything.'"[7] The approach was as appropriate for the parents of affected children as it was for scientific and medical professionals. The work of professionals and of parents is not, in the end, as different as we have been led to believe. For example, the leading journal of autism research, then called the *Journal of Autism and Childhood Schizophrenia*, ran a remarkable column between 1974 and 1985, "Parents Speak," edited by the first two presidents of the National Society for Autistic Children. Park reviewed books for the journal, arguing for the importance of reading parent memoirs not only as historical documents but as clinical evidence, "raw data in the fullest sense."[8]

To be clear, love may not protect against harm. People who love routinely commit acts of violence. Consider three apparent murders of children with autism by their parents in 2006. The editor of a daily Internet autism clipping service and father of a child with autism agonized, "I have been struggling with trying to find a response that does justice to these situations, and I don't think I've been doing such a good job of it because the subject hurts so, the heart can get too much in the way."[9] These were not isolated instances. In one, grieving relatives of the parent called a murder-suicide "an act of love."[10] Different groups interpret such acts in line with their own beliefs. Some blame the lack of support services. Others curse promised cures that fail to deliver, "[leaving] the parents of a half-million autistic children feeling like failures."[11] Some parents will admit that they have also considered violence in spite of, or perhaps alongside, their love for their children.[12] Such acts and the agony that precedes and follows them resist simple explanations.

In focusing on parental love, I am not suggesting that only parents can provide the particular kind of attentive care that I am interested in. Many parents do not love their children. They are completely absent from their children's lives. Some actively and intentionally harm their children. There are also many caregivers in residential facilities or employed by families who are more intimately involved in children's lives than are their parents.

When I discuss the love that is part of effective care and treatments, I am less concerned with biological relatedness than with attitudes of investment in and devotion to another's well-being. Counselors, nurses, and teachers are often the ones providing this care.

Clara Park listed the advantages that parents have in treating their own children, leaving one quality of parental care, "a parent's love for his child," until the very end of her list. Park's hesitant attention to the necessity of attachment and caring, even in instances where doctors and parents are expected to impartially evaluate different treatment options, points to a tension that affects medical research and treatment in general. Love is not a panacea, and "we must be aware of the ways to go wrong in loving, ways that help not the person we love but ourselves." Nevertheless, "there are millions of parents—as well as teachers, and social workers, and doctors, and ministers, and psychiatrists, and ordinary men and women—who practice this love daily, knowing that love is a technique as well as an emotion."[13]

Understanding Autism pursues Park's insight about love as a technique in biomedical knowledge and practice. It is about why love is the last item on Park's list, and why it is the most important.

Thinking about Caring: Theories of Love in Biomedicine

Research programs in autism, as in many areas of the life sciences, have been defined largely by the passions and commitments that have informed them. These commitments inform not only the broad theoretical framing of investigations but also the day-to-day practices of research. My interest in love is a consequence of taking seriously the commitment to analyze science as a social system. It is indebted to work in science studies on reason, rationality, and objectivity. If science is a culture, it should be possible to analyze the rituals and modes of behavior that enable scientists to comprehend and trust each other, and to produce facts that the community recognizes as valid. Sociologists have analyzed the behavioral norms that have allowed scientists to see their work as insulated from the pressures of politics, social aspirations, and commercial enterprise.[14] Even when those norms are not followed to the letter, they have provided models for how scientists believe they ought to behave.

In addition to observing rules of conduct, scientists have also used representational techniques to establish their distinctive identities. They have adopted styles of observation that emphasize impartiality and objectivity, extending to the way that they write up experimental results and illustrate their findings.[15] As scientific work became more collaborative, the problem of knowing whether or not to trust an individual's observations or experimental results became a crucial one. Scientists solved this problem in many ways, but one important way was by making clear distinctions between appropriate and inappropriate attitudes and behavior.[16] Because there is such a close connection between the identities of scientists and their ideas about what constitutes reliable knowledge, one way to learn about epistemology is to study scientists' own statements about acceptable behavior and attitudes. I am interested in particular about claims regarding the emotional content of scientific and biomedical practices.

Love has mattered to feminist science studies scholars for some time. It has been a focus of their work on the role of passion and commitment in maintaining careers and research programs, on the importance of both caring and pleasure in scientific work, and on the way that expectations about gender have influenced scientific investigations.[17] Love also reminds us of the gendered structures of labor in American society, including the institutions of domestic life and the division of domestic labor, as well as ideologies of motherhood and parental work. Caring labor most frequently falls to women, and because women are socialized to accept that obligation, they develop moral systems that are more attentive to matters of care and dependence.[18] Beliefs about gender and its connections to affective behavior inspire speculations into the biology of sex and cognition, as well as psychological theories about cognitive normality and typical functioning in social interactions.[19] These are especially salient in view of the brute demographic fact that boys are diagnosed with autism four times more frequently than girls. Ideas about gender color ideas about "autism moms" and dads who "fix things."

Gender runs deeper than the division of labor, to what we could call gendered economies of care—types of labor can retain their gendered associations no matter who is performing the work. Parent memoirs of autism begin and end with love, while practitioners speak of parents' diligence and devotion. In this view, commitment explains their ascent to near-professional levels of expertise. This praise is not disingenuous, but it still is worth questioning because it goes to the heart of how American society categorizes caring labor and daily commitments. The top professions for women have changed little in the past fifty years, with low-status "pink collar" jobs in elementary and secondary education, nursing, and administrative work still ranking highest.[20] In addition, women continue to provide much of the child care in the United States, although many fathers of children with autism work as hard as mothers on advocacy and treatment. However, caring labor continues to be devalued because of its associations with women, and the expertise associated with it is often considered suspect. To begin to understand the hidden forms of labor in science and medicine, we need to consider the erasure of the research, long hours of therapeutic work, and advocacy that the care of a child with autism entails. It is significant that the serious effort required to know a person well or care about them effectively is often described as a spontaneous expression of affection rather than conscious work.

The fact that caregiving is hard but also intellectually and emotionally demanding work is key to understanding the arguments that this book makes about the ethics of autism treatment. It is also important to understanding how the philosophy of disability can deepen our understanding of the affective components of biomedical practices.

Moral Personhood, Families, and Dependence

Through much of this book, I present the primary act of intervening on the bodies and behaviors of children with autism as relatively unproblematic. Specific practices draw criticism in retrospect as poorly justified, but from the 1950s through the 1980s, few questioned the idea of treating autistic children or of recovery as a goal, whether attainable or not. This has not been the case from the 1990s onward. A growing number of adults with autism have joined a self-advocacy movement modeled on gay rights and Deaf advocacy, arguing for the validity of autistic experience and autistic culture. For this reason, I want to address what treating autism can mean in terms of respecting and acknowledging the personhood and rights of people with disabilities. I return to this question in more practical terms in an interlude midway through the book.

The ethics of treating autism turns on a question of personhood: whether or not one sees it as a disabling condition, something that it would be better not to have or to be. As Evelyn Fox Keller has argued, the definition of autism as a pathology rather than a normal difference rests on the conviction that the ability to relate to other people is not only developmentally necessary but morally necessary as well. It is a component of personhood. Someone cannot be a "whole person" without it.[21] Many disabilities scholars argue in the same vein. Michael Bérubé, in a memoir about his son who has Down syndrome, suggests that it is Jamie's ability to relate to others, his sensitivity to the needs of people, and his sense of humor that reveal his intelligence and his value as a person. Eva Kittay, writing about her daughter who has multiple physical and cognitive impairments, argues that it is her membership in a network of relationships of caring, kinship, and love that grants her "personhood," the quality that makes it ethically necessary for society to protect people like her and provide for their care. One way that society can respect the personhood of people like her daughter is by providing for her caregivers, those who attend to her physical needs, but also those who care for her as a person.[22]

Autism, though, poses a problem. There is no definitive model for how cognition functions—or fails to function—in autism. The dominant psychological and neurological models continue to emphasize the absence of empathy. If Leo Kanner first framed autism in terms of a lack of affective contact, contemporary scientists describe the disorder in terms of lacking the "theory of mind" that allows people to imagine others' mental states. Neuroscientists point to malfunctioning mirror neuron systems, the part of the brain that helps us understand the behaviors of others by providing us with a mental model of their actions. In essence, we understand the behaviors of others in part by imagining ourselves doing the same things.

Although the terms may be more sophisticated, the argument remains the same: people with autism fail at empathy. Adults with autism disagree, but they do so within the terms already set. They say they experience empathy but arrive at it and express it in ways that are difficult for neurotypicals to recognize.[23] This dissent is significant, and the scientific claims about autism and empathy have obvious limitations. It remains true, however, that autism can mean, in practical terms, that an individual is less tightly bound into the network of relationships that sustain most of us.

This is not the place to enter into a complex discussion of the human rights of people with disabilities and why people with autism deserve support and respect as full, rights-bearing humans and citizens.[24] It is clear that many parents have little trouble committing themselves to the wellbeing of their child and seeing their child as a complete person, even if their child does not reciprocate their caring in familiar ways. The question that is relevant to this book is whether researching cures for autism or choosing an intervention with the expectation that it can treat or cure autism—and by doing so, help people with autism participate more fully in the give and take of human relationships—can be an ethical choice. I demonstrate that people who provide services for or do research on or spend their time caring for children and adults with autism make ethical decisions about treatment. This is not a claim about the efficacy of particular treatments or the rightness of specific choices. What I mean is that they weigh their decisions in terms that are familiar to students of ethical philosophy. Some of those decisions are life-changing in the sense that they entail therapies that can alter or eliminate the symptoms of autism. I will argue that these actions, whenever observers do describe them as effective and beneficial, begin and end with close, attentive relationships.[25]

These types of ethical thinking are important beyond the specific question of autism treatments. Alasdair MacIntyre has argued that disability and dependence characterize our lives; and, to the same extent that our ability to reason depends on our intelligence, our humanity is characterized by inevitable periods of profound dependence on the care of others.[26] Nevertheless, many philosophers have begun their descriptions of social relations by assuming that humans are autonomous, independent agents. We need to think harder about our obligations to those with disabilities, including those who are entirely dependent or unable to speak for themselves. The reality of dependence without the prospect of eventual autonomy has an additional implication. Inevitably some members of society will be charged with making good decisions about the care of dependent people.

This book argues that parents think about these decisions in ethical terms, and that their love for their children is something that they cite as central to their ability to choose wisely. The two, love and ethics, may be related. To care well, Kittay argues, caregivers must not only go through the motions of care, but they must also care about the person who depends on them, because without it "the open responsiveness to another that is so essential to understanding what another requires is not possible." In order to do a good job with the rational, arduous, daily labor of caring, an "affective bond" is necessary.[27]

Think of the decision to choose residential care for a child for the long-term benefit of both child and family. In the short term, the decision is utterly wrenching for both. Or the decision that a parent makes to begin a regimen of behavioral therapy, against a child's immediate wishes, because the child may flourish as a result of the temporarily unpleasant drills and repetitions. Children with cognitive disabilities are especially vulnerable to wrong decisions about their care and depend on the caring of others. The problem is that people rarely talk about these decisions in public. Such parents have few guidelines. In the United States, where pregnancy and motherhood represent "a private dimension of public life," in Rayna Rapp's phrase, parents must act as "moral pioneers" in their decisions about the justifiable limits of parental obligations.[28] Put bluntly, parents are utterly on their own.

What ensures a coincidence of interests between the child and his or her caregiver? Our ability to reflect on our actions, values, and beliefs is necessarily tempered and guided by our ability to love. The philosopher Harry Frankfurt calls love an act of "volitional necessity." It is something we experience if not involuntarily than at least unavoidably. It is also a choice, a relation that is entered into willingly, not instinctively or unconsciously. Humans may have a unique and near-compulsive capacity to reflect on their actions, values, and beliefs, but constant reflection would be paralyzing without an equal capacity to love. Reflexive thought and reason matter crucially to functioning in the world, but if we are to survive and "get it right," that is, live a meaningful life, we need to care deeply about particular things in order to make choices about our goals and actions.[29] Reason has no practical application without love, and reason has no fit with lived experience without the winnowing power and narrowed focus that love confers.

Because of the close connection between reason and love, "the ultimate source of practical normative authority lies not in reason but in the will," meaning our choices about what or whom we will care about most deeply.[30] The psychologist Erich Fromm made the same point fifty years ago when he described the art of loving as a practice that involves technical demands of "discipline, concentration, and patience." For Fromm, love required "rational faith," that is, a future-oriented focus on the object of love, not only as it is, but as it might become given the opportunity to flourish. This nurturing attitude could describe the focus and passion required for fostering scientific research as well as child development.[31] An orientation toward the future is central to the care of children with disabilities. It is why parents may accept the calculated risk of choosing a treatment plan that places more demands on their child but offers the prospect that he or she will have access to more experiences as they grow older.

Frankfurt's description of a necessary alliance between reason and love may not apply to everyone, but it fits many parents of children with disabilities. Consider those engaged in the type of everyday moral philosophy that Rayna Rapp suggests is fostered by their unique position. Although Rapp discusses prenatal testing in particular, parents typically continue to wrestle with difficult questions of dignity, respect, and rights long after making the decision to carry a pregnancy to term. Parents decide what is most important in their child's life. Where a child does not ask for a greater range of experiences but seems content with a sharply circumscribed set of activities, what ethical imperative allows parents to demand more of the child? Eva Kittay and others suggest that imagining independence as the exclusive goal can be both damaging and unattainable for many. However, parents are obliged to increase their children's "capacities to experience joy," which can best be done by broadening their range of possible experiences—for instance, by pushing a child who does not process visual information well to learn to watch and enjoy movies, because learning how will eventually broaden that capacity.[32] It is hard to disagree.

I draw on these philosophical concepts in order to more accurately represent the people that I care about, the families and children who are the central concern of this book. Many children with autism have language delays. Others are nonverbal. Even those considered "high-functioning" or mildly affected may have difficulty serving as advocates for their own cause. They have more effective representatives among the hundreds of thousands of parents, practitioners, and researchers devoted to autism.[33] Of necessity, much of my story centers on actors, technologies, and knowledge systems that affect these children. The children themselves play a limited role in the debates that swirl around them.

Adults with autism are a different story. These often highly effective self-advocates matter to arguments about the appropriate and ethical treatment of children with autism, and I agree that they are better equipped than others are, myself included, to represent their experience. Self-advocates have enjoyed greater visibility and a bigger voice within parent organizations in recent years. Organizations such as Autism Network International, the Global and Regional Asperger Syndrome Partnership, and the Autistic Self-Advocacy Network, founded both by and for autistic people, are an important presence within the world of autism advocacy. Children, adults in institutions, parents who feel that the state and the medical industry disregard their complaints, and researchers excluded from mainstream biomedical research are all silenced in one form or another.[34] The burden for all of us who do have an audience is to act as adequate witnesses for those who are not speaking and to avoid the temptation to assume that their silence is equivalent to agreement or assent.

As should be clear, I am centrally concerned with how parents understand their children in biomedical and affective terms, and what they do with that understanding. I am interested in how the different identities of parents and professionals work in the scientific field, especially when it comes to making claims about effective treatments. Much of the time, the social mechanisms through which scientists maintain their cultural authority—desire for credit from their peers, willingness to share and dispassionately critique each other's results, and a collective belief in the project of increasing knowledge about the natural world—help produce reliable information. However, struggles for authority in autism research have not enabled practitioners to progress steadily toward increasing independence from external interests.[35] The central role of parents in the history of autism research helps illustrate how investments and commitments from outside have shaped the sphere of scientific research.

Autism in History

Like other disorders, autism has become a site for evocations of the stresses, tensions, and catastrophes of modernity. Professionals have described autism as a symptom of postindustrial and suburban modernity, and a range of techniques and specializations have developed to define and serve the population. The literature on autism brims over with metaphorical as well as technical uses of the idea of autistic isolation, and autism has become, in popular culture, a generic synonym for emotional isolation and conceptual solipsism.[36]

Autism has proven almost infinitely mutable. For a mother struggling to implement a behavioral therapy program in the 1960s without the support of her skeptical, sometimes hostile husband, and plagued by fears that she caused her son's illness through unconscious rejection, the disorder is a behavioral anomaly that can be cured through hard work. If the head of an autism genetics project were to read that mother's memoir, however, he or she might pay more attention to the husband's aloof personality and difficulty articulating his emotional states. This reader might also pick up on the mother's chain smoking and lupus as indicators of compulsive behavior and tendencies toward autoimmunity, possible familial risk factors.[37] For others, autism has been a metaphor. Bruno Bettelheim's famous account of "Joey: A 'Mechanical Boy'" detailed how a patient's fantasy of himself as a machine was so effective that "not only did he himself believe that he was a machine, but more remarkably, he created this impression in others." Joey's case was a parable of "emotional development in a mechanized society," ripe for psychoanalytic dissection.[38] It looks different to a contemporary reader. Joey's obsessions and adherence to ritual, his idiosyncratic use of language, and his alarm at human contact characterize almost perfectly a person with Asperger syndrome, another disorder on the autism spectrum.

Some contemporary autism researchers speak of "secular trends" in autism, noting that the emphasis on early intervention has changed the natural history of the disorder itself.[39] Like children with Down syndrome, many of whom have blossomed under the combined influence of improved medical management and heightened expectations of their intellectual capacities, children with autism today don't "look" like the children that these researchers remember from the early years of their work. Anecdotally, they are less like Leo Kanner's original descriptions of isolated children consumed by repetitive behaviors. They struggle more with communication impairments, social reciprocity, and according to some doctors, systemic illnesses.

The shifts in the symptoms that constitute autism tell us much about how different professional and social communities understood psychology, neurodevelopment, and disability during the second half of the twentieth century. They tell us even more about the practical aspects of medical treatment and the ways that physical acts and interpersonal relationships have contributed to knowledge of bodies, development, and relationships. Parents' and caregivers' accounts can provide valuable insights into informal aspects of care in the history of intellectual and developmental disabilities. That history has often been written from the perspective of professionals and institutions, with a focus on the way that diagnostic labels have been used to control populations, rather than on how disabilities have been experienced by individuals and families.[40]

The history of the autism diagnosis is also an inseparable part of a larger story about biomedicine. Autism may have begun as a category in child psychology, but it is an increasingly *biomedical* diagnosis. Biomedicine itself is more than a static system of knowledge. It is also a powerful way of perceiving and altering the world. When I use the term I mean the particular complex of social and technical practices that emerged after World War II at the intersection of molecular biology, genetics, immunology, and clinical applications derived from this laboratory-based knowledge.[41] This research in universities and corporations fostered the development of new medical technologies, including pharmaceutical research in particular. It also provided the context for doctors' increasing focus on diagnostic standardization as the first step toward characterizing a disease in terms of its underlying biological causes. Standard diagnoses became, in turn, a key way that managed-care organizations determined insurance coverage and reimbursement schedules. These trends in research, health coverage, and product development encouraged clinical and laboratory researchers to develop a mania for "specificity," the idea of a perfect correspondence between pathological mechanisms, diagnostic categories, and disease-specific treatments.[42]

Research on autism spectrum disorders took shape within a late-twentieth-century scientific culture shaped by the cold war, dreams of precise control over life processes, and the dominance of biological models in psychiatry.[43] All of these intellectual trends shaped the scientific culture of which autism research is a part, lending models from computing, cybernetics, defense systems, and behavioral research to investigators' theoretical frameworks. The successes of the American pharmaceutical industry have encouraged popular acceptance of an idea of neurochemical imbalances as the main cause of mental illnesses. Brain imaging techniques and the wide circulation of computer-enhanced images of diseased and typical brains have reinforced public belief in mental illness as something firmly lodged in brain structure and function, rather than as having its source in early childhood experiences or interpersonal relations.[44] One challenge of understanding patient advocacy groups involves placing them within a broader history of American biomedical knowledge. Likewise, it is important to understand parent advocates in terms of the illness-based groups that preceded them in areas like HIV/AIDS treatment activism.[45]

The American culture of scientific parenting plays a role in autism's history as well. Parenting in the twentieth-century United States was influenced by a fascination with psychoanalysis and by ideologies of childhood and child development that emphasized both autonomy and fragility.[46] Mothers did not always submit willingly to the intrusion of medical experts into the domestic sphere, but the pronouncements of medical authorities nonetheless shaped American childrearing practices.[47] Likewise, mothers themselves helped create a culture of competitive parenting that incorporated expert ideas about child development and parental obligations.[48] The experience of autism in the twentieth and early twenty-first centuries is difficult if not impossible to disentangle from ideas about the nature of a "good childhood" and beliefs about normal patterns of socialization, development, and relationships.[49] That said, families of different social and economic classes have not always been subject to the same expert recommendations. There is no single history of American childhood.

Biosociality and Contested Illnesses

Autism is one of a number of contemporary contested illnesses, including Gulf War syndrome, multiple chemical sensitivity (MCS), chronic Lyme disease, and breast cancer. We find similarities in explanations for all of them, from changing human environments and toxic burdens to individual vulnerabilities. Patients have similar difficulties finding professionals who will accept the reality of their symptoms when they don't correspond to generally recognized disease entities.[50] All reflect contemporary trends toward patient networking via new communication technologies, even if in the case of autism such networks predated the Internet. They are also all "embodied health movements" in the sense that disagreements focus on the reality and nature of physical suffering. Treatment strategies often involve tinkering and experimentation, and knowledge about the cause and cure of the disorders is built up in close relationships between doctors and patients, making that knowledge particularly difficult to test or standardize.[51]

Battles over the identity of biomedical groups are one type of classification struggle.[52] These disputes emerge not only from differences in access to material or symbolic capital but also from different ways of using empirical evidence and affective knowledge. The profusion of interest groups surrounding autism research includes autistic self-advocates who see the search for a cure as devaluing their own unique abilities. Psychologists use autism as a platform for constructing theories of cognition and gender. There are parent advocates who are committed to a theory of vaccine-triggered autism, and other parents equally convinced that autism is a genetic disease. Representatives of all these groups push for their positions as much through politics as through mustering empirical evidence. They counter the evidence of their opponents by raising questions about conflicts of interest, compromised objectivity, and suspect funding sources. When what is at stake is the question of who has the authority to act in the name of vulnerable populations, research methods can become as contentious as the findings themselves.

It would be naïve to suggest that access to resources and political power play no role in parents' pursuit of innovative treatments or their founding of advocacy groups. Researchers have long observed that autism is more frequently diagnosed among children of wealthier and more educated parents, although they have disagreed about whether this points to better access to health care or a genuinely higher incidence. Family experiences of autism in different cultural and socioeconomic contexts deserve more study, especially as those experiences are shaped by variable diagnostic standards and different diagnostic expectations among parents.[53] Nevertheless, if middle-class parents may be more likely than those in lower income brackets to trawl Medline, the National Library of Medicine's bibliographic database, in search of promising leads and confront their doctors for access to experimental treatments, skepticism about the prognoses and therapies offered by medical experts crosses class boundaries.[54] Parents' capacity to choose different treatment possibilities within a biomedical framework may be limited by their access to scientific information and professional guidance. However, the choice to acquire these capacities is less an indicator of social class than it is a form of participation in the biomedical community of parents of children with autism. It is difficult if not impossible to reduce disputes among parents over how to treat children with autism to simple differences in their access to economic resources.

Contested illnesses are especially useful for exploring the ways people mobilize around illness categories. Any illness category can destabilize when debates emerge about when and how to intervene and with what tools, or on the possibility and desirability of preventative measures. Medical diagnoses share a second characteristic, however, to which I have tried to remain attentive. Scholars have long recognized processes of "closure" regarding scientific facts about medical conditions.[55] Stability in biomedical facts is achieved at a cost, so that what seems to be a triumph of understanding in the present may in the future turn out to have led to the abandonment of otherwise fruitful approaches. Even the supposedly irrefutable evidence of a medical cure can look quite dubious in retrospect. Throughout this book I am concerned with theoretical and therapeutic stability as well as change in biomedicine, and the extent to which both theory and practice are necessary for a community to believe that a particular intervention is effective.

Scholars in the anthropology of science and medicine have observed the tendency of people to form social groups based on illness. Their work sometimes implies that it is the disorder itself that leads groups to form or that the biological similarities among members of an illness category are what bring them together. My work on autism leads me to question the spontaneity implied by terms like "biosociality."[56] Disorders like autism do not act as agents that construct the social or biological identities associated with them. Designers of research programs and clinical trials, on the one hand, and organizers of advocacy groups, on the other, must all work hard to construct illness-based identities. Communities form around the diagnostic as much as the biological reality of the medical condition that comes to define them.[57]

Genetic research in autism has developed alongside increasing knowledge about other disabilities with genetic components and the formation of patient groups around those diagnoses. Autism's ambiguous status as a genetic disorder and the immense heterogeneity contained under the diagnostic label make it different from these disorders and related forms of "genetic citizenship."[58] Ways of relating based on the idea of genetic kinship have certainly influenced autism advocacy. However, the purposefully experimental approach adopted by many parents suggests that they resist the "pastoral" care that medical and genetic authorities offer those with well-defined genetic conditions.[59] Parents' sense that their obligations to their children extend beyond nurturance to systematic monitoring and medical interventions is nevertheless in keeping with accounts of ethical responsibilities engendered by new genetic technologies and individualized medicine.

By virtue of its status as both a developmental and, mistakenly, a childhood disorder, autism can teach us about the political economy of disability in the contemporary United States. Medical and popular understandings of development both reflect and promote invisibilities in care and lapses in services. The definition of autism as a disorder of childhood has had tragic consequences for families of adults with disabilities who have fallen outside the purview of state-sponsored educational or therapeutic programs. Diagnostic requirements under disabilities legislation have influenced autism advocacy and the framing of autism as a developmental disorder.[60] We can go beyond an understanding of biosociality as the motivating force for forming patient organizations and move toward understanding the political and economic context that makes it necessary to organize around illnesses and biomedical facts in the first place. Biosociality might best be thought of as one kind of politics that interest groups use, rather than as a fundamentally new form of social organization.

Parent advocates in autism research have argued for an authority grounded in their particular perspective and degree of investment. One source of their beliefs is the economics of contemporary U.S. health care. Behavioral therapies and other interventions not covered by insurance or supplied by school districts must be administered in the home by parent experts or by assistants that they have trained. The unpaid, home-based labor of parents that is required by our health care system also contributes to parents' legitimacy as experts about their children. These same parents argue that producing better biomedical knowledge in a world full of visible and invisible risks requires us to learn more about the commitments and passions involved in producing knowledge about bodies. The goal is not some kind of more dispassionate knowledge but a better understanding of passion's importance to producing reliable knowledge about individuals as well as populations.

Affective investments can bolster claims of commitment and entitlement and at the same time weaken claims of objectivity and knowledge. Parent activist groups find the scientific work that they support marginalized because of their nonobjective, nonneutral position. Their work nonetheless suggests that partiality and objectivity are techniques that are not always in conflict. Rather, the networked interactions of parents constitute one dispersed laboratory in which a type of situated knowledge is produced.[61]

Methods, Questions, Interactions

Understanding Autism engages with both texts and communities. I pay attention both to the factual explanations that participants offer for their actions and the embedded meanings that they attach to practices. I treat these practices, whether contemporary or decades old, as taking place within a particular culture of parenting and biomedical knowledge, so even when I work with texts, I treat them as artifacts that provide insight into a particular culture.

Although I spent time with a wide range of professionals, I focused on the role of parent advocates in autism research. These extraordinary individuals act as proxies and representatives for their children. They work to mobilize networks for information sharing and lobbying, and they serve as citizen-scientists arguing for changes in the criteria required for credible scientific research. They do so even while devoting the vast share of their energy and resources to the daily work of caring for their own children. Parents who work as activists do not represent all parents of all children diagnosed with a spectrum of disorders that affect as many as one in every 110 children in America, but many more act as advocates, if only for their own children.[62] Taken together, activists' statements represent a broad range of ways of thinking about autism. Although not all parents have extra resources or time to spend on advocacy, those who do can tell us about the ways that parenting in contemporary America involves an investment of love together with other more scarce resources.

I carried out research for this book in many different places.[63] Over the course of five years, I spent time with designers of diagnostic and assessment tools, screeners who employ these tools, primary care practitioners with diverse orientations and beliefs about autism etiology and treatment, and members of an interdisciplinary team designing and implementing a Centers for Disease Control–funded epidemiological project to establish valid prevalence and incidence rates. I attended conferences on medical interventions for autism. I participated in intensive workshops on these interventions, and I visited practitioners who use these techniques at their homes and offices.

I interviewed linguistic psychologists, geneticists, and neuroscientists at their laboratories and clinics in the United States and United Kingdom and attended talks and conferences in the fields of autism research and neuroscience. I spent time at integrated treatment and research centers. I observed National Institutes of Health meetings on funding and priorities for autism research and on coordinating research programs. I also attended Institute of Medicine hearings on the connection between vaccines and autism, conferences devoted to biomedical treatments for autism, and neuroscience meetings where autism was only one topic on the agenda. I subscribed to listservs for parents and for practitioners who treat autism spectrum disorders. I visited schools for children with autism, biotechnology corporations specializing in treatments for autism spectrum disorders, laboratories with specialized tests for food sensitivities and other conditions associated with autism, and the offices of a gene bank. I spent time at a retreat for adults and children with autism diagnoses, and joined in a fundraising walk for a major autism organization. I wrote articles, corresponded, commiserated, and joked with any number of astonishing, resilient, and utterly brilliant parents, practitioners, scientists, and people with autism.

Autism has a history as both a diagnostic and clinical entity. Some of that history is told here for the first time. I worked in special collections in Chicago and New Haven. I spent a week in the then-uncatalogued Bruno Bettelheim papers and spoke with Jacquelyn Sanders, Bettelheim's successor as director of the Orthogenic School. I studied Amy Lettick's correspondence and followed up by interviewing her and Bernard Rimland. I read memoirs and publications devoted to autism and developmental disorders dating from the first years of autism research through the present.

"Studying up," or "studying at home," by concentrating on highly educated participants in knowledge production who are frequently aware of the limitations in their own work, entails a unique set of hurdles.[64] Scientists are obviously not a "vulnerable population." They spent some time and energy trying to shape my account. Parents are like scientists in this regard. I enjoyed it. I also realized early on that it would not be possible to maintain the position of detached observer. My temperament played a part, but so did my growing understanding of the process of research. Resistance seemed out of keeping with the work, especially when I saw my collaborators and subjects producing good knowledge in the midst of and through their own affective commitments.

Love Stories

I was trying not to watch and I couldn't help watching, the way it always is with pain. I thought that I could learn about diagnostic screening for autism spectrum disorders by sitting in on sessions in a university clinic. Although diagnostic screeners lack the authority to provide an official diagnosis, the doctor across the hallway was in a position to do so, and clearly had. I remember a mother weeping and I think that the father took their daughter, who had just been diagnosed as "on the spectrum," for a walk down the hallway out-side the doctor's office. Their pain was palpable. Even though they had been living with their daughter's disabilities, a diagnosis can change everything.

I was standing in the exhibit hall of a meeting for a group promot-ing biomedical approaches to treatment for autism spectrum disor-ders. Even though I had been lurking on a listserv connected with this group, and even though I had been starting to hear about these interventions, I was nervous and found myself unprepared for the experience. Parents wore photographs of their children tucked under the plastic covers of their conference badges. I listened in on one lecture on the health benefits of omega-3 fatty acids marketed by the speaker, another that directed listeners to recipes for gluten-free/ casein free chicken nuggets, and another on the myriad hazards of vaccination. It didn't matter that I had immersed myself in the sci-entific literature on autism. Like many of the "first time" or "newly diagnosed" parents there, I didn't know what to believe. Someone asked me if I had an affected kid, maybe because I was standing in front of a table of supplements, fingering the packets of samples, looking lost, or maybe just because I was there.

We drove a couple of hours through the Florida marshes to visit the offices of a medical practice that specialized in treating kids with autism spectrum disorders, including the son of one of the two owners. The shelves were lined with nutritional supplements bearing a biblical allusion for a brand name. One of the doctors invited us to watch while he demonstrated a quantitative EEG technique on a boy with severe autism. The boy's parents and a visiting politi-cian stood nearby. The child watched videos of animated vegetables narrating bible stories while my colleague and I discussed disease definitions with the doctor and environmental health with the wor-

ried father, who had a degree in toxicology and wondered about the substances that might have affected his son's development.

More than a year later, I watched the same politician give a speech at an Institute of Medicine meeting on vaccines and autism. The published guest list included lawyers, congressional aides, pharmaceutical sales representatives, medical doctors, researchers, administrators from the Centers for Disease Control, antivaccination advocates, and a number of people who listed their institutional affiliation simply as "parent" or "mom" or "mother of a five-year-old autistic child." During the brief public comment period at the end, one mom stood up at the back of the auditorium and spoke to the committee members while her friends held up a poster of the heavy metals excreted from her son's tissues during chelation, a process for binding and removing metals from the body. A father stood up. He was long-limbed and looked like a person who was used to laughing easily. During his allotted time of two minutes he said, "You have friends; you have fallen in love. I want my son to have friends, to fall in love." He had waited through the entire meeting to say this.

These descriptions are from notes I made while researching this book. I offer them here as a way of explaining how love functions in this book not only as an object of analysis for my subjects and a description of practices that are invisible in biomedical research, but also as a description of my position as an observer. I try to be honest about my affection for and caring about my subjects, my emotional responses to the stories that they shared with me, and my own identity as an imperfect and invested observer of the human interactions that make up autism research.

The chapters that follow are loosely chronological accounts. They are love stories, although some of them contain elements of tragedy. They are about the late, beloved psychologist and parent advocate Bernard Rimland, who diagnosed his son's autism using an old college textbook; anthropologists visiting the homes of "disturbed" children to observe the interactions between parents; mothers forming lasting friendships on the strength of exchanged letters and shared grief; and the hundreds of newly diagnosed "little professors" with Asperger syndrome in Silicon Valley. Some books about autism use the conventions of genre fiction. Having autism is like a detective story, where the task is to understand an impenetrable maze of social norms, or like science fiction, where people inhabit other worlds.[65] Some researchers describe autism as a disorder of narrative. Therapeutic techniques like Carol Gray's "social stories" teach people with autism to craft accounts of human relationships.[66] I use stories to call attention to the fact that most explanations draw on the conventions of narrative in order to shore up the connections between disparate observations.[67]

Although I have organized the next eight chapters around key political, practical, and epistemological battles, it is important to remember that lines were not always so sharply drawn. Parents of children diagnosed with autism, from at least the 1960s through the present, explored treatments ranging from holding therapy and psychoanalysis through operant conditioning, megavitamin therapies, and heavy metal detoxification. Membership in social and research networks overlapped. Eric Schopler, who founded the TEACCH program in North Carolina, joined other prominent researchers to work alongside parents in founding the National Society for Autistic Children (now the Autism Society). In the 1960s, the psychologist Bernard Rimland collated the scattered evidence for the nonpsychogenic and possibly genetic origins of autism, but he was as active in studying behavioral treatments for autism as he was in promoting megavitamin therapy. Uta Frith, Lorna Wing, Edward Ritvo, and Michael Rutter pioneered autism research in England. Rosalind Oppenheim, a mother in Illinois, read all of them as she developed educational programs.

Just as it is wrong to see affiliations or research commitments as exclusive or fixed, it is wrong to imagine that understandings of autism have evolved in a linear fashion, from psychogenic to neurological to genetic models. It is wrong not only because Bruno Bettelheim was able to review both Ivar Lovaas and Bernard Rimland in *The Empty Fortress*. Parents struggling with autism diagnoses in the 1970s and 1980s read Bettelheim and heard their pediatricians speak in psychogenic terms, but they implemented behavioral programs anyway. While it may be appealing to represent autism research as a succession of theories, it is more accurate to consider it as a series of temporary configurations made unstable and more theoretically diverse by the variety of disciplines involved, the centrality of parental participation in research, and changes in the population that the term "autism" represented. As I show, the continuities that have existed have been at the practical level, in terms of courses of action, modes of relating to children with autism, and in the language that has been used to describe autism and autism treatment. This language has continually incorporated ideas about love and its role in human development. The shared language of love is the key to understanding continuities among practices—all require caring labor.

Each chapter in this book illustrates an intersection between structured, formal knowledge and daily life, and in doing so highlights the way that emotional commitments allow biomedical knowledge to become part of caring labor, of telling stories and of putting lives together. Each deals with the practical problems that people encounter when they try to transfer expert knowledge and techniques—whether psychotherapeutic milieu therapy, behavioral therapies, genetics, biomedical interventions, or immunizations—into the messy and indeterminate realm of everyday life. In almost all of these instances, the participants have discovered that their affective commitments—their love—played a crucial part in the efficacy of their techniques or comprised an important element in their beliefs. Love made their techniques make sense, but it was also what made them difficult to explain, transfer, or justify.

This book is divided into two parts. Part One covers the history of theories and treatment practices. Part Two brings us to the present. In chapter 1, I track the evolution of the concept of autism from its first characterization as a rare emotional disturbance in 1943 to its present status as a potential epidemic. The point is that autism, as a diagnostic and clinical entity, has never *not* been a subject of debate with respect to its parameters, its utility as a distinct diagnostic category, and its relationship to an underlying population characterized by a distinct biological identity.

In chapter 2, I describe what happened when the child psychologist Bruno Bettelheim, director of the Orthogenic School at the University of Chicago, designed a research program for training counselors based on the idea that autism represented a form of halted ego development. I analyze the particular social system in which counselors at the School experienced their treatment efforts as worthwhile and effective.

Chapter 3 considers parents emerging from the experience of wide-ranging psychogenic theorizing about autism during the 1950s and 1960s, of which Bruno Bettelheim's work was but one, well-known example. Parental efforts to help their children by training themselves in treatment practices became part of the formal methods of behavioral therapies as described by experts in the field. In both the case of the Orthogenic School's milieu therapy and parental work in behavioral therapies, the affective involvement of "semiprofessionals" was key to what was experienced as the success of the interventions.

In a brief interlude, I describe how advocacy for disability rights has influenced parents' understandings of their children's needs and how parents have justified their desire for treatments in ethical and experiential terms.

I begin the second part of the book in chapter 4, where I tell the story of two parent groups and their efforts to promote genetic research on autism. Parents have argued with self-advocates about the status of kinship as entailed by genetic relationships and the meaning of genetic research.

Chapter 5 turns to the longstanding practice of biomedical interventions. These treatments rely on intensive observation and commitment. My analysis emphasizes how parents describe their ways of knowing about their child's distinct physical symptoms and metabolic needs as a particular form of knowledge.

In chapter 6 I address the contested issue of the relationship between childhood vaccines and autism. As parents make claims about the environmental causes of autism, I consider their explanations about the onset of their children's symptoms and the ideological importance of intervening in processes of injury rather than disease. In my conclusion, I briefly discuss some consequences of this work for other research on advocacy groups before returning to the general question of love's relationship to responsibility and to biomedical knowledge.

Autism research is a volatile field, not only because of the high political stakes involved or the ubiquity of love and related passions, but because of the often unexpected ways that knowledge and focused interests can come together to make accepted facts about the world change quite abruptly.

I am attending a meeting of a NIH committee devoted to coordinating autism research across the different member institutes. The members of the committee are drawn from a number of government agencies, member institutes, and parent organizations. A presenter from a major autism organization unveils a new advertising campaign designed to achieve the same level of prominence as a series of public service announcements from the 1980s that we all still remember. The new ad is meant to change minds, and its message is: the odds of getting autism are far higher than most parents realize. It could easily be your child, and all parents should be aware of the warning signs. A later presentation is devoted to diagnosing autism at ever-younger ages—researchers think that they can perceive the risk of autism in a six-month-old. A parent advocate is standing next to me at the break, and I mention to him that, if the number of children with autism has already dramatically increased, a campaign to increase diagnoses will be sure to strain overburdened educational and support systems. He shakes his head: "They have no idea what they are bringing on."

Before I can begin to answer how a parent organization—or anyone else—changes the life of child and a family by encouraging parents to ask about typical development or doctors to recognize and diagnose a case of autism, I have to explain how autism became a condition that could be diagnosed. Psychiatrists and parent advocates worked over many decades to establish the autism diagnosis. Despite their continuing efforts to craft an objective and stable category, the characteristics of autism have shifted over time, and diagnosticians have had to combine intimate knowledge with standard protocols to arrive at reliable diagnoses. It is this history that I turn to in the next chapter.

One

1

Research Programs, "Autistic Disturbances," and Human Difference

Historians of medicine like to make the point that explanations for disease reflect the historical moments in which those explanations were produced. They incorporate not only clinical observations but also notions of the "good life" or of the "typical person," and anxieties about the pressures and stresses to which human bodies and minds are subject.[1] Diagnostic categories are mutable things. They make groups of subjects visible and distinct by describing them, but they then set them free to carry on their business, to resist, reshape, and reform that definition through their own actions. In other words, disorders constitute a modern process for creating types of humans, or what Ian Hacking calls "making up people."[2]

Disorders are useful ways for doctors to think about medical categories, but just what symptoms—or type of person—a disorder refers to may change a great deal over time, whether through bureaucratic fiat or through the activism of groups who adopt or reject a medical definition. In this respect, autism is like many other disorders. Practitioners may maintain that through the course of their long careers they have gained the ability to recognize autism on sight as, one expert suggested, one might learn by studying a range of examples to recognize the distinctive style of a particular artist.[3] Still, much about the diagnostic criteria, practices of identification, modes of treatment, and daily experience of autism has changed, and changed radically.

Autism has commanded increasing international attention since the early 2000s, to judge from the press coverage, books, weblogs, and specialized research publications. The increase parallels the growth in federal funding authorizations for autism-related research in the United States.

The Children's Health Act of 2000 called for the coordination of autism research efforts across the National Institutes of Health and authorized unprecedented federal support for investigations in the area. These provisions increased under the 2006 Combating Autism Act. This fascination and concern with autism is by no means unprecedented. *Time* magazine profiled Leo Kanner, who first wrote about autism, in 1960.[4] *Life* magazine reported on O. Ivar Lovaas's work with autistic children in 1965. And Bruno Bettelheim's 1967 *The Empty Fortress* met with both critical acclaim and immense popular interest. These are works that I will return to in later chapters.

By most standards autism is a new disorder. It is startlingly recent in origin compared to familiar conditions like tuberculosis or kidney failure, but it is even recent compared to bipolar disorder or schizophrenia, which originate in descriptions dating from the mid to late nineteenth century. There are some historical descriptions of "feral children" that are likely candidates for retrospective autism diagnoses. Nineteenth-century medical records also depict children with symptoms that might fit present-day criteria. Yet the authors of those descriptions did not believe that they had identified a unique set of pathological symptoms or that they were pioneering the diagnosis of a new disorder.[5] They made no difference to medical practice. They certainly didn't cause parents to look at their remote or late-talking child and wonder whether they ought to bring him or her in for an evaluation.

Autism is also a very *modern* disorder, with all of the implications of that term. It is characterized by expert knowledge. It is subject to systems of measurement and quantification. It became visible through attention to language and communication failures, and it has been framed in terms of numerous overlapping systems: the family, sensory feedback loops, brain damage, biochemistry, and metabolism. Because the symptoms of autism could seem so obviously the result of atypical development and yet simultaneously so amenable to explanations that assumed an environmental cause, it came to share shelf space with other childhood disorders of uncertain etiology like attention deficit hyperactivity disorder or even severe childhood allergies.

In order to represent the emergence of autism as both a diagnostic category and a term applied to specific sets of people, it is necessary to explore several issues. The first is the development of standard descriptions of autism and their relationship to different theories of causation. The second is the application of these criteria to the practice of epidemiological surveys. I look at the effects that changes in criteria have had on findings about autism rates. The third is the use of published screening and diagnostic instruments.

The neutral tone of this list belies the significant emotional consequences of each of the practices. Theories about the cause of autism have been sources of wrenching pain for parents, just as authoritative and often dire descriptions of autistic limitations have confused and frustrated the people to whom they have been applied. The possibility that the rising reported incidence of autism represents an epidemic has been the subject of fervent editorials, irate hallway confrontations at otherwise sedate conferences, and several full-length books. Meanwhile, the question of early diagnosis and the potentials and dangers that this represents is a source of real concern to many professionals and parents.

Much of the early research on autism originated in the disciplines of child psychiatry and abnormal psychology. Researchers often consciously or unconsciously incorporated the elements of theories that were popular in their discipline at the time into their descriptions of autism. Later, new tools for studying the brain came to be seen as potential keys to autism. Experts were also concerned with identifying research populations and constructing broad-based cognitive theories, using their study of atypical development as a window onto typical development.

Real populations are messy and difficult to manage, epistemologically and institutionally. A diagnosis describes some shared characteristics, but it is mute on the matter of individual difference. The children that were most useful to researchers were "pure types," those who expressed the social, behavioral and communicative deficits in autism without the complication of comorbid medical or genetic conditions or impairments so severe as to render testing impractical or impossible. The difficulty, as with many research populations, is that such pure types did not always reflect the needs of clinicians and parents—who must treat children of all types—or the natural history of the disorder in human populations.[6] By framing autism as a behavioral syndrome, researchers have elaborated on the nature of many of the deficits but few of the underlying causes. They have produced even fewer insights into intermediary mechanisms, and less still into the tasks of managing daily life.

A few elements in the history of autism distinguish it from other psychiatric or neurological disorders that have been affected by the same overall trends in theory or diagnosis. First, autism has often been construed as a disorder of love. Researchers spoke of the absence of "affective contact" in children, others of the lack of bonding in parents. Second, parents have never been far from expert discussions about autism treatment and autism research. They have been incorporated into theories of etiology and built into research programs as well as the daily practices of treatment. Third, the history of autism has been resolutely experimental. Although some published histories tend toward the view that autism research progressed over time toward more empirical and experimentally based work, both autism researchers and the parents who consumed, modified, and translated the researchers' work for their own purposes have seen themselves as experimentalists from the beginning. As the ethologist Niko Tinbergen and his wife Elisabeth put it, in the course of daily life, "'experiments by nature' happen all the time to autistic children. Parents, visitors, strangers met in the street, and last but not least doctors perform them, but usually without being aware of it."[7]

Describing Autism

Autism has been treated alternately as a psychological, neurological, behavioral, or genetic disorder, often paralleling trends in medical research and popular interest. Leo Kanner, a pioneer in the field of child psychiatry who headed the Behavior Clinic for Children at Johns Hopkins University in Baltimore, introduced the diagnostic category of autism to the world of medicine in his 1943 case series of eleven children, published in the second issue of the journal *Nervous Child*. During the next two decades, while the number of children receiving the diagnosis was still quite small, child psychologists and psychiatrists recognized the need to standardize use of the term.

It is hard to fault Kanner's descriptions, which were models of careful observation, but the category and the range of interpretations that "autism" could encompass quickly slipped beyond his control. As a disorder that seemed to straddle the divide between the psychological and the neurological, between affect and brain chemistry, autism became a subject about which biologically oriented psychiatrists and their more psychoanalytically inclined colleagues struggled to find common ground. Kanner should not have been surprised. The confusion began with his original descriptions of children who seemed to represent "pure-culture examples of *inborn autistic disturbances of affective contact*," a psychological problem that nonetheless seemed to have its origins in disordered biology.[8]

Leo Kanner was in a good position to discover a new disorder. He was born in the Ukraine and immigrated to the United States from Germany in 1924 after receiving his medical degree and doctorate. Although he had avoided the depredations of Nazi Germany, he had a keen sense of the injustice of conventional approaches to treating people with intellectual disabilities, and he became an advocate for their rights. Kanner argued that research on mental deficiency ought to be placed firmly within the concerns of child psychiatry, education, and guidance, as an issue central to the study of all human development, and not "merely an appendix."[9] As the author of a definitive textbook in the field, Kanner had virtually invented the specialty of child psychiatry. The Behavior Clinic for Children that he was tapped to head in 1931 became a model of its kind. As the director of a teaching clinic that was part of a department of pediatrics, Kanner developed a style of instruction based on case consultations with interns. This meant that the most difficult and complex cases were usually referred to him or to a close colleague, leaving Kanner with a wealth of examples to draw on in his writing.[10]

In the introduction to the issue of *Nervous Child* that featured his article, Kanner distinguished between studying inborn inabilities to form affective contact and studying intelligence. " 'Mind' has much too often been identified with 'intelligence.' "[11] Kanner and his colleagues were interested instead in the formation of emotional relations and in the idea that some children might have difficulties in this area in much the same way that some children had physical or mental impairments.

Kanner opened his article with an epigraph by child psychologist Rose Zeligs that suggested at least one source of his fascination with these children:

> To understand and measure emotional qualities is very difficult. Psychologists and educators have been struggling with that problem for years but we are still unable to measure emotional and personality traits with the exactness with which we can measure intelligence.[12]

His ambitions stretched beyond defining a specific disease entity, "autism," a term he borrowed from Swiss psychologist Eugen Bleuler, who had used it back in 1910 to describe symptoms of schizophrenia.[13] Kanner hoped to point the way to a subfield dealing with a range of emotional deficiencies. Nonetheless, the article did not suggest precise mechanisms through which children might become affectively impaired, but merely described eleven cases in exacting detail.

The publication straddled two perspectives on children exhibiting deviant or perplexing behavior. Nervous conditions, or those syndromes that seemed to stem from aberrant mental processes, had once been the province of private neurologists. Children who were "feebleminded" were generally treated with the assumption that their condition was permanent and lifelong, and not on the whole caused by psychodynamic processes.[14] By 1943, both categories were becoming the province of psychiatrists. Psychiatrists had struggled for status within the medical profession and had often found themselves stuck in bureaucratic positions within asylums rather than winning prestigious research appointments. As they began to adopt methods that combined the techniques of psychoanalysis with clinical medicine, they became newly confident of their security within the institutional structure of hospitals and clinics.[15]

Perhaps because Kanner largely abstained from presenting any explicit theory about the causes of autism in his careful description, scientists and advocates have found in it support for a range of positions in the debates that emerged since the publication of his work. They have interpreted it as a condemnation of unresponsive parenting, as a prescient identification of genetic or hereditary aspects of autism, as a careful documentation of the many medical conditions that can occur alongside autism, and as a chronicle of symptomatic and diagnostic unity in the context of clinical heterogeneity.

Kanner himself leaned toward an organic interpretation of autism. He thought that it was caused by an innate, structural difference in the brains of the children, but his writing left the possibility open for multiple interpretations. Starting in 1938 a set of children had arrived at the clinic at Johns Hopkins with symptoms that stood out "so markedly and uniquely from anything reported so far" that each case deserved an independent discussion. Instead, he offered a "condensed" description of the history and behavior of the eight boys and three girls. His presentation of these eleven cases as a group worked to establish them as a meaningful set that might be tracked over time to better establish the existence of this new diagnostic entity.[16] As a colleague of his would later write, Kanner's "genius" was to identify a set of stable traits in the midst of such vast individual variation. Later generations of psychiatrists would modify these criteria with consequences for the number of children diagnosed and for theories of the causes of the disorder, but they would maintain that it was Kanner himself who had "recognized the essential core of the disorder."[17]

The children who had arrived at the clinic were a remarkable group. None appeared to have any intellectual disability, although one, Virginia, had been "dumped" in a state school for the feebleminded where she stood out as unlike any of the other children. Donald, the first case, had exceptional memorization skills, but rarely used language to communicate, instead repeating nonsense phrases like " 'Chrysanthemum'; 'Dahlia, dahlia, dahlia'; 'Business;' 'Trumpet Vine'; 'The right one is on, the left one is off';

'Through the dark clouds shining.'" He seemed uninterested in the people around him and didn't desire affection. He had trouble with pronouns like "you" or "I," so that when he wanted a bath, he would say "Do you want a bath?" repeating the phrase that his mother would use with him. He hummed to himself and flicked his fingers in the air, was fascinated by spinning objects, and liked to line up beads and blocks according to color. He hated deviations from routine and demanded that his mother adhere to certain "rituals," repeating a precise verbal exchange with him, for instance, at every mealtime. Nevertheless, in the three years following Donald's initial visit, he gradually became more oriented to his surroundings and his mother expressed surprise at how well he was doing when she visited his classroom at school.[18]

The other children in Kanner's case series behaved in similar ways. Frederick was terrified of egg beaters and vacuum cleaners, and he repeated questions that were put to him rather than answering them directly, a symptom called echolalia. While it was hard to get him to cooperate on intelligence tests, he performed well on tasks that required recognizing and manipulating geometric shapes. Richard, who seemed physically healthy on the whole, was drawn to light switches and didn't seem to speak at all until, at four years old, he said "good night" to his foster mother. Elaine "independently went her own way" at nursery school, "not doing what the others did." For instance, she "drank the water and ate the plant when they were being taught to handle flowers." When she was placed in a residential school, she learned the names, eye colors, and other features of all of the children, but "never entered into any relationship with them."[19]

Although many of the similarities among the cases emerged through his simple reiteration of details, Kanner waited until the end of his paper to discuss the similarities among the cases in depth. The central feature of these children, Kanner believed, was their "*inability to relate themselves in the ordinary way to people and situations from the beginning of life.*" Their "autistic aloneness" appeared to have been present from birth—the children had not so much withdrawn as failed to establish relationships in the first place. Kanner emphasized that all of the children seemed to come from "highly intelligent families" in which both parents were often exceedingly accomplished.[20]

Kanner limited his interpretation of the cases, restricting his discussion of causation to only a few comments, a choice that probably contributed to the durability of his article.[21] Although he took care to record the phrases that the children chose to repeat, unlike many of the psychologists who followed him, he did not try to ascertain a hidden meaning in lines like Donald's "Dahlia, dahlia, dahlia." He believed that many of the children's behaviors could be explained in terms of their profound resistance to intrusions upon their isolation, and that this was the source of the feeding difficulties that so many of them had. Food represented only the earliest and most persistent intrusion upon their solitude. Inanimate objects, in contrast, did not threaten their seclusion, and the children related to them easily and comfortably. Kanner also emphasized that there was a "great deal of obsessiveness in the family background," some of which had actually aided his research because the parents were able to provide detailed accounts of their children's development and skills.

"One other fact," Kanner wrote, "stands out prominently. In the whole group, there are very few really warmhearted fathers and mothers. . . . Even some of the happiest marriages are rather cold and formal affairs. Three of the marriages were dismal failures. The question arises whether or to what extent this fact has contributed to the condition of the children," although it was hard to believe that it was caused entirely by the parents since the children seemed different "from the beginning of life."[22] For this reason, Kanner concluded that the disorder was innate and inborn, not acquired.

In the present, autism is generally described as a lifelong disorder that is treatable but not curable. Few clinicians talk about cases of autism resolving over time, and the American Psychiatric Association's *Diagnostic and Statistical Manual of Mental Disorders* (*DSM*) has not included a classification for a "residual state" of autism since 1987. In contrast, Kanner argued that the condition of the children he had observed seemed to improve as they developed. If the children's "basic desire for aloneness and sameness has remained essentially unchanged," follow-up visits and reports of the children showed that they had also gradually learned to recognize and tolerate some people, to vary their routines, and to use language to communicate and express ideas. Their tendency to panic and obsess seemed less severe, and if they never really learned to play with a group, they at least seemed comfortable "on the periphery *alongside* the group," enough so that their parents felt that real progress had been made.[23]

Kanner's article is routinely cited as the first description of classic autism, sometimes called "Kanner autism." His account of a child who created his own vocabulary for items and insisted that they be referred to in these terms alone, of another obsessed with spinning objects or parts of objects, and of another who reversed pronouns are recognizable to anyone who has worked with children with autism. The article gives the impression of sketching out a previously unrecognized and invisible natural kind, identified and set out so skillfully that it would henceforth be difficult to ignore. After Kanner, autism became visible. Yet the similarity between Kanner's cases and cases of autism in later places and times may be specious because of investigators' reliance on particular diagnostic criteria for classic autism. This apparent similarity has led generations of theorists to propose global theories of autism that downplay the possibility of variation within the diagnosis.

When Kanner published his findings, Hans Asperger, a doctor working at the University Children's Hospital in Vienna, was carrying out a strikingly similar analysis of another set of children, also borrowing Bleuler's term to describe them.[24] Asperger's case series resembled Kanner's, with some important exceptions. Like Kanner, Asperger found his cases because they were referred to a psychiatric clinic where he worked. He also believed that the syndrome was characterized above all by isolation and self-sufficiency, and like Kanner, Asperger noted the children's unusual and idiosyncratic use of language. Asperger did not describe the syndrome as a disability but rather as an "abnormal personality structure," and took pains to emphasize the talents and potential of the children that he described in his 1944 article on the subject.[25]

Even though Asperger described the syndrome in terms of personality, he suggested that it was biological in origin and might even be heritable. He saw qualities in the parents similar to those of their offspring, noting for instance that one mother who "seemed strange and rather a loner" took care to point out the ways that she and her son were alike.[26] He thought that these children could grow to be successful in professional life despite their social oddities, and that they showed no evidence of cognitive disability. Rather, they demonstrated potential for great creativity and originality in their thought processes, "as if they had compensatory abilities to counter-balance their deficiencies," such as their ability to focus narrowly on topics of special interest.[27] Most important, Asperger's cases did not evince the same difficulties with language that Kanner had found. While their language at times did not seem to be used to communicate, they could speak well, a few with the vocabulary and pedantic qualities of academics. Many of the children in Asperger's clinic were obsessed with topics of special interest to them and could discuss them at length, often past the point of exhaustion on the part of the listener.

Whereas Asperger believed that "autistic psychopathy" was not only organic, but also quite possibly heritable, Kanner left the matter of etiology more open to interpretation. The ambiguities in his early writings make it easy to see how readers interpreted his characterizations of parents as explicit claims about pathology and causation:

I have dwelt at some length on the personalities, attitudes, and behavior of the parents because they seem to throw considerable light on the dynamics of the children's psychopathologic condition. Most of the patients were exposed from the beginning to parental coldness, obsessiveness, and a mechanical type of attention to material needs only. They were the objects of observation and experiment conducted with an eye on fractional performance rather than with genuine warmth and enjoyment. They were kept neatly in refrigerators which did not defrost. Their withdrawal seems to be an act of turning away from such a situation to seek comfort in solitude.[28]

Elsewhere, Kanner explicitly rejected the idea that autism was a heritable disorder. In 1954 he wrote that, while it was tempting to "think of a familial trend toward detached, obsessive, mechanical living," still, "it should not be forgotten that the emotional refrigeration which the children experience from such parents cannot but be a highly pathogenic element in the patients' early personality development, superimposed powerfully on whatever predisposition had come from inheritance." Two years later he argued that "the emotional frigidity in the typical autistic family suggests a dynamic experiential factor in the genesis of the disorder in the child."[29] From Kanner's early characterizations, the authors of popular articles drew the term "refrigerator mothers," a term that, in all its potent suggestiveness, persisted in the popular imagination long after researchers, Kanner included, had abandoned the hypothesis.

By the 1960s, both new research on autism and the growing consensus of practitioners who used behavioral therapies suggested that autism was neurological in origin. Nevertheless, popular discourse and practitioners in medical fields outside of psychiatry continued to emphasize the psychogenic theory, associated most in the public mind with Bruno Bettelheim and his 1967 best-selling *The Empty Fortress: Infantile Autism and the Birth of the Self.* Kanner himself became aware of the considerable suffering that the psychogenic theory had caused. Ruth Christ Sullivan, the first elected president of the National Society for Autistic Children, recalled that Kanner delighted the assembled parents at their meeting in 1969, declaring that "I hereby acquit you people as parents" while dismissing Bettelheim and his "empty book."[30] In later years, he distanced himself from theories of psychogenic causation, both in public speeches and in print. In a 1971 follow-up essay on his first eleven cases, Kanner noted his original claim that autism seemed to be organic in nature, "*innate*" and "*inborn*." "Some people," he wrote, "seem to have completely overlooked this statement, however, as well as the passages leading up to it and have referred to the author erroneously as an advocate of postnatal 'psychogenicity.'"[31]

At the time, the question of causation interested parents and had potential relevance for treatment, but it did not seem urgent given the rarity of the condition. During the period from the 1940s through the 1970s, autism remained an uncommon diagnosis. Kanner's diagnostic criteria, described in collaboration with Leon Eisenberg in 1956, delineated the syndrome narrowly. A diagnosis required extremely aloof behavior, repetitive and circumscribed activities, and near-typical intelligence.[32] This appeared to describe a very small set of children. Researchers had made few efforts to ascertain either the prevalence (the number of cases in a given population at a particular time) or incidence (the number of new cases) of autism. Diagnostic practices were far from standardized. Doctors tended to rely on prior experience, if any, of children with autism and their knowledge of Kanner's descriptions.

Nevertheless, by 1971, there was sufficient interest in autism among psychologists and other specialists in development that Leo Kanner could found the *Journal of Autism and Childhood Schizophrenia* to promote collaboration across the disciplines of child psychiatry, psychology, psychometrics, and neurology. The original editorial staff and editorial board included the leading names in autism research and child psychiatry: Leon Eisenberg, Carl Fenichel, Michael Rutter, Lauretta Bender, Stella Chess, Bernard Rimland, Edward Ritvo, D. Arn Van Krevelen, and Eric Schopler, who would eventually succeed Kanner as editor. The board included psychiatrists, psychologists, and psychoanalysts, and the articles that they included in the journal reflected their often sharply divergent approaches to the disorder.

In his early writing, Kanner had left open the question of the relationship between infantile autism and childhood schizophrenia, and the name of the new journal reflected that diagnostic flexibility. In 1949, he had explained that autism was the "earliest possible manifestation of childhood schizophrenia" and doubted that it would ever be "separated from the schizophrenias." Indeed, autism offered proof that "schizophrenic withdrawal can and does begin as early as in the diaper stage."[33] Although some authors thought that childhood schizophrenia was a distinct entity, characterized by psychotic and possibly delusional behavior, most followed Kanner's lead and used the terms "childhood schizophrenia" and "autism" interchangeably. Through the 1960s, infantile autism was seen as a promising model for adult schizophrenia, because of the "briefer environmental history" of the psychosis present in autistic children.[34] In other words, if both types of schizophrenia were caused by exposure to pathogenic family environments, childhood schizophrenia was less difficult to study because of the relatively shorter experience of children compared to their adult counterparts. For the next decade, articles in the *Journal of Autism and Childhood Schizophrenia* referred to "psychosis," "childhood schizophrenia," and "infantile autism" virtually interchangeably, although choices did occasionally reflect commitments to psychodynamic or neurological explanations.

By the time he founded the journal, however, Kanner had abandoned the idea that infantile autism was related to adult forms of schizophrenia. Unfortunately, the fact that infantile autism was not a form of psychosis "had not quite percolated" to the editors of the *DSM*, then in its second edition. As a result, the diagnosis of "schizophrenia, childhood type" remained "the only available legitimate port of entry" for children with autistic symptoms. The 1968 *DSM*-II described "schizophrenia, childhood type" as a condition that "may be manifested by autistic, atypical, or withdrawn behavior; failure to develop identity separate from the mother's; and general unevenness, gross immaturity, and inadequacy in development." The entry specified that "these developmental defects may result in mental retardation, which should also be diagnosed."[35] During the 1960s and 1970s, psychiatrists and other clinicians not working specifically on autism were more likely to use a diagnosis of childhood schizophrenia or mental retardation "with autistic features" than a diagnosis of autism.

The situation was different by the end of the 1970s. Eric Schopler, now editor of the renamed *Journal of Autism and Developmental Disorders*, explained the change to readers in 1979. The new name responded to a revised understanding of the distinction between autism and schizophrenia and the growing recognition that autism was a developmental disorder that affected individuals throughout their lives.[36] The articles published in the journal's first eight years had reflected the fertility of the field, but also the confusion that inevitability resulted from overlapping and sometimes conflicting diagnostic frameworks and treatment modalities. The editors also nodded to the growing recognition that the category of autism consisted of different subtypes, including groups with mental retardation, a family history of language disorders, problems with motor control, or genetic diseases regularly associated with autism such as Lesch-Nyhan syndrome, each of which might have different educational and treatment needs. The shift in focus for the journal also reflected trends in psychiatry more generally. By the mid-1960s, armed with newly available psychopharmaceuticals, many psychiatrists had begun to see most behavioral anomalies as neurological or neurochemical in origin, even in advance of any concrete evidence that this was the case.

Theories and Mechanisms

When the inaugural issue of the *Journal of Autism and Childhood Schizophrenia* was published in 1971, most researchers had concluded that environmental influences in general, and the personalities of parents in particular, were not the primary cause of autism. When psychologists studied parents to identify the sources of psychogenic influences, they instead found that the parents of autistic children were not particularly different from the parents of other children with developmental problems. "Such parental abnormalities as do occur are at least as likely to result from pathology in the child as the other way around."[37] Surveying the state of research in 1996, Michael Rutter observed that "old controversies over the supposed relationship between autism and schizophrenia, and over its postulated psychogenic causation, have disappeared as the evidence has made it clear that autism is a neurodevelopmental disorder, involving basic cognitive deficits, with genetic factors strongly predominant in etiology."[38]

While explanations of this kind might have seemed adequate to researchers within the field, the accumulation of evidence alone was not sufficient to change professional thinking about the causes of autism. I discuss the relationship between theories of causation and treatment practices at length in later chapters. Here I briefly survey major theories about autism's cause and their connections to more general trends in psychological, genetic, and neurological research.[39]

Bruno Bettelheim was only the best known among researchers who located the cause of autism in the family environment. Specialists insisted that they did not "blame" parents for pathogenic attitudes toward their children. Their feelings were, after all, products of unconscious motivations, physical illnesses, or their own flawed upbringing. They were simply acknowledging the parental component in the causation of autism.[40] For many parents, that distinction was hard to perceive, if not entirely meaningless.

Three years before Bruno Bettelheim published *The Empty Fortress*, Bernard Rimland had already amassed a book-length summary of evidence against the psychogenic theory and in support of a definition of autism as a neurological disorder. He tentatively hypothesized that the disorder originated in the reticular formation, a region of the cerebellum associated with attention and wakefulness.[41] Leo Kanner wrote a complimentary introduction to Rimland's *Infantile Autism*, criticizing his profession's use of autism as a "pseudodiagnostic wastebasket for a variety of unrelated conditions" and praising Rimland's willingness to suggest a theory of biological causation that "lends itself to respectfully sober scrutiny."[42]

Rimland did not so much produce new data on autism as analyze and synthesize existing data in such a way that it became difficult to deny autism's biological, as opposed to psychological, causes. He observed that psychotherapy rarely helped children with autistic symptoms, and he reinterpreted psychoanalysts' observations about the parents of autistic children. "Since many of these practitioners are deeply committed to the psychogenic point of view," he wrote, "they tend to see the parents as highly pernicious. As a consequence, the use of terms like 'compulsive,' 'narcissistic,' 'rigid,' etc., in their reports is not unexpected."[43] Returning to these descriptions, much could be explained by parents' uncomfortable interactions with psychologists—it was hard to appear relaxed and socially comfortable when you were dealing with a professional who thought that you had irreparably damaged your own child. However, Rimland wanted to hold on to the claim that the parents of autistic children had unusual personalities. When you dropped the assumption that parents were pathogenic, the features that stood out were their objectivity, their unemotionality, and their goal-directedness, cognitive (as opposed to affective) attributes that could in many cases be viewed as assets.[44] These same traits seemed to be expressed in extreme versions in their offspring, as though a genetic predisposition to a particular cognitive style had somehow been amplified.

The tension between primarily psychodynamic theories and those proposing an underlying biological cause continued for decades. Years after Rimland published *Infantile Autism*, psychiatrists like Margaret Mahler still explained autism as a disorder of ego development and differentiation, albeit one that arose early in infancy, and possibly as a result of a child's disposition rather than its mother's. She considered autism a variety of psychosis resulting from a child's failure to relate normally to its mother early in development. Unable to use their mothers as formative reference points for the idea of self and other, children with infantile autism retreated from human relations altogether.[45] In England, Frances Tustin developed similar ideas about autism, locating the origin of the syndrome in an abnormal closeness between mother and child following the child's birth that led to trauma and withdrawal as a child became aware of its separate existence.[46]

Researchers at major autism treatment centers continued to employ psychodynamic explanations for autistic behaviors through the 1980s.[47]

In experimental settings, behaviorists like Ivar Lovaas, Laura Schreibman, and Robert Koegel were developing theories that interpreted autistic behavior patterns in terms of "stimulus overselectivity." They based their ideas on the observation that children with autism often seemed to favor one sensory modality, for instance, vision or hearing, over others. In cases where they were presented with a number of stimuli in one modality, multiple sounds, for instance, they tended to "overselect" one to the exclusion of others, despite the fact that they did not seem to have a hearing impairment. These patterns seemed to explain the difficulty that children with autism had comprehending speech and their "unresponsivity" in general, especially when they were distracted by another source of information. The finding had obvious implications for how educational programs were designed and appeared to extend to problems that autistic children had with social learning.[48]

Ivar Lovaas believed that the causes of autism did not matter to treating the disorder. Children with autism did not experience social stimuli as rewarding and so failed to seek them or respond to them. It mattered little why their response was absent for the purposes of teaching them how to respond appropriately.[49] Nevertheless, many other researchers remained interested in autism as a potential key to other developmental and communication disorders and in terms of its own biological and behavioral features. Although in the early 1970s genetics had not seemed like a promising avenue—research was at yet "disappointingly limited and inconclusive"—some researchers had taken a cue from Rimland's observations about autism's likely neurological and genetic underpinnings.[50] For instance, Michael Rutter and Susan Folstein moved beyond suggestive but isolated case reports of autism in twins to look at large numbers of twin pairs.[51] They found a significant degree of concordance between identical twins, meaning that both twins had autism. This suggested that autism had a genetic component, although the higher rates in twins could also have been caused by birth complications that affected both children. Lacking more powerful techniques for genetic research, studies were fairly limited, enough so that a definitive review of the field was titled "The Genetics, If Any, of Infantile Autism and Childhood Schizophrenia." The authors came down firmly against genetic involvement, arguing that the weight of evidence suggested that the syndromes were "biological but not genetic."[52]

As consensus grew that autism had to arise from some fundamental cognitive difference, researchers turned to comparing autistic and typical brains. Advances in computing and radiography yielded new techniques, including computed tomography in the 1970s and magnetic resonance imaging in the 1980s. These new tools allowed researchers to look with increasing clarity at the brains of people with autism for evidence of structural abnormalities.[53] Early research seemed to confirm the suspicion that most autistic children were "brain damaged," a catchall term that could refer to any number of conditions that affected brain structure and function. They appeared to have abnormalities in brain structure, although the range of abnormalities that the researchers found gave no clear indication that any difference was consistently associated with autism.[54]

In 1985, two major articles from very different disciplines suggested new ways of thinking about the relationship between brain and behavior in autism. A team at Harvard took tissue from the brain of a young man with autism who had died and compared it with tissue from a developmentally typical brain. They found numerous microscopic differences between the two brains. In the autistic man's brain, the neuronal cells in portions of the brain associated with the limbic system were smaller and more densely packed, and there seemed to be less of the Purkinje cells, which form a layer of the cerebellum. It seemed that they had died off or never formed in the first place. The researchers saw no evidence of damage in the region and concluded that the changes had occurred during development.[55] Their research, and findings by another team that pointed to abnormal enlargement of parts of the cerebellum in autism provided justification for further research on structural variation in autistic brains. For a time it appeared that the cerebellum might play a central role in the genesis of autistic behaviors.[56]

Meanwhile, a team of social psychologists proposed that individuals with autism lacked a "theory of mind," a concept that had been developed years earlier to describe the ability to infer mental states in others. Children with autism were largely unable to pass a simple test for theory of mind in a laboratory setting, unlike the groups of typically developing children and children with Down syndrome that the researchers used as a comparison. The resulting article, "Does the Autistic Child Have a 'Theory of Mind'?" remains one of the most-cited articles in the autism research literature even decades later.[57]

Theory of mind seemed poised to replace communication as the primary deficit in autism. Researchers wondered whether difficulty with "mindreading" might exist alongside a problem with executive function, the ability to plan and carry out goal-directed actions. Others proposed that the disorder resulted from weak central coherence, that is, the ability to organize and synthesize information.[58] They argued that these dysfunctions could cause difficulties in understanding and participating in social interactions and might also lead to the other behavioral characteristics typical of autism. These differences in cognition might help explain the otherwise confusing observation that children with autism outperformed typical children on certain tests, for instance those that required them to recognize or construct patterns. Most important, cognitive and social psychologists joined those whose research focused on brain structures in their conviction that all of the symptoms of autism, including those that affected emotional understanding, resulted from brain damage or "brain abnormalities" that might be genetically determined.[59]

Others struggled to explain the gender gap in autism diagnoses, another feature that might elucidate biological mechanisms of the disorder. Kanner and Asperger both described more male than female patients— Kanner and Eisenberg reported a ratio of four boys to every girl in their clinic, and that estimate has remained fairly stable in the decades since.[60] Female patients seemed more likely to have severe autism alongside mental retardation, and Asperger syndrome appeared more common in males. How much of this difference had to do with self-referral, diagnostic biases, and a tendency for autism to manifest differently in girls remained unclear.[61] Psychiatrists, despite their determined focus on failures of mothering as a causal factor, seemed disinclined to regard the disparity in cases as anything other than evidence of underlying biological causes. Those biological causes, however, were described in terms that expressed researchers' beliefs about gender differences.[62] Contemporary clinicians have only gradually moved to consider how girls' upbringings may result in milder social disabilities and lower rates of diagnosis. Although boys with autism may have more difficulty early on, adolescent girls experience a distinctive agony when they are unable to keep up with their peers socially.[63]

Asperger considered the overrepresentation of male cases important, suggesting that the syndrome reflected a "sex-linked or at least sex-limited mode of inheritance." He claimed that he had seen no female patients with the full syndrome, and those that did fit the pattern seemed to have developed the disorder as a result of illness. However, he did note that he had "seen several mothers of autistic children whose behavior had decidedly autistic features."[64] Taking his cue from Asperger, Simon Baron-Cohen wrote extensively on autism as the "extreme male brain." He observed that all individuals have a spectrum of abilities in the domains of empathizing and systemizing. Those characteristics that cause social impairments in people with autism and Asperger syndrome diagnoses, meaning a high degree of systemizing ability and poor empathizing skills, Baron-Cohen saw in milder form in most males, although he pointed out that some women also have "male brains."[65]

If in 1971 a genetic etiology for autism had seemed unlikely, researchers came to markedly different conclusions by the 1980s. Higher rates of diagnosis had revealed that siblings of children with autism had at least a 3- to 4-percent risk of having autism themselves, and researchers were paying more attention to the association of a number of genetic disorders, for instance tuberous sclerosis, with autism.[66] By the mid-1990s, most experts agreed that autism was a highly heritable neurological disorder with a genetic basis. This certainty had its source in Rimland's carefully argued case for research into the genetics of autism, but Rimland's research had been followed by a slowly accumulating set of studies that appeared to provide solid evidence for genetic causation.

Researchers also began to consider the possibility that autism might comprise multiple, distinct genetic disorders that corresponded to different symptomatic subgroups or "endophenotypes." Wing and Gould's introduction of the concept of an "autism spectrum" in their epidemiological research of the late 1960s had anticipated the idea. These groups might display severe symptoms or milder ones, associated with the increasingly recognized categories of Asperger syndrome and pervasive developmental disorder not otherwise specified (PDD-NOS). Groups might also manifest different combinations of the standard deficits. Geneticists began talking about a "broader autism spectrum" or "broader phenotype" for the purpose of genetic studies, in order to take into account autistic traits in close relatives of people with autism.[67]

Epidemiologists and diagnosticians also came to recognize a subcategory of children with "regressive autism," who developed typically, or at least with fewer symptoms, for the first few years of life, and then lost skills.[68] Not only had researchers placed less emphasis on the pattern of onset, in some cases they dismissed the reports of parents who described their children as having regressed.[69] Yet the idea that autism could develop after a period of apparently normal development was not new. As early as the 1950s, Kanner and Eisenberg noted cases of regression, confirmed by other researchers.[70] By the 1970s, many recognized multiple possible patterns of onset for the disorder, which might each be connected to different modes of causation.[71] Parents drew attention to a feature of autism that investigators had noted but not emphasized. They also provided the evidence, via home movies, of children who regressed after their first birthdays.[72]

As parents began to think about autism as a medical condition, they returned to Kanner's original case series. Almost all of the children Kanner described had feeding problems of some sort, including constant vomiting during the first year of life, an inability to tolerate breastfeeding, and disinterest in or refusal of food; one child needed to be fed through a tube for her entire first year.[73] Although Kanner had interpreted these difficulties with food in terms of the children's autistic psychology, parents now saw them as evidence of possible digestive difficulties, allergies, or immune dysfunction. The child whose mother had described him as developing normally for his first year and then having gradually "gone backward mentally" had suffered diarrhea and fever following his smallpox vaccination at twelve months. Another seemed to have regressed after a fever. One child suffered from recurring colds and ear infections, while another seemed to never get sick at all—both possible signs of immune problems.[74] Finally, parents who were concerned about vaccines as a possible causative agent in autism returned to another of Kanner's observations. The parents of the first cases were all educated and middle class, which could indicate that these parents were more likely not only to have identified developmental problems in their children, but also to have had them vaccinated completely and on schedule.

Counting Autistic Children: Categories, Refinements, and Standards

Early estimates of autism prevalence put the figure at approximately 4 children with autism in 10,000, and possibly lower.[75] Experts considered autism interesting but not a matter of urgency. Starting in the late 1990s, however, rates of autism began increasing dramatically. Depending on the study, epidemiologists began reporting rates as high as 1 in 175, 1 in 150, or even 1 in 86 children with an autism spectrum disorder broadly defined, and from 1 in 500 to 1 in 257 children with the narrower diagnosis of autistic disorder.[76] This increase in rates occurred in all of the countries that had been recording cases, including the United States, Sweden, and England, although the precise level of increase appeared to vary. Although rates of other childhood disorders had also increased during this time period, the increase in autism incited far more public and professional concern and interest.[77]

The majority of epidemiologists working on autism, including those who have been central in measuring the increase, believe that the rise is a result of broadened diagnostic criteria, more thorough identification of cases in epidemiological research ("ascertainment" in the literature), and better detection because of improved public and professional awareness.[78] Others have argued that introducing autism as a category in special education records in the United States and the social stigma of mental retardation led parents to push for autism diagnoses and doctors to accede to parents' wishes, encouraging the false perception of a real increase in autism as one diagnosis was substituted for another.[79] They are joined in these arguments by a number of specialists in psychiatry, psychology, and genetics, and also by self-advocates with autism diagnoses.[80]

In 1966, Victor Lotter conducted the first epidemiological survey of autism prevalence in a large population in the English county of Middlesex. Lotter used a combination of criteria that "aimed to clarify the behavioral descriptions and avoid interpretations of behaviors." He found a prevalence rate of 4.5 "autistic" children in 10,000, and noted that when he applied behavioral criteria evenly, without following Kanner's practice of excluding children with intellectual impairments, he found a large proportion of children with autistic symptoms alongside evidence of developmental delay and "brain abnormalities," perhaps warranting a separate category for prognostic purposes.[81]

Starting in the 1970s, Lorna Wing began an epidemiological study in the London borough of Camberwell with her colleague Judith Gould. They restricted their subject population to children under the age of fifteen "who were known to the local health, education, or social services for reasons of physical or mental handicap or behavior disturbance." They then conducted their own assessments of the children. Like Lotter, Wing and Gould concluded that the "boundaries [were] not as rigid" as Kanner had thought. Autism seemed to occur along a "spectrum" of severity, perhaps encompassing many different conditions. And, contrary to Kanner's beliefs and those of many researchers at the time, there was no "bias" toward the middle class in autism cases. The two authors called for a revised definition in terms of a "triad" of deficits in social communication, social ability, and social imagination, accompanied by a restricted pattern of activities.[82]

The work of Lotter, Wing, and Gould transformed psychologists' images of the autistic child. The children's intellectual skills and behaviors varied widely. They came from a diversity of class backgrounds. Even their symptoms varied, from "aloof" children who seemed genuinely uninterested in social contact and often had considerable cognitive delays, to "active but odd" ones who desired connections but seemed unable to decipher the unwritten rules of social interactions. Wing and Gould began to question the "usefulness of regarding childhood autism as a specific condition," although the long-term effect of their work led researchers not to question the integrity of the diagnosis, but to broaden its parameters.[83] Their findings also suggested that, contrary to Kanner's assertion that autistic children seemed to be of normal or above-average intelligence, autistic symptoms often occurred alongside significant cognitive impairment. By the 1990s, the conventional wisdom was that the majority of children with autism had some degree of intellectual disability, although the claim was based on intelligence tests that provided few accommodations for autistic children's social and communicative differences.[84]

As experts turned to studying autism as a subject in its own right as opposed to a model for understanding other disorders, they recognized the need for more accurate and consistent diagnoses. During the 1940s and 1950s, doctors had diagnosed autism largely through their own clinical experience. Kanner did not produce formal criteria until 1956, when he and Leon Eisenberg identified two factors as central to the category: "extreme self-isolation" and "the obsessive insistence on the preservation of sameness."[85] Nearly two decades later, in 1978, Michael Rutter brought the centrality of language impairments in Kanner's original observations and in his own experience to bear on the matter of diagnosis. He argued for the inclusion of language and communication as a third diagnostic factor.[86] These were essentially the criteria included in the 1980 *DSM*-III, the first time that autism was included by name in the *DSM*.[87]

The choice to include language use as a symptom altered the way that clinicians thought about autism. By removing the disturbed, absent, or idiosyncratic language associated with autism from the realm of meaningful behavior, symptoms such as pronominal reversal (e.g., substituting "you" for "I") lost their value as meaning-laden statements, where psychologists had previously devoted significant efforts to their close study and analysis. For child psychologists who followed Kanner, speech provided important clues to emotional disturbances. For later researchers, lack of speech signaled developmental delays or sensory processing problems, and for neurologically inclined researchers, it indicated the presence of localizable brain dysfunction. It would take nearly three decades for the speech and writing of children and adults with autism to be analyzed closely for particular meanings tied to individual experience, and this time this attention would come from parents as much as from brain researchers.[88]

While professionals worked to refine the category of autism for diagnostic purposes, parent advocates sought to alter its definition for political ends. In 1975, the National Society for Autistic Children (NSAC, later the Autism Society of America,) lobbied to include autism as one of the developmental disabilities covered under the Education for All Handicapped Act. They succeeded. The bill, later revised and renamed the Individuals with Disabilities Education Act, entitled children with autism and other developmental disabilities to a "free, appropriate, public education."[89] The NSAC also demanded autism's inclusion in the Developmental Disabilities Act, a bill authorizing services and support. The group's effective lobbying for a "noncategorical definition" of developmental disabilities rather than simply a list of eligible conditions ultimately won them the admiration of other parent groups and helped NSAC establish a presence in Washington.[90] In 1981, members of the society helped convince the U.S. Department of Education to take autism out of the category of "severe emotional disturbance," a characterization that had only served to reinforce professional biases against the parents of children with autism.[91]

Lorna Wing, the psychiatrist whose epidemiological work was so instrumental in pushing researchers to recognize a spectrum of autistic conditions, also helped bring Asperger syndrome to the English-speaking world. In the early 1970s, Wing, who was also raising a daughter with autism, came across a paper by D. Arn Van Krevelen in the first issue of the *Journal of Autism and Childhood Schizophrenia*. Van Krevelen argued that those psychiatrists who knew of Asperger's work assumed incorrectly that he and Kanner had described the same population. In fact, Asperger had defined a syndrome distinct from Kanner's early infantile autism. Asperger's work had been largely neglected in the English-language literature, although Japanese and European researchers had been aware of it for decades.[92] His descriptions fit the patients in the psychiatric ward where Wing was practicing at the time. The diagnosis made sense for those patients unable to comprehend social cues, some of whom had been misdiagnosed as having schizophrenia. In 1991, Uta Frith published a full translation of Asperger's paper, which began the process of establishing Asperger syndrome as a diagnostic category for clinicians in the United States and United Kingdom and a new research area for those interested in the autism spectrum and the role of social learning in typical development.[93]

Asperger had not read Kanner's work when he wrote his case series in 1944, but he had read it by the late 1970s, when he and Lorna Wing met and discussed the relationship between the two syndromes. They "cordially agreed to differ." Asperger believed that he had described a distinct syndrome, while Wing thought that Asperger syndrome represented the high-functioning end of the autism spectrum.[94] The "agreement," needless to say, did not end the debate in the research community at large, and to this day diagnostic practices for Asperger syndrome remain frustratingly inconsistent. Asperger thought that the children he observed seemed to "delight in malice" and in making their parents and teachers suffer, a characteristic that is quite absent from contemporary descriptions of the disorder.[95] Lorna Wing, in contrast, would describe people who "give the impression of fragile vulnerability and a pathetic childishness, which some find infinitely touching and others merely exasperating."[96] In the present, even among those who agree about the validity of the diagnosis, some clinicians decide what label is appropriate based on when a child began speaking, others on a child's current level of language skills, or on their social abilities, their intelligence, or their personality.[97]

The failure to identify reliable biomarkers, consistently recognizable biological indicators, for the disorder has reinforced a behavioral definition of autism. The behavioral slant fit well with the premises of the post-1980 versions of the American Psychiatric Association's DSM, which sacrificed causal hypotheses about disorders' origins in favor of diagnostic reliability.[98] The editors of the 1980 DSM-III used field trials to establish the accuracy and precision of their categories, and they dispensed with psychoanalytic diagnoses like neurosis. Psychiatrists working independently needed to agree on a diagnosis based on the DSM criteria, ensuring that a single patient could reasonably expect to receive the same diagnosis at different places and times. These changes accompanied the first mention of "infantile autism" in the DSM, under the DSM-III category of "pervasive developmental disorders."[99] Since then, shifts in the criteria for autism in the DSM have subtly impacted the contours of the autism category and the features of admissible cases.

The DSM-III criteria for autism were fairly stringent. They were oriented toward identifying severe cases in young children. The DSM-III-R (1987) had a broader scope. "Infantile autism" became "autistic disorder," "in tacit recognition of the fact that most autistic individuals continue to exhibit the disorder after early childhood and in recognition of the need for a more developmental orientation to the diagnosis."[100] The revised edition both standardized and broadened the set of impairments required for diagnosis.[101] The editors hoped to ensure that "the entire spectrum of dysfunction," including a range of cognitive abilities, would be represented by the category. In practice, the changes may have encouraged psychiatrists to diagnose more children with autism spectrum disorders.[102]

The editors of the DSM-IV (1994) tightened the criteria somewhat by reintroducing the DSM-III's requirement for early onset in autistic disorder. They also included additional categories, including "childhood disintegrative disorder" (previously called Heller's syndrome), a rare disorder characterized by at least two years of typical development followed by a rapid and severe loss of skills; "Rett syndrome," a genetic disorder affecting primarily girls; and "Asperger's disorder" under the broad category of "pervasive developmental disorders."[103] Although practitioners thought that the Asperger's disorder category was too close to autism to have any utility, in practice Asperger syndrome became an increasingly common diagnosis.[104]

The *DSM*-5 will be published in 2012. The authors plan to replace the *DSM*-IV category of "autistic disorder" with a broad new category of "autism spectrum disorders," encompassing all subtypes of pervasive developmental disorders. They explain that the change is a response to the ambiguity surrounding distinctions among different subcategories like Asperger's disorder and pervasive developmental disorder not otherwise specified (PDD-NOS). The new category makes room for the range of strengths and weaknesses that any individual may possess.[105] The proposal was met with dismay by some psychologists, who argue that Asperger syndrome has not been studied for long enough to confirm or discount its existence as a separate entity, and geneticists, who think that a single category incorrectly downplays the biological heterogeneity of the syndrome.[106] Self-advocates are concerned that association with people with more significant impairments will undermine their demands for self-determination and respect. They value the way that Asperger syndrome works to succinctly explain their differences.[107]

The successive editions of the *DSM* established autism as a behaviorally defined disorder, one that experts understood to be biologically based, but for which they had yet to locate convincing biological explanations. As a result, diagnosis came to rely exclusively on the ability of practitioners to recognize the symptoms of autism and distinguish them from other developmental disorders. Despite the clarifications of the *DSM*-IV, the extent to which administrative records have included PDD-NOS and Asperger syndrome cases as "autism" remains unclear, making the job of epidemiologists tasked with retrospectively determining autism prevalence that much more difficult. Although epidemiologists generally accept Wing and Gould's finding that autism is not significantly more common in wealthier families, more affluent parents are likelier to have their children evaluated and diagnosed. This means that children in lower-income families remain underdiagnosed and underreported, and that autism rates will continue to rise as these cases are identified.[108]

As I noted, most epidemiologists believe that changes in formal diagnostic parameters coupled with increased awareness on the part of pediatricians and the general public fully account for the increases in autism rates seen since the 1990s. Lorna Wing still has the computer dataset of the original Camberwell study. She periodically reanalyzes the data as formal criteria change. By applying the current diagnostic criteria from the *International Statistical Classification of Diseases and Related Health Problems,* 10th edition (*ICD*-10), the World Health Organization's guide, and *DSM*-IV, she found a prevalence rate three or four times higher than her original rate. That is, the result suggested that with each successive modification of criteria, epidemiologists coded more children with autism in their studies.[109]

For others, although these factors may explain the phenomenon in part, a real increase cannot be ruled out because it is impossible to establish a reliable and comparable data set of past cases. As one epidemiologist concluded in 2006, "given the behavioral basis of the autism diagnosis, the lack of knowledge about autism's underlying etiology, and the limitations of retrospective analyses, we are not likely to develop a conclusive body of evidence to either fully support or fully refute the notion that there has been some real increase in autism risk over the past two decades."[110]

In contrast to the more reserved statements of epidemiologists and psychological professionals, parents have become forceful advocates of the idea that increases in autism rates represent an epidemic. Doing so has gained them political recognition and social capital. It has also functioned as a shorthand way to demand that scientists and the public acknowledge that their children's autism is not a matter of chance and heredity, but is a preventable and treatable environmental illness demanding accommodation, remediation, and political attention. They have worked hard to raise public awareness about autism rates, but they have spoken up in professional circles as well, publishing articles refuting the idea that changes in criteria or the substitution of diagnoses of mental retardation for autism were sufficient to account for the increase.[111] In at least one case parents challenged the authors of an article published in the *Journal of Autism and Developmental Disorders* effectively enough that the authors conceded their mistaken interpretation of their own data.[112]

Parents connect their arguments about an increase to claims about causation, but the diagnostic category itself says nothing about the cause of autism. While many contemporary psychiatrists presume that all disorders of the mind have their origins in the brain, from the *DSM*-III onward the editors took no position on the matter of etiology. Nevertheless, psychopharmaceuticals need to be targeted to specific diagnoses in order to be medically valid, and the *DSM* provides the clear boundaries between conditions that psychiatrists need, even if such boundaries ignore the blurry distinctions among real populations.[113]

The practices of autism diagnosis reflect these assumptions about specificity. They also tend to reinforce the view of researchers who think autism is a single disease entity that will eventually resolve into a condition with a specific treatment. Such an outcome would be more manageable than finding that autism represents a cluster of syndromes, multiple "autisms" that share behavioral but not necessarily biological features, a concept supported by the claims of many parents that their children suffer from a range of medical conditions associated with their autism.[114] Even this view of multiple autisms may be too simple. There is good evidence that not all children diagnosed with autism have all of the same features in the three categories of impairment, and closer segmentation could reveal multiple behavioral syndromes.[115]

Although explanations that focus on the way epidemiologists work or bureaucratic institutions maintain records may be compelling, they do not necessarily explain changes in diagnostic practice more broadly. Clinical settings matter more than research settings to understanding the history of autism diagnoses. We need to explain psychiatrists' increasing tendency over the past two decades to describe noncommunicative children with severe behavioral problems as having autism, and we need to explain their choice to see the development, educability, and social relationships of these children in terms of a standard set of cognitive impairments associated with that disorder.

Testing Instruments: Diagnosis as Practice and Product

Diagnostic codes in the *DSM* both standardize therapeutic practices and determine insurance coverage and educational accommodation, matters of central importance for children with neuropsychiatric disorders. A majority of children still receive an autism diagnosis from their pediatricians or developmental specialists who use the criteria set out in the *DSM* as a general guide without employing a published diagnostic instrument. Conventions are different in research settings where, to ensure a consistent population, investigators use assessment tools. The Autism Diagnostic Interview (ADI) and the Autism Diagnostic Observation Schedule (ADOS), the current gold standard for autism diagnoses, were designed using the *DSM*-IV criteria. For clinical and basic research studies and for epidemiological studies, the most reliable diagnoses are those generated by these proprietary instruments.[116] The instruments have been increasingly used in clinical settings as well.[117]

An international team headed by Catherine Lord and Michael Rutter designed the two instruments and released them in 1989.[118] Both investigators had worked on autism for decades. They had designed the ADOS and ADI to conform to the *DSM*-IV and *ICD*-10 criteria for autism, but built in a degree of rigor that would not be found in a clinical diagnosis based on observation and simple knowledge of the criteria. The objective was to guarantee that a population of subjects would be consistent across different study sites or even different studies, and to ensure that findings could in theory be generalized to people with autism as a group.

The two instruments differ in key respects and were meant to complement each other. Lord and Rutter's team designed the ADI to be administered to a child's primary caregiver. It consists of an extensive list of questions, and knowledgeable parents often arrive at an appointment for the ADI with pages of notes and recollections. In contrast, the ADOS is a carefully structured, timed test that is optimized toward children and adults on what practitioners call the higher-functioning end of the autism spectrum. It is best used for distinguishing among pervasive developmental disorders, or for diagnosing autism in a person with significant language skills and the ability to navigate certain social situations. The test is organized as a series of "pushes" or challenges, which are intended to provoke a range of responses or examples of skills on the part of the subject. The screener must rate these responses on a scale of one to three in terms of the degree to which the person being screened exhibits features of autism.

The screener's skills in administering and scoring both instruments matter a great deal. Both instruments also depend on the direct knowledge that comes from interacting with an individual. In the ADI, the interviewer needs to learn to use questions as prompts to elicit very precise descriptions of behaviors from caregivers. The key is to obtain the type of specific and textured details that come from living with someone and being attentive to their needs. For the ADOS, interaction is such a key component that the designers of the instrument discovered the test did not work unless the examiners performed the "pushes" themselves, making requests of the children and playing with them. If they stayed in the room and observed another investigator performing the test, their scores were not as accurate.[119]

The ADOS, which yields the most reliable diagnoses of autism, requires an elaborate system of checks to ensure interrater and test-retest reliability. It involves almost no active recollection on the part of the parents, although their presence and occasional participation is necessary for the exam, especially when it is administered to severely affected children. In order to become certified to use the ADOS, screeners must complete an intensive three-day program, which they begin at home by watching videotapes of sample exams. To ensure that workers use the instrument in the same way at each site that adopts the test, videotapes of children receiving an ADOS screening are sent to outside raters to code. Their diagnoses are matched against those of the technician who administered the test. These outside raters are either the designers of the test or trained by them, creating a technique in which perception and interaction with subjects are as consistent as possible.[120] Although some screeners are skeptical that the built-in degree of oversight is actually reached in practice, it may be more important that screeners understand that their reliability depends on adhering to the routines that they have learned. Their confidence in their diagnoses comes from faith in the instrument and their sense that an experienced screener or diagnostician can recognize a case of autism immediately, even though the diagnostic schedule is necessary to maintain the level of reliability that research requires.

Although psychological testing was once primarily a domain of male professionals, many trained screeners are young women. Screening may be a low-status occupation, but it is hardly trivial work. Like the intensive behavioral therapies used to treat children with autism, testing requires not only extensive training but also the ability to adapt to a widely variable population. It also requires what might be called emotional labor. A typical ADOS screen requires the person performing the assessment to engage empathically by trying to share pleasure and conversation with the subject. Testers must laugh, tickle, make faces, applaud, and occasionally console a distraught subject. The fine labor of diagnosis has become a type of work that demands exquisite skill, and one in which the rewards of questioning the design of the instruments are relatively low.

I observed a number of ADOS screenings at a children's hospital. The tester recognized the difficulty in determining how an individual performs in a familiar daily environment via a single screening session. She was potentially under evaluation as well, because her judgments could be measured against their fit with or deviation from those of external reviewers. She had learned to train her observations and interpretations in line with the requirements of the test. It was a matter of job performance and also of pleasure. The ability to distill forty-five minutes of close observation into a diagnosis has its rewards, even if revealing the diagnosis might cause pain. Parents, however, did not see the tester as the diagnostician. Although she coded the test and thus knew the outcome, the parents instead believed that a doctor would arrive at a conclusion at a later date, and the examiner said nothing to contradict their assumption.

Although most clinicians and epidemiologists use the ADI-R (a revised version of the ADI) and ADOS to screen study candidates, these two instruments are only a few of the available tests that might be administered to a child with autism as specialists evaluate him or her.[121] Psychologists might administer a standard IQ test in order to assess cognitive abilities, although many experts acknowledge that IQ testing may not accurately measure the cognitive abilities of people with autism. The Weschler Adult Intelligence Scale, for example, assumes a certain level of attention and that the subject is willing to attempt the test. Adaptive behavior scales like the Vineland look at an individual's ability to carry out skills involved in daily life like answering the telephone or getting dressed, as well as the ability to communicate and interact on a basic level. A whole series of specialized neuropsychiatric tests might be used to measure specific abilities. Other tests are optimized for different purposes, like the Gilliam Autism Rating Scale (also based on the *DSM*-IV), and the Childhood Autism Rating Scale, both of which take far less time to administer than the ADOS or ADI, or the Checklist for Autism in Toddlers (CHAT) developed by Simon Baron-Cohen and colleagues, which helps clinicians and researchers identify potential cases of autism before children are old enough to receive an official diagnosis.

Diagnostic Consequences

Although diagnostic instruments are designed simply to identify individuals who would also be recognized by an experienced pediatrician familiar with autism, tools like the ADI and the ADOS inevitably incorporate assumptions about the nature of the disorder, if only by virtue of what they are not designed to assess. Despite the precision with which researchers can characterize cognitive and developmental abnormalities, very few techniques exist for measuring the outcome of treatments for autism because autism is understood to be a relatively static and lifelong disorder, with symptoms that are stable over time. In some cases, tests like the Childhood Autism Rating Scale developed by Eric Schopler are revised to enable raters to measure treatment outcomes. In theory, children can be retested using an instrument like the ADOS to see if they continue to qualify for an autism diagnosis. Some specialists argue that true outcome measures need to be developed in order to measure improvement as a direct result of different therapeutic interventions. Many parents, caregivers, and professionals believe that symptoms, behaviors, and abilities can change dramatically, either as a result of intensive therapeutic measures or as the result of development and maturation.[122]

Screening instruments also have a popular life beyond their utility for experts. Simon Baron-Cohen, who heads the Cambridge University Autism Research Centre, has developed a questionnaire used to identify milder forms of neurological variation that would not qualify for a diagnosis of autism or Asperger syndrome. The Autism Questionnaire, or AQ, is available on the Internet and appears in excerpted form in mass market magazine articles.[123] Although it is not presented as a diagnostic instrument, the design of the AQ encourages self-diagnosis and suggests that anyone can be located somewhere in a spectrum of neurological types. As Baron-Cohen and his colleagues wrote, "The AQ is thus a valuable instrument for rapidly quantifying where any given individual is situated on the continuum from autism to normality."[124]

Sociologists of medicine have pointed out the possibility that diagnostic categories, made stable and rendered consistent and standard by tests, can serve to reinforce the appearance of disease entities as simple facts about nature. The effect is to hide the underlying truth that the categories themselves have been shaped by social and political considerations, and in some cases the needs of researchers, rather than the best interests of patients.[125] By introducing an apparently objective scale, diagnostic instruments can erase many of the subjective elements of diagnostic practices and the theories of illness and disability that inform them. One question is what symptoms are required for a diagnosis—for instance, communication deficits versus feeding problems or sensory disturbances. Another is what constitutes a symptom versus a benign difference—for instance, a failure to express interest in social interaction. In other cases, diagnostic instruments are incorporated into educational or health care bureaucracies such that screeners are rewarded for producing the kind of consistent and clear-cut diagnoses that conform to the requirements of record-keeping, but are less able to highlight important individual variations that are relevant to an individual's needs or prognosis.

As an experienced test designer explained to me, neuropsychological tests have a tendency to "reify the diagnoses" that they seek to measure, taking a constellation of characteristics and making it seem as though they support a more general claim about what causes and constitutes a cognitive disorder. The same is true of many screening instruments. It is difficult to design an instrument that measures cognitive abilities without building in a theory about the source of deficits or their relationship to one another. The result is that diagnostic tests contribute to the as-yet-unproven assumption that "autism" is a uniform disorder, with a consistent presentation of symptoms and a single cause. They also, intentionally or not, lead to a diagnosis that many parents experience as a final pronouncement that suggests no logical or necessary next step, and in which their own input and questions are often effectively silenced.[126]

This impression that a diagnosis of autism is both static and justified by a structural difference in the brain has both therapeutic and theoretical implications. In terms of brain research, the belief encourages specialists in the field to design research programs that assume that the symptoms of autism are caused by specific, focal deficits rather than dysfunctions in, say, the relationships among different cognitive domains or pervasive factors like inflammation that affect the brain as a whole. Although exams like the ADI or ADOS do not presume any particular cause for autistic behaviors, they can also encourage researchers to think of the behaviors that they test for as the basis for autism, the central facts of the disorder, rather than the results of more fundamental neurological processes. Autism acquires an identity as a set of "core deficits," rather than a syndrome that happens to be identifiable by those deficits but is not identical to them. As we have seen, researchers have spent a great deal of time working to precisely characterize the central deficits in autism. In most cases, they have been conceptualized in very similar terms to Kanner's original descriptions of disturbed social affect, repetitive behavior, and resistance to change; or the "triad" of deficits in social communication, social ability, and social imagination, accompanied by a restricted pattern of activities, that Lorna Wing and Judith Gould abstracted from their own observations during the 1960s and 1970s; or the impairments in social interaction and communication and the "stereotyped patterns of behavior" of the DSM-IV and ICD-10.

Theories that explain autism in terms of poor executive function, weak central coherence, or problems with attention all describe the syndrome in terms of properties that are more basic to cognitive function than complex activities like communication, behavior, and sociability. Researchers, however, have only recently begun to connect these processing dysfunctions to actual changes in brain structure, changes that may be distributed rather than localized.[127] It is much easier to think about the connection between modular theories of brain function—those that assume that particular areas of the brain are designated from birth for particular functions—and brain structure. It makes intuitive sense, given the symptoms of many brain injuries, which when they occur in adults are known to impair specific brain functions. Think of the way that a stroke can cause paralysis or language loss, depending on where it occurs. This is one of the reasons that many researchers working on brains and autism continue to look for localized lesions, using ever more powerful imaging techniques to try to identify sites of structural difference in autism, just as they have been doing since the late 1960s. The problem is that although such approaches provide compelling theories about how and why autism occurs, they may not be the best way to discover what is actually occurring in autistic brains.

I have provided this discussion of the history of the autism diagnosis and contemporary diagnostic techniques for two reasons. The first is to explain how researchers have described autism and how their assessments of the key features of that syndrome have changed over time. In many instances, those changes have reflected researchers' interests in new technologies, such as CT scans, or in growing areas of research, like genetics. It was not always the case that new evidence or a conclusive refutation of some earlier theory determined a new course of investigation. In these respects, the history of the autism diagnosis resembles many other modern psychiatric and developmental disorders. Autism has been constituted as a neurological and genetic disorder and this belief is supported by a broad consensus among the research community, but the precise mechanisms of causation remain obscure. This history of diagnostic parameters and investigative techniques serves as introduction and background to the story that I tell in the next chapters about how knowledge about autism has been produced.

The second reason is to clarify that, while autism is a disorder of social relationships, diagnoses cannot take place without the fact of intense, even intimate human interaction. A diagnosis depends on skillful observation and close interaction with a patient. Test designers have understood this, crafting instruments like the ADI that make use of parents' and caregivers' intimate knowledge of children with autism. In the case of the ADOS, they designed an instrument that creates an environment that simulates and condenses a long series of social interactions. Treating the disorder requires the same close contact.

The rest of this book traces the knowledge that grows out of intense involvement with children with autism. Symptoms are closely observed, recorded, and interpreted, but those symptoms tell the men and women in this story not what children with autism "are," or "have," but how to engage them, what they need, and how best to approach, understand, and respond to them.

2

Love Is Not Enough: Bruno Bettelheim, Infantile

Autism, and Psychoanalytic Childhoods

Bruno Bettelheim once rivaled Montessori, Piaget, and Anna Freud in popularity and influence in the fields of child psychology and development. He is probably best known among the general public for his 1975 study of fairy tales, *The Uses of Enchantment*. Eight years earlier, he had written an enormously influential book on treating autistic children, *The Empty Fortress: Infantile Autism and the Birth of the Self*. Although both books captivated the public at the time of their publication and for years afterward, many readers have since focused on flaws in these works and Bettelheim's questionable research methods. After Bettelheim's suicide in 1990 at the age of eighty-six, his reputation plummeted. He was accused of substantially plagiarizing his groundbreaking work on fairy tales. Observers claimed that he had beaten and verbally abused both children and staff during his thirty-year tenure as director of the Sonia Shankman Orthogenic School at the University of Chicago. He had reinforced, if not invented, the cruel and harmful portrayal of the mothers of children with autism as "refrigerator mothers."[1] Most damning of all, he had refused to alter his position even as evidence accumulated against the psychogenic theory of autism. This was indeed a sharp decline in status for "a hero of our time," the man who was daring and compassionate enough to work with children whom others considered "hopeless and worthless."[2]

These controversies ought not to confuse us about the weight Bettelheim's books, magazine articles, reviews, and public presence carried in the 1950s and 1960s. Bettelheim popularized psychotherapy in a postwar America hungry for the vision of humanity offered by psychoanalysis, with its humanistic emphasis on what Freud had called "a cure through love."[3]

The country's fascination with psychoanalysis could itself be called a "romance."[4] Countless magazine articles referenced psychoanalytic terms. Popular books on psychotherapy and psychoanalysis enjoyed high sales. Film plots featured virtuoso performances of therapeutic interpretation and cures. Psychoanalytic training was a standard part of medical education, while psychologists enjoyed growing influence in public policy.[5]

Postwar Americans, especially those in the middle class, imagined that the science and art of psychoanalysis could be applied to children to manage their development into healthy and well-adjusted adults.[6] Psychoanalysts and popular promoters of psychoanalytic theories responded to their interest, adding to an already substantial collection of childrearing advice and parenting manuals.[7] Nor was psychoanalysis the only movement to argue for the influence of mothers' actions on the early development of children and to offer conflicting statements about good mothering either as an innate or acquired skill. "Parenting," understood as a technical practice best carried out with input from experts, became part of the American vernacular as both pediatricians and advertisers urged mothers to seek guidance on childrearing.[8]

As early as the 1940s, experts themselves cautioned against an excess of expert authority in childrearing. In 1941, Leo Kanner wrote the short handbook *In Defense of Mothers*, and in 1945 Simon & Schuster published *Dr. Spock's Baby and Child Care*, the best seller that reassured rattled mothers that "you know more than you think you do."[9] Spock's matter-of-fact advice, unfortunately, provided few suggestions for parents struggling with the work of raising children with developmental disabilities. Nevertheless, postwar theories of childrearing affected how parents treated children with disabilities as well as their siblings. Dr. Spock's *Baby and Child Care* shared shelf space with Bettelheim's *Love Is Not Enough* in the homes of families of both disabled and typically developing children.

The story of Bettelheim's involvement with autism illustrates the ambivalent and sometimes tragic qualities of the affective, institutional, and professional commitments that drive research and therapeutic programs. Psychoanalytic approaches to autism were not a developmental stage through which treatment strategies had to progress before more effective approaches could be found, but neither were they an accident or aberration. They have existed alongside behavioral and medical approaches, sharing vocabularies, methodologies, and, often, ideological commitments with them. Understanding why participants believed that they worked, and how they worked, can do much to illuminate the ways that attention, affective commitments, and techniques work together to create a cohesive belief system and sense of efficacy.

Autism functioned as a focal point for ideas about motherhood, childhood, and development in twentieth-century America. Bettelheim's writings on the Orthogenic School and on autism served as meditations on human experience and existential dilemmas, as "a passionate description of *deliverance*, as it may be achieved for one child and denied to another," as much or more than as accounts of clinical treatment.[10] They became part of a national conversation about "natural" forms of love, caring, and bonding. Understanding the appeal of this work inevitably involves writing a kind of psychohistory, not only of Bettelheim, but also of a profession that drew on psychoanalytic theory in treating autism, and of the parents who accepted a vision of childhood as a vulnerable experience best managed by experts. Although the Orthogenic School was a unique institution, Bettelheim's desire to use ideas from psychoanalysis to understand and treat autism was not unusual. He was one of a significant number of psychologists and psychiatrists who shared the ambition to decode autistic language and interpret children's symptoms as effects of their family environments.

Bettelheim's great literary and personal appeal reflected the culture of cold war America, as well as mid-century beliefs about childhood and about the forms of emotional labor called parenting and therapy. As such, his work is very much part of the history of autism as one of love and labor. Both were present in the work of Bettelheim's Orthogenic School counselors, and both were the focus of discussion when Bettelheim attributed failures to the mothers of autistic children. Counselors provided the kind of receptive and responsive interactions that Bettelheim imagined mothers had failed at. Bettelheim has also been remarkably hard to escape. The view of autistic children and their families that he popularized has remained both a reference and a foil for generations of parents. His claims resonate in contemporary psychological literature and in the corridor-talk of practitioners and policymakers.

Bettelheim and the Orthogenic School

The Sonia Shankman Orthogenic School, Bettelheim's main institutional home at the University of Chicago, was founded in 1915 as a school for cognitively disabled children. The university purchased it in 1931, converting it to a laboratory school for studying human development in collaboration with the Department of Education. They renamed the school, choosing a term meant to evoke the idea of straight growth.[11] By 1944, the school was foundering as the acting director struggled to transform a custodial institution into a residential treatment program for emotionally disturbed children and youth. Bettelheim had been working part time for the University of Chicago, and he was effectively forced into the director's position after agreeing to evaluate the school and suggest improvements. He initially considered it beyond repair.[12]

When Bettelheim took over, he was just beginning to achieve prominence with the 1943 publication of "Individual and Mass Behavior in Extreme Situations," an account of the psychological effects of concentration camps. The text drew on Bettelheim's personal experience as a prisoner in Dachau and Buchenwald, where he was held for about a year during 1938–1939.[13] The article took on "instant authority" as one of the first analyses of what had happened inside the concentration camps.[14] Bettelheim had no background in child psychology and no formal training in psychoanalysis. He had attended the University of Vienna where he received a doctorate in Philosophy and Aesthetics. After escaping to the United States, he held a variety of jobs, which included designing art appreciation tests for schoolchildren and teaching part time at a women's college. Although he did not seek out the director position at the Orthogenic School, it represented a great improvement in terms of job security and the route to the academic prominence that Bettelheim sought.

Bettelheim traced his interest in helping troubled children, and those with autism in particular, to his experience with an American child who came to stay with him and his first wife in Vienna. The child psychologist Anna Freud had determined that the child's only hope was a "psychoanalytically organized environment." Whether Bettelheim, at the time working in his father's lumber business, could have provided that has been a matter of debate. Years later, Bettelheim explained how "the severe pathology of [the child's] case permitted observing a phenomenon also seen in normal behavior but as if it were under microscopic enlargement, or thrown into bold relief by a bright light." He "carefully respected her wish to be left alone, while still trying to take careful, loving care of her, before she moderated her total isolation and permitted occasional approaches, although she did not respond to these in any discernable way." After a year and a half of gentle child's games that helped her accept and acknowledge other people, she spoke her first sentence in perfect English. Bettelheim concluded that her condition, which he believed to be autism, resulted from her fatherless upbringing and rejection by her mother.[15] He hoped to continue to work with her when he arrived in the United States. The opportunity fell through, but his experience with the child intrigued him and his sense of the importance of the attention that he and his wife had provided gave him confidence in pursuing a career treating emotionally disturbed children.

The contrast between Bettelheim's unorthodox training and the significant public authority he later enjoyed as a child psychologist led later writers to question his credentials. After his death, some suggested that he allowed potential employers to understand that he had earned a degree in psychology. He had also never undergone a full psychoanalysis. The credentialing of psychoanalysts by local psychoanalytic societies in the 1950s required a training analysis, although it was not a requirement for practice as a clinical psychologist, a title that more closely fit Bettelheim's work. Nevertheless, counselors who worked with Bettelheim recollect that it was "common knowledge" among them that Bettelheim's degree was not in psychology.[16] He eventually became a "non-therapist member" of the Chicago Psychoanalytic Society, a position that reflected his lack of formal training and perhaps also the ambiguous position of child psychology at the time.[17] Bettelheim may have intentionally misled various publics about other aspects of his past, including his connections to Freud and the nature of his internment in concentration camps. However, biographers also note that Bettelheim's generation might have regarded this type of untruth as an exigency. Among millions of displaced persons, each felt the need to make themselves as desirable to employers in the States as possible.

Bettelheim instituted sweeping changes at the Orthogenic School. He demanded an increased level of training for, and dedication from, the school's counseling staff and a larger budget from the University of Chicago.[18] He remade the school into a physically welcoming space in which the entire staff focused on the recovery of the students. At the same time, he sought alternative placement for all of the children there who he believed had neurological impairments. He wanted the school population to comprise only "emotionally disturbed" children whom he and the counselors might reasonably expect to help using the methods at hand.[19]

Through his accounts of work at the school, Bettelheim also became a public intellectual. Positioned as both scientist and observer of the traumatic events of the present, he appeared uniquely suited to speak to the trials facing children and parents in a culture that he approached as both an admiring outsider and engaged participant. Bettelheim published as much or more in popular venues than in professional journals, sometimes borrowing liberally and without attribution from more academic sources.[20] He wrote about the changing role of women in the home and workplace, the student antiwar movement, educational problems for normal children, and childrearing. He returned to the themes of autonomy and of children's self-authorship achieved through infantile desires for gratification and, later, their self-conscious assertion of their needs and identities. Magazine profiles reflected Bettelheim's own self-fashioning. They frequently opened with a physical description and included a photo. His bald head, prominent ears, and the heavy frames of his glasses became immediately recognizable.

Bettelheim linked his claims regarding the malleability of the human psyche to his observations of behavior during wartime, particularly that of his fellow inmates in the labor camp. As a survivor, Bettelheim enjoyed a unique, almost anthropological authority. As a witness, he could speak to the motivations underlying fascism and authoritarianism, and as therapist, he could claim a theory that transmuted the negative power of the camps into a positive therapeutic insight, just as Ivar Lovaas recalled that witnessing fascism made him realize how malleable the human psyche might be.[21] Bettelheim claimed that, in contrast to other prisoners, he had been able to avoid "a disintegration of his personality" and pathological identification with prison guards by maintaining a scientific attitude of detached observation.[22] Bettelheim's claims about the therapeutic possibilities of a "total environment" and the importance of autonomy to the growth and preservation of a sense of self resonated with a contemporary movement toward milieu therapy as well as with public interest in moral autonomy and the social environment's role in shaping subjective experience.

The Empty Fortress Enchants America

Most accounts of the Orthogenic School at the University of Chicago, whether by former students, staff members, or participants in the larger world of twentieth-century psychotherapy and psychology, reflect long-standing loyalties and commitments. As with many therapeutic practices in the history of mental illness, it is hard if not impossible to speak in absolute terms about the effectiveness of the therapeutic activities that took place within the walls of the school, judged against other treatments at other times.[23] In the case of the Orthogenic School, as in other cases that I describe, the institutional location and the interactions between practitioners and subjects mattered, as did the forms of social learning and tacit knowledge used to reproduce particular interventions. Therapies changed both patients and practitioners, as each became increasingly committed to the therapeutic program, a mutual influence that has parallels in other biomedical treatments.[24] Unlike the majority of modern diagnostic and treatment strategies, which derive much of their authority from the appearance of what Charles Rosenberg has called therapeutic "specificity," psychotherapy as practiced by Bettelheim never placed much weight on diagnostic accuracy or on treatments tailored to a diagnostic group. The salient categories were the universal human psyche and the individual sufferer.[25]

When it appeared in 1967, *The Empty Fortress: Infantile Autism and the Birth of the Self* became a best seller, featured in major national newspapers and magazines, from the *New York Times* and the *Saturday Evening Post* to the *New Yorker* and *The New York Review of Books*. Reviewers greeted it as a philosophical rather than a technical work, a meditation on the drama of childhood and the triumphant "search for self" that Bettelheim claimed to both facilitate and chronicle. Few readers cared about or took the time to evaluate Bettelheim's accounts of his specific methods for treating autism or his rates of success. A reviewer in the *New York Times* invoked Bettelheim's account of a year spent in German concentration camps, proclaiming that "it is evidence that the informed heart is possible and that the alienations in our age—whether they are the planned dehumanization of the concentration camps or the unintentional dehumanization of modern mass society or the still largely mysterious dehumanization of individual psychosis—need not be accepted as the permanent condition of man."[26] Other reviewers wrote of Bettelheim's compassion and generosity, of the mothers "who believe in him" and seek his advice, and of Bettelheim's "real love, warmth, understanding, and years of infinite patience and hope."[27]

With the encouragement of his publisher, Bettelheim chose to write *The Empty Fortress* for a broad audience, avoiding jargon and technical terminology. He wrote with a comfortable and resoundingly self-confident style, an approach that he also brought to his public appearances and magazine columns.[28] His intended audience was not looking to investigate treatment options for their own children or patients, but instead wanted to comprehend their anxieties about their own, typically developing children and the "problem of parental preoccupation and indifference" as a uniquely modern risk to child development.[29] For such readers, autism represented not a practical concern but a metaphor for American anxieties about childrearing, the changing roles of women, and the formative power of love.[30] Bettelheim seemed to offer a series of salvation stories, a promise of help for the previously untreatable.

Not all parents of autistic children who read the book agreed. Amy Lettick, the founder of Benhaven, a residential program for developmentally disabled children and adults, asked the director of the Nassau Center for Emotionally Disturbed Children whether she had read the book yet.

> Fascinating. I think this book alone is enough to have him committed. He has marvelous descriptions of autistic behavior, but the reasoning he ascribes to it is unbelievable. Wait till you read how 12 year old Joey cured himself by giving birth to himself out of a chicken egg. Mira Rothenberg [another promoter of psychotherapeutic techniques] should have rushed out to Chicago with her incubator![31]

Another mother, Judy Barron, recalled that she and her husband "fumed" when they read the book and wondered how anyone could believe Bettleheim, then were astonished to discover that "almost everyone did."[32]

Like Lettick and other parents, reviewers in clinical journals noted the failure of the book to offer pragmatic advice or specific treatments. They also questioned Bettelheim's tendency to interpret any behavior through the lens of psychoanalysis, often in the absence of detailed clinical descriptions of the behavior in question. One frustrated reader complained that Bettelheim's complex interpretation of the unwillingness of children with autism to be treated by dentists failed to mention—or perhaps to recognize—that such problems were common with other "non-verbal subnormal children." Similarly, Bettelheim's theory that the actions of mothers were perceived by their autistic child as a "threat to his very existence" failed to explain why some mistreated children developed autism and some developed normally. Others simply wished that he had addressed the neurological aspects of the disorder.[33]

By 1967, the psychiatric community had in fact abandoned many of the ideas about autism upon which Bettelheim based his treatments, as Jacquelyn Sanders, a counselor who later became director of the school, has noted.[34] Most had concluded that there was "little evidence that psychotherapeutic treatment of a child influenced prognosis."[35] Nevertheless, Bettelheim presented *The Empty Fortress* as the culmination of work funded by a 1956 Ford Foundation grant. He divided the book into sections devoted to theory, case studies, and an extensive review of the published literature on autism. He situated autism as a theoretical problem within developmental psychology, contrasting typical human development and ego differentiation with the failures of ego formation in the three cases that he described.

To the contemporary reader of his work, Bettelheim's relentless psychoanalytic interpretation of behavioral and physiological symptoms can be perplexing. He described "twiddling," pronominal reversal, rocking, dietary restrictions, obsessions with order and with organizing time, sensory abnormalities, and head-banging, all symptoms familiar to contemporary diagnosticians and parents.[36] However, he believed that through the "process of personality integration" at the School, "psychosomatic manifestations of long standing—such as allergies, neuro-dermatitis, ocular-motor disturbances, mucous colitis and other disorders of the digestive tract—also disappeared spontaneously."[37] The physical symptoms were merely epiphenomena, incidental to autism's root cause. Readers encountering the text at the time of its publication, like Peter Gay, a biographer of Freud, admired these curative feats without questioning them.

> Obviously (Bettelheim is enough of a Freudian to be convinced of this) all aspects of autistic behavior are meaningful; all of it—the twiddling, the peculiar modes of defecating, the silent rocking, the refusal to eat—is a kind of language, even if it is directed at no one. But since symptoms vary so enormously, and since the therapist has no way of checking his hunches with the patient, as he does in psychoanalysis, the interpretation of the "language" autistic children have available to them demands the utmost concentration, intelligence, empathy, and persistence.[38]

Despite his readiness to rely on psychoanalytic interpretations of autistic behavior, Bettelheim had read widely not only in the psychoanalytic literature but in child development. His characterizations of autism drew on theories of development as an interactive process in which parents were central. He began with Sigmund Freud. But Bettelheim also turned to John Dewey's work on education and to the psychoanalysts Erik Erikson, August Aichhorn, and Anna Freud.[39] For accounts of abnormal ego development, he relied on René Spitz's studies of institutionalized children who showed emotional withdrawal. Spitz had concluded that even typical children regressed when they were deprived of their emotional connection to a "love object, such as the mother" but recovered when their mother or a "substitute love object" was returned to them.[40] Perhaps most important, he drew inspiration from Leo Kanner's arresting image of children "kept neatly in refrigerators which did not defrost," and parents who attended them with the "mechanized service of the kind which is rendered by an overconscientious gasoline station attendant."[41]

Harry Harlow's experiments on infant monkeys served as an important source for the devastating effects of deprivation, establishing for both scientific colleagues and the readers of *Life* magazine the idea of "natural" childrearing as characterized by an abundant supply of maternal warmth. Harlow's ability to simulate innate disorders of affect through sensory deprivation seemed to support Bettelheim's psychoanalytic theories. By isolating young rhesus monkeys in a stainless-steel chamber, Harlow and his colleague Stephen Suomi believed that they had produced something akin to the "well of despair" described by humans suffering from depression.[42] Harlow noted the "striking" similarities of the monkeys to autistic children, referring to the "coldness, ambivalence, double binding messages and lack of physical contact" that caused some children to develop "infantile autism, other forms of childhood psychosis, or severe behavioral disorders."[43] Harlow's chilling images of baby monkeys clinging desperately to wire "mothers" looked to popular audiences like icons of childhood instinct. For Bettelheim, the failures of these monkeys to develop normally demonstrated the necessity of what he elsewhere called "dialectics of hope" between mothers and children.[44]

People typically misremember Bettelheim in *The Empty Fortress* as having compared mothers of children with autism to concentration camp guards. Although Bettelheim's descriptions of the mothers were hardly generous, he had first reached for the concentration camp in explaining the milieu therapy used at the Orthogenic School. He argued that personality change could be effected through the institution of a total environment, a claim based on observations of his fellow inmates in a labor camp.[45] A decade before publication of *The Empty Fortress* he had concluded that the stunted ego development of a child with autism resulted from the child's unconscious sense of a deep ambivalence on the part of the mother. Children responded with terror to their mothers' mixed feelings. Unlike real prisoners, Bettelheim stressed, infants lacked the capacity to make rational judgments and merely had to believe that their lives were in danger. Perhaps, Bettelheim conceded, the mother's rejection was itself a response to a child who had failed to bond with her. "All children are born with differential sensitivities and react differently to their environment. . . . In the realm of interaction, it really matters little who makes the first move, who begins the interaction, or even the nature of the action. What counts is whether the action is interpreted correctly and meets an appropriate response," a complex choreography in which a single misstep in breastfeeding an especially sensitive child might precipitate a cascade of developmental maladies.[46]

Following the case studies, Bettelheim provided two literature reviews, explaining that they were not "systematic" but replicated his own reading into the "nature of the disturbance" in the children that he had treated. The first section, "Etiology and Treatment," began with Leo Kanner's 1943 monograph and proceeded to Bernard Rimland's *Infantile Autism*, published in 1964, just a few years prior to Bettelheim's book. Rimland wrote *Infantile Autism* primarily to refute the psychogenic theory of autism, and Bettelheim dismissed it as an argument without merit. Rimland's careful compilation of evidence mattered little because "even if a specific neurological dysfunction should some day be found to correlate highly with the syndrome of infantile autism, it would still be compatible with the psychogenic hypothesis.[47]

Bettelheim did not entirely dismiss the possibility of organic correlates for autistic behaviors. "While I do not accept the hypothesis that autism is due to an original organic defect, I do not feel I can rule out its later appearance. On the contrary, I tend to believe that far from being organic in origin, infantile autism, when persisting too long, can have irreversible effects.[48] It was through psychotherapy, however, that he hoped to offer treatment, and a psychogenic theory implied malleability and the potential for healing.[49] Writing at Bettelheim's death in 1990, a former counselor at the school explained that "Bettelheim's view was that until mental health professionals came up with a specific neurological disorder that was responsive to medication, psychotherapists had little choice but to continue with treatment efforts.[50] This confidence in the prospect of curing the disorder through psychiatric treatment faced relentless opposition from Rimland and other advocates of research into organic factors. So did his dismissal of the behavioral treatment methods developed by Ivar Lovaas, which Bettelheim said reduced autistic children "to the level of Pavlovian dogs" or made them into "more pliable robots" with new symptomatic behaviors.[51]

In practice, Bettelheim's commitment to a psychogenic framework appeared neither understanding nor humanistic. Richard Pollak, one of Bettelheim's most critical biographers, recounts a meeting in which Bettelheim, years after the deaths of Pollak's autistic brother and his mother, maintained that the brother had committed suicide in response to his mother's hatred. "'What *is it* about these Jewish mothers, Mr. Pollak?' he asked. I was stunned by this casual anti-semitism, coming as it did from a Jew who had suffered in the camps, and by the ferocity of his antagonism two decades after Stephen's death.[52] His brother had fallen from a hayloft. The accident filled Pollak with guilt and drove him to exonerate both his mother and his brother. Bettelheim never stopped insisting that children with autism suffered from a deficit of affective contact on the part of their mothers. He did not see this as a conscious or blameworthy act on the part of parents: "They did as they did because they could not help themselves to do otherwise. They suffer more than enough in having such a child. To make them guilty will only add to the misery of all and help none."[53]

The Empty Fortress represented both a synthesis of Bettelheim's experience with autism at the Orthogenic School and one work in a corpus that Bettelheim clearly regarded as interconnected. Throughout the text, he referred to his books on the structure of the Orthogenic School, *Truants from Life* (1955) and *Love Is Not Enough* (1950), to explain the creation of the therapeutic milieu. Likewise, he referenced his work on authoritarian aspects of contemporary society in *The Informed Heart* (1960) and his research on childrearing and personality development on the kibbutz (published later as *Children of the Dream,* 1969). The work that led to *The Empty Fortress* used treating children with autism as a way to understand the course of typical human development. Bettelheim alluded to this objective in his interim reports for the Ford Foundation, writing that their hope was to "arrive at a much better understanding not only of the nature of this disorder and its appropriate therapy, but also of certain, so far poorly understood, aspects of early personality development," and later that "clarification of some still very baffling problems of the earliest ego development forms the core of the research."[54] For Bettelheim, claims about children with autism were intimately connected to claims about the efficacy of his school and the theories behind it.

Bettelheim built *The Empty Fortress* around four lengthy case studies. The best-known chapter dealt with "Joey: A 'Mechanical Boy,'" an account that he had published earlier in *Scientific American.* Joey's symptoms lent themselves to easy interpretation. "Machine-like" in his movements and speech, Joey drew engines and described himself as a mechanical person. Bettelheim offered the case as proof of his success in treating autistic children. Joey's emergence into the human world was an allegory for "emotional development in a machine age."[55] Contemporary writers have suggested that the metaphorical richness of Joey's conversations about power sources, emissions, and the like, let alone his art, reflected the kind of symbolic reasoning that children with autism are now seen as lacking, but he also tended to reverse his pronouns, insist on routine, had difficulties with eating, and lacked a useful emotional vocabulary. These are all characteristics of what psychiatrists would now call high-functioning autism or Asperger syndrome.

Bettelheim and the counselors realized that Joey wanted badly to be "reborn," and that doing so would require him to progress through an infant's developmental stages.[56] They helped Joey come to terms with his early and strict toilet training by encouraging him to defecate in a wastebasket and later to "eliminate freely wherever he happened to be," and were rewarded by Joey's increasing willingness to picture himself as an integrated human being and not a machine.[57] His emerging ego and personality development culminated in an interview with Bettelheim at the time of his graduation from high school three years later. The interview itself demonstrated a certain psychoanalytic subjectivity. Prompted by Betttelheim, Joey spoke about his fear of expressing his emotions and about the importance to him of his intimate connections with the staff. He recalled in particular that counselors had held him like a child and fed him in the School's dining room. It is hard to tell whether Joey had only mastered Bettelheim's vocabulary and view of the self or if Bettelheim and the counselors had indeed cured him. Within the terms of the Orthogenic School's milieu therapy, it was difficult to tell the two transformations apart.[58] Joey's paintings are preserved in the Bettelheim archives, and in picking up and examining each cracked and fragile page, I did indeed gain a palpable sense of one boy's transformation.[59]

In a second case, "Laurie," Bettelheim elaborated his theory of the origins of autism.

> Throughout this book I state my belief that the precipitating factor in infantile autism is the parent's wish that his child should not exist. While the same wish may not cause the same disturbance in other children, and while at some future time we may learn that some organic factor is a precondition of autism, the fact is that almost all organic conditions that have so far been linked to this disease are also present in nonautistic children.[60]

In the case of children who had already developed autism, their apparent lack of interest made their parents further ambivalent, which would then make the child turn away entirely.[61] Bettelheim understood autism as a kind of feedback between infant withdrawal and inadequate parental response precipitated by factors that could only become legible through psychotherapeutic intervention. Mothering became the careful management of libidinal impulses and drives, because their expression could exact real harm on the developing child. The mere thought of rejection became a harmful act. Hence, mothers needed to be constant interpreters of their children's struggles, for autonomy on the one hand and for affirmation on the other. Failures at reading became failures at love.

The Romance of Bettelheim: Motherhood, Ambivalence, and Psychological Expertise

If Bettelheim exercised a particular appeal among the public, he was not the only psychologist to do so at a time when the profession sought public influence by "giving psychology away."[62] Freud traveled to the United States for the first and only time in 1909, and in the intervening decades Freudian psychology was modified and adapted to the needs and tastes of the American population. Americans were more interested in ego psychology and in applying psychoanalytic theory to problems of human management and child and adult development than in the unconscious. Interest groups and activists adapted Freudian theories to provide support for a variety of issues, from autonomy and self-determination to women's liberation and social equality. During the 1950s, American psychologists wedded Freudian theory to behaviorism, drive theory to theories of conditioning. Individual experiences of psychotherapy, likewise, took place within an American—and frequently middle-class—milieu, where people were concerned with the trajectories of their careers and questions of social performance.[63]

Just as psychologists sought to become purveyors of expert advice during the 1950s, they also worked to expand their clinical influence to reach not only the emotionally disturbed, but also healthy "normally neurotic" individuals seeking help for a variety of problems in their daily lives.[64] The treatment of war neuroses and preventative measures aimed at keeping troops psychologically healthy had provided a means for psychological professionals to argue for their specialized skills during the war.[65] Afterward, the reintegration of soldiers into American society was framed as a problem in "readjustment." The GI Bill was a means for providing the tools for this reintegration into American society and for filling the ranks of the mental health professions through specialized training.[66]

While soldiers enrolled in campus courses in psychology, their spouses looked to incorporate psychological expertise into their own work as mothers and wives. To meet this demand, Bettelheim ran a series of "Mothers Meetings" in the Hyde Park area near the Orthogenic School and University of Chicago. They were transcribed and edited as *Dialogues with Mothers*.[67] The transcripts show concerned mothers and some fathers eager to inspect their interactions with their children. The mothers themselves seemed comfortable employing a psychoanalytic perspective in their childrearing, transforming their concerns about normality into questions about strategies for developing healthy children. The interpretive framework of psychoanalysis could be applied as easily to typical children as to highly disturbed ones. Bettelheim's dialogues, which some critics called "diatribes," encouraged mothers to examine their part in problematic interactions with their children in order to determine their contributions to their children's difficult behaviors. No action on the part of a child was carried out in emotional isolation from his or her family, but mothers were also to understand their children's actions as autonomous expressions of desire and frustration. Love was an intuitive technique, but one that could be honed, tested, and critiqued. Love was innate but it could be improved and refined, carried out reflexively, and on occasion, skewed or corrupted.

Bettelheim argued against the belief that there existed a single, correct method of parenting guaranteed to produce desirable results. As the title of his book on childrearing stressed, borrowing a phrase from the child development expert D. W. Winnicott, one need not be perfect, but merely "good enough." "Whatever we do with and for our children ought to flow from our understanding of and our feelings for the particular situation and the relation we wish to exist between us and our child."[68] He addressed his frequent columns in women's magazines to a psychoanalytically literate readership, one accustomed to understanding individual development as a series of moral achievements by parents, children, and the wider culture. In the predictable daily battles over appropriate clothing, learning to read, and toilet training, life history and desire mattered more than biological or cognitive limitations. Bettelheim wrote for two separate groups, one, "intelligent and highly motivated mothers of more or less normal youngsters," and the other, counselors such as the staff of the Orthogenic School. Both groups might benefit from insights into the "ever-changing situations in which they find themselves as the adult raises a child and as the child reacts to being raised."[69] The parents of children suffering from "severe psychological impairments" were a different case. Bettelheim never imagined them as an audience. Treating their children was the domain of the properly trained.

If Bettelheim placed high demands on mothers, his positions reflected broader trends in 1950s psychoanalysis and public discourse.[70] Ideals of "scientific motherhood" increasingly clashed with the many other demands on women in the postwar era.[71] Philip Wylie's "momism" was one extreme portrayal of mothers as a suffocating menace to the autonomy of their sons, but milder versions of such theories proliferated. Nevertheless, women embraced psychoanalysis, although during the late 1960s they would begin to offer their own critiques of psychoanalysts' and psychiatrists' contributions to inequality between the sexes.[72] A public culture of psychoanalytic discourse gained ground even as so-called "traditional" roles strained under the weight of women's entry into the workforce and the professions.

The 1950s also witnessed an explosion in referrals for parents—mainly mothers—of children diagnosed with autism. Bettelheim was far from the only expert insisting that those who treated autistic children should realize "that the child's behavior no matter how bizarre or seemingly isolated has meaning." For instance, a 1957 article in the *American Journal of Orthopsychiatry* advocated simultaneously treating both parents and children. As the authors, staff members at a Massachusetts treatment center, explained, "the core anxiety of the parents and their schizophrenic child is fear of annihilation," which mothers managed by rigidly separating the roles of "mother, housewife, working woman," leading to their refusal to acknowledge their child's identity as a separate person.[73]

Parents submitted to psychoanalytic treatment because their doctors told them that the best way to improve the welfare of their child was to be treated themselves.[74] One mother recalled how

> they never were interested in really seeing the child, but they had my husband and I come in forever—really doing the trick on us. We both thought we loved each other before we went there, and after that things have never been the same—even though it was fifteen years ago . . . but I never accepted Bettelheim. No. Nobody ever loved anything or anybody like I love this kid. I would gladly, at a moment's notice, give my life for the slightest improvement in him—I mean that. I'm doing it every day.[75]

Another, writing in 1992, described an encounter with a psychotherapist at a residential school.

> "How did you feel when you discovered you were pregnant?" he asked. "Did you want this child?"
>
> I felt the heat of rage rising to my head. "Yes. I did want Sean. *I still do.*" I stared at him. His eyes shifted, and he smiled slightly at something just to the left of my ear.
>
> "Ah, sometimes we think we want something we really don't want at all. Sometimes, you see, we are afraid of the truth."[76]

Bettelheim's Ford Foundation grant funded the anthropologist Jules Henry's research on the home environments of children with autism. Henry brought a "social-anthropological" perspective to studying the role of culture and family in the disorder.[77] The ensuing book-length report demonstrated his commitment to Bettelheim's approach. Each chapter described a pathogenic family environment, in which the ambivalence of parents generated emotional disturbances in their offspring. Henry had come to the conclusion that "we are not loving our children right."[78]

What is most striking is the complete absence of the children from Henry's account. Henry knew the children but seldom observed them interacting with their parents. He crafted explanations based on family dynamics through what one reviewer described admiringly as the work of an "intuitive psychologist."[79] As he entered their homes to observe the families, the mothers underwent psychoanalysis. At the end of the first year of the study, Bettelheim reported:

> According to our findings their most characteristic attitude is either one of "towering rage" against everyone in their family, or "humiliation run rampant," directed most of all against the child who becomes autistic. Unable to act in accordance with this rage because of guilt, they try to protect the child by emotionally totally removing themselves from him, often using empty but rigidly enforced schedules as a device to protect the child from their anger. Matters are compounded by the fact that the fathers seem to show uniformly an implacable paranoid distance from their wives.[80]

In the second year of the study, Bettelheim expanded its scope to include parents of schizophrenic children who were not in the school. By comparing them to the parents of children living at the school Bettelheim hoped to answer the question of "whether it is the nature and degree of the disturbance of the child that makes placement in a treatment institution necessary, or whether the psychology of the parents is decisive for whether or not a schizophrenic child can be treated ambulatory or requires hospitalization."[81]

While some parents resisted psychoanalytic interpretations of autism, others accepted responsibility for their child's problems—after all, if they had consciously or unconsciously caused the disorder, they might also possess the key to a cure.[82] Jules Henry wrote with some admiration of one mother's knowledge of current psychoanalytic theory.

> Mrs. Wilson—who never studied psychology and who never attended college—has such fine insight into the causes of primary infantile autism that I sometimes think I may have gotten my own theory of it from her. Her description of Donald's isolation—of his general "stimulus impoverishment"—also describes my view of the cause of this disease perfectly. And because she believes it, because she blames herself, guilt is a devil riding on her back; she gets very

little sleep, even with the aid of pills. She blames herself for leaving Donald alone, for following the directions of the pediatrician and for leaving him for two days with the sitter. Meanwhile her husband brushes all her explanations aside, as he does his own guilt. He is calm; she is almost beside herself.[83]

Henry's work enjoyed considerable influence both in his profession and in the culture at large. A reviewer in *Time* magazine zeroed in on his portrayal of families who, although they seemed "quite average," were in fact seething below the surface with poorly expressed anger. To an acute observer like Henry they offered prime examples of "shamming" performances of false emotions and love promised but ultimately withheld.[84] Henry himself emerged as "a brilliant, sensitive student of human behavior," a "prophet and scientist" who saw the human sciences as instruments of social reform.[85]

The efforts of mothers to convince professionals that their autistic children were truly—consciously and unconsciously—"wanted children" were never sufficient, as long as experts felt confident of their theories. Within the confines of the Orthogenic School, however, the origins of disability were less a concern than the needs of the individual child and the training of the therapists who worked with them.

The Therapeutic Milieu: Treating Children and Training Counselors

Bettelheim explained his approach to treating autistic children as an outcome of his life experiences, including observations of "total environments" and what he learned about human behavior in the face of powerlessness and fear. He believed that an environment that encompassed all aspects of life could produce psychological change, working as a "concentration camp in reverse," where the children were free to wander outside, but outsiders were barred from entering.[86]

> A total therapeutic setting implies a separation of the child from his family and protection against those influences coming from the outside which led to that mortal anxiety which caused the child to withdraw to the autistic position. It also demands careful study of his behavior in order to understand the hidden motives which cause it and a therapy based on this understanding.[87]

Bettelheim borrowed the idea of the therapeutic milieu together with the prescription that children should be removed from the home environment from the Austrian psychoanalyst August Aichhorn, a source that he acknowledged.[88] Bettelheim was among the first in the United States to employ a treatment milieu with emotionally disturbed children, but by the 1950s others were trying the method in a variety of settings, and with a range of disorders from schizophrenia to "mental deficiency." Psychologists in the 1950s and 1960s understood themselves as members of a profession that acted on the basis of an established body of theories and methods. Milieu therapy was one reputable, if experimental, practice that received serious attention, although the number of centers declined in later decades, partly owing to the monumental devotion required of the staff.[89]

The approach deviated significantly from the methods previously used at the Orthogenic School. Bettelheim described the school's framework for treating students and training staff in a series of articles that he coauthored with Emmy Sylvester, a consulting child psychiatrist, near the time of his appointment. Bettelheim emphasized psychoanalytic theory, but largely ignored traditional psychoanalytic technique. Instead of maintaining the school as a custodial institution, he turned it into a therapeutic and experimental environment, a place where the practice of milieu therapy could be refined but also a place where systematic insights into the children's emotional development might be obtained. Counselors worked both in child care and as research assistants. Bettelheim referred to them as "participant observers," simultaneously his protégés, research assistants, technicians, and instruments of observation.[90] Although students at the Orthogenic School had been research subjects before Bettelheim's arrival, those studies had not focused on specific diagnoses.[91] As his work at the school progressed, Bettelheim saw the opportunity for a research program built around the unique constellation of symptoms associated with one particular syndrome, autism.

In retrospect, Bettelheim's claims to have successfully treated a number of autistic children seem questionable if not willfully false. However, as Jacquelyn Sanders has suggested, autism "in the field at large" at the time was not so different from autism at the Orthogenic School, either in terms of clinical understanding or treatment practices.[92] It was Bettelheim's refusal to alter his position over time that eventually relegated him and his approach to the margins of the profession. Sanders argues that it is important to understand the context in which Bettelheim and his staff attempted to treat children with autism and other emotional disturbances. These interventions, directed at children who to readers today clearly suffered from neurological disorders, were carried out with the utmost seriousness and sincerity. Most significantly, in their work as both trained counselors and surrogate parents, the staff of the Orthogenic School did not emphasize Bettelheim's framework of mortal fear and maternal ambivalence. Caught up in the daily effort of caring for and working to understand autistic children, their labor drew on their empathy and identification with the children.

Bettelheim's practices at the school came under attack after his suicide, when counselors came forward to condemn his violent disciplinary techniques.[93] Former counselors at the Orthogenic School, troubled by the degree of vitriol directed at Bettelheim and by implication their own work, have situated their mentor's beliefs and their own in the context of the therapeutic milieu, their training as counselors, and the specific program Bettelheim committed to under the terms of his Ford Foundation grant. Jacquelyn Sanders was a "counselor and assistant" for fourteen years, during which time she received a doctorate in psychology. She succeeded Bettelheim as director of the school.

> In November of 1952 I began my first intensive engagement with an autistic child. My first memory is of his back as he leaned over the drinking fountain and Joanne, a senior counselor, spoke gently to him while I watched with admiring fascination, both the counselor and the child. At that time what autism meant to me was simply the extreme of my own deeply introspective tendencies, coupled with a refusal to engage in communication. I was convinced that guided by my empathic understanding I would overcome that refusal. I was one of a group of unrealistic but devoted optimists.[94]

Most exciting of all, "the least trained—the counselors (i.e., childcare workers)—were viewed as being pivotal in the success of this wonderful enterprise. It was thrilling to be a part of it." The end of the experiment was heartbreaking.[95] After years of intensive therapy children that she had worked with closely were transferred to custodial institutions. Her observations suggest that Bettelheim did not persist in his beliefs merely out of stubbornness. For the school staff, the approach to autism was part and parcel of a worldview that gave profound meaning to their hours of work and guided decisions from the choice of art on the school walls to the arrangement of seats in the dining room.

Bettelheim drew on the cases of the school's autistic children in his writing on the school, but what he and the counselors meant by "autism" is complicated, as Sanders's recollection suggests. As we saw in chapter 1, many clinicians used the terms "childhood schizophrenia," and, as in the case of

Joey, "autistic tendencies," almost interchangeably until at least the late 1970s, much to the consternation of professionals concerned with psychiatric nosology. Karen Zelan, a counselor who worked with many of the children, maintained that Betteleheim's criteria fit Kanner's 1943 definition of autism, including children who were "symptomatic" but not mentally retarded.[96]

However, Bettelheim and his staff treated autism as a symptom rather than a biological category. The school depended on the ability of the counselors to "put themselves in the position of the children" meaning that the symbolic worlds of the children could be comprehended and that they mattered to treatment. For example, Bettelheim praised Karen Zelan for adapting her footsteps to those of "Marcia," an autistic girl who feared crossing the street.[97] Similarly, the staff knew not to disturb Joey's elaborate system of motors and wires. Bettelheim explained the children's language problems as the outcomes of emotional blockages. This attention to the symbolic meanings of actions made heavy demands on the patience of therapists who had to attend to every nuance of a child's behavior. Ultimately, the counselors' practices and the quality of their interactions mattered more than theories about disease mechanisms, with the exception of the foundational assumptions that behaviors had meaning and that healing required a process of interaction between counselors and children.

Autistic children cultivated what Bettelheim identified as "passionate indifference." They only appeared unconcerned with their surroundings and relationships, where in fact they cared so deeply that they feared expressing it. Likewise, Bettelheim urged his counselors to develop an equivalent attitude of committed detachment, which would permit them to withstand physical assaults from the children while maintaining an absolute devotion to the project of curing them. Bettelheim believed that the counselors would do so in part because of "all the narcissistic and interpersonal rewards" they received from their central role in the children's treatment.[98] Bettelheim and Emmy Sylvester encouraged counselors to see themselves as the primary therapists for the children, the "crucial ones" who "got all the credit for whatever happened to the kids."[99] Many former counselors testified to their participation in the life of the school as a learning experience of the utmost value. A shared psychoanalytic perspective, evident in their interpretation of cases at the time as much as in their recollections decades later, shaped the collective ethos. Bettelheim saw these two components—total devotion on the part of the counselors and a "consistent therapeutic philosophy"—as critical to the creation of the school's unique milieu.[100]

In Bettelheim's reports to the Ford Foundation, he presented autism as a means to understand typical development. All twelve of the original children in the study—Bettelheim referred to having observed "over forty" children overall—were given a clinical diagnosis of "childhood schizophrenia, autistic type," and Bettelheim and his staff observed them closely, sometimes filming them. Because Bettelheim believed that autism represented an instance of development halted early in life, a successful cure would allow children to resume a normal course of progress. The counselors spent their days recording the steps the children took toward health, and in doing so observed a process that was normally hidden or at least unobserved, because changes happened quickly in typical children, and at a much younger age.[101] If Bettelheim could understand the halted developmental pathway in autism he would be capable of inferring from this to the progress of typical personality and ego development.[102] According to the models of psychological development current at the time, personality and ego development proceeded in much the same fashion as physiological development, along a predefined course. Deviations from this course, whether as a result of heredity, faulty parenting, or injury, inevitably led to harmful outcomes.

The five-year Ford Foundation grant of $342,500 (about $2,685,000 in 2008, a significant sum for the school) awarded in 1956–1962, involved several components. Bettelheim and his team would study "formation of personality in autistic children" and the "family background" of the children. "But," noted an interim progress report, "the most important study will simply seek to learn what it is that this school does that works, so that its success in dealing with a tragic problem may be duplicated more readily elsewhere."[103] In other words, Ford had funded a study not of autism but of treatment methods. Bettelheim thus may have felt pressured to present positive results to the grant committee in his yearly reports and in his research culminating in *The Empty Fortress* in 1967.[104]

The total environment of the school—the commitment and emotional labor required of the counselors, the emphasis on the ability of the environment to alter both students and teachers alike, and the holistic focus on daily life as an avenue to healing—all made the school a special type of social and therapeutic technology. Turning the school into an environment that seemed more like a home than a hospital represented a fundamental change in treatment strategy. Bettelheim and his colleagues also took seriously the idea that "the primary agents of treatment were the people who were with the children in their daily activities—the counselors who were with the children during all of their waking out of class hours, and the teachers."[105] Psychiatrists served as consultants, but played a supportive rather than central role at the school.[106] In addition, Bettelheim brought his charismatic personality and his desire to make meaningful contributions to studies of treatment methods, although he insisted that research not overshadow the goal of individualized treatment.

There is little doubt that the Orthogenic School was a unique environment. Some former students have written warmly of their experiences. Bettelheim explained that for a student "to live in an institutional setting which protects him against the vagaries of life, and in which contrary to his past experiences, those people important to him are characterized by a deep commitment to his physical and emotional needs—this in a slow process should heal his diseased mind."[107] The physical space of the school reflected Bettelheim's vision: beautiful grounds, a welcoming interior, and fine china used to serve meals. Bettelheim believed that the surroundings encouraged the children to treat their environment with care. At the same time, they might feel respected in a way that many did not in their lives outside the school. Bettelheim worked to create "a setting whose smallest detail was inspired by the recognition [of] psychoanalysis that implicit meanings must be made explicit in terms of their significance for the lives of children." Staff at the school recalled that they "sort of fell in love with the place."[108]

The therapeutic milieu produced a strange kind of asylum, a fact not lost on observers. The Orthogenic School had roots in the design of Victorian-era mental institutions that equated a calming built environment with mental order, but Bettelheim introduced some crucial modifications and revisions.[109] The children could leave the grounds at any time, but visitors needed permission to enter. The institution protected those living there from real and imagined threats outside the gates, even as the staff encouraged independence. Bettelheim's school had none of the oppressive restraints common to other institutions. Classrooms were bright and cheerful spaces, and students could keep toys and other belongings with them in the dormitories.[110]

Bettelheim stood unquestioned at its center, exerting what all accounts agree was an awesome force in his overlapping roles as parent figure, interpreter, disciplinarian, instructor, and architect, a "cross between a janitor . . . and a policeman," he said.[111] As a former counselor reported,

> Bettelheim functioned as a sort of superego. He expected every child to work hard to solve its problems. He oversaw the institution as a whole, for example, by making rounds every evening as the children were put to bed and by conducting daily staff meetings where he not only searched a child's behavior for meaning but also brilliantly instructed the child's "central persons."[112]

This absolute authority may explain the extreme reactions to Bettelheim on the part of staff members. As I noted, they tended either to treat him with great loyalty, crediting him with aiding in the formation of their present selves, or to reject him entirely.[113]

The counselors were frequently young, unmarried, and female, adept at the work of emotional involvement and attentiveness. Child care was considered "a woman's job."[114] They often had little prior experience in the psychoanalytic or psychiatric professions. Some, like Jacquelyn Sanders, went on to obtain clinical degrees. Others married and moved on. Still others spent their entire careers at the school. At a facility that was as much an educational environment for the teachers as it was a therapeutic environment for the students, some had difficulty identifying the boundary between training and therapy.

Each staffer underwent daily debriefings with "Dr. B," and given Bettelheim's propensity to regard any conflicts arising between students and counselors as a dyadic process involving contributions from both parties, the distinction between debriefing and psychoanalysis may have been a thin one. Bettelheim encouraged his staff members to see how their own emotional lives affected interactions with the students. As the "ego supports" for children whose ego functioning had "lapsed," they were literally incorporated into the emotional and psychological structure of the school.[115] Bettelheim suggested that transference, that is, the projection of unresolved issues in a counselor's unconscious life onto Bettelheim, began inevitably from the moment of the initial employment interview.

Bettelheim wanted teachers to review their interactions with children in terms of their own anxieties and fears. In some cases, he used psychological tests to evaluate them as their work progressed.[116] Counselors were taught that in the course of their work they might undergo countertransference, acting out their own unresolved emotional issues with the students. They learned to assume that a student's misbehavior might be a response to his or her counselor's own disordered behavior. Many remember feats of interpretive virtuosity on the part of Bettelheim, in which he helped staff members realize that a student's aggressive action resulted from their own failures to act in accordance with the child's needs. Bettelheim relentlessly criticized his teachers and they in turn measured his confidence in their performance by the harshness of his critiques.

If the work of the counselors resembled the routine of an introspective and responsive parent, it brought with it the same hazards that Bettelheim often ascribed to parental love. *The Empty Fortress* recounts Laurie's "collapse" and "total withdrawal from the world," precipitated by a counselor's ambivalence. The counselor's "bondage to her own needs and desires" led her to "misread" Laurie's intentions.[117] Bettelheim purposely chose counselors who had not undergone analysis themselves because he believed that their unresolved conflicts with their parents enabled them to identify with the students in ways that ultimately helped both to learn and mature. He explained the surprise of one counselor, "Jane," to a student's relief after being disciplined. Jane had been overly permissive in the past because she empathized with the girl's feelings of anger toward her mother.[118] Jane gained confidence as a therapist, but only by coming to terms with the unfinished business of her own childhood.

Jules Henry, the anthropologist who observed the staff as part of his research on "ideo-emotional" factors in institutional membership, and whom Jacquelyn Sanders remembered from her early years at the school, saw the social structure of the Orthogenic School as a welcome antidote to the detachment of staff members in the "contemporary psychiatric hospital."[119] The milieu model was a remedy for the disinterest and detachment chronicled by observers of state institutions of the period, one of many shortcomings that seemed to justify their wholesale closure in the following decade.[120] Ten years after Henry's visit, another group comparing the effectiveness of state institutions against therapeutic milieus came to a similar conclusion. Compared to custodial care, the intimate setting of a "psychoanalytically-oriented day-care unit which emphasizes the emotional relationship between staff and children" offered a far better opportunity for behavioral improvements. It did not appear to matter that many of the program's theoretical premises fit autistic children poorly if at all.[121]

Henry concluded that success at an institution like the Orthogenic School required absolute emotional and personal commitment to the therapeutic project. He argued that the intense involvement of the counselors in the lives of their patients was the only thing that could explain their long tenures at a school that paid them little, yet made relentless emotional and psychological demands.

> Another consequence of the deep mutual involvement of counselor and child is that most of the counselor's energies go into the children. The following question must now be answered: Given the exacting nature of the counselor's task, from where does she derive the necessary strength and incentive to carry on?[122]

Counselors found rewards in the form of their own growing autonomy through the process of "self-seeking" as they worked with the children. The school formed a system in which children, director, and counselors all played critical and interrelated roles. "In the School the children are in the center of the therapeutic and *emotional* interest; for the successful counselor the child remains the focus of her emotional life for a long time."[123]

Jacquelyn Sanders described the functioning of the educational aspects of the school under her guidance in terms that reflected Bettelheim's own accounts. In the introduction to her book, evocatively titled *A Greenhouse for the Mind,* Sanders recalled that "we created a world for them based on our understanding of the theory of psychoanalytic ego psychology, on anything else that any of us might know, and on the dictates of our hearts."[124] For Sanders, techniques emerged intuitively, based on evolving self-understanding and close observations of the counselor's own interactions with troubled children. The children established strong connections with individual workers, with whom the long-term therapeutic relationship progressed day and night. If these relationships were understood both by workers and students in psychoanalytic terms, it was still the relationship that held meaning and resided at the center of the school's practices.

The Politics of Treatability

Bettelheim made autism stand for childhood disorders in general—as the model through which the therapeutic milieu would be tested—and, through his interpretations, for modern forms of psychopathology. Thus, any concessions to arguments about the neurological basis of autism potentially undermined his entire research program. His commitments were not only to his theory of autism, but to a psychoanalytic perspective on development and survival. If autism was organic, it was also fixed and inalterable, a failure of neurons and not attachment. For Bettelheim, there really was no choice. Even though he allowed that vulnerabilities might predispose one child and not another to develop autism, his successes in treating the disorder proved the correctness of a psychogenic interpretation. "It is only when, after years of frustrated attempts, these children begin slowly to respond to treatment efforts based on psychoanalytically oriented hypotheses on the nature of the disturbance, that the psychogenic explanation becomes more and more convincing."[125]

Bettelheim nonetheless found others much less convinced than he was by his account of autism. Bernard Rimland was one. Following the 1964 publication of *Infantile Autism,* Rimland emerged as a major figure in his own right, who, unlike Bettelheim, defined himself by the heterogeneity of his theories and practical commitments rather than by his adherence to a single approach.[126] Bettelheim seemed relatively unconcerned with how his theories were applied within the psychoanalytic community or by general practitioners in their interactions with parents of autistic children. As a parent himself, Rimland knew how parents' encounters with medical authorities who saw in their hunger for information only further evidence of their "cold intellectuality" deprived them of the confidence they needed to help their children.[127]

The two engaged in an uncomfortable correspondence between 1965 and 1966 in which they debated how best to treat autism. For Rimland, the stakes were high. Psychotherapeutic approaches competed with behavioral treatments and biomedical research for scarce resources and professional attention. In a lecture that he presented to chapters of the National Society for Autistic Children between 1967 and 1970, Rimland rehearsed the conclusions of a number of experts that parents were not the cause of learning and behavioral disorders, and that psychotherapy had failed to help children with autism.

> The psychogenic theory has cast blame on the parents, and thus immobilized the child's strongest ally in what should be his struggle to recover. It has caused stagnation in research—which biochemist wants to analyze a "fractured oedipus complex?" It has caused educators to shrug their shoulders and leave the problem in the hands of the psychiatrists, psychologists and social workers. It has cost families untold fortunes in money, time, convenience and human dignity. And, worst of all, it has cost far too many children their lives. Such children are not medically dead—just psychologically dead, existing like human vegetables in institution after institution.[128]

Bettelheim and Rimland's correspondence began before Bettelheim published *The Empty Fortress*. Rimland sent Bettelheim a version of his "Diagnostic Check List for Behavior Disturbed Children," a device initially designed to refine diagnoses, but which Rimland hoped would eventually guide treatment based on a child's unique symptom profile.[129] It signified Rimland's conviction that an "impersonal checklist" was an instrument equivalent in worth to a "personal clinical impression," the authority that Bettlheim relied on for his own diagnoses.[130] He asked Bettelheim to help him obtain blood samples from autistic children. Bettelheim refused. "I regret to inform you that I am very critical of the approach that you are using to study infantile autism. In my opinion your book contains gross errors and misstatements. I therefore shall give you no help in a study of autistic children which I consider ill-conceived and based on erroneous and biased judgments."[131] In response to another letter, he told Rimland that "since you seem committed to the convictions that infantile autism is an inborn disease and incurable, no matter what the contrary evidence may be, I see little point in discussing treatment results. Suffice it to say that better than eighty-five percent of our former students have made an adequate adjustment to life, including some who are your and my colleagues as Ph.D.'s in psychology."[132] Despite the fact that Rimland was indeed quite interested in treating autism, Bettelheim found it impossible to believe that he could be genuinely committed to identifying treatment strategies given his view that autism was a neurological disorder.

After publishing *Infantile Autism* in 1964, Rimland began working on a follow-up volume on treatments, and he wrote to Bettelheim in 1966 with another request: "I propose that we set the precedent—pretty nearly unheard of in polemics—of granting each other a small section of response room [at] the end of each of our forthcoming books."[133] Bettelheim's angry response stood in marked contrast to his customary cordial style with parents and former patients. "The idea that after you have written a book, I should write something within its covers to detract from it is repellent to me. You see, feelings are unimportant to you, and to me they are the most important thing in dealing with human beings. But the most important reason is that I abhor arguments. I firmly believe that scientific progress is best made by each man stating his opinions and allowing the present and future generations to decide on their merits."[134]

His position was unchanged in the late 1970s when he co-taught a graduate seminar at Stanford. In one exchange, Bettelheim responded to a question asked by "Dan Berenson," a child psychiatrist working with autistic children, modeled on the child psychologist Bryna Siegel.[135] Siegel was planning a study of symptomatically similar autistic children with the hope of identifying an underlying biochemical marker. Bettelheim criticized this approach because it required an experimental protocol that, he suggested, treated the children merely as a means of fulfilling the researchers' agenda. The discovery of a "molecular oddity" would legitimize the tendency to view these children as "alien." If this happened, their actions could be seen as unsusceptible to sympathetic and individualized interpretation. Declaring these children biologically abnormal would be an unforgivable demonstration of the "laziness of the heart." "Isn't that laziness what prevents people from having empathy with these children's terrible suffering?"[136]

Eric Schopler, a clinical psychologist who went on to found Division TEACCH, the first statewide autism treatment program in the United States, said Bettelheim similarly "rebuffed" and "ridiculed" him when he asked for help with his doctoral research on neurological factors in autism.[137] After visiting the Orthogenic School, Schopler concluded that Bettelheim had "scapegoated" parents to make up for a lack of empirical research about the condition.[138] By 1974, as editor of the *Journal of Autism and Childhood Schizophrenia*, Schopler's editorial policies effectively downplayed psychogenic theories of autism by emphasizing "objective experimental studies" and "objective clinical data," and by directly soliciting parents' insights and responses to research.[139]

Why Bettelheim so adamantly refused to alter his position with respect to autism is a difficult question to answer. He oversaw an apparently productive research program in autism at a moment when psychology was struggling to create an identity for itself as a scientific profession with proven outcomes.[140] He had invested considerable time and money to build a staff trained in and committed to his treatment method. The Orthogenic School and its students was a rich resource that the prolific writer continued to exploit. Not least, his methods appeared to do some good, both for the students and for Bettelheim and the staff. This efficacy matters a great deal to understanding Bettelheim within his own milieu. It is not necessary to dismiss the pain that Bettelheim's theories caused parents to recognize that if he ruled harshly, his realm was still very small, and others bear responsibility for the broader application of psychogenic theories.

Other Psychotherapies, Other Autisms

By the 1970s claims about the efficacy of any therapy had to contend with the assumption that damage to brains in autism was congenital. Even before autism was reclassified in the educational system from an emotional to a developmental disorder, parents had come to understand their children's disabilities as outcomes of brain function rather than psychology. The transition from a psychoanalytic interpretation of the disorder to neurological and genetic accounts of etiology represented a new way of relating to these children and thinking about interventions on their behalf. The gradual decline of psychoanalytic thought in American culture makes it difficult to imagine a context in which inquiring and observant adults believed in milieu therapy as an effective treatment or believed that parents of autistic children needed psychotherapeutic treatment themselves. That a child need only eat from a counselor's hand or that a counselor need only listen sympathetically to a child's private language to effect positive change nevertheless made sense within the context of Bettelheim's school.

Our desire to avoid similar mistakes is one reason that it is important to understand Bettelheim's work, but there are other reasons why it is crucial to look at the role of Bettelheim, the popular appeal of his work, and the social organization of the Orthogenic School. Bettelheim epitomized the psychological perspective on autism during the first two decades that the diagnosis existed. This perspective encouraged an attitude toward the mothers of children with autism that exists even now and that informs the contemporary activities of parent advocacy groups. Unlike parents of children with other disorders more clearly marked as genetic or due to pre- or neonatal injury, such as cerebral palsy, parents of children with autism dealt with stigma through the 1950s, 1960s, and much of the 1970s. That stigma continues to exist albeit with subtle variations. Today professionals may suggest that parents manifest mild symptoms of autism themselves, and that their seeking after cures is a kind of "perseveration." Other experts continue to see parents as unresponsive, if only as a result of their child's own detachment. These writers understand rage, distress, and energetic self-education as defenses against the obvious fact of a child's disability, symptoms rather than reasonable responses.

The ideas that underpinned Bettelheim's experiment in Chicago and that helped to legitimize his work, including attachment theory, maternal deprivation, milieu therapy, and the role of parent–child interaction in cognitive development, all existed prior to Bettelheim's influential run as an authority on autism. They persisted long after his reputation in that field declined. That complex legacy has cast a long shadow over the tradition of psychoanalytic work with autism in the United States. Its proponents have understood their theories about the social or familial environment as a cause of mental illness to be a progressive alternative to those that emphasized an individual's temperament or heredity. In contrast, their theories seemed to offer the possibility of successful treatment through interventions in the family or educational environment, drawing scrutiny away from the individual patient's deviance. Symptoms might represent a logical response to a pathogenic situation.

The specter of Bettelheim may haunt autism research and advocacy, but psychoanalytic approaches to treating autism were never his project alone. Bettelheim's worldview was one among many examples of postwar attitudes toward childrearing, including an intense focus on development of selfhood and the growth of autonomy, and critiques of behaviorism's focus on innate tendencies and patterned responses. Many others shared a psychoanalytic perspective on mental disorders, of which autism was understood to represent a classic case. The child psychologists Mira Rothenberg and Virginia

Axline, like Bettelheim, located the source of autism in early experiences that made children either literally or metaphorically fear for their lives. Both published books that were warmly received by professional colleagues and popular audiences and remained in print for decades.[141] Contemporary psychiatric approaches to autism still seek to interpret symptoms as meaningful communicative behavior and to unpack the effect of parent–child bonding. In other countries, psychoanalytic approaches to autism remain standard and institutionalized, into the present, even when psychiatrists have adopted a biological interpretation of autism's causes.[142] Bettelheim's protégé, Karen Zelan, uses many of his methods in her own therapeutic work, abandoning only his insistence on a purely psychogenic explanation for autism.[143]

For Bettelheim, the counselors at the Orthogenic School, and his many readers, love took work and, even then, it was often "not enough" unless combined with interpretive acumen and clear-eyed introspection. Bettelheim did not question that parents loved their autistic children. He merely, devastatingly, maintained that they loved them incorrectly. Counselors at the school, in contrast, might not even have described their relationships with the students in terms of love, but they almost certainly would have identified the detailed, empathic responsiveness of their interactions with the students as key to any successes they witnessed. Jacquelyn Sanders pointed to underlying similarities between different approaches when she recalled films of a treatment based on operant conditioning, where "the therapist practicing a conditioning protocol would treat the youngster in very much the same way as we would at the Orthogenic School in terms of respect and empathic sensitivity, but . . . would report only on the conditioning techniques," suggesting a difference of emphasis and perspective more than of practice.[144] Indeed, while the Orthogenic School continues to provide individualized psychotherapy, small classroom environments, and resident counselors, it has now "adapted its milieu" to incorporate both the positive reinforcements more often associated with behavior modification techniques and "detailed psychopharmacological assessment and treatment."[145]

We can also read Bettelheim's story as a cautionary tale about analytical frameworks and passionate commitments in biomedicine today. It reminds us that social and environmental contingencies affect the perceived efficacy of any therapeutic modality. Despite claims for universality and objectivity, biomedical knowledge can be both situated and pluralistic in practice, drawing on multiple and contradictory ways of thinking about disease and difference. Bettelheim's conviction that one might temper reason with love and his insistence that emotion stood at the heart of rational scientific practice might sound unfamiliar to practitioners of contemporary autism research.

Observers inclined to equate reliance on affect with the abdication of reason might even see the seeds of Bettelheim's downfall in the claim. Still, we should consider seriously his conviction that his methods worked and that affective work lay at the heart of their efficacy. "The daring heart must invade reason with its own living warmth, even if the symmetry of reason must give way to admit love and the pulsation of life." [146] While this might sound like an impractical demand to those committed to a view of biomedicine that divorces reason from affective commitments, it remains a reasonably accurate description of biomedical and therapeutic work in practice.

Psychoanalysis offered an explanation for autism that worked until it failed to cure. That failure notwithstanding, it founded research schools, generated funds for investigators, and offered a systematic means of comprehending previously inexplicable, severe disorders of development. An emphasis on the contingent rather than fixed factors in development recurs in contemporary discussions of both gene–environment interactions and therapeutic modalities. Sanders believes that "the accounts that describe reliable treatment are remarkably similar to the practices of the Orthogenic School with autistic children. Shock treatment, facilitated communication and the like come and go, but the need for an intense involvement of a whole environment over a long period of time remains." [147] She is not alone. Another psychoanalytically oriented clinician, Bertrand Ruttenberg, argued in 1976 that "among good programs—i.e., those which were sensitive to the behaviors and needs of the children and which were skillfully implemented by a dedicated and attentive staff—there was little evidence of differences in therapeutic effectiveness regardless of whether the therapy was behavior modification, education, psychoanalytically oriented relationship therapy, or activity therapy." [148]

As Bettelheim noted, at a time when his colleagues still believed him, love alone could not secure such intense involvement. The work required discipline and expertise. Structured therapeutic techniques and the caring and labor involved in creating them are the topic that I turn to next.

3

Expert Amateurs: Raising and Treating Children with Autism

This is a love story, and it begins with a sensitive child. Benjamin ("Ben") Lettick was born on April 7, 1955. He was the fourth child of Amy and Birney Lettick of New Haven, Connecticut. Amy Lettick had trained as a schoolteacher before her marriage to Birney, a portrait artist. Their son Ben suffered from severe food allergies almost from birth. Amy Lettick took the susceptibilities of her youngest in stride. Dealing with the allergies of her three older children had armed her with strategies for treating him, including keeping a detailed record of diet, immunizations, and reactions. Her diary entries indicate the delicate balances that had to be achieved.

> Feb. 17 David—one pimple on cheek. Had liver today??
> Mar 17 Gave Sharon cooked carrot. Skin on arms & legs improved.
> June 7 S had ¼ c. raisins. <u>Terrible</u> hives all over body.
> Gave benedryl.
> No more raisins for anybody![1]

It soon became clear that Benjamin Lettick had developmental problems far beyond those of a typical, if delicate, child. Although he developed on schedule for the first six months, he then "grew very quiet" and began to sleep for most of the day. Lettick, trained in education, knew what normal behavior looked like. The "peppy, smiling, chubby baby" turned into an unsmiling child who no longer seemed to recognize anyone, including his mother.[2] At eight months, Ben's pediatrician told Lettick he suspected that her son was retarded and referred him to the Yale Child Study Center in New Haven for evaluation.

After the doctor's crushing assessment, Lettick was relieved when the director of the Autism Unit at the Child Study Center diagnosed Ben with autism. At the time most parents, Lettick included, had little understanding of the disorder save that it seemed better than the more serious and irreversible diagnosis of mental retardation. Ben received psychotherapy, the standard practice at the time, between the ages of two and a half and six, when his therapist recommended discontinuing the treatment. His behavior and responsiveness to people had improved, but he had failed to learn to talk, and it was unclear whether he understood spoken words at all.[3]

For Lettick, this admission of defeat by the staff at the Yale Child Study Center seemed more devastating than the original diagnosis, but it led her to learn more about autism and eventually to seek advice and training from Newell Kephart at Purdue University. Kephart, in turn, inspired Lettick to found a school and then a residential program for her son and others like him. Over the course of the next four decades, Lettick developed an educational program for Ben through her own research at the Yale University Library and information provided by other mothers of children with autism, many of whom were seeking help for their children through early versions of behavioral therapy. She helped found the National Society for Autistic Children (NSAC, later the Autism Society of America), and she founded Benhaven, one of the first lifespan-oriented residential programs for children and adults with autism.

Although Lettick's energy and determination were exceptional, her experiences were tied to those of many parents during the 1960s and 1970s who often found themselves with few resources other than each other in learning to treat their children. During the 1950s, parents of children diagnosed with mental retardation had successfully lobbied for special education classrooms and other forms of support in their efforts to keep their children at home and out of institutions, often against the recommendations of psychologists.[4] Parents of children with autism in the 1960s and 1970s faced many of the same difficulties, made worse because autism was still viewed as an emotional disorder rather than a cognitive disability. Several founded schools and treatment programs in response to the overwhelming lack of resources.[5] Lettick's work as an institution builder distinguishes her. However, she consistently described her efforts as a succession of pragmatic responses to Ben's needs as he grew older—in other words, as the understandable consequences of her commitment to her child.

Parents' accounts of their work during a period when the diagnostic category of autism was in flux identify their unique authority as caregivers and "amateur" therapeutic practitioners. They claim an expertise that is well defined, but never quite professional. The most successful behavior programs took place in highly controlled environments. Parents did the work of translating them into elements of daily life in domestic spaces. In many cases, this transformation of everyday familiarity into everyday authority began as an opposition to psychologists who ignored them and experts who offered only dire prognoses. However, even as parents were developing their own therapeutic strategies, psychologists were working to incorporate parents into the programs that they were designing themselves.

Lettick said that she and other parents were compelled to become "paraprofessionals."[6] This idea lies at the center of the practice of what is now called applied behavior analysis (ABA) and related behavioral therapies derived from operant conditioning, as well as other developmental education programs. In the 1970s, professionals in child psychology adopted the methodology of parental participation. Leo Kanner recognized that

> parents are beginning to be dealt with from the point of view of mutuality, rather than as people standing at one end of a parent–child bipolarity; they have of late been included in the therapeutic efforts, not as etiological culprits, nor merely as recipients of drug prescriptions and of thou-shalt and thou-shalt-not rules, but as actively contributing cotherapists.[7]

Amy Lettick never published the story of her son's development and her search for treatments, although she wrote several books about Benhaven.[8] Other parents did write about their own experiences of raising children with autism, using terms that are remarkably similar despite the distance of decades that separated them. Noah Jiro Greenfeld, the subject of Josh Greenfeld's memoir *A Child Called Noah*, was born a decade after Benjamin Lettick in 1966. Raun Kahlil Kaufman, the subject of *Son-Rise* and its sequel, was born in the early 1970s, and Catherine Maurice's memoir *Let Me Hear Your Voice* takes place in the mid 1980s—and these are only a representative sample of some of the most widely read books. These books show that the transformation of parents into technicians is far from straightforward. Indeed, they make visible some longstanding contradictions in the distinction between what Americans understand to be therapeutic expertise and what they call acts of love. Parents both gain and lose when they use the category of personal experience to emphasize their authority, just as there can be contradictions in therapeutic programs that train parents as "cotherapists" and "paraprofessionals," amateurs at research but experts on their own children.

The term "amateur" has been central to parents' accounts of their work. It serves at once as a demure renunciation of expertise and a claim about commitment and particularity of knowledge. Catherine Maurice recalled,

> Once when I sent a mother to one of the early-intervention pro-grams in New York to try to recruit some therapists for her home program, she reported back to me that the director had informed her that it was "illegal and unethical" for "amateurs" to be attempt-ing this kind of work.
>
> We parents *are* amateurs, in the true sense of the word: ama-teurs are lovers. We are lovers of our children, and until the profes-sional community can offer us more effective programs, we will often have to take matters into our own hands.[9]

More than two decades earlier, Clara Claiborne Park wrote about the differences between parents and professionals as she reflected on her daughter Jessy's first eight years. When daily life constitutes a series of on-going, experimental interventions, determining who is a reliable witness of a child's behavior or the efficacy of a treatment can be complicated.[10] Parents seem both materially and emotionally invested in the develop-ment of their own children, while professionals seem dispassionate and uninvolved. However, Park intimated, professionals' interest in autism as a clinical entity gave them commitments far more dangerous than the car-ing partiality of parents.

When Park wrote in 1967, psychiatrists and psychologists would "sel-dom welcome parents as co-workers" or see them as potential therapists because of the "handicaps inherent in their position," when "detachment is necessary for wise action." Nevertheless, Park continued, the handicaps of parents may be "counterbalanced by special advantages that even the most gifted psychiatrists cannot match." Park listed these advantages, including a familiarity with their child's developmental trajectory and current be-haviors that rivaled any doctor's, the continuous therapeutic opportunities offered by the activities of daily life, and their own biological kinship with the child, including shared personality traits and milder forms of the same symptoms. Conscious that they were not professionals and constantly made aware of the variety and changeability of their child's behavior, the also had a "certain humility" that professionals often lacked.[11]

Park left the most important asset until last, not even quite including it in her list. "I have not dared to set down in my list of advantages a parent's love for his child. Love is not only not enough—we have almost been per-suaded to admit that it is a disadvantage. Yet I cannot think that we are disqualified for working with our child because we love her. Detachment and objectivity are techniques too and can be learned."[12] Park reflected on her own experience interacting with professionals, noting that Bettelheim may have been right in claiming that "love is not enough"—certainly, and "one must know *how* to love as well." Love is a form of expertise or, in Park's words, a "technique" that is given the name of empathy, transference, or knowledge when it translated into expert terms. It is, above all, an attitude of reflecting on the needs of another and translating those inner states into facts that can be acted upon, and it is a skill that can be refined. Park wrote that "physicians of the soul do the thousands of afflicted children no service if they undermine the confidence of their parents in what they can accomplish by intelligent love. Intelligence and love are not natural enemies. Nothing sharpens one's wits for the hints and shadows of another's thinking as love does—as anyone who has been in love can testify," and she concluded that "love is a technique as well as an emotion."[13]

In a book about the daily operation of Benhaven, Amy Lettick included a talk on raising a severely disabled child at home. In choosing to keep one's child at home and with the family, parents were left with little support, isolated in their decisions about how best to care for their children.

> The last thing I want to say is that what *all children but particularly ours need is love.* About four weeks ago a young teacher came to school and she was telling us about her school. She said that the key word in their school, the word that guided them through everything, was the word "Love."
>
> I told her that that wasn't the key word in our school. The key word was "help."
>
> We were really both saying the same thing, except that I think that "Help" is more positive, a more positive way of expressing your love than just showing affection. Love can't really accomplish much unless it is fed into action.[14]

For Bettelheim, the insufficiency of love pointed the way to the reflexive and interactive healing processes of psychoanalytic principles applied in a therapeutic milieu. Amy Lettick's emphasis was similarly site specific and pragmatic. Love was essential, but it was ineffective without appropriate application and practice. Lettick reminded her audience that the techniques that helped children were acts of caring empathy backed by knowledge of a child's needs, not mere affection. Simple and unpracticed affection might actually cause harm. As Josh Greenfeld, another parent-turned-author concluded, "Love is caring enough to teach obedience."[15]

The work of parents entailed incorporating expert knowledge and research into daily routines. Commitment in the form of love helped justify shaping everyday life around therapeutic techniques, but it was not necessarily the substance of the treatments themselves. Like the work of counselors at the Orthogenic School, parents' work was characterized by situated efficacy. They achieved results through emotional and cognitive labor in particular settings, among specific communities.

Although many parents have written about professionals who resented their intrusion into expert domains, designers of treatment programs also emphasized the centrality of parental involvement in the daily tasks of treatment. Eric Schopler, who with Robert Reichler pioneered a therapeutic program during the 1970s that explicitly incorporated parents' insights, thought that a number of factors explained the reluctance of professionals to speak frankly with parents. Professionals may have intuited that parents would "resist" their psychoanalytic interpretations of parental culpability in their children's autism. They also believed that telling parents about "indications of brain damage" in addition to autistic symptoms would discourage them. Not least, professionals felt the need to preserve their status by maintaining terms of the art such as IQ scores as "top secret," even if IQ scores ideally correlate to performance in everyday life, something that is "usually no secret from parents anyhow." Knowledge about their child's condition and explicit involvement in their treatment enabled parents to "react, think, and feel more rationally about their child." Parents' initial dismay at their child's diagnosis caused far less harm than ill-advised "professional attempts to protect them."[16]

O. Ivar Lovaas's research at the UCLA Psychology Department's Autism Clinic beginning in the mid-1960s formed the direct or indirect basis for much of the work done on structured behavior modification with autistic children. For Lovaas and his team in the Young Autism Project, parents offset the "situationality" of children's gains, a liability of a largely clinic-based approach. Without including the home environment, children would never learn to generalize the skills that they were taught. Furthermore, parents were already a "child's primary language teachers."[17]

Martin Kozloff, arguing in 1973 for the importance of parent training, explained that "systematic efforts are made to teach parents to be teacher-therapists in programs for educating, treating, or socializing their children." Parental involvement was necessary for psychosocial development and treatment as were parents' "extensive and detailed *practical* knowledge of their children's strengths, impairments, capacities, learning needs and preferences." In the absence of "timely and adequate parent training," there was a danger that a child's impairments might worsen as a family's re-sources and strength wore thin. There were also simply not enough trained professionals to serve autistic children.[18]

As skilled practitioners who nevertheless lacked a professional iden-tity, parents have had to justify their credibility and authority in order to be taken seriously. They often used conventional, well-established meth-ods, for example, behavioral programs. Their work was informed by then current beliefs about normal bonding, child development, learning, and communication. The work also depended on highly specific knowledge of particular children. In this sense, successful behavioral programs required both affective commitment and "situated knowledge" formed through a close relationship with one child. This type of knowledge is by definition partial in both senses of the term, where partial refers to both an incom-plete point of view and the state of caring and being invested.[19] Although the content of parental expertise depends on context, the terms are re-markably similar: attention, the quotidian patterns of care, and the impor-tance of similarities among family members. Love is an advantage and a technique rather than a liability.

Life's Work

Amy Lettick saw her diary as a record not only of her son's growth but also of her own progress from young mother to parent of a child with autism to determined educator and eventual administrator. Ben Lettick, she wrote, was possibly the best-documented autistic child of all time.

> But there was a life of sorts outside of Ben. There were birthday celebrations, trips to the dentist, and dinner parties; I worked vig-orously as my husband's research assistant, and compiled his ex-tensive picture file, handled the billing for his art classes. I froze corn, polished silver, and ironed shirts. What is apparent, though, from the diaries, is that as the demands of caring for Ben became overwhelming, my husband and my other children had to take sec-ond place in my life, even in my thoughts. It never occurred to me that I had a choice; the others could help themselves, while Ben could not.[20]

Lettick's diary documented experimental care, research, and training—her "life's work"—produced at a time when little was known and even less was standardized about treating children with autism. She described Ben's development in terms of a series of authorities who exerted a formative influence on her life and her perception of her son's development. "The intense scrutiny and documenting of my existence over the past four decades was required of me by the three people who shaped my life."[21] The pediatrician Morris Krosnick had encouraged her to record every environmental variable in her household in order to manage her son David's extreme allergies. Sally Provence, a pediatrician at the Yale Child Study Center, had requested records of Ben's behavioral development. Newell Kephart, the director of the Achievement Center for Children at Purdue University had, starting in 1962, developed an educational program for Ben that required careful records of his daily activities.[22]

Lettick's journals chronicled "how little professional help was available in the decades following Leo Kanner's first article on autism." They also demonstrated "what could be accomplished by a low-functioning, classically autistic person with optimum education," and the cost of those accomplishments to the child's family.[23] Lettick's attitude was eminently pragmatic. She rarely speculated, in writing at least, about the cause of Ben's condition. She saw her role as one of enabling development and growth at whatever level was possible. The nineteenth and twentieth century ideal of scientific motherhood dictated that women turn to experts for advice on every aspect of child care. Lettick, like other mothers before her, was selective about the advice that she followed.[24] Ben's needs also meant that Lettick went beyond the mandate that she merely seek and follow expert guidance. She reinterpreted and adapted the information she found in order to develop methods that were suited to her child.

In her efforts to synthesize ongoing research on behavioral interventions that might help Ben, Lettick sought consultations with rising experts in the field. However, she also kept detailed reading lists and gained access to the Yale library, where she devoured books on educational methods for typically developing children as well as remedial educational techniques. In one of her few references to psychoanalysis she mentioned the one useful piece of advice from Bettelheim's *Love Is Not Enough*: keep a jar of candies available, from which the child can help himself freely. She didn't mention Bettelheim's complicated psychological rationale based on denial and fulfillment, but she did leave a jar of M&Ms out for Ben and noted his delight.

Lettick experimented with a range of educational techniques. She devised visual puzzles where Ben was required to match identical pieces in a row, exercises to increase his fine motor coordination, tactile routines that required him to manipulate forms, and a wide variety of techniques to teach Ben to form spoken consonants with the hope that he might eventually learn to speak. Although she speculated about Ben's responses to one educational trial or another and sometimes recorded that he was "having a bad day" (or that they both were), she rarely interpreted Ben's behavior in any terms other than pleasure, frustration, anger, or boredom. She persisted in working to develop Ben's verbal skills until, when he was eleven, she decided to have his hearing tested—none of his doctors had thought to check on this—and discovered that he had severe hearing loss, probably significant enough to prevent him from distinguishing speech as anything but "noise."[25] Lettick promptly refocused her teaching methods.

In the summer of 1961, a student in her husband's art class sent Lettick an article from the *Saturday Evening Post* by Rosalind Oppenheim, "They Said Our Child Was Hopeless."[26] By then, the staff at the Yale Child Study Center had concluded that there was no way to help Lettick's son. Oppenheim's article offered Lettick hope that she might teach herself to treat Ben, and she began corresponding with Oppenheim.[27] Although their relationship was not always personally close, they shared a series of troubling and revelatory experiences. For many of the same reasons that Lettick founded Benhaven, Oppenheim founded and directed two schools, the second of which she named the Bernard Rimland School for Autistic Children. She also wrote a book on teaching methods for parents and professionals.[28] Lettick would write of Oppenheim that "she was my first mentor, and a more capable one could not have existed."[29]

Oppenheim had trained herself as a teacher after finding Newell Kephart, a specialist at Purdue working on a treatment for brain-damaged children. Contrary to the beliefs of doctors influenced by psychoanalytic theory, Kephart said that Oppenheim would not "irreparably damage Ethan's psyche by making demands on him (advice which was, incidentally, diametrically opposite to everything we had been told by every clinician we had consulted prior to Dr. Kephart)."[30] Her son Ethan was six years old and nonverbal, but after using a "home-training program" designed to teach him pre-academic skills, the Oppenheims had discovered that he was capable of communicating by writing. After publishing her article, Oppenheim was "besieged by hundreds of letters from distraught parents from several continents who were seeking help." Professionals wanted to cite it. Oppenheim told Lettick, "I wish I had a secretary!"[31] Most inquiries she answered only once, but Lettick's enthusiasm, energy, and, above all, persistence led her to continue the correspondence.[32] Lettick described reading Oppenheim's response to her first letter as a transformative moment: "I put down Roz Oppenheim's wonderful letter, took Ben by the hand, walked him upstairs to the table in his bedroom and began his first classtime."[33]

Rosalind Oppenheim encouraged Lettick to attend Kephart's summer camp, which trained parents in behavioral techniques, and she reassured Amy when Ben's progress was slow: "Don't be discouraged by Ben's seeming lack of progress. Kep says all children have learning plateaus during which they seem to be standing still, or even regressing; but are actually consolidating their previous gains."[34] Lettick placed a great deal of weight on Oppenheim's advice and support, persisting in her efforts to gain access to Kephart at Purdue. This turned out to be a lengthy process, requiring her first to convince Sally Provence to write a referral to Kephart and then wait for Kephart to respond and agree to treat Ben.[35]

The week before the Letticks planned to travel to Indiana to visit Kephart, Rosalind Oppenheim warned Lettick that she might have misunderstood what Kephart could offer. While Kephart's techniques helped immensely in educating Ethan, Ethan's behavior and social skills were still far from normal. Oppenheim thought that she might not have written the article had she understood how slow progress would be:

> Learning to read and write, for Ethan, and, when it happens, for Ben, was no more remarkable than it is when a normal child learns to read and write. *Because this has nothing to do with their basic problem.* I hope you won't hate me for telling you this. But, oh God, what a letdown we suffered! This is not to imply, I hasten to add, that the situation is hopeless; but Ethan's social progress—while there *is* some—continues at what seems to us to be a snail's pace. He is still very deviant. [36]

While Ethan's testable performance might have improved, his ability to function socially did not—he was still autistic.[37] Ethan, moreover, was generally more responsive than Ben, and had considerable receptive language abilities to begin with. Where Ben tended to be lethargic, Ethan was hyperactive. Lettick almost cancelled the trip, writing that the letter "knocked the heart right out of me."[38]

Luckily, Kephart designed individualized programs geared toward increasing children's overall "flexibility" and skill in integrating sensory information, rather than their performance in any specific area.[39] The methods depended on a view of developmental domains as fundamentally related to each other. It was a perspective in keeping with Lettick's desire to see Ben acquire skills that he could take out of the classroom and into the outside world. The group in Indiana that the Letticks joined included two other autistic children, who were a recent research interest for Kephart. Lettick noted that Ben performed better than many of the other children, and she took Kephart's encouragement seriously. The Letticks returned from their visit to Indiana optimistic:

> Basically, what we came away with was a completely new under-
> standing of why Ben acts the way he does and what we have to do.
> I realize that what I have been doing with Ben hasn't harmed him,
> but his needs go far, far, backward to much more basic behavior,
> and now of course I shall concentrate on those needs. Being forti-
> fied with understanding is the greatest strength we received.[40]

Lettick also felt that she now had the skills to act alone, "as though the cord tying me to Roz has been cut."[41] She began a wide correspondence, and she became part of a small but growing network of parent activists, including Bernard Rimland, who wrote to Lettick about a study of high-dose vitamin B6 that was recruiting participants through the new National Society for Autistic Children.[42] Years later, what most struck Lettick was the divergent paths that Ben's and Ethan's lives had taken, even though their mothers were equally determined and "she had the bright boy, I had the retarded boy."[43] After Oppenheim's death, Ethan was placed in a residential facility, where he regressed to the point that he interacted with no one and did not appear to recognize Lettick when she visited. Meanwhile, Ben was "flourishing" in adulthood, living at Benhaven and working at a supervised job, surrounded by people who "enjoyed, even loved him."[44]

The two mothers had both begun by contacting the same doctor, Newell Kephart, an expert on teaching children with diagnoses of brain damage. The amorphous category referred less to a discrete injury in an adult brain than to the recognition that an alteration early in development could lead to multiple disabilities later in life. For many parents of children given diagnoses of autism or "autistic tendencies" during the 1960s and 1970s, "brain damage" might have seemed the most adequate description of the difficulties that their children experienced, including developmental regressions and unusual combinations of strengths and deficits in cognitive abilities.[45]

Kephart's approach concentrated on "perceptual motor skills." He based his techniques on the premise that children's cognitive development occurred in parallel to their ability to coordinate the movements needed to explore and learn from their environments.[46] He thought that children who had developed atypically were often pressured by parents or schools to develop "splinter skills" that they memorized as a series of movements rather than integrated as organic reflexes.[47] Although Kephart's method deviated from the behaviorist approaches now standard in treating children with autism, it shared with them an emphasis on parents as "prime coordinators of and contributors to their child's development and learning."[48] He avoided technical descriptions of his methods and stressed the importance of training parents in general concepts that they could apply themselves.[49]

Not all experts offered the same level of hope and encouragement. Much of Lettick's daily work involved seeking teachers for Ben and then training them, an intellectually and emotionally demanding process. At one point, the Letticks met with a man at Southern Connecticut State College who claimed to be a psychologist who had recovered from autism through the help of yet another recovered autistic man.[50] At their initial meeting, the psychologist identified Lettick as "classically neurotic" and told her that she was pressuring her child to behave as a typical person when he was unable to conform to her expectations. Autistic children had to be met at their own level and in their own language. He spoke of rolling on the floor and growling and of his own lack of empathy for other human beings. The Letticks listened in fascination and dismay. After telling them that they were utterly unable to love or care for their son, he said that he had no time to treat Ben and that treatments took two years. They did not bring Ben back for an evaluation.

Ben had appointments at the Yale Child Study Center twice a week and was enrolled in their preschool for a time. As he neared the age of seven, Lettick discovered that Ben would no longer be eligible for treatment when his doctor casually asked Lettick about her plans for the future. The center had "no procedure for helping parents find successive placement, nor did they have lists of existing facilities elsewhere."[51] The Association for Retarded Children (now the ARC) was starting a chapter in New Haven, and a group of parents set up a day care center that Ben attended for a time, although Lettick was saddened to place Ben with "defective children" when his limitations seemed so different from theirs.[52]

Starting in 1962, Lettick worked with other parents to set up an autism class at the public school.[53] In 1966, the New Haven public school system hired a new teacher, Gilbert Freitag, for the autism class. Lettick found Freitag's behaviorism difficult to countenance. Although he had been highly recommended by Bernard Rimland, Lettick wondered whether Freitag knew anything about child development.[54] Lettick decided to start a new school as a nonprofit corporation, with a year-round schedule so as not to "leave too much of the day to regress in for children who don't know how to use free time or whose parents are not able or free to cope with their needs." The public educational system offered mainly frustrations and no residential schooling options apart from institutionalization for children who had graduated from elementary school and who could no longer live with their families. Lettick would, as she put it, turn her "remaining energies to creating rather than adapting."[55]

She envisioned the new residential program, Benhaven, as a developmentally organized environment. The goal for students was not normality but achievement and growth within the boundaries set by their disability. Lettick's choice of a name for the school echoed New Haven, Connecticut; the idea of a safe home for children like Ben; and the name of Newell Kephart's school, the Glen Haven Achievement Center, in Fort Collins, Colorado. It was to be a year-round facility, based on Kephart's ideas and practices, although Lettick differed with Kephart on the question of parent training.[56] Kephart felt that there was "no adequate substitute for parent participation in the training program," while Lettick believed it crucial to serve parents who might not have the ability or the time to fully participate or who divided their attention among many children. Other advisors to the school argued against parent volunteers, but Lettick disagreed. "The one basic difference between me and all my advisors is that in addition to being a teacher, I am a mother of a child like this. I don't intend that this shall be a handicap to the development of Benhaven. Rather I feel that my experience in this double capacity can contribute to the endeavor."[57]

Benhaven was an experimental site where, during a typical six months, behavioral programs for any given student might be tried and, if necessary, abandoned.[58] The tools used at Benhaven included diagnostic inventories imported from developmental psychology, forms for rating improvement, behavioral methods, and other "developmentally designed" psychoeducational approaches. Teachers set goals according to each child's abilities rather than a predetermined trajectory. A child might be taught sign language as an alternative to verbal speech. Employees sometimes had to stop students from engaging in self-injurious behaviors and occasionally used restraints.[59] One student had been expelled from all of his previous schools and arrived in restraints, requiring two grown men to control him. Behaven's treatment program, which emphasized his skills and downplayed restraints, helped him to leave as one of the school's first graduates.

Benhaven became "a place that everyone who works with severely handicapped people should see," and "an inspiration," but it could not become a home to all, and not all residential treatment programs reflected the values of an Amy Lettick.[60] From the outset, she envisioned her approach as one that could be replicated, and the National Society for Autistic Children agreed, naming her methods "essential reading" for people who worked with autistic children in any capacity.[61] She was open about both the strategies that worked and those that failed, earning her books a warm review in the *Journal of Autism and Developmental Disorders*.[62] In contrast to psychoanalytic treatment programs that emphasized relationships between children and staff, the Benhaven philosophy stressed "immediate work with the child, with the idea that through work, relationships will be formed."[63]

Lettick's honorary degree from Yale, a doctorate of humane letters awarded in 1975, made implicit and perhaps even wry reference to the legacy of training—from "training schools" for disabled children in the early part of the century to the promises of discrete trial training and the professional training offered by universities. The citation read:

> The haven you provided for autistic children is recognized as one of the most advanced schools for those so tragically impaired. You were not willing to accept the dehumanizing institutions available for such children. The accomplishment of Benhaven is the result of your extraordinary effort to train yourself, teach others and perfect existing knowledge about the autistic child. Through love and action you have earned the admiration of all who work in your field.[64]

Technologies of Change: NSAC and Behavioral Therapies

Bernard Rimland, an experimental psychologist with an autistic son, founded the National Society for Autistic Children (NSAC) in 1965 with a group of concerned parents, including Amy Lettick. The organization would be "a means for parents of autistic and schizophrenic children to meet and work for better schools and facilities for their children."[65] By promoting the idea that autism was incorrectly classified as a severe emotional disturbance (SED) when it was in fact an "organic" neurological disorder best treated through specialized educational programs, NSAC influenced a transition in the disease category of autism from psychological to neurological disorder. A large proportion of the early work of NSAC involved making the autism diagnosis visible to educators, legislators, and physicians.[66]

These efforts took place prior to the Education for All Handicapped Children Act of 1975 (renamed the Individuals with Disabilities Education Act [IDEA] in 1990) and other legislation that made developmental disorders a bureaucratically visible entity.[67] The laws extended the principle of equal protection or what the legislation termed a "free and appropriate public education," in the "least restrictive environment" possible for a given child. Parents played a role in their passage, motivated in part by the reprehensible and often debilitating conditions in institutions for the mentally and developmentally disabled. Despite the existence of NSAC, parents of autistic children lagged behind parents of children with other cognitive disabilities in their efforts to organize. One reason was the assumption of their culpability by a generation of medical professionals.[68] They banded together to secure educational supports, in response to the prospect of effective interventions, and because of the sense of accomplishment and agency they derived from therapies that worked.

Even though autism was not yet an entirely stable medical category, those diagnosed with the disorder had become an orphaned population in terms of care and support services. NSAC reflected the realization among parents that they comprised a population with shared experiences, among them an arduous journey through clinics and expert consultations en route to a diagnosis. Although psychiatrists began to develop standard guidelines for autism diagnosis by the late 1970s, the majority of autism diagnoses during that decade, as in the present, were based on clinical observation and judgment. The Society enlisted the help of a professional advisory board in crafting a new, standard definition of autism that was suited for use in schools and in writing legislation. In 1975, they successfully pushed for autism's inclusion in the Developmental Disabilities Act, procuring entitlements to developmental opportunities and education for their children.[69] Children with autism deserved the same services available to other developmentally disabled children. Protection alone was not enough. Autistic citizens had the right to education within the bounds of their capacities, and professionals and parents alike, under the influence of current research, saw those capacities broadening.

After he helped reshape research approaches to autism with his 1964 book *Infantile Autism*, Bernard Rimland became an important proponent of biomedical treatments. Rimland saw the founding of NSAC primarily as a means to promote behavior modification therapies based on the work of O. Ivar Lovaas, who was just then developing educational methods for use with autistic children. Rimland was willing to consider any treatment not premised on psychotherapy, and which made room for the neurological and biological differences of children with autism.

In the late 1960s, when Lovaas began his research on Skinnerian operant conditioning techniques for use with autistic children, many specialists viewed behavior analysis as antithetical to the developmentalist progression of other structured learning techniques. The method treated skills in isolation rather than as interlinked in cumulative developmental patterns. Although applied behavior analysis (ABA) was becoming established as a method for addressing problem behaviors in educational settings, it met with significant opprobrium from within the educational and medical communities devoted to autism. Bruno Bettelheim described operant conditioning disparagingly as "a method where small (or even severe) punishments, and rewards, are used to induce the subject to do what the experimenter wants him to do, and this without any consideration of why the subject chose to do what he did, or not to do what he does not do."[70]

Parents oriented toward whatever might work and hungry for practical advice worried less than others about theoretical inconsistencies. Lovaas's techniques suggested that skills could be acquired separately, using positive and negative reinforcements to establish basic imitation and language abilities. For children who had failed to acquire these skills in a typical pattern, sometimes a counterintuitive progression worked better. Bernard Rimland, although initially skeptical of operant conditioning techniques because it seemed unlikely that children would generalize beyond the laboratory or classroom, became convinced that children could acquire skills beyond those they were taught by therapists. They were literally learning how to learn through techniques that parents could apply themselves.[71] In 1965, Rimland visited Lovaas's laboratory at UCLA and arranged a meeting with some parents of "autistic-type" children.

> It was the beginning of a worldwide movement for active and vigorous parent participation in their children's training.
>
> As a result of that meeting, Dr. Lovaas set up an experimental workshop at UCLA in which the mothers were taught to use operant methods to teach their children speech, simple arithmetic, imitation, and other things. Before the one-hour daily sessions got underway the parents' letters to me were full of misgivings. Professionals had advised them for years to be permissive and loving and to accept anything the children did, in the hope that they would, someday, somehow, realize that they were *really* loved and accepted.[72]

These new techniques produced "spectacular" results. Although none of the children had been "made normal," many had improved in their communicative abilities and had fewer destructive and ritualistic behaviors. Lovaas, "impressed and pleased at the skill and determination the mothers showed in their work," invited them to lecture in his classes and made parent workshops part of his program.[73] Rimland immediately saw the promise of the technique and its mode of delivery, but he "felt that unless a grass roots (consumer's) movement of parents was started, it might take 20 years or more for behavior modification to filter through the walls of the ivory towers and begin to replace psychoanalysis and play therapy as the preferred treatments for autistic children."[74] At the founding meeting of NSAC, Rimland introduced the concept of behavioral treatment and went on to promote it in meetings across the country. However, it was not until 1987 that Lovaas published results on the use of discrete trials in treating autism and established ABA as a legitimate intervention for autism in the eyes of psychiatrists and policymakers.[75]

ABA used "discrete trial training," which required a child to perform a simple task in return for positive reinforcement in the form of applause, food, or a favorite toy. A child might initially be required simply to sit in a chair for a period of time or establish eye contact or respond to his or her name. If the child failed to complete the task, the therapist could give a physical prompt by guiding the child's hand to match a puzzle piece or deliver a requested object.[76] Tasks would then grow more complex. ABA primarily focused on language, drawing on B. F. Skinner's idea of language as a "stimulus function." Lovaas treated language as the basis for other social interactions. If children came to understand speech as a way to get what they wanted, they would begin to employ it spontaneously. Thus initial sessions often involved verbal prompts. Lovaas wrote that "we were interested in learning how the child's language might regulate his own behavior. In the back of our minds we had some notion that if the child learned to talk, somehow a conception of himself would emerge, that he might become more defined as a person, that he might show more self-control," a view of autism not entirely remote from psychoanalytic concerns with ego formation, although Lovaas's approach drew on learning theory instead.[77]

Throughout his work, Lovaas emphasized parents' participation. "We have been unable to help a child meaningfully in language development without the parent's active involvement."[78] Lovaas's handbook, *Teaching Developmentally Disabled Children: The ME Book*, became something of a bible for a generation of parents teaching themselves the techniques of behavioral analysis. The book had a warm and instructive tone: "You want to teach your child to listen more, to talk more, and to take more care of his personal needs." When Lovaas introduced new terms like "rewards" and "punishments," he repeated them so that readers would "understand them like an expert" by the time they had finished the book.[79] The book taught parents the technique of discrete trial training, guiding their efforts to employ contingent rewards in calculated rather than intuitive ways. The mother of one of the first children enrolled in Lovaas's Young Autism Project worried that she was expected to participate in the therapy when she had no professional training. Years later, she observed that while her son "seems to take his normality for granted," she did not. "Many years after his autistic behavior was extinguished, I find myself watching Drew, seeking opportunities to further his socialization."[80] She went on to earn a degree in learning disabilities and became a special education teacher.

If Oppenheim's 1961 *Saturday Evening Post* article showed that children with autism could be educated, the 1965 *Life* magazine article that made Lovaas's work visible to the American public had an even more immediate and far-reaching effect. While for many parents the story made education appear as a real possibility for their autistic children, the "Screams, Slaps and Love" of the title also made clear that Lovaas sometimes used violent aversive techniques—and demanded that the audience recognize those techniques as acts of loving intervention.[81] In a choice that Lovaas and his team perhaps should have anticipated, the editors selected photographs that showed "aversive events": a graduate student shouting only a few inches from a boy's face, his hand a blur as he moved to slap the child; a girl in a flowered dress cringing as her bare feet touched an electrified grid.[82] Lovaas and his team were surprised and dismayed at the editorial choices.[83] Immersed in their experimental work, they had not imagined how their techniques might look to observers. The *Life* article left a lasting impression, enough so that when Rimland began actively promoting behavior modification starting in 1966, "the hands would shoot up" and concerned audience members would demand his response to the images.[84] Even after he had discontinued the use of most aversives, an approving article in *Rolling Stone* in 1979 featured one of Lovaas's students using an "aversive no" delivered at a volume that made the reporter "jump a foot out of my chair."[85]

Many parents and therapists saw aversives as crucial to the care of autistic children, even with the risk that they might harm a child. Untreated, the child's behaviors might lead to far more severe injuries or death. Parents described children who dashed out into the street in front of cars and others who banged their heads ceaselessly and without discernable cause.[86] The debates within NSAC and among professionals illustrate how both groups understood the ethics of the emerging behavioral therapies. Their values and attitudes did not segment neatly across group lines, and instead suggest the centrality of experiential knowledge for individuals' decisions. In 1975 the board of directors of NSAC issued a white paper on behavior modification that gave "qualified support" to the use of aversive techniques to alleviate severely self-injurious behaviors. Responding to reports of abuses, the society adopted a "Position on the Abuse of Aversives" in 1985, stating that "many conscientious and concerned practitioners are aware that occasionally they must make judicious use of short-term, well-designed, and carefully monitored interventions that include aversive elements."[87] However, in 1988, the board of directors of the renamed Autism Society of America passed a resolution effectively calling for a ban on "aversive techniques" across the board.

This move provoked an extended letter-writing campaign by board members including Amy Lettick and Bernard Rimland, as well as by experts in the field such as Eric Schopler, former editor of the *Journal of Autism and Developmental Disabilities*, and Donald Cohen, director of the Yale Child Study Center. They argued that those who sought to ban these practices failed to understand the technical aspects of behavior modification. They suggested that critics, perhaps because of their lack of experience, did not recognize that even the daily routines for educating severely handicapped children would in some cases cause the children emotional distress, and that sometimes children had to be restrained. Schopler's support for the limited use of aversives mattered because his North Carolina-based program, Division TEACCH, emphasized the "culture of autism" and respect for the different ways that children with autism perceived the world. He suggested that those who opposed aversives made the same mistake as those who had once argued for psychotherapeutic treatment. They assumed that children with autism were "essentially normal" and therefore required only "normal experiences."[88]

In an exchange with Bernard Rimland in *The Advocate*, the newsletter of the Autism Society of America, Marcia Datlow Smith argued that "We have always had a technology of behavior change for even the most challenging behaviors. It has never been necessary to use strategies which are dehumanizing or cause discomfort or injury."[89] For Datlow Smith, a "functional analysis" of behavior in the context of a child's environment would allow practitioners to understand why problem behaviors occurred in the first place. "Misbehavior has a purpose," and identifying that purpose allowed therapists to address problems without resorting to aversives. Rimland disagreed. He countered that "the prohibitionists are mistaken in claiming that positive reinforcements *always* work. . . . Is a lifetime of blindness, of self-injury, or of being drugged insensible 24 hours a day—

often the real alternatives to aversives—more humane?" Although aversives could be misused, the results of "regulated and monitored" aversive techniques were lasting, were not to be confused with abuse, and in any event, "aversives are a fact of everyday life, quite unavoidable by any living creature," making the Autism Society of America resolution unnecessarily restrictive.[90]

The *Rolling Stone* reporter that Lovaas had startled with his "aversive no" wrestled with the idea that "conditioners" like Lovaas were merely imposing a "culturally relevant sense of order" on autistic children. After visiting families, special education classrooms, and speaking with Lovaas in Los Angeles, he came to a different conclusion:

> One transparent, unmystical giggle from one of these strange kids—one laugh that seems to exist in relation to something funny makes you see it: behaviorism as applied to autism is a stopgap, a methodology of convenience, but autism, like war, is hell, and until somebody produces that magic pill it seems to be all there is.[91]

Precisely because of their imperfections, behavioral techniques required parental support networks not only for knowledge about implementation but also for support and reassurance. With behavioral therapies, care became even more technical, the demands on the energy of therapists and parents even greater. Looking back on her daughter's early years, prior to the wide use of behavioral techniques, Clara Park described how "no one person, or family, could provide all that Jessy needed to grow. There was always someone else working with her in those days. . . . None had any training in special education or developmental psychology, but I claim for them the word 'therapist' without hesitation."[92] Behavioral therapies transformed some of those informal therapists into trained technicians. However, the alterations ran in both directions. Essentially laboratory techniques, behavioral therapies required social work to transform them into a viable intervention for use with disabled children.

Theorizing Child Development, Brain Injury, and Parental Work

From the start, biological theories of autism fit well with behavioral techniques. Even before researchers began to look for structural abnormalities in the brains of developmentally disabled children or to treat childhood disabilities through pharmacological therapies, books like Newell Kephart's *The Slow Learner in the Classroom* began with introductory chapters on neuroscience. Biological reasoning helped child psychologists establish their professional authority. Their approaches were methodologically diverse in ways that mattered to their designers and to parents, but the programs shared certain elements. They nodded to behaviorism in that they focused on discrete goals and did not assume specific mechanisms of neurological impairment. Their authors did not consciously avoid hypotheses about the neural or psychological basis for autism, but they also did not depend on them. They also shared an even more crucial element, which architects of behavioral programs recognized and documented as a clinical innovation: Parents played as large a part in therapy as the counselors had at the Orthogenic School in the 1950s and 1960s.

Ivar Lovaas had begun research on reinforcement techniques in 1961, and by 1966 he had enough data to report on the work in a peer-reviewed journal.[93] In their initial study, Lovaas and his team at UCLA found that all of the twenty children treated responded in some degree to behavior modification. Therapy worked better when it was practiced intensely over a longer period of time.[94] The UCLA group discovered something else in their follow-up research. Children treated in institutions improved, but their gains evaporated when they left the institution. There was an obvious solution.

> More and more we became involved in parent-training because the parents, as the child's therapists, could overcome these problems. That is, they could restructure the child's total environment and provide him with continuous treatment, which protected against the situational effects of reversibility.[95]

Lovaas realized some of the same things as Bettelheim, although their techniques were markedly different. Both spoke about the need for a "total environment" for treating children. In this case, the milieu was transported into the home. Lovaas saw other benefits in transforming parents into "explicitly trained cotherapists." The controversies surrounding behavioral therapies made it "absolutely essential, for both moral and legal purposes, that the parents be intimately familiar with how their child is treated." Parents who learned the techniques became "semi-professionals." In cases where parents placed their children in therapeutic group homes instead of providing therapy themselves, Lovaas referred to the caregivers as "*professional* parents."[96] Other behavior analysts likewise found that parents, nonscientists, could be trained in behavioral techniques with results superior to when children were treated in clinics isolated from their homes. Lovaas reached his conclusion alongside a growing number of other researchers and parents.

As a behaviorist, Lovaas thought that therapies should be used to eliminate problem behaviors in order to attain "normal functioning," not the more elusive "normality." His well-known 1987 study, portentously titled "Behavioral Treatment and Normal Intellectual and Behavioral Functioning in Young Autistic Children," involved an experimental group of nineteen compared with forty control children, all of whom had a clinical autism diagnosis consistent with the criteria in *DSM*-III. The researchers "sought to maximize behavioral treatment gains by treating autistic children during most of their waking hours for many years. Treatment included all significant persons in all significant environments."[97] Because the study demonstrated that a control group of children receiving less therapy had poor outcomes, and a follow-up study on the children receiving behavioral treatment indicated that they retained their skills, the publication helped justify wide implementation of Lovaas's methods. It did so despite Lovaas's warning that parents and teachers might find it difficult to achieve the level of intensity that his group had maintained in a laboratory setting with almost unlimited resources.

Many professional objections to the study focused precisely on this question of the relationship between success in the laboratory setting and in the far more complex environment of everyday life. Eric Schopler was concerned about Lovaas's use of aversive techniques and about the near-prohibitive expense of a forty-hour-a-week program. He warned parents to wait for definitive research on outcomes before demanding ABA programs under special education legislation.[98] Schopler and his colleague Gary Mesibov questioned the validity of Lovaas's 1987 study on several grounds, including the outcome measures, which involved IQ testing and placement in a classroom with typical children. These measures might have reflected a child's compliance on the one hand and school policy on the other, neither of which were relevant to the central communicative and behavioral features of autism.[99] Schopler and Mesibov also disagreed with Lovaas's criteria for subject selection and the composition of the control group.[100] Finally, they criticized Lovaas's willingness to move from his experimental results to the claim that autism did not have a basis in neurological impairment.[101] Despite their criticisms, the 1987 study established ABA as a gold standard for the treatment of children with autism.

During the late 1960s and early 1970s when Lovaas and his team at UCLA were developing their program, Eric Schopler and Robert Reichler were completing a pilot study and five-year experimental program based on related principles.[102] The University of North Carolina–based psychologists called their program Division TEACCH (Treatment and Education of Autistic and Communication-related handicapped CHildren). Although they designed their program only to test the efficacy of using parents as the "primary developmental agents" in educating children with autism, parents successfully petitioned the North Carolina state legislature for permanent funding.[103] The TEACCH system relied on "high external structures" organized around educational tasks, but unlike the program Lovaas had developed, Schopler and Reichler's program emphasized individualized developmental goals based on extensive diagnostic testing, the cognitive strengths of the child, and a nuanced understanding of the child's home and family environment.[104]

Like Kephart and Lovaas, Schopler and Reichler understood that parental work mattered to their program and that parents were the "primary experts" in the needs of their children.[105] Lovaas required that parents sign a formal "work-contract" that committed them to the program and its demanding schedule of therapy sessions. Schopler and Reichler were less regimented in their approach, opting for a treatment contract that allowed parents to define the focus of work. Treatments began by observing parents working with their child on an "organized activity" that would be similar to the tasks in the program.[106] Following this first session, parents and therapists took equal shares of the work. Along with a "parent consultant"—all staff members acted as both therapists and parent consultants, although not with the same family—parents observed therapists working with their child through a one-way screen, placing parents in literally the same position as professional clinical observers.[107]

Making the therapists try activities themselves kept them from suggesting tasks that sounded reasonable but were impossible to execute in practice. More important, the practice downgraded "the mystique and unfounded authority of the therapist who reports to parents from only private observations of the child" and allowed the parents to see the therapist, like them, suffer through failures, missteps, and frustrations.[108] In addition to the sessions observing therapists, parents developed and implemented home programs for their children, solving the problem of helping children—and their parents—generalize from the clinical and experimental setting. Martin Kozloff used a similar design for his parent-training program, including an "experimental" phase in a laboratory setting followed by a home program.[109]

Schopler and Reichler emphasized that their demonstrations were meant to help parents "develop a degree of self-consciousness inappropriate to normal child rearing. Indeed, they need to become experts on their own autistic child." Like Lovaas, they were impressed by the dedication of parents who drove up to four hours for visits, assiduously maintained daily logs, and often outdid trained therapists in the effectiveness of their work. Schopler and Reichler concluded that using parents as cotherapists and experts was not merely an expedient in the face of staff shortages.[110] Given confidence in their expertise, parents were often more capable than trained professional staff in working with their own children.

From Schopler's perspective, the stage had long been set for parents to participate fully as cotherapists for their children, even by treatment approaches that consciously excluded them. By identifying parents as the cause of their children's autism, Schopler argued, psychoanalytically inclined practitioners made observing and altering parental behavior through psychotherapy the focus of autism treatment for their children.[111] The experts in learning theory and behaviorism who arrived on the scene in the 1960s with experimental approaches to behavior modification identified children rather than parents as the target of intervention. However, many of the techniques they developed still demanded that parents alter their interactions with their children. Behaviorists worked with typical and brain-damaged children to establish methods for reinforcing behavior. In the process, they also established that parents made effective therapists. Despite the status of behavioral techniques as the province of skilled professionals, with training, parents might be in a position to surpass their efforts.[112]

Lovaas and his team had shown that in order for children to maintain the skills that they gained through behavioral programs and transfer them from the laboratory setting to their daily lives, parents had to become actively involved in therapy, even to the extent of setting agendas and carrying out experimental observations in their own homes.[113] These findings did not come out of the blue. Rather, they reflected a decade of experience by specialists in the wider field of mental health and children's behavior problems. Several factors had combined to increase involvement by parents in behavioral therapies. More children required services, and the number of trained mental health workers in a traditionally low-paid industry could not satisfy the demand. At the same time, behavioral therapies were becoming more intensive, leading researchers to consider the feasibility of using "nonprofessionals" in a range of mental health fields.[114] Researchers had first demonstrated that "untrained psychotherapists" like child-care workers and teachers could apply operant conditioning methods to treating autistic children in the early 1960s, and it was this work that directly inspired Lovaas's own research.[115]

Investigators also broadened the scope of behavioral therapies. They wanted to go beyond "contrived settings" in which "highly trained professional personnel" worked with children who were then left to their own devices when they returned home, and who often regressed. The evidence suggested that training had to be done in the "natural environment" for behavior change to take place, a finding that "inevitably leads to the parents." The techniques that had worked so well in the laboratory setting worked equally well in the home.[116] In some cases, parents could use the same social reinforcements that worked with their typical children, only systematizing their habitual responses to each of their child's actions. Investigators realized that generalization was not only a problem for the children. Parents might need help implementing techniques that they had learned in the laboratory.[117] Given an appropriate initiation into the techniques of behavioral therapy, however, even siblings could be trained as "behavior modifiers," with their parents acting as reliable experimental observers. Far from being unable to report objectively on improvements in their child, parents proved to be "at least as good as outside observers."[118]

In summary, a number of factors hastened the move from the clinic to the home and from expert personnel to parents as cotherapists. Clinicians cared about practical matters: children's ability to generalize skills in different settings, the pressing shortage of trained professionals to administer intensive therapy, and, later, the discovery that parents could indeed be expert, objective experimental observers of their own children. Learning theory, experimental psychology, and behaviorism had taught researchers to pay close attention to the naturally occurring "reinforcers" in a developmentally disabled child's environment. It was a short, if not always intuitive step to move from scrutinizing parents to engaging them as therapeutic practitioners who could be taught to behave in regularized and experimentally reliable ways.[119] Parents, as we have seen, were happy to receive guidance and support in their efforts to treat their children. Indeed, they worked hard to promote behavioral approaches.

Researchers sought to establish the validity of their techniques not only as therapeutic methodologies but also as components of general models. For parents, what they already knew to be effective from their experiences raising their typical children—knowledge about bodily states, preferences, and commonplace reinforcement and persuasion—formed the basis for a therapeutic relationship with their child. Not all parents had access to Newell Kephart, TEACCH, the Young Autism Project at UCLA, or any number of other site-specific programs, however, through which they might have learned the finer points of behavioral techniques. For the majority, their transformation into semiprofessionals and their incorporation of the techniques of behaviorism into their daily lives drew on more eclectic sources, working through trial and error.

Tales of Love and Labor

Accounts by parents make clear that expert knowledge and private life have continually intersected in the families of autistic children. Although some memoirs report startling transformations that could be compared to "conversion narratives," not all tell triumphant stories of total recovery.[120] Religion or spirituality plays a role in some, but they are mostly about hard work. A few examples among many published accounts illustrate the ways that parents have described their complicated roles as experts and caregivers, their views on the ethics of treatment, and the effort it took to transform laboratory techniques into practical interventions and homes into therapeutic environments.

Barry Kaufman describes his son, Raun, as a beautiful, seemingly typically developing child who regressed after a severe ear infection. Spinning objects fascinated him, and he grew increasingly remote. The Kaufmans became concerned about Raun's development while he was still quite young, and in the early 1970s they could not find programs willing to accept or even diagnose him at such an early age. Instead they began a vigorous process of self-education. They "contacted a dedicated specialist in behaviorism in California with a major university and a Federal grant to study and research autism"—probably Lovaas. They "investigated psycho-pharmacology. Psychoanalysis. Behaviorism. Vitamin Therapy. Nutritional analysis. The CNS (central nervous system) factor. The genetic theory. There were many opinions and non-opinions, many unsubstantiated theories and debatable assumptions."[121] They eventually turned to the Option Method, as taught by a "short, round, monk-like Friar Tuck sipping Coke and smoking one cigarette after another."

> As I listened, I felt a surging from within. Understanding a knowledge that always seemed to have been there, but that I had never really put into focus. As it crystallized rapidly for me, I began to recognize that my feelings and wants did come from my beliefs and that those beliefs could be investigated. And this pursuit of exposing and choosing beliefs was the subject of the Option Attitude:

"To love is to be happy with." It was not merely a philosophy, but a vision that would become the basis for our way of life and a foundation from which we would try to help Raun.[122]

Kaufman's book, published in 1976, is infused with the language of acceptance, withholding judgment, and consciously inspecting the origins of desires and needs. The Kaufmans brought in caregivers from among their extended community of yoga teachers, movement instructors, and mother's helpers. They became virtual members of the family. Resisting the idea that Raun's behaviors could be modified directly, the Kaufmans decided that the best intervention was to "join" Raun in his behaviors:

> Sometimes there would be as many as seven of us spinning with him, turning his isms into an acceptable, joyful and communal event. It was our way of being with him ... of somehow illustrating to him that he was okay, that we loved him, that we cared and that we accepted him wherever he was.[123]

Kaufman contrasted this approach with the methods of behavior modification advocated by Lovaas and others, which, although effective as an "educational tool," failed as the basis for a rehabilitation program. "The behaviorist, at the outset, makes many judgments about an autistic or deviant child and his behavior. Some activities are categorized and labeled as 'bad' or undesirable while others are deemed good. The underlying reasons for the behavior would not be considered applicable in treatment."[124]

The Kaufmans designed an alternative, three-phase program. The first phase required an attitude of total acceptance that would accompany any attempt to communicate with Raun. They envisioned the second phase as a "motivational/therapeutic experience" designed to "show Raun that our world was beautiful and exciting." Suzi Kaufman directed the third phase of treatment, a summer of intensive intervention with Raun, putting in seventy-five hours a week and nearing exhaustion at times.

> Often, we were asked how we felt about being deprived of other activities and interests. The word "sacrifice" was even suggested. If a painter or sculptor begins a piece and works year after year on it, no one would ask him how deprived he feels.[125]

The Kaufmans periodically sought the advice of professionals, with disappointing results. None of the doctors knew the research that Kaufman had been able to locate on his own.[126] Kaufman was dismayed at their lack of familiarity with the work of researchers like Lovaas and Kozloff. And while they opted to go it alone and had markedly different ideas about the reasons underlying successful treatments, they also learned much from the research at UCLA and elsewhere, sharing with other programs an emphasis on positive reinforcement and intensive parental involvement.[127] Other parents, likewise, heard about the Kaufmans' method and took what they could use from it. While Judy Barron didn't think that the method would have worked for her son, in their joint memoir *There's a Boy in Here*, she and her son Sean remembered how watching a TV special on Son-Rise led them to have their first honest conversation about his autism and their feelings for each other.[128]

Josh Greenfeld reacted with some skepticism to Kaufman's widely read account, to which he referred indirectly:

> I read of a parent who claims to have cured his autistic son through love, by accepting the kid the way he was. But when I read closely I realized the kid wasn't too developmentally disabled—never had any toilet problems, for example; and that the autism diagnosis came from the parent himself. The number of miracle workers who are quick to generalize from a false specific is frightening. And the effect is cruel beyond words on other parents.[129]

Greenfeld's *A Client Called Noah* covered the period during which his son Noah was placed in what Greenfeld called the "Operant Conditioning Center (OCC)," an unnamed residential school in the Southern California desert outside their home in Pacific Palisades, where Greenfeld worked as a screenwriter. The Center was run by a "strict Skinnerian," who "carries operant conditioning to its nth degree, and evidently that sometimes gets her into a lot of trouble." As Noah's time at the Center lengthened, the Greenfelds became concerned that "OCC is too committed to a program bent on breaking the kids spiritually through aversives," some of which bordered on physical abuse.[130] In response to their inquiries, the Center's president gave the Greenfelds an ultimatum: remove Noah from the Center or agree not to contest the Center's use of aversive techniques. They removed Noah.

Catherine Maurice, the pseudonymous author of *Let Me Hear Your Voice*, adhered to the fundamentals of ABA in treating her two children. By the 1980s, the family had access to therapy aides who used the principles of behaviorism and discrete trial instruction but were not directly affiliated with the UCLA program. The approach had found increasing acceptance. Still, Maurice found professionals inclined to counsel resignation and acceptance, an attitude that she "wasn't buying," especially after her own "crash course" in autism and her growing skill at identifying targets for therapy and problem behaviors. She saw an important difference between herself and professionals.

> They, with their clinical distance, were comfortably resigned; I was torn apart. Worse, they could delude themselves, with their degrees and their windy verbosity, that they were "helping." I could afford no such pretensions.[131]

However, even after reading *The ME Book*, Ivar Lovaas's manual for parents, she found videos of ABA "dehumanizing" and avoided watching her daughter's therapy. She nevertheless found herself drawn into the routine.

> It was ironic that I had mentally castigated Bridget [her child's therapist] for doing just this, when she had asked me to draw up my lists, but here I was learning how to look at my daughter's weaknesses and daily note all her autistic behaviors, just as Bridget did in the session logs. This clinical objectivity about something that a month ago had caused me the most searing pain was rendered possible, I suppose, by the simple fact that she was making sure and steady progress on all fronts.[132]

Such splintering of opinion among parents regarding even a single category of treatment such as behavioral therapies suggests autism's heterogeneity as a syndrome. It also points to the difficulty of conveying the practicalities of a home-based program in a memoir intended to persuade rather than instruct. However, these disagreements should not be read as demonstrating the fundamental incoherence of parents' ideas and accounts, but rather as evidence of their resourcefulness and willingness to draw on a range of methods in developing the programs best suited for their own children and families.

A Nation of Caregivers

Parents from the 1960s to the present have encountered a bewildering proliferation of techniques and practices for treating autism, including a range of distinct methods broadly categorized as early intensive behavioral intervention (EIBI). Their advocacy groups, like parents themselves, have balanced an attitude of acceptance with one of aggressive treatment-seeking in the face of highly variable evidence. Children with autism respond inconsistently to treatments, necessitating an experimental approach in each case. Parents of children with autism have weighed their desires for recovery against the apparent contentment of their children. In doing so against a shifting landscape of treatment options, they navigate terrain as unfamiliar as the "research frontier" of reproductive technologies that Rayna Rapp memorably describes. Clara Park wrote that contrary to the claims then current in psychoanalytic theory, it was always clear that her daughter was happy. But Park still refused to "leave Jessy to her empty serenity."[133]

Like many others, the Parks came to behavior modification in the context of using other therapeutic strategies and found that it solved some problems beautifully and failed to address others. Within the field of disability studies, aggressive efforts to cure are often seen as normative efforts at social control on a micro level. Such a perspective assumes that enlightened accommodation and intrusive rehabilitative technologies are easily distinguished from each other. Critics often view disability as a social construct in the deepest sense, the failure of a society that demands excessive standardization and consistency from its citizens and penalizes those who fail to conform. As proxies and spokespeople for their affected children, parents who seek to apply behavioral or biomedical techniques make the opposite determination, that their children must want to become more interactive, communicative, and socially cognizant.

Daily life with a child with autism does not often assume a stable pattern. It is more frequently a matter of finding tentative workable arrangements in the context of chronic difficulties. Problem behaviors are brought under control with one approach just as new ones emerge, demanding alternative strategies. The onset of adolescence can present both social and biological challenges after a period of relative calm. In a broader national context, thresholds are crossed as educational systems become overburdened with children with complex social and cognitive needs. These processes can lead to the systematic abandonment of populations, especially those who "age out" of educational systems or other types of support. Amy Lettick founded Benhaven at the height of deinstitutionalization, a process begun in 1963 but that picked up speed with changes in medical entitlements brought about by Medicaid and Medicare and the growth of the mental patient's rights movement.[134] The absence or deterioration of both community and institutional supports leaves families as exclusive providers of ongoing care for disabled relatives. This structural failure to recognize the uncompensated labor of familial caregivers contributes to untold hardships on an individual level. The families of disabled children, like those who care for the chronically ill, the elderly, or people with severe mental illnesses, have few options for their continuing care.

Behavioral techniques for treating autism have been subject to continual criticism. Skeptical experts in other areas of autism research have questioned their ability to effect meaningful changes in developmental trajectories, while psychological and educational professionals have criticized the techniques for their harshness and failure to take into account the communicative or functional meanings of behaviors. Others have questioned the lack of standard certification for practitioners. Therapists, often students employed at low wages, frequently cannot stay with families for the full course of treatment, making outcomes uncertain. Self-advocates with autism and Asperger syndrome have called the techniques abusive. Indeed, self-advocates have targeted ABA in particular for withering criticism. In the United States, insurance companies often refuse to cover ABA as an "un-proven" treatment, although both the Autism Society and the National Academies of Science recommend twenty-five hours a week of ABA as a best practice for treating autism.[135]

Parents played a key role in developing behavioral therapy methods during the 1960s and through the 1980s through their advocacy, their participation in experiments, and through teaching themselves the techniques and teaching others about them. To a significant extent, those who developed these techniques did so with just this type of participation in mind. Indeed, the intensive approaches literally required the participation of parents in the therapeutic process, and the redesign of the home as a therapeutic environment. State-run Early Intervention programs continue to situate parents as ambiguously authoritative semiprofessionals, reiterating their right to serve as "service coordinators" for their children, while simultaneously framing families as "targets of intervention" and professional scrutiny.[136] Promoters of behavioral therapies have framed them as a means of transitioning children into educational settings, but that fact does not negate the intensity of demands on parents for the duration of their use.[137]

When insurers refuse payments for behavioral therapies, citing the failure to reproduce the rates of success in Lovaas's original studies, parents are left to pay out of pocket or seek treatment through the special education programs in their child's school district.[138] Some parents, frustrated with the lack of quality or consistency in the therapists that they employed, have earned master's degrees in behavioral therapy in order to run their children's programs themselves.[139] Children with autism are often eligible for treatment in a public educational setting through the 1990 Individuals with Disabilities Education Act. However, school districts may resist providing behavioral therapies like ABA because of the expense involved, as much as $40,000–$80,000 per child each year, and so parents have become experts of another kind, legal representatives for their children at the annual meetings required by law to settle the terms of a child's Individualized Education Program (IEP).[140] Although school districts argued that parents "lack professional experience and judgment and are 'emotionally invested in the outcome of the case,'" the Supreme Court ruled that parents had a legitimate personal interest in their children's education, rendering it both acceptable and constitutionally mandated that they be allowed to represent their children.[141]

Behavioral therapies, as everyday semiprofessional activities on the part of parents, established two important precedents in the history of the autism diagnosis and the population that it defined. By making parents technicians, they provided structural and pragmatic support for what parents had argued all along and what they would come to argue more energetically: Parents were experts on their own children, in terms of their individual symptoms and their idiosyncratic responses. By establishing that children with autism could be educated and that such practices could take place in the context of a theory of neurological difference and sensory atypicality as much as one of meaningful behavior, they provided a context for later developments.

In the ensuing years, an emphasis on surveillance, early identification, and intervention meant that parents spent less time seeking explanations before they were able to act. An increasingly standardized diagnosis and growing empirical support for treatment gave parents better guidance in their decisions about their child. And research in genetics and neuroscience provided a foundation for understanding children with autism as biologically different from typical children. However, parental knowledge remained central to daily life.

Parents Speak: The Art of Love and the Ethics of Care

Disability studies in the university emerged from the disability rights movement of the 1970s and 1980s. Conversations about autism are inevitably also about issues that have occupied both scholars and activists. They range from philosophical questions about defining disability and the ethics of treatment to policies regarding access to health care and living supports, deinstitutionalization and patient's rights, the Individuals with Disabilities Education Act (IDEA), and inclusive education.

A history of autism focused specifically on parental experience and knowledge cannot hope to incorporate all the lessons that disability studies teaches us, in particular, that we take seriously the accounts of people with disabilities themselves. As I mentioned in the introduction, there are many women and men with autism diagnoses who are capable spokespeople. A number of them are passionate advocates of neurodiversity, the concept of accepting and accommodating atypical cognitive styles and personality types as valuable elements of human difference.[1] Advocates insist on the importance of respecting the desires of the person with the disability, first and foremost, in policies and treatments directed at them, a position best expressed in the imperative "nothing about us without us."[2]

Many draw on their experience of autism to question not only policies but also psychiatrists' assumptions, maintaining, for example, that the diagnostic distinction between "low" and "high-functioning" autism is specious. This segmentation fails to acknowledge the range of strengths and weaknesses of any individual. Dividing the autism spectrum, needless to say, divides people. Self-advocates reject the claim that those able to communicate and live without assistance are not qualified to weigh in on interventions directed toward those who are unable to care for them-selves. Self-advocates have routinely argued that attempts to ameliorate or cure autism are motivated by parents' self-interest. Parents, they say, long for a typical child who conforms to dominant standards of normal functioning. Their pursuit of cures can make them oblivious to their chil-dren's own desires or needs.[3] Self-advocates have also criticized federal allocations of research funds on similar grounds. Funding for studies of autism's causes and treatment eclipses outlays for research into services and supports.[4]

In making such claims, they invoke arguments from the disability rights movement.[5] The movement has tended to view medical discourse about disabilities suspiciously and with often well-deserved scorn. The dominant medical model of disability emerged from rehabilitation medi-cine for wounded soldiers that aimed to return them to their pre-injury level of functioning. As a consequence, many doctors learned to view dis-abilities against a concept of normality or normal functioning. Activists in the 1960s and 1970s began to challenge this concept of disability. It valued individuals only in terms of their productivity, framing disability in terms of barriers to participation in the workplace, and it automatically assumed that a disabled person was less than whole or complete. Disability stud-ies offered an alternative, the "social model," which holds that the experi-ence of disability emerges from a person's social and physical environment rather inhering in an individual. Accommodations in the built and human environments are the way to address disability. The burden should not be on the individual but on society, which effectively creates the experience of disability by failing to accommodate human variations.

In the United States, the history of autism cannot be written without reference to the history of cognitive disabilities more generally. The idea that parents caused their children's autism or that autism was a product of the child's will resembled other moral explanations for disability common in the nineteenth and early twentieth centuries. Although expressed in a psychotherapeutic language, the demand that both children and parents achieve a cure through self-understanding had much in common with ear-lier theories of intellectual disability that saw cognitive deficits as failures of character. The association that professionals drew between criminal-ity and intellectual disabilities further stigmatized those conditions, and current arguments over the presence or absence of intellectual disabilities associated with autism attest to the persistence of that stigma.[6] Parents' work to create the National Society for Autistic Children (NSAC) and find effective treatment methods during the late 1960s and 1970s took place at a time when parents of children with many types of disabilities had begun to cooperate to obtain educational rights for their children. Current developments take place in a system defined by legislation enacted during the 1970s, including the Education for All Handicapped Children Act, which transformed the experience of many childhood disabilities.[7]

By focusing on interventions intended to cure, ameliorate, or reframe autism as a medical condition, my discussion may seem remote from the concern in disability studies with recognizing each individual's fundamental value as a whole person with a right to autonomy over decisions about his or her care. If anything, mine is an account of the relentless medicalization of autism. Parents adopted and integrated expert discourses from behaviorism, biochemistry, psychology, and genetics in their efforts to treat their children. In the process, their advocacy work centered more on raising awareness and funds than on examining the social factors that have contributed to the perception of autism as a severe disorder in need of treatment. I focus on caregivers because understanding how they make distinctions between their knowledge and that of professionals helps show how acts of love are part of biomedical work. This means telling a story about the shaping of autism through different sets of biomedical discourses and practices as opposed to a history of the social production of autism as a disability.

The "semiprofessional" parents who have intervened in the production of autism demonstrate facility with medical terminology and practices and argue for their own situated expertise on their children. They may be aware of self-advocates' arguments, but they also act knowing that their choices early on may affect their child's entire life. Some children with autism will become adults with the same needs and limitations that they had as children, while others will go on to live more independent lives. However, *all* children remain absolutely dependent on their caregivers and unable to express their needs with complete freedom, at least for their first few years. This is significant for thinking about the decisions that parents must make.

Chapters 2 and 3 identified a number of sites in which love has functioned as a form of practice or technique in interventions to address the syndrome of autism. I want to take a step back and revisit the idea of love as an introduction to the chapters that follow. Love relates to practical knowledge, the ethics of care, and concepts of "moral personhood," familial commitments, and dependence, themes I introduced at the beginning of this book. It also matters to treatment choices and to the ethics of interventions, all of which are central to the final three chapters on genetics research, biomedical interventions, and immunizations. Gail Landsman has described how

> mothers of disabled infants and toddlers also suggest that mothers, because of their commitment to their child rather than to a stated prognosis or to their own professional ego, have the passion and freedom to gather the *same* biomedical information as physicians do, and in some instances, to come to know more than a particular medical practitioner not only about their child but about their child's disability and treatment options.[8]

Throughout this book, I extend Landsman's insight by describing how caregivers have applied their expertise not only in providing therapies for the child in their care, but also in helping to shape research programs and treatment options within the biomedical community devoted to that child's diagnosis. Here I provide additional examples of how they have accomplished this and how professionals have responded.

I hope to accomplish two things by taking the time to discuss how parents think about treatment. The first is to draw attention to the practical forms of bioethical reasoning used by parents and practitioners in the course of everyday life and work. Disability studies can help draw attention to the practice of caregiving and affective work as central to biomedical practices and, therefore, crucial to debates about the ethics of those practices. The second goal is to show how studying the application of medical interventions matters for disability studies, a discipline that has traditionally been concerned with normative questions that are not always the focus of work by sociologists of science and medicine. To do this, I need to begin by discussing how experts have represented parents' ability to reason and make decisions.

The Demands and Desires of Parenting

As we have seen, parents of children with autism have been scrutinized nearly as much as their children. Psychologists and anthropologists studied them for clues about a child's "choice" of symptoms.[9] Beginning with Leo Kanner, experts also noted interesting parallels between parents' personalities and those of their children, although it was hard to determine whether these shared traits reflected common genetic factors or parents' reactions to their child's unusual behavior and emotional remoteness. Behavioral therapists sought to harness parents' knowledge, but focused on the therapeutic interaction rather than on the minutiae of daily life with an autistic child. Professionals finally realized that therapies could take place within households rather than the laboratory, but homes came with their own set of pitfalls. Behavioral programs often broke down under the stress and, at moments, chaos of daily life.[10]

Stress is a recurring theme in writing about these parents. Researchers distinguish it from the predictable stress of raising a child with a severe disability.[11] Young children with autism often appear typical to onlookers, who then tend to blame parents for their children's "misbehavior."[12] Some researchers think that raising a child with autism is uniquely taxing because the children have a difficult time relating socially and emotionally.[13] If part of parents' stress stems from their children's difficulties with social reciprocity and part from stigma, a significant portion comes from managing behavioral issues, including problems with eating and sleep and emotional outbursts.[14] Parents of children with autism report more extreme experiences of isolation and loneliness than do parents of children with other developmental disabilities. The loneliness is no doubt reinforced when doctors tell them that their child can learn to mimic appropriate behaviors but will never share feelings with them, and that what they believe about their child's sociability and capacity to interact with them is an illusion.[15]

Given the levels of parental demands and stress, it is not surprising that even sympathetic researchers characterize much of what parents do as coping strategies. Their turns to religion or use of support services and, in particular, their activism are ways of coming to terms with a harrowing diagnosis and uncertain prognosis.[16] There is a cost, however, to seeing such actions as determined exclusively by parents' involuntary reactions to their child's symptoms rather than by their intelligence or beliefs—a mistake similar to seeing every act carried out by a child with autism as a symptom of the disorder: It robs conscious actions of their value and intentionality. As Gail Landsman explains, when parents disagree with doctors about applying the label of developmental "delay" rather than "disability" to their child, they are not denying the obvious but making a strategic choice about their own level of investment. Their choice to believe that their attention and nurturance can continue to shape their child's development yields concrete results.[17] It is no accident that parents describe their own actions as those of knowledgeable observers and rational actors.

Parents Speak

In 1974, the *Journal of Autism and Childhood Schizophrenia*, then the only journal devoted exclusively to research on autism, began publishing a section called "Parents Speak." It ran for slightly over a decade, until 1985. It was a remarkable column, coming at a time when the majority of research that focused on the parents of children with autism did so only in order to assess the parents' level of pathology and identify exactly how parents had caused their child's disability.[18] In the course of the column's life, contributors used their own experiences to identify significant characteristics of autism that researchers would not investigate for another three decades. More important, they demonstrated that alongside their technical acumen, they were willing to address problems relating to the ethics of treatment. In contrast, practitioners without autistic children tended to define those ethical problems as outside their area of concern, when they acknowledged their existence at all.

The influence of Eric Schopler, the new editor-in-chief, was evident in the decision to begin "Parents Speak." He had to defend the choice to at least one skeptical reader who feared that "the scientific level might well be lowered as a result."[19] As a founder of Division TEACCH, Schopler favored an ecological approach to autism predicated on seeing parents as cotherapists with professionals. The first editor of the column, Mary S. Akerley, then president of the National Society for Autistic Children (NSAC), wanted to encourage dialogue as a way to counteract the increasing specialization among autism researchers, often at the expense of a comprehensive view of the child in their care. She valued parents' perspectives in particular because "their observations, interpretations, and suggestions for research and/or treatment are perhaps more likely to represent the problems of the autistic child than the specialized professional concerns."[20]

It turned out that parents had quite a bit to say. One discussed the "Near-Normal Autistic Adolescent," a "subgroup of autistic persons with unique problems and needs, not previously given separate attention." [21] These young people were often hungry for social interaction but unsure of how to seek it. David Park, Clara Claiborne Park's husband and Jessy Park's father, described trying operant conditioning with his daughter, years before the publication of Lovaas's 1987 study on efficacy.[22] In another article, Park marveled at the mathematical complexity of his daughter's scheme to order her world. Working to understand the "entirely personal kind of meaning" of these intellectual structures might, at the very least, provide a source of shared interest and conversation with an autistic child that could help them to develop speech.[23] Parents debated the use of aversive techniques and reviewed books and memoirs by other parents. There was even a selection of poems about children with autism.[24] Throughout, they insisted on the irreducible importance of their own observations as a kind of data that experts were incapable of providing.

The column also provided a forum for parents to suggest directions for research and treatment, often before professionals showed interest in the same areas. Parents noticed responses in their own children that seemed like promising avenues for investigation. In a 1975 column titled "Hunches on Some Biological Factors in Autism," Ruth Christ Sullivan wondered whether there might be a connection linking rheumatoid arthritis, celiac disease (an immune reaction to wheat protein), and autism, as the three seemed to run in families. She was particularly interested in the gastrointestinal symptoms that parents reported in their children.[25] A section of a column titled "Why Do Autistic Children. . .?" commented on the routine observation that children with autism seemed much calmer, more communicative, and better oriented when they were running a fever. Might this be a clue to some underlying biological mechanism of the disorder? Only decades later would researchers systematically investigate these connections, in both cases finding that the parental observations were largely correct.[26]

The column also became a place to explore the ethics of treatment. At one point, Mary Akerley proposed the subtitle "Values in Conflict," since so many of the entries dealt with the often wrenching process of weighing a child's health against his or her freedom, or a child's needs against those of the family.[27] One article about the successful use of a diet to treat a child's "cerebral allergies" occasioned short commentaries by Eric Schopler, the Nobel Prize–winning chemist Linus Pauling, an allergist, and a psychiatrist on the responsibilities of practitioners and national organizations like NSAC in publicizing promising but unproven treatments.[28]

As editor, Mary Akerley took the opportunity to suggest some ways that the doctor–patient or, more accurately, the doctor–parent relationship might be improved. In the mid-1970s, long after researchers had putatively abandoned psychogenic theories of causation, psychological professionals still had the unsettling habit of blaming parents for their children's autism. Others sought to protect parents by delaying diagnosis, withholding prognoses, and discouraging them from doing their own research. Most parents, Akerley pointed out, were doing their own research anyway. Doctors needed to understand that "hard as it is to live with one's mistakes, it is infinitely more terrible to have to live with someone else's." She also called for professionals to take a more active role alongside parents in advocating for services for autistic children.[29] Professionals responded approvingly to the column, although few believed that the criticisms applied to them. Rather, they described other "incompetent" psychiatrists who "would not survive in most of our therapeutic programs," or doctors who had unsuccessfully treated their patients in the past.[30]

The column also brought parents into debates that originated on the research pages of the journal. One of the most anguished discussions of the period concerned the use of negative reinforcement or "aversives" in treating children with intractable behavior problems including self-injury, aggression, and running away—sometimes into traffic. A 1976 review article on the use of shock in autism treatment triggered responses, often heartfelt, from both parents and professionals that continued for two years.[31] One of the most telling came from a North Carolina parent who had been forced to place her son in an institution. She wrote, "Every 10 days I make the 200 mile trip to visit him. I have glimpsed competence. Risk/benefit?"[32] A decade later, as activists called for full rights and education for people with cognitive disabilities, professionals took up the appropriateness and content of sex education. Parent respondents reminded readers that they were already making decisions about what their children needed to understand about sex and providing the instruction themselves, at home.[33]

In 1977, Ruth Christ Sullivan took over the editorship of the "Parents Speak" column, leading off with an article by Katharine Sangree Stokes about "Planning for the Future of a Severely Handicapped Child." It was an issue that was largely absent from the journal and neglected by experts on the whole. Nonetheless, Christ Sullivan reminded readers, Stokes spoke to a concern "that parents (and truly concerned professionals) talk about when they are speaking with their hearts."[34] Like other parents, Stokes had "worked to find, to support, and to create the necessary educational and social opportunities" for her child. Although these were the immediate concerns, she wanted to address the thinking "that occupies parents in the long nights after their more immediate cares are set aside."[35]

Stokes questioned the readiness of any institution to provide what the family setting did for her son, namely, connecting with and valuing him as an individual. For instance, a school's efforts to teach her adult son age-appropriate behaviors might actually work against his interests. She imagined a situation in which an otherwise dangerous encounter with a police officer unaware of his condition might be mitigated by his thumb-sucking.[36] Other parents chimed in, suggesting that the best possible environment for their children might not be one that superficially appeared normal, but rather one that provided for their particular developmental needs in ways that allowed them to continue to grow and learn. An autism label served their children only in some contexts. It might sometimes be useful to "consider efforts to unlabel our children."[37] One of the respondents, Clara Park, concluded that those who helped her daughter grow were "those who take her where she is, responding warmly to both woman *and* child, continually alert to the possibilities for normalization, but recognizing their limits, and warmly responding to her simple humor and guilelessness, her charm."[38] The care that parents and other primary caregivers provided was profoundly difficult to replicate in a standard or conventionalized format. Nevertheless, they knew that someone would eventually have to learn to do their work for them.

Deinstitutionalization and "normalization" were important trends in the care of children with autism and other developmental disabilities during the 1970s. Professionals wrote about these issues in the pages of the journal, but parents also weighed in, urging researchers to recognize the gulf between daily realities and the ideal of disabled children experiencing the typical rhythms of daily life rather than the artificial routines of institutions.[39] In this instance, career employees of treatment centers and others who worked with autistic children on a daily basis also commented. The portrait of normalization as a rigid and prescriptive set of practices offered by Gary Mesibov, a psychologist, had failed to take into account the flexibility of such programs in practice.[40]

Community care came up again in the 1980s as the column became a place where the "autism family" could air opposed views on the desirability of deinstitutionalization and the degree to which the approach made room for the individualized programs that seemed to work for many severely affected children. Christ Sullivan summarized the responses to a new NSAC resolution in favor of closing residential institutions.[41] Amy Lettick, who had founded Benhaven in 1967, opposed it, pointing out that for many children with autism, the best, least restrictive environment was not necessarily the one with the least structure.[42] Ivar Lovaas and Corinne Fredricks, another parent, believed that the resolution provided important support for the movement toward group homes where people with developmental disabilities could live alongside other members of the community, having new experiences and learning skills that they would never have acquired in an institution.

The long run of columns in the *Journal of Autism and Childhood Schizophrenia / Journal of Autism and Developmental Disorders* revealed parents eager to share their knowledge and ideas in an academic forum, aware that they had data that clinicians and researchers didn't possess. That information came in part from parents' ability to see their children as whole persons and to observe them throughout their daily lives. Although parents wanted treatments, they were also the first to promote the then-controversial view of autism as a static condition to be dealt with by recognizing the value of their child's unique attributes and, where feasible, accommodating their special needs. Others were the first to suggest interventions that became standard practice. This focus on everyday life and a child's immediate needs shows parents, through their entanglement with their child, charting a complicated course between treatment and acceptance.[43] Finally, the contributions to the "Parents Speak" column remind us that many who contributed were also professionals who had entered the field in part due to their experience as parents.

The social role of parent provides no assurance that a person will make the best of all possible decisions for his or her child, nor does it make that individual a better authority than the child on questions about that child's own condition. It certainly does not grant a person sudden and effortless medical and neurological expertise. What the identity can signify is a very specific and intimate understanding of a child's physical and emotional character, born of years of close observation and experience. In most cases, it also signifies insights gained as a result of the special attentiveness that comes from love. Parents learn to understand their child both as an individual and as a member of their family unencumbered by assumptions about what the child's particular diagnosis or symptoms may mean. As Gail Landsman explains,

> In one's own home, alone with the child and apart from the stresses of "competitive mothering" or medical diagnoses, a mother comes to understand her child as simply himself/herself, neither terribly unusual nor comparable to other children on any scale that makes sense.[44]

Landsman's insight is particularly relevant to questions about the ethics of treatments designed to ameliorate the symptoms of autism. Those debating the ethics of interventions tend to assume that the choice is between two alternatives, to act aggressively to cure the disorder or to respect the integrity of autistic personhood by eschewing treatment altogether.[45] This yields little practical advice for those considering treatments designed to ameliorate elements of autism but unlikely to cure it. Landsman's interviews with mothers of children with a range of disabilities also demonstrate that few see the choices so starkly. Most of the women that Landsman spoke with effortlessly negotiated the tensions between apparently opposed perspectives.[46] They saw their child as a complete person, worthy of value and respect, not despite but in terms of his or her disability. At the same time they were committed to working to increase their child's opportunities for pleasure and new experiences in ways that often involve efforts to alleviate some of their impairments.[47] Their position, and that of many parents of children with autism, is not far from more recent writing in disability theory. Scholars like Tom Shakespeare now argue that the social model of disability unfairly disregards both the reality of bodily suffering and the fact that impairments do inevitably alter individual experience, sometimes in painful ways.[48]

Contemporary Developments

As we have seen, for parents of children with autism, experimentation is central. I describe the types of parental knowledge that have mattered in the context of a series of successive, competing, and often incommensurable arguments about autism's causes and about the correct course of treatment. I do so largely for ease of exposition. In reality, parents range across theories, practices, and paradigms in treating their children. Their approaches reflect a kind of biomedical syncretism, where they are behaviorists one moment, biochemists another, and homeopaths later, often unconcerned about the degree of fit among rival theories. Their choices can seem irrational to experts who proceed from theory to treatment, but they reflect a pragmatic logic rooted in caregiving and defined by practice. Even more than other professional groups that treat children with autism, parents are technicians first, although some may become theorists. Their attitude toward their children is caring, but it is also experimental—as most childrearing is.

The relationship between affective commitment and specific, practical knowledge unites places as disparate as the Orthogenic School at the University of Chicago and Defeat Autism Now! conferences. The young female counselors at the Orthogenic School were "repeatedly bitten, kicked, defecated upon or otherwise abused," but they tolerated these behaviors out of devotion to the students and a belief that they had provoked them, at least in part.[49] Similar motives drive parents who, decades later, administer taxing schedules of nutritional supplements and detoxification agents to their children. Both therapies raise troubling ethical questions, at least for some. Parents and counselors consider their affective commitment an advantage, while critics say that devotion blinds them to consequences. Love is never enough, but those parents and counselors might argue that at times it, or other forms of affective knowledge, accounts for the difference in decisions that are otherwise too hard to make. Medical practitioners and even some sociologists see parents' choices as reactive, motivated by their despair at a diagnosis. Parents have a more subtle understanding of the knowledge and values that they bring to determining the right course of action. Despite their frequent need to choose among undesirable alternatives in order to care for their children, they indeed weigh the ethical consequences of their actions.

Recognizing parents' ethical agency is crucial because parents often have to make decisions for children who are unable to do so for themselves. Such choices are sometimes shaped by parents' hopes for a typical child but more often by deep appreciation of their child's individuality and unique strengths. Parents also understand that while some adults with autism lead lives in which they experience their autism as a source of strength rather than a liability, many more of them, the majority, remain dependent on extensive services and support, often in highly restrictive environments where they have limited autonomy.[50] In a sense self-advocates represent another set of experts that parents may call on for inspiration. I take up some of their arguments in the next chapter on genetic and neurological models of autism.

Although the number of individuals diagnosed with autism is increasing, the vast majority of people in the United States and elsewhere are neurotypical. The task for most of us in the years ahead, as researchers, educators, journalists, neighbors, and voters, is to learn how to interact with autistic people in an ethical and honest fashion, even if their perceptual and emotional worlds are different from ours. Parents have longer experience in this task than the rest of us. When we stop thinking about them as limited by their commitments to and love for their children and start thinking of them as rational actors whose knowledge is enhanced by the attentiveness that love encourages, it seems clear that they represent one community that has already thought long and hard about the ethics of treatment, the desirability of normalization, and the difficulty of balancing respect, protection, and care.[51] The rest of us are compromised, too, by our anxieties, commitments, and desires. Parents have thought more than many of us about what these feelings do and the help that they might provide in the production of knowledge.

The remainder of this book considers different perspectives on autism treatment, theories of etiology, and the implicit and explicit ethical concerns that influence both theory and professional practice. As parents enter into professional areas of authority they do so by claiming that their love helps them determine how best to understand and treat their children. These claims about love are strong and sometimes risky.

Two

Brains, Pedigrees, and Promises:

Lessons from the Politics of Autism Genetics

Patricia Stacey is a memoirist who attributes her son's recovery from autism to "floor time," an intensive program of early behavioral intervention. Like many parents' accounts, Stacey's story of her child's diagnosis and treatment includes an explanation of autism's causes. In her version, seemingly unaffected parents exhibit, in milder form, the same behaviors and sensitivities as their children. Autism "runs in the family."[1] When Stacey describes how a therapist's passing comment about her tendency to "space out" during sessions with her son helped her recognize her own sensory oversensitivities and defensiveness, she is speaking to a wider community of parents for whom genetic claims make obvious sense. "Sometimes the children we are working with are just exaggerated versions of their parents," her son's therapist observes.

> Time and again when I have been talking to women with children with autism, I hear a resonant story. I heard nearly the same story twice from two different mothers who had never met. The couple goes to a lecture on autism or visits a therapist shortly after their child receives a diagnosis. The couple learns that people with autism have systematic minds, like things in certain orders, have trouble with transitions—that people with autism are not social—that they may be good with math and music, or they are highly visual. The husband walks out of the classroom, or office, and says, "My God, they've just been describing me."[2]

That shock of recognition concerning the heritability and genetic nature of autism comes at a moment when the category has been rendered relatively stable through standardized behavioral screening tools and an entry in the *Diagnostic and Statistical Manual of Mental Disorders*. It probably could not have happened at an earlier moment. Parents might have noted similarities between themselves and their children in passing, but they and their children's doctors would not have shared an understanding of autism as a genetic syndrome of unknown origin, among the "most heritable" of disorders of its kind.[3] For parents to raise millions to fund genetic research and donate blood and tissue samples from themselves and their children to fuel that research, autism first had to become a genetic disorder. That process occurred in tandem with diagnostic standardization. However, clearer diagnostic boundaries were not sufficient to make autism visible as "genetic." That process required that researchers learn to exchange psychological explanations for genetic ones, while characterizing the disorder in terms of broadly defined behavioral symptoms that could be identified in family lineages. They had to exchange their reservations about the existence of environmental causes for certainties about prenatal origins and faith in evocative animal models of behaviorally similar syndromes.

Organizational spokespersons, self-advocates, and relatives of people with autism work in a landscape shaped by the history of autism genetics. Autism has become genetic, but it has become so in the wake of the long history of theorizing about autism as a form of organic affective deficit in those diagnosed or as caused by a deficit of emotion in their parents. In the present, acts of speaking for people with autism are often legitimated by the idea of heritability as much as by claims of parental caring and involvement. Likewise, when self-advocates speak from the perspective of their identities as autistic people, they ground their claims in presumed neurological and genetic likeness to other autistic people. The idea of genetic similarity in autism research and advocacy provides ethical legitimacy and entitlement. In stories such as this one, where individuals choose one definition of a disorder (as "genetic"), thereby excluding others (for instance, theories of environmental etiology, psychological frameworks, or purely behavioral descriptions), it is important to acknowledge the workings of desire. Self-advocacy groups and parents are not merely pawns, expressing the genetic optimism of scientists because that is what they have been told to believe. They want autism to be genetic and they invest financially and emotionally in a definition of it as such.

Genetics provides an effective vocabulary for expressing responsibilities and experiences of membership that develop out of love, friendship, and loyalty. These connections have been established in a number of ways. Parent groups and researchers reframed autism as a neurological and genetic condition during the 1960s as an alternative to psychogenic theories of autism. In the 1990s, parent groups began to dispute the proper organization of research on biological materials from themselves and their children. Two of these groups were able to mobilize the partiality associated with their status as parents as an asset as they constructed new institutions for producing facts about autism genetics. In the process, they mobilized representations of ideal scientific practice drawn both from scientists' accounts and from popular representations of science to demand acceptable behavior from the scientists that they sought to enlist.

In the present, advocates for autism and Asperger syndrome (AS) accept a genetic and neurological definition of the syndrome, but protest the use of behavioral and sometimes medical interventions. Even as they embrace genetic characterizations of autism, they fear the possible outcomes of genetic research applied to prenatal testing or treatment. They argue that aggressively seeking interventions devalues autistic traits and tendencies. Autism represents a type of neurological diversity that becomes a disability only due to discrimination and stigma.

Advocates' efforts to define an "autistic culture" and "autistic voices" remind us that genetic identities are only as fixed as the meanings attached to them. For instance, it is not entirely clear what it means to be "a little autistic" when psychiatrists or genetics researchers use the term in casual conversation to describe a family member of a child with full-spectrum autism. That researchers and increasingly the general public understand what this means, that "a little autism" grants one a certain attention to detail combined with more limited social skills, reflects a social consensus crucial for the shaping of identity and relationships.[4] Put slightly differently, the presumed genetic status of autism permits certain kinds of kinship relations—seeing a relationship of likeness between "high" and "low" functioning autistic individuals or recognizing similarities between parents and children with autism—as well as expressions of commitment and obligation, while excluding others. Meanwhile, brain research and genetics research in autism work synergistically, each contributing to an explanatory framework in which autism is a genetic disorder that affects the brain and cognition exclusively, effectively precluding research on mid-level explanations focused on disease mechanisms.[5] Who gets caught up in the genetic relations of autism, then, becomes a question of research politics, with both practical and ethical consequences.

Making Autism a Genetic Disease

Since the 1960s, disease has been largely conceived of in genetic terms, reflecting the gradual "realization of an idea," in Susan Lindee's words, "that all human disease is a genetic phenomenon subject to technological control."[6] Genetics is also understood in a particular way, in which genes are not multiple, interacting sources of vulnerability but discrete sites for potential therapeutic intervention.[7] Peter Conrad has called this "the mirage of genes."[8] "Genes for" complex psychiatric disorders are increasingly the focus of corporate, government, and activist attention. "Gene talk" in expert discourse helps to heighten public expectations.[9] This "genetic" status of many contemporary disorders required social and intellectual work. Acknowledging the labor required to link a disease primarily to genetic knowledge, as opposed to physiological or behavioral knowledge or the "familial knowledge" of caregivers, does not deny the reality of genetic causes for disorders.[10] It simply takes into account the multiple possible ways of describing a disorder and the active choice of genetics as the preferred explanation. Disorders become genetic through research programs that help to certify them as such.

While the tendency of autistic traits to run in families has been of interest to researchers since the category was first described, research into the heritability of autism constituted a relatively small proportion of work through the 1970s. Since the mid-1990s, autism genetics has enjoyed a massive increase in prominence via private and government-funded research programs.[11] From its origins in a series of twin studies, research has come to focus successively on sibling pairs and multiplex families, and more recently on full-genome scans paired with candidate gene studies. Researchers operate with the implicit assumption that high-throughput genetic research will eventually yield results.[12] The vast majority of these studies rely on families in which multiple members have autism diagnoses, despite the fact that the vast majority of autism cases—about 90 percent—are sporadic, meaning that they occur in families in which there was no prior history of the disorder.[13] Publications in autism genetics have transformed autism from a disorder with hereditary components to a complex genetic disorder, a shift that has impacted the direction and funding of autism research. The change reflects an increasing focus on psychiatric genetics in general and a deepening conviction that autism treatment is necessary, that it will involve the use of pharmaceuticals, and that developing these techniques depends on locating autism genes.

Familial Tendencies

Speculation about the relationship between familial traits and autism has a history as long as that of the diagnosis. Depending on the perspective of the expert who observed them, what looked like affective distance on the part of parents was a causative factor in autism or evidence of underlying genetic likeness in parents. As we saw in chapter 1, Leo Kanner observed that parents of children with autism were often highly educated and seemed aloof and removed. In a 1960 *Time* magazine profile, he described parents as "just happening to defrost long enough to produce a child," although he later regretted that characterization.[14] Kanner's ideas shaped the way that child psychiatrists and psychologists first understood and treated autism in the 1950s and 1960s. The idea that parents might have caused their child's autism offered the hope that it might be treated. The allure of psychology eclipsed the study of heredity, with its uncertain prospects.

In 1964, Bernard Rimland published *Infantile Autism*, the first point-by-point refutation of the psychogenic theory of autism. The book reflected mounting skepticism among many psychologists, if not among the pediatricians and other health-care professionals that had been trained on their earlier work, of the idea that parental rejection—or even outright mistreatment—was an important causal factor in autism. Rimland revisited Kanner's original characterizations of his eleven cases and their parents, suggesting that these observations offered clues to a genetic etiology. Rimland argued that "despite the presence of a few borderline cases . . . the evidence overwhelmingly supports Kanner's unprecedented early report that the parents of autistic children form a unique and highly homogeneous group in terms of intellect and personality."[15]

Genes promised parents, Rimland included, both exculpation and the prospect of targeted medical intervention, the kind of therapeutic specificity on which modern medical knowledge is premised.[16] Psychological experts had thought that genetic reasoning precluded interventions into children's behavior and development. The growing promise of behavioral therapies helped to separate the practice of successful treatment from psychological theory. Rimland played a role in this shift as well, founding the National Society for Autistic Children (later the Autism Society of America) in 1965 with the aim of promoting behavioral therapies.

Psychologists like Bruno Bettelheim saw little difference between causal theories that implicated genetics and parental psychopathology. Since parents caused harm to their children through the operation of unconscious processes of rejection, whether their faulty genes or their flawed psyches damaged their children didn't affect parents' culpability. Treatment remained the same. For parents, however, the moral valence of genetic theories appealed more than their psychogenic equivalents. By the 1970s, the most influential researchers in the field agreed that "such parental abnormalities as do occur are at least as likely to result from pathology in the child as the other way around."[17] As researchers largely rejected the idea of parental attitudes playing a role in triggering autism, their certainty about the heritability of autism increased. Twin studies provided the justification for describing autism in genetic terms, but familial tendencies toward autism were the means through which these genes would be identified. The fact that the majority of autism cases are sporadic, with no previous family history, was a methodological hindrance, not an indication of potential limitations in the genetic framework. Some parents embraced a view of autism's genetic underpinnings. Others held back, observing that even when there is no family history of mental illness or cognitive disorders, "this diagnosis is like a metal detector, beeping on harmless bits of trash that appear more tantalizing when underground."[18]

Producing Certainty

Twin studies played a crucial role in convincing researchers of the hereditary nature of autism, although they said little about the mechanism through which genetic differences resulted in the behavioral syndrome. The impetus for these studies came from a number of published case reports of monozygotic, or identical, twin pairs that were concordant for autism, meaning that both twins fit the requirements for diagnosis. The results seemed suggestive enough that in the 1971 inaugural issue of the *Journal of Autism and Childhood Schizophrenia*, Michael Rutter and Lawrence Bartak allowed that that there might be a "genetically determined type of autism that constitutes a small subgroup of autistic disorders." They also thought that the evidence weighed "rather against a decisive hereditary element."[19] Others agreed. A 1976 review article argued against a significant genetic contribution to autism, although the authors were fairly certain that autism was caused by biological factors, perhaps pre- or postnatal brain injury.[20] At the time, it seemed possible that autism could be caused by a rare spontaneous mutation, although the under-100-percent concordance in monozygotic twin pairs seemed to contradict this, or by an interacting set of genes, but that so few family members of autistic children were affected made this seem unlikely.

By 1977, Rutter and Susan Folstein's study of twenty-one twin pairs had found a 36-percent concordance rate for autism in monozygotic twins. This finding hardly served as evidence that hereditary factors explained all cases of autism, although when researchers asked whether nonautistic identical twin siblings of children with autism had any kind of cognitive or social impairment, they found higher rates of concordance. These milder traits would later become important for theories of a "broader autism spectrum." At the time, Rutter and Folstein concluded that "the hereditary influences are concerned with a variety of cognitive abnormalities and not just with autism," noting that although the nonautistic twin siblings were more likely to have "delays or disorders in the acquisition of spoken language," it was impossible to draw "firm conclusions" on the heritability of "social and emotional difficulties." Rutter and Folstein also thought that the higher autism rates in twins might reflect their increased likelihood of perinatal complications. They had observed that when they took account of such "biological hazards" as delayed breathing or congenital abnormalities in cases where both twins did not have autism, the sibling with autism invariably was the one who had suffered the complication.[21] It seemed possible to researchers that autism might only develop after an experience that rendered children especially vulnerable. It might be a consequence of delayed development but not necessarily itself a developmental disorder.

During the 1980s, geneticists began conducting twin studies using broadened concepts of an "autism spectrum," including participants who tested within the typical range for IQ. They found concordance rates above 90 percent in monozygotic twins. Still, in 1986, an article on the early developmental backgrounds of autistic and mentally retarded children emphasized their preconception histories, including parental exposure to chemicals and maternal viral infections. "To the extent that not only direct infection by the mother but mere exposure to viruses, either in the workplace or in the household, can have an adverse effect on the developing embryo and fetus, we need much more research in this critical area," the authors argued.[22] Autism had yet to become a "genetic disease" as late as 1991, when Susan Folstein, the coauthor of the important 1977 twin study, wrote in a review article that "autism is a behavioral syndrome with multiple etiologies. Within the subgroup where hereditary factors play a significant role it is likely that there is genetic heterogeneity as well."[23]

By the late 1990s, twin studies had given way to other approaches designed to locate susceptibility genes, although researchers continued to cite concordance rates from earlier twin studies as evidence for the heritability of autism. Researchers argued for the use of affected-sibling-pair research designs and candidate gene studies, most of them focused on genes associated with the central nervous system.[24] Changes in diagnostic practices, meanwhile, reflected attempts by researchers to produce behaviorally (and presumably genetically) homogeneous populations for research. The ADI-R and ADOS, diagnostic tools developed during the mid-to-late 1990s, offered promise for creating standardized populations for genetic studies. Researchers also adopted the concept of a "broader autism phenotype," arguing that in family studies this approach might "increase the power to find genes" by allowing researchers to take into account family members who did not quite meet the criteria for autism.[25] Geneticists knew that siblings of children with autism had about a 4.5-percent chance of developing the disorder themselves.[26] Broader criteria would help researchers make use of the similarity among family members. They could also use new tools for genetic analysis, including automated sequencing, linkage studies, and full genome scans.

These new efforts also met with limited success. A review article in 2001 found that the eight published whole-genome scans for autism available at the time "yielded a fairly large number of suggestive linkage signals, only a few of which overlap from one study to the next."[27] An accompanying figure made the point clear: when signals from the majority of studies were collated, candidate loci appeared on all but three chromosomes. Nevertheless, the authors believed that "on the basis of the past few decades of research, genetic factors have clearly emerged as the most significant aetiology for autism spectrum disorders." Based on candidate gene studies combined with animal models and studies of human brain tissue, "we can afford to be optimistic that important progress will soon be made in our understanding of this most puzzling of conditions."[28] Even if autism disease genes had "proven elusive" to researchers who now admitted that autism was unlikely to be caused by any single genetic mutation, researchers tended to view the problem as an "impasse," which they would surmount through the use of ever-more-innovative techniques.[29] Another review of the molecular genetics of autism simply stated that "autism is one of the most heritable complex disorders, with compelling evidence for genetic factors and little or no support for environmental influence."[30] Yet by 2008, even the most successful studies using genome scans of multiplex families could use their findings to explain 1 percent of autism cases at best.[31]

Although researchers maintain a genetic focus in autism research for multiple reasons, at least one is the conviction that genetics will lead to treatment. "Locating susceptibility genes is the first step in developing

medical and genetic interventions for individuals with autism, and ultimately it is hoped that genetic findings may lead to the development of
new and more effective drug treatments for autistic individuals.[32] This
ever-receding genetic horizon is not unique to autism research. Adam
Hedgecoe has described how limits to genetic explanations are incorporated into the discourse of genetics in Alzheimer's disease research in what
he has called a "narrative of enlightened geneticization," in which findings
that apparently contradict the idea of Alzheimer's as a genetic disease are
simply built into the dominant framework.[33] Most recently, researchers
have looked to copy number variations, small segments of the genome
that are reproduced or deleted, to explain the preponderance of cases of
sporadic autism. Other teams have looked at families with a high degree
of intermarriage to implicate a set of genes involved in brain development
and language.[34] Although the findings are suggestive, none offers the prospect of a single explanation for autism. Rather, they raise the possibility
that different cases of autism are likely to be associated with different genetic factors.

As further evidence suggests that multiple genes and genetic pathways
may contribute to autism, experts often invoke an "additive model" popular
with researchers working on mental illnesses, in which the number of atypical genes that an individual has determines how much they are affected by
a disorder. Siblings of children with autism show "subsyndromal" impairments of social responsiveness.[35] Within this discourse, genetics goes hand
in hand with the expectation of future treatments. Genes are made to seem
fundamental. Other points of entry into the pathophysiology of autism, in
contrast, come to seem less reliable and less worthy of investment.

Meanings from Mice: Rett Syndrome and Animal Models

Based on the limited findings in autism genetics, one might have expected
parent groups to grow skeptical of the promise of therapeutic targets in the
near future. However, the opposite was true. Financial support for research
on autism genetics from parent groups like the National Alliance for Autism Research and the Cure Autism Now Foundation ballooned during
the 1990s. Successes in other disorders held out the promise of genes for
autism, sometimes even appearing on the timelines of autism genetics research used by parent organizations in their educational materials.[36]

A number of genetic disorders are associated with autistic features in
some individuals, including Fragile X syndrome, tuberous sclerosis, and

neurofibromatosis. By far the most significant of these is Rett syndrome. Huda Zoghbi, a researcher at Baylor College of Medicine, identified a gene for Rett syndrome, MECP2, in 1999 while funded by the International Rett Syndrome Association.[37] Rett syndrome is a relatively recently described disorder, first identified in a 1966 case series of twenty-two children.[38] It only affects girls, and it is characterized by a period of typical development followed by a rapid and often extreme loss of motor and communication skills around age two. Rett syndrome is a pervasive developmental disorder, linked diagnostically to autistic disorder, Asperger syndrome, childhood disintegrative disorder (CDD, a severe neurodegenerative condition), and pervasive developmental disorder not otherwise specified (PDD-NOS).

As with autism, the parents of children with Rett syndrome became aggressive and savvy advocates for research into their children's condition. The International Rett Syndrome Association (IRSA) consisted of a group of dedicated, tireless, and, in their own telling, somewhat obsessive parents. IRSA provided funding for Dr. Zoghbi, who, through a series of hunches and experiments, isolated the gene for Rett syndrome in 1999. Two factors aided Zoghbi in her investigation. The first was the existence of one family with heritable Rett syndrome—most cases are caused by spontaneous mutations, making linkage studies difficult. She was also aided by the knowledge that the syndrome was likely to be caused by a gene involved in the form of gene regulation called methylation, an epigenetic process that selectively activates or inactivates portions of the genome.

After they identified the gene, Zoghbi and her colleagues produced a mouse model for the syndrome. In order to produce a reliable laboratory organism, the model featured an important deviation from the syndrome in humans. Rett syndrome is only seen in girls because the MECP2 gene is on the X chromosome. Boys with the genotype generally do not survive beyond birth, because they experience the full impact of the mutated gene. In girls, the phenomenon of X chromosome inactivation—common to all women—makes the expression of Rett syndrome highly variable. Because each cell has only one active X chromosome, all girls with Rett syndrome have at least some cells in their bodies with functioning copies of the gene.[39] In contrast to the syndrome in humans, when researchers created the mouse model they introduced a nonfatal "knockout" of the gene in male mice, thus limiting the variability of the phenotype. "Male mice have consistently more severe symptoms than female mice and more uniform symptoms," making the severely affected male mice a better testing ground for "new medications or therapies."[40] A characteristic trait of girls with Rett syndrome is their almost continuous hand-wringing; the icon for IRSA was a line drawing of clasped hands. The trait was poignantly reproduced in the model mice.[41]

Dr. Zoghbi gave a keynote address at the 2002 International Meeting for Autism Research. Her speech left few doubts about the ideological power of the successful hunt for MECP2 for autism researchers. While she spoke, a video of Rett model mice was projected onto a large screen. The mice stumbled off a balance rod that wild-type mice can navigate without difficulty. An unseen researcher then dangled them by their tails and the mice began wringing their forepaws. Many in the audience gasped. The video froze for a few seconds on the final frame of the Rett mice with paws clasped together, as Dr. Zoghbi continued speaking, noting that in most cases members of her laboratory can reliably genotype knockout mice by picking them up by their tails and observing their behavior.[42]

Despite its appeal as a herald of promised advances in autism genetics research, the relevance of Rett syndrome research for autism is not entirely clear. Like many disorders in which epigenetic factors play a role, the route through which mutation leads to disorder in Rett syndrome is still unknown. Researchers cannot explain why a gene involved in so many physiological pathways seems to affect primarily neurological function without causing other major systemic problems in affected girls.[43] Because in Rett syndrome phenotypes vary as a result of X-inactivation, different girls and even different tissues in individual girls have varying levels of the damaged gene, whereas genes on the X chromosome have not been significantly implicated in autism. Another major source of phenotypic variation is the multiple spontaneous mutations that can occur in MECP2, leading to subtly different symptoms.[44] Still, a preponderance of cases of Rett syndrome —around 85 percent— occur as a result of mutations in MECP2, making it close to a monogenic disorder. This scenario is unlikely in autism, where genetics researchers suspect that the heterogeneity of the condition stems in part from a pattern of multiple, interacting genes.

Zoghbi's success, though significant, has yet to lead to specific therapies for affected children. It also offered few investigative techniques that could be incorporated into autism research. The gene was not found through the relatively blunt instrument of linkage or genome-wide association studies, the two favored forms of genetics research in autism. In linkage studies, samples from families with high rates of autism are screened for markers that indicate portions of the genome that are inherited consistently from generation to generation. The identified sites indicate places to seek out candidate genes. In association studies, many samples are screened in search of any genetic variant present in affected children but absent in a control population. In both methods, researchers proceed without any precise idea of the locations of genes of interest. In contrast, Dr. Zoghbi already had a good idea of the type of gene involved in the disorder. Although the genetic test for Rett syndrome does not offer any information to guide treatment, it nonetheless gave parents some measure of relief—"once we had the gene, they could see it was not their fault"—in an equation where the existence of a defective gene definitively exonerated parents from guilt and worry.[45]

Autism organizations encouraged Zoghbi to pursue further research in autism genetics, hoping that the success with Rett syndrome might be replicated. The Cure Autism Now Foundation awarded Zoghbi a $100,000 "genius grant" for autism research, but, according to one report, it might have been the $2.2 million grant from the Simons Foundation that "actually prompted Dr. Zoghbi's foray into autism research."[46] James Simons, a mathematician turned hedge-fund manager, and Marilyn Simons, parents of a girl diagnosed with a "mild form of autism," decided to use their considerable wealth to promote autism genetics research after bringing together a group of "renowned academic figures" and determining that the "one solid lead" in autism research was the results of twin studies.[47]

The appeal of Rett syndrome as a model genetic disorder and a symbol of the desires of autism genetics researchers increased with a 2007 report on success in reversing neurological deficits in a mouse model of Rett syndrome. In this case, researchers engineered mice to have their MECP2 genes conditionally silenced by an allele that could itself be inactivated with timed injections of the drug tamoxifen. If the symptoms of Rett syndrome were due to the inactivation of the gene during development, causing irreversible damage to neural architecture, then reactivating the gene would have had little effect in mature mice already showing symptoms. Instead, the researchers observed what they called "robust phenotypic reversal, as activation of MECP2 expression leads to striking loss of advanced neurological symptoms in both immature and mature adult animals."[48] In other words, genetic neurological disorders that affect children early in their development may carry the potential for reversibility. They are not, strictly speaking, developmental disorders marked by permanent changes in brain architecture.[49]

Although the researchers cautioned that the results "do not suggest an immediate therapeutic approach to RTT," the families speaking in videos on the Rett Syndrome Research Foundation Web site made the potential connection to therapies explicit. One father said that he would be delighted to teach his daughter to walk at the age of fifteen, given the opportunity.[50] Reports of the experiment in the news followed the lead of the families by further broadening the applicability to autism spectrum disorders in general. A headline on the *Scientific American* Web site read "Reversal of Fortune: Researchers Erase Symptoms of Autism Spectrum Disorder."[51]

Meanwhile, researchers have continued their attempts to construct a plausible mouse model for autism in all of its behavioral features, many of which are inconveniently human in character. Despite the "long and illustrious history" of rodent models for human neuropsychiatric disorders, it is not easy to create mouse analogs for communication difficulties, lack of a theory of mind, or failure to engage in imaginative play, nor has it proven easy to design tasks to test these capacities in mice.[52] Some models involving selective gene "knockouts" have succeeded in mimicking specific behavioral abnormalities such as "impaired social learning," but animals with these features often turn out to have clearly visible neuropathology of a kind rarely associated with autism in humans.[53] When researchers have attempted to use primates to study the importance of specific brain structures in autism, results have been similarly disappointing. The amygdala seemed to be an important component of the "social brain" that might be impaired in people with autism, but primates with damage to this structure did not behave in ways that fully supported that conclusion.[54]

Neurological Difference

Studies of the brain in autism consistently failed to locate any specific impaired structures, even on a microscopic level. Nevertheless, researchers still imagined that impairments in autism would eventually correlate to damaged brain structures. Studies of brain tissue during the 1990s indicated that cells in the cerebellum might be missing in the brains of people with autism, but the original research team eventually concluded that they had been mistaken.[55] Scientists have also speculated about the potential role of mirror neurons in autism, referring again to primate studies. Findings in humans have indicated structural abnormalities in the mirror neuron system, which seems to play a role in understanding and imitating the actions of others, forming "a possible neural substrate of empathy."[56] This ability to comprehend the actions of others as though they were our own is what psychologists have referred to as a "theory of mind."[57] However, the connections linking these structures and their specific malfunctions to any set of genes have yet to be determined.

Many researchers working on brain research in autism assume that findings in the brain tissue of people with autism should, like the ideal genetic findings, locate specific domains that are structurally atypical. However, one of the most reliable findings in the brains of people with autism is that they seem to experience a period of rapid early brain growth and then a slowing down that leads to a statistically higher brain volume in young children with autism, concentrated in the white matter of those portions that developed after birth.[58] This pervasive change does not lend itself to any simple genetic interpretation and has inspired some scientists to begin thinking in terms of disrupted developmental systems and chronic disease processes rather than malformed structures.[59] The neurological differences involved in autism seem literally to pervade the brains of affected people.[60]

When researchers use imaging techniques such as functional MRI or psychometric tests from social and cognitive psychology to study brain function, their results seem to support the finding of pervasive, nonspecific brain changes. People with autism may have an atypical excitation/inhibition ratio, a measure of brain activity that relates to the ability to screen out irrelevant information. Many have difficulties shifting their attention on cognitive tasks and perform better when their attention is focused rather than divided, perhaps as a paradoxical result of their difficulties screening out irrelevant stimuli.[61] The psychologist Simon Baron-Cohen distinguishes between "empathizing" and "systemizing," with systemizing seen as a function of autistic strengths that can co-occur with a deficit in empathizing.[62] Researchers have wondered whether these findings might relate to altered patterns of brain connectivity due to brain overgrowth during early development, leading to a pattern of overconnectivity between neurons in smaller regions and underconnectivity over larger expanses.[63] Some researchers note that this pattern of cognition shades easily into autism "endophenotypes," or characteristics associated with autism but not diagnostic of the syndrome, such as the ability to focus on one task to the exclusion of others. These patterns are present within the cognitively typical population and might relate to genetic models of a "broader autism phenotype."[64]

Brain research in autism requires its own system of tissue repositories and sample sharing protocols. Since individuals with autism have a normal lifespan, brains can be difficult for researchers to acquire. Even researchers who succeed in obtaining brain tissue contend with sample sizes far smaller than would be acceptable in many other areas of research, especially given the acknowledged variability among people with autism. Scientists must collaborate to acquire material for research. The LADDERS clinic outside Wellesley, Massachusetts, an interdisciplinary autism research and treatment clinic, "works closely" with the Harvard Brain Tissue Resource Center, a brain donation program and repository, which is in turn partnered with the Autism Tissue Program, funded by the National Institutes of Health and the parent organization Autism Speaks.[65]

Beyond supporting the Autism Tissue Program, parents have made fewer attempts to influence brain research relative to their work funding genetics. This could be due to the difficulty of obtaining research materials compared to genetics research or because researchers had already established a system for sharing samples. Although autism researchers have tended to present brains as the site of pathology, they have not presented them as likely points of direct intervention, and that may also have made the stakes in brain-based research seem less high. They present visible brain pathology as the product of prenatal developmental processes, rather than as resulting from an ongoing process of chronic illness. Despite evidence suggesting that brains retain elements of plasticity, or the ability to heal, into adult life, many people view brain pathology as less alterable than genetic abnormalities.

Although researchers have had trouble finding localized structural changes, autism has retained its identity as a genetic disorder of the brain. Those few findings that are produced, from unusual activation of the amygdala to differences in the mirror neuron system, assume an almost iconic value.[66] Like findings in genetics, they invite multiple interpretations on both a functional and ethical level. Opponents of treatment see pervasive brain differences as evidence of fundamental differences in autistic brains that should be treated as a form of "neurodiversity." Advocates concerned about environmental causes welcome evidence that inflammatory processes may trigger the behavioral differences seen in autism. Brain researchers and social psychologists focus on the possibility that the malfunctioning systems in autistic brains might yield insights into the nature of social knowledge, learning, or even gender.[67]

Parenthood, Pedigrees, and Partiality in Autism Genetics

In a 2003 speech, Jonathan Shestack, who founded the Cure Autism Now Foundation (CAN) with his wife, Portia Iverson, spoke about fatherhood and autism. He implicitly referenced histories of parent-blaming as he explained his devotion to research:

> Dov is now eleven, and I'm still trying to figure out how best to love him. All the ways they teach men to be—loud, fast, aggressive—aren't effective with an autistic kid. You come home from the office and make a big commotion, looking for a big reaction, like you're the greatest, most fun dad, but that's just not going [to] get you any closer. They say autistic kids don't imitate very well, but their parents imitate quite well and after a couple of years of nonresponsiveness sometimes you just sort of check out.

Shestack more easily expresses his commitment to his son through advocacy than through conventional expressions of paternal devotion: "That's what I know how to do for Dov. That's how I know best to love him."[68]

Genetics operates as a powerful resource for parent organizations. It provides leverage with autism researchers and the ability to speed sluggish research timelines. The authors of a 2004 review in *Pediatrics* admonished, "Parents need to understand that they and their affected children are the only available sources for identifying and studying the elusive genes responsible for autism," but the urging was unnecessary.[69] Parents of children with autism had taken up the idea of genetic research and embraced their unique position to foster that research nearly a decade earlier, with the founding of the New Jersey–based National Alliance for Autism Research (NAAR) in 1994 and the California-based CAN in 1995. Both organizations committed millions to autism research over the following decade. More important, both groups exploited the identities of their members as parents to influence the direction of genetics research in autism. CAN believed that "with enough determination, money and manpower, science can be hurried." Science meant genetics, and genetics signaled the means to repair families as much as it was a sign of familial likeness.[70]

The founders of CAN, Portia Iverson and Jonathan Shestack, are Hollywood insiders who bring a certain charisma and aptitude for pitching a story to their work in autism advocacy. They founded CAN in 1995, shortly after their son, Dov, was diagnosed. Shestack and Iverson realized that they could shift researchers' priorities by leveraging control over genetic materials and the social networks of parent autism communities to influence researchers. HIV/AIDS treatment activists had used similar strategies in the 1990s, and Iverson and Shestack drew inspiration from the Los Angeles–based Pediatric AIDS Foundation in particular.[71] Elizabeth

Glaser, who founded the organization in 1988, argued that in a context of funding neglect for AIDS research as a whole, researchers had ignored the fact that the virus developed and progressed differently in children. CAN also followed a number of groups that had organized in the 1990s around the goal of locating disease genes, including the Dysautonomia Foundation, Inc., PXE International, and the Hereditary Disease Foundation.[72]

All of these groups understood that professional researchers would not necessarily share their priorities or interests. Realizing this, they made use of their funds and human contacts to create novel institutions. Parents demanded that scientists adhere to the standards of "good research" and the ideal of researchers as driven by the altruistic goals of broadening knowledge and treating illness, rather than by their desire for recognition or commercial gain. As observers of scientific practices often note, day-to-day behavior often deviates from the scientific norms of disinterestedness and communal sharing of data.[73] Such lapses dismayed Iverson and Shestack.

Controlling the Coin of the Realm

The founding of CAN's Autism Genetic Resource Exchange (AGRE) in 1997 is one of the more visible success stories in autism research and advocacy. According to most accounts, Portia Iverson and Jonathan Shestack met with experts and determined that genetics offered the most promise in autism research. They also learned that effective genetic research would require DNA samples from at least 100 multiplex families, that is, families with two or more family members with the condition. This requirement proved difficult because families with one case of the disorder are more common. When they began contacting genetics researchers, they discovered that "as as group, the scientists had collected DNA from the necessary 100 families. Individually, however, no single team had DNA from anywhere near that number." The researchers refused to share their samples. Shestack explained that "everyone wanted to be the first to find the genes—their careers depended on being first—and they didn't want anyone else to get a competitive advantage."[74]

The solution was to control "the coin of the realm: DNA." Iverson and Shestack formed their own gene repository, using their status as a parent organization to reach and recruit families. They eventually produced a sample of over 400 multiplex families, more than four times the original requirement.[75] By the summer of 2006, the collection totaled 12,000 families.[76] The acronym for the Autism Genetic Resource Exchange, pronounced like the word "agree," makes explicit CAN's objective of accelerating collaborative work on shared samples. Qualified researchers could access AGRE's samples, including purified DNA, serum samples, and immortalized cell lines approximately at cost. A team that included pediatricians, geneticists, and neurologists gathered phenotypic information through home visits designed to minimize inconvenience to the families. AGRE supplied the results to participant researchers via a built-to-purpose database, the Internet System for Assessing Autistic Children (ISAAC), designed by the father of a child with autism. Private donors contributed more than $6 million to the project, which also received a substantial grant from the National Institute of Mental Health in 2002.

AGRE was set up as a necessary destination for genetic researchers who wished to work with the best possible samples.[77] In the process, CAN made researchers behave in ways that matched the interests of parents. By 2004 the National Institutes of Health (NIH) followed suit by requiring that grant recipients provide "explicit details" on their plans for sharing materials with other researchers.[78]

Where CAN/AGRE chose to exploit parental networks to create a material resource in the form of a genetic repository, the genetics initiative headed by NAAR used a different strategy. The Autism Genetics Cooperative (AGC) incorporated the professional and social worlds of the scientists into the architecture of their program. The desire for recognition and the fear of preemption by competing researchers mattered to genetics researchers in the same way that speed and treatment targets mattered to parents. The founders of NAAR, like the founders of CAN, reasoned that the combined effects of the NIH funding structure, academic career trajectories, tenure considerations, and the increasing commercialization of genetic information had created a climate of intense competition and secrecy. In an attempt to overcome this barrier, NAAR directly addressed the culture of autism genetics research, using its status as a parent organization as a tool for organizing scientific work. For NAAR, research was better organized by those with personal, indeed affective and familial, stakes in the outcome than by the purportedly neutral scientific collective.

In the words of one staff member, NAAR-AGC acted as an "honest broker" for autism geneticists.[79] NAAR selected twenty-two international sites that included the most experienced researchers with the objective of encouraging them to pool their samples and work collaboratively. Researchers attended an annual, invitation-only retreat in Atlanta, Georgia. Several ground rules set the tone for the meetings. Researchers could only present unpublished work, discussions were strictly confidential, and researchers agreed to respect priority, meaning that if an individual had staked out a particular area of research, other participants would not encroach on that area. The organizers insisted on democratic participation, meaning that junior researchers worked alongside more experienced colleagues.[80]

The organizers established an atmosphere of trust among members, although it took about four years. Although it was made up primarily of parents, NAAR nonetheless developed credibility as an organization capable of promoting collaborative research insulated from the routine pressures of scientific careers. It emphasized its status as an "honest broker," gaining the confidence of researchers and fostering trust among them. The resulting arrangement served the interests of both the parent organization and the scientists.

In different ways, CAN and NAAR turned their identities as parent groups to their advantage in acting on and reshaping the social worlds of scientists. They capitalized on their cultural and biological role as parents by acting as brokers and intermediaries, transforming family connections, biological likenesses, and emotionality into a resource. For both CAN and NAAR, the partiality that comes with parenthood was an asset rather than a liability. Although experts on advisory boards ensured that proposals were evaluated based on the standards of the research community, parents added an essential component of affective investment. [81] They evaluated proposals not only in terms of the work's scientific interest, but also for its potential to improve the lives of their children.

With support from the NIH, the NAAR-Autism Genome Project (AGP) Consortium launched in 2003. The project incorporated most of the major autism genetics research networks, including AGRE, into a consortium, or a "collaboration of collaborations."[82] Having altered the terrain of autism genetics research, the initiatives of CAN and NAAR were effectively absorbed into the normal practices of government-funded research. In 2005, NAAR announced that it was merging its operations with the newly formed Autism Speaks. In 2006, CAN followed suit, bringing its gene bank AGRE with it. As of February 2006, the three groups had merged into a single entity.[83]

Meanwhile, genetics researchers adapted their language to reflect the unpromising results of the multiple genome scans that they had conducted on the newly abundant genetic material. They recognized that the time had come to "give up" on finding a single gene for autism.[84] By 2004, the NAAR Autism Genome Project began to refer to "autism susceptibility genes," contributing to an "inherited risk of autism" that implicitly worked together with environmental factors to create autistic symptoms.[85] For parents and researchers with commitments to genetics research, the failure to produce results has been a function of genetic complexity, technological lags, and the breakdown of collaboration in the quest for ever-larger sample populations for research. It is not a problem with the underlying assumptions guiding the research. Parents could make researchers cooperate by helping to reorganize research programs and sample-sharing. They imagined that the complexity of the genetics would yield to high-throughput technologies, improved sample sizes, and alternative genetic models.[86]

Making Use of Genetics: Kinship along the Spectrum

For organizations that have invested in genetic research, the question has been not whether a cause for autism can be found, but how long it will take. Their certainty contributes to fears on the part of adults with autism that people like them will eventually be eliminated through prenatal testing and selective abortion. The concerns are not unfounded.[87] Bioethicists worry that future genetic tests for autism could lead parents to choose against having a child who might have become a future version of Bill Gates, Thomas Jefferson, or Lewis Carroll, who all retrospectively seem to "fit the profile" for Asperger syndrome.[88]

Organizations like CAN, NAAR, and the Autism Society invoke broken family relations in their fundraising appeals, reinforcing the idea that children with autism are, like the changelings in fairy tales, fundamentally unlike their typical family members.[89] A Web site sponsored by the Autism Society of America featured family photographs torn into two pieces, isolating one child.[90] These popular images of alienation are nevertheless at odds with the genetic research programs that the organizations sponsor, since such research often makes use of the existence of autistic traits in direct family members. Many parents recognize these traits in themselves and obtain diagnoses only after their child is found to have autism.[91] Like the parents of children with other disabilities, parents of children with autism spend a great deal of time thinking about the ways that their children resemble them and explaining that resemblance to the world.[92]

Genetic research has so far failed to produce information with concrete implications for screening or treatment and it has done little to illuminate the underlying biological mechanisms of autism. When parents, the popular media, and self-advocates use genetics as support for their arguments about the nature of autism, they make little use of ongoing linkage or association studies. Instead, they draw on a wider set of genetic discourses, although they may not do so consciously. These include ideas about the relationship between modern life and genetic degeneration, notions of kinship that go beyond shared lineages, and fears of eugenics programs.

Autism, Asperger Syndrome, and Autistic Cousins

An emerging autism self-advocacy movement uses genetics as a basis for an entirely different kind of appeal than that made by parents. For those who describe themselves as supporters of neurodiversity, the genetically defined population with an autism diagnosis matters to a set of claims about representation and entitlement. By emphasizing kinship across the spectrum, adults with autism can argue for recognition as spokespeople and biologically ideal translators for children who may seem unlike their parents.[93]

Autism self-advocacy as a visible social force emerged as a result of at least three factors. A resurgence of professional interest in the Asperger syndrome diagnosis and the broader autism spectrum in the 1990s led more adults and people with "higher functioning" forms of autism to be diagnosed. The growth of Internet mailing lists made communication among people with autism easier. And an already established framework of parent organizations allowed connections to be formed among people "on the spectrum."[94] Although what self-advocates call the neurodiversity movement originated partly in parent organizations, by the early twenty-first century self-advocates had become increasingly critical of these groups.

In 2005, when the Autism Society of America, which called itself "The Voice of Autism," launched a new campaign for early diagnosis and treatment, complete with a Web site, "Getting the Word Out," self-advocates with autism responded indignantly.[95] The Web site www.autistics.org changed its slogan to "The Real Voice of Autism," arguing that people with autism ought to speak for themselves and that a diagnosis rather than familial connections was the more significant requirement for spokespersons.[96] Amanda Baggs, another self-advocate, posted a parody of the site and those of other organizations that used images of suffering in their fundraising. She scored points in noting that the images of stricken families used on the site were not real families with autistic children but instead stock photographs of models posing as sad children and miserable parents.[97] The parody was only one instance of an ongoing conflict in which parents of children with autism and self-advocates battle over who gets to "speak for" autism, and most importantly, what that speech says about the value of autistic persons and the meaning of their symptoms.

Jim Sinclair's essay "Don't Mourn for Us," written in 1993, continues to express the sentiments of a segment of the autism community. He writes that the sadness that parents experience upon their child's diagnosis and their subsequent search for a cure reflect "grief over the loss of the normal child the parents had hoped and expected to have," but that to focus on this grief is damaging.

> Push for the things your expectations tell you are normal, and you'll find frustration, disappointment, resentment, maybe even rage and hatred. Approach respectfully, without preconceptions, and with openness to learning new things, and you will find a world you could never have imagined.[98]

Sinclair does not merely claim genetic-cum-ethnic kinship with children with autism. He downplays their ties to their parents, explaining that parents must first accept that their child "is an alien child who landed in my life by accident," someone who is "stranded in an alien world."[99] Meanwhile, adults with autism also have children, and they reflect on the connections that result from a shared diagnosis and biology. They can offer their children "something fundamental" as parents and advocates: "the capability—and importance—of pointing out *meaning* in autistic behavior, sensory and aesthetic sensibilities, cognitive patterns, and emotional processing—and of asserting their legitimacy."[100]

Advocates base their arguments on a framing of autism as neurological and genetic rather than contingent and environmental.[101] In some cases, they are vocal critics of hypotheses of environmental etiology. They are often joined by parents who resent professional and media portrayals of autism as a tragedy. These parents focus on acceptance and accommodation, arguing through advocacy groups and research that nonautistic parents of children with autism need to learn to adapt to their children rather than the reverse.[102] The self-advocacy community has forced the question of legitimate representation for the genetically different. They demand that genetic likeness, which is presumed to unite the population that shares a diagnosis of autism, trumps familial relations in the contest over who gets to speak for children with autism. They may reshape not only how autism is represented but also the normal practices of autism research and treatment.

Many of the implications of these new ways of valuing people will only be worked out through practices that require intense, intimate relationships among people. One way requires inviting autistic people to participate in designing research programs. Others involve learning to create spaces, both professional and casual, where people with autism can have their differences accommodated and even valued. Jim Sinclair founded the annual Autreat in 1996 to provide a space for autistic people from any point on the spectrum where they were not expected to " 'act normal' or to behave like a neurotypical person."[103] The Internet provides another social space in which autistics (the preferred term for many self-advocates) arrange dating or interact at a pace and in a medium that is less intrusive and overwhelming in emotional or sensory terms.[104] For children, schools have been created that encourage the "perseverations" of their "Aspie" pupils, while their families may come to embrace their shared autistic traits.

There are also parents who find no contradiction between identifying with their child's autism diagnosis and trying to help their child recover or participating in genetics research.[105] They credit their persistence, ability to synthesize information, and broad knowledge of technical literature to an autistic attention to details bordering on the obsessive. Genetics researchers note with pleasure that unlike "ADHD parents," "autistic parents" show up on time for appointments. Their studies take into account the existence of relatives with "communication difficulties" or "social impairments," or the fact that some parents of children with autism have "distinct" ways of judging emotions from facial expressions.[106] Hans Asperger, after all, speculated about the similarities between the children that he studied and their mothers, describing the way one mother-and-child pair walked down the street as though they did not know each other.[107] By the late 1950s, researchers were noting that the fathers of many autistic children were "obsessive, detached and humorless individuals," accomplished in their professional lives but uncomfortable with social encounters.[108] Later researchers emphasized the number of engineers among the fathers and grandfathers of children with autism, speculating that the "assortative mating" of computer engineers in places like California's Silicon Valley led to locally increased autism rates.[109] Hearing the theory, one journalist worried that the "hidden cost" of the growing technology industry "may be lurking in the findings of nearly every major genetic study of autism in the last 10 years."[110]

In some forms of childhood disability such as Down syndrome, the visible physical differences between parents and children can disrupt the experience of kinship. In autism, genetic kinship is defined in terms of disability.[111] Within the parent community, jokes about the milder symptoms of autism that many parents exhibit are common. Their more serious conversations touch on familial histories of autoimmune syndromes, allergies, and other characteristics that might have acted as risk factors for their children. At the same time, researchers can turn those similarities against parents, accusing them of symptomatically "perseverating" on unproven treatments and cures—although researchers have also been known to accuse colleagues of acting on autistic impulses if they don't agree with the focus of their research.[112]

Autism's Genetic Futures

Both parent organizations and self-advocates are eminently pragmatic in their efforts to promote their interests. Their allegiances, in the end, are to specific goals of representation, accommodation, or treatment, not to broadly conceived research programs in genetics or psychology. During the 1970s and 1980s, parents learned to invest their time and energy in behavioral therapies for their children even as they explored the potential of megavitamin therapies and dietary modifications. During the 1990s and early 2000s, parent organizations diversified their investments, waiting for genetic therapies in the long term while focusing in the short term on addressing the pathophysiology of possible genetic difference using a similarly broad range of interventions. The majority of parents are committed to no perspective on autism as strongly as they are devoted to the idea that their children can be helped in some way.

For this reason, the differences between self-advocates and parent advocates are more ethical than epistemological. They are characterized as much by disputes over appropriate courses of action as they are by disagreements about the biological facts of autism. Ideals of neurological diversity and acceptance do not mesh well with research programs devoted to eventually treating or eradicating neurological disabilities. In contrast, as we have seen, the genetic models that are used to support both advocacy for neurological diversity and research on neurological disability display similar themes and invoke similarly linear models of causation.

As genetic knowledge develops beyond the more reductive or deterministic models that characterized earlier expectations of finding an "autism gene," the social groups that reference genetics may need to reconsider using it as a basis for claims about community or representation. Direct lines between genetics and identity will seem far more contingent. For example, the ethical implications of genetic identities will become uncertain as researchers become more knowledgeable about how genes and environments interrelate.[113] In addition, forms of autism may be found to share common molecular mechanisms with other seemingly unrelated disorders, bringing children into new relations of surveillance and care.[114] Self-advocates who understand their autism as a benign genetic variation may also need to see their present identities as shaped by their past experiences and surroundings. Parents who count on intensive behavioral therapies and medical interventions as a way of treating intractable symptoms of the disorder might have to allow that other elements of autism will prove to be fixed and settled from birth, and could even present advantages or sources of pleasure for their child.[115]

The idea of autism genetics has been used to claim that the disorder is an untreatable constant in human populations that ought to be accepted and not treated. It is also seen as a way of repairing kinship ties in affected families or as the path to a cure in the near future. All of these ways of thinking view genetics as a determinant of disorder, and disorders as unified wholes for which treatments are either useless or fully curative. The perspective leaves little room for complex causation or for treatments that modulate some traits and leave others alone. Meanwhile, autism genetics has been a waiting game tied to the future prospects of research.

In reality, few parents can wait for definitive answers. Some push for increases in funding for translational research that has the ability to act as a bridge between studies of disease mechanisms and treatment applications.[116] In the absence of a satisfying explanation for autism, many others become experimenters and investigators. In doing so, they do not necessarily deny the plausibility of genetic studies—in fact, many are convinced that genes play a large role in autism susceptibility. However, they believe that genotypes are merely the starting point for developmental processes that take place in response to an environment. Processes that are controlled by genes can still be modulated through individualized treatments. This plasticity is nowhere more evident than in disorders diagnosed in childhood, where early intervention has the potential to literally reshape the neurology and biology of a syndrome.[117]

My next chapter is about the choice of parents to take on the task of trying to shape their child's development. These parents have come to regard their children's behaviors in terms of underlying biological processes. They have incorporated this perspective into their daily life, restructuring their schedules, diets, attention, and habits into the work of caring for their children through biomedical interventions. They do this without the factual certainty that genetics has promised but not yet delivered.

Desperate and Rational: Parents and Professionals in Autism Research

In fact, the journey grows longer than expected—and
steeper—
           and perplexing
How many times have you, now almost nine, sent us back to our
           lovers' laboratory
Dark with dashed expectations, challenging us to let go and try
again?

                                        —Jack Zimmerman[1]

Jack Zimmerman is the husband of Dr. Jacquelyn McCandless, the author of *Children with Starving Brains*, a guide to biomedical treatments for autism spectrum disorders. In the poem that prefaces McCandless's book, Zimmerman addresses his granddaughter Chelsea, the subject of those "dashed expectations" and the inspiration for their "lovers' laboratory." Zimmerman's and McCandless's focus on treating an individual child, the affective and rational challenges of treatment, and the idea that the process of healing is a "journey" are all components of a perspective they share with an international network of doctors and parents. Although McCandless entered the world of autism treatment after a lengthy career in anti-aging medicine and psychiatry, the couple joins evangelical Christians, functional and integrative medicine practitioners, parents with nursing degrees, and university-based pharmacologists in their efforts to transform the syndrome of autism. The laboratory that they describe is both private and connected to hundreds of similar places. These include commercial testing sites, the homes of individual parents, the collaborative hum of a doctor's listserv, and lone researchers trawling medical databases for useable entries late into the night.

In this chapter, I describe the production of biomedical knowledge in one parent-practitioner community. I discuss the process of persuasion and affective involvement whereby parents and new practitioners come to take part in the practice of treating autism. I emphasize the ways that social relations based on affect alter vision, create trust, and change measures of therapeutic success. Such a community neither arises spontaneously nor remains entirely stable over time. Members come and go, and they identify with its main premises to varying degrees. However, despite the fact that biomedical treatments for autism are considered to be "alternative" practices, this community does not operate "outside" the forms of expertise and representations of biological systems accepted by conventional practitioners. What makes them distinct is a conscious shift in perspective as opposed to an appeal to a different knowledge system altogether. They are an experimental community within biomedicine.

The treatments employed by this community remain controversial, but parents of children with autism are exploring them at increasing rates. Between 30 percent and 74 percent of all parents use alternative treatments.[2] Investigators report different rates depending on the scope of their survey instruments. Some include a wide range of treatments under the umbrella designation of complementary and alternative medicine (CAM). Even when a broad definition is used, parents seem to turn to "biologically based" treatments about 70 percent of the time they go outside the treatments defined as "conventional" or "mainstream." Parents of younger and more severely impaired children appear more inclined to explore a range of treatments.[3]

Biomedical treatments encompass a range of conventional and unconventional therapies, all premised on the idea that autism is a treatable medical condition. In using the term "biomedical," participants emphasize that these interventions employ biomedical models of physiological systems. At the same time, they distinguish biomedical interventions from treatments focused on altering behaviors alone (e.g., applied behavior analysis), and from approaches that focus on single bodily systems (e.g., the gastrointestinal tract) without recognizing that different parts of the body share common regulatory mechanisms and biochemical pathways. Since metabolic processes can be described in conventional scientific terms, community members would distinguish efforts to manipulate them from, for instance, homeopathy, although many families explore such treatments as well.

Members of the community that uses these methods speak in terms of "recovering" and "curing" autism, ideas that contradict established models of autism as a lifelong condition. Their practices also involve a fragmenting of the diagnostic category that, if taken seriously, might be quite disruptive to established research programs. Because it is defined behaviorally, autism is a syndrome, a set of related symptoms. It is not a single disease with a known pathophysiological mechanism. Observable autism symptoms may be secondary to a range of other underlying causes, rather than associated with a single, definitive disease process.[4] Autism may not be only one disorder. Individuals running carefully constructed research programs that assume an underlying biological homogeneity in autism might find such a statement difficult to accept.

The Food and Drug Administration (FDA) has currently approved only one medication as a treatment for autism, risperidone, an atypical antipsychotic marketed as Risperdal by Johnson & Johnson. The medication is not considered to treat the "core" behavioral symptoms of autism, but rather the "irritability" associated with the condition in children. Most practitioners recognize that its metabolic and psychiatric side effects, including often-dramatic weight gain, make it far from ideal.[5] The paucity of approved medical treatments coupled with the severity of many cases of autism and its categorization as a lifelong condition almost inevitably lead members of the medical profession and the journalists who consult them to question the ethical standing and emotional state of those making claims about treatment or recovery.

To speak of treating autism, let alone curing the disorder, is to invite accusations of desperation on the part of parents and charlatanism on the part of practitioners. A *New York Times* cover story in December 2004 read "Autism Therapies Still a Mystery, But Parents Take a Leap of Faith." It opened with the line, "Desperate parents of autistic children have tried almost everything—hormone injections, exotic diets, faith healing—in the hope of finding a cure." Experimenting with alternative treatments made it difficult to ascertain the benefits of more established forms of behavioral therapy. An expert in the field said that the use of alternative treatments was a "grief response."[6] Another article, "Desperate Parents Seek Autism's Cure," in the *Providence Journal* in August 2005 quoted an internist at the National Center Against Health Fraud as saying, "It's a group of people preying upon the desperate."[7] A third described autism as a battle, "parents vs. research," and noted expert concerns about "a raft of unproven, costly, and potentially harmful treatments—including strict diets, supplements and a detoxifying technique called chelation—that are being sold for tens of thousands of dollars to desperate parents of autistic children as a cure for 'mercury poisoning.'"[8] A 2004 *Boston Globe* story quoted the director of a noted residential treatment center who, despite having said he understood "why 'desperate' parents might consider various treatments" beyond behavioral therapy, explained, "We don't see these kids as experimental guinea pigs for the latest cure *du jour*.... We want parents to be informed advocates for their kids, and to choose wisely."[9] Doctors tell reporters that parents are "willing to believe anything" as an alternative to "expensive and difficult" behavioral treatments.[10]

When physicians write for their peers, they explain parents' use of alternative treatments as "an attempt to gain a sense of control over their child's chronic illness or disability and to improve quality of life," or as a form of "stress reduction" in the face of a severe diagnosis. While they emphasize respect for parental choices, they also underscore the importance of the pediatrician as a "medical home" and the site of primary care.[11] They worry that alternative treatments may be harmful and that support for them is based on practitioners' "subjective" reports rather than peer-reviewed studies.[12]

Yet despite the prevalent view that parents who use alternative treatments are irrational, ignorant about their child's condition, and too easily persuaded by false claims, a 2006 survey found a mild association between the use of CAM and higher parental education level, longer time since diagnosis, and a greater degree of disability.[13] Those who use biomedical treatments may have more time and ability to learn about the diagnosis. Parents talk about desperation too, but they portray themselves as emphatically reasonable, at once skeptical and willing to experiment. Their accounts emphasize experience. A mother speaks with other parents, and

> they give me copies of exotic recipes, show me cupboards full of pure honey, molasses, and nuts, freezers full of game meats and bizarre flours. By nightfall, Jonah is off all milk, butter, cheese, bread, crackers, pasta, and cookies. Five days after our talk with Jane, we have begun the gluten-free/casein free diet with sheer desperation as the catalyst.[14]

When physicians write for parents, they draw sharp boundaries between "sound, systematic, and well-conducted research," and "hype, dramatic claims, and wishful thinking," as Laura Schreibman does in *The Science and Fiction of Autism.*[15] Schreibman's examples of theories and treatments that "waste time, money, and emotional energy" range widely, from the psychogenic theory of autism and facilitated communication to biomedical treatments, but she explains to readers that "the principles of science" will enable them to distinguish these from legitimate research. Like other doctors, she uses secretin, a pancreatic hormone that had once seemed like a promising therapy but failed to show benefits in clinical trials, as an example of how resources can be misspent following up on parents' hunches.[16] One "need not be a scientist" to separate reliable claims from false ones, but her readers had best rely on the judgment and systematic analyses of people other than themselves.[17] Some of these critical physicians are themselves parents. Michael Fitzpatrick, a general practitioner whose teenage son has autism, accuses parents who opt for biomedical treatments of resisting the idea that no one is to blame for their child's disability. Practitioners who offer the treatments are opportunists and parents who focus on their children's medical symptoms harm the cause of autism acceptance by using "metaphors of toxicity and disease" to describe their child.[18]

Parents describe their use of biomedical interventions in caring for their affected children as an act of love. There are costs in doing so. If knowledge of the affective, the anecdotal, and the everyday lends efficacy to treatments for autism, it also makes it difficult to translate them into conventional medical terms and to replicate their effects.

The Autism Research Institute, Defeat Autism Now!, and Biomedical Interventions for Autism

Most parents who seek biomedical treatments for autism learn about the techniques from the Autism Research Institute's publications and Defeat Autism Now! (or DAN!) conferences.[19] The Autism Research Institute is neither the largest nor the best-funded of the parent groups involved in research on the autism spectrum disorders, and it is one of several that advocate biomedical interventions. However, it is the only one that not only promotes but also develops the techniques. It has therefore become broadly identified with biomedical treatments for autism by both parents and practitioners.[20] Understanding Defeat Autism Now! is crucial for understanding the ways in which families with autism intervene in medical knowledge production and the complicated ways in which familial, scientific, therapeutic, and professional interests converge in an organization that seeks to recruit practitioners as well as parents.

Defeat Autism Now! conferences are a project of the Autism Research Institute (ARI) in San Diego, California, founded by Bernard Rimland, who also cofounded the National Society for Autistic Children (renamed the Autism Society of America). Rimland was a Ph.D. in experimental psychology and spent his career in the Navy, working as the director of the Personnel Measurement Research Department at the Training Research Laboratory in Point Loma, California. As a parent of a child with autism and a scientist, Rimland represented the paradigmatic parent activist, using his set of prior skills in autism research while ironically and publicly referencing his own "autistic" tendencies. In his experience, "parents of autistic children are often people able to concentrate deeply," an ability that served them well in research careers.[21]

The story of Bernard Rimland's entry into the field has been told many times. His son Mark cried constantly from birth and did not speak a meaningful sentence before the age of eight. Mark cared less about who was taking care of him than whether they were wearing a "certain flowered dress," so Rimland's wife, Gloria, ordered them from a catalog for his grandmothers to wear while they babysat.[22] Gloria remembered reading about children like Mark in one of her textbooks, and Rimland "went out to the garage, found the dusty box of old college texts, and there, five years after I had earned a Ph.D. as a research psychologist, I saw the word 'autism' for the first time."[23] Rimland obtained behavioral therapy for his son and maintained that this was largely responsible for his significant improvements. Nevertheless, as early as 1972 in an article promoting operant conditioning therapies for autism, Rimland noted that "the ultimate answer to the problem of severe behavior disturbances in children—and adults—will come from the biochemistry laboratory, in the form of a drug or a special diet, like the one for phenylketonuria (PKU)." In other words, an intervention tailored to a disorder's underlying biological mechanisms could prevent symptoms of the disorder from appearing.[24]

Rimland formed the National Society for Autistic Children in 1965 in part to promote applied behavior analysis (ABA), then being developed by O. Ivar Lovaas at UCLA. As we have seen, proponents of psychotherapeutic treatments regarded ABA as a form of conditioning tantamount to abuse, but Rimland saw promise in the techniques. He also began his own research program, leading to the publication in 1964 of *Infantile Autism*, which won the Appleton Century Psychology Series publishing award. Rimland's work earned praise for offering a fresh perspective in a field in which experts' lack of interdisciplinary knowledge kept them from drawing on new research.[25] Rimland challenged the psychogenic theory of autism promoted in the work of Kanner, Bettelheim, and others, proposing an alternative theory of etiology and directions for future research.

In 1967, two years after founding NSAC, Rimland set up the Institute for Child Behavior Research, later the Autism Research Institute (ARI), as a clearinghouse for treatment-based research. He began publishing the *Autism Research Review International*, a review of promising and new treatments, to which many parents subscribed over the years.[26] To this end, Rimland spent decades refining diagnostic measures of factors left out of the standard definition of autism. The original Autism Behavioral Checklist he included in *Infantile Autism* asked about developmental regression, pregnancy complications, and the child's eating habits, in addition to questions about behavioral symptoms.[27] His instructions for a system of monitoring and ambition to develop individualized care have become part of the practice of the Defeat Autism Now! community.

The idea of treating mental and developmental disabilities using nutritional supplements did not begin with Defeat Autism Now! conferences or even ARI. Roger J. Williams's work on "biochemical individuality" and the variability of patients' nutritional needs inspired Rimland to frame autism as a chronic illness, as did Linus Pauling's idea of a "molecular disease" that could be treated through nutrient supplementation.[28] In practical terms, parents and practitioners began experimenting with high doses of B-vitamins for autism during the 1960s, following studies of phenylketonuria patients and controversial attempts to use nutritional supplements to treat Down syndrome.[29] Elsewhere, experiments with megadoses of vitamin B3 seemed promising in treating adults with schizophrenia.[30] Despite equivocal results in the syndromes studied and the resistance of medical organizations, parents and practitioners remained interested in experimenting with nutritional therapies in autism.[31]

Rimland began investigating megavitamin therapies and orthomolecular medicine through his Institute for Child Behavior Research in San Diego. During the mid-1960s, parents had begun contacting him about the therapy.

> Even though few of the parents were acquainted with each other and each was trying quite a variety of vitamins, the same small group of

vitamins was being mentioned again and again. As the number of parent-experimenters grew, it began to include more parents whom I knew personally to be intelligent and reliable people. At that point I contacted a number of doctors in California and on the East Coast who had been experimenting with vitamin therapy. The combined information from the doctors and parents convinced me that I could not, in good conscience, fail to pursue this lead.[32]

Rimland conducted his initial study on megavitamins with the help of parents in the National Society for Autistic Children. Linus Pauling advised on the project. While the long-term affiliation between ARI and Kirkman Laboratories, which manufactured the vitamin mixture, might represent a conflict of interest to some, Rimland noted that of "all 26 vitamin manufacturers in the *Thomas Register,*" Kirkman was the only company willing to experiment with autism treatments. His results suggested that when combined with magnesium to prevent deficiencies associated with high doses of B6, the therapy helped a subset of children.[33] The fact that only some children responded to any treatment suggested problems with current psychiatric nosology:

> I am firmly convinced that very little progress may be expected in finding cause and treatment for mental illness in children until the total group of children now loosely called "autistic," "schizophrenic," "psychotic," or "severely emotionally disturbed" can be subdivided in a scientific way into smaller homogeneous subgroups. . . . I believe the children loosely called "autistic" or "schizophrenic" actually represent a dozen or more different diseases or disorders, each with its own cause.[34]

This multiplicity of causes might correspond to an equally large number of interventions that would be effective for only some children. Although Rimland preferred to evaluate treatments through parent responses rather than eliminate an option merely because it was unfamiliar, he was hardly indiscriminate in his support of therapeutic techniques. For example, he disputed the claims of those who promoted "facilitated communication" as a means of enabling people with autism to use language. The technique, developed first to help people with cerebral palsy, required a facilitator to support the arm of a person with autism while they typed. Rimland argued against the approach in the *Autism Research Review International* and later published an article suggesting that it involved a significant degree of prompting on the part of the facilitator that its supporters confused with independent action on the part of autistic children.[35] Research by others corroborated the finding.

Rimland convened the first Defeat Autism Now! meeting in Dallas, Texas, in January 1995, with Sidney Baker, a physician with a background in functional medicine and Jon Pangborn, an industrial biochemist and parent of a child with autism. The Dallas meeting helped to define the Defeat Autism Now! mission: to go beyond merely describing autism to "identify treatments—safe treatments—for which there is credible evidence of efficacy." Once found, "an attempt would be made to find why they work, so their efficacy could be improved."[36] Those among the thirty or so participants at the first Defeat Autism Now! meeting remember it as exhilarating, a moment when physicians from research universities shared the floor with alternative medicine practitioners experimenting with promising therapies, and where parents of autistic children, many of them also scientists, were taken seriously. Defeat Autism Now! elevated the commitment to listening to parents to the level of principle. Rimland observed that "as the years went on, I continued to find, repeatedly, that the parents, especially the mothers, were remarkably effective at identifying treatments that were helpful to their autistic children. They were also very observant in detecting factors that caused their children to become worse."[37]

Following the conference, Rimland and Baker published a brief report in the *Journal of Autism and Developmental Disorders*. Developing effective interventions would require physicians to consider the potential of alternative treatments for which there existed "abundant clinical evidence," despite the difficulty of testing them in placebo-controlled studies. The Defeat Autism Now! group saw a number of interrelated factors contributing to autism, among them food allergies and intolerances, microbial infections, and immune dysregulation. The interventions they advocated in 1996 included

> gluten- and casein-free diets; avoidance of allergenic foods; antifungal, antimicrobial, and antibacterial drugs; normalization of bowel flora; improvement in gut mucosal nutrition and permeability; biochemical support with nutrients that are important in intermediary metabolism (B6, Mg) and in detoxification chemistry (sulfur amino acids, reduced glutathione, treatment of phenosulfotransferase deficiency).[38]

This set of treatment types, individualized for each child, has, with the exception of an increasing emphasis on detoxification, remained much the same. Pangborn, Baker, and Rimland all grew more concerned about rising rates of autism diagnoses in the mid-1990s and began to emphasize the possibility that immunizations could be triggering the disorder. A decade later, most Defeat Autism Now! practitioners and conference speakers tended to treat vaccines as one among a range of environmental causes, an opinion shared by many parents. Rimland maintained that his own son, a successful artist whose whimsical paintings are exhibited in a gallery next to ARI's headquarters, differed from the younger children who accounted for the recent increase. That is, he did not regress and did not appear to have suffered ill effects from vaccines.

Bernard Rimland passed away in 2006 after a long illness. He earned wide and well-deserved recognition for having transformed the professional perspective on autism.[39] Stephen Edelson took over as director of ARI. Edelson, referred to Rimland as a graduate student in the 1970s by Rimland's friend Ivar Lovaas, had become the director of the Oregon affiliate of ARI, the Center for the Study of Autism. He had spent many years working with Rimland in assessing various treatments, and remembered him as "not just a professional mentor but also a kind and generous friend."[40] Rimland's death came at a transitional time for ARI/Defeat Autism Now!, as other founding members moved closer to retirement. It served to emphasize the need to train new practitioners and publicize the dual messages of autism's treatability and the role of biochemical individuality in the disorder.

Despite the stability of ARI's commitment to promoting systematic medical evaluations and collaboration with parents in designing treatment programs, Defeat Autism Now! conferences have evolved to reflect parents' new concerns and the shifting research agendas of its members and the autism research community at large. By the end of the first decade of the twenty-first century, many presenters emphasized the interactive effects of multiple environmental and genetic factors. Ten years earlier a majority might have argued that vaccines alone accounted for the bulk of new autism cases. ARI/Defeat Autism Now! had drawn the line at the understanding of autism promoted by the neurodiversity community, which rejects the idea that autism should be treated. Lately they have begun working to reconcile the two approaches by addressing the medical problems that adults with autism report and by engaging directly with some self-advocates.[41] As of 2011, the organization announced that it would refer to future meetings as "ARI conferences," partly because so many self-advocates objected to the Defeat Autism Now! name.[42] However, Defeat Autism Now! practitioners resolutely see autism as a treatable result of chronic medical conditions. They believe that improvement and sometimes recovery are both desirable and possible.

An Experimental Community: Biomedicine as Practice

ARI organizes twice-yearly Defeat Autism Now! conferences along with periodic parent or practitioner training workshops in cities across the United States. Both parents and practitioners attend conferences, rubbing shoulders during sessions, at coffee breaks, and in the exhibitor hall. At the center of the Defeat Autism Now! conferences and the broader parent community that they inspire is the Defeat Autism Now! guide, *Biomedical Assessment and Treatment Options for Autism Spectrum Disorders*. It has grown from a spiral-bound sheaf of suggestions distributed at the first meeting in Dallas to a commercially produced manual that parents and practitioners take home from conferences along with a "syllabus" of the PowerPoint slides from presentations. Presenters urge parents to share the guide with their children's doctors.

The Defeat Autism Now! treatment method involves an explicit, though often individualized, set of tests and regimens, which proceed stepwise through levels of difficulty and sometimes cost. More complex treatments require monitoring by a medical professional. The first stage is an elimination diet, removing foods that parents and doctors have associated with sensitivities in autistic children. Two popular diets are the gluten-free/casein-free (gf/cf) diet and the specific carbohydrate diet (SCD). In some cases, a practitioner will feel that a child might do well on a diet designed to address an overgrowth of yeast (*Candida albicans*) by eliminating sugar, yeast-containing foods, and dairy products. They may supplement that diet with antifungal medications like Nystatin or Diflucan. Many parents report that such diets ameliorate typical symptoms such as "stimming" (self-stimulatory behavior like hand-flapping) and acting "drunk" or "silly." They also improve their child's level of awareness and visibly result in improved physical symptoms. "His skin is smoother too—the small white bumps on his cheeks are gone. His fiery cheeks faded with the diet, but now he isn't really red-cheeked at all. . . . We've come to realize how sharply his behavior deteriorates when he gets sugar."[43]

The second stage aims at repairing metabolic processes through nutritional supplements. Defeat Autism Now! doctors speak of an "emerging picture" of the biochemistry of autism. They do not believe that the children they treat have nutrient deficiencies. Rather, they use supplements to promote or "drive" metabolic processes that may be slower or less effective in children with autism because of problems at multiple points in a reaction. For example, a child might have a functional but slower form of an enzyme required to metabolize nutrients like vitamin B6.[44] These problems may be caused by oxidative stress, the overproduction of reactive oxygen species, molecules that can kill or injure cells. They could also be caused by environmental factors combined with genetic predispositions. In some cases, doctors will also prescribe antiviral medications and treatments designed to support children's immune systems, such as intravenous immunoglobulin (IVIG). They use these drugs because of concerns about persistent measles virus infections acquired from vaccines and because of symptoms that seem generally consistent with immune dysregulation, such as recurring ear infections.[45]

Chelation (pronounced key-LAY-shun), the third stage of treatment in the guide, is also the most contentious. Originally developed as a treatment for acute heavy metal poisoning, it involves the oral, transdermal, or intravenous administration of molecules with a selective binding affinity for heavy metals, which are then excreted in urine along with the captured metals.[46] The process is time-consuming and unpleasant. Treatments take place throughout the day, during which parents need to measure and monitor their child's urine to ensure that metals are being excreted. Only certain doctors, usually those with a background in functional or environmental medicine, will oversee chelation treatment because of the risks involved. At some level, most who offer the treatment believe in a mercury or heavy metal hypothesis of autism etiology. While a majority of Defeat Autism Now! doctors maintain that autism involves some form of toxic etiology, many have shifted in their public statements from describing autism as a vaccine-caused epidemic to emphasizing heterogeneous causes and symptoms, effective treatments, and outcomes.

Laboratory and clinical studies of nutrition and metabolism in children with autism seem to confirm parents' routine reports of improved functioning and behavior and the remission of allergies and gastrointestinal problems after beginning biomedical treatment. Some recent studies suggest a biological basis for altered immune responses to certain foods in children with autism. Additional studies point to the presence of oxidative stress and impaired methylation, both of which can slow the removal of toxic substances from bodies. Others have found potential functional impairment or even genetic vulnerabilities in detoxification enzymes such as methionine synthase or glutathione transferase. Still others highlight evidence of recognized pathological processes, including neuroinflammation and overt gastrointestinal pathologies.[47] Defeat Autism Now! doctors see in these studies children with bodies unable to sustain the daily burdens of metabolizing and removing complex modern foodstuffs and toxic environmental substances—who retain rather than excrete elements that are harmful to their bodies.[48]

For the parents associated with Defeat Autism Now! these biomedical interventions entail laborious experimentation and therapeutic trials followed by incremental improvements and occasional sudden leaps in functional behaviors. A parent quoted in the Defeat Autism Now! treatment guide says that the most important thing "is daily record keeping."[49] Parents track the treatments that they have tried, recording minute variations in their child's mood, behavior, and physical symptoms in thick binders with elaborate charts. One parent posted her recording method to the ARI Web site as an example to others. She monitors eleven variables, from stool quality to eye contact, using a five-point scale to rate responses to twenty separate treatments. She explains that this strategy helps her with the different kinds of attentiveness and sensitivity required by biomedical treatments because it "allows me to adjust one treatment at a time without rushing into different things. It also allows me to see subtle differences over a relatively long period of time and helps me go back and ask: 'When did I see that behavior last?' "[50]

Motherhood often involves this type of intense care and watchfulness. In this sense, parents using biomedical treatments take part in a longstanding U.S. culture of childrearing. Historians and sociologists have documented the tendency of American mothers in particular to seek expert scientific advice. The time-consuming practices that Defeat Autism Now! doctors recommend—or that parents discover on their own—become a type of biomedical "intensive motherhood." As Sharon Hays points out, women accept that the emotional rewards of mothering will compensate for the sacrifices of time and energy.[51] Love is both the impetus and the outcome. Christina Adams makes the point even more plainly. The mothers of some children with autism diagnoses become not mere mothers but "Autism Mommies."

> This is a slender tier of women who do everything that sounds remotely reasonable. They do the diet. They draw vials of blood from

their children and test it for signs and deficits, like oracles looking to foretell the future. They run twenty-five- or thirty-hour-a-week home programs, and send their kids to the special ed classroom twice a week to keep the school district happy. They make the immediate round of specialists, trudge to occupational and speech therapy twice a week. They share gf/cf recipes, educate relatives, and generally walk the intervention treadmill for years.[52]

Like many parents, Adams sees her entry into intensive motherhood as a transformation by choice and necessity. It is a full-time job driven by love, but accomplished through reason and experience, because "This is our work. Everything else vanishes."[53]

Defeat Autism Now! conferences act primarily to disseminate knowledge about biomedical treatments. Advocacy for services and support play a secondary role at best. Parents share experiences and encourage others. Still, the circulation of knowledge in the Defeat Autism Now! community is political in that it involves an active choice about how to conceive of autism. That choice is informed by more than the facts that medical authorities can provide by citing studies or arguing from expertise. It comprises personal craft knowledge about the specifics of interventions. The Defeat Autism Now! community sees diets as a form of targeted biomedical intervention because they address the pathophysiology of the disorder rather than the symptoms alone. In this sense diets are more appropriate treatments than psychopharmaceuticals. However, parents undertake diets not because the underlying rationale is convincing but because the results reinforce the practice. This framing of an experimental approach in which parents are the technicians as a pathway to an authentic understanding of autism is reflected in discussions among doctors and in promotional literature.

Beyond the Defeat Autism Now! conferences and guide lies a broader constellation of message boards, discussion groups, and newsletters. Doctors use one listserv to share insights, seek guidance on difficult cases (withholding identifying information about patients) and how to interpret unexpected laboratory results, and circulate references to journal articles. A group closely connected to Defeat Autism Now! is a Yahoo-based listserv called the Autism Biomedical Discussion Group (ABMD), with over 5,000 members. A parent set up the list in early 2000 to share information about using the pancreatic hormone secretin as a treatment for autism, and it later expanded to cover the range of biomedical interventions.[54] Not all participants on ABMD are parents. Doctors told me that they tracked the list for information about possible treatment side effects or the general tenor of parent discussions and concerns.

The listserv discussions occasionally reference key texts that circulate within the biomedical treatment community, including Karen Seroussi's *Unraveling the Mystery of Autism and Pervasive Developmental Disorder: A Mother's Story of Research and Recovery*, which promotes elimination diets, and Lynn Hamilton's combined memoir and handbook, *Facing Autism: Giving Parents Reasons for Hope and Guidance for Help*.[55] Lisa Lewis's *Special Diets for Special Kids* guides readers through dietary modifications and Stephen Edelson and Bernard Rimland's *Treating Autism* includes parent testimonials about their children's sometimes-tentative improvements.[56] A fifth book, Jacquelyn McCandless's *Children with Starving Brains*, details her journey from psychiatrist to autism treatment specialist as a result of her granddaughter Chelsea's diagnosis.[57] McCandless's book is sold at Defeat Autism Now! conferences and members consistently reference it as central to their approach. McCandless and her husband, Jack Zimmerman, use the language of love as one explanation for what they see as a reciprocal process of healing opposed to the conventional medical model of treatment:

> The children with starving brains challenge our capacity to love— particularly in regard to the qualities of patience and perseverance, devotion beyond the usual parental call of duty and the capacity to think and act creatively "out of the box." Often, it is only after a profound challenge to our capacity to love, such as the rearing of an ASD child, that we come to realize how much more there is to discover about loving.[58]

While Seroussi and Hamilton both say that treatment led to their children losing their diagnoses, McCandless offers a more guarded appraisal of her granddaughter's progress.[59]

Crossing Over

> I was once a "very mainstream" physician. I did everything by the book. I was taught, "if it is not a drug, it doesn't work," and "parents know absolutely nothing." And I truly believed this.[60]

The organizers of Defeat Autism Now! conferences see them as a means to recruit and train new doctors and parents. For many years, ARI maintained a registry of clinicians offering biomedical treatments, but it abandoned the practice in 2011 because it was too difficult to review each applicant to ensure that he or she was reliable and had the requisite training. ARI now suggests that parents contact local support groups for referrals.[61] As is the case in many medical or scientific communities, parents decide to trust practitioners based on their physical presence; their self-presentation, including signs of their devotion to research; and their commitment to evaluating evidence in a disinterested manner. Parents' trust also hinges on how well a doctor can muster facts on demand and demonstrate mastery of the specialized language of biomedical treatment. Conferences and meetings help build this trust.

The daily routine of monitoring and care trains parents to view their children's symptoms as mutable via interventions. The same methods affect practitioners through seeing children "actually respond" for the first time since beginning to treat children with autism. Their experiences with parents and patients lead to membership in the group. Onstage at a banquet held at a Defeat Autism Now! conference, one father offered "the top ten reasons that you know that you are the parent of an autistic child": You cheer when your child has a normal bowel movement. You have alarms installed in your home to alert you when someone has *left* rather than entered without warning—a reference to the ordeal of lost or missing children shared by many parents—and you find that you have packed for a trip with only the things that your child needs. You are also able to "sit for hours listening to scientific theories—and understand it." Others in the room nodded and, despite the heartwrenching details, laughed along with him.[62]

One of the most vivid accounts of parenting a child with autism while immersed in biomedical interventions is the comic "The Chelation Kid" by Robert Tinnell and Craig Taillefer. Many of the strips deal with the skepticism that accompanies biomedical treatments, first on the part of the father when his wife suggests that they explore alternatives in treating their son, and then on the part of the therapists, teachers, and doctors who work with their son. When a doctor advises them to stop using nutritional supplements and continue on only the gf/cf diet, their child is transformed from the relatively calm and happy "Chelation Kid" to the angry and violent "Autism Lad."[63]

Defeat Autism Now! treatments depend on a network of commercial laboratories with specialized tests for measuring baseline and posttreatment levels of various enzymes, nutrients, antibodies, and heavy metals.

A typical set of tests will check for allergies, nutrient levels, and both immediate and delayed allergic reactivity.[64] Conventional practitioners tend to regard these tests skeptically. At worst, they exploit parents desperate for information, and at best they are too poorly standardized an instrument to be useful. Insurance companies often fail to cover the costs of laboratory work. Nevertheless, Defeat Autism Now! doctors argue that genetic vulnerabilities in conjunction with environmental triggers might cause a variety of symptoms. These complex responses may not be visible at thresholds conventionally recognized as indications of disease processes. From this perspective, doctors have been quietly characterizing the biochemistry of autism for at least two decades. One researcher explained that

> it is IMPORTANT, if present models are to change, that concrete data about the chemistry of those with autism is made a public record. Professionals with whom I have shared my own daughter's chemical workup have been miffed by what they've seen, because this sort of workup is not usually done; since these sorts of results are unfamiliar they are viewed as only a curiosity when they are seen individually. How can a neurologist become convinced he needs to know about his patient's immune/metabolic status unless the results of a great many of these workups are put to public inspection? [65]

At one Defeat Autism Now! conference, I attended a meeting organized to introduce "mainstream" practitioners from the local community to the framework promoted by the Autism Research Institute. The Defeat Autism Now! practitioners each gave short presentations on the metabolic and nutritional differences between individuals with autism and typically developing children. They suggested that in principle it was possible to intervene at these points of variation to produce behavioral changes. Each presentation focused on a different metabolic system. During the question period, one audience member, an experienced chemist but not a Defeat Autism Now! doctor, asked for a sheet of butcher paper and demonstrated how the various implicated biochemical pathways formed an interlocking series of reactions. One could intervene at various points in order to produce effects throughout the entire body. The point is one that Defeat Autism Now! practitioners regularly make, but the chemist came up with it on his own after hearing the presentations on single disease mechanisms. The presentations hardly addressed treatment philosophy. They reported pathological findings, and the chemist made the connection himself. If this practitioner chose to become involved in Defeat Autism Now!, he would have found a dispersed community united less by their association with Defeat Autism Now! than by their interest in alternative treatment methods, their practical attitude of experimentation, and their individual commitment to that particular vision of bodies as dynamic convergences of fundamentally interlinked systems.[66] The rest is open for discussion.

Defeat Autism Now! doctors and families focus on treating children and on converting qualified practitioners to their vision of autism. With increased experience, doctors and families also work a process of transformation on themselves. This is not indoctrination into an "irrational" nonscientific belief system. Rather, it means joining a community acutely aware of how social relationships help to define the boundaries of rationality, of the difficulties inherent in translation and proof, and of how expectations and prior assumptions can govern how experts read scientific texts, seeing some connections and overlooking others. Reflexivity is the dubious privilege of a marginal group. People who face continuous questions about their decisions build up arsenals of sources and arguments and become skilled at explaining why they believe what they do. Defeat Autism Now! practitioners struggle with the conflicting demands of treating children based on parent reports, maintaining credibility and certification, and establishing biomedical facts legible and credible to regulatory agencies and medical associations.

While I have argued that shared practical and affective dimensions of autism treatment rather than a specific theory of etiology unite this emerging community, a collective vision of autism as a treatable and mutable syndrome does indeed emerge from these practices. The vision is a practical one. It involves attending to dimensions of the disorder that could be described as medical rather than behavioral. These include skin ailments, levels of stimming and self-injury, exacerbations of gut disturbances, and variations in mood, all of which may be correlated with different dietary or other biomedical regimens. Tracking these associations leads parents and practitioners to reframe the diagnostic category. The same Defeat Autism Now! researcher quoted earlier expressed this idea well in an e-mail to a parent that focused on funding genetic research on autism.

You and I probably would agree about the need for autism to become a diagnosis of biochemical certainty rather than one built around behavioral things that may change as people respond to a whole host of different sorts of therapy. I think that the only thing you and I may see differently is what may be the fastest and most effective method at getting to a "physical marker" which could replace current methods of diagnosis. I very much feel that studying the measurable factors in the immune, endocrine and metabolic systems would yield faster results, as opposed to looking at something as incredibly large as the human genome, and looking at only those persons from multi-incidence families who may not represent at all those whose autism appears without precedent in a family.[67]

While it is possible to seek genetic analogs for behavioral characteristics, the search for metabolic biomarkers by doctors who insist that "every child is biochemically unique" points to a reframing of both disease concept and research practice. Seeking explanations for autism at the level of cellular signaling involves a choice of perspective, away from a monolithic diagnosis and toward autism as a "final common outcome" (a perspective that, ironically, genetic research may also eventually adopt). In similar fashion, research programs that look to treatment response to identify potential disease mechanisms revise the investigative process by enrolling caregivers' observations and designing studies around the work of community-based clinicians.[68]

The Heart of the Matter: Commitment, Trust, and the Work of Recovery

At my first Defeat Autism Now! conference, I experienced what many other newcomers feel. I was utterly overwhelmed. I didn't know whom or what to trust.[69] First-time parents sometimes leave the room in tears during a lecture, overcome by the prospect of healing a child diagnosed as untreatable or else by the onslaught of biochemical jargon and PowerPoint slides.

One of the premises of the field of science studies is that contemporary science and biomedicine are built on trust as well as claims to truth. If I wanted to understand the Defeat Autism Now! community, it followed that I needed to learn how practitioners' claims were persuasive. As I spent more time at Defeat Autism Now! meetings, I realized that the problem

involved not unwavering trust in medical authorities as much as persuasion, followed by provisional commitments. Parents can decide to try one
intervention, rather than accept a wholesale shift in viewpoint. I started to
spend less time squeezing myself into huddles of doctors and more time
chatting with moms in the lobby, asking them why they tried biomedical
interventions. One parent showed me a photograph of her dreamy-eyed
daughter. When she first considered biomedical treatments her friends
said that only the desperate would try diets and supplements. She said that
she reached that point when her daughter, who had taken to wandering
out of the house mid-winter in her nightgown, tried to jump out of their
car into traffic.

Parents certainly grow skeptical when experts cannot solve their most
pressing concerns, but doubts about conventional forms of medical authority are something of a tradition in the United States. The transition
from home- to hospital-based care followed on doctors' claims that medical treatment required expert knowledge and extended training, what Paul
Starr terms the "legitimate complexity" of American medicine.[70] Recipe
books for special diets, an emphasis on home-based care, and mistrust of
medical professionals by parents who would rather do their own research
are predictable and enduring responses to the limitations of accepted
treatment modalities and the difficulty of contending with symptoms
that conventional models of disease do not recognize or acknowledge.[71]
While the rationales for biomedical interventions are often as complex as
those for conventional treatments, the mode of interaction between practitioners and parents is decidedly different. Defeat Autism Now! doctors
depend on parental reports, and this compels them to regard parents as
collaborators as much as clients. Parent reports are something to be taken
seriously and shared with colleagues, because it is through them that doctors can evaluate interventions and learn about the behavioral effects of
different treatments.

Their acknowledged debt to parents' observations of their children
and their descriptions of parents as competent technicians and insightful partners in treatment can put Defeat Autism Now! doctors at odds
with the prevailing public depictions of "autism parents." The image of the
desperate parent often trumps the professional identities of researchers,
practitioners, or reporters. Members of the Defeat Autism Now! community accept that observations of one's own child, professional practices,
and clinical experimentation often run together. Elsewhere, researchers
will go to significant lengths to downplay the fact that their research fol-

lows upon their own child's diagnosis, especially when the work might be associated with a "hysterical" parent's belief about vaccines or environmental toxins. Parents are acutely aware that their status compromises their claims for objectivity and disinterestedness. Objectivity, understood as the ability to evaluate experiments without any personal stake in the outcome, is what theorists have called a technique of social position, a way of seeing that has historically been associated with certain identities and not with others.[72] At different moments, women, employees, parents, or anyone else whose well-being was too tightly dependent on another person have been seen as unreliable observers. Some parent-researchers operate within mainstream science by insulating their public, professional identities from their roles as parents. Others situate themselves outside the center of scientific culture, citing eclectic educations, the demands of parenting, or a deeply felt critique of conventional medicine.

In 1964, a reviewer of *Infantile Autism* noted Rimland's comparison between his perspective and that of an observer putting an eye to a keyhole and finding a magnified landscape beyond.

> Yet maybe because he has come from the other side of the door the author has been able to see things which were obscured to those in the room, obscured in part because they were too close to the problem, in part because doctrinaire viewpoints prevented them from perceiving the obvious, and in part because their obscure notions of genetics, neurophysiology, motivation and cognition did not permit them to make use of the latest research findings from these rapidly expanding sciences.[73]

If theorizing autism treatment requires a view "from the other side of the door," then accepting the idea of complete recovery from those treatments requires a still greater shift, even as many researchers have begun to accept that a small percentage of children do in fact lose their autism diagnoses.[74] A 2004 video produced by ARI, "Recovered Autistic Children," featured a series of children interacting with their parents and speaking directly to the camera. Not all of the children would be likely to meet a diagnostician's standard of developmental typicality, but the parents in the video seemed thrilled nonetheless about how far their children had progressed. For some parents, recovery promises a respite from behaviors that disrupt daily life, the parts of autism that prevented them from "having a family," in the words of one parent. They might refer to chronic physical problems like diarrhea or eczema as the real source of discomfort to the child, far more disabling than a lack of social reciprocity. Or they might accept the premise that recovery is possible for some children but see their own use of biomedical treatments as simply one more way that they are working to improve their child's prospects for a good life.[75] Parents also highlight changes too subtle to record in a standard interview like "the length of their sentences, their empathy and sense of humor," traits that are so tightly woven into the fabric of family interactions and the individual quirks of a personality that it may take an intimate to register them.[76]

Visceral Issues: "Sick Kids" and Diagnostic Vision

The complexities of symptom identification, interpretation, and diagnostic modes of seeing involved in alternative treatment practices come together in the case of gastrointestinal issues in autism. Other examples would serve the same purpose: vitamin B6 and magnesium, or subcutaneous injections of methyl-B12, or the elimination diet laid out in *Special Diets for Special Kids* by Lisa Lewis. Members of the medical community consider each approach equally dubious. Adherents have had an equally hard time establishing the existence of a specific pathological mechanism and the efficacy of the corresponding treatments. This is partly because all of these treatments, depending on a functional approach to physiological systems, do not involve the clear correlations between brain chemistry and behavior that the broader medical community expects to see in autism treatments. It is also because only a subgroup of children seems to respond to each treatment. This confuses analysis when investigators base their studies of treatment efficacy on an assumption that all cases of autism are caused by the same underlying biology.

The broader medical community is only now coming to accept that children with autism can experience significant gastrointestinal symptoms, although they disagree about whether these symptoms represent a distinct diagnostic category of "autistic enterocolitis," as some doctors associated with Defeat Autism Now! have contended.[77] Doctors have arrived at this recognition of the reality of digestive symptoms often despite, not because of, a long history of parents complaining about allergies and gastrointestinal issues in their children. According to the testimony of parents in the on-line biomedical discussion group and at conferences, often the first—and sometimes the only—effect of an elimination diet is that their child finds relief from chronic diarrhea or constipation. Researchers who want to confirm the reports confront the additional problem of identifying a disease process, which may not be visible without invasive diagnostic exams, in children who do not communicate well.

Some physicians are willing to treat children empirically, that is on the basis of reported symptoms and without medical evaluations that can require procedures like colonoscopies. The problem is that in general a clearly defined set of symptoms must be present to justify invasive tests. Patients need to report that they have cramps, or they need to have bloody stool or unexplained weight loss. Often children with autism present none of these indicators, and doctors are more likely to consider their bowel issues consequences rather than causes of the child's neurological disturbance. A child might simply be refusing to defecate or be experiencing stomach upset as a result of stress. Likewise, the physicians are likely to view self-injurious behaviors as an isolated problem, rather than a result of underlying physical discomfort. The problem of gastrointestinal illnesses in autism literally had to acquire diagnostic visibility.

In 1998, Andrew Wakefield, a gastroenterologist at the Royal Free Hospital in London, published a paper with colleagues describing a novel intestinal pathology in children with autism and developmental regression.[78] Although the paper was discredited and eventually withdrawn by the journal (an episode I discuss in chapter 6), doctors have since increasingly accepted that gastrointestinal issues could affect the behavior of individuals with autism spectrum disorders. These symptoms may be due to allergies, food intolerances, inflammatory processes, behavioral issues, or functional problems with the gastrointestinal tract.[79] However, taking gastrointestinal symptoms seriously requires a change in perspective. Without this, members of the Defeat Autism Now! community have argued, they are literally invisible.

When I first met one pediatric gastroenterologist at a Defeat Autism Now! conference, he preferred to avoid explicit speculations about the causal relationship between gut pathology and regressive autism. He suggested that stress associated with the inability to communicate might be the cause of the problems parents reported.[80] Certainly, many of the children he treated had exceptionally difficult gastrointestinal symptoms. At a subsequent meeting, having spent more time with the Defeat Autism Now! community, he remained skeptical about the existence of any distinct gastrointestinal condition associated with autism. However, he was convinced of the need to teach pediatricians to look for medical issues underlying a host of behavioral problems. He showed a video clip of a child screaming and writhing on the floor, pressing his hands into his stomach.[81] An audience primed to the underlying condition reacted as expected. That is, they responded empathically to a case of agonizing pain, visibly expressed, where others might have said that the child was merely "tantrumming."

Another gastroenterologist illustrated his talks with photographs that parents provided of their own children angling their bodies over chairs and placing pressure on their abdomens, behaviors that would be dismissed as "posturing" or forms of stereotyped behavior by an uninitiated audience. He talked about the limitations of conventional gastroenterologists when they encounter these kids in their practices. Their training dictates that gastrointestingal disorders will follow a recognizable pattern, including persistent diarrhea or rectal bleeding, and so they fail to recognize important signs like growth retardation and don't even think to ask parents about constipation.[82] In some cases, parents have to work hard to find doctors willing to use techniques like colonoscopies or X-rays to examine superficially healthy children, although it is often these techniques that yield the definitive visual evidence of pathology that many practitioners refer to when they explain why they began considering gut issues in their patients with autism. Diagnostic moments like this require both empathy and detailed knowledge. Without them, it is as if professionals literally cannot see a child's pain.

Symptoms of children with autism that are dismissed as comorbidities or "just the autism" by many conventional practitioners can also be reinterpreted as food sensitivities that lead in turn to gastrointestinal disturbances. Although many doctors are primarily attuned to the acute immune-mediated allergic reactions that children can have to problem foods (think peanut allergies), many parents are more concerned about food sensitivities and intolerances. These conditions may not be mediated by the same immune responses as typical food allergies or may not involve immune reactions at all. At one conference I joined a group of young mothers from Louisiana while they talked among themselves, mainly about their children's bowel problems. One participant confided, "If you hang around autistic parents enough, all we talk about is poop." For a community that understands their children's problems to arise at least partially from gut dysfunction, the specifics of foul-smelling bowel movements and chronic diarrhea or constipation are important observational diagnostic tools that are a special province of parents. Parents share the common currency of experience, filtered through their conviction that these experiences can be interpreted in medically significant terms.

The first step toward embracing a biomedical framework is learning to view children with autism as suffering from physiological dysfunctions that can affect their entire bodies, as opposed to purely neurological problems manifested mainly in behaviors. In conversations with practitioners about deciding whether to incorporate biomedical treatments into their practices, many referred to the threat of liability for using "unproven" treatments. Even recommending elimination diets as a treatment for autism can lead to losing one's license to practice medicine. Vitamin and mineral supplementation carry a lower risk, while chelation and intravenous therapies are higher risk. The riskiest move in personal terms may be altering the way one weighs available information in treating a condition that is supposedly localized in and expressed by the brain and its dysfunctions.[83]

The case history becomes an important way of learning to see autism differently, that is, to see children with autism as "sick kids" who are in need of treatment. Martha Herbert is a pediatric neurologist at Massachusetts General Hospital who, although not a Defeat Autism Now! doctor, has emphasized thinking about the brain in autism as often "downstream" of other physiological problems. She described her own shift in perspective:

> A key transition in my own understanding of this disorder has been taking careful and thorough medical histories of my autistic and other neurobehavioral patients, and taking their physical complaints seriously. These complaints, once one learns to ask about them, turn out to be so common that it has become impossible for me to ignore them or assume that they are less important than the behavioral features. These children cannot be assumed to have nothing more than brain and behavior problems, since so many of them are also physically ill. A critical question is whether—and if so how—these things are related.[84]

Doctors associated with Defeat Autism Now! are converts if only in the sense that their diagnostic perspective is dramatically different from the one that they learned in medical school. This change can complicate their sense of identity as doctors.[85] They emphasize the importance of listening to parents for clinical insights and research suggestions.[86] Some see themselves as part of a movement with the objective of altering medical practice in order to improve the prospects for children with autism and other neurodevelopmental disorders. Others emphasize the disciplinary and investigational aspects of their work as neurologists, psychiatrists, gastroenterologists, or immunologists, thereby maintaining their identities as specialists and primary researchers, even if, like Martha Herbert, they draw on insights from biomedical approaches. Those who are less concerned with institutional status may come increasingly to identify themselves as "DAN! docs." These are not a homogeneous group by any means.

At one conference, I joined a conversation between two doctors whom I had known for several years. One explained how he had become interested in nutritional medicine after traditional training in pediatrics and medical genetics. He had gone to school in the 1960s and acquired the habit of questioning conventional wisdom. This might have primed him to listen when a family returned to his office with a child that he had known years before, a small boy with severe autism. The child was thriving, nearly typical in behavior. The parents said that the child was on an elimination diet and asked him to watch a video of the child being fed a piece of pizza. Within hours, the child "went to pieces," giggling and running in circles, shedding his clothes. Later still, he was curled in a fetal position on the floor, moaning. In the background, offscreen, it was possible to hear his father saying that he knew that it hurt, but they had to make this video so that the doctors would know that they were telling the truth. The doctor showed me a copy of the video on his laptop. It was indeed hard evidence to ignore.

Biomedical Pluralism, Invisible Labor, and the Practice of Love

The combination of compromised witnessing and daily attentiveness associated with biomedical interventions in autism suggests a problem that must be dealt with in discussing contemporary illness-based communities in general. Sociologists of medicine and science have underscored the importance of social position in the construction of credible witnessing. They have documented how hard it can be to establish lay expert claims to knowledge. Clumsy descriptive terms like "semiprofessional" and "amateur" remind us that parental knowledge always seems unreliable, compromised, and partial, never more so than when parents make forays into more technical aspects of biomedicine or when practitioners rely on their reporting of technical details to establish their own claims to truth.[87] Because parents have a primary commitment to their child rather than to generalizable knowledge, their understanding is not only colored by their emotional involvement. It is also limited to their subjective observations of one child. But as we have seen, that partiality, attention to individual variation, and unwavering commitment may also have a lot to do with the efficacy of biomedical treatments for the families that have chosen to use them.

Just as some versions of "biosociality" seem to discount the active work that renders certain disease categories "genetic" in the first place, the concept of biosociality can also make social organization around disease categories appear spontaneous, as though illnesses themselves cause communities to form. We tend to naturalize the forms of labor and care associated with chronic illness. We also ignore how the decision to manage it experimentally, using unproven medical interventions, may produce an experience of membership and belonging. It is important to recognize these as choices based on reason and experience, rather than passive reactions to any particular diagnosis. What types of language are appropriate to the rich circulation of techniques, information, craft knowledge, inquiry, and passion that attend membership in these groups? If this is not scientific investigation, but it takes place inside of biomedicine—if it is standardized practice on bodies, but is not legitimate science—then what is it? Doctors and parents refer to their work as "biomedical interventions" because they identify it with techniques and models drawn from biomedicine's system of reason and rationality.

Deciding to value treating metabolic processes over identifying genes, environment over "innate biology," development over hardwiring, and cell over protein entails a shift in perspective and emphasis that renders certain processes more or less visible, certain interventions more or less possible, but that does not negate any specific approach. Defeat Autism Now! practitioners seamlessly incorporate genomics, psychopharmacology, and behavioral therapies into their practices. They may do so as a result of their education and background, of witnessing the effects of treatment, or out of a desire to help affected children. For parents, therapeutic pragmatism is one after-effect of engaging in the practical operations associated with learning to manage the disrupted biochemistry and difficult behaviors of their children. Members of the Defeat Autism Now! community have tried to reach other researchers and clinicians by using the techniques of contemporary biomedicine: peer-reviewed articles, clinical trials, published case reports, and readily legible theories of pathological mechanisms. The persuasive power of such techniques can only do so much against the resistance of autism, as a category, to resolve into a clear population in biological terms.

Psychiatrists can promise at least the prospect of a specific treatment for many of the disorders that they see in their practices, and this expectation is an incentive to produce accurate and clearly defined diagnoses. [88] Autism diagnoses using techniques like the ADOS and ADI or early screening methods like the CHAT have become standardized at least partly in the interest of developing treatments, but the monolithic definition of autism may in fact hinder the identification of successful therapies. Directed efforts to destabilize rather than refine the category, supported by unlikely alliances of functional medicine practitioners, not-for-profit research institutes, nutritional supplement manufacturers, maverick researchers, and independent laboratories, have encountered marked resistance from investigators whose research programs depend on the stability and reality of autism as a "true" population.

The efforts of parents and professionals using biomedical treatments to reframe autism as a chronic illness rather than a fixed genetic and neurological condition are, in some sense, aided by the absence of generally recognized biomarkers for autism. No genes or distinctive patterns of metabolites or dysmorphology have been consistently identified to establish children with autism as a visibly separate population. The work that constructs autism as a stable population occurs largely at the level of behavioral observations, diagnostic questionnaires, and checklists. Even researchers working outside of the world of biomedical interventions have become frustrated by the heterogeneity within the diagnostic category of autism. They have hinted at the need to consider the possibility that not one, but multiple forms of pathophysiology lead to the behavioral syndrome known as autism. As Martha Herbert and others put it, there is not one "autism" but multiple "autisms."[89] These might involve different genetic backgrounds as well as different patterns of onset and metabolic markers. Those who made the testimonies of parents part of their data set came to this conclusion earlier and more emphatically.

In one world, parents sit with their child in a doctor's office somewhere in the United States, hearing a diagnosis that they have probably already suspected. They are told that the term describes a mostly fixed and lifelong condition with a neurological basis, which will someday, through the efforts of academic research and the pooling of genetic material, become susceptible to pharmacological interventions or prenatal di-agnostic screening. They are directed toward early intervention programs and behavioral therapies. They may be encouraged to take part in one of the autism genetics initiatives currently in progress. Time passes, the child's behavior deteriorates, life becomes unmanageable, and the parents enter another world, seeking help through handbooks, the Internet, or exchanges with other parents. In this other world, parents trade diet tips and learn to administer vitamin injections. They attend conferences and talk tentatively about improvements and recovery. There are few reports of miracles, but considerable optimism. In both worlds, parents' massive efforts of attention, monitoring, care, and observation are described as acts of love.

While it might seem that this story describes parents gradually accu-mulating experience and knowledge about autism, the subjective experi-ence of moving from a conventional framework to a biomedical frame-work for understanding autism entails a more radical shift in perspective. The experience of joining a community devoted to biomedical treatment can involve learning to see familiar phenomena through different eyes. It's not unlike those random-dot stereograms that resolve from a mass of disconnected pixels into pictures of dolphins and palm trees if you stare hard enough. Learning to see in this new way requires physical effort, the affective labor involved in the private, home-bound work of treatment and care, and committing to an experimental attitude that yields results only sparingly and often without the comfort of expert support.

Making this claim, that learning to see autism in biomedical terms involves both reinterpreting daily life and transfiguring one's own beliefs about autism as an entity, requires that I take a position about what autism really is. The doctors and researchers involved with Defeat Autism Now! want to recruit colleagues and supporters with the objective of chang-ing medical practice in tangible ways. A sympathetic description of them that takes seriously their claim that really listening to parents, taking case histories, and thinking about the individual before the syndrome can all work to change the clinical entity of autism means that I am necessarily participating in their system of values and judgments.

The psychologist Erich Fromm wrote that our preoccupation with ro-mantic love leads us to regard love as a state of being, when it ought to be regarded as an art or a practice. It is one that demands techniques that might be familiar to parents: "discipline, concentration, and patience."[90] For Fromm, the practice of love required "rational faith," based on a productive and future-oriented focus on the potential of the object of love, be it one's child, oneself, or, he suggested, the subject of a scientific investigation.[91] Maybe it is all three. Passionate investment is characteristic of scientific practice, but it is also not far from parenting, especially at a moment in which intensive motherhood has become common practice, to sometimes problematic and sometimes transformative ends.

6

Pandora's Box: Immunizations,

Parental Obligations, and Toxic Facts

The November 2003 "Autism Summit" conference of the Interagency Autism Coordinating Committee occupied a large lecture hall in the new Washington Convention Center in Washington, D.C. Heads of the three major autism advocacy organizations joined the rest of the audience to watch presentations on research, advocacy, and education. Officials from the National Institutes of Health (NIH), geneticists, database administrators, parents, and legislators listened to the speakers attentively and mingled in the building lobby. I had been spending a lot of time thinking about the concept of risk as I followed the ongoing debates about the appropriate management of the National Immunization Program (now the National Center for Immunization and Respiratory Diseases [NCIRD]), vaccine safety, and autism. Parents and public health officials routinely talk about the relative risks associated with vaccines in children. One side in the debate connects the risk of developing autism with vaccines. The other side stresses the higher risk associated with the diseases that vaccines are designed to prevent and the risk to the public health and confidence in immunization programs that could result from sustained public discussions about autism and vaccines.

One speaker momentarily confused me by projecting a slide that divided NIH-funded projects by level of risk—"low," "moderate," and "high." In an area where studies often involve children, wasn't risk to research subjects rigorously controlled? That was when I realized that the presentation referred to projects "at risk" of not being completed.[1] Many of the studies described in speeches and presentations were as yet unfunded, existing only as proposals and potentialities. At best, Congress had authorized funds for the general purpose of research in a given area, but had not yet appropriated them. As it turned out, that risk that research will remain frozen at the discussion stage in the absence of meaningful support or funding also affects arguments about autism and vaccines.

The Interagency Autism Coordinating Committee (IACC), which organized the Autism Summit, coordinates all autism-related activities of the various member agencies of the U. S. Department of Health and Human Services, including the Centers for Disease Control (CDC), the Centers for Medicare and Medicaid Services, the NIH, and the FDA. The IACC was initially authorized by the Children's Health Act of 2000 and renewed in accordance with the Combating Autism Act of 2006. In addition to coordinating the autism spectrum disorder–related work of different agencies and facilitating information-sharing between groups, it provides a public forum "for discussions related to ASD research, screening, education, and interventions" at its committee meetings.[2] The broad range of activities and participants represented at the IACC meetings and the Autism Summit, where even the most banal laboratory research is scrutinized for political undertones, makes controversy inevitable.

The organizers of the Autism Summit designed the meeting along the lines of a scientific conference, but it operated more like a market. Presenters sold their rival projects to the audience as more urgent and thus more deserving of scarce funds and attention than others. As speaker after speaker emphasized the "bipartisan" nature of autism, I saw approaches to a neurodevelopmental condition transformed into commodities. Since advocacy groups, politicians, government administrators, and judges, like parents themselves, do not have the luxury of waiting for closure on debates about the cause or treatment of autism before they act, facts alone do not necessarily determine their choices. Needless to say, each of these constituencies interprets evidence differently. Many parents and at least some clinicians grant the most weight to personal, subjective, and experiential knowledge. Those who make immunization policy or measure the health outcomes of immunizations, in contrast, see good knowledge as objective, abstract, and based on large population samples. The different sides in the debate do not disagree with each other's arguments. They find them unfathomable.

The organizers may not have intended it, but the issue of childhood immunizations surfaced repeatedly at the Autism Summit. The Indiana Republican congressman Dan Burton's talk featured video clips showing neural cells in a petri dish retreating and degenerating when treated with thimerosal, a solution of approximately 49 percent ethylmercury that was used as a preservative in multidose vaccines until 2001. Representative Burton is a prominent advocate of theories that link autism cases to thimerosal, and he has stated in public that vaccines caused his grandson's autism.[3] The slides he used conveyed the idea of autism overtaking a brain at the cellular level—the neural cells seemed literally to recoil as they reacted to the solution.[4] Some scientists in the audience squirmed. While dramatic, Burton's presentation had little standing based on their standards of proof. The cells in solution seemed a poor substitute for a child receiving a vaccine.

Other presentations, held in breakout sessions the day after the packed plenaries, argued the case for environmental causes of autism with more subtlety. One researcher's talk covered example after example of the dangers associated with low doses of environmental toxins when combined with genetic susceptibility and exposure during a vulnerable developmental period. He then turned to the ways that persistent infections could be implicated in neurological disorders. In the final portion of his talk, he described a study of the measles, mumps, and rubella (MMR) vaccine and autism, mentioning in passing that he didn't feel strongly about the subject or outcome of the study. Unlike some other presenters, he wanted the audience to know that he hadn't made up his mind.[5] As the audience filed out, the presenter remained to answer questions. Behind him, his final slide featured an image of a woman lifting the lid of a chest to peek inside. The name of his study, the Pandora's Box Program, appeared above the picture.[6] Although the slide served mainly to provide his contact information, it wasn't hard to imagine a connection between his talk and his choice of name, an allegory about unintended consequences.

That idea, presented as ambiguous afterword in a talk that was a model of rigor and restraint, also happened to reflect the sentiments of many parents of children diagnosed with autism. They are certain that the world has become a dangerous place as a result of human activities and that their children are paying the price. Their children began life developing typically and regressed into autism as a result of their childhood immunizations, in some cases helped along by severe allergies, too many courses of antibiotics, or environmental toxins like lead and arsenic.

On the whole, these parents do not receive a particularly sympathetic hearing in scientific, policy, or media circles, although they do receive a great deal of attention.[7] Critics portray them as people grasping at an otherwise implausible explanation out of anger, disappointment, and frustration at their child's disability. They point out that language delays often become visible around the age that children receive a number of vaccines, leading parents to mistakenly identify immunizations as the cause of their child's autism. Indeed, many parents do want an explanation that will indicate not only how their child acquired autism, but how to treat the condition. Parents are also angry, not only at the possibility that they might have prevented their child's disorder, but also at the inadequacy of educational accommodations, the failings of insurance companies, and the lack of support services.

A preponderance of evidence suggests that vaccines are not responsible for the upsurge of autism cases over the past two decades, although the matter is not closed and may never be. Still, parents who nonetheless believe that vaccines caused their child's autism are not impaired, in denial, or unable to comprehend statistical correlations. Their individual experiences and observations contradict the claims of scientists and the evidence against an association between immunizations and autism. There is much that we can learn from the claims that parents make and little to be gained by ignoring them.

Parent Advocacy and Vaccine Fears

The modern public health systems in the United States, Great Britain, and most other industrialized nations rely on childhood immunizations. Although they administer and enforce them differently, all of these countries have programs to ensure that children are vaccinated against diseases that were some of the worst killers and causes of permanent disability during infancy and childhood. These diseases included measles and rubella (German measles), mumps, pertussis (whooping cough), and tetanus. Despite the great gains in health associated with immunization campaigns, these public enterprises have also inspired public suspicion and fear since their inception. During the nineteenth and early twentieth centuries, women's groups campaigned against vaccination as an unwelcome government intrusion into the private sphere of family life and an unhealthful violation of children's bodies.[8] Victorian methods of immunization were not nearly as safe or as hygienic as contemporary methods, and activists produced pamphlets with chilling photographs of children allegedly disfigured by vaccines.[9]

Like many debates over the appropriate use of technologies, arguments about vaccination have never been about the technique alone. They have also reflected anxieties about entrusting the health of one's family to authorities. In nineteenth-century England, the antivaccination movement engaged antivivisectionists, supporters of women's suffrage, and religious dissenters. Early activists emphasized that mothers knew more than vaccination enforcers about the health and needs of infants.[10] Contemporary parents may place more trust in medical professionals, but they react strongly if they believe that this trust has been violated. As one mother explained, when she first gave birth to her son, she understood an implicit division of labor: "My job is to love him; your job is to keep him well." After her son developed autism and she became convinced that his immunizations had played a role, her understanding changed, "my responsibility as his mother expanding to include advocacy—even activism—along with love."[11]

Contemporary parents concerned about the link between neurodevelopmental disorders and immunizations share some of their predecessors' mistrust of authority, but it is not the act of immunization itself or the loss of privacy that motivates them. They also rely less on sensational imagery and more on the language of science in articulating their concerns. During debates in the 1980s about risks associated with the diphtheria, pertussis, and tetanus (DPT) vaccine, activists like Barbara Loe Fisher, the cofounder and president of the National Vaccine Information Center, found success with a strategy of couching reservations about vaccines in terms of concerns over lapses in the vaccine safety and monitoring system.[12] In their role as autism advocates, parents have published journal articles and authored white papers on public health policy, and they have succeeded in recruiting scientists and medical practitioners to their cause.

Bernard Rimland, a cofounder of the National Society for Autistic Children (renamed the Autism Society of America) and founder of the Autism Research Institute (ARI), was not initially concerned about vaccines and never implicated them in his son's autism, which was present from birth. The published handbook of methods recommended by doctors associated with ARI's Defeat Autism Now! project mentions vaccines as one of many possible factors involved in autism. It emphasizes the value of immunizations and focuses instead on practical approaches to autism treatment.[13] However, after hearing the concerns among a newer generation of parents, Rimland began to focus on vaccines as a possible cause of autism. Defeat Autism Now! conferences featured talks devoted to immune dysfunction and detoxification. In the years before his death in 2006, Rimland took to asking the audience at Defeat Autism Now! meetings for a show of hands on whether their children had regressed and whether they believed that their child's regression had been caused by one or more vaccines. Rimland would look to the back of the room to be certain that the response was noted or filmed by any reporters present.

Professional epidemiologists would argue that Rimland's poll, based on an association of like-minded parents, is just the kind of nonsystematic measurement that has led to fears about vaccines in the first place. Public health officials worry that parental concerns about immunizations are a type of mass hysteria, where yellow journalism and opportunistic medical professionals fuel the fears of vulnerable and impressionable parents. Their concerns are only heightened when news programs, determined to report on controversies, devote equal time to antivaccine activists and their critics within the medical profession or when popular television programs feature a "ripped from the headlines" story of an autism–vaccine trial, with the lawyer for the parents positioned clearly on the side of good.[14]

When parents describe their own understanding of their child's regression in terms of vaccines, they often reference their growing awareness of news reports and organizations promoting the association. That the association only occurred to them after hearing other reports doesn't matter. One parent recalled leaving her house for an autism conference:

> Before I left I went through Connor's photo album. I did this soon after he was diagnosed, but perhaps I was too close to him and too ignorant of autism to recognize dramatic changes. This time, I saw it: Connor at 11 months, smiling for the camera, looking into his daddy's eyes, touching his mommy's hair. Connor on his first birthday, after his morning visit to the doctor's office and MMR vaccinations, no longer looking at anyone, no longer smiling. And perhaps the most revealing picture: Connor walking on his toes, one of the most common behaviors in autism. Within a day he had changed.[15]

Although each parent has a unique account of their child's regression, published theories about autism and vaccines generally propose two different possible etiologies, sometimes presented in combination. The first theory, relating to the connection between autism and MMR vaccine, has received slightly more attention in the U.K. Theories linking autism and the preservative thimerosal, produced by Eli Lilly and Company since the 1940s and containing 49.6 percent ethylmercury by volume, have received more attention in the United States.[16] Many parents believe that the combination of vaccines, or "two hits," triggered their child's regression. A mercury-containing vaccine weakens the immune system of children with a genetic susceptibility. When followed by an MMR vaccine that, because of the child's vulnerable state, leads to a chronic measles infection and intestinal inflammation, it can produce the behaviors and cognitive symptoms characteristic of autism. Parents are certainly well versed in the evidence in support of various theories; however, what they more often talk about are their child's complex and difficult-to-manage medical symptoms, the temporal association of those symptoms with vaccines, and the importance of detoxification, dietary changes, or anti-inflammatory medications in their child's treatment.

The MMR Vaccine and Autism as a Chronic Disease

The idea that the MMR vaccine might be associated with autism emerged prior to concerns about mercury as a preservative. In 1998, a team of researchers headed by Andrew Wakefield, a gastroenterologist at the Royal Free Hospital in London, published a paper in the British medical journal *Lancet* about a group of twelve children with regressive autism. Their parents had brought them in for consultations related to their painful gastrointestinal symptoms, although the article also noted that a number of the parents had connected their children's symptoms to the MMR vaccine. Colonoscopies revealed that the children had chronic gut inflammation and a set of symptoms that Wakefield began to term "autistic enterocolitis."[17]

Wakefield would have been primed to see a connection between the measles vaccine and gut disturbances in these children. His previous research had looked at a possible connection between measles and Crohn's disease, a chronic bowel disorder with autoimmune components.[18] The new research made him an ardent advocate of a theory linking autism to the MMR vaccine. Following the publication of the article, he held a press conference at which he suggested that parents seek out single shots rather than the combined MMR vaccine for their children.[19] His continuing willingness to go public made him a hero to many parents and an outcast among his colleagues, culminating in his departure from the Royal Free Hospital in 2001.[20] In February 2004, the *Lancet* issued a public retraction of its decision to publish Wakefield and his coauthors' article, stopping short of actually retracting the article from the published record. The editor explained that a previously unrevealed "fatal conflict of interest" had come to light, leading the editor to regard the findings of the study as "entirely flawed."[21] A few days later, the *Sunday Times* revealed that Wakefield had received support from the Legal Aid Fund, an agency that provided financial support for families engaged in litigation against vaccine manufacturers. The association may have compromised the referral process for the *Lancet* study.[22]

By 2007, Wakefield had joined Thoughtful House, a Texas clinic founded by parents. He continued to conduct research on the potential role of the measles vaccine as a causative agent in autism spectrum disorders.[23] He also continued his public role as advocate, testifying before congressional committees on the associations among the MMR vaccine, enterocolitis, and autism, and serving as an expert witness in lawsuits against the pharmaceutical industry.[24] He spoke with intensity and conviction about the importance of listening to parents. Meanwhile, immunization rates in the U.K. began to decline, and Wakefield and two of the coauthors of the *Lancet* study faced the prospect of losing their medical licenses. In January 2010, the U.K.'s General Medical Council reprimanded Wakefield for unethical conduct, including medically unnecessary investigative procedures performed on the children in his study.[25] The *Lancet* then retracted in full the article that they had partially retracted in 2004.[26] In May 2010, Wakefield lost his license to practice medicine. He promised to continue his research nonetheless. "These parents are not going away. . . . The children are not going away. And I am most certainly not going away."[27] In January 2011, the journalist who wrote the initial *Sunday Times* exposé reported that Wakefield also appeared to have fabricated details of his initial cases. The story received wide coverage.[28]

Wakefield was neither the first researcher to link viruses to autism nor the only one to argue that autism involved abnormal immune responses. Doctors generally accept that there are connections between maternal exposure to rubella and autism in children, and there is some evidence linking autism to other viruses, as a result of either chronic or acute infections.[29] Studies have found evidence of autoimmune reactions in autism, including the presence of antibodies against the brain in children's blood. At least one lab associated autoantibodies with the presence of measles virus antibodies, although this finding has been strongly contested.[30]

Scientists know that molecules associated with inflammation called cytokines also have a role in neural signaling and brain development. They seem to be elevated in children with autism, especially in those who experienced a developmental regression, suggesting that regression may be tied to an inflammatory process. Researchers have hypothesized that children who later develop autism have an abnormal innate immune response that might make them react to immunizations in idiosyncratic ways.[31] Of more interest to practitioners concerned about potential environmental causes is accumulating evidence of "an active neuroinflammatory process" in the brains of children with autism.[32] Inflammatory processes are often associated with infections. That observation encourages practitioners who might otherwise be skeptical to consider the possibility that some as-yet-unidentified infectious process could lead to the symptoms that parents attribute to the MMR vaccine.

Wakefield's supporters asked why enrolling children whose parents believed that their autism was vaccine-related constituted a source of bias, when, for example, journals routinely publish papers by experts who receive funding from pharmaceutical manufacturers. Had Wakefield acted unethically by misinterpreting his own results? The multiple coauthors and peer-review process presumably protected him. Was the problem the funding that Wakefield received from lawyers who were directly interested in supporting their clients' cases? The study's coauthors maintained that ongoing research supported their initial findings, yet the retraction led many to assume that all of the article's claims had been rejected.[33] In fact, ten of the thirteen authors of the original article had issued a highly unusual partial retraction, or "retraction of an interpretation." They maintained that the original findings of an "unexpected intestinal lesion" in children with autism were valid but sought to make clear that "no causal link was established between MMR vaccine and autism."[34] Few commentaries noted that the new disease entity remained a source of concern, as did the more general question of whether children with autism had gastrointestinal symptoms that required treatment. In the end, Wakefield's credibility was compromised because he was seen as allied with parent groups rather than the research community.

Wakefield crossed a line by making a policy recommendation as a bench scientist, a choice that disturbed many of his colleagues. He consistently maintained that the new pathological entity he identified was real, as was its association with measles virus.[35] For many of his medical colleagues, this alone was enough to discredit him and his associates. Research in 2008 failed to replicate Wakefield's findings of measles virus in the gut tissue of children with autism and enterocolitis, meaning that the laboratory that evaluated Wakefield's samples might have inadvertently contaminated the materials.[36]

None of this mattered much to parents. That is, theories implicating MMR in autism seemed to offer concrete possibilities for treatment and an explanation for their children's gut disturbances and even for apparently unrelated behavior problems. Children could be treated with antivirals, restriction diets, and anti-inflammatory medications, and parents reported that they saw improvements. Because the broader medical community rejected the theory guiding these treatments, research on their effectiveness has been slow to arrive.

Thimerosal and Detoxification

The second theory connecting the onset of autism to vaccinations concerns thimerosal, an ethylmercury-based preservative used to prevent contamination in multidose vaccines and flu shots. Thimerosal was not considered highly toxic when it was first developed in the 1920s, although manufacturers acknowledged by the 1970s that some consumers had severe reactions to high concentrations of the substance.[37] The convenience and apparent safety of thimerosal kept it in production through the 1990s, even as parents began to report concerns. In 1999, an FDA team tallied the amount of mercury that a child would have received following the recommended vaccine schedule and found that the total easily exceeded the maximum safe dosage for methylmercury, another form of mercury, as set by the Environmental Protection Agency. There was no standard for exposure to ethylmercury, the kind in thimerosal. A vaccine safety expert at Johns Hopkins University admitted his surprise at the finding because "what I believed, and what everybody believed, was that it was truly a trace, a biologically insignificant amount."[38] While he believed that the possible association between mercury and developmental delay ought to be investigated, he did not believe that there was any association with autism.

Since the 1990s, evidence has increasingly linked methylmercury, the type of mercury associated with environmental contamination, to neurodevelopmental disorders. Reports on historical incidents in which populations received accidental exposure to high levels of environmental mercury through contaminated food or pollution present disturbing evidence of brain damage, severe cognitive deficits, and developmental delays.[39] Lower exposures to mercury over time can affect intelligence, and it is possible that there are long-term effects on motor skills and attention, which are poorly measured by IQ tests. Even prenatal exposures seem to cause problems.[40] Toxicologists have found that individual responses to methylmercury vary, and that even pollution that doesn't necessarily affect food supplies can have significant effects.[41] Specifically, methylmercury is a potent developmental neurotoxin, especially dangerous to developing brains. The FDA monitors mercury levels in commercial fish and shellfish and recommends that women who are pregnant or planning to become pregnant, nursing mothers, and young children limit their consumption of fish with higher levels of mercury in their tissues.[42]

These emerging associations may have encouraged parents to consider a connection between the ethylmercury in vaccines and developmental disorders.[43] Beginning in 2000, parents formed a number of organizations focused specifically on mercury in vaccines, most prominently The Coalition for SafeMinds (Sensible Action for Ending Mercury-Induced Neurological Disorders), Moms Against Mercury, and Generation Rescue.[44] Older organizations like the National Vaccine Information Center, which were concerned with the phenomenon of vaccine injury more broadly, joined forces with parents of children with autism after those parents sought them out. Although ARI describes its primary mandate as one of promoting clinical research and treatment, speakers focused on both thimerosal and MMR toxicity have found a warm reception at Defeat Autism Now! conferences. Members of all of these groups have played a role in making the thimerosal debate part of public discourse and therapeutic practice, from running an early listserv called "Chelating Kids" to funding published studies of hair mercury levels and encouraging congressional and IOM hearings. Almost any account of the origins of public unease about thimerosal in childhood vaccines cites parents as the first and most vocal proponents of this view. Medical practitioners and laboratory researchers signed on later, as parents actively recruited them to the cause.

In 2001, Sally Bernard, Lyn Redwood, Albert Enayati, and Teresa Binstock, three parents of children with autism and an independent researcher with a diagnosis of Asperger syndrome, published a paper in the journal *Medical Hypotheses* that argued that regressive autism might be a "novel form of mercury poisoning." The authors observed that victims of mercury poisoning and individuals with autism shared symptoms such as lack of pain perception and odd behavior. The effects of low-dose mercury exposure even appeared to parallel the sex ratios found in autism. The spread of autism spectrum disorders also seemed to follow the increasing use of thimerosal-containing vaccines in the United States, with the first reported cases of autism emerging shortly after the introduction of thimerosal-containing vaccines.[45] Although the article was not published in a peer-reviewed medical journal and autism researchers criticized its central claims, it became a rallying point for parents who already suspected a causal association between their child's regression and their immunizations.[46]

Those concerned about thimerosal received a boost from investigative journalist David Kirby's 2005 book *Evidence of Harm*, which followed the stories of a number of founding members of SafeMinds from the moment they first noticed problems with their children's development to their transformation into political activists. Kirby emphasized parents' sense of betrayal at their discovery that the CDC had misjudged the true amount of ethylmercury that children received cumulatively through their vaccinations. He portrayed the researchers and clinicians associated with Defeat Autism Now!, who were willing to explore the link and consider possible mechanisms of toxicity, as sympathetic allies of parents.[47]

The CDC has never found any association between thimerosal and autism spectrum disorders. Rather, it has produced a number of epidemiological studies demonstrating a lack of association between thimerosal-containing vaccines and developmental disorders. The destructive potential of ethylmercury, the form of mercury used in thimerosal, is difficult to characterize. Many scientists argue that the substantial evidence against methylmercury does not apply to ethylmercury, the form in thimerosal, which differs in a small but very significant way in its chemical composition. The reality is that the biological activity of ethylmercury is not well understood. Toxicity estimates have drawn mainly on studies of exposure to methylmercury.[48] We know relatively little about the differences in the ways that bodies respond to the two forms of mercury, differences that could render thimerosal either more dangerous than organic mercury or entirely benign.[49]

Evaluating those studies that have focused on ethylmercury is complicated. Disputes over results have turned on the putative affiliations and loyalties of those interpreting them. Investigators sympathetic to the claims of parents have gradually built a theory about the relationship between thimerosal and neurodevelopmental harm, although many of them are conscious of maintaining their credibility and refrain from making any direct claims about vaccines and autism in their published work. It is up to the press, to parents, and to practitioners to guess at the work's practical implications.

Some studies have directly examined the toxic effects of thimerosal on neural cells. Exposure can lead to a process that looks much like apoptosis or "programmed cell death." A healthy body normally uses apoptosis in the process of development and in removing dead or aging cells. If thimerosal causes cell death that mimics apoptosis, it may not leave the clear evidence of injury that investigators would otherwise expect with a toxic exposure— this was the research that caused such a dramatic reaction at the Autism Summit in 2003.[50] Thimerosal may also act to inhibit intercellular signaling at concentrations even lower than those that are lethal for cells in culture.[51] Subgroups of children may be genetically vulnerable to thimerosal toxicity because of differences in the metabolic pathways devoted to detoxification and managing oxidative stress, a source of cellular damage.[52]

One major way that genes are regulated is through the selective attachment and removal of methyl groups, methylation and demethylation. Researchers have connected a number of diseases, including cancer, autoimmune diseases, and neurodegenerative disorders, to problems with DNA methylation. Thimerosal, like the two known developmental neurotoxins ethanol and lead, appears to affect an enzyme, methionine synthase, which plays a significant role in methylation and in the manufacture of glutathione, another chemical important in mercury detoxification.[53] When researchers exposed neural cells to toxic levels of thimerosal they found depleted levels of glutathione, lending further weight to the hypothesis.[54]

Although critics invariably point to the limits of any attribution of symptoms of autism to animal models, a well-publicized 2004 study found that a strain of mice that had been engineered with a tendency to develop autoimmune conditions appeared far more vulnerable than typical laboratory mice to behavioral and brain structure changes resulting from injections of thimerosal during crucial developmental periods.[55] A 2007 study found that thimerosal itself was capable of altering immune responses.[56] That the susceptible mice were those with a genetic vulnerability fueled claims that children who developed autism reacted differently to mercury than typical children, although a later study failed to reproduce the findings.[57] Several studies funded and in some cases coauthored by parents found significantly lower rates of mercury in first baby haircuts of children with autism compared to those of typical children. Children with autism might have a reduced capacity to excrete mercury, but other groups of investigators have disputed that result as well.[58]

Mercury and Detoxification Therapies

The findings from laboratory studies suggest to some researchers the beginnings of a plausible integrated picture of autism as a chronic illness induced in vulnerable individuals by even relatively low doses of thimerosal. These potential mechanisms have inspired practitioners to experiment with biomedical treatments based on the affected metabolic pathways. In some cases, they have also served as post hoc justifications for treatments that practitioners were already using to address suspected cases of toxic exposures to thimerosal. They include supplementation with either glutathione or methylcobalamine, methyl-B12, which parents usually administer to their children through subcutaneous injections. Both chemicals are part of the methionine synthase pathway that is affected by thimerosal. The treatments are intended to increase rates of methylation in affected children by providing extra doses of substances in order to drive chemical reactions.

By far the most notorious treatment for thimerosal toxicity is chelation, a therapy commonly used to treat individuals suffering from the acute effects of heavy metal poisoning. It works by chemically binding toxins so that the body can excrete them. Although dimercaptosuccinic acid (DMSA) is the best known of the chelating agents, doctors have also used other substances, including ethylene diamine tetraacetic acid. EDTA is sold as edetate calcium disodium under the brand name Versenate. The Autism Research Institute's mercury detoxification consensus statement does not mention or advocate EDTA, but this meant little to critics when, in a widely covered incident, a doctor inadvertently caused the death of a five-year-old boy by giving him an infusion of edetate disodium, another form of EDTA.[59] Although investigators concluded that he had used the substance in error, the doctor eventually faced a charge of involuntary manslaughter. Critics of detoxification therapies saw the tragedy as further evidence that practitioners and parents who opt for these interventions do not have the best interests of affected children at heart.[60] Self-advocates with autism, appalled by the incident, said it proved that pro-cure parents would willingly risk the lives of their offspring in exchange for the prospect of normal development. Even if the doctor had administered the correct substance, the procedure still carried risks.

News that the National Institute of Mental Health (NIMH) had decided to fund a clinical trial of chelation as part of a study of novel treatments buoyed proponents of detoxification therapies. The NIMH initiative aimed at better understanding autism subtypes such as regressive autism.[61] Critics warned that that the safety and potential utility of DMSA was not established enough to warrant a trial, although thousands of parents were already treating their children with it. Then, an institutional review board refused to approve the trial after the release of a new study showing that DMSA might cause lasting cognitive harm if prescribed unnecessarily. To the dismay of a number of advocacy organizations, in July of 2008 the NIMH cancelled the trial.[62] Nevertheless, parents continue to pursue chelation. They are encouraged by laboratory reports that show high rates of mercury and other heavy metals in their children, especially after an initial "provocation" with a chelating agent, although some results show the same levels in typically developing children following provocation.[63]

Parent advocacy groups like SafeMinds have proved particularly skilled at recruiting supporters from within the medical professions and the government. They have targeted those already suspicious of immunizations because of their own children's medical problems, lawmakers opposed to government interference in private life, and people who distrust experts or pharmaceutical manufacturers. Republican congressman Dan Burton was one early recruit. His grandson developed autism following his childhood immunizations, and Burton became a convinced opponent of mercury in vaccines as well as a supporter of disabilities-related legislation. A second Republican in Congress, Dave Weldon, a medical doctor, signed on as well. Weldon had spoken publicly about his belief in the importance of immunizations but warned that "the failure to get answers to the many questions concerning vaccine safety is beginning to undermine public confidence" in the CDC and immunization program.[64]

Supporters spanned party and ideological lines. The environmental lawyer and member of the first family of the Democratic Party, Robert F. Kennedy Jr., wrote an impassioned article in *Rolling Stone* about the thimerosal controversy, which came down largely in support of parents. The controversial radio host and political independent Don Imus championed *Evidence of Harm*, the book by David Kirby about vaccines and autism.[65] Critics charged both Kirby and Kennedy of opportunism, speculating in Kennedy's case that he might pursue tort cases against vaccine companies. Kirby allegedly just wanted the free publicity.[66] Meanwhile, Rick Rollens, the former secretary of the California State Senate, who believes his son's autism is vaccine-related, helped raise more than $5 million to fund the MIND (Medical Investigation of Neurological Disorders) Institute, an autism research center at the University of California, Davis.[67]

Parents are not a homogeneous group. Those who implicate immunizations in autism take that position for a variety of reasons. Many others remain skeptical of hypotheses that environmental factors, including childhood immunizations, play a role in autism. They ally themselves with medical authorities in their interpretations of the symptoms and probable causes of autism, and they focus on educational services and accommodation, in line with self-advocates. Some help to fund research on the genetics and neurobiology of autism but have largely refrained from criticizing or seeking to influence scientists' underlying assumptions about the biological underpinnings of the disorder.

To some parents, however, it is hardly necessary to test for a possible connection between vaccines and autism. They know through experience that an association exists. They worry less about a study's design than whether its conclusions support their beliefs and can be used to mobilize support for alternative treatments and vaccine policy reform. Even the most sympathetic researchers tend to interpret their results conservatively. They care more about what those findings can tell them about disease mechanisms than their implications in the vaccine debate. Parents, in contrast, see published articles as political tools.

Testimony versus Epidemiology

In February of 2004, as the news was breaking about Andrew Wakefield's potential conflict of interest and as the *Lancet* issued its first retraction, the Institute of Medicine (IOM) in Washington, D.C., convened a meeting of its Immunization Safety Review Committee. It was held in a spacious lecture hall at the National Academies of Science building and, like the Autism Summit a few months earlier, it was open to the public. A wide range of interested parties attended—young women wearing jeans and "Moms Against Mercury" T-shirts, lawyers and epidemiologists, laboratory scientists who looked distinctly uncomfortable on stage, congressional interns, and reporters with notepads. The participants had assembled to address the question of the relationship between immunizations and autism. The committee, which was composed of experts in immunization, public health, and pediatrics, although not necessarily specialists in autism, sat at the front of the room and listened to a full day of presentations before retiring to write its report.

Wakefield's absence from the hearings stood out. Other researchers, especially those sympathetic to him, cited his work as evidence of the potential danger of the MMR vaccine. The experts who presented at the meeting reflected two distinct research traditions and, not coincidentally, the two main positions in the controversy. The majority, who did laboratory work using blood samples and animal models and who reasoned from the perspective of biochemistry, molecular biology, and toxicology, tended to argue that the risk associated with immunizations had yet to be conclusively determined. One toxicologist with little background in autism research seemed surprised by the contentiousness of the hearing. Ethylmercury was quite possibly a developmental neurotoxin, with its precise level of toxicity not yet established. The problem clearly required further research. The epidemiologists insisted the opposite, that their population studies demonstrated that immunizations with the MMR or thimerosal-containing vaccines carried negligible risk. No correlation existed between immunizations and autism spectrum disorders. The two sides turned out to be debating two different, if related, questions.

Released four months later, the final committee report made clear which question the panel considered relevant. Although noting cases of autism in which children had regressed and that autism was a complex, heterogeneous disorder, it concluded that no credible evidence existed to connect autism with immunizations. Although scientists conducting laboratory research in vitro had suggested some potential, biologically plausible mechanisms, the findings were not sufficiently strong, and it was more important that research funds be "channeled to the most promising areas." [68] Opponents of the decision saw the statement as an explicit attempt to close down debate. The decision dismayed parent groups. Committee members seemed to have let their concern about the integrity of a powerful public health program override any reservations they might have had about the effect of vaccines on individual children.[69] To the more disillusioned parents, the decision also reflected a willingness to bend to the desires of pharmaceutical companies and bureaucrats in the CDC concerned about their public images.

It was not the first time that the IOM had tackled the issue of public mistrust of childhood immunizations, nor was it the first time that parents had felt cheated by a committee that had ignored crucial evidence. Three years earlier, in 2001, the IOM had called two separate meetings of the Immunization Safety Review Committee on the topics of the MMR vaccine and autism and thimerosal-containing vaccines and autism. Their report, issued in 2001, found no direct evidence of thimerosal leading to developmental disorders or other neurological symptoms in children, but that the hypothesis warranted further study. They had drawn similar conclusions about the MMR vaccine.[70] Parent groups began to respond by challenging the methods and findings of the studies upon which the IOM had relied.

SafeMinds, the most forceful promoters of the mercury–autism hypothesis, worried that scientists at the CDC had suppressed positive epidemiological results. The organization had obtained transcripts of a June 2000 IOM scientific meeting at the Simpsonwood Retreat Center in Norcross, Georgia. The attendees discussed the preliminary results of a study using data from the Vaccine Safety Datalink, a database created through a partnership between the CDC and several private health maintenance organizations (HMOs). The study's authors met with other experts in epidemiology and immunizations to confirm their interpretation of the results and to address possible flaws in advance of meetings of the IOM review committee and the CDC's Advisory Committee on Immunization Practices.

At the closed session, the authors presented their analysis of the data, which associated thimerosal with a risk for some neurological disorders. After a tense discussion, the authors decided to exclude some groups from the sample and add others, which resulted in the weakening of thimerosal effects in the revised models. They brought younger children who were less likely to have been diagnosed into the analysis. One decision in particular concerned parents in SafeMinds. In massaging the data (or, as the authors understood it, improving the model) the researchers had excluded from the sample children who had received little or no exposure to thimerosal at an age when children typically receive the majority of their shots. The authors reasoned that these children were from atypical families. If the families had been unwilling or unlikely to have them vaccinated, they were probably also unwilling or unlikely to bring them in for a developmental evaluation. In other words, the low rate of neurological disorders in the sample resulted from underdiagnosis rather than from low exposure to thimerosal.[71]

It is possible to read the transcripts and construct an account of the meeting that differs from that of SafeMinds. Paul Offit, a University of Pennsylvania professor of vaccinology and author of *Autism's False Prophets*, finds an instance of routine scientific practice. Researchers commonly have their findings and methods critiqued by panels of their peers prior to publication.[72] Parents focused on the negotiations recorded in the transcripts and the decision to revise the sample set. It convinced them that CDC officials had made protection of the nation's vaccination program a priority even at the cost of exposing children to a potent developmental neurotoxin.

Decisions to include or exclude sets of children from epidemiological studies can reflect underlying ideas about the nature of reliable research and about disease mechanisms. Many epidemiological researchers assume that a good study should answer the question: were previously healthy children more likely to develop autism if exposed to either thimerosal or the MMR vaccine? Thus, the strongest evidence against an association between autism and immunizations comes from population-level studies that compare children who received vaccines with those who did not. Since 2000, epidemiologists have conducted a number of these studies on several data sets in the United States, Denmark, and Canada, and the majority failed to demonstrate any association.[73] Based on a study design that seeks to eliminate confounding factors, researchers exclude children likely to have other underlying health conditions. From the perspective of parent advocates, such decisions make no sense. Children with underlying vulnerabilities—genetic conditions, preexisting health problems, family histories of illness—are more likely to be harmed by vaccine-related exposures. Excluding these children from the sample set only proves that researchers are not really listening to their ideas about the causes of autism.

During the IOM meeting in February 2004, when toxicological and laboratory analyses of potential vaccine toxicity clashed with epidemiological analyses of their evident safety, it became evident that participants understood the idea of a "conflict of interest" in very different ways. The formal requirement that presenters disclose their potential financial conflicts might have seemed like a rule with self-evident justification to the many who understood conflicts of interest as arising from private and, in particular, corporate funding for research, while viewing their own government funding as a primary safeguard of disinterested and objective scholarship. At the meeting, however, some participants who had obtained seed funds from parent organizations implied that employment by the CDC or funding through that agency constituted a far more egregious conflict of interest. It did not matter that one branch of the CDC oversaw the national immunization program and another the safety evaluations of vaccines. These participants and their supporters took conflict to mean any affiliation that might lead the investigator to favor a particular set of results over others. In other words, parent groups viewed financial ties as only one of many possible impediments—including institutional, ideological, or political commitments on the part of an individual investigator—to the ideal of "good science."[74] The dispute may have led the CDC to restructure the offices responsible for safety monitoring of vaccines in the following year.[75]

Any possibility of measuring the relationship between immunizations and autism rates depends on the availability, integrity and, ultimately, reliability of different databases. Countries with nationalized health care have more readily available records of immunizations, including adverse outcomes. In the United States, most researchers rely on the Vaccine Adverse Events Reporting System database and the Vaccine Safety Datalink. In 1990, in accordance with a legislative mandate that the CDC monitor the post-market safety of vaccines, the Immunization Safety Branch of the Epidemiology and Surveillance Division of the National Immunization Program established the two databases.[76]

The Vaccine Adverse Events Reporting System database (VAERS) is a voluntary reporting system in which primary care practitioners, patients, and insurance companies can register adverse events associated with immunizations.[77] Epidemiologists do not have a particularly high regard for the quality of the VAERS data, both because reporting is voluntary, which leads to underreporting of incidents and poor identification of cases, and because no standardized criteria exist for reporting symptoms. In one instance, following publication of an article that used the VAERS data, the American Academy of Pediatrics issued a statement declaring that that the data were never intended for use to test hypotheses about connections between immunizations and illnesses.[78] At best, the VAERS database could aid in the post-market monitoring and oversight of vaccines and might occasionally serve to identify issues for further study. Mark and David Geier, a father-and-son team that has turned out a steady stream of epidemiological studies on vaccines and autism, have relied almost exclusively on the VAERS data.[79] Most epidemiologists ignore their work because of its methodological problems. The willingness of parents to hold up work by the Geiers only reinforces critics' belief that parents do not understand the mechanics of reliable research design.

The second database, the Vaccine Safety Datalink (VSD), is a collaborative project run by the CDC and a consortium of HMOs. Participants voluntarily report on a broad set of variables in their patient populations that can then be correlated with vaccination schedules. The VSD data suffer some significant shortcomings of their own. The HMOs have historically used different reporting systems with poorly standardized measures to report health outcomes, and no method exists to distinguish differences in health care utilization, income levels, and other significant variables among populations in the various HMOs. The VSD also includes detailed information on variables that could be linked to individual patients, including geographic location, genetics, and exact dates and times of doctor visits and procedures. As a result, the CDC tightly restricts access to the data, requiring that potential researchers submit a formal proposal in addition to obtaining the approval of an institutional review board before they begin their study. Researchers must travel to the Research Data Center (RDC) in Atlanta in order to access the data. The many inconsistencies in the data also make it difficult to interpret and, the CDC suggests, subject to misinterpretation by ill-informed or poorly trained researchers.

Parent organizations did not find those arguments convincing. Although they have differed on the importance of investigating the relationship between autism and vaccinations, they have agreed on the desirability of greater public access to the VSD data and the need for further safety research on vaccines in general. A joint statement issued in 2003 by organizations including the Autism Society of America, the Cure Autism Now Foundation, SafeMinds, and the Autism Research Institute demanded that the VSD "must be made available to all qualified research scientists in a timely manner. The current practice of restricting access to the database to a limited group of possibly biased individuals is not acceptable."[80]

Accounts and Explanations

Parents may be more sympathetic than researchers to the idea that vaccinations affect specific vulnerable populations because of their experiences with the medical complaints of their own children. Critics have suggested that parents create retrospective narratives about vaccines only after hearing similar claims from others or after watching news reports that, some say, overrepresent the potential role of vaccines.[81] However, to read accounts by parents of their child's precipitous developmental regression following a set of immunizations or to read the transcripts of the Autism Omnibus Proceedings of the U.S. Court of Federal Claims is to appreciate the degree to which parents' testimonies reflect their intimately observed understanding of the onset of symptoms. The accounts also reflect their utter certainty, retrospectively, about the cause of their child's illnesses.

Parents tell stories of acute reactions to vaccines, including clear declines in overall health, which began with enough of a delay following a child's immunizations that doctors reject any association between the two. Parents, however, insist on the connection. According to one parent, "eleven days after Ryan's DPT he had a sudden, rapidly rising fever (to 105°) and a stiff neck and body. He screamed and pitched for 24 hours, having convulsions, his eyes rolling."[82] Another writes that "shortly after his 18-month shots, RJ seemed to shut down right before our eyes. His first words stopped abruptly and he wouldn't do anything to communicate except point and grunt. He stopped interacting, smiling, and laughing altogether."[83] Another remembers that

> two years ago, shortly before his second birthday, our son William went to his doctor's office and received a standard set of "catch-up" shots. . . . During the following summer William suffered from constant diarrhea, unexplained bumps and welts, reduced speech, bloating, binge eating, bloody lesions, "croup attacks," and lost interaction and eye contact.[84]

Other parents describe their growing certainty in the wake of medical tests that confirmed for them that their children suffered from an environmental illness caused by the immunizations that they had received:

> So you see, I've had some successes here and there, and I've gained much knowledge, but I have a lot more to think about. We just received test results showing that the kids have antibodies to almost all of their brain proteins and neurotransmitters. They have anti-

bodies to myelin, serotonin and receptor sites, catecholamines and neural axon filament proteins. You cannot tell me that these children are just psychologically involved; they are *systematically ill*.[85]

The nutritionist ordered a hair test to see how Augie was metabolizing minerals. The test results showed that Augie's mercury level was literally "off the chart," and that he also had some aluminum in him. . . .Dr. Zbylot then gave us the name of another doctor who specialized in chelation, and that doctor started Augie on a very low dose of DMSA. Augie remained on DMSA in varying doses for a year and a half. Each time we gave it to him, we thought we saw him take a little developmental jump forward.[86]

Many doctors dispute the validity of unorthodox or unfamiliar tests that examine antibody levels, measure amounts of organic acids in the blood, look for the possibility of yeast overgrowth, and calculate the amount of heavy metals excreted following chelation treatments. For many parents, those same laboratory printouts provide documentary evidence of the foreign substances that their children harbor as a result of their vaccines and of the real physical changes that underpin their behavioral regressions. The situation of these parents resembles that of other communities brought together by their experience of disorders that doctors do not universally recognize as "real" disease entities with characteristic patterns of onset. Examples include multiple chemical sensitivity and Gulf War syndrome, among other environmental illnesses.[87] Even though epidemiologists and parents agree on the existence of autism as a valid and generally recognized disease entity, this agreement counts for little. Parents view gut symptoms, body rashes, food intolerances, and an inability to concentrate as important ways that the disease manifests in their children, whereas researchers persist in describing autism in terms of impairments or abnormalities in communication, behaviors, and social reciprocity.

Many of the public health and policy experts who arbitrate on issues of vaccine safety recognize experimental biomedical treatments as "complimentary and alternative treatments" but not as practices intimately bound up with the vaccine issue. For many parents, however, the two are closely connected. Part of the significance of these treatments for parents is the role that they play in a causal narrative, one that ends with the prospect of healing. What matters is that, instead of having to depend on the instructions of medical personnel, parents take an active role in monitoring their child's condition. Many parents first learn to understand their child's autism as a chronic disease. They later begin to see it as a result of immunizations, based on their successes with treatments or meeting other parents with similar concerns.

Detoxification therapies appear to work, as evidenced by the toxins excreted from their children's bodies, the repair to their compromised digestive and immune systems, and their behavioral improvements. Providers of specialized therapies operate on the assumption, based on clinical observations or on laboratory work, that children with immune over- or underactivity, gut disturbances, and inflammation differ in clinically important ways from children with heavy metal toxicity, oxidative stress, and impaired methylation capacity.[88] Parents talk about "mercury kids" being "zoned out" and "spacey," possibly as a result of their chronic yeast infections, while "measles kids" have chronic diarrhea and gastrointestinal pain, weak immune systems, food sensitivities, and obsessive symptoms.

To parents, the CDC is as incapable of recognizing these distinctive illnesses as it is the risks associated with vaccines. One parent explained that he believed that CDC officials were quite conservative and careful in their initial approval of new vaccines—it was what came after they were introduced to the market that troubled him. Although officials were cautious about adding new vaccines to the schedule, they paid little attention to the possibility of cumulative effects or interactions among vaccines. Vaccine critics worry in particular about the neglect of chronic diseases in post-market monitoring practices. Bernadine Healy, a former head of the NIH, came forward in 2008 with her concerns that the CDC might prefer epidemiological studies as a way of identifying possible adverse effects of vaccines, even though they had a more limited ability to tease out vulnerable subgroups. Although she recognized that many colleagues would criticize her for saying it, she was inclined to be thankful for the vaccine court, where even concerns about widely accepted practices could receive a hearing.[89]

Defining Science in Court

About a year before the strange confluence of political and medical discussions at the November 2003 Autism Summit, angry references to the Homeland Security Act appeared on parent listservs. Members took aim not at the act itself but at a rider attached to it, designed to limit litigation in cases of vaccine injury. The National Vaccine Injury Compensation Program (VICP), begun in 1988, already restricted litigation on vaccine injuries, but parents could still bring legal cases against vaccine manufacturers outside the structure created by the National Childhood Vaccine

Injury Act. They used a loophole that allowed them to focus on thimerosal, a preservative, rather than on the vaccine itself. They could sue vaccine manufacturers over their use of thimerosal without first bringing their cases before the VICP.

These civil suits also offered some recourse for children who had found their cases excluded under the three-year statute of limitations set by the VICP, a considerable number given that many parents did not draw an immediate connection between vaccines and their child's illness. Authorities designed the rider to insulate the pharmaceutical industry from litigation on the grounds that protecting the national vaccine supply took priority, an argument that parents considered to be transparently flimsy. Congress eventually dropped the rider from the bill. The uproar helped to publicize the parents' concerns and also suggested how much manufacturers would have liked to shut down the ongoing discussions about autism and vaccines.

The Office of Special Masters of the U.S. Court of Federal Claims, colloquially the "vaccine court," is an unusual institution. It exists exclusively to hear cases brought to the VICP. "Special masters" rather than career judges preside. They are lawyers vested with provisional judicial powers in order to execute the requirements of the Vaccine Injury Compensation Act.[90] The VICP was brought into being through activism by parents who believed that their children had been injured by the whole-cell pertussis vaccine used in the DPT shot in the 1980s. When companies reported a vaccine shortage due to the burden of lawsuits related to this concern, Congress passed the National Childhood Vaccine Injury Act of 1986 (NCVIA), which established the VICP. In 1990, in accordance with the requirement that the CDC monitor post-market safety of vaccines, the Immunization Safety Branch of the Epidemiology and Surveillance Division of the National Immunization Program also established the two key databases, the VAERS and the VSD.

The VICP turned out to be a lucky legislative move for the CDC and vaccine manufacturers, and a Pyrrhic victory for parent advocates of injury compensation.[91] By incorporating parents' objections and arguments about vaccine safety into the very fabric of vaccine-related legislation, lawmakers effectively silenced them and all but ended the possibility of large-scale civil suits against vaccine manufacturers. Congress created the VICP explicitly as a "no-fault alternative" to tort litigation on vaccine proceedings. While parents benefited from a standardized hearing and compensation process, vaccine manufacturers gained a "less adversarial" legal process, in which findings that children were owed compensation did not lead to penalties for manufacturers.

In the summer of 2007, that is, eighteen years after its creation, the VICP finally began to hear cases brought by the families of children with autism. These constituted the Omnibus Autism Proceeding, a series of "test cases" to determine the validity of parents' claims. At the time, there were over 5,000 cases related to autism filed under the VICP, none of which had gone to trial.[92] The court selected the test cases in order to examine the evidence for claims about injuries caused by the MMR vaccine, thimerosal-containing vaccines, or a combination of the two. The testimony brought into sharp focus the many conflicts that pitted parents concerned about vaccines and the minority of doctors that allied with them against the majority of other medical practitioners concerned with autism. Many families attended the open sessions, while others listened in via teleconference or later downloaded and read the transcripts. They already knew the arguments if they had been following discussions of vaccines and autism through Defeat Autism Now! conferences, parent list-servs, or other publications.

The first autism case heard by the Office of Special Masters involved Michelle Cedillo, a then twelve-year-old girl with multiple health problems. She had been a healthy and sociable toddler before receiving thimerosal-containing vaccines followed by the MMR vaccine. Her parents claimed that she regressed dramatically, became nonverbal, and developed a variety of severe medical problems including inflammatory bowel disease. But some of Michelle's otherwise unexplained and self-injurious behavior, which included repeatedly hitting herself in the chest, began to abate once she received treatments for a stomach ulcer and gut inflammation. Parents in other test cases told similar stories.

All of the families also produced videotapes of their children before their first birthdays, and these videos played a major role in the hearings. For the parents, they represented clear evidence that their children had developed typically up until a sudden and dramatic regression. The lawyers representing the government's case brought witnesses in to reinterpret the tapes. The witnesses explained that they saw early signs of autism that the parents failed to identify. Why? Parents lacked special training. They did not have a typically developing child as a reference point. They were "actually compensating in their behavior [for] the lack of response in the child, but they are not aware of that."[93] One expert witness pointed to Michelle Cedillo's "hand regard," a type of self-stimulatory behavior, as evidence that her autism predated her vaccinations. Theresa Cedillo disagreed. It was only Michelle blowing kisses. "He's referring to where she pulls her hand back to look at it, but what you're probably not aware is that my mom, her grandmother, had been teaching her to blow kisses. Of course, when babies blow kisses, you know, she was just doing that."[94]

As the Omnibus Autism Proceeding began, an epidemiologist and a professor of psychiatry participating in an NIH-funded autism program appeared as guests on *Talk of the Nation*, a National Public Radio call-in show. The two specialists assured listeners of vaccines' safety. Minimal evidence existed to prove an association with autism.[95] They feared the adverse consequences of parents refusing to vaccinate their children. In the United Kingdom, where compliance with vaccination is voluntary, the rate of immunizations with the MMR vaccine declined following public concerns about its safety, and this could have contributed to a measles outbreak in 2007.[96]

The speakers on the program, like many of their colleagues, may also have worried that listeners would not understand how evidence was used in the vaccine court. In the Omnibus Autism Proceeding, the claimants only had to demonstrate that a "preponderance of evidence" supported their case, not that it was true "beyond a reasonable doubt." The standard conforms to civil law but seems markedly looser than that supplied by conventional use of evidence in court cases.[97] The families needed to prove to the court's satisfaction that their argument was plausible for their particular case. They had no need to demonstrate that immunizations caused autism as a general rule, the standard that would apply within most of the scientific community. Nevertheless, they served as "test cases" for the latter, wider claim.

One caller asked the radio guests whether the studies used to reject the claim that immunizations caused autism had been conducted by groups affiliated with either vaccine manufacturers or government agencies charged with overseeing immunization programs. The guest assured the caller that "of course" there were no connections, although the claim may have been based on his own convictions rather than certain knowledge. The CDC had relied on a set of Danish studies. The advocacy organization SafeMinds argued that many of the lead researchers had ties to vaccine manufacturers.[98] The problem is that it is quite difficult to find researchers with adequate expertise in the area of vaccine safety that are not in some way affiliated with either the government or a vaccine manufacturer.

The Omnibus Proceedings provided a perhaps unintended forum for both sides to explain what they understood to be sound science. On the plaintiff's side, the expert witnesses talked about the importance of entertaining all possible theories of causation in the interest of treating children and of crediting parents' understandings of their own child's development, regression, and recovery. "It's not scientific certainty," a lawyer for Michelle Cedillo explained, "because, frankly, the science is in dispute."[99] An epidemiologist appearing as a witness for the plaintiffs argued that existing studies would not have been able to identify a small set of children with "clearly regressive autism" if such a group existed. For that reason the studies refuting a link between autism and vaccines might not apply to the test cases.[100]

The lawyers representing the Department of Health and Human Services responded by distinguishing between "good science" and "junk science," as defined by the Supreme Court. "What has no place here are experts at the margins of legitimate science" whose theories were no better than guesses.[101] In the hearing regarding the thimerosal causation theory, a lawyer for the Department of Health and Human Services declared that

> there is no scientific debate. The debate is over. There's no scientific controversy. The only controversy is the media controversy, propelled by those groups who were founded on the premise that vaccines cause autism or by those groups who promote and advocate experimental therapies for autism such as chelation. The credible scientific community has already spoken on this issue and has rejected it.[102]

In conclusion, the respondents warned that the Special Masters' decisions would be taken as guides not only by the vaccine court, but by parents in general, who might look to them as they decided whether their own children should receive vaccines.[103]

Parents grew hopeful after the 2008 finding by the vaccine court for Hannah Poling, a child with autism that was related to a mitochondrial disorder. The court had accepted that the disorder might have been triggered by vaccines.[104] Then, in February 2009 the vaccine court ruled against the arguments of the first three test cases and the theory that MMR vaccine and thimerosal-containing vaccines could together lead to autism.[105] In March 2010 the court ruled against the second three test cases on the theory that thimerosal alone could cause autism, effectively concluding the proceedings.[106]

Throughout the series of test cases, the lawyers for the Department of Health and Human Services questioned the credibility of the expert witnesses who supported the theories that vaccines could cause autism. They challenged the witnesses' qualifications to speak on toxic injury or neurological malfunction given that many of them were pediatricians rather than clinical researchers. The Special Master for the Cedillo case concluded his decision by observing that the parents sincerely believed that Michelle had been injured by vaccines, but had been "misled by physicians who are guilty, in my view, of gross medical misjudgment."[107]

Paul Offit, a vaccine expert present at the hearings, suggested that Michelle Cedillo's lawyers had established an antagonistic tone early on in the hearings by alleging that the government had stood "shoulder to shoulder" with vaccine manufacturers.[108] By the conclusion of the hearings both sets of lawyers were decidedly confrontational. Everyone involved took pains to acknowledge the devotion and care on the part of the parents as entirely distinct from their efforts to demolish the arguments of the parents' allies. No one was questioning whether the parents were attentive, responsible, and devoted to their children. For the parents the distinction might not have been so clear. The witnesses whose competence was being called into question were also the doctors that they had chosen to trust, and who were treating their children with what the parents saw as definitive success.

Risk, Particularity, and Responsibility

The beliefs that parents hold about vaccine injuries and autism spectrum disorders matter to them for their explanatory power. The vaccine hypothesis validates a course of treatments, but it also identifies a cause of their children's condition, answers the question of who or what is to blame, and opens up the issue of compensation, including support for their children's continuing care. Officials worry instead about the consequences for the health of present and future generations if the courts or the medical research communities ultimately side with parents. Public health professionals see vaccination programs as victims of their own success, where declining rates of infectious diseases have made parents complacent. Complications from diseases like measles can be life-threatening or disabling.[109] The solution is more and better information delivered through a trusted government body.

Sociologists of medicine are concerned with recent trends in vaccine use as well, but their analyses challenge those of the public health officials on a number of grounds. First, parents of typical children don't differ all that much from parents of children with autism when it comes to evaluating risk and the possibility of harm. Both act rationally, in ways consistent with the way they understand their obligations. Second, the focus on reassuring the public through information campaigns cannot solve the problem of trust in interactions with medical authorities. Parents see the choice to vaccinate, especially when there is no way to know with absolute certainty about the associated risks, as a "leap of faith" of the type that takes place in the context of any close relationship between two trusting individuals. A general mistrust of government that may seem initially un-related to medical issues compounds the problem.[110] Third, doctors miss something important when they dismiss all objections of vaccines as prob-lems of misunderstanding or "bias." Many parents come to their decisions as a result of broader ideological commitments to holistic medicine or at-tachment parenting.[111]

For many mothers and fathers, good parenting constitutes a type of "moral imperative" that obliges them to seek out additional information and not take authorities' assurances as fact.[112] Many groups that are criti-cal of vaccinations want to encourage parents to come to conclusions for themselves, and the statements of parent groups reflect this sense that "the process of education and learning is more important than the eventual de-cision and that trust, (or at least blind faith) is . . . itself a source of risk."[113] Immunizations remind parents how much they must, as citizens and con-sumers, trust in "systems of expertise" that can potentially fail.[114] Many parents emphasize their child's particular vulnerability to vaccines and the need to conduct case studies on specific populations. Even if epidemio-logical findings offer convincing evidence of a lack of association, "these findings in and of themselves lack the rich meaning offered by the narra-tive accounts found in parents' description of their children changing."[115]

Sociologists also point to the problems created by the perceived divide between the assumed rationality of medical professionals and the emo-tionality of parents. Indeed, doctors and nurses themselves have expressed reservations about the demand that they express absolute certainty when they tell parents that vaccines are safe, rather than admit the complexities of the issue.[116] Doctors also do not have an "exclusive claim to rationality" in their concern about the potential for disaster if a child goes unvacci-nated. Parents too engage in a style of "worst-case" thinking when they worry about autism or other adverse outcomes of vaccines.[117] Rather than viewing parents who choose not to vaccinate as part of an "antivaccination movement" with the potential to seriously undermine public health pro-grams, it might be more reasonable to understand them as "vaccine crit-ics." They do not necessarily oppose vaccines but demand more research on safety and on the potential existence of vulnerable populations. By cul-tivating respect between the two sides and recognizing the claims to ratio-nality of each, there is a better chance of creating the trust that underpins decisions to vaccinate.[118] In some cases this is easier said than done, and public health experts and researchers have reason to be discouraged and angered when they receive threats or find their work misrepresented.[119]

The CDC and the public health community will have to work harder to solve the problem of the decline in vaccination rates. To claim that immunizations carry absolutely no risk or to contrast the risk in choosing not to vaccinate with the risk of contracting a disease like measles can have the effect of lessening parental confidence. Parents understand that herd immunity protects their child. If a disease were to appear, it would probably be contained because most people have been vaccinated. Educational messages instead ought to emphasize the idea of vaccination as a social responsibility. Those parents unwilling to expose their child to any risk are effectively threatening others, and public health officials are correct that such decisions are both unsafe and unfair.

The public also needs better information about the safety research built into vaccine development, even if drawing attention to safety can have the unintended effect of raising concerns about risks. Parents of children with autism have highlighted some problems with the way that the CDC has worked in the past. A critical one is the markedly smaller amount of resources devoted to post-market research and vaccine safety. Another is the appearance of conflicts of interest in research on vaccine safety. The CDC needs to vet authors of the studies it funds and consider rejecting those that have plausible conflicts, including connections to vaccine manufacturers. The increased costs will return dividends in the form of restoration of public trust in immunizations. Officials have fallen into the habit of assuming that public trust is a given, something inherent in the authority of medical experts, rather than something earned and assiduously maintained.

Parents of children with autism, at least some of them, differ from other parents in their conviction that immunizations brought on their child's disability. They are witnesses to an adverse reaction to a vaccine or set of vaccines. Public health officials therefore have little to gain and much to lose by disputing their accounts, or, worse, questioning their sanity. Parents are not all driven by desperation. In some cases, their testimony needs to be questioned as part of an investigative process, as in the case of Michelle Cedillo, where her baby videotapes potentially contradicted her parents' account of her first year's "typical" development. However, the arguments of parents have served to highlight problems with standard claims about the onset and progression of autism, and they have led researchers to pay greater attention to symptoms that may hold significant clues to the disorder's underlying causes and mechanisms.

The Limitations of Certainty

When parents talk about thimerosal or the MMR vaccine, they employ an alternative framework for thinking about etiologies and disease mechanisms for autism. The terms do not imply a static condition or an exclusively genetic form of causation. Parents see the MMR vaccine and thimerosal either as distinct causes or as part of a cumulative series of "hits" to the bodies of children with an underlying genetic predisposition. They link theories about the synergistic effects of vaccines with concerns about antibiotic overuse, perhaps as a result of chronic ear infections brought on by an impaired immune system. They implicate maternal illnesses; Rho-Gam injections; environmental mercury, lead, and arsenic; and organophosphate pesticides, to name just a few of the possible environmental factors that have been suspected of causing autism. Epidemiologists have been unable to rule out environmental factors as a partial cause of the continuing increase in autism rates.[120] Therefore, it is important to take these concerns seriously, as impossible as it may be to determine with any certainty the effects of such a broad set of potential causative factors and associated disease mechanisms.

It is easy to dismiss the arguments for all of the reasons enumerated by critics—the frustration and anger of parents trying to raise children with disabilities in a social climate that provides too little meaningful support, the negative or at best ambiguous results of epidemiological studies, the division among parents themselves when it comes to the question of autism's cause or causes, and the antagonism of many adults on the autism spectrum to hypotheses that link autism to environmental factors. In practice, though, respectful dialogue ought to be possible. Indeed, the situation demands it because all of these groups—parents, self-advocates, researchers, and clinicians—need to share their particular insights to arrive at the best ways to understand, respect, and nurture people on the autism spectrum.

Parents concerned about vaccines have pointed to features of autism that might otherwise have received little attention and which may have significant implications for treatment regardless of their relevance for understanding causation. Prior to 1999, a handful of articles made passing reference at best to a subgroup of children who seemed to lose skills over time. No researchers devoted themselves to identifying unique features of this group. Beginning around 2001, an increasing number of articles began to deal explicitly with regression in autism and ask whether or not children with the "regressive phenotype" shared distinctive biological or behavioral features. Likewise, following Wakefield's 1998 study, more published studies focused on gastrointestinal symptoms in autism as a problem worthy of attention, even apart from any possible association with the MMR vaccine.[121]

Parental testimony has also provided valuable clues to those clinicians and laboratory researchers who are now thinking about autism as a chronic disease. In many cases parents have pointed researchers toward paths that would have been invisible without their intimate knowledge of the bodies and behaviors of affected children. For these researchers, worries about appearing to validate the concerns of vaccine critics and the tendency to dismiss parental reports of successful treatments as "desperate foolishness" act as barriers to serious consideration of autism's underlying neurological and biological mechanisms.[122] The polarization of opinion that has characterized so much discussion about the possibility of a genuine increase in autism cases and the role of environmental factors can lead investigators to neglect very real and potentially promising avenues of research. Conversely, those researchers who were attentive early on to the possibility that environmental factors played a role in autism have cleared a path for investigators from a wide range of backgrounds and institutional affiliations who are studying intermediate mechanisms in autism, rather than focusing exclusively on genes, brain structure, and behavior. Their findings suggest that oxidative stress and neuroinflammation, which can be caused by toxic agents, infections, or autoimmune processes, can act early on to disrupt neurodevelopment, playing a significant role in some cases of autism.[123]

It seems unwise, unreasonable even, to dismiss the claims of parents who are so specific in their delineation of the physical symptoms that affect their children, the ear infections, the gut symptoms, the allergies, and the insensitivity to pain. Not all parents have the technical vocabulary, the social authority and status, and the scientific expertise to articulate these concerns in ways that pass muster in the world of formal academic publications or even committee hearings at the National Academies of Science or in Congress. It would be a great mistake, however, to conclude, as many writers have, that because their explanations are not always theoretically consistent or because they place too much weight on hypotheses and speculation as opposed to peer-reviewed publications, it follows that their experience contains nothing of value. Those observations and informal trials can, in their attention to symptomatic particularities and individuality, help researchers incorporate some of the passionate particularity of parental commitment and love into their own devotion and commitment to research programs and experimental facts.

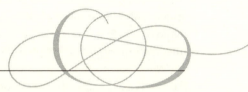

What the World Needs Now:

Learning About and Acting on Autism Research

None of the debates that I describe in this book has ended. Despite periodic promises that researchers are "closing in" on a comprehensive understanding of autism's causes, the distance still appears formidable.[1] Many researchers now agree with parents that although autism is a useful term for describing a common behavioral syndrome, it is one that offers few insights into the particular biology of individual children. It may say even less about adults because, in addition to the biological and cognitive differences among them, they have been shaped by experiences over a lifetime. For the foreseeable future, both the facts about autism and the politics of treatment will remain contentious.

In this conclusion, I return a last time to the question of love as both a subject and a method for research on autism. I revisit the evidence for its centrality to the work of producing knowledge about autism and in particular the importance of parents' caring as a source of insights about children. I then turn to the issues that these arguments raise about knowledge production in the field of science studies. I conclude by discussing how we can move forward from here to include other neglected voices in autism research, in particular people on the autism spectrum.

Love at Work

Certain researchers have devoted themselves to predicting the onset of autism in its earliest stages. They analyze social behavior using videos of the younger siblings of children with autism, deemed "high-risk" infants because of the genetic contributions to the syndrome.[2] Some of the children are only a few months old. The researchers have become connoisseurs of babies' smiles and gurgles. They talk about "beautiful joint attention" behaviors and "gorgeous" social gazes. They are learning to distinguish among subtle indicators of derailed development and to predict future pathology before a formal diagnosis is possible. With earlier diagnoses, interventions might be initiated at ever-younger ages.

Work like this represents the cutting edge of research, combining standardized diagnostic instruments, behavioral studies, epidemiology, genetics, and brain imaging. It promises early treatments and support. It also reminds us that, despite the practical and epistemological differences among the many programs developed over the past half century, autism research and treatment are syncretic processes.[3] Technicians identify subjects of genetic research using cognitive measures. Biomedical treatments take place in the context of structured behavioral therapy programs through which parents track and record the progress of their child. In addition to the functional interdependence of these programs, they all demand affective as well as intellectual and financial resources.

Some may argue that I have perseverated on love, conjuring it where there really is nothing more than the routines of medical research and treatment. They would be wrong. Love is a vexed term that is nonetheless central to a discussion that ranges from the mechanisms of social movements to the daily preparation of meals and to state-level education and early intervention programs. My choice arose from some concern that the technical vocabularies of science studies, while useful, can alienate some readers and obscure a relatively clear point. I also respect the categories of my actors and the work that they do. Love captures the social processes at work in contemporary biomedicine so well because it is common property.

Autism research depends on it. Love has been incorporated into those diagnostic instruments that demand the attentive, detailed knowledge of caregivers. Emotional work kept the Orthogenic School running during Bruno Bettelheim's tenure as director, and it was part of what made parents some of the most effective behavioral therapists. Parents have argued for its importance in the criteria for selecting research projects. It matters to all those biomedical treatments that rely on parents. It also shapes the vaccine debate, in ways that may be dangerous but are even more risky when ignored. Biomedicine is increasingly important to arguments about citizenship, entitlement, and governance, so it is crucial that we do our best to understand how it works and what can be done to improve it. Love is a central, if often overlooked, component of biomedical knowledge. It is also part of work in the social sciences. Neglecting my own affective responses would be akin to placing myself impossibly outside of this system.

Guidelines for Caring

In the 1990s, academics across the United States and Europe launched what became known as the "science wars," that is, a set of debates about who has a right to weigh in on the conduct and content of scientific research and on the conceptual tools to be used in their analysis. Did it make sense to bring the methods of literary studies to scientific texts? Could an anthropologist suggest that scientists, like members of other social and professional cultures, hold beliefs shaped by their values in addition to the incontrovertible evidence of the material world? While I entered the field of science studies after the dust had settled, I benefited enormously from the hostilities, above all from Donna Haraway's questioning how "commitment, anger, hope, pleasure, knowledge, and work all come together in the practice of love we call science? And science studies?"[4]

One consequence of this project is that some of my own writing has become part of the phenomena that I describe, simply through my commenting in print on activist strategies and research priorities. There is no consensus on the rules for social scientists working on a contested illness. We do know that representations are potent instruments for shaping reality.[5] Studying autism made me ask whether good scholarship in science and technology studies can include statements about appropriate action.[6] It also made me question how my own affective commitments to friends, informants, and colleagues colored my interpretations. Researchers often confront this question as members of the communities that they are studying, as I would be, for instance, if a family member or I had an autism spectrum diagnosis. Did I have the right to argue for what I thought best, in addition to representing what I believed was true? What was an appropriate ethical position for a researcher investigating a condition that has had such power to shape lives and families?

Many social scientists have come to believe that one obligation of scholarship in contemporary professional and activist communities is faithful representation of and engagement with their technical and political arguments.[7] While many of the professionals and advocates I studied are less vulnerable than other, more marginal populations, they have a stake in my findings and the ability to appraise the ways in which a positive representation benefits them. It is easy to become involved in the "projects and interests" of the researchers that we study. We can lose sight of what Paul Rabinow has described as "the ethical task [of] finding the mean" between identifying with our subjects as scientists and becoming an uncritical promoter of research agendas or technological products.[8] With communities that include parents and patients who can be simultaneously savvy and vulnerable, we need to consider what obligations our relationships produce. There is no real option of deferring affiliations until after completing our research.[9] Scientific work involves interpersonal relationships, and in order to comprehend these relationships we have to form some ourselves.

A secondary part of work at home is the additional requirement—long recognized by cultural anthropologists—to contribute to the community studied. Subjects of ethnographic research increasingly expect a reciprocal investment from ethnographers. When they offer themselves as willing subjects of research, they want to know what the knowledge generated by this research can do for them. They may ask what they can expect in exchange for serving as research subjects, contributing their time, instructing the researcher, and offering potentially risky revelations. Those in large clinical trials customarily receive compensation for contributing their time to the projects. For families with members affected by a genetic disorder, participation holds out the promise of an eventual treatment or cure. It is harder to portray the ultimate deliverables of research in the social sciences in the same hopeful light.

At one point, I imagined producing a handbook for health-based social movements. Activists for research reform borrow strategies from other kinds of movements. I would survey the most productive approaches used by a range of groups, including autism advocates. Many of the advocates I had interviewed were self-conscious about their role in creating knowledge about autism and presenting their ideas using a language valued by those setting research policy. I gave up the idea. I wasn't enough of a participant or insider to write compellingly about strategy. Instead, as a sympathetic outsider, I could strive to portray the members of these communities in a comprehensive and contextualized way.

Our choices are not always limited to joining those we study or eschewing all involvement. For instance, social scientists are uniquely positioned to promote dialogue among groups that are otherwise at odds.[10] At various points in my research I served as an informal translator among activist groups, between activist groups and scientists, and among scientists in different disciplines. Now, at the end of a long research project, I have joined an ongoing conversation about autism research, doing my best to raise questions as a researcher and also as a caring person where I think that the choices being made are wrong ones.

Rights, Wrongs, and Awkward Alliances in Autism Research

We measure the efficacy of actions in biomedicine by using bodies and minds. Doing so exposes men and women to potentially tragic risks. Even interventions that carry a minimal possibility of bodily harm, like behavioral therapies, can have irreversible, life-altering consequences. Thus, those who serve as spokespeople for communities or for particular forms of treatment exercise tremendous power. The stakes are high for those faced with the choice of whom to believe. When geneticists design a research program or funding agencies support a particular line of inquiry or parents decide on one intervention over another, they are all choosing whom to trust regarding what is best for people with autism.

Central to both feminist epistemologies of science and theories of autism treatment is a view of empathy as a learned skill—something to be struggled for and achieved laboriously, partially, and imperfectly. Autism is a uniquely good place to listen in on conversations about the role of affect in biomedicine and about the ethics of empathy. It is, however, far from the only place where these conversations take place. They happen every time children develop in ways different from what their parents expected and the parents seek out experts for guidance. These exchanges are especially tough since parents, doctors, and at times policymakers all must make decisions affecting children who may not be able to communicate fully their own thoughts and desires, and who are, by definition, changing every day.

Mark Osteen, in confronting this problem, has proposed what he calls "empathetic scholarship." Researchers should try "speaking *with* those unable to communicate entirely on their own," by "combining rigorous scholarship with the experiential knowledge" acquired through kinship and friendships with autistic people.[11] As a matter of both method and ethics, in writing about disabilities like autism it is important not only to acknowledge but also to build those relationships so critical to knowledge production.[12]

Treatments for autism cannot be understood apart from their specific historical and social contexts, just as autism must be understood as having evolved over time through communities constituted by practice. Each of the techniques that I have described is a site of ethical and technical controversy where the boundaries between the two are often hard to make out. I focused on what participants have had to say about various therapies rather than just the theories of etiology that informed them, since theories are never sufficient to describe the full range of experiences that constitute treatment.

When I write about pluralism in American biomedicine, I am making essentially the same argument. Different ways of engaging with autism are site specific and involve practices that are *both* affective and rational, but these practices are not "alternative," if by alternative one means opposed to biomedical reason. Positioning unconventional medical practices outside of mainstream medicine invites analysts to ignore or to diminish them—as "culturally bound" or a product of desperation rather than research and rational evaluation. Contests over autism treatment are nearly always arguments over what counts as medical knowledge and who can produce it. For this reason, ethical debates do not occur in parallel to but as a constitutive part of biomedical choices and contests. What do we talk about when we talk about love—especially in regard to biomedicine? One thing is ethics—the ethics of communication, of position, of dependence, responsibility, obligation, and commitment.

One issue that almost everyone involved with autism agrees on is the need for better services for people with autism across the lifespan. Currently, insurance companies cover educational and behavioral treatments only inconsistently if at all. Parents pay for treatments, including nutritional supplements and the expenses associated with special diets, out of pocket. Although the law requires school districts to provide appropriate educational supports, in practice, as many parents know, these vary widely by region. As a result, families are often forced to move in search of better services. Educational services also evaporate once a child ages out of the school system around age twenty-one. Even parents of young children fear for the future of their children were they to die or become ill and incapable of caring for them. Parents of adult children face the additional, continuing trial of finding stimulating occupations and care for people who may need constant and watchful supervision.

The neurodiversity movement has made a difference in several areas. Many national autism advocacy organizations understand that they cannot adequately represent the needs of people with autism without including people with autism diagnoses in their decision-making and on their supervisory boards. Adults with autism who serve in executive positions may not be representative of the full spectrum of people with autism, but that is not a justification for exclusion. If they cannot speak for children and adults unable to communicate their own wishes, their demands for changes in conventional representations of autism and in the services that the national organizations push for are different enough from existing priorities to make their inclusion not only ethical but also productive.

Self-advocates, together with parent activists, have contributed to changing public awareness and popular representations of autism. People with autism continue to be the subject of misunderstanding and discrimination in public and in the workplace. Strangers still stop parents in the street to offer suggestions about managing their child's "misbehavior" and teenagers with autism face exclusion by their peers. Nonetheless, more people now understand the basic facts about autism and are prepared to learn more. The impact on research priorities may be even greater in the long run. While the opposition of self-advocates is unlikely to halt studies on autism genetics, biomedical treatments, environmental causation, or behavioral therapies, some researchers are now listening to people with autism when designing new research projects, asking what aspects of the experience of autism ought to be considered and which areas might be of interest to them and useful in their daily lives.

More inclusive research and public awareness will not, however, solve all the ethical dilemmas that surround autism. The most unsettling of them stem from the reality of dependency and of suffering that can't be ameliorated by changes in the social or physical environment. All children with autism and those adults who are most severely affected rely on others for their care and for the decisions that impact their treatment. The particular theory of autism that their caregivers subscribe to, as I have shown, matters to the choice of treatment, including the decision not to intervene. No specific form of treatment, however, necessarily follows from a view of autism as genetic, biochemical, psychological, a benign form of neurological diversity, or the result of an injury. Many genetic conditions are labile, susceptible to all manner of nutritional and pharmacological interventions, whereas many injuries are just as "fixed" as genetic errors.[13] In other words, the degree to which beliefs about fundamental causes and mechanisms of autism do continue to guide treatment is further evidence—if any is needed—of the ethical and social valences of scientific and biomedical facts.

Parents who want simultaneously to love and heal their children are old hands at finessing the fact that caring requires that we believe incompatible things at the same time. That is, parents can accept the value and importance of their child's obsessions and the beauty of their different ways of experiencing the world around them, even as they work to free them from restrictions that their impairments impose on them. As Clara Park observed, parents often learn, after all, that they "can have it both ways." At the beginning of her memoir of her daughter's adult years, Park writes that

> the world we share, the only world we had to offer that wordless baby, is our common world of risk, frustration, loss, of unfulfilled desire as well as of activity and love. We could not leave Jessy to her empty serenity. We would not, as was often recommended in those days, institutionalize her "for the sake of the other children," to spend her days somewhere in a back ward, rocking. We would keep her with us, entice, intrude, enter where we were not wanted or needed.[14]

Caring for her reminds the Parks that just as Jessy's autistic traits can contain things of value for both Jessy and the people that surround her, the world of typical behaviors and sociability is not an entirely good or desirable place. It contains no assurance of right action or a superior understanding of reality compared to their daughter's "secret life." Yet, despite grappling with the possibility that they are stepping in where no change is wanted or needed, the Parks persist in framing their obligation in terms of providing the best possible circumstances for their daughter to flourish. Perhaps that tentativeness is part of the moral of these love stories. Devotion is ideally an experimental procedure. It is especially so when, as parents often feel in the case of autism, it impels us to consider the object of our love as both a biological being, subject to manipulation and harm, and a person, precious and complete in his or her own right.[15]

NOTES

Note on Sources and References

I consulted the Bruno Bettelheim Papers at the Special Collections Research Center, University of Chicago Library; and the Amy L. Lettick Papers at the Manuscripts and Archives Collection, Sterling Memorial Library, Yale University.

In order to provide ease of access to readers, in the notes to this book I have included full citations to both archival sources and published primary sources that I cite a single time. The notes also contain short references to secondary sources. These sources are listed in the bibliography. Readers interested in finding a general guide to secondary literatures (e.g., in the social sciences) can consult the bibliography.

Introduction

1. Rose (1983, 83).
2. Haraway (1997a, 124).
3. Slogan on a T-shirt, CafePress, http://www.cafepress.com/buy/autism/-/pv_design_details/pg_4/id_9298831/opt_/fpt_/c_360/.
4. It can also refer to a type of person (e.g., "autistic child") or a syndrome that a person has ("child with autism"). Throughout this book, I observe the convention of "person-first" language advocated by the disability rights movement when referring to children with autism in the present, but I use the terminology appropriate to any given historical period when describing children in that period. In keeping with the preference of most self-advocates in the present, I do not use person-first language when referring to them.
5. There is a growing body of anthropological scholarship that does focus on informal practices of care with children with autism. See, in particular, Park (2008) and Solomon (2010).

6. Bruno Bettelheim cited Freud's statement that "Psychoanalysis is in essence a cure through love," in *Freud and Man's Soul* (New York: Knopf, 1983). Cited in Zelan (1993, 97).

7. Park (1967, 188).

8. Park (1985, 115).

9. Lenny Schafer, "Autistic Children Murdered: Outrage vs. Sympathy," *Schafer Autism Report* 10, no. 89 (May 23, 2006).

10. Alexandra Wood, "Mother's Bridge Death Plunge with Her Son Was an Act of Love, Say Sisters," *Yorkshire Post,* May 22, 2006, http://www.yorkshiretoday.co .uk/ViewArticle.aspx?SectionID=55&ArticleID=1517218. Alison Davies jumped off a bridge into the River Humber with her son, Ryan. Ryan was diagnosed with Fragile X syndrome, which is often associated with autism; news coverage referred to both diagnoses.

11. Cammie McGovern, "Autism's Parent Trap," *New York Times,* June 5, 2006. The full quote read "In mythologizing recovery, I fear that we've set an impossibly high bar that's left the parents of a half-million autistic children feeling like failures."

12. Josh Greenfeld, the author of three books (1970, 1978, 1986) about his son Noah, who has autism, has said that "We're always on that edge of violence when we're on that edge of intense concern and intense love or intense— whatever word you want to use," and mentioned that he wanted to write about that impulse so "once I've said them, I can't do it" because he would be accountable. Greenfeld was quoted in a 1978 *60 Minutes* interview. "Noah's Story," http://www.cbsnews.com/stories/2000/05/09/60II/main193439 .shtml#1978.

13. Park (1967, 194–95).

14. Merton (1973); Mulkay (1976); Shapin (1994).

15. Daston and Galison (1992); Daston (1992, 609).

16. Shapin (1996).

17. For example, Haraway (1989, 1991, 1997b), Rose (1994), and Keller (1983, 1992).

18. Cowan (1983); Wajcman (1991). Gibbon (2007, 92–94) provides an insightful analysis of gendered "care work" in the context of testing for genes associated with increased risk of breast cancer. On gendered divisions of caring labor, see Gilligan (1982).

19. For example, Baron-Cohen (2003).

20. According to the Women's Bureau of the Department of Labor, the top five occupations for women in 2009 were secretaries and administrative assistants, registered nurses, elementary and middle school teachers, cashiers, and nursing, psychiatric, and home health aides. United States Department of Labor, Women's Bureau, "20 Leading Occupations of Employed Women: 2009 Annual Averages," http://www.dol.gov/wb/factsheets/20lead2009.htm.

21. Keller (2007, 355–56).

22. Bérubé (1996, xviii, 145–46, 249); Kittay (2001, 560–61, 567–68).

23. For example, adults with autism may arrive at moral judgments by applying rules or a repertoire of models of people's behaviors. Kennett (2002, 352).

24. But for a discussion of some of these questions, see Barnbaum (2008).

25. Stacy Clifford (2006, 131–32), writing as the sibling of a person with severe autism, argues that just as people with autism strive for "local coherence" as a way of coping with an otherwise chaotic perceptual world, caregivers should think about solutions to the ethical questions of caregiving "at the local level, contextualized into the local realities of dependency situations."

26. MacIntyre (1999). Also see Nussbaum (2006).

27. Kittay (1999, 557–79).

28. A "philosophy of the limit" is Eva Feder Kittay's term for the types of decisions that women must make, quoted in Rapp (1999, 3, 308–9).

29. Frankfurt (2006, 40–43, 2–5, 24–26).

30. Ibid., 3.

31. Fromm (1956, 93,103).

32. Kittay (1999, 172–73).

33. A rough estimate, based on the fact that as of 2002 the Department of Education reported that there were 120,000 children with autism being served under the Individuals with Disabilities Education Act (IDEA). Because the CDC reported in 2009 that approximately one in 110 children in the U.S. has an autism spectrum disorder, "hundreds of thousands" might in fact be closer to millions. U.S. Government Accountability Office, "Special Education: Children with Autism" (January 14, 2005), http://www.gao.gov/products/GAO-05-220, Autism and Developmental Disabilities Monitoring Network Surveillance Year 2006 Principal Investigators and Centers for Disease Control and Prevention (CDC), "Prevalence of Autism Spectrum Disorders—Autism and Developmental Disabilities Monitoring Network, United States, 2006," *MMWR Surveillance Summaries* 58, no. 10 (2009): 1–20.

34. On the silencing of parents in encounters with health professionals, see Noah Feinstein, "Silenced by Science? Parents of Autistic Children Finding Their Voice" (paper presented at the Society for Social Studies of Science, Vancouver, British Columbia, November 2006).

35. Bourdieu's (1975/1999, 19) description of science as a system of productive labor, the outcome of which is "the objective truth of the product," and of scientific careers as a "competitive struggle" for authority are reflected in much of autism research, but the field has not always progressed steadily toward increasing autonomy or independence from external interests.

36. Murray (2008).

37. These accounts can be found in Johnson and Crowder (1994).

38. Bettelheim (1959, 117). See the thoughtful critique of Bettelheim's analysis in Jurecic (2006, 8–10).

39. The specific phrase comes from an interview with Francesca Happe conducted on June 21, 2005, although others echoed the general observation.

40. Ferguson (1996, 25). Ferguson noted that populations seen as "chronic" and "unteachable" were particularly neglected in historical work on disability. There have been notable exceptions since he wrote, in particular Trent (1994) and Noll (1995).

41. Some scholars contrast biomedicine with other, non-Western knowledge systems, an assumption that fails to recognize the many differences in how biomedicine is practiced in different places. In fact, biomedical knowledge often has to accommodate or incorporate other adjacent or prior ways of knowing about the world, what Susan Lindee (2005) calls "moments of truth" in biomedicine. On the rise of molecular biology following World War II, see de Chadarevian (2002).

42. Rosenberg (2002).

43. Kay (1993, 2000); Luhrmann (2000).

44. Dumit (2003).

45. Epstein (1996).

46. Apple (2006).

47. On the tension between trust in scientific authority and traditions of lay participation in biomedicine, see Starr (1982).

48. Hays (1996, 9). In making the connection between Hays's work and parenting children with autism, I draw on Stevenson (2008, 199).

49. The classic text exploring the historical contingence of "childhood" as a category is Ariès (1962).

50. Murphy (2000, 88; 2006) has described how people suffering from multiple chemical sensitivity (MCS) come together not due to their symptoms, which vary, but due to their shared experience of bodies that don't fit the explanatory frameworks that their doctors have to offer them. Also see Kroll-Smith and Floyd (2000). Brown, Zavestoski, McCormick, Linder, et al. (2001) describe how disputes over Gulf War syndrome have followed similar lines.

51. Brown, Zavestoski, McCormick, Mayer, et al. (2004, 54–55). Also see discussions of myalgic encephalitis and Lyme disease in Aronowitz (1998). Dumit (2000) describes some contested illness categories as "the new socio-medical disorders," which are characterized by their "biomental" nature, causal indeterminacy, biosocial organization, legal explosiveness, therapeutic heterogeneity and diversity, interrelationships between categories, and the disputed use of brain imaging techniques in establishing their "objectivity."

52. Bourdieu (1984, 479) uses the term to describe struggles over the identity of groups and particular social practices.

53. Apart from the finding that in the United States, autism is more frequently diagnosed among children in higher-income families, relatively little research has been done on how the experience of the diagnosis differs across socioeconomic contexts. See Maureen S. Durkin, Matthew J. Maenner, F. John Meaney, Susan E. Levy, et al., "Socioeconomic Inequality in the Prevalence

of Autism Spectrum Disorder: Evidence from a U.S. Cross-Sectional Study," *PLoS One* 5, no. 7 (2010): e11551. There is a growing body of work, however, on autism in different cultural contexts. Grinker (2008) describes how families in India, Korea, and South Africa often must oppose social and institutional norms in order to obtain diagnoses and treatment for their children. Also see Daley (2002, 2004). Shaked (2005) and Shaked and Bilu (2006) describe how mothers use religious discourse strategically to push for their children's inclusion in the Jewish ultraorthodox community. Ochs and Solomon (2010, 74–76) observe intersections among cultural, sociological, and symptomatic aspects of a child with autism's experience of sociability.

54. More research is needed on the exact relationships among income, education, and choice of therapies. Here I refer to three things: first, the finding that use of alternative treatments for autism is very high overall, perhaps as high 74 percent or even 92 percent of all children diagnosed; second, that this seems to be consistent across income levels; and, third, that mothers with a range of educational levels are willing to question doctors' developmental prognoses. See Ellen Hanson, Leslie A. Kalish, Emily Bunce, Christine Curtis, et al., "Use of Complementary and Alternative Medicine among Children Diagnosed with Autism Spectrum Disorder," *Journal of Autism and Developmental Disorders* 37, no. 4 (2007): 628–36, 628; John W. Harrington, Lawrence Rosen, and Ana Garnecho, "Parental Perceptions and Use of Complementary and Alternative Medicine Practices for Children with Autistic Spectrum Disorders in Private Practice," *Developmental and Behavioral Pediatrics* 27, no. 2 (2006): S156–61, S160; and Landsman (2009, 6).

55. Fleck's (1979) account of how syphilis stabilized as a disease category and Jack Pressman's (1998) work on the emphatic—if temporary—adoption of psychosurgery are only two of the best accounts of this type. On studying the achievement of closure on matters of scientific fact more generally, see Latour (1988).

56. Rabinow (1996).

57. Hacking (1998, 1999, 2007) has called this tendency of populations to shape and be shaped by medical categories "dynamic nominalism" or the "looping effect," a phenomenon that he has suggested applies to autism spectrum disorders. As he has observed (1999, 170), no two instances of "making up" people are the same.

58. On the concept of genetic citizenship, see Heath, Rapp, and Taussig (2004).

59. In the absence of predictive testing for autism risk, parents do not enter into the type of potentially coercive relations with genetic counselors and other professionals that Rose (2007, 27–29, 73–76, 217) describes as an "ethopolitics" that influences conduct by appealing to people's "sentiments, beliefs, and values." However, what Rose calls "somatic experts" do have authority in the field of autism, through advising, for example, on the crucial importance of early intervention as a future-shaping technology (e.g., Leiter [2004]).

60. Amsterdamska and Hiddinga (2004) have argued that provisions in American disabilities legislation encouraged practitioners to emphasize autism spectrum disorders' status as developmental disorders.
61. My use of "partiality" and "situated knowledges" depends on Haraway's (1991, 183–202) foundational use of the terms.
62. In addition, advocacy for one's own child often leads to work that is better described as social activism. Ryan (2009, 52).
63. Marcus and Fischer (1986) advocate "multi-sited ethnographies" for studying cultural practices that occur at multiple scales, locations, and levels of organization, such as commodities markets and biomedical research. The method works well for examining the tight connections between local and global economies of knowledge production and the "emergent forms of life" made possible by new sciences and technologies. Also see Marcus (1998), and for considerations of the potential applications of ethnographic techniques in science studies, see Fischer (1999; 2000).
64. Nader (1972); Forsythe (1999, 7).
65. Two examples are Haddon (2004) and Moon (2003).
66. Belmonte (2008, 168–69); The Gray Center for Social Learning and Understanding, http://www.thegraycenter.org.
67. This claim has been made more than once, but I am thinking in particular of Joan Didion's (1990, 11) observation that stories are both essential and an "imposition" of meaning upon the overwhelming clutter of images and events that constitute "actual experience."

Part One
Chapter 1

1. See, for instance, any of the essays in Rosenberg and Golden (1992).
2. Hacking (1999; 2007, 303–4; 2009a) has applied his own analysis to autism spectrum disorders, describing how people with autism are and are not like other "kinds of people." Autistic autobiographies, Hacking argues, have helped develop a language to describe what is distinct about autistic experience.
3. Frith (1991, 1).
4. "Medicine: The Child Is Father," *Time,* July 25, 1960.
5. For instance, Lane (1979), Happe (1994), Houston and Frith (2000), Frith (2003), and Waltz and Shattock (2004).
6. Rosenberg (2002).
7. "An observer even slightly trained in ethology cannot help seeing such 'experiments by nature' happen all the time to autistic children." Tinbergen and Tinbergen (1983, 75).
8. Kanner (1943, 250).

9. Neumärker (2003); Leo Kanner, *A History of the Care and Study of the Mentally Retarded*, (Springfield, IL: Charles C. Thomas, 1964), 143.

10. Kanner first worked in South Dakota, then moved to Johns Hopkins University, where he spent the rest of his career. Neumärker (2003); Edwards A. Park, "A Child Psychiatric Clinic in a Paediatric Department," *Canadian Medical Association Journal* 38, no. 1 (1938): 74–78, 76.

11. Leo Kanner, "Co-Editor's Introduction," *Nervous Child* 2 (1943): 216.

12. Rose Zeligs, *Glimpses into Child Life: The Twelve-Year Old at Home and School* (New York: W. Morrow & Co., 1942), quoted in Kanner (1943, 217).

13. Bleuler also coined the term "schizophrenia" in 1908, to describe the disorder that had previously been called "dementia praecox." Kuhn and Cahn (2004).

14. Trent (1994).

15. Grob (1994); Hale (1978, 303–4).

16. Kanner (1943, 217).

17. Leon Eisenberg, "Preface," in *Childhood Psychosis: Initial Studies and New Insights*, by Leo Kanner (Washington, DC: V. H. Winston & Sons, 1973), xi.

18. Kanner (1943, 249, 219, 221–22).

19. Ibid., 222–24, 226, 239–40.

20. Kanner (1943, 242, 248).

21. "Nevertheless, the usefulness of Kanner's original observation persists today when many of the other diagnostic formulations have faded into obscurity. This is precisely because Kanner relied on careful and systematic clinical observations rather than on theoretical dicta." Eric Schopler, Michael Rutter, and Stella Chess, "Editorial: Change of Journal Scope and Title," *Journal of Autism and Developmental Disorders* 9, no. 1 (1979): 1–10, 2.

22. Kanner (1943, 250).

23. Ibid., 249–50.

24. For a discussion of Bleuler's understanding of psychopathology and the sense in which he used the term "autism," see Kuhn and Cahn (2004, 364).

25. Asperger wrote in Austria during World War II, in the shadow of Nazi eugenics programs, and Frith (1991, 90) has suggested that this inspired him to downplay the idea that the syndrome was a disabling condition. Asperger (1944/1991, 38).

26. Ibid., 41.

27. Aperger (1944/1991, 88).

28. Leo Kanner, "Problems of Nosology and Psychodynamics in Early Infantile Autism," *American Journal of Orthopsychiatry* 19 (1949): 416–26, 425.

29. Leo Kanner, "To What Extent Is Early Infantile Autism Determined by Constitutional Inadequacies?" in *Childhood Psychosis: Initial Studies and New Insights* (Washington, DC: V. H. Winston & Sons, 1973), 69–75, 75, revised from the original published in D. Hooker and C. C. Hare, *Genetics and the Inheritance of Integrated Neurological and Psychiatric Patterns* (Baltimore, MD: Williams and Wilkins, 1954, 378–85); Leo Kanner and Leon Eisenberg,

"Early Infantile Autism, 1943–1955," *American Journal of Orthopsychiatry* 26 (1956): 556–66, 561.

30. Ruth Christ Sullivan, "Presentations from Experts in the Field" (round-table discussion), The Autism Summit Conference: Developing a National Agenda, Washington, DC, November 19–20, 2003; Warren (1984, 109).

31. Kanner (1971, 141).

32. Wing (1993, 63).

33. Leo Kanner, "Problems of Nosology and Psychodynamics in Early Infantile Autism," *American Journal of Orthopsychiatry* 19 (1949): 416–26, 420.

34. C. B. Ferster, "Positive Reinforcement and Behavioral Deficits of Autistic Children," *Child Development,* 32 (1961): 437–56.

35. *Diagnostic and Statistical Manual of Mental Disorders,* 2nd ed. (Washington, DC: American Psychiatric Association, 1968), 35; Leo Kanner, "Follow-Up Study of Eleven Autistic Children," *Journal of Autism and Childhood Schizophrenia* 1, no. 2 (1971): 119–45, 141. Interestingly, in 2009 researchers again proposed a connection between childhood schizophrenia and autism, noting the high degree of comorbidity between the two conditions, with many cases of childhood-onset schizophrenia initially receiving diagnoses of pervasive developmental disorder. Judith Rapoport, Alex Chavez, Deanna Greenstein, Anjene Addington, et al., "Autism Spectrum Disorders and Childhood-Onset Schizophrenia: Clinical and Biological Contributions to a Relation Revisited," *Journal of the American Academy of Child and Adolescent Psychiatry* 48, no. 1 (2009): 10–18.

36. Eric Schopler, Michael Rutter, and Stella Chess, "Journal of Autism and Childhood Schizophrenia. Change of Journal Scope and Title," *Journal of Autism and Developmental Disorders* 9, no.1 (1979): 1–10.

37. Michael Rutter and Lawrence Bartak, "Causes of Infantile Autism: Some Considerations from Recent Research," *Journal of Autism and Childhood Schizophrenia* 1, no. 1 (1971): 20–32, 24.

38. Michael Rutter, "Autism Research: Prospects and Priorities," *Journal of Autism and Developmental Disorders* 26, no. 2 (1996): 257–75, 257.

39. Nadesan (2005) provides a more thorough analysis in her history of the social construction of the autism diagnosis.

40. Tinbergen and Tinbergen (1983, 12).

41. Rimland (1964, 87–92).

42. Leo Kanner, "Foreword," in Rimland (1964, v).

43. Rimland (1964, 149).

44. Ibid., 151, 155.

45. Margaret S. Mahler and Manuel S. Furer, "Child Psychosis: A Theoretical Statement and Its Implications," *Journal of Autism and Childhood Schizophrenia* 2, no. 3 (1972): 213–18, 214.

46. Frances Tustin, "Revised Understandings of Psychogenic Autism," *The International Journal of Psychoanalysis* 72, no. 4 (1991): 585–91. Tustin began writing on autism in the late 1960s and published a book-length study, *Autism*

and Childhood Psychosis (London, UK: The Hogarth Press, 1972). See also Nadesan (2005, 99–101).

47. For example, researchers at the Yale Child Study Center conceptualized the anxiety that children with autism experienced in terms of "the persistent possibility of ego disorganization" in a 1987 paper. Sally Provence and E. Kirsten Dahl, "Disorders of Atypical Development: Diagnostic Issues Raised by a Spectrum Disorder," in Donald J. Cohen, Anne M. Donnellan, and Rhea Paul, eds., *Handbook of Autism and Pervasive Developmental Disorders* (Silver Spring, MD: V. H. Winston and Sons, 1987), 677–89, 682.

48. O. Ivar Lovaas, Laura Schreibman, Robert Koegel, and Richard Rehm, "Selective Responding by Autistic Children to Multiple Sensory Input," *Journal of Abnormal Psychology* 77, no. 3 (1971): 211–22, 211; Laura Schreibman, "Effects of Within-Stimulus and Extra-Stimulus Prompting on Discrimination Learning in Autistic Children," *Journal of Applied Behavior Analysis* 8, no. 1 (1975): 91–112; Robert L. Koegel and Arnold Rincover, "Some Detrimental Effects of Using Extra Stimuli to Guide Learning in Normal and Autistic Children," *Journal of Abnormal Child Psychology* 4, no. 1 (1976): 59–71; Barry S. Reynolds, Crighton D. Newsom, and O. Ivar Lovaas, "Auditory Overselectivity in Autistic Children," *Journal of Abnormal Child Psychology* 2, no. 4 (1974): 253–63; Laura Schreibman and O. Ivar Lovaas, "Overselective Response to Social Stimuli by Autistic Children," *Journal of Abnormal Child Psychology* 1, no. 2 (1973): 152–68.

49. O. Ivar Lovaas, "Contrasting Illness and Behavioral Models for the Treatment of Autistic Children: A Historical Perspective," *Journal of Autism and Developmental Disorders* 9, no. 4 (1979): 315–23, 318; O. Ivar Lovaas and Tristram Smith, "A Comprehensive Behavioral Theory of Autistic Children: Paradigm for Research and Treatment," *Journal of Behavior Therapy and Experimental Psychiatry* 20, no. 1 (1989): 17–29.

50. Michael Rutter and Lawrence Bartak, "Causes of Infantile Autism: Some Considerations from Recent Research," *Journal of Autism and Childhood Schizophrenia* 1, no. 1 (1971): 20–32, 25.

51. Susan Folstein and Michael Rutter, "Infantile Autism: A Genetic Study of 21 Twin Pairs," *Journal of Child Psychology and Psychiatry* 18, no. 4 (1977): 297–321, 308.

52. Partly because in the 1970s so few cases of autism were diagnosed, it was hard to find many instances where there were multiple cases in one family. This seemed to argue against genetic involvement. D. R. Hanson and I. I. Gottesman, "The Genetics, If Any, of Infantile Autism and Childhood Schizophrenia," *Journal of Autism and Childhood Schizophrenia* 6, no. 3 (1976): 209–34.

53. A single 1975 study used the older technique of pneumoencepholography to image the brains of eighteen children with autistic behavior, a surprising choice given that the procedure was notoriously painful and quite dangerous. Stephen L. Hauser, G. Robert DeLong, and N. Paul Rosman, "Pneu-

mographic Findings in the Infantile Autism Syndrome. A Correlation with Temporal Lobe Disease," *Brain* 98, no. 4 (1975): 67–88.

54. Christopher Gillberg and Pal Svendsen, "Childhood Psychosis and Computed Tomographic Brain Scan Findings," *Journal of Autism and Developmental Disorders* 13, no. 1 (1983): 19–32; Gary R. Gaffney and Luke Y. Tsai, "Brief Report: Magnetic Resonance Imaging of High Level Autism," *Journal of Autism and Developmental Disorders* 17, no. 3 (1987): 433–38. Others researchers produced evidence that there were asymmetries between the size of structures in the left and right hemispheres of autistic brains, although findings were inconsistent. The earliest report on brain asymmetries in autism was Daniel B. Hier, Marjorie LeMay, and Peter B. Rosenberger, "Autism and Unfavorable Left-Right Asymmetries of the Brain," *Journal of Autism and Developmental Disorders* 9, no. 2 (1979): 153–59; and the later study that failed to replicate the finding was Judith M. Rumsey, Helen Creasey, Jennifer S. Stepanek, Robert Dorwart, et al., "Hemispheric Asymmetries, Fourth Ventricular Size, and Cerebellar Morphology in Autism," *Journal of Autism and Developmental Disorders* 18, no. 1 (1988): 127–37.

55. Margaret Bauman and Thomas L. Kemper, "Histoanatomic Observations of the Brain in Early Infantile Autism," *Neurology* 35 (1985): 866–74, 871. Also see Margaret L. Bauman, "Brief Report: Neuroanatomic Observations of the Brain in Pervasive Developmental Disorders," *Journal of Autism and Developmental Disorders* 26, no. 2 (1996): 199–203.

56. Eric Courchesne, R. Yeung-Courchesne, G. A. Press, J. R. Hesselink, et al., "Hypoplasia of Cerebellar Vermal Lobules VI and VII in Autism," *New England Journal of Medicine* 318, no. 21 (1988): 1349–54.

57. Simon Baron-Cohen, Alan M. Leslie, and Uta Frith, "Does the Autistic Child Have a 'Theory of Mind'?" *Cognition* 21, no. 1 (1985): 37–46. The group built on Premack and Woodruff's concept and Alan Leslie's application of the idea to developmental theory. David Premack and G. Woodruff, "Does the Chimpanzee Have a 'Theory of Mind'?" *Behavioral and Brain Sciences* 4 (1978): 515–26.

58. On executive function and autism, see Sally Ozonoff, Bruce F. Pennington, and Sally J. Rogers, "Executive Function Deficits in High-Functioning Autistic Individuals: Relationship to Theory of Mind," *Journal of Child Psychology and Psychiatry* 32, no. 7 (1993): 1081–1105. On weak central coherence, see Amitta Shah and Uta Frith, "Why Do Autistic Individuals Show Superior Performance on the Block Design Task?" *Journal of Child Psychology and Psychiatry* 34, no. 8 (1993): 1351–64.

59. Ibid., 1353.

60. Lorna Wing, "Sex Ratios in Early Childhood Autism and Related Conditions," *Psychiatry Research* 5, no. 2 (1981): 129–37, 129; Leon Eisenberg and Leo Kanner, "Childhood Schizophrenia: Symposium, 1955. VI. Early Infantile Autism, 1943–55," *American Journal of Orthopsychiatry* 26, no. 3 (1956): 556–66, 560.

61. For example, researchers theorized that autistic girls' relatively superior early social development was aided by higher expectations from parents, while their later difficulties resulted from their "difficulty negotiating peer relationships that rely heavily on conversation." John D. McLennan, Catherine Lord, and Eric Schopler, *Journal of Autism and Developmental Disorders* 23, no. 2 (1993): 217–27, 225. On current efforts to provide support for girls with autism, see Emily Bazelon, "What Autistic Girls Are Made Of," *New York Times*, August 5, 2007.

62. Kristin Bumiller (2008, 972–74, 977–78) provides a more extended analysis of the role of gender in autism research and advocacy, arguing that the neurodiversity movement, in arguing for acceptance of autistic traits, also argues against normative gender expectations built into autism research and treatment.

63. Nichols, Moravcik, and Tentenbaum (2009, 21, 24, 26–27).

64. Asperger (1944/1991, 84–85). Asperger thought that autism might be "an extreme variant of male intelligence."

65. Baron-Cohen (2003); Simon Baron-Cohen, "The Cognitive Neuroscience of Autism: The Psychology and Biology of a Complex Developmental Condition," *Journal of Neurology, Neurosurgery, and Psychiatry* 75 (2004): 945–48; Simon Baron-Cohen and Matthew Belmonte, "Autism: A Window onto the Development of the Social and the Analytic Brain," *Annual Review of Neuroscience* 28 (2005): 109–26.

66. Susan L. Smalley, Robert F. Asarnow, and M. Anne Spence, "Autism and Genetics: A Decade of Research," *Archives of General Psychiatry* 45, no. 10 (1988): 953–61.

67. Geraldine Dawson, "Defining the Broader Phenotype of Autism: Genetic, Brain, and Behavioral Perspectives," *Development and Psychopathology* 14, no. 3 (2002): 581–611.

68. Catherine Lord, Cory Shulman, and Pamela DiLavore, "Regression and Word Loss in Autistic Spectrum Disorders," *Journal of Child Psychology and Psychiatry* 45, no. 5 (2004): 936–55.

69. For instance, some researchers argue that even regressive autism produces visible signs in infants, implicitly denying parents' claims that their children were developing typically before developing autism, and that the dramatic quality of their regression is central to the syndrome. Rebecca Landa commented on "progression" versus "regression" in autism at an NIH Interagency Autism Coordinating Committee (IACC) meeting on May 9, 2006, in Washington, DC. Also see Rebecca J. Landa, Katherine C. Holman, and Elizabeth Garrett-Mayer, "Social and Communication Development in Toddlers with Early and Later Diagnosis of Autism Spectrum Disorders," *Archives of General Psychiatry* 64, no. 7 (2007): 853–64.

70. Michael Rutter, "Diagnosis and Definition of Childhood Autism," *Journal of Autism and Childhood Schizophrenia* 8, no. 2 (1978): 139–61, 140.

71. Juliet Harper and Sara Williams, "Age and Type of Onset as Critical Variables in Early Infantile Autism," *Journal of Autism and Childhood Schizophrenia* 5, no. 1 (1975): 25–36.

72. Emily Werner and Geraldine Dawson, "Validation of the Phenomenon of Autistic Regression Using Home Videotapes," *Archives of General Psychiatry* 62, no. 8 (2005): 889–94.

73. See Dan Olmstead, "The Age of Autism: Backward," UPI, May 4, 2005, http://www.upi.com/Science_News/2005/05/04/The_Age_of_Autism_Backward/UPI-18211115179500/.

74. Kanner (1943, 225, 239, 237, 236).

75. Edward R. Ritvo, B. J. Freeman, Carmen Pingree, Anne Mason-Brothers, et al., "The UCLA-University of Utah Epidemiologic Survey of Autism: Prevalence," *American Journal of Psychiatry* 146, no. 2 (1989): 194–99, 199. The authors found that their rate of 4 in 10,000 was "remarkably close" to those found by a range of studies from different countries dating from 1966 to 1984.

76. L. A. Shieve, C. Rice, C. Boyle, S. N. Visser, et al., "Mental Health in the United States: Parental Report of Diagnosed Autism in Children Aged 4–17 Years, United States, 2003–2004," *Morbidity and Mortality Weekly Report* 55, no. 17 (2006): 481–86; Autism and Developmental Disabilities Monitoring Network Surveillance Year 2002 Principal Investigators, "Prevalence of Autism Spectrum Disorders—Autism and Developmental Disabilities Monitoring Network, 14 Sites, United States, 2002," *Morbidity and Mortality Weekly Report* 56, no. SS-1 (2007): 12–28; Gillian Baird, Emily Simonoff, Andrew Pickles, Susie Chandler, et al., "Prevalence of Disorders of the Autism Spectrum in a Population Cohort of Children in South Thames: The Special Needs and Autism Project (SNAP)," *Lancet* 368, no. 9531 (2006): 210–15 ; Eric Fombonne, "Epidemiology of Autistic Disorder and Other Pervasive Developmental Disorders," *Journal of Clinical Psychiatry* 66 Suppl. 10 (2005): 3–8.

77. On increased rates of hospital admissions for a number of childhood psychiatric disorders, see David Mandell, William W. Thompson, Eric S. Weintraub, Frank DeStefano, et al., "Trends in Diagnosis Rates for Autism and ADHD at Hospital Discharge in the Context of Other Psychiatric Diagnoses," *Psychiatric Services* 56, no. 1 (2005): 56–62.

78. A typical argument is made in Eric Fombonne, "Is There an Epidemic of Autism?" *Pediatrics* 107, no. 2 (2001): 411–12.

79. Paul T. Shattuck, "Diagnostic Substitution and Changing Autism Prevalence," *Pediatrics* 117, no. 4 (2006): 1438–39. An important related argument, put forward by Eyal, Hart, Onculer, Oren, et al. (2010), is that the perceived increase resulted from the convergence of changing diagnostic standards for autism, the deinstitutionalization of children previously diagnosed with mental retardation, changes in developmental disabilities legislation, and parent activism.

80. For example, Morton Ann Gernsbacher, Michelle Dawson, and H. Hill Gold-smith, "Three Reasons Not to Believe in an Autism Epidemic," *Current Directions in Psychological Science* 14, no. 2 (2005): 55–58.

81. Victor Lotter, "Epidemiology of Autistic Conditions in Young Children. I. Prevalence," *Social Psychiatry* 1, no. 3 (1966): 124–37, 125, 133–34.

82. Lorna Wing and Judith Gould, "Severe Impairments of Social Interaction and Associated Abnormalities in Children: Epidemiology and Classification," *Journal of Autism and Childhood Schizophrenia* 9, no.1 (1979): 11–29, 13; Interview with Lorna Wing on June 10, 2005; Eric Schopler, "On Confusion in the Diagnosis of Autism," *Journal of Autism and Childhood Schizophrenia* 8, no. 2 (1978): 137–38.

83. Wing (2001, xiii–xiv, 14–16); Lorna Wing and Judith Gould, "Severe Impairments of Social Interaction and Associated Abnormalities in Children: Epidemiology and Classification," *Journal of Autism and Childhood Schizophrenia* 9, no. 1 (1979): 11–29, 27. In referring to "unwritten rules," I am thinking of a book by two adults with autism, Temple Grandin and Sean Barron, *Unwritten Rules of Social Relationships: Decoding Social Mysteries through the Unique Perspective of Autism* (Arlington, TX: Future Horizons, 2005).

84. On the lack of empirical support for claims about the association between autism and mental retardation, see Meredyth Goldberg Edelson, "Are the Majority of Children with Autism Mentally Retarded?" *Focus on Autism and Other Developmental Disabilities* 21, no. 2 (2006): 66–83. Individuals with autism may also perform significantly better on tests that showcase their cognitive strengths, such as Raven's Progressive Matrices. The test demands that the subject recognize patterns and infer rules, and it is considered an'excellent measure of fluid intelligence (the ability to solve problems and reason). Michelle Dawson, Isabelle Soulieres, Morton Ann Gernsbacher, and Laurent Mottron, "The Level and Nature of Autistic Intelligence," *Psychological Science* 18, no. 8 (2007): 657–62, 658.

85. Leo Kanner and Leon Eisenberg, "Early Infantile Autism, 1943–1955," *American Journal of Orthopsychiatry* 26 (1956): 556–66, 557. This is also discussed in Lorna Wing, "The Definition and Prevalence of Autism: A Review," *European Child and Adolescent Psychiatry* 2, no. 2 (1993): 61–74.

86. Michael Rutter, "Diagnosis and Definition," in *Autism: A Reappraisal of Concepts and Treatment* (New York: Plenum Press, 1978), 1–25.

87. Lorna Wing, "The Definition and Prevalence of Autism: A Review," *European Child and Adolescent Psychiatry*, 2, no. 2 (1993): 61–74. The *DSM-III* also specified that schizophrenic features must be absent in patients in order to qualify for an autism diagnosis.

88. For example, Ralph Savarese's memoir, *Reasonable People: A Memoir of Autism and Adoption* (New York: Other Press, 2007).

89. Warren (1984, 103–5).

90. Mary S. Akerley, "Parents Speak: The Politics of Definitions," *Journal of Autism and Developmental Disorders* 9, no. 2 (1979): 222–31, 230–31.

91. Warren (1984, 105).

92. D. Arn Van Krevelen, "Early Infantile Autism and Autistic Psychopathy," *Journal of Autism and Developmental Disorders* 1, no. 1 (1971): 82–86, 83; Lorna Wing, "Asperger's Syndrome: A Clinical Account," *Psychological Medicine* 11 (1981): 115–29. On the use of Asperger syndrome diagnoses in Japan and Europe, see Kohei Inose and Masato Fukushima, "Asperger's Solitary Ally: Psychiatric Debate and the Educational Policy on Autism in Postwar Japan" (presentation at the Society for Social Studies of Science [4S], Pasadena, CA, October 2005); and Lorna Wing, "Reflections on Opening Pandora's Box," *Journal of Autism and Developmental Disorders* 35, no. 2 (2005): 197–203. Bruno Bettelheim, an Austrian, was aware of Asperger's work during the 1960s, according to Jacquelyn Sanders (personal communication, November 27, 2005).

93. Lorna Wing, "Asperger's Syndrome: A Clinical Account," *Psychological Medicine* 11 (1981): 115–29, 118, 121; Asperger (1991).

94. Wing, "Reflections on Opening Pandora's Box," 198.

95. Asperger (1944/1991, 77).

96. Wing, "Asperger's Syndrome: A Clinical Account," 117.

97. On the variations in everyday diagnostic practices, see Victoria Shea, "Letter to the Editor: Lumpers, Splitters, and Asperger Syndrome," *Journal of Autism and Developmental Disorders* 35, no. 6 (2005): 871–72. The relationship of Asperger syndrome to autism continues to be debated, with some structural brain imaging studies suggesting that the disorders may be behaviorally similar but anatomically distinct. See Linda J. Lotspeich, Hower Kwon, Cynthia M. Schumann, Susanna L. Fryer, et al., "Investigation of Neuroanatomical Differences between Autism and Asperger Syndrome," *Archives of General Psychiatry* 61, no. 3 (2004): 291–98.

98. For an analysis of these changes, see Kirk and Kutchins (1992) and Kutchins and Kirk (1997).

99. American Psychiatric Association, "Pervasive Developmental Disorders," in *Diagnostic and Statistical Manual of Mental Disorders*, 3rd ed. (Washington, DC: American Psychiatric Association, 1980).

100. Fred Volkmar, Joel Bregman, Donald J. Cohen, and Domenic V. Cicchetti, "*DSM*-III and *DSM*-III-R Diagnoses of Autism," *American Journal of Psychiatry* 145, no. 11 (1988): 1404–8, 1405; Lynn Waterhouse, Lorna Wing, Robert Spitzer, and Bryna Siegel, "Pervasive Developmental Disorders: From *DSM*-III to *DSM*-III-R," *Journal of Autism and Developmental Disorders* 22, no. 4 (1992): 525–49.

101. American Psychiatric Association, "Pervasive Developmental Disorders," in *Diagnostic and Statistical Manual of Mental Disorders*, 3rd ed., rev. (Washington, DC: American Psychiatric Association, 1987). The *DSM*-III-R defi-

nition included only "pervasive developmental disorder not otherwise specified" (PDD-NOS) along with "autistic disorder" under the umbrella of "pervasive developmental disorders," eliminating the categories of "infantile autism—residual state," "childhood onset developmental disorder—residual state," and "atypical disorder" altogether.

102. Volkmar et al., "*DSM*-III and *DSM*-III-R Diagnoses of Autism," 1405.

103. American Psychiatric Association, "Pervasive Developmental Disorders," in *Diagnostic and Statistical Manual of Mental Disorders*, 4th ed. (Washington, DC: American Psychiatric Association, 1994).

104. Susan Dickerson Mayes, Susan L. Calhoun, and Dana L. Crites, "Does *DSM*-IV Asperger's Disorder Exist?" *Journal of Abnormal Child Psychology* 29, no. 3 (2001): 263–71.

105. American Psychiatric Association, "American Psychiatric Association: *DSM*-5 Development," http://www.dsm5.org/ProposedRevisions/Pages/proposedrevision .aspx?rid=94#. Also see Roy Richard Grinker, "Disorder out of Chaos," *New York Times*, February 9, 2010.

106. Simon Baron-Cohen, "The Short Life of a Diagnosis," *New York Times*, November 9, 2009. For one geneticist's objections, see David A. Greenberg, "Letter to the Editor," *New York Times*, February 14, 2010.

107. Claudia Wallis, "A Powerful Identity, A Vanishing Diagnosis," *New York Times*, November 2, 2009; Jon Hamilton, "Asperger's Officially Placed within Autism Spectrum," National Public Radio broadcast, http://www.npr.org/ templates/story/story.php?storyId=123527833&ft=1&f=123527833.

108. Maureen S. Durkin, Matthew J. Maenner, F. John Meaney, Susan E. Levy, et al., "Socioeconomic Inequality in the Prevalence of Autism Spectrum Disorder: Evidence from a U.S. Cross-Sectional Study," *PLoS One* 5, no. 7 (2010): e11551, 7. The authors do not rule out "the possibility that factors associated with socioeconomic advantage might be causally associated with the risk for developing autism."

109. Lorna Wing, personal communication, June 10, 2005.

110. Craig J. Newschaffer, "Commentary: Investigating Diagnostic Substitution and Autism Prevalence Trends," *Pediatrics* 117, no. 4 (2006): 1436–37. Michael Rutter made much the same claim, concluding in his review of the epidemiological literature that "a true rise over time in the incidence of ASD cannot be entirely ruled out," Michael Rutter, "Incidence of Autism Spectrum Disorders: Changes over Time and Their Meaning," *Acta Paediatrica* 94, no. 1 (2005): 2–15, 13.

111. Mark Blaxill reviewed the epidemiological literature published up to the point of his article, comparing the stated diagnostic criteria used in each of the studies. M. Blaxill, "What's Going On? The Question of Time Trends in Autism," *Public Health Reports* 119, no. 6 (2004): 536–51.

112. For the exchange in the *Journal of Autism and Developmental Disorders*, see Lisa A. Croen, Judith K. Grether, Jenny Hoogstrate, and Steve Selvin, "The

Changing Prevalence of Autism in California," *Journal of Autism and Developmental Disorders* 32, no. 3 (2002): 207–15; Mark F. Blaxill, David S. Baskin, and Walter O. Spitzer, "Commentary: Blaxill, Baskin and Spitzer on Croen et al. (2002), 'The Changing Prevalence of Autism in California,'" *Journal of Autism and Developmental Disorders* 33, no. 2 (2003): 223–26; and Lisa A. Croen and Judith K. Grether, "A Response to Blaxill, Baskin and Spitzer on Croen et al. (2002), 'The Changing Prevalence of Autism in California,'" *Journal of Autism and Developmental Disorders* 33, no. 2 (2003): 227–29.

113. On the concept of therapeutic specificity, see Rosenberg (1992). Lakoff (2005, 10–14) discusses the importance of therapeutic specificity to psychiatrists in particular, and the concept's effects on the evolution of the *DSM* and psychopharmacology. On biological psychiatry as a dominant approach, see Luhrmann (2000).

114. Martha Herbert (2005a, 2005b) has suggested the concept of multiple "autisms." For parent reports of medical problems, see, for instance, Edelson and Rimland (2003).

115. On the importance of recognizing that autism may not only contain biological subgroups but also multiple behavioral syndromes, see Francesca Happe, Angelica Ronald, and Robert Plomin, "Time to Give Up on a Single Explanation for Autism," *Nature Neuroscience* 9, no. 10 (2006): 1218–20.

116. Any research group or practitioner who wishes to use the ADOS or ADI in published research must purchase them from Western Psychological Services, which in addition to publishing the tests also runs the required training sessions.

117. Catherine Lord, Susan Risi, Linda Lambrecht, Edwin H. Cook, et al., "The Autism Diagnostic Observation Schedule-Generic: A Standard Measure of Social and Communication Deficits Associated with the Spectrum of Autism," *Journal of Autism and Developmental Disorders* 30, no. 3 (2000): 205–23, 206.

118. Ann Le Couteur, Michael Rutter, Catherine Lord, Patricia Rios, et al., "Autism Diagnostic Interview: A Standardized Investigator-Based Instrument," *Journal of Autism and Developmental Disorders*, 19, no. 3 (1989): 363–87; Catherine Lord, Michael Rutter, Susan Goode, Jacquelyn Heemsbergen, et al., "Autism Diagnostic Observation Schedule: A Standardized Observation of Communicative and Social Behavior," *Journal of Autism and Developmental Disorders* 19, no. 2 (1989): 185–212.

119. Ibid. (187, 192–93). The authors write that "first, the ADOS is an *interactive* schedule. What is standardized in the ADOS are the contexts that provide the background for all observations and, more specifically, the behaviors of the examiner, not the sample."

120. Once trained in this way, screeners can enable colleagues at their site to "establish reliability" under their guidance, but only if they are in daily contact. University of Michigan Autism and Communication Disorders Center, "Es-

tablishing Reliability on the ADOS," http://www.umaccweb.com/education/adosreli.html.

121. Catherine Lord, Michael Rutter, and Ann Le Couteur, "Autism Diagnostic Interview-Revised: A Revised Version of a Diagnostic Interview for Caregivers of Individuals with Possible Pervasive Developmental Disorders," *Journal of Autism and Developmental Disorders* 24, no. 5 (1994): 659–85.

122. Molly Helt, Elizabeth Kelley, Marcel Kinsbourne, Juhi Pandey, et al., "Can Children with Autism Recover? If So, How?" *Neuropsychology Review* 18, no. 4 (2008): 339–66; Herbert (2009).

123. The AQ was reproduced in Carolyn Abraham, "Is There a "Geek" Syndrome?" *Globe and Mail*, October 12, 2002.

124. Simon Baron-Cohen, Sally Wheelwright, Richard Skinner, Joanne Martin, et al., "The Autism-Spectrum Quotient (AQ): Evidence from Asperger Syndrome/High-Functioning Autism, Males and Females, Scientists and Mathematicians," *Journal of Autism and Developmental Disorders* 31, no. 1 (2001): 5–17, 5.

125. See, for instance, Nelkin and Tancredi (1994).

126. On the "silencing" of parents during encounters with professionals concerning their child's autism diagnosis, see Feinstein (2006).

127. Martha R. Herbert, "Neuroimaging in Disorders of Social and Emotional Processing: What Is the Question?" *Journal of Child Neurology* 19, no. 10 (2004): 772–84.

Chapter 2

1. Pollak (1997); Richard Bernstein, "Ideas and Trends: Accusations of Abuse Haunt the Legacy of Dr. Bruno Bettelheim," *New York Times,* November 4, 1990. Not all accounts of Bettelheim's tenure are as critical as Pollak's. More favorable ones include biographies by Sutton (1996) and Raines (2002), and a memoir by Stephen Eliot (2002, 53), a former student at the school.

2. See, for instance, Robert Coles, "A Hero of Our Time," *New Republic* 156, no. 9 (1967): 23–24; the assessment of Bettelheim and the counselors as "heroes" in Peter Gay, "Books: *Per Ardua*," *New Yorker*, May 18, 1968, 160–73; Jacquelyn Sanders, quoted in Martin Weil, "Pioneering Psychologist Bruno Bettelheim Dies; Scholar Known for Imaginative Techniques in the Study of Children," *Washington Post,* March 14, 1990; and Robert Coles, quoted in Jacobsen (2004, 216).

3. Freud's statement to Jung is quoted in Karen Zelan, "Bruno Bettelheim, 1903–1990," in *Prospects: The Quarterly Review of Special Education* (Paris, UNESCO: International Bureau of Education) XXIII, no. ½ (1993): 85–100, 98.

4. Herman (1995). On the importation of psychoanalysis to America and the early history of the profession, see Hale (1978), and see Lunbeck (1994) on the

gendered division of labor involved in establishing psychiatric reasoning as a form of American cultural common sense. Luhrmann (2000) discusses psychoanalytic training in American medical schools and its gradual displacement by biological psychiatry.

5. See, for instance, Alfred Hitchcock's *Spellbound* (1945), which features Freudian analysis and dream sequences designed by Salvador Dalí. Hollywood's fascination with psychoanalysis proved to be enduring. The director Woody Allen featured Bettelheim playing a version of himself in the 1983 film *Zelig*. On the expanding ranks of clinical professionals during the postwar period, see Herman (1995, 259).

6. Herman (1995, 259).

7. On the history of parenting advice manuals, see Grant (1998) and Stearns (2003).

8. The ideology of scientific motherhood gave women responsibility for their families while simultaneously demanding that they turn to expert advice (Apple 1995, 176, 178). Watsonian behaviorist principles dominated expert advice before psychoanalytic ideas were introduced to the United States. Apple (2006, 83–85).

9. Leo Kanner, *In Defense of Mothers: How to Bring Up Children in Spite of the More Zealous Psychologists* (Springfield, IL: Charles C. Thomas, 1941); Benjamin Spock. *Dr. Spock's Baby and Child Care* (New York: Simon & Schuster, 1945/1998), 1–2.

10. Coles, "A Hero of Our Time," 23.

11. Sutton (1996, 199–200).

12. "As he later told the story, his advice was, 'There's only one thing to be done with that school: burn it down.'" Sutton (1996, 222).

13. Bettelheim's obituary in the *New York Times* stated that Bettelheim was held for "almost two years," but Bettelheim said that he was in the two camps for "approximately one year." Daniel Goleman, "Bruno Bettelheim Dies at 86; Psychoanalyst of Vast Impact," *New York Times,* March 14, 1990; Bettelheim (1943, 417).

14. Sutton (1996, 244); Roazen (1992, 225).

15. Bettelheim (1987, 199–201).

16. Jacquelyn Sanders, personal communication, December 10, 2005.

17. Roazen (1992, 233); Raines (2002, 488). During the 1950s, the question of who would be entitled to offer psychotherapy was far from settled, especially between psychologists and psychiatrists. The matter was further complicated by uncertainty over what, exactly, psychotherapy entailed. Buchanan (2003, 226).

18. Sutton, (1996, 223).

19. On the transition in the school's population, see Gayle Janowitz, quoted in Jacobsen (2004, 202–3).

20. Alan Dundes (1991, 80) notes that while Bettelheim might be credited with bringing the psychoanalytic treatment of fairy tales to "the attention of the

general public," he both failed to consult relevant sources in the folklore literature and failed to cite sources from which he borrowed substantially, specifically Julius E. Heuscher's *A Psychiatric Study of Fairy Tales: Their Origin, Meaning and Usefulness*, published in 1963 by Charles C. Thomas. Dundes notes that while Bettelheim mentioned Heuscher in a footnote, he appears to have "borrowed" entire passages.

21. Ivar Lovaas commented on this during "Presentations from Experts in the Field" (roundtable discussion), The Autism Summit Conference: Developing a National Agenda, Washington, DC, November 19–20, 2003.

22. Bettelheim (1943, 420–21).

23. For a discussion of the problem of retrospectively discussing therapeutic efficacy in psychiatric disorders, and the argument that "efficacy" must be understood not only in terms of biological mechanisms but also in terms of social, professional and institutional interests, see Braslow (1996) and Pressman (1998, 194–235).

24. See for instance Kramer's (1993/1997) speculations about how treating patients with SSRIs caused him to view the specifics of his patients' lives differently.

25. Rosenberg (1992, 2002) describes how, as medicine became increasingly committed to a scientific ideal over the course of the nineteenth century, therapeutic specificity became increasingly important. However, in psychoanalysis, nosology could be less important than general theories about the causes of psychological distress. Bettelheim thought that extensive considerations of diagnoses and even abstract discussions of psychodynamics ran the risk of distracting staff members at the Orthogenic School from the real, emotional, problems at hand concerning the children in their care. Bruno Bettelheim, "Psychiatric Consultation in Residential Treatment: Workshop, 1957. 1. The Director's View." *American Journal of Orthopsychiatry* 28, no. 2 (1958): 256–65, 262.

26. Eliot Fremont-Smith, "Children Without an 'I,'" *New York Times*, March 10, 1967.

27. Carol Kleiman, "A Total Commitment to Children," *Chicago Tribune*, January 22, 1967.

28. For an analysis of Bettelheim's rhetorical strategies, see Severson, Aune, and Jodlowski (2008, 72–74). Because of his lack of ease with English, Bettelheim relied on the help of an editor, Ruth Soffer Marquis, to produce finished work. (Raines, 173–76). Nevertheless, he was committed to accessible writing: "He was determined not to get bogged down in highly technical and overly specialized questions, not to write in jargon." Fisher (1991, 256). Jacquelyn Sanders, likewise, remembers that he "not only wrote without jargon, he talked without jargon—he would say that if you can't explain something so that ANYONE can understand it, then you don't understand it yourself" (personal communication, December 10, 2005).

29. Jacquelyn Sanders wrote that controversies about the book "clouded a more fundamental contribution to the study of personality development focusing on the significance of the relationship between parent and child for the child's development of self. Bettelheim also pointed to the problem of parental preoccupation and indifference which he and other critics believed unique to our own time, and which had important implications for the child's subsequent adjustment." Bertram J. Cohler and Jacquelyn Sanders, "Obituary: Bruno Bettelheim, (1903–1990)," *International Journal of Psychoanalysis* 72 (1991): 155–58.

30. Stearns (2003, 39) describes how expert discourse about psychological risks, changes in the environmental context of children's development, and the displacement of adult anxieties about their own lives contributed to the growth of the concept of the "vulnerable child" during the twentieth century. For changes in labor and insurance policies that placed increasing weight on children's physical wellbeing and protecting children from risks, see Zelizer (1985).

31. Letter from Amy Lettick to M. J. Shodell, dated January 11, 1967. "Shodell, M.," Box 2, ACC 92-M-41, Amy L. Lettick Papers, 1920–2006, Yale University Library Special Collections, New Haven, CT (henceforth, "Lettick Papers"). Margaret Shodell, the director of the Nassau Center for Emotionally Disturbed Children, had written to accept a position as an advisor to Benhaven in a letter to Amy Lettick dated January 3, 1967. "Shodell, M.," Box 2, ACC 92-M-41, Lettick Papers. Mira Rothenberg was another noted promoter of psychotherapeutic techniques for treating children with autism, as chronicled in her book *Children with Emerald Eyes: Histories of Extraordinary Boys and Girls* (New York: The Dial Press, 1960).

32. Barron and Barron (2002, 111).

33. J. K. Wing, "Family and Society: The Empty Fortress" (review), *British Journal of Psychiatry* 114, no. 511 (1968): 788–91, 789–90; Zelan (1993, 93). Wing also noted that the methods of counselors at the school "seem very similar to those used by other workers and adopted by sensible parents."

34. My discussion of Jacquelyn Sanders's reflections on treating autistic children at the Orthogenic School relies on Sanders (1996), email correspondence with Dr. Sanders, and an interview conducted on April 3, 2003, in Chicago, IL.

35. Michael Rutter, "The Influence of Organic and Emotional Factors on the Origins, Nature and Outcome of Childhood Psychosis," *Developmental Medicine and Child Neurology* 7, no. 5 (1965): 518–28, 521–22, quoted in Bernard Rimland, "Freud Is Dead: New Directions in the Treatment of Mentally Ill Children," *Distinguished Lecture Series in Special Education* (Los Angeles: University of Southern California, 1970), 33–48, 44. Adapted from a lecture presented to chapters of the National Society for Autistic Children in various cities, 1967–1970.

36. Bettelheim's description of autism for a Collier's Encyclopedia entry was similarly detailed. Bruno Bettelheim, letter to Miss Barbara Crowell, Life Sciences Department, Colliers Encyclopedia, September 15, 1971. Bruno Bet-

telheim Papers, Special Collections Research Center, University of Chicago Library, Chicago, IL (unprocessed; henceforth, "Bettelheim Papers").

37. Bruno Bettelheim and Emmy Sylvester, "Physical Symptoms in Emotionally Disturbed Children," reprint in folder marked "The Psychoanalytic Study of the Child" (probably *Psychoanalytic Study of the Child* [New Haven: Yale University Press, 1948 or 1950]), Bettelheim Papers. Elsewhere, Bettelheim interpreted sensory disturbances such as preferring one sensory modality (seeing, hearing, touch, etc.) over others in terms of lacking a "body ego" and having poorly integrated ego functions. Bruno Bettelheim, second interim report to Mr. Joseph McDaniel Jr., Secretary, Ford Foundation, July 17, 1958, folder marked "Ford Foundation Reports," Bettelheim Papers.

38. Gay, "Books: *Per Ardua*," 169.

39. Zelan (1993, 85).

40. René A. Spitz, *Dialogues from Infancy: Selected Papers* (New York: International Universities Press, 1983); Lucy Freeman, "Emotions of Baby Held First to Gain," *New York Times,* May 14, 1949.

41. Leo Kanner, "Problems of Nosology and Psychodynamics in Early Infantile Autism," in *Childhood Psychosis: Initial Studies and New Insights* (Washington, DC: V. H. Winston and Sons, 1973), 61, 59. Originally published in *American Journal of Orthopsychiatry*, 19 (1949): 416–26, 425, 424.

42. The investigators reported that although they "did not ask our subjects if they felt helpless and/or hopeless, their posture and lack of activity seemed to indicate an attitude of 'giving up,'" in addition to "profound and persistent behavioral abnormalities" that lingered after the experiment. Harry F. Harlow and Stephen J. Suomi. "Production of Depressive Behaviors in Young Monkeys," *Journal of Autism and Childhood Schizophrenia* 1, no. 3 (1971): 246–55, 247, 253.

43. Harry F. Harlow and William T. McKinney Jr., "Nonhuman Primates and Psychoses." *Journal of Autism and Childhood Schizophrenia* 1, no. 4 (1971): 368–75, 371.

44. Bettelheim (1967, 32, 74–75). Donna Haraway's (1989, 231–43) treatment of Harlow's experiments using terrycloth "false" mothers situates the peculiar cruelty of Harlow's experiments within the context of biological theories of both motherhood and gender as reproduced within primatology.

45. Bettelheim (1943).

46. Bettelheim (1967, 68, 129). Bettelheim wrote in an earlier article that "severe as the impact of the mother may be, the child also responds all along in terms of his nature, his personality." Bruno Bettelheim, "Childhood Schizophrenia; Symposium, 1955. III. Schizophrenia as a Reaction to Extreme Situations," *American Journal of Orthopsychiatry* 26, no. 3 (1956): 507–18, 508.

47. Bettelheim (1967, 385, 401).

48. Ibid., 403. Bettelheim thought that if "certain neural systems are not appropriately stimulated within a specific period of life, they may suffer permanent

impairment," a suggestion that his opponents might have agreed with in content if not in implications. Bettelheim (1967, 401).

49. Elsewhere, Bettelheim wrote that "as long as those who hold the view that schizophrenia is organic in nature do not present us with methods of therapy that are more successful than those based on psychoanalysis, it is justified if, for the time being, we neglect the organic factor, about which we can do nothing as yet, and concentrate instead on that psychological understanding and treatment which yields some quite worth-while results." Bettelheim, "Childhood Schizophrenia; Symposium, 1955. III. Schizophrenia as a Reaction to Extreme Situations," 508.

50. Zelan (1993, 93).

51. Bettelheim (1967, 410, 412).

52. Pollak (1997, 10).

53. Bettelheim (1967, 404).

54. Bettelheim, first interim report to Mr. Joseph McDaniel Jr.; Bettelheim, second interim report to Mr. Joseph McDaniel Jr., 2.

55. Bettelheim (1959, 117).

56. Ibid., 127.

57. Bettelheim (1959, 122, 124).

58. Critics have argued that Joey's sophisticated imaginary world suggests that he would not be given an autism diagnosis in the present. Grinker (2008, 81–82) suggests that the children described in *The Empty Fortress* might, indeed, have been victims of severe child neglect, rather than children with autism.

59. "Joey" was a pseudonym but the paintings were reproduced in Bettelheim's book and were easily recognizable.

60. Bettelheim (1967, 125).

61. A "liminal action of the autistic child—and most of their actions are liminal or subliminal—evokes ambivalence, or a negative response in the caretaker. To this the child responds with massive withdrawal." Ibid., 126.

62. Herman (1995, 313).

63. Matthews (1967, 61–62); Lemov (2005, 127); Gifford (1991).

64. Herman (1995, 259) "During the years after 1945, ordinary people sought therapeutic attention more insistently than ever before and for more reasons than ever before" (257).

65. Ibid., 82–83.

66. Herman (1995, 257, 259, 82–83, 238–39). The official name of the GI Bill was the Soldiers' Readjustment Act of 1944.

67. Bruno Bettelheim, *Dialogues with Mothers* (New York: Free Press of Glencoe, 1962).

68. Bettelheim (1987, xi and 17).

69. Ibid., 4–5.

70. See Molly Ladd-Taylor and Lauri Umansky, "Introduction," in Ladd-Taylor and Umansky (1998).

71. Of course, mother-blaming and the idea of "bad" mothers extended before and after the 1950s and 1960s in America. Ladd-Taylor and Umansky (1998, 2) argue that it is important to ask why mothers in particular have been the focus of public discourse about a range of social and economic problems. Jennifer Terry's (in Ladd-Taylor and Umansky, 1998, 169–90) survey of "momism" in psychiatric discourse during the 1950s focuses on the claim that dissatisfied or overvigilant mothers caused their children to become homosexuals, but these beliefs were related to arguments about "failures of development" more generally.

72. Wylie produced a vitriolic and psychologically inflected critique of what he perceived to be the effects of mothers who attempted to control their male offspring. Philip Wylie, *Generation of Vipers* (New York: Rinehart, 1942). On the acceptance of "momism" within the psychiatric establishment and on emerging feminist critiques in the late 1960s, see Herman (1995, 278–79, 281–84).

73. Irving Kaufman, Eleanor Rosenblum, Lora Heims, and Lee Willer, "Childhood Psychosis: 1. Childhood Schizophrenia: Treatment of Children and Parents," *American Journal of Orthopsychiatry* 27, no. 4 (1957): 683–90, 685, 683, 684.

74. There are a number of poignant, firsthand accounts in the documentary *Refrigerator Mothers* (Kartemquin Films, 2002).

75. Donald R. Katz, "The Kids with the Faraway Eyes: The Strange Secret World of Autism," *Rolling Stone*, March 8, 1979, 48–53.

76. Barron and Barron (2002, 247).

77. As Bettelheim wrote, "It is the parents who, in our opinion, make a significant contribution to the development of the autistic disturbance in their children." Bruno Bettelheim, second interim report to Mr. Joseph McDaniel Jr.

78. Not all of the families in Henry's book had autistic children; some are given no specific diagnosis. Henry (1971, 195).

79. John M. Townsend, review of *Pathways to Madness* by Jules Henry and *On Sham, Vulnerability and Other Forms of Self-Destruction* by Jules Henry, *American Anthropologist*, New Series 77, no. 3 (1975): 623–24, 623.

80. Bettelheim, second interim report to Mr. Joseph McDaniel Jr.

81. Ibid.

82. Eric Schopler and Gary B. Mesibov, "Professional Attitudes toward Parents: a Forty-Year Progress Report," in *The Effects of Autism on the Family*, eds. Eric Schopler and Gary Mesibov (New York, Plenum Press), 11.

83. Henry (1971, 298).

84. Horace Judson, "Five American Families (Review of *Pathways to Madness* by Jules Henry)," *Time*, March 12, 1973.

85. H. A. Gould, "Jules Henry, 1904–1969," *American Anthropologist*, 73, no. 3 (1971): 788–97, 788, 792.

86. The term comes from an obituary for Bettelheim. Rudolf Ekstein, "Bruno Bettelheim (1903–1990)," *American Psychologist* (October 1991). Bettelheim

wrote that "if residential treatment makes any sense, it must come about through the creation of a milieu that is therapeutic in its totality, in all aspects and not just some of its aspects." Bruno Bettelheim, "Training the Child-Care Worker in a Residential Center," *American Journal of Orthopsychiatry* 36, no. 4 (1966): 694–705, 695. The fact that residents could leave freely but visitors required permission to enter is repeated in several accounts, among them Daniel Goleman, "Bruno Bettelheim Dies at 86; Psychoanalyst of Vast Impact," *New York Times,* March 14, 1990; and Gayle Janowitz, quoted in Jacobsen (2004, 208).

87. Bruno Bettelheim, letter to Miss Barbara Crowell, Life Sciences Department, Collier's Encyclopedia, September 15, 1971, Bettelheim Papers.

88. Zelan (1993, 85); Bruno Bettelheim and Emmy Sylvester, "A Therapeutic Milieu," *American Journal of Orthopsychiatry* 18 (1948): 191–206.

89. Earl Saxe and Jeanetta Lyle, "The Function of the Psychiatric Residential School," *Bulletin of the Menninger Clinic* 4, no. 6 (1940): 162–71; Fees (1998).

90. Jacquelyn Sanders explained how counselors were hired as child-care workers and "research assistants" in a personal communication, December 10, 2005. As an attitude on the part of the teachers in the school, participant observation (called a "marginal interview" by Fritz Redl, a colleague of Bettelheim's) meant a kind of critical or interpretive distance that did not preclude interaction. It was "interpretive in character but does not need to interfere with the momentary activity of the group or individual." Bettelheim (1950, 35). I have also drawn on Raines's (2002, 178–90) excellent explanation of the milieu at the Orthogenic School.

91. Helen Robinson, an "eminent professor involved in remedial reading," used the students in research before Bettelheim's arrival. Jacquelyn Sanders, personal communication, December 10, 2005.

92. Sanders (1996).

93. Counselors and therapists spoke out about how Bettelheim used to slap children when they were dangerous to themselves or others. He said that it was "utterly necessary that the kids feel secure in the school and that to feel secure from one another, which was the hardest thing to arrange, there had to be absolutely enforced rules about their not hurting one another." Robert Bergman, interviewed in Jacobsen (2004, 195). Also see the comments from "Stephen Eliot," a former student at the school, also quoted in Jacobsen (2004, 210), and Richard Bernstein, "Ideas & Trends; Accusations of Abuse Haunt the Legacy of Dr. Bruno Bettelheim," *New York Times,* November 4, 1990.

94. Sanders (1996, 2).

95. Ibid., 2–3. Sanders's phrase is that she "watched with breaking heart" as the children were sent away.

96. Zelan (1993, 93).

97. Raines (2002, 266–67).

98. Bettelheim (1967, 89–90); Bruno Betteheim, "Training the Child-Care Worker in a Residential Center," *American Journal of Orthopsychiatry* 36, no. 4 (1966): 694–705, 705.

99. Gayle Janowitz, interviewed in Jacobsen (2004, 203).

100. Bettelheim (1974, 5).

101. Jacquelyn Sanders, personal communication, December 10, 2005.

102. At the time, the diagnosis of "childhood schizophrenia" and "infantile autism" would have been virtually interchangeable among most practitioners. According to Jacquelyn Sanders, "the most widely accepted notion was that, though there may be some organic propensity or predisposition, there was a significant component of environmental etiology. The firmness of this assumption was reflected in the nature of the grant awarded to Bettelheim by the Ford Foundation. Its purpose was not an investigation into autism, but an exploration of normal development." Sanders (1996, 6).

103. "The Unhappiest Children," Ford Foundation Annual Report (1958?), 26, Bettelheim Papers.

104. Sutton (1996, 303–4).

105. Jacquelyn Sanders, personal communication, December 10, 2005.

106. Bruno Bettelheim, "Psychiatric Consultation in Residential Treatment: Workshop, 1957. 1. The Director's View," *American Journal of Orthopsychiatry* 28, no. 2 (1958): 256–65, 262.

107. Bettelheim (1974, 4). For descriptions by former students, see Eliot (2002) and the semifictionalized account by Lyons (1983).

108. Bertram J. Cohler and Jacquelyn Sanders, "Obituary: Bruno Bettelheim, (1903–1990)," *International Journal of Psychoanalysis* 72 (1991): 155–58; Robert Bergman, quoted in Jacobsen (2004, 195).

109. Tomes (1981).

110. Sanders (2005).

111. Bruno Betteheim, "Training the Child-Care Worker in a Residential Center," 697.

112. Zelan (1993, 86).

113. See Jacquelyn Seevak Sanders, "Defending Bruno Bettelheim," *The New York Review of Books* 50, no. 18 (November 20, 2003). Sanders was writing in response to Robert Gottlieb's description of her apparently ambivalent relationship with Bettelheim in Robert Gottlieb, "The Strange Case of Dr. B," *The New York Review of Books* 50, no. 3 (February 27, 2003).

114. Gayle Janowitz, interviewed in Jacobsen (2004, 207).

115. Zelan (1993, 85). On staff meetings, Bettelheim's teaching methods, and reports of Bettelheim treating counselors, see Raines (2002, 191–201).

116. Bettelheim, "The Role of Residential Treatment for Children; Symposium, 1954. 8. Staff Development in a Treatment Institution," *American Journal of Orthopsychiatry* 25, no. 4 (1955): 705–19, 711–15.

117. Bettelheim (1967, 129).
118. Bruno Bettelheim, "The Role of Residential Treatment for Children: Symposium, 1954. 8. Staff Development in a Treatment Institution," 706–7, 709–11.
119. Jules Henry, "The Culture of Interpersonal Relations in a Therapeutic Institution for Emotionally Disturbed Children," *American Journal of Orthopsychiatry* 27, no. 4 (1957): 725–34, 734.
120. For an example of the sociological critique of state hospitals in the early 1970s (approximately a decade after Henry wrote about this, but conditions had only worsened), see Rosenhan (1973). For a retrospective consideration of the political economy of deinstitutionalization in the 1960s and early 1970s, see Mechanic and Rochefort (1990).
121. Charles Wenar, Bertram A. Ruttenberg, M. L. Dratman, and Enid J. Wolf, "Changing Autistic Behavior: The Effectiveness of Three Milieus," *Archives of General Psychiatry* 17, no. 1 (1967): 26–35, 35.
122. Jules Henry, "The Culture of Interpersonal Relations in a Therapeutic Institution for Emotionally Disturbed Children," 727.
123. Ibid., 728.
124. Sanders (1989, xiii).
125. Bettelheim (1967, 412).
126. Some of Rimland's wide-ranging interests can be seen by exploring the archived issues of the *Autism Research Review International*, which Rimland edited beginning in 1987. Rimland was willing to report on and at least consider most potential theories or treatments, although he was skeptical of some. See archived issues online at http://www.autism.com/ari/newsletter/index_a.asp.
127. The phrase is from Park (1967, 190).
128. Bernard Rimland, "Freud Is Dead: New Directions in the Treatment of Mentally Ill Children," *Distinguished Lecture Series in Special Education* (Los Angeles: University of Southern California, 1970): 33–48.
129. Bernard Rimland, letter to Bruno Bettelheim, March 22, 1965, Bettelheim Papers.
130. Sanders (1996, 11).
131. Bruno Bettelheim, letter to Bernard Rimland, March 25, 1965, Bettelheim Papers.
132. Bruno Bettelheim, letter to Bernard Rimland, April 9, 1966, Bettelheim Papers.
133. Bernard Rimland, letter to Bruno Bettelheim, April 25, 1966, Bettelheim Papers.
134. Bruno Bettelheim, letter to Bernard Rimland, April 29, 1966, Bettelheim Papers.
135. Steve Silberman, "The Geek Syndrome," *Wired* 9, no. 12 (2001); Bruno Bettelheim and Alvin A. Rosenfeld, *The Art of the Obvious* (New York: Alfred A. Knopf, 1993), xv.

136. Ibid., 141–42. Bettelheim is referring to *The Laziness of the Heart* (trans.) by Jacob Wasserman, which recounts the story of Kaspar Hauser, a socially deprived child who became a celebrity of sorts in nineteenth-century Germany.

137. Gary B. Mesibov, "A Tribute to Eric Schopler," *Journal of Autism and Developmental Disorders* 36, no. 8 (2006): 967–70. 968.

138. Ibid., 968; Eric Schopler and Robert J. Reichler, "Parents as Cotherapists in the Treatment of Psychotic Children," *Journal of Autism and Childhood Schizophrenia* 1, no. 1 (1971): 87–102.

139. Eric Schopler, "New Publisher, New Editor, Expanded Editorial Policy— Goal: An Improved Journal," *Journal of Autism and Childhood Schizophrenia* 4, no. 2 (1974): 91–92, 91.

140. Buchanan (2003, 225).

141. Mira Rothenberg, *Children with Emerald Eyes: Histories of Extraordinary Boys and Girls* (New York: The Dial Press, 1960); Virginia M. Axline. *Dibs: In Search of Self* (New York: Random House, 1964).

142. According to Jacquelyn Sanders, Bettelheim was very popular in France, and she was invited to speak in Columbia, Argentina, France, and Italy on the basis of Bettelheim's reputation and her association with him. Jacquelyn Sanders, personal communication, December 10, 2005. Also see Chamak (2008a, 81, 85).

143. Karen Zelan, *Between Their World and Ours: Breakthroughs with Autistic Children* (New York: St. Martin's Press, 2003). Also see Raines (2002, 267–70).

144. Sanders (1996, 12).

145. "Treatment Methods," Web site for the Sonia Shankman Orthogenic School, http://orthogenicschool.uchicago.edu/treatment/ (accessed June 13, 2006; no longer available).

146. Bruno Bettelheim, quoted in Zelan (1993, 90).

147. Sanders (1996, 17).

148. C. Wenar and Bertram Ruttenberg, "The Use of BRIAC for Evaluating Therapeutic Effectiveness," *Journal of Autism and Childhood Schizophrenia* 6, no. 2 (1976): 175–91, 175.

Chapter 3

1. Excerpted entries from Amy Lettick's diary, 1953, 5–7, folder marked "Diaries of Amy Lettick, 1953, 1955–1957: transcription, 1991," Box 1, ACC 92-M-79, Amy L. Lettick Papers, Manuscripts and Archives, Sterling Memorial Library, Yale University, New Haven, CT (henceforth, "Lettick Papers," with finding information).

2. Amy L. Lettick, *Ways and Means* (Tempe, AZ: The Behaven Press, 1998), 1.

3. Sally Provence, letter to Newell Kephart, March 27, 1962, folder marked, "Kephart, Newell C.," Box 2, ACC 92-M-41, Lettick Papers.

4. See James Trent's description of this process in Trent (1994, 225–68), and for an excellent brief history of parent activism around services and education, see Leiter (2004).

5. Lettick was not the only mother to found a treatment program. In addition to Lettick's correspondent Rosalind Oppenheim, who founded the Rimland School for Autistic Children in 1971, Ruth Christ Sullivan founded the Autism Training Center at Marshall University in Huntington, West Virginia, in 1983. See http://www.marshall.edu/coe/atc/about_us/history_of_atc/default.asp and http://www.rimland.org/history.htm.

6. Lettick (1979a).

7. Leo Kanner, "Follow-Up Study of Eleven Autistic Children." *Journal of Autism and Childhood Schizophrenia* 1, no. 2 (1971): 119–45, 145.

8. She did circulate a short, self-published account of her experiences to colleagues and friends, which she kindly shared with me. Lettick, *Ways and Means*.

9. Maurice (1993, 307).

10. On identifying reliable witnesses for experiments as an enduring problem, see Shapin (1999).

11. Park (1967, 179, 180–86).

12. Ibid., 188. Park is referring to Bettelheim's *Love Is Not Enough* (Glencoe, IL: Free Press, 1950).

13. Park (1967, 195).

14. Lettick (1979a, 303–4).

15. Greenfeld (1986, 138–39).

16. Eric Schopler, "Toward Reducing Behavior Problems in Autistic Children," *Journal of Autism and Childhood Schizophrenia* 6, no. 1 (1976): 1–13, 6.

17. "The parents, of course, greatly expanded the efficiency of the project in a number of ways." Lovaas (1977, 184, 3).

18. Kozloff, (1998, 11–12).

19. On "partial perspectives" see Haraway (1991, 183–202).

20. The record included not only daily classroom sessions, but also videotapes and voice recordings. "Amy Lettick's Diaries: Introduction," folder marked "Diaries of Amy Lettick, 1953, 1955–1957: transcription, 1991," Box 1, ACC 92-M-79, Lettick Papers.

21. Ibid.

22. Ibid. Benjamin Lettick was a client at Newell C. Kephart's Achievement Center for Children from 1962 to 1969. Lettick, *Ways and Means*, foreword.

23. "The Daily Records of a 6-Year Educational Program Designed for a Severely Autistic Boy" (Manuscript), Milford, Connecticut, 1990, Folder 19, Box 1, ACC 92-M-79, Lettick Papers.

24. Apple (2006, 123–25).

25. Lettick, *Ways and Means*, 45–46.

26. Rosalind C. Oppenheim, "They Said Our Child Was Hopeless," *Saturday Evening Post* 23 (June 17, 1961): 56–58.

27. Amy Lettick, "Notes for Speech at Dinner in Honor of Rosalind Oppenheim, Evanston, Ill., Dec. 9, 1990, 20th Anniversary of Rimland School," folder marked "Oppenheim," Box 2, ACC 92-M-41, Lettick Papers.

28. Lettick, *Ways and Means*, 34–35; Oppenheim (1974).

29. Lettick, "Notes for Speech at Dinner in Honor of Rosalind Oppenheim."

30. Oppenheim (1974, 34).

31. Ibid., 10; Letter from Rosalind Oppenheim to Amy Lettick, May 28, 1962, Box 1, ACC 92-M-79, Lettick Papers. Clara Claiborne Park (1967, 188) was also inspired by Oppenheim's article.

32. Oppenheim regularly apologized to Amy Lettick for lapses in the correspondence, or for simply taking too long to reply—at one point she reassured Amy that "you are the only mother I am corresponding with regularly." Letter from Rosalind Oppenheim, May 28, 1962, folder marked "pgs. 306–399," Box 1, ACC 92-M-79, Lettick Papers.

33. Lettick, "Notes for Speech at Dinner in Honor of Rosalind Oppenheim"; Amy Lettick, diary entry, October 27, 1961, folder marked "pgs. 1–103," Box 1, ACC 92-M-79, Lettick Papers.

34. Letter from Rosalind Oppenheim, May 28, 1962, folder marked "pgs. 306–399," Box 1, ACC 92-M-79, Lettick Papers.

35. Dr. Provence did eventually provide a referral for Benjamin, in a letter to Newell Kephart dated March 27, 1962. Folder marked "Kephart, Newell C," Box 2, ACC 92-M-41, Lettick Papers.

36. Letter from Rosalind Oppenheim, October 18, 1962, folder marked "pgs. 400–483," Box 1, ACC 92-M-79, Lettick Papers.

37. Parents continue to remark upon this distinction. See, for instance, Iverson (2006).

38. Amy Lettick, diary entry, October 23, 1962, folder marked "pgs. 400–483," Box 1, ACC 92-M-79, Lettick Papers.

39. Kephart (1960, 83–84).

40. Amy Lettick, "Our Trip," Nov. 11, Nov 17, 1962, folder marked "pgs. 400–483," Box 1, ACC 92-M-79, Lettick Papers.

41. Ibid.

42. The treatment under investigation became Super Nu-Thera™, a product still available from Kirkman Laboratories. Bernard Rimland, Institute for Child Behavior Research, letter to Vitamin Study Parents and Physicians, folder marked "Rimland, B.," Box 2, ACC 92-M-41, Lettick Papers.

43. Lettick, *Ways and Means*, 35.

44. Ibid, 45.

45. Lettick, *Ways and Means*, 36.

46. An announcement for the 1969 schedule of a "Workshop for Teachers and Therapists Conducted under the Supervision of N. C. Kephart Ph.D." offered "practical experience in the diagnosis of perceptual motor problems and in teaching to the diagnosis." Folder Marked "Kephart, N. C.," Box 2, ACC

92-M-41, Lettick Papers. A film series produced by the Purdue University Department of Education proceeded from *Atypical Child in the Classroom* (Film 1) through *Motor Development I* (Film 2), *Laterality* (Film 6), *Body Image* (Film 7), *Perceptual Processes I* (Film 8), and *Teaching Generalization I* (Film 12), and concluded with *Time* (Film 20). Folder marked "Kephart, N. C.," Box 2, ACC 92-M-41, Box 2, Lettick Papers.

47. Kephart (1960).

48. "The Passing of a Giant: N. C. Kephart" *The N. C. Kephart Glen Haven Achievement Center Feedback* 3, no. 2 (Spring 1973). Kephart died on April 12, 1973. He continually emphasized the participation and knowledge of parents, arguing that "too often, the parent is the most forgotten element in the entire complex. We forget that he has the same problems we have but he has them in greatly magnified intensity. Whereas we have this child for a few hours a day in a limited and controlled situation, he has him twenty-four hours in all kinds of situations and all types of demands. Much valuable information can be gained from parents and much valuable aid in the child's handling can be obtained from them if one can only learn to communicate." Quoted in publication from N. C. Kephart Glen Haven Achievement Center, folder marked "Kephart, N. C.," Box 2, ACC 92-M-41, Lettick Papers.

49. Sylvia Kottler, foreword to "The Daily Records of a 6-Year Educational Program Designed for a Severely Autistic Boy."

50. Lettick related the incident in a letter to Rosalind Oppenheim, October 11, 1962, folder marked "Diary," folder marked "pgs. 400–483," Box 1, ACC 92-M-79. Lettick Papers.

51. Lettick, *Ways and Means*, 22.

52. Ibid., 22. As Benjamin matured, Lettick came to describe him as mentally retarded as well as autistic. The ARC, founded in 1950, was a coalition of parent groups that had been gathering since the 1930s as a means of support and activism for education for children with intellectual disabilities.

53. Amy Lettick, diary entry, Wednesday, June 6, 1962, folder marked "pgs. 306–399," Box 1, ACC 92-M-79, Lettick Papers.

54. Amy Lettick, diary entry, Wednesday, Sept. 21, 1966, "Original Journal, 1966, July 28–Nov. 30," Folder 17, Box 1, ACC 92-M-79, Lettick Papers.

55. She planned for the board of her school to consist of Dr. Kephart, Mrs. Margaret Shodell of the Nassau Center, and Dr. Carl Fenichel of the League School in Brooklyn. Amy Lettick, draft letter, undated, folder marked "Kephart, N.C.," Box 2, ACC 92-M-41, Lettick Papers.

56. Lettick, *Ways and Means*, 37

57. Ibid., 44–45.

58. Lettick wrote, "We believe that an intensive, driving dynamic program involving measurement, diagnosis and adjustment of techniques is the force that propels our children on the roads we would have them travel." Amy L.

Lettick, "The Philosophy behind Benhaven's Program," folder marked "All Writings, 1931–69," Box 3, ACC 92-M-79, Lettick Papers; Lettick (1979a).

59. Lettick (1979b).

60. Gary Mesibov, review of *Benhaven Then and Now* and *Benhaven at Work, Journal of Autism and Developmental Disorders*, 10, no. 2 (1980), 248–50, 248.

61. Lettick, *Ways and Means*, 51.

62. Mesibov, review of *Benhaven Then and Now* and *Benhaven at Work*.

63. Lettick, "The Philosophy behind Benhaven's Program."

64. Quoted in the *Connecticut Jewish Ledger*, March 29, 1975.

65. "Rimland Family Year-End Newsletter: 1968," folder Marked "Rimland, B.," Box 2, ACC 92-M-41, Lettick Papers. The British equivalent of the NSAC, the National Autistic Society, was founded two years earlier, in 1962.

66. Sula Wolff (2004, 205) writes that in both the U.S. and the U.K., "the greater awareness of the condition is largely attributable to the activities of parent organisations."

67. The Education for All Handicapped Children Act, PL 94-142, became the IDEA, PL 105-17, in 1990. "History: Twenty-Five Years of Progress in Educating Children with Disabilities through IDEA," Washington, DC: U.S. Office of Special Education Programs, http://www2.ed.gov/policy/speced/leg/idea/history.html.

68. Eric Schopler and Robert Reichler argued that parents of children with autism were slower to form advocacy groups because of their presumed guilt. Schopler and Reichler (1971, 89).

69. Mary S. Akerley, "The Politics of Definitions," *Journal of Autism and Childhood Schizophrenia* 9, no. 2 (1979): 222–31. The Developmentally Disabled Assistance and Bill of Rights Act, PL 94-103, was passed in 1970, amended in 1975, and amended again in 1978 to focus on functional limitations rather than specific diagnoses.

70. Bruno Bettelheim, letter to Miss Barbara Crowell, Life Sciences Department, Collier's Encyclopedia, September 15, 1971, Bruno Bettelheim Papers, Special Collections Research Center, University of Chicago Library, Chicago, IL.

71. Rimland (1972, 576).

72. Ibid., 582.

73. Ibid., 583.

74. Bernard Rimland, "Parents Speak: A Risk/Benefit Perspective on the Use of Aversives," *Journal of Autism and Childhood Schizophrenia* 8, no. 1 (1978): 100–104, 101.

75. O. Ivar Lovaas, "Behavioral Treatment and Normal Educational and Intellectual Functioning in Young Autistic Children," *Journal of Consulting and Clinical Psychology* 55, no.1 (1987), 3–9. In current usage, some parents and practitioners distinguish between ABA in general and the "Lovaas technique," meaning intensive ABA methods involving discrete trial training as they are applied to autism and other developmental disabilities.

76. Lovaas (1981, 9).

77. Lovaas explained that the operant learning theory upon which he based his work was premised on the idea that "aspects of the child's environment must acquire certain stimulus functions which serve to regulate the occurrence of his verbal behavior." Lovaas (1977, 11, 13).

78. Lovaas (1977, 3).

79. Lovaas (1981, 9).

80. Johnson and Crowder (1994, 177).

81. "Screams, Slaps and Love: Surprising, Shocking Treatment Helps Far-Gone Mental Cripples," *Life* 58, no. 18 (May 7, 1965): 90–101.

82. Ibid. Aversives were a fairly routine part of experimental practice. In one study, "pain was induced by means of an electrified grid on the floor upon which the children stood. The shock was turned on immediately following pathological behaviors. It was turned off or withheld when the children came to the adults who were present. Thus these adults 'saved' the children from a dangerous situation." O. Ivar Lovaas, Benson Schaeffer, and James Q. Simmons, "Building Social Behavior in Autistic Children by Use of Electric Shock," in *Perspectives in Behavior Modification with Deviant Children,* eds. O. Ivar Lovaas and Bradley D. Bucher (Englewood Cliffs, NJ: Prentice-Hall, Inc., 1974), 109.

83. Rimland, "Parents Speak: A Risk/Benefit Perspective on the Use of Aversives," 100. Rimland noted that the program in fact used primarily positive reinforcement—the standard practice in behavior modification programs.

84. Ibid., 101.

85. Katz, "The Kids with the Faraway Eyes," 53.

86. "Parents Speak: Risks and Benefits in the Treatment of Autistic Children," *Journal of Autism and Childhood Schnizophrenia* 8, no. 1 (1978): 99–113. See especially Ann Jepson, "Ethical Use of Aversives," 104–5; and Nancy McClung, "Risk/Benefit?" 107–8.

87. Kenneth Laureys with Roy Morgan, "Abuse of Aversive Therapy Opposed by NSAC," *The Advocate* (Jan./Feb. 1986): 6–7.

88. Schopler wrote that "some older Board members will remember that the psychoanalysts argued that people with autism are essentially normal and need only psychotherapy. The ASA today seems to want to go them one better by suggesting they only need normal experiences. This seems to bring us full cycle for denying their special problems and needs." "Letter to the Editor," *The Advocate* 20, no. 4 (Winter 1988). Donald Cohen was concerned that language regarding avoiding "physical side effects" of therapies might be construed as arguing against the use of medications in treatment, and that in many cases, routine activities could elicit "emotional stress." See Donald J. Cohen, letter to Edward Ritvo, August 31, 1988, second of two folders marked "ASA, NSAC," Box 1, ACC 92-M-41, Lettick Papers. On the contemporary incarnation of Division TEACCH, see http://www.teacch.com/.

89. Marcia Datlow Smith, "Response to Dr. Rimland's *Don't Ban Aversives*," *The Advocate* 20, no. 4 (Winter 1988): 14.

90. Marcia Datlow Smith and Bernard Rimland, "Pro and Con Arguments Regarding the ASA Resolution on the Use of Aversives," *The Advocate* 20, no. 4 (Winter 1988).

91. Katz, "The Kids with the Faraway Eyes," 53.

92. Park (2001, 77).

93. Lovaas's first report on the use of reinforcers in training children with autism was a paper presented in 1964, with Gilbert Freitag, the teacher hired, with little success, by the New Haven school system. The experience of the parents in New Haven only serves to underscore the point that laboratory techniques were difficult to translate into less formal settings, and using them successfully in homes and schools possibly required different forms of expertise. Probably the earliest account of Lovaas's work in this area was O. I. Lovaas, G. Freitag, M. I. Kinder, et al., "Experimental Studies in Childhood Schizophrenia—Establishment of Social Reinforcers" (paper delivered at Western Psychological Association, Portland, OR, April, 1964). Another study was published in 1966 on the acquisition of language: O. I. Lovaas. J. P. Berberich, B. F. Perloff, and B. Schaeffer, "Acquisition of Imitative Speech by Schizophrenic Children," *Science* 151, no. 3711 (1966): 705–7.

94. O. Ivar Lovaas, Robert Koegel, James Q. Simmons, and Judith Stevens Long, "Some Generalization and Follow-Up Measures on Autistic Children in Behavior Therapy," *Journal of Applied Behavior Analysis* 6, no. 1 (1973): 131–66.

95. O. Ivar Lovaas, "Parents as Therapists," in *Autism: A Reappraisal of Concepts and Treaments,* eds. Michael Rutter and Eric Schopler (New York: Plenum Press, 1978): 366–78, 371.

96. Ibid., 376–77.

97. O. Ivar Lovaas, "Behavioral Treatment and Normal Educational and Intellectual Functioning in Young Autistic Children," *Journal of Consulting and Clinical Psychology* 55, no. 1 (1987): 3–9

98. Eric Schopler, "Ask the Editor: Will Your Journal Support Parents Advocating for Intensive Behavior Therapy (the Lovaas Method) as an Entitlement under Part H of the Individuals with Disabilities Education Act?" *Journal of Autism and Developmental Disorders* 28, no. 1 (1998): 91–92.

99. Eric Schopler, Andrew Short, and Gary Mesibov, "Relation of Behavioral Treatment to 'Normal Functioning': Comment on Lovaas," *Journal of Consulting and Clinical Psychology* 57, no. 1 (1989): 162–64.

100. They thought that the children selected were higher-functioning than most children with autism and that children were placed in the control group because of the severity of their problems or because their parents were unable to participate fully in the treatment, meaning that the control and experimental group had different selection criteria. Ibid., 163. Lovaas responded that entirely arbitrary subject selection had been impossible because of parent

protests and that they had used the best available outcome measures. O. Ivar Lovaas, Tristram Smith, and John J. McEachin, "Clarifying Comments on the Young Autism Study: Reply to Schopler, Short and Mesibov," *Journal of Consulting and Clinical Psychology* 57, no. 1 (1989): 165–67, 165.

101. Schopler, Short, and Mesibov, "Relation of Behavioral Treatment to 'Normal Functioning': Comment on Lovaas," 164.

102. Schopler and Reichler (1971).

103. Gary Mesibov recalled this in his two obituaries for Schopler. Gary B. Mesibov, "A Tribute to Eric Schopler," *Journal of Autism and Developmental Disorders* 36, no. 8 (2006): 967–70; Gary B. Mesibov, "Eric Schopler (1927– 2006)," *American Psychologist* 62, no. 3 (2006): 250.

104. Gary Mesibov assumed the directorship of the program after Schopler partially retired in 1993. On the structure of the experimental program, see Schopler and Reichler (1971, 90–98). On the basic premises of Division TEACCH, see Lee M. Marcus, Margaret Lansing, Carol E. Andrews, and Eric Schopler, "Improvement of Teaching Effectiveness in Parents of Autistic Children," *Journal of the American Academy of Child Psychiatry* 17, no. 4 (1978): 625–39; Eric Schopler, Gary B. Mesibov, and Kathy Hearsey, "Structured Teaching in the TEACCH System," in *Learning and Cognition in Autism,* eds. Erich Schopler and Gary B. Mesibov (New York: Plenum Press, 1995): 243–68.

105. Eric Schopler, "Toward Reducing Behavior Problems in Autistic Children," *Journal of Autism and Childhood Schizophrenia* 6, no. 1 (1976): 1–13, 10.

106. Schopler and Reichler (1971, 92). Lovaas explains how he emphasized the idea of a "work-contract" in O. Ivar Lovaas, "Parents as Therapists," 372. For Schopler's focus on parental control in contrast to Lovaas, see Eric Schopler, "Changing Parental Involvement in Behavioral Treatment," in Michael Rutter and Eric Schopler, eds., *Autism: A Reappraisal of Concepts and Treatment* (New York: Plenum Press, 1978), 416.

107. Schopler and Reichler (1971, 92).

108. Ibid., 93

109. Lee M. Marcus, Margaret Lansing, Carol E. Andrews, and Eric Schopler, "Improvement of Teaching Effectiveness in Parents of Autistic Children," *Journal of the American Academy of Child Psychiatry* 17, no. 4 (1978): 625–39, 627. Kozloff's program was based on social exchange theory. Kozloff (1998, 55–95).

110. Schopler and Reichler (1971, 93, 99).

111. Eric Schopler, "Changing Parental Involvement in Behavioral Treatment," 414.

112. Gerald R. Patterson, R. A. Littman, and W. C. Hinsey, "Parental Effectiveness as Reinforcers in the Laboratory and Its Relation to Child Rearing Practices and Adjustment in the Classroom," *Journal of Personality* 32, no. 2 (1964): 180–99; G. R. Patterson, R. Jones, J. Whittier, and Mary A. Wright, "A Behavior Modification Technique for a Hyperactive Child," *Behaviour Research and Therapy* 2, no. 2–4 (1965): 217–26. O'Dell refers to behavioral techniques

as a "technology" throughout his review, which called for the training of parents in multiple domains. O'Dell (1974, 430). Examples of books that encouraged parents of typically developing children to try behavioral techniques included Gerald R. Patterson, *Families: Applications of Social Learning to Family Life* (Champaign, IL: Research Press, 1971) and Wesley C. Becker, *Parents Are Teachers: A Child Management Program* (Champaign, IL: Research Press, 1971).

113. O. Ivar Lovaas, Robert Koegel, James Q. Simmons, and Judith Stevens Long, "Some Generalization and Follow-Up Measures on Autistic Children in Behavior Therapy," *Journal of Applied Behavior Analysis* 6, no. 1 (1973): 131–66. The comments of reviewers summarized by the journal following the article criticized Lovaas et al.'s argument that children who were institutionalized fared considerably less well on follow-up than those who stayed at home and received treatment from their parents, noting that "many factors" could account for differences between the two groups.

114. O'Dell (1974, 418, 430).

115. The first "systematic application of operant conditioning" as a treatment for autism was probably that of Marian K. DeMyer and C. B. Fester, according to Edward K. Morris, Charryse M. Fouquette, Nathaniel G. Smith, and Deborah E. Altus, "A History of Applied Behavior Analysis in the Treatment of Autism: Fathers, Originators, and Founders" (poster presented at the meeting of the International Society for the History of the Behavioral and Social Sciences, Toronto, Canada, June 26–29, 2008). Morris et al. note that this was not an example of ABA, the first use of which is rightly attributed to other researchers. See "Teaching New Social Behavior to Schizophrenic Children," *Journal of the American Academy of Child and Adolescent Psychiatry* 1, no. 3 (1962): 443–61; and C. B. Ferster and Marian K. DeMyer, "A Method for the Experimental Analysis of the Behavior of Autistic Children," *American Journal of Orthopsychiatry* 32, no. 1 (1962): 89–98.

116. Vey Michael Nordquist and Robert G. Wahler, "Naturalistic Treatment of an Autistic Child," *Journal of Applied Behavior Analysis* 6, no. 1 (1973): 79–87, 79, 85; O'Dell (1974, 418).

117. Benjamin L. Moore and Jon S. Bailey, "Social Punishment in the Modification of a Pre-School Child's 'Autistic-Like' Behavior with a Mother as Therapist," *Journal of Applied Behavior Analysis* 6, no. 3 (1973): 497–507; Margaret Wulbert, "The Generalization of Newly Acquired Behaviors by Parents and Child Across Three Different Settings: A Study of an Autistic Child," *Journal of Abnormal Child Psychology* 2, no. 2 (1974): 87–98.

118. Gep Coletti and Sandra L. Harris, "Behavior Modification in the Home: Siblings as Behavior Modifiers, Parents as Observers," *Journal of Abnormal Child Psychology* 5, no. 1 (1977): 21–30, 29.

119. Moore and Bailey, "Social Punishment in the Modification of a Pre-School Child's 'Autistic-Like' Behavior with a Mother as Therapist," 498.

120. James Fisher (2007) has described some of these memoirs as part of the literary genre of "conversion narratives," where the search for a child with autism's lost selfhood takes the form of a religious journey with a recovery as the goal. I am interested in a parallel set of claims about love and expertise that are compatible with the types of narrative structure that Fisher has aptly identified, and that are present even in memoirs that do not conform to the structure of a conversion narrative.
121. Kaufman (1976, 29–31).
122. Ibid., 39.
123. Ibid., 63.
124. Ibid., 63.
125. Ibid., 96.
126. Ibid., 143. In addition to writing several books about their techniques, Barry and Suzi (now Samahria) Kaufman now offer a range of services and instruction to families of children with disabilities at the Option Institute, where their son Raun is a facilitator.
127. Observers of the program at a later date noted that "Option states that no behavior is judged, yet in practice some behaviors are deliberately misinterpreted, or almost ignored, while others are welcomed and acted upon enthusiastically." Rita Jordan and Stuart Powell, "Reflections of the Option Method as a Treatment for Autism," *Journal of Autism and Developmental Disorders* 23, no. 4 (1993): 682–85, 684.
128. Barron and Barron (2002, 227–28).
129. Greenfeld (1986, 39).
130. Ibid., 79–83, 322.
131. Maurice (1993, 56–57).
132. Ibid., 104, 128.
133. Rapp (1999, 3, 146); Park (2001, 10).
134. Mechanic and Rochefort (1990).
135. A 2001 study by the National Academies of Science found that intensive behavioral therapies for autism were generally effective, and that the specific type of intervention mattered less than the number of hours of therapy received per week, ideally at least twenty-five hours. *Educating Children with Autism*, Commission on Behavioral and Social Sciences and Education (CBASSE; The National Academies Press, 2001). At least one self-advocate has testified in court against behavioral therapies. See Michelle Dawson, "The Misbehaviour of Behaviourists: Ethical Challenges to the Autism-ABA Industry," http://www.sentex.net/~nexus23/naa_aba.html; and Michelle Dawson, "An Autistic Victory: the True Meaning of the Auton Decision," http://www.sentex.net/~nexus23/naa_vic.html. For a description of one family's struggles to implement a behavioral therapy program, see Susan Sheehan, "The Autism Fight," *New Yorker*, December 1, 2003.

136. Leiter (2004) describes how parents contested their position as targets of professional authority, succeeding in changing the terminology used in Early Intervention programs but not the distribution of power within the programs.
137. Rimland (1972, 573).
138. Milt Freudenheim, "Battling Insurers over Autism Treatment," *New York Times*, December 21, 2004.
139. Jane Gross, "Continuing Education: A Master's in Self-Help," *New York Times*, April 20, 2008.
140. There are different reported ranges for the cost of a year of behavioral therapy. Benedict Carey, in "To Treat Autism, Parents Take a Leap of Faith" (*New York Times*, December 27, 2004), reported $40,000–$60,000. An article in the APA *Monitor* (Lea Winerman, "Effective Education for Autism," http://www.apa.org/monitor/deco4/autism.html), reported $40,000–$80,000.
141. The National School Board Association, quoted in Linda Greenhouse, "Legal Victory for Families of Disabled Students," *New York Times*, May 22, 2007.

Interlude

1. The term was probably first used in print by Judy Singer (1999), who says that she coined the term in 1997.
2. Charlton (1998). I have also referred to Shapiro (1994) for the history of the disability rights movement, and Lennard Davis's (2006) essay on the emergence of the concept of normality in the nineteenth century.
3. A number of scholars have written about the neurodiveristy movement from a social science perspective. For summaries of claims made by self-advocates (and thoughtful analyses and critiques of the movement), see Orsini (2009) and Ortega (2009).
4. Durbin-Westby (2010); Robertson (2010).
5. Bagatell (2010, 36).
6. On the invention of the "moral idiot" and "moral imbecile" and associated treatment programs during the latter half of the nineteenth century, see Trent (1994, 20–23).
7. The act was originally the Education for All Handicapped Act, PL 94-142, of 1975. On the growth of advocacy groups for parents of children with cognitive disabilities and a history of the theories that have been applied to the education of children with cognitive disabilities, see Trent (1994).
8. Landsman (2009, 99).
9. Bruno Bettelheim and Emmy Sylvester, "Notes on the Impact of Parental Occupations: Some Cultural Determinants of Symptom Choice in Emotionally Disturbed Children," *American Journal of Orthopsychiatry* 20, no. 4 (1950): 785–95.

10. Sandra L. Harris, "The Family and the Autistic Child: A Behavioral Perspective," in "The Family with Handicapped Members," special issue, *Family Relations* 33 no. 1 (1984): 127–34, 132; Lisa A. Osborne, Louise McHugh, Jo Saunders, and Phil Reed, "Parenting Stress Reduces the Effectiveness of Early Teaching Interventions for Autistic Spectrum Disorders," *Journal of Autism and Developmental Disorders* 38, no. 6 (2008): 1092–1103; Richard P. Hastings and Emma Johnson, "Stress in U.K. Families Conducting Intensive Home-Based Behavioral Intervention for Their Young Child," *Journal of Autism and Developmental Disorders* 31, no. 3 (2001): 327–36, 328.

11. Interestingly, a child's need for support in daily activities or his or her level of intellectual disability seems to have little to do with parents' reported stress. Annette Estes, Jeffrey Munson, Geraldine Dawson, Elizabeth Koehler, et al., "Parenting Stress and Psychological Functioning among Mothers of Preschool Children with Autism and Developmental Delay," *Autism* 13, no. 4 (2009): 375–87, 383; Patricia A. Rao and Deborah C. Beidel, "The Impact of Children with High-Functioning Autism on Stress, Sibling Adjustment, and Family Functioning," *Behavior Modification* 33, no. 4 (2009): 437–51.

12. David E. Gray, "Perceptions of Stigma: The Parents of Autistic Children," *Sociology of Health and Illness* 15, no. 1 (1993): 102–20, 111.

13. Estes et al., "Parenting Stress and Psychological Functioning among Mothers of Preschool Children with Autism and Developmental Delay," 376.

14. Specifically, stress was associated with "regulatory problems" (e.g., problems managing sleep, eating, and emotions), and "externalizing behavior," which can include hyperactivity, explosive outbursts, or aggression. Naomi Ornstein Davis and Alice S. Carter, "Parenting Stress in Mothers and Fathers of Toddlers with Autism Spectrum Disorders: Associations with Child Characteristics," *Journal of Autism and Developmental Disorders* 38, no. 7 (2008): 1278–91. One study did find that maternal stress, in particular, was related to a child's level of social skills. Mary J. Baker-Ericzen, Lauren Brookman-Frazee, and Aubyn Stahmer, "Stress Levels and Adaptability of Toddlers With and Without Autism Spectrum Disorders," *Research and Practice for Persons with Severe Disabilities* 30, no. 4 (2005): 194–204, 201.

15. Gray (1993).

16. Gray (1994) found parents using a variety of strategies, including religion and activism, to cope with stress. Ryan and Cole (2009, 51) write that "activism, then, may be a mechanism for expressing, in a 'selfless' way, the mothers' aspirations and needs."

17. Landsman (2003, 1950).

18. Schopler and Mesibov (1984, 7).

19. E. James Anthony, "Editorial Query," *Journal of Autism and Childhood Schizophrenia* 4, no. 2 (1974): 93. This particular entry was brought to my attention through a reference in Eyal, Hart, Onculer, Oren, et al. (2010, 181).

20. Mary S. Akerley, "Parents Speak: Introduction," *Journal of Autism and Childhood Schizophrenia* 4, no. 4 (1974): 347.

21. Ibid., 347; Margaret A. Dewey and Margaret P. Everard, "The Near-Normal Autistic Adolescent," *Journal of Autism and Childhood Schizophrenia* 4, no. 4 (1974): 348–56, 351. The article was written by a "correspondence panel of parents and professionals from the British and American National Society for Autistic Children" who exchanged observations via airmail (348).

22. Eric Schopler introduced the article, noting that "parents' use of behavior modification techniques predates that of the behavioral scientists, and no doubt has played a part in the scientific formulation." David Park, "Parents Speak: Operant Conditioning of a Speaking Autistic Child," *Journal of Autism and Childhood Schizophrenia* 4, no. 2 (1974): 189–91.

23. David Park and Philip Youderian, "Light and Number: Ordering Principles in the World of an Autistic Child," *Journal of Autism and Childhood Schizophrenia* 4, no. 4 (1974): 313–23.

24. Ruth Christ Sullivan, "Poems on Autism: Beyond Research Data," *Journal of Autism and Childhood Schizophrenia* 7, no. 4 (1977): 397–407.

25. Ruth Christ Sullivan, "Hunches on Some Biological Factors in Autism," *Journal of Autism and Developmental Disorders* 5, no. 2 (1975): 177–84.

26. Ruth Christ Sullivan, "Why Do Autistic Children...?" *Journal of Autism and Developmental Disorders* 10, no. 2 (1980): 231–41.

27. Mary S. Akerley, introduction to Henry A. Beyer, "Parents Speak: Changes in the Parent–Child Legal Relationship—What They Mean to the Clinician and Researcher," *Journal of Autism and Childhood Schizophrenia* 7, no. 1 (1977): 83–108.

28. Mr. and Mrs. M. Fields, "Parents Speak: The Relationship Between Problem Behaviors and Food Allergies: One Family's Story" and comments by Charles H. Banov, Linus Pauling, and Morris A. Lipton, *Journal of Autism and Childhood Schizophrenia* 6, no. 1 (1976): 75–91.

29. Mary S. Akerley, "Springing the Tradition Trap," *Journal of Autism and Childhood Schizophrenia* 5, no. 4 (1975): 373–80, 376, 379.

30. "Springing the Tradition Trap Continued," *Journal of Autism and Childhood Schizophrenia* 6, no. 1 (1976): 93–100. Stella Chess wrote that "I find myself in substantial agreement with the points made by Ms. Akerley. Since a number of children with autism or strong autistic features come to me for evaluation, after having been seen by others, I have duplicated in my clinical experience her examples of subjective and insufficiently substantiated interpretations of symbolic meanings of the children's behavior—interpretations which have been of little help as a guide to management" (94). William Goldfarb wrote that "Ms. Akerley's 'traditional' psychiatrist can probably be better described as incompetent and he would not survive in most of our therapeutic programs" (98). Leon Eisenberg was the only respondent who seconded Aker-

ley's call for "the therapist to become a social advocate," although Stella Chess saw "no principled professional objection to involvement in community activity and education regarding children's needs of any kind" (97, 95).

31. Kenneth L. Lichstein and Laura Schreibman, "Employing Electric Shock with Autistic Children: A Review of the Side Effects," *Journal of Autism and Childhood Schizophrenia* 6, no. 2 (1976): 163–73; Mary S. Akerley, "Parents Speak: Reactions to Employing Electric Shock with Autistic Children (Introduction)," *Journal of Autism and Childhood Schizophrenia* 6, no. 3 (1976): 289; "Parents Speak: Comments," *Journal of Autism and Childhood Schizophrenia* 6, no. 3 (1976): 290–94; Kenneth L. Lichstein, "Reply to Reader Comments on 'Employing Electric Shock with Autistic Children,'" *Journal of Autism and Childhood Schizophrenia* 7, no. 3 (1977); "Parents Speak: Comments," *Journal of Autism and Childhood Schizophrenia* 7, no. 2 (1977): 199–202.

32. Nancy McClung, "Risk/Benefit," in Ruth Christ Sullivan, "Risks and Benefits in the Treatment of Autistic Children," *Journal of Autism and Childhood Schizophrenia* 8, no. 1 (1978): 111–13, 108.

33. Dan Torisky and Connie Torisky, "Parents Speak: Sex Education and Sexual Awareness Building for Autistic Children and Youth: Some Viewpoints and Considerations," *Journal of Autism and Developmental Disorders* 15, no. 2 (1985): 213–27. This was the only column edited by the Toriskys and the last "Parents Speak" column featured in the journal. The Toriskys wrote, "In modifying this behavior, it is we who must forget that this is the emotionally charged subject of sexual behavior, and treat this educational process in much the same manner that we deal with table manners, how to cross the street, or what to say to the waiter in the restaurant." Dan and Connie Torisky, "Response," *Journal of Autism and Developmental Disorders* 15, no. 2 (1985): 221–23, 222.

34. "It addresses problems that parents (and truly concerned professionals) talk about when they are speaking with their hearts: *Who* will care for our severely handicapped children when we're gone?" Ruth Christ Sullivan, "Parents Speak: Needs of the Older Child," (Introduction), *Journal of Autism and Childhood Schizophrenia* 7, no. 3 (1977): 287–88, 287.

35. Katharine Sangree Stokes, "Planning for the Future of a Severely Handicapped Autistic Child," *Journal of Autism and Childhood Schizophrenia* 7, no. 3 (1977): 288–98, 289.

36. Ibid., 291.

37. Leonard G. Berger, "Working within the System (Response to Katharine Sangree Stokes, "Planning for the Future of a Severely Handicapped Autistic Child")," *Journal of Autism and Childhood Schizophrenia* 7, no. 3 (1977), 299–301, 301.

38. Clara Claiborne Park, "The Limits of Normalization (Response to Katharine Sangree Stokes, "Planning for the Future of a Severely Handicapped Autis-

tic Child")," *Journal of Autism and Childhood Schizophrenia* 7, no. 3 (1977): 301–2, 302.

39. Mesibov explained that normalization was developed by Wolfensberger (1972) as a principle to guide the design of programs for individuals diagnosed with mental retardation, but it began to be applied to autism as well. The concept was incorporated into law in the 1975 Education for All Handicapped Children Act's requirement that educators provide the "least restrictive environment" possible. A "Parents Speak" column on the concept of normalization included comments from both professionals and parents and ran in conjunction with the article by Gary Mesibov, "Implications of the Normalization Principle for Psychotic Children," *Journal of Autism and Childhood Schizophrenia* 6, no. 4 (1976): 360–65; Mary S. Akerley, "Parents Speak: Introduction," *Journal of Autism and Childhood Schizophrenia* 6, no. 4 (1976): 359.

40. "Responses" to Gary Mesibov, "Implications of the Normalization Principle for Psychotic Children," *Journal of Autism and Childhood Schizophrenia* 6, no. 4 (1976): 365–72, especially James P. Chapman, "Normalization a Philosophy, Not a Treatment Strategy," 365–66.

41. Ruth Christ Sullivan (with contributions from Corinne Fredricks, O. Ivar Lovaas, Norris G. Haring, Amy L. Lettick, Eric Schopler, Robert J. Reichler, Donald J. Cohen, Sheridan Neimark, Ellen L. Wike, Anne M. Donnellan, and Gary W. LaVigna), "What Does Deinstitutionalization Mean for Our Children?" *Journal of Autism and Developmental Disorders* 11, no. 3 (1981): 347–56.

42. Amy Lettick, "Letter to the Editor: Dissent from NSAC Deinstitutionalization Resolution," *Journal of Autism and Developmental Disorders* 12, no. 1 (1982): 95–96; Ruth Christ Sullivan, "What Does Deinstitutionalization Mean for Our Children?" 350–51.

43. This is also true of contemporary parents of children with disabilities. Landsman (2005, 139) writes that "mothers' understandings, fitting neatly into neither the medical nor the social model but steeped in the everyday experience of interdependency, may yet converge with efforts within disability studies to reexamine the identity of disability and create a more inclusive world."

44. Landsman (2005, 138).

45. Deborah Barnbaum (2008, 204–7) argues that "autistic integrity" is violated by efforts to cure autism in adults, but she spends very little time discussing the ethics of treatments that may ameliorate but not cure autism.

46. Landsman (2009, 212).

47. Barnbaum (2008, 161) refers to the concept of a child's right to an "open future" to argue for the ethical acceptability of a genetic test used to prevent autism. Landsman's (2009, 183–87) findings suggest that parents may reference their child's future as they consider treatment options, but that other

factors, including social pressures to provide treatments, also figure in their considerations.

48. Landsman (2009, 213); Shakespeare (2006).

49. Bruno Betteheim. "Training the Child-Care Worker in a Residential Setting," *American Journal of Orthopsychiatry* 36, no. 4 (1966): 694–705, 705.

50. Patricia Howlin, Susan Goode, Jane Hutton, and Michael Rutter, "Adult Outcome for Children with Autism," *Journal of Child Psychology and Psychiatry* 45, no. 2 (2004): 212–29.

51. As Landsman (2009, 213) argues, their understanding that dependence is consistent with human dignity allows them to move beyond existing theoretical models of disability.

Part Two
Chapter 4

1. "At the time I was born, we had no idea autism ran in the family." Zaks (2010).

2. Stacey (2003, 254–55).

3. Jeremy Veenstra-VanderWeele, Susan L. Christian, and Edwin H. Cook Jr., "Autism as a Paradigmatic Complex Genetic Disorder," *Annual Review of Genomics and Human Genetics* 5 (2004): 379–405, 379.

4. Uta Frith (1991, 32) affirmed Hans Asperger's comment that many scientists could wish that they had a "dash" of autism.

5. Herbert (2005a).

6. Lindee (2005, 2).

7. A number of studies exist on the history of research in molecular biology and genetics, as well as the markets for and ideological stakes involved in genetics research in the present. This discussion was informed in particular by Doyle (1997), Haraway (1997b), Keller (1995, 2000), Kay (2000), and Lindee (2005).

8. Conrad (1999, 236).

9. Keller (2000, 10).

10. Lindee (2005, 2) explains how lay knowledge about genetic disorders is incorporated into published, authoritative knowledge about the disorders.

11. Government-funded autism research takes place at a number of sites. The NIH funds the Collaborative Programs of Excellence in Autism (CPEAs) through member institutes, as well as the Studies to Advance Autism Research and Treatment Centers Program (STAART) network, in addition to individual researcher grants, through funding provided in the Children's Health Act of 2000. A joint NIH and CDC program called Centers of Excellence for Autism and Developmental Disabilities Research and Epidemiology (CADDRE) is devoted to epidemiological research. The 2006 Combating Autism Act authorized Congress to appropriate $860 million in funding over

five years to autism research, although individual pieces of legislation must be passed to actually provide the funds. As part of the 2007 Defense Appropriations Act, the Department of Defense began funding autism research in order to attempt to help military families that have children with autism, with an emphasis on developing treatments.

12. Sunder Rajan (2003).

13. Jonathan Sebat, quoted in Nikhil Swaminathan, "Autism Risk May Lie in Fragile Areas of Genetic Code," *Scientific American*, March 16, 2007. Attempts have been made to develop a "unified theory" that will tie together sporadic cases of autism with the far less common inherited cases. See Xiaoyue Zhao, Anthony Leotta, Vlad Kustanovich, Clara Lajonchere, et al., "A Unified Genetic Theory for Sporadic and Inherited Autism," *Proceedings of the National Academy of Science* 104, no. 31 (July 2007): 12831–36.

14. "The Child Is Father," *Time*, July 25, 1960.

15. Rimland (1964, 38).

16. Rosenberg (1992).

17. Michael Rutter and Lawrence Bartak, "Causes of Infantile Autism: Some Considerations from Recent Research," *Journal of Autism and Childhood Schizophrenia* 1, no. 1 (1971): 20–32, 24

18. Adams (2005, 214).

19. Rutter and Bartak, "Causes of Infantile Autism," 25.

20. D. R. Hanson and I. I. Gottesman, "The Genetics, If Any, of Infantile Autism and Childhood Schizophrenia," *Journal of Autism and Childhood Schizophrenia* 6, no. 3 (1976): 209–34.

21. Susan Folstein and Michael Rutter, "Infantile Autism: A Genetic Study of 21 Twin Pairs," *Journal of Child Psychology and Psychiatry* 18, no. 4 (1977): 297–321, 308, 298, 304. Also see Susan Folstein and Michael Rutter, "Genetic Influences and Infantile Autism," *Nature* 265, no. 5596 (February 1977): 726–28.

22. M. Mary Konstantareas, "Early Developmental Backgrounds of Autistic and Mentally Retarded Children: Future Research Directions," *Psychiatric Clinics of North America* 9, no. 4 (1986): 671–88.

23. Susan E. Folstein and Joseph Piven, "Etiology of Autism: Genetic Influences," *Pediatrics* 87, no. 5, pt. 2 (1991): 767–73. The two twin studies are E. R. Ritvo, B. J. Freeman, A. Mason-Brothers, A. Mo, et al., "Concordance for the Syndrome of Autism in 40 Pairs of Afflicted Twins," *American Journal of Psychiatry* 142 (1985): 74–77; and S. Steffenberg, C. Gillberg, and L Holmgren, "A Twin Study of Autism in Denmark, Finland, Iceland, Norway, and Sweden," *Journal of Child Psychology and Psychiatry* 30, no. 3 (1986): 405–16.

24. These have included the serotonin transporter gene, the reelin gene (which is involved in neuronal migration), dopamine-related genes, and MECP2, the gene found in the majority of girls with Rett syndrome, another pervasive developmental disorder. See Janine A. Lamb, Jeremy R. Parr, Anthony J. Bailey, and Anthony P. Monaco, "Autism: In Search of Susceptibility Genes," *Neu-*

roMolecular Medicine 2, no. 1 (2002): 11–28, 19. Candidate gene approaches are also discussed in Jeremy Veenstra-VanderWeele and Edwin H. Cook Jr., "Molecular Genetics of Autism Spectrum Disorder," *Molecular Psychiatry* 9, no. 9 (2004): 819–32.

25. Catherine Lord, Bennett L. Leventhal, and Edwin H. Cook Jr., "Quantifying the Phenotype in Autism Spectrum Disorders," *American Journal of Medical Genetics* 105, no. 1 (2001): 36–38, 37. The ADI-R was published in 1994, the ADOS in 1999. On the use of the "broader autism phenotype" in genetic studies, see Susan E. Folstein, Erica Bisson, Susan L. Santangelo, and Joseph Piven, "Finding Specific Genes That Cause Autism: A Combination of Approaches Will Be Needed to Maximize Power," *Journal of Autism and Developmental Disorders* 28, no. 5 (1998): 439–45; Geraldine Dawson, Sara Webb, Bernard D. Schellenberg, Stephen Dager, et al., "Defining the Broader Phenotype of Autism: Genetic, Brain, and Behavioral Perspectives," *Development and Psychopathology* 14, no. 3 (2002): 581–611; and Thomas H. Wassink, Linda M. Brzustowicz, Christopher W. Bartlett, and Peter Szatmari, "The Search for Autism Disease Genes," *Mental Retardation and Developmental Disabilities Research Reviews* 10, no. 4 (2004): 272–83.

26. L. B. Jorde, S. J. Hasstedt, E. R. Ritvo, A. Mason-Brothers, et al., "Complex Segregation Analysis of Autism," *American Journal of Human Genetics* 49, no. 5 (1991): 932–38.

27. Susan E. Folstein and Beth Rosen-Sheidley, "Genetics of Autism: Complex Aetiology for a Heterogeneous Disorder," *Nature Reviews Genetics* 2, no. 12 (2001): 943–55.

28. Ibid., 953.

29. Wassink et al., "The Search for Autism Disease Genes," 272, 281.

30. The authors cited a concordance rate of 60 percent–91 percent for monozygotic twins "depending on whether a narrow or broad phenotype is considered," which by the conclusion of the article was transformed into "the less than 10% of variance that is not genetic." Veenstra-VanderWeele et al., "Autism as a Paradigmatic Complex Genetic Disorder," 380, 396.

31. Laurena A. Weiss, Yiping Shen, Joshua M. Korn, Dan E. Arking, et al. "Association between Microdeletion at 16p11.2 and Autism," *New England Journal of Medicine* 358, no. 7 (2008): 667–75.

32. Lamb et al., "Autism: In Search of Susceptibility Genes," 13.

33. Hedgecoe (2001). Bumiller (2009, 878) has also noted the similarities between the rhetoric of scientists involved in autism genetics and Hedgecoe's observation that Alzheimer's researchers have capitalized on the "complex nature" of the disorder to justify continued research despite unpromising results.

34. Jonathan Sebat, B. Lakshmi, Dheeraj Malhotra, Jennifer Troge, et al., "Strong Association of De Novo Copy Number Mutations with Autism," *Science* 316, no. 445 (2007): 445–49. The Autism Genome Project Consortium, "Mapping Autism Risk Loci Using Genetic Linkage and Chromosomal Rearrange-

ments," *Nature Genetics* 39, no. 3 (2007): 319–28, used a combination of methods, including a genome scan of multiplex families and analysis of copy number variations. A study that used families with high rates of intermarriage to identify genes related to learning in association with autism cases was Eric M. Morrow, Seung-Yun Yoo, Steven W. Flavell, Tae-Kyung Kim, et al., "Identifying Autism Loci and Genes by Tracing Recent Shared Ancestry," *Science* 321, no. 218 (2008): 218–23.

35. Conrad (1999, 236); John N. Constantino, Clara Lajonchere, Marin Lutz, Teddi Gray, et al., "Autistic Social Impairment in the Siblings of Children with Pervasive Developmental Disorders," *American Journal of Psychiatry* 163, no. 2 (2006): 294–96.

36. A genetics education site sponsored by NAAR included the identification of Rett syndrome on its timeline, "A Look at the Genetics of Autism," although it is not clear that the two disorders are related by anything but their shared features of impaired communication and interaction. http://www.exploringautism .org/history/index.htm.

37. Ruthie E. Amir, Ignatia B. Van den Veyver, Mimi Wan, Charles Q. Tran, et al., "Rett Syndrome Is Caused by Mutations in X-linked *MECP2*, Encoding Methyl-CpG-Binding Protein 2," *Nature Genetics* 23 (1999): 185–88.

38. Andreas Rett, "Uber ein eigenartiges hirnatrophisches Syndrom bei Hyperammonamie im Kindesaler," *Wiener Medizinische Wochenschrift* 116 (1966): 723–26, cited in Neumarker (2003).

39. Ruthie E. Amir, Ignatia B. Van den Veyver, Rebecca Schultz, Denise M. Malicki, et al., "Influence of Mutation Type and X Chromosome Inactivation on Rett Syndrome Phenotypes," *Annals of Neurology* 47, no. 5 (2000): 670–79.

40. "Mouse with Rett Syndrome May Provide Model for Testing Treatments, Understanding Disorder," (NIH News Release), National Institute of Child Health and Human Development, July 29, 2002.

41. This research is described in Mona D. Shahbazian, Juan I. Young, Lisa A. Yuva-Paylor, Corinne M. Spencer, et al., "Mice with Truncated MeCP2 Recapitulate Many Rett Syndrome Features and Display Hyperacetylation of Histone H3," *Neuron* 35, no. 2 (2002): 243–54.

42. This was not only a feature of the public presentation of this research. In the publication reporting the creation of a mouse model for Rett syndrome, the extraordinary recapitulation of symptoms in the mouse was also emphasized. Ibid., 246. A video of the Rett syndrome mice can be found at http:// www.hhmi.org/biointeractive/neuroscience/rett_mouse.html.

43. "It is difficult to comprehend how dysfunction of this protein, which might be predicted to cause derepression of hundreds or thousands of genes, leads to primarily neurological phenotypes. To investigate this paradox and understand the disease mechanism, animal models should prove useful." Shahbazian et al., "Mice with Truncated MeCP2 Recapitulate Many Rett Syndrome Features," 243.

44. Amir et al., "Influence of Mutation Type and X Chromosome Inactivation on Rett Syndrome Phenotypes," 671.

45. Claudia Dreifus, "A Conversation with Huda Zoghbi: Researchers Toil with Genes on the Fringe of a Cure," *New York Times*, March 22, 2005.

46. The exact figure was $2,246,817. Antonio Regalado, "Wealth Effect: A Hedge-Fund Titan's Millions Stir Up Research into Autism—James Simons Taps Big Stars from Outside Field to Find a Genetic Explanation—Three Personal DNA Tests," *Wall Street Journal*, December 15, 2005.

47. Simons's growing conviction that genetics research was the key to autism was given support when, according to Simons, he discovered that James Watson was of the same opinion when they met at a dinner party. Ibid.

48. Jacky Guy, Jian Gan, Jim Selfridge, Stuart Cobb, et al., "Reversal of Neurological Defects in a Mouse Model of Rett Syndrome," *Science* 315, no. 5815 (2007): 1143–47.

49. The precise phrasing is "Our data show that developmental absence of MeCP2 does not irreversibly damage neurons, suggesting that RTT is not strictly a neurodevelopmental disorder." Ibid., 1145.

50. The generalization to other autism spectrum disorders (accomplished by emphasizing the status of RTT as an autism spectrum disorder) was reflected in the press release on the research "Reversal of Symptoms in an Autism Spectrum Disorder: Rett Syndrome is Reversed in Genetic Mouse Model," Rett Syndrome Research Foundation, http://www.rsrf.org/reversal_experiment/index.html; and a video, *Families Comment on the Experiment*. Both were posted on the Rett Syndrome Research Foundation Web site. The International Rett Syndrome Association and the Rett Syndrome Research Foundation merged in 2007 to form the International Rett Syndrome Foundation; the Web site is no longer active.

51. Nikhil Swaminathan, "Reversal of Fortune: Researchers Erase Symptoms of Rett Syndrome," *ScientificAmerican.com* (February 8, 2007), http://www.scientificamerican.com/article.cfm?id=reversal-of-fortune-resea.

52 Jacqueline N. Crawley, "Designing Mouse Behavioral Tasks Relevant to Autistic-Like Behaviors," *Mental Retardation and Developmental Disabilities Research Reviews* 10, no. 4 (2004): 248–58.

53. Chang-Hyuk Kwon, Bryan W. Luikart, Jing Zhou, Sharon A. Matheny, et al., "Pten Regulates Neuronal Arborization and Social Interaction in Mice," *Neuron* 50, no. 3 (2006), 377–88; and commentary, Joy M. Greer and Anthony Wynshaw-Boris, "*Pten* and the Brain: Sizing Up Social Interaction," *Neuron* 50, no. 3 (2006): 343–44.

54. David G. Amaral, Margaret D. Bauman, and C. Mills Schumann, "The Amygdala and Autism: Implications from Non-Human Primate Studies," *Genes, Brain and Behavior* 2, no. 5 (2003): 295–302.

55. See, for instance, Margaret Bauman and Thomas L. Kemper, "Histoanatomic Observations of the Brain in Early Infantile Autism," *Neurology* 35,

no. 6 (1985): 866–74; Margaret Bauman, "Microscopic Neuroanatomic Abnormalities in Autism," *Pediatrics*, 87, no. 5 (1991): 791–96; Margaret Bauman, "Brief Report: Neuroanatomic Observations of the Brain in Pervasive Developmental Disorders," *Journal of Autism and Developmental Disorders* 26, no. 2 (1996): 199–203; and Margaret L. Bauman and Thomas L. Kemper, "Observations on the Purkinje Cells in the Cerebellar Vermis in Autism," *Journal of Neuropathology and Experimental Neurology* 55, no. 5 (1996): 613. On reconsiderations of the results, Elizabeth R. Whitney, Thomas L. Kemper, Margaret L. Bauman, Douglas L. Rosene, et al., "Cerebellar Purkinje Cells are Reduced in a Subpopulation of Autistic Brains: A Stereological Experiment Using Calbindin D28k," *The Cerebellum* 7, no. 3 (2008): 406–16.

56. Nouchine Hadjikhani, Robert M. Joseph, Josh Snyder, and Helen Tager-Flusberg, "Anatomical Differences in the Mirror Neuron System and Social Cognition Network in Autism," *Cerebral Cortex* 16, no. 9 (2006): 1276–82, 1276.

57. Baron-Cohen (1997).

58. Eric Courchesne, "Brain Development in Autism: Early Overgrowth Followed by Premature Arrest of Growth," *Mental Retardation and Developmental Disabilities Research Reviews* 10, no. 2 (2004): 106–11; Martha R. Herbert, David A. Ziegler, Nikos Makris, Pauline A. Filipek, et al., "Localization of White Matter Volume Increase in Autism and Developmental Language Disorder," *Annals of Neurology* 55, no. 4 (2004): 530–40.

59. Martha R. Herbert, "Large Brains in Autism: The Challenge of Pervasive Abnormality," *Neuroscientist* 11, no. 5 (2005): 417–40. On changing programs in brain imaging research in autism, see Herbert (2004).

60. Diana I. Vargas, Caterina Nascimbene, Chitra Krishnan, Andrew W. Zimmerman, et al., "Neuroglial Activation and Neuroinflammation in the Brain of Patients with Autism," *Annals of Neurology* 57, no. 1 (2005): 67–81.

61. J. L. R. Rubenstein and M. M. Merzenich, "Model of Autism: Increased Ratio of Excitation/Inhibition in Key Neural Systems," *Genes, Brain and Behavior* 2, no. 5 (2003): 255–67; Rajesh K. Kana, Timothy A. Keller, Nancy J. Minshew, and Marcel Adam Just, "Inhibitory Control in High-Functioning Autism: Decreased Activation and Underconnectivity in Inhibition Networks," *Biological Psychiatry* 62, no. 3 (2007): 198–206.

62. Simon Baron-Cohen and Matthew Belmonte, "Autism: A Window onto the Development of the Social and Analytic Brain," *Annual Review of Neuroscience* 28 (2005): 109–26.

63. Matthew K. Belmonte, Greg Allen, Andrea Beckel-Mitchener, Lisa M. Boulanger, et al., "Autism and Abnormal Development of Brain Connectivity," *Journal of Neuroscience* 24, no. 42 (2004): 9228–31.

64. Matthew K. Belmonte, Edwin H. Cook Jr., George M. Anderson, John L. R. Rubenstein, et al., "Autism as a Disorder of Neural Information Processing: Directions for Research and Targets for Therapy," *Molecular Psychiatry* 9, no. 7 (2004), 646–63.

65. The Autism Tissue Program was founded by the National Alliance for Autism Research. Brains are kept at the Harvard Brain Tissue Resource Center. Information on brain donations on the LADDERS Web site can be found at http://www.ladders.org/pages/Brain-Donations.html. The Autism Tissue Program Web site is located at http://www.autismtissueprogram.org/site/c.nlKUL7MQIsG/b.5183271/k.BD86/Home.htm.

66. On the iconic power of images of brains, especially those that seem to bring the visible differences of disordered brains into sharp relief, see Dumit (2003).

67. Their suggestions are taken up by sociologists and psychologists, for instance Christopher Badcock (2004), who follows Simon Baron-Cohen in viewing autism as an extreme of male cognitive characteristics.

68. Quotes are from a CAN fundraising pamphlet, sent December 2003 (Los Angeles, CA: Cure Autism Now).

69. Rebecca Muhle, Stephanie V. Trentacoste, and Isabelle Rapin. "The Genetics of Autism," *Pediatrics* 113, no. 5 (2004): e472–86, e473.

70. From the CAN Web site, http://www.cureautismnow.org/about/index.jsp (accessed August 4, 2005; no longer available).

71. On the range of strategies used by HIV/AIDS treatment activists, see Epstein (1995, 1996). For an account of the founding of the Pediatric AIDS Foundation, see Elizabeth Glaser (1991). Elizabeth Kilpatrick at CAN mentioned the connection during an interview in June 2003.

72. On the importance of families in driving research into familial dysautonomia, and the centrality of their experiential knowledge in the process of caregiving, see Lindee (2005, 156–87).

73. These normative practices are described by Merton (1973). On deviations from these norms in the practice of scientific work, see Mulkay (1976).

74. Aaron Zitner. "Whose DNA Is It, Anyway?" *LA Times*, July 18, 2003. In another account, there were six researchers, but the general terms of the account are the same. See Allan Coukell, "You Can Hurry Science," *Proto: Massachusetts General Hospital Dispatches from the Frontiers of Medicine* (Winter 2006), http://protomag.com/assets/you-can-hurry-science.

75. This came to over 800 samples from individuals with autism spectrum disorders, or over 1,000 samples including family members. Daniel H. Geschwind, Janice Sowinski, Catherine Lord, Portia Iversen, et al., "The Autism Genetic Resource Exchange: A Resource for the Study of Autism and Related Neuropsychiatric Conditions," *American Journal of Human Genetics* 69, no. 2 (2001): 463–66. General information on AGRE is available at www.agre.org. My information also comes from a visit to CAN/AGRE headquarters in August 2003 and an interview with Portia Iverson in November 2002.

76. CAN press release, http://www.cureautismnow.org/site/apps/nl/content2.asp?c=bhLOK2PILuF&b=1289185&ct=2676321&tr=y&auid=1771171 (accessed May 18, 2007; no longer available).

77. In this sense, AGRE functioned as a kind of "obligatory passage point" through which CAN became "indispensable" for other researchers because it succeeded in incorporating their interests. On the concept of the "obligatory passage point" in actor-network theory see Callon (1987). Heath, Rapp, and Taussig (2004, 164) make a similar point regarding Sharon and Patrick Terry's work to "insure their status as obligatory passage points," by assembling a collection of biological materials and family pedigrees, and by using intellectual property rights to the PXE gene identified in 2000 to compel researchers to follow rules of data-sharing.

78. Although it is difficult to draw a causal line from AGRE to the NIH's decision, Shestack and Iverson's work was arguably a precedent for this type of data-sharing, as one of the first advocacy efforts concerned specifically with sharing biological materials. Nelkin and Andrews (2001, 40–41) suggest that their approach was unique at the time. However, Iverson and Shestack were not the first activists to use their positions as parents and access to materials to manage the behavior of scientists—in addition to Sharon and Patrick Terry's work through PXE International, parent members of DEBRA (founded in 1979) assembled a tissue bank in order to promote research on epidermolysis bullosa. For descriptions of these organizations and other strategies for "organizing access" to genetic material, see Taussig (2005, 232) and Heath, Rapp, and Taussig (2004). On the revised NIH rules, see Charles Jennings, "Universities Unnerved by Revised Rules for Sharing NIH Research," *Nature* 430, no. 7003 (August 2004): 953. For "Final NIH Statement on Sharing Research Data" dated February 26, 2003, see http://grants.nih.gov/grants/guide/notice-files/NOT-OD-03-032.html.

79. NAAR staff member, interview, August 26, 2003.

80. For information on the structure of the program, see National Alliance for Autism Research, "NAAR Autism Genome Project: Frequently Asked Questions," http://www.autismspeaks.org/inthenews/naar_archive/largest_autism _genetics.php.

81. NAAR used a two-tiered review process for proposals, with a first review carried out by a board of advisors, after which a "lay review committee" consisting of members of the board of trustees who were parents or family members of people with autism reviewed the proposals again. CAN maintained similar provisions for input from parents, although the members of their Scientific Review Council were required *both* to have scientific degrees and be parents of people with autism. Alycia Halladay (associate director of research and programs, NAAR), personal communication, December 27, 2005; Therese Finazzo (grants officer, CAN), personal communication, January 6, 2006.

82. These included the Centers for Professional Excellence in Autism (CPEA), the International Molecular Genetic Study of Autism Consortium (IMGSAC), the Autism Genetics Cooperative (AGC), the Collaborative Programs of Excellence in Autism Research (CPEA), and AGRE. National Alliance for

Autism Research. "NAAR Autism Genome Project: Fact Sheet," www
.autismspeaks.org/docs/agp1a.pdf. Four institutes of the NIH were involved:
the National Institute of Mental Health (NIMH), National Institute of Child
Health and Human Development (NICHD), National Institute of Neurological Disorders and Stroke (NINDS), and National Institute of Deafness and
Other Communication Disorders (NIDCD).

83. NAAR, "Autism Speaks and the National Alliance for Autism Research
(NAAR) Complete Merger" (press release, 2005), http://www.autismspeaks
.org/press/autism_speaks_naar_merger.php; CAN, "Autism Speaks and Cure
Autism Now Complete Merger: Combined Operations of Leading Autism Organizations Will Lead to Enhanced Research, Treatment and Advocacy Programs" (press release), http://www.autismspeaks.org/press/autism_speaks
_can_complete.php).

84. Francesca Happe, Angelica Ronald, and Robert Plomin, "Time to Give Up on a
Single Explanation for Autism," *Nature Neuroscience* 9, no. 10 (2006): 1218–20.

85. Autism Speaks, "Autism FAQ: NAAR Autism Genome Project: Frequently
Asked Questions" (July 19, 2004), http://www.autismspeaks.org/inthenews/
naar_archive/largest_autism_genetics.php.

86. "Everything changed with the introduction of the Affymetrix GeneChip®
Mapping 10K Array. It finally gave researchers the ability to see these tiny
little genetic changes that will ultimately help them figure out what happens
to the DNA of those affected with autism." Autism Speaks, "Autism FAQ:
NAAR Autism Genome Project: Frequently Asked Questions"; The Autism
Genome Project Consortium, "Mapping Autism Risk Loci Using Genetic
Linkage and Chromosomal Rearrangements."

87. For instance, a program at the MIND Institute, an organization founded
by parents at the University of California, Davis, aims to develop tests for
"prospective parents." See Diana Hu-Lince, David W. Craig, Matthew J.
Huentelman, and Dietrich A. Stephan, "The Autism Genome Project: Goals
and Strategies," *American Journal of Pharmacogenomics* 5, no. 4 (2005):
233–46.

88. Art Caplan, "Would You Have Allowed Bill Gates to Be Born? Advances in
Genetic Testing Pose Tough Questions," msnbc.com, http://www.msnbc.msn
.com/id/7899821.

89. On the possibility that stories about "changelings," fairy children hidden in
typical families, are historical accounts of autism, see Lorna Wing and David
Potter, "The Epidemiology of Autistic Spectrum Disorders: Is the Prevalence
Rising?" *Mental Retardation and Developmental Disabilities Research Reviews* 8, no. 3 (2002): 151–61, 151.

90. http://www.gettingthewordout.org/ (accessed May 27, 2007; no longer available).

91. Amy Harmon. "Finding Out: Adults and Autism: An Answer, but Not a Cure,
for A Social Disorder," *New York Times*, April 29, 2004.

92. Rapp (2000); Rapp and Ginsburg (2001).

93. Of course, adults with autism are not a homogeneous group, and some identify as activists while resisting the notion that they can speak for other people with autism. In particular, see Durbin-Westby (2010).

94. Martijn Dekker, "On Our Own Terms: Emerging Autistic Culture" (online essay), http://trainland.tripod.com/martijn.htm (accessed October 14, 2004; no longer available); Jim Sinclair, "Autism Network International: The Development of a Community and Its Culture," http://www.autreat.com/History _of_ANI.html.

95. http://www.gettingthewordout.org/home.php (accessed December 26, 2005; no longer available). For a description of a later protest against a 2007 NYU "public service campaign," which served as a rallying point for the neurodiversity movement, see Kras (2010).

96. http://www.autistics.org/.

97. Although the site was initially published anonymously, Baggs later began writing a blog, including videos that make her identity clear as the author of the Web site.

98. Jim Sinclair, "Don't Mourn for Us," originally published in the Autism Network International newsletter, *Our Voice* 1, no. 3 (1993), based on a presentation given at the 1993 International Conference on Autism, Toronto, Canada, http://www.autreat.com/dont_mourn.html.

99. Ibid. Ian Hacking (2009b, 57) has taken the alien metaphor seriously in an essay on its use by both self-advocates and others, noting that the cognitive differences characteristic of autism make autistic ways of inhabiting the world appear truly "alien" to neurotypical humans. Bridging this difference may require effort on both sides of relationships.

100. Phil Schwartz, "Wearing Two Hats: On Being a Parent and On the Spectrum Myself." The article first appeared in the MAAP newsletter, vol. 2 (2004), http:// www.grasp.org/new_art.htm. Schwartz is not the only person to reflect on the experience of parenthood on the autism spectrum. Another notable account is Prince-Hughes (2005). Also see the description of parents recognizing autism in themselves after their child was diagnosed in Harmon, "Finding Out."

101. Kristin Bumiller (2008, 971–72; 2009, 882) writes that spokespeople for neurodiversity not only are clear that "autistic differences are genetic variations found in the general population," but also that many "readily subscribe to" Simon Baron-Cohen's theory about autism as an example of the "extreme male brain."

102. See, for instance, the Autism Acceptance Project, a parent-run organization online at http://www.taaproject.com/, as well as Gernsbacher (2006).

103. Autreat orientation materials, quoted in Jim Sinclair, "Autism Network International: The Development of a Community and Its Culture," http://www .autreat.com/History_of_ANI.html.

104. Joyce Davidson (2009, 795–97, 802) describes how a distinctive autistic culture has emerged through online communities.

105. See, for instance, Adams (2005, 191).
106. Happe, Ronald, and Plomin, "Time to Give Up on a Single Explanation for Autism."
107. Asperger (1944/1991, 41).
108. Leon Eisenberg, "The Fathers of Autistic Children," *American Journal of Orthopsychiatry* 27, no. 4 (1957): 715–24, 721.
109. Bruno Bettelheim and Emmy Sylvester, "Notes on the Impact of Parental Occupations: Some Cultural Determinants of Symptom Choice in Emotionally Disturbed Children," *American Journal of Orthopsychiatry* 20, no. 4 (1950): 785–95; Simon Baron-Cohen, Sally Wheelwright, Carol Stott, Patrick Bolton, and Ian Goodyer, "Is There a Link between Engineering and Autism?" *Autism* 1, no. 1 (1997): 101–9; Ralph Adolphs, Michael L. Spezio, and Morgan Parlier, "Distinct Face-Processing Strategies in Parents of Autistic Children," *Current Biology* 18, no. 14 (2008): 1090–93.
110. Steve Silberman, "Is There an Epidemic of Autism in the Silicon Valley?" *Wired* (December 2001).
111. Rapp (2000).
112. "The field of complex genetics is replete with many researchers and reviewers who want to promote their overly focused interest in one method at the exclusion of others. However, it is essential that the restricted interests of patients with autism not be reflected in overly restrictive genetic approaches if we are to better understand the genetics of autism in the most expeditious and thorough manner." Veenstra-VanderWeele et al., "Autism as a Paradigmatic Complex Genetic Disorder," 379.
113. See, for instance, studies that link elevated levels of certain metabolites in children with autism to genetic polymorphisms, such as S. Jill James, Stepan Melnyk, Stefanie Jernigan, Mario A. Cleves, et al., "Metabolic Endophenotype and Related Genotypes are Associated with Oxidative Stress in Children with Autism," *American Journal of Medical Genetics Part B: Neuropsychiatric Genetics* 141, no. 8 (2006): 947–56. This work was based on findings of elevated levels of biomarkers associated with oxidative stress in children with autism versus controls, a finding that could be interpreted as evidence that environmental factors combined with genetic factors affect the clinical manifestations of autism. See S. Jill James, Paul Cutler, Stepan Melnyk, Stefanie Jernigan, et al., "Metabolic Biomarkers of Increased Oxidative Stress and Impaired Methylation Capacity in Children with Autism," *American Journal of Clinical Nutrition* 80, no. 6 (2004): 1611–17. Current studies such as the Early Autism Risk Longitudinal Investigation (EARLI) Study and the Autism Birth Cohort (The ABC Project) aim to correlate a range of environmental factors, including substances to which mothers were exposed, with genetic variations and autism symptoms. The EARLI Study, based at multiple U.S. sites, tracks pregnant women who already have a child with an autism spectrum disorder. See http://www.earlistudy.org/ and http://www.abc.columbia

.edu/Home.html. Thanks to Martine Lappe for educating me about current developments in this area.

114. See Jennifer Singh's (2010, 162, 134–47) discussion of the ethical implications of research on copy number variations (CNVs) in autism, one of which has revealed a link between some cases of autism and cancer risk, meaning that children must be more closely monitored for signs of the disease. Singh's dissertation also brings the history of genetic research on autism to the present, including an insightful discussion of the politics of scientific and public investment in genome-wide association studies.

115. For instance, Tyler Cowen writes that "I refer to autistics as the 'infovores' of modern society and I argue that along many dimensions we as a society are working hard to mimic their abilities at ordering and processing information. Tyler Cowen, "Autism as Academic Paradigm," *Chronicle of Higher Education*, August 13, 2009, http://chronicle.com/article/Autism-as-Academic-Paradigm/47033/.

116. "This trend in the science of autism is consistent [with], if not due to, political lobbying and independent funding of U.S. advocacy groups." Singh, Illes, Lazzeroni, and Hallmayer (2009, 793).

117. On the questions raised by seeing ourselves as "simultaneously biological things and human persons—when 'the biological' is fundamentally plastic," see Landecker (2005).

Chapter 5

1. Jack Zimmerman, in McCandless (2003, preface).

2. These surveys are most frequently conducted by groups troubled by the rate of complementary and alternative medicine (CAM) use. See Susan E. Levy, David S. Mandell, Stephanie Merhar, Richard F. Ittenbach, et al., "Use of Complementary and Alternative Medicine among Children Recently Diagnosed with Autistic Spectrum Disorder," *Journal of Developmental and Behavioral Pediatrics* 24, no. 6 (2003): 418–23, which reported a rate of 30 percent; and Susan L. Hyman and Susan E. Levy, "Introduction: Novel Therapies in Developmental Disorders—Hope, Reason, and Evidence," *Mental Retardation and Developmental Disabilities Research Reviews* 11, no. 2 (2005): 107–9. A survey of 112 families of children with an autism spectrum disorder found a rate of use of CAM of 74 percent, using a broad definition of CAM. See Ellen Hanson, Leslie A Kalish, Emily Bunce, Christine Curtis, et al., "Use of Complementary and Alternative Medicine among Children Diagnosed with Autism Spectrum Disorder," *Journal of Autism and Developmental Disorders* 37, no. 4 (2007): 628–36.

3. Helen H. L. Wong and Ronald G. Smith, "Patterns of Complementary and Alternative Medical Therapy Use in Children Diagnosed with Autism Spec-

trum Disorders," *Journal of Autism and Developmental Disorders* 36, no. 7 (2006): 901–9; Vanessa A. Green, Keenan A Pituch, Jonathan Itchon, Aram Choi, et al., "Internet Survey of Treatments Used by Parents of Children with Autism," *Research in Developmental Disabilities* 27, no. 1 (2006): 70–84.

4. This observation has been made by a number of researchers, but I am drawing mainly on Martha Herbert's ideas, for example, Herbert (2011).

5. "FDA Approves the First Drug to Treat Irritability Associated with Autism, Risperdal." (October 6, 2006), http://www.fda.gov/NewsEvents/Newsroom/PressAnnouncements/2006/ucm108759.htm. Also see Benjamin Chavez, Mapy Chavez-Brown, and Jose A. Rey, "Role of Risperidone in Children with Autism Spectrum Disorder," *The Annals of Pharmacotherapy* 40, no. 5 (2006): 909–16.

6. Benedict Carey, "Autism Therapies Still a Mystery, But Parents Take a Leap of Faith," *New York Times*, December 27, 2004.

7. Jennifer Levitz, "Desperate Parents Seek Autism's Cure," *Providence Journal*, August 27, 2005.

8. Gardner Harris and Anahad O'Connor, "On Autism's Cause, It's Parents vs. Research," *New York Times*, June 25, 2005.

9. Emily Shartin, "Difficult Choices. Variety of Treatments Face Parents of Autistic Children," *Boston Globe*, January 25, 2004.

10. James Mulick, quoted in Jeff Grabmeier, "As Autism Diagnoses Grow, So Do Number of Fad Treatments, Researchers Say," *Research News,* Ohio State University (August 20, 2007), http://researchnews.osu.edu/archive/fadaut.htm. Similar views were expressed in Jane Brody, "Trying Anything and Everything for Autism," *New York Times*, January 20, 2009.

11. American Academy of Pediatrics Committee on Children with Disabilities, "Counseling Families Who Choose Complementary and Alternative Medicine for Their Child with Chronic Illness or Disability," *Pediatrics* 107, no. 3 (2001): 598–601. On CAM as a means of "stress reduction," see Hanson et al., "Use of Complementary and Alternative Medicine among Children Diagnosed with Autism Spectrum Disorder," 634. A 2003 survey of CAM use in autism noted correctly that these treatments are often used to address "associated medical difficulties that standard treatments do not address," but did not linger on the possibility that such treatments might "affect autism-specific behaviors," despite parental beliefs. Their main concern was that if practitioners appeared dismissive, parents might avoid standard treatments. Levy et al., "Use of Complementary and Alternative Medicine among Children Recently Diagnosed with Autistic Spectrum Disorder," 418, 422.

12. On the potential risks of elimination diets, see Georgianne L. Arnold, Susan L. Hyman, Robert A. Mooney, and Russell S. Kirby, "Plasma Amino Acids Profiles in Children with Autism: Potential Risk of Nutritional Deficiencies," *Journal of Autism and Developmental Disorders* 33, no. 4 (2003): 449–54; and on concerns about the lack of evidence supporting biomedical interven-

tions, see Susan E. Levy and Susan L. Hyman, "Novel Treatments for Autistic Spectrum Disorders," *Mental Retardation and Developmental Disabilities Research Reviews* 11, no. 2 (2005): 131–42, 132.

13. Hanson et al., "Use of Complementary and Alternative Medicine Among Children Diagnosed with Autism Spectrum Disorder," 631–32. A second survey likewise found an association between both maternal and paternal education level and CAM use. Wong and Smith, "Patterns of Complementary and Alternative Medical Therapy Use in Children Diagnosed with Autism Spectrum Disorders," 907.

14. Adams (2005, 61).

15. Schreibman (2005, 7).On the practice of demarcating between science and nonscience as an "ideological style" adopted in scientists' public statements, see Gieryn (1983).

16. Schreibman (2005, 7, 10–12). Levy and Hyman write that "it is ironic that the intervention for treatment of children with Autistic Spectrum Disorders that has been most carefully studied is an alternative, off-label treatment that gained in popularity prior to adequate scientific scrutiny." Levy and Hyman, "Novel Treatments for Autistic Spectrum Disorders," 132.

17. Schreibman (2005, 4, 7).

18. Fitzpatrick (2009, xvi). Also see Roy Richard Grinker, "Review of *Defeating Autism: A Damaging Delusion*," *International Journal of Epidemiology*, 38, no. 5 (2009): 1415–17.

19. This chapter is based on fieldwork conducted from 2002 to 2008 at Defeat Autism Now! conferences and through interviews with practitioners and researchers who either use biomedical treatments or conduct research related to biomedical frameworks for understanding autism. I have referred to ARI/Defeat Autism Now! by name because it is a unique organization that would be immediately identifiable if I used a pseudonym. Because my fieldwork ended in 2008, my descriptions should not be taken as documentation of current ARI/Defeat Autism Now! recommendations or practices. In this discussion, I occasionally employ the abbreviation DAN! in favor of spelling out "Defeat Autism Now!" because this is the conventional spoken usage at conferences, although the abbreviation never appears in ARI's official materials. The organization dropped the Defeat Autism Now! name in 2011, but I have retained it because it was current at the time of my fieldwork.

20. For example, Levy and Hyman, "Novel Treatments for Autistic Spectrum Disorders," 132, who reference the "DAN!™ approach" as an example of "biological treatments" in general. Others sites that promote biomedical interventions include Autism One conferences and Talk About Curing Autism (TACA).

21. Patricia Morris Buckley, "Dr. Bernard Rimland Is Autism's Worst Enemy," *San Diego Jewish Journal*, October 2002; Bernard Rimland, quoted in Noel Osment, "Keying In on the Secret of Autism: Father Is Devoted to His Son, and

to Finding an Answer," *San Diego Union*, July 10, 1988. At one Defeat Autism Now! conference (Fall 2002, San Diego), Rimland told a joke that fell—resoundingly—flat. After a moment of embarrassed silence, the audience erupted in laughter, realizing that his inability to deliver the joke was in fact the joke itself.

22. Buckley, "Dr. Bernard Rimland is Autism's Worst Enemy"; Osment, "Keying In on the Secret of Autism."

23. The diagnosis was later confirmed by their pediatrician. Bernard Rimland, "The History of the Autism Research Institute and the Defeat Autism Now! (DAN!) Project," in Edelson and Rimland (2003, 13).

24. Rimland (1972).

25. Osment, "Keying In on the Secret of Autism"; Alan O. Ross, review of *Infantile Autism: The Syndrome and Its Implications for a Neural Theory of Behavior* (Appleton-Century-Crofts, 1964), *American Journal of Mental Deficiency* 69, no. 4 (1965): 592–93.

26. Rimland, "The History of the Autism Research Institute and the Defeat Autism Now! (DAN!) Project," 14. For the *Autism Research Review International*, see index of volumes 1 to 18, http://www.autism.com/ari/newsletter/index_a.asp.

27. See "Appendix: Suggested Diagnostic Check List" in Rimland (1964, 219). The checklist included questions about gut problems, reactions to "bright lights, bright colors, unusual sounds," "unusual cravings" for foods, loss of verbal skills after acquiring them, and fine motor coordination, along with more conventional diagnostic measures for autism. "Form E-2," a parent assessment of pharmaceutical therapies, biomedical treatments and special diets, has been produced and collated by ARI since 1967. They report that they have collected over 40,000 of these forms, designed to contrast the efficacy of a variety of treatments. Also see http://www.autism.com/pro_parentratings.asp, "Parent Ratings of Behavioral Effects of Biomedical Interventions," updated March 2009.

28. Williams (1956/1998, 5) drew on Archibald Garrod's idea of "chemical individuality" and "genetotrophic diseases" caused by interactions among genetic variation, unique nutritional needs, and environment leading to functional deficiencies. Murphy (2000, 101–3) describes how the idea of "biochemical individuality" was also important for clinicians developing the field of clinical ecology in the 1960s.

29. The two doctors treating Down syndrome were Ruth Harrell and Henry Turkel. Bernard Rimland, "Vitamin and Mineral Supplementation as a Treatment for Autistic and Mentally Retarded Persons" (presentation to the President's Committee on Mental Retardation, Washington, DC, September 20, 1984), 5.

30. Megadoses are defined as doses above the nutritional requirements for an average person. Bernard Rimland, "The History of the Autism Research Institute and the Defeat Autism Now! (DAN!) Project," 15.

31. Turkel's study was repudiated in a one-page critique in the *Journal of the American Medical Association*, while a 1981 paper by Harrell was the subject

of a negative policy statement by the American Academy of Pediatrics. Rim-land, "Vitamin and Mineral Supplementation as a Treatment for Autistic and Mentally Retarded Persons."

32. Rimland (1976, 200).

33. Pauling offered to answer questions from physicians wary of supporting their patients' participation in a Vitamin B6 study. Letter from Bernard Rimland to vitamin study participants, December 8, 1968, Institute for Child Behavior Research, San Diego, CA. The letter includes contact information for Linus Pauling in the Chemistry Department at the University of California, San Diego. Folder marked "Rimland, B." Box 2, ACC 92-M-41, Lettick Papers. Also see Rimland, "The History of the Autism Research Institute and the Defeat Autism Now! (DAN!) Project," 16; and Bernard Rimland. "The Effect of High Dosage Levels of Certain Vitamins on the Behavior of Children with Severe Mental Disorders," in *Orthomolecular Psychiatry*, eds. D. R. Hawkins and Linus Pauling (San Francisco: W. H. Freeman, 1973).

34. Rimland (1976, 203). Rimland's work on subtyping also dates from this period. See Bernard Rimland, "The Differentiation of Childhood Psychosis: An Analysis of Checklists of 2,218 Psychotic Children," *Journal of Autism and Childhood Schizophrenia* 1, no. 2 (1971): 161–74.

35. Facilitated communication (FC) was developed by Rosemary Crossley as a way to help people with dyspraxia caused by disorders like cerebral palsy to communicate. Rimland argued that Douglas Biklen's later claims about the capabilities of children with autism were exaggerated and needed to be subjected to testing in "Facilitated Communication: A Light at the End of the Tunnel?" *Autism Research Review International* 7, no. 3 (1993): 3; and Stephen M. Edelson, Bernard Rimland, Carol Lee Berger, and Donald Bill-ings, "Evaluation of a Mechanical Hand-Support for Facilitated Commu-nication," *Journal of Autism and Developmental Disorders* 28, no. 2 (1998): 153–57. For a critical review of facilitated communication studies since see Mark P. Mostert, "Facilitated Communication Since 1995: A Review of Pub-lished Studies," *Journal of Autism and Developmental Disorders* 31, no. 3 (2001): 287–313.

36. Rimland, "The History of the Autism Research Institute and the Defeat Au-tism Now! (DAN!) Project,"18.

37. Ibid., 16. Presenters at Defeat Autism Now! conferences continue to empha-size this point. During a talk at the spring 2005 Defeat Autism Now! confer-ence (Quincy, MA, April 14–17, 2005), Sidney Baker described listening to parents as an "ethos" that involved being conscious of the fact that there are "two people in the room," and he spoke movingly of the need to learn to "translate" the intuitions of parents into "technical language."

38. Bernard Rimland and Sidney M. Baker, "Brief Report: Alternative Ap-proaches to the Development of Effective Treatments for Autism, *Journal of Autism and Developmental Disorders* 26, no. 2 (1996): 237–41, 240.

39. Benedict Carey, "Bernard Rimland, 78, Scientist Who Revised View of Autism, Dies," *New York Times*, November 28, 2006.

40. Stephen M. Edelson, "Following the Vision of Dr. Rimland," *Autism Research Review International* 20, no. 3 (2006).

41. Valerie Paradiz, with an introduction by Stephen Edelson, "When the Twain Shall Meet: Biomed and Self-Advocacy," *Autism Research Review International* 24, no. 2 (September 2010): 3, 7. Paradiz, a self-advocate and parent, is married to ARI's director, Stephen Edelson. She writes that "many of us are practicing biomedical approaches without even knowing that we are, simply by avoiding foods we know make us feel bad."

42. Stephen M. Edelson and Jane Johnson, "Moving Forward in 2011," *Autism Research Review International* 24, no. 4 (2010): 3, 7.

43. Adams (2005, 178).

44. For instance, one study conducted by a researcher affiliated with Defeat Autism Now! found abnormally high levels of plasma B6 in children with autism compared to controls (neither group was taking supplements at the time). The researchers hypothesized that the raised levels might have been due to a polymorphism in the enzyme that modifies B6 into its biochemically active form; supplementation of further B6 might bring the intracellular concentration to a level at which the enzyme would be activated. James B. Adams, Frank George, and T. Audhya, "Abnormally High Plasma Levels of Vitamin B6 in Children with Autism Not Taking Supplements Compared to Controls Not Taking Supplements," *Journal of Alternative and Complementary Medicine* 12, no. 1 (2006): 59–63.

45. Sudhir Gupta, "Immunological Treatments for Autism," *Journal of Autism and Developmental Disorders* 30, no. 5 (2000): 475–79. "Dysregulation" can refer to either overactive or underactive immune functioning. A number of parents report chronic ear infections in their children, even prior to their diagnoses. See, for instance, Debbie Bayliss, "Dillon's Story," and Karyn Seroussi, "We Rescued Our Child from Autism," in Edelson and Rimland (2003, 92–96, 299–305).

46. See "Treatment Options for Mercury/Metal Toxicity in Autism and Related Developmental Disabilities: Consensus Position Paper," Autism Research Institute (February 2005), http://www.autism.com/pro_mercurydetox.asp.

47. See, for instance, Harumi Jyonouchi, Sining Sun, and Hoa Le, "Proinflammatory and Regulatory Cytokine Production Associated with Innate and Adaptive Immune Responses in Children with Autism Spectrum Disorders and Developmental Regression," *Journal of Neuroimmunology* 120, no. 1–2 (2001): 170–79; S. Jill James, Paul Cutler, Stepan Melnyk, Stefanie Jernigan, et al., "Metabolic Biomarkers of Increased Oxidative Stress and Impaired Methylation Capacity in Children with Autism," *American Journal of Clinical Nutrition* 80, no. 6 (2004): 1611–17; Diana L. Vargas, Caterina Nascinbene,

Chitra Krishnan, Andrew W. Zimmerman, et al., "Neuroglial Activation and Neuroinflammation in the Brain of Patients with Autism," *Annals of Neurology* 57, no. 1 (2005): 67–81; and Theodore Page, "Metabolic Approaches to the Treatment of Autism Spectrum Disorders," *Journal of Autism and Developmental Disorders* 30, no. 5 (2000): 463–69.

48. A number of studies support the conclusion that children with autism have trouble removing toxic substances from their bodies, including heavy metals. See Amy S. Holmes, Mark F. Blaxill, and Boyd E. Haley, "Reduced Levels of Mercury in First Baby Haircuts of Autistic Children," *International Journal of Toxicology* 22, no. 4 (2003): 277–85; Janet K. Kern, Bruce D. Grannemann, and Madhukar H. Trivedi, "Sulfhydryl-Reactive Metals in Autism," *Journal of Toxicology and Environmental Health, Part A* 70, no. 8 (2007): 715–21.

49. Katie, a parent, quoted in Pangborn and Baker (2005, 17).

50. Chart and explanation by Brenda Kerr, http://www.autism.com/ind _trackprogress.asp. See Murphy (2000, 114–18) on how sufferers from multiple chemical sensitivity (MCS) similarly track their own symptoms and correlate them with minute changes in their environments.

51. Hays (1998).

52. Adams (2005, 188–89).

53. Christina Adams, "Guest Blog: I Am an Autism Mom," http://blog.washingtonpost .com/onbalance/2006/06/guest_blog_i_am_an_autism_mom.html>.

54. The secretin discussion group, founded in 1999, became inactive as of June 23, 2000, and readers were encouraged to join ABMD. While ABMD was founded as a forum for parents to discuss using infusions of the pancreatic hormone secretin as a treatment for autism, many members of ABMD were also once members of the "St. John's" list, which one former participant described as a kind of "big city" for autism. There were discussions of many biomedical treatments, as well as participants with autism diagnoses.

55. Seroussi (2003); Hamilton (2000).

56. Lewis (1998); Edelson and Rimland (2003).

57. The most recent edition includes an extensive additional literature review and discussion by Teresa Binstock, an independent researcher diagnosed with Asperger syndrome who is active in the Defeat Autism Now! community and widely respected by both parents and practitioners. McCandless (2003).

58. Jack Zimmerman, in McCandless (2003, 194).

59. Hamilton (2000).

60. Amy S. Holmes, "My Son, the King of Metals," in Edelson and Rimland (2003, 185).

61. Autism Research Institute, "Defeat Autism Now! U.S. Clinicians," http:// www.autism.com/pro_danlists_results.asp?list=US&type=1.

62. Scott Bono, "Top Ten List" (presentation given at the spring Defeat Autism Now! conference, Quincy, MA, April 14–17, 2005), cited with permission.

63. Robert Tinnell and Craig A. Taillefer, "The Chelation Kid, Episode 107," http://www.webcomicsnation.com/taillefer/chelation_kid/series.php?view=single&ID=49934.

64. One doctor whom I spoke with will not see patients until they have run a battery of allergy and metabolic tests. She maintains that she needs these as a baseline, along with the requirement that a child be entirely gluten-free and casein-free before starting any other therapy.

65. Susan Costen Owens, posting on St. John's List for Autism and Developmental Delay on July 6, 1997, AUTISM@MAELSTROM.STJOHNS.EDU, quoted with permission of author.

66. While Herbert (2009) is not a Defeat Autism Now! doctor, her description of some autism cases as possibly involving "chronic dynamic" processes that may lend themselves to intervention is an excellent description of how this model can apply to research programs.

67. Letter from Susan Costen Owens to Jonathan Shestack, dated 1997 (shared by author and quoted with permission).

68. Jon Pangborn and Sidney Baker both use the phrase "biochemically unique" in talks and presentations and may be implicitly or explicitly referencing Williams (1956/1998, 201) on differences in vitamin requirements between individuals.

69. Although I thought about my dilemma at the time in terms of trust in a very mundane sense, my uncertainty regarding who could be relied on to provide valid information consistent with experimentally supported evidence is also very much part of the modern experience of scientific knowledge. Shapin and Schaffer's (1989) and Shapin's (1994; 1999, 492) work on the problem of trust and witnessing in the creation of modern science is my reference point here, as well as Haraway's (1997a, 23–39) discussion of how Shapin's descriptions relate to feminist science studies.

70. Starr (1982).

71. Murphy (2000, 109) notes similar attitudes in the efforts of MCS sufferers to manage their "personal ecology" and create chemical-free "safe" homes.

72. On the career of the concept of "objectivity" in science, from visual metaphor to moral achievement, see Daston and Galison (1992).

73. Ross, review of *Infantile Autism*.

74. Molly Helt, Elizabeth Kelley, Marcel Kinsbourne, Juhi Pandey, et al., "Can Children with Autism Recover? If So, How?" *Neuropsychology Review* 18, no. 4 (2008) 339–66.

75. Prussing, Sobo, Walker, and Kurtin (2005, 593) observe that this is the case for some parents of children with Down syndrome, who see "CAM as a means of maximizing personal potential," and part of their role as "authoritative advocates and service coordinators for their children."

76. Jill Neimark, "Autism: It's Not Just in the Head," *Discover* (April 2007): 75.

77. Timothy Buie, Daniel B. Campbell, George G. Fuchs, Glenn T. Furuta, et al., "Evaluation, Diagnosis, and Treatment of Gastrointestinal Disorders in

Individuals with ASDs: A Consensus Report," *Pediatrics* 125 Suppl. (January 2010): S1–18. This consensus report did not affirm the existence of unique gastrointestinal symptoms in individuals with ASDs but did acknowledge that further research was warranted.

78. Andrew J. Wakefield, Simon H. Murch, A. Anthony, J. Linnell, et al., "Ileal-Lymphoid-Nodular Hyperplasia, Non-Specific Colitis, and Pervasive Developmental Disorder in Children," *Lancet* 351, no. 9103 (1998): 637–41.

79. Timothy Buie, "Gastrointestinal Issues Encountered in Autism," in *The Neurobiology of Autism* (2nd ed.), eds. Margaret L. Bauman and Thomas L. Kemper (Baltimore, MD: Johns Hopkins University Press, 2004), 103–17.

80. He cited Michael Gershon's (1998) arguments in *The Second Brain*, a book that emphasizes gut-brain connections while remaining firmly situated in neurology—the objective of the book is to describe the gut nervous system rather than theorize how gut pathology might affect neurological functioning indirectly.

81. Timothy Buie, "Processing and Pain in the Gut and Brain" (talk given at the spring Defeat Autism Now! conference, Quincy, MA, April 14–17, 2005).

82. For examples of posturing and self-injury connected to GI pain, see Arthur Krigsman, "Gastrointestinal Pathology in Autism: Description and Treatment," *Medical Veritas* 4 (2007): 1528–36, 1531, 1532. Also see Andrew J. Wakefield, Carol Stott, and Arthur Krigsman, "Getting It Wrong," *Archives of Disease in Childhood* 93, no. 10 (2008): 905–6.

83. The bias toward the brain in autism is even more specific: researchers have focused almost exclusively on the central nervous system, overlooking signs of autonomic nervous system dysfunction in autism, including sleep disorders, difficulty regulating temperature, and gut disturbances. Xue Ming, Peter O. O. Julu, Michael Brimacombe, Susan Connor, and Mary L. Daniels, "Reduced Cardiac Parasympathetic Activity in Children with Autism," *Brain & Development* 27, no. 7 (2005): 509–16.

84 Martha Herbert, personal communication, September 19, 2010. For further development of these concepts see Herbert (forthcoming).

85. Erving Goffman (1959) suggested that medical identities can be understood as a kind of "costume drama" in terms of the role-playing necessary and the specific requirements for attire and equipment. These roles are compromised when practitioners choose to abandon sources of their authority, for instance by admitting their ignorance about causes of certain illnesses. Paul Wolpe (1990, 1994) describes holistic medicine's proposal of an alternative framework for understanding pathology as a form of "medical heresy" that leads to an "ideological battle" in which the orthodoxy's responses can range from cooptation to isolation and outright suppression.

86. Parents have sometimes gone on to coauthor papers with researchers. For example, Sydney Finegold attributed his research program on gut microbiology to the observations and research of Ellen Bolte, the mother of a child with au-

tism. Bolte contacted Feingold while trying to find a doctor to treat her child with vancomycin, an antibiotic, based on her hypothesis that some of her son's symptoms were due to neurotoxins produced by gut flora. Both publications resulting from this research listed Bolte as a coauthor. See Sydney M. Finegold, Denise Molitoris, Yuli Song, Chengxu Liu, et al., "Gastrointestinal Microflora Studies in Late-Onset Autism," *Clinical Infectious Diseases* 35 Suppl. 1 (2002): S6–16; and R. H. Sandler, Sydney M. Finegold, Ellen R. Bolte, Cathleen P. Buchanan, et al., "Short-Term Benefit from Oral Vancomycin Treatment of Regressive-Onset Autism," *Journal of Child Neurology* 15, no. 7 (2000): 429–35.

87. Again, I am using the term "partial" here in Donna Haraway's (1991, 183–201) sense, to mean situated in particular bodies and necessarily incomplete, but also passionate and committed.

88. However, even stabilizing psychiatric categories requires work and is often market-driven. Lakoff (2005, 18–42).

89. Francesca Happe, Angelica Ronald, and Robert Plomin, "Time to Give Up on a Single Explanation for Autism," *Nature Neuroscience* 9, no. 10 (2006): 1218–20. Happe et al. argue that both behavioral and neurological impairments in autism suggest that multiple, independent features may be involved to a different degree in different individuals, although they still consider autism primarily in genetic terms, where behavioral features are potentially separable and attributable to different genes. On Herbert's comments, see Jill Neimark, "Autism: It's Not Just in the Head," *Discover* (April 2007); and Herbert (2005a, 2009, forthcoming).

90. Fromm (1956, 93).

91. Ibid., 103

Chapter 6

1. See the 2003 version of the autism research matrix, which uses risk designations to identify projects that are either more or less likely to be completed in the short or long-term, http://iacc.hhs.gov/reports/2006/evaluating-progress-autism-matrix-nov17.shtml#research-matrix.

2. Announcement for IACC full committee meeting, November 21, 2008. Online at: http://www.nimh.nih.gov/research-funding/scientific-meetings/recurring-meetings/iacc/events/2008/november/iacc-full-committee-meeting.shtml.

3. Brian Vastag, "Congressional Autism Hearings Continue: No Evidence MMR Vaccine Causes Disorder," *Journal of the American Medical Association* 285, no. 20 (2001): 2567–69.

4. There is also published research on the toxicity of thimerosal solution to neural cells in vitro: David S. Baskin, Hop Ngo, and Vladimir V. Didenko,

"Thimerosal Induces DNA Breaks, Capase-3 Activation, Membrane Damage, and Cell Death in Cultured Human Neurons and Fibroblasts," *Toxicological Sciences* 74, no. 2 (2003): 361–68.

5. The study, when it was completed, found no association between the MMR vaccine and autism. Mady Hornig, Thomas Briese, Timothy Buie, Margaret Bauman, et al., "Lack of Association between Measles Virus Vaccine and Autism with Enteropathy: A Case-Control Study," *PLoS ONE* 3, no. 9 (2008): e3140–40, http://www.plosone.org/article/info:doi/10.1371/journal.pone.0003140 .

6. W. Ian Lipkin, presentation at The Autism Summit Conference: Developing a National Agenda, Session on Epidemiological and Environmental Research, Washington, DC, November 19–20, 2003.. The official title for Lipkin's grant was the Pandora's Box Project.

7. Singh, Hallmayer, and Iles (2007, 157) write that "despite a relatively long and intricate history of autism, millions of dollars of funding and thousands of papers in the peer-reviewed literature to explore causes, symptoms and possibilities for intervention, the selective reporting of the press was in sharp contrast to the focus of research and funding," in particular, the emphasis in the press on environmental causes and on vaccines in particular.

8. Durbach (2002).

9. Ibid., 59; Durbach (2005, 114–17).

10. Durbach (2005, 44–46 and 61).

11. Lesli Mitchell, "Secrets and Lies: Is the Astonishing Rise in Autism a Medical Mystery or a Pharmaceutical Shame?" *Salon.com,* August 2, 2000, http://archive.salon.com/mwt/feature/2000/08/02/autism/index.html.

12. Johnston (2004, 279).

13. The treatment guide (Pangborn and Baker 2005, 49–55; 60–64) largely refrains from offering explicit input on detoxification therapies (it details one option), but it does direct readers to a 2005 consensus statement on mercury toxicity and treatment options, including various methods of chelation, available at the ARI Web site. "Treatment Options for Mercury/Metal Toxicity in Autism and Related Developmental Disabilities: Consensus Position Paper" (February 2005), http://www.autism.com/pro_mercurydetox.asp.

14. The first season of the ABC television program *Eli Stone* featured an episode (aired on January 31, 2008) in which a parent sued a vaccine maufacturer for compensation for her son's injury and subsequent autism due to the use of a preservative called "mercuritol" in a flu vaccine. A January 8, 2009, episode of another ABC drama, *Private Practice,* painted a very different picture when a child died of measles because his mother refused to have him vaccinated, believing that an older child had developed autism as a result of the MMR vaccine he received.

15. Mitchell, "Secrets and Lies."

16. Concerns relating to the more familiar form of mercury, methylmercury or organic mercury, are also current in the parent community and public dis-

course. In particular, parents consider the methylmercury accumulated in placental blood as a result of fish consumption and environmental mercury a source of possible cumulative effects.

17. In particular, the researchers claimed that the children showed a characteristic set of bowel changes termed ileo-colonic lymphoid-nodular hyperplasia, an enlargement of the intestinal lymph nodes that by itself is not necessarily pathological, but which seemed to be associated with (or at least occur in conjunction with) physical discomfort and active gut irritation in these children. Andrew J. Wakefield, Simon H. Murch, A. Anthony, J. Linnell, et al., "Ileal-Lymphoid-Nodular Hyperplasia, Non-Specific Colitis, and Pervasive Developmental Disorder in Children" *Lancet* 351, no. 9103 (1998): 637–41.

18 Anders Ekbom, Peter Daszak. Wolfgang Kraaz, and Andrew J. Wakefield, "Crohn's Disease After In-Utero Measles Virus Exposures," *Lancet* 348, no. 9026 (1996): 515–17.

19. Jo Revill, "Scientist's Warning Prompts Fears over Measles Vaccine," *Evening Standard*, February 26, 1998.

20. Kamran Abbasi, "Man, Mission, Rumpus," *British Medical Journal* 322, no. 7281 (2001): 306; Brian Deer, "Secrets of the MMR Scare: How the Measles Crisis Was Meant to Make Money," *British Medical Journal* 342 (2011): c5258.

21. "Reid Calls for Probe into MMR Report," *Mail on Sunday*, February 22, 2004. The editor of the *Lancet* wrote that "had we appreciated the full context in which the work reported in the 1998 *Lancet* paper by Wakefield and colleagues was done, publication would not have taken place the way it did." Richard Horton, "The Lessons of MMR," *The Lancet* 363, no. 9411 (2004): 747–49.

22. Brian Deer, "Revealed: MMR Research Scandal," *Sunday Times*, February 22, 2004; Glenn Frankel, "Charismatic Doctor at Vortex of Vaccine Dispute: Experts Argue over Findings, but Specialist Sees Possible MMR Link to Autism," *Washington Post*, July 11, 2004. The Legal Aid Fund serves to provide legal services in the U.K. to those who cannot afford them. It is now called the Community Legal Service Fund and is run by the Community Legal Services Commission, which replaced the Legal Aid Board. See http://www.clsdirect.org .uk/legalhelp/clscharges.jsp.

23 However, the only research article Wakefield produced after 2006 was withdrawn before publication by the journal *Neurotoxicology* for unspecified reasons (a version of the article was published a year later, without Wakefield listed as a coauthor). For earlier work, see Andrew J. Wakefield, "Enterocolitis in Children with Developmental Disorders," *American Journal of Gastroenterology* 95, no. 9 (2000): 2285–95; Andrew J. Wakefield, "Enterocolitis, Autism and Measles Virus," *Molecular Psychiatry* 7 Suppl. 2 (2002): S44–46; and H. Kawashima, T. Mori, Y. Kashiwagi, K. Takekuma, et al., "Detection and Sequencing of Measles Virus from Peripheral Mononuclear Cells from

Patients with Inflammatory Bowel Disease and Autism," *Digestive Diseases and Sciences* 45, no. 4 (2000): 723–29.

24. See, for instance, testimony reproduced in Neil Z. Miller, *Vaccines, Autism and Childhood Disorders: Crucial Data That Could Save Your Child's Life* (Santa Fe, New Mexico: New Atlantean Press, 2003); and Abbasi, "Man, Mission, Rumpus," 306.

25. James A. Wright and Clare Polack, "Understanding Variation in Measles-Mumps-Rubella Immunization Coverage—A Population-Based Study," *European Journal of Public Health* 16, no. 2 (2006): 137–42; Press Association, "MMR Doctor 'Failed to Act in Interests of Children,'" *Guardian*, January 20, 2010.

26. The *Lancet* editors pointed in particular to the facts that children had not been "consecutively referred" to Wakefield's clinic as had originally been reported, and that the study had not been approved by the "local ethics committee." The Editors of the *Lancet*, "Retraction—Ileal-Lymphoid-Nodular Hyperplasia, Non-Specific Colitis, and Pervasive Developmental Disorder in Children," *Lancet* 375, no. 9713 (2010): 455. See also Gardiner Harris, "Journal Retracts 1998 Paper Linking Autism to Vaccines," *New York Times*, February 2, 2010.

27. The council also barred one colleague of Wakefield's, John Walker-Smith, but cleared another, Simon Murch. John F. Burns, "British Medical Council Bars Doctor Who Linked Vaccine with Autism," *New York Times*, May 25, 2010. The council referenced the fact that Wakefield had paid healthy children for blood samples at his son's birthday party. The interview with Wakefield quoted in the article above aired on NBC's *Today* show on May 24, 2010.

28. Brian Deer, "Secrets of the MMR Scare: How the Case against the MMR Vaccine was Fixed," *British Medical Journal* 342 (2011): c5347; Deer, "Secrets of the MMR Scare: How the Measles Crisis Was Meant to Make Money," c5258.

29. Jane E. Libbey, Thayne L. Sweeten, William M. McMahon, and Robert S. Fujinami, "Autistic Disorder and Viral Infections," *Journal of NeuroVirology* 11, no. 1 (2005): 1–10.

30. Vijendra K. Singh, Sheren X. Lin, and Victor C. Yang, "Serological Association of Measles Virus and Human Herpesvirus-6 with Brain Autoantibodies in Autism," *Clinical Immunology and Immunopathology* 98 (1998): 105–8; Vijendra K. Singh, Sheren X. Lin, Elizabeth Newell, and Courtney Nelson, "Abnormal Measles-Mumps-Rubella Antibodies and CNS Autoimmunity in Children with Autism," *Journal of Biomedical Science* 9, no. 4 (2002): 359–64.

31. Harumi Jyonouchi, Sining Sun, and Hoa Le, "Proinflammatory and Regulatory Cytokine Production Associated with Innate and Adaptive Immune Responses in Children with Autism Spectrum Disorders and Developmental Regression," *Journal of Neuroimmunology* 120, no. 1–2 (2001): 170–79.

32. The study did not draw any explicit connections to vaccines. Diana L. Vargas, Caterina Nascimbene, Chitra Krishnan, Andrew W. Zimmerman, et al.,

"Neuroglial Activation and Neuroinflammation in the Brain of Patients with Autism," *Annals of Neurology* 57, no. 1 (2005): 67–81. Markers of inflammation were unexpectedly absent in samples of serum and cerebrospinal fluid. Andrew W. Zimmerman, Jarumi Jyonouchi, Anne M. Comi, Susan L. Connors, et al., "Cerebrospinal Fluid and Serum Markers of Inflammation in Autism," *Pediatric Neurology* 33, no. 3 (2005).

33. The coauthors who retracted their interpretation stated that "further evidence has been forthcoming in studies from the Royal Free Centre for Paediatric Gastroenterology and other groups to support and extend these findings." Simon Murch, Andrew Anthony, David H. Casson, Mohsin Malik, et al., "Retraction of an Interpretation," *Lancet* 363, no. 9411 (2004): 750.

34. Murch et al., "Retraction of an Interpretation," 750. The *Lancet's* later decision to retract the article in its entirety in February 2010 effectively overrode the earlier, partial, retraction.

35. A. J. Wakefield, "Autistic Enterocolitis: Is It a Histopathological Entity?" *Histopathology* 50, no. 3 (2007): 380–84.

36 However, the study did find elevated rates of regression among children who also had GI disturbances, suggesting an association between the two. Mady Hornig, Thomas Briese, Timothy Buie, Margaret L. Bauman, et al., "Lack of Association between Measles Virus Vaccine and Autism with Enteropathy: A Case-Control Study," *PLoS ONE* 3, no. 9 (2008): e3140–50. An earlier study failed to find measles virus in the immune cells of children with autism. Yasmin D'Souza, Eric Fombonne, and Brian J. Ward, "No Evidence of Persisting Measles Virus in Peripheral Blood Mononuclear Cells From Children with Autism Spectrum Disorder," *Pediatrics*, 118, no. 4 (2006): 1664–75.

37. Baker (2008, 246).

38. Arthur Allen, "The Not-So-Crackpot Autism Theory," *New York Times* Magazine, November 10, 2002. Allen quotes Neal Halsey, head of the Hopkins Institute for Vaccine Safety and a prominent supporter of childhood immunizations, on the growth of his own concerns regarding thimerosal during a June 1999 visit to the FDA.

39. These incidents included industrial pollution that contaminated fish in Japan, leading to outbreaks of Minamata disease in the 1950s and 1960s, and an episode in 1971–1972 in which thousands of people in Iraq consumed bread made from grain treated with a methylmercury fungicide. National Research Council (2000). On the poisoning in Iraq, see T. W. Clarkson, L Amin-Zaki, and S. K. Al-Tikriti, "An Outbreak of Methylmercury Poisoning due to Consumption of Contaminated Grain," *Federation Proceedings* 35, no. 12 (1976): 2395-99.

40. See National Research Council (2000); Daniel A. Axelrad, David C. Bellinger, Louise M. Ryan, and Tracey J. Woodruff, "Dose-Response Relationship of Prenatal Mercury Exposure and IQ: An Integrative Analysis of Epidemiologic Data," *Environmental Health Perspectives* 115, no. 4 (2007): 609–15;

Philippe Grandjean, Pal Weihe, Roberta F. White, Frodi Debes, et al., "Cognitive Deficit in 7-Year-Old Children with Prenatal Exposure to Methylmercury," *Neurotoxicology and Teratology* 19, no. 6 (1997): 417–28.

41. National Research Council (2000, 72); Raymond F. Palmer, Stephen Blanchard, Zachary Stein, David Mandell, et al., "Environmental Mercury Release, Special Education Rates, and Autism Disorder: An Ecological Study of Texas," *Health Place* 12, no. 2 (2006): 203–9.

42. See the FDA Web site, "Mercury Levels in Commercial Fish and Shellfish," http://www.cfsan.fda.gov/~frf/sea-mehg.html, and their "Advisory on Mercury in Seafood," http://www.cfsan.fda.gov/~dms/admehg3.html.

43. Baker (2008, 246).

44. SafeMinds, Sensible Action for Ending Mercury-Induced Neurological Disorders Web site, http://www.safeminds.org/. Generation Rescue, founded by J. B. and Lisa Handley, has also been a vocal proponent of these views since its founding in 2005—the actress Jenny McCarthy is its most visible member. Generation Rescue Web site, http://www.generationrescue.org/.

45. Sally Bernard, Lyn Redwood, Albert Enayati, and Teresa Binstock, "Autism: A Novel Form of Mercury Poisoning?" *Medical Hypotheses* 56, no. 4 (2001): 472–81.

46. Karin B. Nelson and Margaret L. Bauman, "Thimerosal and Autism?" *Pediatrics* 111, no. 3 (2003): 674–79. Nelson and Bauman argued that there was no epidemiological evidence of a connection and that the biological (as opposed to behavioral) signs of methylmercury toxicity were very different from autism. The two authors discuss the *Medical Hypotheses* piece as well as a later article, in which the group made an even more emphatic case for the thimerosal-autism hypothesis, Sally Bernard, Albert Enayati, H. Roger, Teresa Binstock, et al., "The Role of Mercury in the Pathogenesis of Autism," *Molecular Psychiatry* 7 Suppl. 2 (2002): S42–43.

47. Kirby (2005, 141–44).

48. Arthur Allen, "The Not-So-Crackpot Autism Theory."

49. "On average, for each 1,000 lb. of environmentally released mercury, there was a 3% increase in the rate of special education services and a 61% increase in the rate of autism." Palmer et al., "Environmental Mercury Release, Special Education Rates, and Autism Disorder," 203–9; Thomas M. Burbacher, Danny D. Shen, Noelle Liberato, Kimberly S. Grant, et al., "Comparison of Blood and Brain Mercury Levels in Infant Monkeys Exposed to Methylmercury or Vaccines Containing Thimerosal," *Environmental Health Perspectives* 113, no. 8 (2005): 1015–21.

50. Damani K. Parran, Angela Barker, and Marion Ehrich, "Effects of Thimerosal on NGF Signal Transduction and Cell Death in Neuroblastoma Cells," *Toxicological Sciences* 86, no. 1 (2005): 132–40. Also see Baskin et al., "Thimerosal Induces DNA Breaks, Caspase-3 Activation, Membrane Damage, and Cell Death in Cultured Human Neurons and Fibroblasts,": 361–68.

51. Parran et al., "Effects of Thimerosal on NGF Signal Transduction and Cell Death in Neuroblastoma Cells," 132–40; Ramuel R. Goth, Ruth A. Chu, Gennady Cherednichenko, and Issac N. Pessah, "Uncoupling of ATP-Mediated Calcium Signaling and Dysregulated Interleukin-6 Secretion in Dendritic Cells by Nanomolar Thimerosal," *Environmental Health Perspectives* 114, no. 7 (2006): 1083–91.

52. Investigators have found evidence of increased oxidative stress in children with autism and possible evidence of impaired DNA methylation. DNA methylation plays a central role in neural development and regulation. S. Jill James, Paul Cutler, Stepan Melnyk, Stefanie Jernigan, et al., "Metabolic Biomarkers of Increased Oxidative Stress and Impaired Methylation Capacity in Children with Autism," *American Journal of Clinical Nutrition* 80, no. 6 (2004): 1611–17; Janet K. Kern and Anne M. Jones, "Evidence of Toxicity, Oxidative Stress, and Neuronal Insult in Autism," *Journal of Toxicology and Environmental Health, Part B* 9, no. 6 (2006): 485–99; S. Jill James, Stepan Melnyk, Stefanie Jernigan, Mario A. Cleves, et al., "Metabolic Endophenotype and Related Genotypes Are Associated with Oxidative Stress in Children with Autism," *American Journal of Medical Genetics Part B: Neuropsychiatric Genetics* 141, no. 8 (2006): 947–56.

53. Kenneth P. Stoller, "Autism as a Minamata Disease Variant: Analysis of a Pernicious Legacy," *Medical Veritas* 3 (2006): 772–80; M. Waly, H. Olteanu, R. Banerjee, S.-W. Choi, et al., "Activation of Methionine Synthase by Insulin-Like Growth Factor-1 and Dopamine: A Target for Neurodevelopmental Toxins and Thimerosal," *Molecular Psychiatry* 9, no. 4 (2004): 358–70.

54. S. Jill James, William Slikker, Stepan Melnyk, Elizabeth New, et al., "Thimerosal Neurotoxicity Is Associated with Glutathione Depletion: Protection with Glutathione Precursors," *NeuroToxicology* 26, no. 1 (2004): 1–8.

55. M. Hornig, D. Chian, and W. I. Lipkin, "Neurotoxic Effects of Postnatal Thimerosal Are Mouse Strain Dependent." *Molecular Psychiatry* 9, no. 9 (2004): 1–13.

56. Anshu Agrawal, Poonam Kaushal, Sudhanshu Agrawal, Sastry Gollapudi, et al., "Thimerosal Induces TH2 Responses via Influencing Cytokine Secretion by Human Dendritic Cells," *Journal of Leukocyte Biology* 81, no. 2 (2007): 474–82.

57. Thomas H. Maugh II, "Study Finds Genetic Link Between Autism, Vaccines," *LA Times*, June 9, 2004. Researchers were unable to reproduce the study—see Robert F. Berman, Isaac N. Pessah, Peter R. Mouton, Deepak Mav, et al., "Low-Level Neonatal Thimerosal Exposure: Further Evaluation of Altered Neurotoxic Potential in SJL Mice," *Toxicological Sciences*, 101, no. 2 (2008): 294–309.

58. Studies that found lower levels of mercury in the hair of autistic children are Amy S. Holmes, Mark F. Blaxill, and Boyd E. Haley, "Reduced Levels of Mercury in First Baby Haircuts of Autistic Children," *International Journal of Toxicology* 22, no. 4 (2003): 277–85; and Janet K. Kern, Bruce D.

Grannemann, Madhukar H. Trivedi, and James B. Adams, "Sulfhydryl-Reactive Metals in Autism," *Journal of Toxicology and Environmental Health Part A* 70, no. 8 (2007): 715–21. The latter article found that children with autism may sequester not only mercury, but also lead, arsenic, and cadmium. Another article argued that the differences between children with autism and their typically developing siblings in levels of hair mercury was not significant. P. Gail Williams, Joseph H. Hersh, AnnaMary Allard, and Lonnie L. Sears, "A Controlled Study of Mercury Levels in Hair Samples of Children with Autism as Compared to Their Typically Developing Siblings," *Research in Autism Spectrum Disorders* 2, no. 1 (2008): 170–75.

59. "Treatment Options for Mercury/Metal Toxicity in Autism and Related Developmental Disabilities: Consensus Position Paper," Autism Research Institute (February, 2005), http://www.autism.com/pro_mercurydetox.asp; Karen Kane and Virginia Linn, "Boy Dies During Autism Treatment," *Pittsburgh Post-Gazette*, August 25, 2005, http://www.post-gazette.com/pg/05237/559756.stm; M. J. Brown, T. Willis, B. Omalu, and R. Leiker, "Deaths Resulting from Hypocalcemia after Administration of Edetate Disodium: 2003–2005," *Pediatrics* 118, no. 2: e534–36. At the time, there was speculation that some of the confusion may have resulted from the similarities between the brand names of the two substances, Versenate (edetate calcium disodium) and Endrate (edetate disodium).

60. Karen Kane, "Drug Error, Not Chelation Therapy, Killed Boy, Expert Says," *Pittsburgh Post-Gazette*, January 18, 2006, http://www.post-gazette.com/pg/06018/639721.stm.

61. National Institute of Mental Health (NIMH),"New NIMH Program Launches Autism Trials," NIMH (September 7, 2006), http://www.nimh.nih.gov/science-news/2006/new-nimh-research-program-launches-autism-trials.shtml; Carla K. Johnson, "Fringe Autism Treatment Could Get Federal Study," *Associated Press Archive,* July 8, 2008.

62. Ibid.; Erik Stokstad, "Stalled Trial for Autism Highlights Dilemma for Alternative Treatments," *Science* 321, no. 5887 (July 2008): 326; Carla K. Johnson, "U.S. Researchers Call Off Controversial Autism Study," *Associated Press Archive,* September 18, 2008.

63. Other groups have produced results that call into question the idea that children with autism have higher heavy metal burdens than typically developing controls, for example, Sarah E. Soden, Jennifer A. Lowry, Carol B. Garrison, and Gary S. Wasserman, "24-Hour Provoked Urine Excretion Test for Heavy Metals in Children with Autism and Typically Developing Controls, A Pilot Study," *Clinical Toxicology* 45, no. 5 (2007): 476–81.

64. See Congressman Dan Burton's Web site, http://www.house.gov/burton/. Burton has been a strong advocate of investigations into both the use of thimerosal and the MMR vaccine, starting with testimony as committee chairman to the House of Representatives Committee on Government Reform on

"Autism: Present Challenges, Future Needs. Why the Increased Rates?" April 6, 2000. A number of parents testified at the hearing, as well as Drs. Andrew Wakefield, Bernard Rimland, Vigendra K. Singh, and Mary Megson, among others. See transcripts included in Miller, *Vaccines, Autism and Childhood Disorders*. Also see Rep. Dave Weldon, "Before the Institute of Medicine" (comments), Institute of Medicine, February 9, 2004, www.iom.edu/~/media/Files/Activity%20Files/.../IOMWeldonFinal2904.pdf.

65. Robert F. Kennedy Jr., "Deadly Immunity: Robert F. Kennedy Jr. Investigates the Government Cover-Up of a Mercury/Autism Scandal," *Rolling Stone*, June 20, 2005, http://www.rollingstone.com/politics/story/7395411/deadly _immunity/ (no longer available); Kirby (2005).

66. Offit (2008, 149–53).

67. Carole Gan, "Four Dads' Passion Leads to New University-Based Institute for Treating Autism and Other Disorders: Team Effort and Relentless Drive Makes Parents' Vision a Reality" (press release, March 19, 1999), http://www .ucdmc.ucdavis.edu/news/MIND_Inst.html.

68. Immunization Safety Review Committee, *Immunization Safety Review: Vaccines and Autism* (Washington, DC: National Academies Press, May 17, 2004).

69. Both the National Vaccine Information Center and SafeMinds immediately issued press releases claiming that the IOM report was biased and incomplete and had ignored evidence in support of the mercury–autism hypothesis.

70. Kathleen Stratton, Alicia Gable, and Marie C. McCormick, eds., *Immunization Safety Review: Thimerosal-Containing Vaccines and Neurodevelopmental Disorders.* (Washngton, D.C.: National Academies Press, October 1, 2001); Kathleen Stratton, Alicia Gable, Padma Shetty, and Marie McCormick, eds., *Immunization Safety Review: Measles-Mumps-Rubella Vaccine and Autism* (Washington, DC: National Academies Press, April 23, 2001).

71. SafeMinds obtained the meeting's transcript through the Freedom of Information Act and posted it, correspondence following the meeting, and their own analysis and summary, "Analysis and Critique of the CDC's Handling of the Thimerosal Exposure Assessment Based on Vaccine Safety Datalink (VSD) Information (October 2003)," on their Web site, http://www.safeminds .org/government-affairs/foia/simpsonwood.html. For the particular points mentioned, see p. 38 as well as Kirby (2005, 168–74).

72. Offit (2008, 91–94).

73. Eric Fombonne, Rita Zakarian, Andrew Bennett, Linyan Meng, et al., "Pervasive Developmental Disorders in Montreal, Quebec, Canada: Prevalence and Links with Immunizations," *Pediatrics* 118, no. 1 (2006): 139–50. Other important studies have been B. Taylor, E. Miller, R. Lingam, N. Andrews, et al.,"Measles, Mumps, and Rubella Vaccination and Bowel Problems or Developmental Regression in Children with Autism: Population Study, *British Medical Journal* 324, no. 7334 (2002): 393–96; and Kreesten Meldgaard Madsen, Anders Hviid, Mogens Vestergaard, Diana Schendel, et al., "A

Population-Based Study of Measles, Mumps, and Rubella Vaccination and Autism," *New England Journal of Medicine* 347, no. 19 (2002): 1477–82; and the study discussed at Simpsonwood, Thomas Verstraeten, Robert L. Davis, Frank DeStefano, Tracy A. Lieu, et al., "Safety of Thimerosal-Containing Vaccines: A Two-Phased Study of Computerized Health Maintenance Organization Databases," *Pediatrics* 112, no. 5 (2003): 1039–48. A metananalysis of studies on autism and MMR vaccine also found no association: Kumanan Wilson, Ed Mills, Cory Ross, Jessie McGowan, et al., "Association of Autistic Spectrum Disorder and the Measles, Mumps and Rubella Vaccine: A Systematic Review of Current Epidemiological Evidence," *Archives of Pediatric and Adolescent Medicine* 157, no.7 (2003): 628–34. A more recent study also took prenatal exposure into account, finding no association. Cristofer S. Price, William W. Thompson, Barbara Goodson, Eric S. Weintraub, et al., "Prenatal and Infant Exposure to Thimerosal from Vaccines and Immunoglobulins and Risk of Autism," *Pediatrics* 126, no. 4 (2010): 656–64.

74. As Epstein (1996) has documented, similar disputes played out around trials of medications for HIV/AIDS, in which patient advocates had very different ideas from investigators about what constituted "good science" in a clinical trial.

75. The National Immunization Program was responsible for overseeing immunization coverage and monitoring safety through the Immunization Safety Branch. In 2005, the Immunization Safety Branch, now the Immunization Safety Office (ISO), was moved to a different branch of the CDC. Nevertheless, a "mismatch in resources" remains, encouraging doubts about the CDC's commitment to vaccine safety—the NCIRD (formerly the National Immunization Program) receives about $3 billion in funds per year, while the ISO was getting about $20 millon as of 2008. Louis Z. Cooper, Heidi J. Larson, and Samuel L. Katz, "Protecting Public Trust in Immunization," *Pediatrics* 122, no. 1 (2008): 149–53, 152.

76. The requirement for post-market monitoring was a provision of the National Childhood Vaccine Injury Act, PL 99-660. The VAERS database was established in cooperation with the FDA and the VSD in cooperation with several HMOs.

77. Johnston (2004) describes a television segment that showed a mother attempting to navigate the forms and paperwork required to file a report, suggesting that the system is anything but streamlined.

78. American Academy of Pediatrics, "Study Fails to Show a Connection between Thimerosal and Autism" (press release).

79. See, for instance, the exchange about a 2003 article, Mark R. Geier and David A. Geier, "Neurodevelopmental Disorders after Thimerosal-Containing Vaccines: A Brief Communication," *Experimental Biology and Medicine* 228, no. 6 (2003): 660–64; Joshua R. Mann, "Questions About Thimerosal Remain," *Experimental Biology and Medicine* 228 (2003): 991–92; and David A. Geier

and Mark R. Geier, "Response to Comments by J. R. Mann," *Experimental Biology and Medicine* 228, no. 9 (2003): 993–94.

80. "Joint Statement on the Use of the CDC's Vaccine Safety Datalink for Thimerosal Investigations," CAN-Alert listserv, November 3, 2003.

81. R. Lingam, A. Simmons, N. Andrews, E. Miller, et al., "Prevalence of Autism and Parentally Reported Triggers in a North East London Population," *Archives of Disease in Childhood* 88, no. 8 (2003): 666–70, 668–69. The authors suggest that some parents changed their accounts of the onset of their child's autism to reflect developmental regression only after Wakefield's first public statements about the MMR vaccine. The article dates this phenomenon to August 1997, seven months before the press conference regarding the *Lancet* study, but close in time to some other reports of statements by Wakefield, e.g., Louise McKee, "New MMR Studies Revive Crohn's and Autism Fears," *Pulse*, August 2, 1997.

82. Kathy Blanco, "Story of Ryan and Stacy Blanco," in Edelson and Rimland (2003, 105).

83. Jason Rowe and Angelene Rowe, "Love Never Fails," in Edelson and Rimland (2003, 279).

84. Tory Mead and George Mead, "Through a Glass Darkly," in Edelson and Rimland (2003, 251).

85. Kathy Blanco, "Story of Ryan and Stacy Blanco," in Edelson and Rimland (2003, 108).

86. Dianne Doggett, "A Very Tough Kid," in Edelson and Rimland (2003, 145).

87. For instance, Murphy (2000) and Brown et al. (2001).

88. Vijendra K. Singh, "Letter to the Editor: Thimerosal is Unrelated to Autoimmune Autism," *Pediatric Allergy and Immunology* 18, no. 1 (2007): 89.

89. Her words were, "Thank goodness for the vaccine court." Bernadine Healy, "Fighting the Vaccine-Autism War," *U.S. News and World Report*, April 10, 2008, http://health.usnews.com/articles/health/brain-and-behavior/2008/04/10/fighting-the-autism-vaccine-war.html.

90. Gardiner Harris, "Opening Statements in Case on Autism and Vaccinations," *New York Times*, June 12, 2007.

91. Johnston (2004). The VICP is administered jointly by the Department of Health and Human Services, the U.S. Court of Federal Claims, and the Department of Justice. The hearing process requires a substantial contribution from each member organization, and even then requires a degree of streamlining, such as the Special Masters, in order to function. Information on the program can be found at http://www.cdc.gov/nip/vacsafe/.

92. The figure is from the Health Resources and Services Administration, part of the Department of Health and Human Services, which administers the VICP. Online at http://hrsa.gov/vaccinecompensation/omnibusproceeding.htm.

93. For instance, in the Cedillo case see U.S. Court of Federal Claims, *Theresa Cedillo and Michael Cedillo, as Parents and Natural Guardians of Michelle*

Cedillo, Petitioners v. Secretary of Health and Human Services, Respondent, Docket No. 98-916V, June 19, 2007, 1364, 1649–51. Also see the dispute over dating the presence of autistic symptoms for Jordan King and William Mead: *Fred and Mylinda King, Parents of Jordan King, a Minor, Petitioners v. Secretary of Health and Human Services, Respondent,* Docket No. 03-584V; and *George and Victoria Mead, Parents of William P. Mead, a Minor, Petitioners v. Secretary of Health and Human Services, Respondent,* Docket No. 03-215V, May 30, 2008, 4221–44. In the Cedillo case, the parents were reluctant to release the complete videotapes rather than excerpts to the respondent's experts, citing privacy concerns, until the Special Master assigned to the case required that they produce the tapes. George L. Hastings, "Ruling on Respondent's 'Motion for Production'" in *Cedillo v. Secretary of Health and Human Services,* filed May 10, 2007. Transcripts for all referenced cases can be found at http://www.uscfc.uscourts.gov/omnibus-autism-proceeding.

94. *Cedillo v. Secretary of Health and Human Services,* 2879.

95. This was David Amaral, director of the MIND Institute at the University of California, Davis, and Peter Hotez, president of the Sabin Vaccine Institute, on the radio program *Talk of the Nation,* June 14, 2007.

96. Rachel Heathcock, "Measles Outbreaks in London, United Kingdom—A Preliminary Report," *Eurosurveillance* 13, no. 15 (2008): 18829.

97. Sugarman (2007, 1277). Cases utilizing scientific evidence delivered by expert witnesses require that the science used reflect the consensus of the scientific community in addition to being testable and relevant to the case at hand. Specifically, under the *Daubert* standard, the testimony of an expert witness must be both "relevant" and "reliable," where reliability is defined in terms of standards that include testability, consensus of the scientific community, and rates of errors. For a thorough discussion of the standards for evidence in federal cases, see Jasanoff (1997).

98. Mark Blaxill, "Something Is Rotten in Denmark," unpublished presentation (May 18, 2004), http://www.safeminds.org/research/commentary.html.

99. *Cedillo v. Secretary of Health and Human Services,* 14.

100. *King and Mead v. Secretary of Health and Human Services,* 72.

101. *King and Mead v. Secretary of Health and Human Services,* 60. The full quote reads "What has no place here are experts at the margins of legitimate science who present untested theories, untested hypothesis [sic], speculation, conjecture, logical fallacies based on post hoc ergo propter hoc reasoning."

102. *King v. Secretary of Health and Human Services* and *Mead vs. Health and Human Services,* 56–57.

103. *King v. Secretary of Health and Human Services* and *Mead vs. Health and Human Services,* 4368–69.

104. Poling's parents are not convinced that she in fact had an underlying disorder, but the court chose to agree with the theory that proposed an underlying disorder as the source of Poling's illness. Gardiner Harris, "Deal in Autism Case Fu-

els Debate on Vaccine," *New York Times*, March 8, 2008; Marie McCullough, "Autism Theory Gains Support: Conceding a Rare Vaccine Tie," *Philadelphia Inquirer*, May 28, 2008, http://www.philly.com/inquirer/home_top_stories/ 20080529_Autism_theory_gains_support.html. Commentators cautioned that it was unlikely that the same mechanism applied to many other cases. Paul Offit, "Inoculated Against Facts," *New York Times*, March 31, 2008.

105. Donald G. McNeil Jr., "Court Says Vaccine Not to Blame for Autism," *New York Times*, February 12, 2009.

106. In the course of the proceedings, the Petitioners' Steering Committee (representing the families) concluded that the information relevant to the MMR-only theory had been presented as part of the joint theory and elected to present cases for only the first two theories. The decision on the part of the petitioners to not seek review of the decisions brought hearings on the second theory to an end, although an appeal on the *Cedillo* case remained pending. On the decisions, see Office of Special Masters, In Re: Claims for Vaccine Injuries Resulting in Autism Spectrum Disorder or a Similar Neurodevelopmental Disorder, *Various Petitioners v. Health and Human Services, Respondent,* Autism Update, March 25, 2010; and on the decision to not seek review, see Office of Special Masters, In Re: Claims for Vaccine Injuries Resulting in Autism Spectrum Disorder or a Similar Neurodevelopmental Disorder, *Various Petitioners v. Health and Human Services, Respondent,* Autism Update, May 20, 2010. For a summary, see Donald G. McNeil Jr., "3 Rulings Find No Link to Vaccines and Autism," *New York Times*, March 12, 2010.

107. George L. Hastings Jr., decision in *Cedillo v. Secretary of Health and Human Services,* 173.

108 *Cedillo v. Secretary of Health and Human Services,* 15; Offit (2008, 160).

109. It follows that educational efforts often focus on perceived "misunderstandings" on the part of parents. See, for instance, a 2008 presentation by a nurse who serves on an advisory committee for the CDC: Patricia Stinchfield, "Effectively Addressing Parents' Concerns about Immunizations," presentation at the Centers for Disease Control and Prevention Vaccine Safety Netconference (June 12, 2008), www.cdc.gov/vaccines/ed/ciinc/downloads/June_08/ Stinchfield.ppt; and Hobson-West (2003, 278). Hobson-West writes that "in a horrific irony, proponents argue, the success of vaccination undermines itself."

110. Brownlie and Howson (2005, 224, 233, 235).

111. Hobson-West (2003, 278); Senier (2008, 219–20).

112. Casiday (2007, 1065); Hobson-West (2007, 211).

113. The full quote reads, "The process of education and learning is more important than the eventual decision and that trust, (or at least blind faith) is constructed as itself a source of risk." Hobson-West (2007, 209, 211–12).

114. Kaufman (2010, 22–24).

115. Casiday (2007, 1067).

116. Brownlie and Howson (2006, 439).

117. Senier (2008, 225).
118. Hobson-West (2007, 203–4); Blume (2006, 637, 640).
119. "Editorial: Silencing Debate over Autism," *Nature Neuroscience* 10, no. 5 (2007): 531.
120. Irva Hertz-Picciotto and Lora Delwiche, "The Rise in Autism and the Role of Age at Diagnosis," *Epidemiology* 20, no. 1 (2009): 84–90.
121. See, for instance, a 2008 study that investigates a possible association between regression and gastrointestinal issues. Maria D. Valicenti-McDermott, Kathryn McVicar, Herbert J. Cohen, Barry K. Wershil, et al., "Gastrointestinal Symptoms in Children with an Autism Spectrum Disorder and Language Regression," *Pediatric Neurology* 39, no. 6 (2008): 392–98. Other studies have looked at the relationship between developmental regression and the severity of autistic symptoms, for instance, A.-A. S. Meilleur and E. Fombonne, "Regression of Language and Non-Language Skills in Pervasive Developmental Disorders," *Journal of Intellectual Disability Research* 53, no. 2 (2009): 115–24.
122. Martha Herbert, "Learning from the Autism Catastrophe: Key Leverage Points," *Alternative Therapies* 14, no. 6 (2008): 28–30.
123. Herbert (2010). A special issue of the *American Journal of Biochemistry and Biotechnology* featured articles on a number of candidate factors in the etiology of autism, including infections, mercury, immune dysfunction, and mitochondrial disorders. Of particular interest were Teresa A. Evans, Sandra L. Siedlak, Liang Lu, Xiaoming Fu, et al., "The Autistic Phenotype Exhibits a Remarkably Localized Modification of Brain Protein by Products of Free Radical-Induced Lipid Oxidation," *American Journal of Biochemistry and Biotechnology* 4, no. 2 (2008): 61–72; and Matthew P. Anderson, Brian S. Hooker, and Martha R. Herbert, "Bridging from Cells to Cognition in Autism Pathophysiology: Biological Pathways to Defective Brain Function and Plasticity," *American Journal of Biochemistry and Biotechnology* 4, no. 2 (2008): 167–76.

Conclusion

1. For instance, "There comes a point in every great mystery when a confusing set of clues begins to narrow." Sandra Blakeslee, "Focus Narrows in Search for Autism's Cause," *New York Times*, February 8, 2005.
2. For example, Sally J. Rogers, "What Are Infant Siblings Teaching Us about Autism in Infancy?" *Autism Research* 2, no. 3 (2003): 125–37; and Lonnie Zwaigenbaum, Susan Bryson, Catherine Lord, Sally Rogers, et al., "Clinical Assessment and Management of Toddlers with Suspected Autism Spectrum Disorder: Insights from Studies of High-Risk Infants," *Pediatrics* 123, no. 5 (2009): 1383–91.

3. In using "syncretic," I am thinking of Lawrence Cohen's (1995) use of the term. While Cohen described the parallel application of incommensurate medical belief systems within modern medical practice in India, I am extending the argument to biomedicine in the United States by observing that it contains multiple, often contradictory, belief systems. Just because behaviorism and genetics are both used by psychiatric professionals, it does not mean that the assumptions that they make about the origins and treatment of disease, or the motivations behind human behavior, are entirely compatible.

4. Haraway (1997a, 128).

5. Hacking (1983, 136).

6. For instance, I cowrote an editorial for *GeneWatch*, the Journal of the Council for Responsible Genetics, with Martha Herbert, in which we argued that genetics was overemphasized and overfunded in the search for autism's causes, and another article with Jeffrey Brosco, a developmental pediatrician, in which we argued that clinicians need to remember how important parental insights have been in developing better understandings of autism and new treatment strategies.

7. Forsythe (1999); Nader (1972).

8. Rabinow and Lowy, quoted in Blume (2000, 142).

9. Ibid., 141–43.

10. Blume (2000, 139, 162).

11. Osteen (2008, 8).

12. One excellent example of research that explicitly asked autistic adults for guidance is Chamak, Bonniau, Jaunay, and Cohen (2008).

13. Eric Schopler made much the same point in criticizing those who claimed that psychogenic theories offered more prospects for improvement—many "organically involved" patients improved while those suffering from "habits formed early in life" might not do so well. Eric Schopler, "The Stress of Autism as Ethology," *Journal of Autism and Childhood Schizophrenia*, 3, no. 4 (1974): 193–96, 195.

14. Park (2001, 201, 10).

15. Landecker (2005) expresses a similar idea when she asks, "What is the social and cultural task of being biological entitities—being simultaneously biological things and human persons—when 'the biological' is fundamentally plastic?"

BIBLIOGRAPHY

Adams, Christina. 2005. *A Real Boy: A True Story of Autism, Early Intervention, and Recovery*. New York: Berkeley Books.

Amsterdamska, Olga, and Anja Hiddinga. 2004, August. "Negotiating Classifications: Autism in the DSM." Paper given at the Society for Social Studies of Science, Paris, France.

Apple, Rima D. 1995. "Constructing Mothers: Scientific Motherhood in the Nineteenth and Twentieth Centuries." *Social History of Medicine* 8 (2): 161–78.

———. 2006. *Perfect Motherhood: Science and Childrearing in America*. New Brunswick, NJ: Rutgers University Press.

Ariès, Philip. 1962. *Centuries of Childhood: A Social History of Family Life*. Trans. Robert Baldick. New York: Vintage Books.

Aronowitz, Robert. 1998. *Making Sense of Illness: Science, Society, and Disease*. Cambridge, UK: Cambridge University Press.

Asperger, Hans. 1991/1944. " 'Autistic Psychopathy' in Childhood." In *Autism and Asperger Syndrome,* ed. Uta Frith, 37–92.Cambridge, UK: Cambridge University Press.

Badcock, Christopher. 2004. "Mentalism and Mechanism: The Twin Modes of Human Cognition." In *Evolutionary Psychology, Public Policy and Personal Decisions,* eds. Charles Crawford and Catherine Salmon, 99–116. Mahwah, NJ: Lawrence Erlbaum Associates.

Bagatell, Nancy. 2010. "From Cure to Community: Transforming Notions of Autism." *Ethos: Journal of the Society for Psychological Anthropology* 38 (1): 33–55.

Baker, Jeffrey P. 2008. "Mercury, Vaccines, and Autism: One Controversy, Three Histories." *American Journal of Public Health* 98 (2): 244–53.

Barnbaum, Deborah. 2008. *The Ethics of Autism: Among Them, But Not Of Them*. Bloomington, IN: Indiana University Press.

Baron-Cohen, Simon. 1997. *Mindblindness: An Essay on Autism and Theory of Mind*. Cambridge, MA: MIT Press.

———. 2003. *The Essential Difference: The Truth about the Male and Female Brain*. New York: Basic Books.

Barron, Judy, and Sean Barron. 2002. *There's a Boy in Here: Emerging From the Bonds of Autism*. New York: Simon and Schuster.

Belmonte, Matthew K. 2008. "Human, but More So: What the Autistic Brain Tells Us about the Process of Narrative." In *Autism and Representation.*, ed. Mark Osteen, 166–79. New York: Routledge.

Bérubé, Michael. 1996. *Life as We Know It: A Father, a Family, and an Exceptional Child*. New York: Pantheon Books.

Bettelheim, Bruno. 1943. "Individual and Mass Behavior in Extreme Situations." *Journal of Abnormal and Social Psychology* 38 (4): 417–52.

———. 1950. *Love Is Not Enough: The Treatment of Emotionally Disturbed Children*. Glencoe, IL: The Free Press.

———. 1959. "Joey: A 'Mechanical Boy.'" *Scientific American* 200 (3): 116–20.

———. 1967. *The Empty Fortress: Infantile Autism and the Birth of the Self*. New York: The Free Press.

———. 1974. *A Home for the Heart*. New York: Knopf.

———. 1987. *A Good Enough Parent: A Book on Child-Rearing*. New York: Knopf.

Blume, Stuart. 2000. "Land of Hope and Glory: Exploring Cochlear Implantation in the Netherlands." *Science, Technology and Human Values* 25 (2): 139–66.

———. 2006. "Anti-Vaccination Movements and their Interpretations." *Social Science and Medicine* 62 (3): 628–42.

Bourdieu, Pierre. 1975/1999. "The Specificity of the Scientific Field and the Social Conditions of the Progress of Reason." In *The Science Studies Reader,* ed. Mario Biagioli, 31–50. New York: Routledge.

———. 1984. *Distinction: A Social Critique of the Judgment of Taste*. Trans. Richard Nice. Cambridge, MA: Harvard University Press.

Braslow, Joel. 1996. "The Influence of a Biological Therapy on Physicians' Narratives and Interrogations: The Case of General Paralysis of the Insane and Malaria Fever Therapy, 1910–1950," *Bulletin of the History of Medicine*. 70 (4): 577–608.

Brown, Phil, Stephen Zavestoski, Sabrina McCormick, Meadow Linder, Joshua Mandelbaum, and Theo Luebke. 2001. "A Gulf of Difference: Disputes over Gulf War–Related Illnesses." *Journal of Health and Social Behavior* 42 (3): 235–57.

Brown, Phil, Stephen Zavestoski, Sabrina McCormick, Brian Mayer, Rachel Morello-Frosch, and Rebecca Gasior Altman. 2004. "Embodied Health Movements: New Approaches to Social Movements in Health," *Sociology of Health and Illness* 26 (1): 50–80.

Brownlie, Julie, and Alexandra Howson. 2005. "'Leaps of Faith' and MMR: An Empirical Study of Trust." *Sociology* 39 (2): 221–239.

———. 2006. "'Between the Demands of Trust and Government': Health Practitioners, Trust and Immunisation Work." *Social Science & Medicine* 62 (2): 433–43.

Buchanan, Roderick D. 2003. "Legislative Warriors: American Psychiatrists, Psychologists, and Competing Claims over Psychotherapy in the 1950s." *Journal of the History of the Behavioral Sciences* 39 (3): 225–49.

Bumiller, Kristin. 2008. "Quirky Citizens: Autism, Gender, and Reimagining Disability," *Signs: Journal of Women in Culture and Society* 33 (4): 967–91.

———. 2009. "The Geneticization of Autism: From New Reproductive Technologies to the Conception of Genetic Normalcy." *Signs: Journal of Women in Culture and Society* 34 (4): 875–99.

Callon, Michel. 1987. "Some Elements of a Sociology of Translation: Domestication of the Scallops and the Fishermen of St. Brieuc Bay." In *Power, Action and Belief: A New Sociology of Knowledge,* ed. John Law, 196–223. London: Routledge and Kegan Paul.

Casiday, Rachel Elizabeth. 2007. "Children's Health and the Social Theory of Risk: Insights from the British Measles, Mumps and Rubella (MMR) Controversy." *Social Science & Medicine* 65 (5): 1059–70.

Chamak, Brigitte. 2008. "Autism and Social Movements: French Parents' Associations and International Autistic Individuals' Organisations." *Sociology of Health and Illness* 30 (1): 76–96.

Chamak, Brigitte, Beatrice Bonniau, Emmanuel Jaunay, and David Cohen. 2008. "What Can We Learn about Autism from Autistic Persons?" *Psychotherapy and Psychosomatics* 77 (5): 271–79.

Charlton, James. 1998. *Nothing About Us Without Us: Disability Oppression and Empowerment.* Berkeley: University of California Press.

Clifford, Stacy A. 2006. "The Politics of Autism: Expanding the Location of Care." Master's thesis, Ohio University.

Cohen, Lawrence. 1995. "The Epistemological Carnival: Meditations on Disciplinary Intentionality and Ayurveda." In *Knowledge and the Scholarly Medical Traditions,* ed. Don Bates, 320–43. Cambridge, UK: Cambridge University Press.

Conrad, Peter. 1999. "A Mirage of Genes," *Sociology of Health & Illness.* 21 (2): 228–41.

Cowan, Ruth Schwartz. 1983. *More Work for Mother: The Ironies of Household Technology from the Open Hearth to the Microwave.* New York: Basic Books.

Daley, Tamara. 2002. "Diagnostic Conceptualization of Autism among Indian Psychiatrists, Psychologists, and Pediatricians." *Journal of Autism and Developmental Disorders* 32 (1): 531–50.

———. 2004. "From Symptom Recognition to Diagnosis: Children with Autism in Urban India," *Social Science & Medicine* 58 (7): 1323–-35.

Daston, Lorraine. 1992. "Objectivity and the Escape from Perspective." *Social Studies of Science* 22 (4): 597–618.

Daston, Lorraine, and Peter Galison. 1992. "The Image of Objectivity." *Representations* 40 (1): 81–128

Davidson, Joyce. 2008. "Autistic Culture Online: Virtual Communication and Cultural Expression on the Spectrum." *Social and Cultural Geography* 9 (7): 791–806.

Davis, Lennard. 2006. "Constructing Normalcy: the Bell Curve, the Novel, and the Invention of the Disabled Body in the 19th Century." *Disability Studies Reader*, 2nd ed. New York: Routledge.

de Chadarevian, Soraya. 2002. *Designs for Life: Molecular Biology after World War II*. Cambridge, UK: Cambridge University Press.

Didion, Joan. 1979/1990. *The White Album*. New York: Farrar, Straus and Giroux.

Doyle, Richard. 1997. *On Beyond Living: Rhetorical Transformations of the Life Sciences*. Palo Alto, CA: Stanford University Press.

Dumit, Joseph. 2000. "When Explanations Rest: "Good-Enough" Brain Science and the New Socio-Medical Disorders." In *Living and Working With the New Medical Technologies,* eds. Margaret Lock, Alberto Cambrosio, and Allan Young, 209–32.. Cambridge, UK: Cambridge University Press.

———. 2003. *Picturing Personhood: Brain Scans and Biomedical Identity*. Princeton, NJ: Princeton University Press.

Dundes, Alan. 1991. "Bruno Bettelhem's Uses of Enchantment and Abuses of Scholarship." *The Journal of American Folklore* 104 (411): 74–83.

Durbach, Nadja. 2002. "Class, Gender, and the Conscientious Objector to Vaccination, 1898–1907." *The Journal of British Studies* 41 (1): 58–83.

———. 2005. *Bodily Matters: The Anti-Vaccination Movement in England, 1853–1907*. Durham, NC: Duke University Press.

Durbin-Westby, Paula C. 2010. "Cultural Commentary: 'Public Law 109-416 Is Not Just About Scientific Research': Speaking Truth to Power at Interagency Autism Coordinating Committee Meetings." *Disability Studies Quarterly* 30 (1).

Edelson, Steven, and Bernard Rimland, eds. 2003. *Treating Autism: Parent Stories of Hope and Success*. San Diego, CA: Autism Research Institute.

Eliot, Stephen. 2002. *Not the Thing I Was: Thirteen Years at Bruno Bettelheim's Orthogenic School*. New York: St. Martin's Press.

Epstein, Steven. 1995. "The Construction of Lay Expertise: AIDS Activism and the Forging of Credibility in the Reform of Clinical Trials." *Science, Technology, & Human Values*. Special Issue: Constructivist Perspectives on Medical Work: Medical Practices and Science and Technology Studies. 20 (4): 408–37.

———. 1996. *Impure Science: AIDS, Activism and the Politics of Knowledge*. Berkeley: University of California Press.

Eyal, Gil, Brendan Hart, Emine Onculer, Neta Oren, and Natasha Rossi. 2010. *The Autism Matrix*. Cambridge, UK: Polity Press.

Fees, Craig. 1998. "'No Foundation All the Way Down the Line': History, Memory and 'Milieu Therapy' From the View of a Specialist Archive in Britain." *Therapeutic Communities: The International Journal for Therapeutic and Specialist Organizations* 19 (2): 167–78.

Feinstein, Noah. 2006, November. "Silenced by Science? Parents of Autistic Children Finding Their Voice." Paper presented at the Society for Social Studies of Science, Vancouver, BC.

Ferguson, Phil. 1996. "Mental Retardation Historiography and the Culture of Knowledge." *Disability Studies Quarterly* 16 (3): 18–31.

Fischer, Michael M. J. 1999. "Emergent Forms of Life: Anthropologies of Late or Postmodernities." *Annual Review of Anthropology* 28: 455–78.

———. 2000. "Calling the Future(s) with Ethnographic and Historiographic Legacy Disciplines: STS@the_Turn_[ ]ooo.mit.edu." In *Late Editions 8: Zeroing in on the Year 2000: The Final Edition*, ed. George E. Marcus, 218–302. Chicago: University of Chicago Press.

Fisher, David James. 1991. "Homage to Bettelheim (1903-1990)." *Psychohistory Review* 19 (2): 255–61.

Fisher, James. 2007. "No Search, No Subject? Autism and the American Conversion Narrative." In *Autism and Representation,* ed. Mark Osteen, 51–64. New York: Routledge.

Fitzpatrick, Michael. 2009. *Defeating Autism: A Damaging Delusion.* New York: Routledge.

Fleck, Ludwik. 1979. *Genesis and Development of a Scientific Fact.* Chicago: University of Chicago Press.

Forsythe, Diana E. 1999. "Ethics and Politics of Studying Up in Technoscience." *Anthropology of Work Review* 20 (1): 6–11.

Frankfurt, Harry. 2006. *Taking Ourselves Seriously & Getting It Right.* Palo Alto, CA: Stanford University Press.

Frith, Uta. 1989/2003. *Autism: Explaining the Enigma.* Malden, MA: Blackwell Publishers.

———. 1991. "Asperger and His Syndrome." In *Autism and Asperger Syndrome,* ed. Uta Frith, 1–36. Cambridge: Cambridge University Press.

Fromm, Erich. 1956. *The Art of Loving.* New York: Harper and Row.

Gernsbacher, Morton Ann. 2006. "Toward a Behavior of Reciprocity." *Journal of Developmental Processes* 1: 138–52

Gershon, Michael. 1998. *The Second Brain: The Scientific Basis of Gut Instinct and a Groundbreaking New Understanding of Nervous Disorders of the Stomach and Intestine.* New York: HarperCollins.

Gibbon, Sahra. 2007. *Breast Cancer Genes and the Gendering of Knowledge: Science and Citizenship in the Cultural Context of the "New" Genetics.* Houndmills, UK: Palgrave Macmillan.

Gieryn, Thomas F. 1983. "Boundary-Work and the Demarcation of Science from Non-Science: Strains and Interests in Professional Ideologies." *American Sociological Review* 48 (6): 781–95.

Gifford, Sanford. 1991. "The American Reception of Psychoanalysis." In *1915, The Cultural Moment: The New Politics, The New Woman, The New Art, and the*

New Theater in America, eds. Adele Heller and Lois Rudnick, 128–45. New Brunswick: Rutgers University Press.

Gilligan, Carol. 1982. *In a Different Voice: Psychological Theory and Women's Development.* Cambridge, MA: Harvard University Press.

Glaser, Elizabeth, with Laura Palmer. 1991. *In the Absence of Angels: A Hollywood Family's Courageous Story.* New York: Berkeley Books.

Goffman, Erving. 1959. *The Presentation of Self in Everyday Life.* New York: Doubleday.

Grant, Julia. 1998. *Raising Baby by the Book: The Education of American Mothers.* New Haven, CT: Yale University Press.

Gray, David E. 1993. "Negotiating Autism: Relations Between Parents and Treatment Staff." *Social Science & Medicine* 36 (8): 1037–46.

———. 1994. "Coping with Autism: Stresses and Strategies." *Sociology of Health and Illness* 16 (3): 275–300.

Greenfeld, Josh. 1970. *A Child Called Noah.* New York: Pocket Books.

———. 1978. *A Place for Noah.* San Diego, CA: Harcourt Brace Jovanovich.

———. 1986. *A Client Called Noah.* New York: Henry Holt and Company.

Grinker, Roy Richard. 2008. *Unstrange Minds: Remapping the World of Autism.* New York: Basic Books.

Grob, Gerald. 1994. *The Mad among Us: A History of the Care of America's Mentally Ill.* Cambridge, MA: Harvard University Press.

Hacking, Ian. 1983. *Representing and Intervening: Introductory Topics in the Philosophy of Natural Science.* Cambridge, UK: Cambridge University Press.

———. 1998. *Rewriting the Soul: Multiple Personality and the Sciences of Memory.* Princeton, NJ: Princeton University Press.

———. 1999. "Making Up People." In *The Science Studies Reader,* ed. Mario Biagioli, 161–71. New York: Routledge.

———. 2007. "Kinds of People: Moving Targets." *Proceedings of the British Academy* 151: 285–318.

———. 2009a. "How We Have Been Learning to Talk About Autism: A Role for Stories." *Metaphilosophy* 40 (3–4): 499–516.

———. 2009b. "Humans, Aliens, and Autism." *Daedalus* 138 (3): 44–59.

Haddon, Mark. 2004. *The Curious Incident of the Dog in the Night-Time.* New York: Vintage.

Hale, Nathan G. 1978. "From Bergasse XIX to Central Park West: The Americanization of Psychoanalysis, 1919–1940." *Journal of the History of the Behavioral Sciences* 14 (4): 299–315.

Hamilton, Lynn. 2000. *Facing Autism: Giving Parents Reasons for Hope and Guidance for Help.* Colorado Springs, CO: Waterbrook Press.

Happe, Francesca. 1994. *Autism: An Introduction to Psychological Theory.* Cambridge, MA: Harvard University Press.

Haraway, Donna. 1989. *Primate Visions: Gender, Race, and Nature in the World of Modern Science.* New York: Routledge.

————. 1991. *Simians, Cyborgs, and Women: The Reinvention of Nature.* New York: Routledge.

————. 1997a. "enlightenment@science_wars.com: A Personal Reflection on Love and War," *Social Text* 50 (The Politics of Sport): 123–29.

————. 1997b. *Modest_Witness@Second_Millenium.FemaleMan©_Meets_Onco-Mouse™: Feminism and Technoscience.* New York and London: Routledge.

Hays, Sharon. 1996. *The Cultural Contradictions of Motherhood.* New Haven, CT: Yale University Press.

Heath, Deborah, Rayna Rapp, and Karen-Sue Taussig. 2004. "Genetic Citizenship." In *A Companion to the Anthropology of Politics,* eds. David Nugent and Joan Vincent, 152–67. Malden, MA: Blackwell Publishing.

Hedgecoe, Adam. 2001. "Schizophrenia and the Narrative of Enlightened Geneticization." *Social Studies of Science* 31 (6): 875–911.

Henry, Jules. 1971. *Pathways to Madness.* New York: Random House.

Herbert, Martha R. 2004. "Neuroimaging in Disorders of Social and Emotional Functioning: What Is the Question?" *Journal of Child Neurology* 19 (10): 772–84.

————. 2005a. "Autism: A Brain Disorder, or a Disorder that Affects the Brain?" *Clinical Neuropsychiatry* 2 (6): 354–79.

————. 2005b. "Autism Biology and the Environment." *San Francisco Medicine* 78 (8): 13–16.

————. 2009. "Autism: The Centrality of Active Pathophysiology and the Shift from Static to Chronic Dynamic Encephalopathy." In *Autism: Oxidative Stress, Inflammation, and Immune Abnormalities,* eds. Abha Chauhan, Ved Chauhan, and W. Ted Brown, 343–87. Boca Raton, FL: Taylor & Francis/CRC Press.

————. 2010. "Contributions of the Environment and Environmentally Vulnerable Physiology to Autism Spectrum Disorders." *Current Opinions in Neurology* 23 (2): 103–10.

————. 2011. "A Whole Body Systems Approach to ASD." In *The Neuropsychology of Autism,* ed. Deborah A. Fein, 499–510. Oxford, UK: Oxford University Press.

Herman, Ellen. 1995. *The Romance of American Psychology: Political Culture in the Age of Experts.* Berkeley, CA: University of California Press.

Hobson-West, Pru. 2003. "Understanding Vaccination Resistance: Moving Beyond Risk." *Health, Risk & Society* 5 (3): 273–83.

————. 2007. "'Trusting Blindly Can Be the Biggest Risk of All': Organised Resistance to Childhood Vaccination in the UK." *Sociology of Health & Illness* 29 (2): 198–215.

Houston, Rab A., and Uta Frith. 2000. *Autism in History: The Case of Hugh Blair of Borgue.* Oxford, UK: Blackwell Publishing Limited.

Iverson, Portia. 2006. *Strange Son: Two Mothers, Two Sons, and the Quest to Unlock the Hidden World of Autism.* New York: Riverhead Hardcover.

Jacobsen, Kurt, ed. 2004. *Maverick Voices: Conversations with Political and Cultural Rebels.* Oxford, UK: Rowman & Littlefield Publishers.

Jasanoff, Sheila. 1997. *Science at the Bar: Science and Technology in American Law.* Cambridge, MA: Harvard University Press.

Johnson, Carol, and Julia Crowder. 1994. *Autism: From Tragedy to Triumph.* Boston: Branden Books.

Johnston, Robert D. 2004. "Contemporary Anti-Vaccination Movements in Historical Perspective." In *The Politics of Healing: Histories of Twentieth-Century Alternative Medicine in North America,* ed. Robert D. Johnston, 259–86. New York: Routledge.

Jurecic, Ann. 2006. "Mindblindness: Autism, Writing, and the Problem of Empathy," *Literature and Medicine* 25 (1): 1–23.

Kanner, Leo. 1943. "Autistic Disturbances of Affective Contact." *Nervous Child* 2: 217–50.

———. 1971. "Follow-Up Study of Eleven Autistic Children Originally Reported in 1943." *Journal of Autism and Childhood Schizophrenia* 1 (2): 119–45.

———. 1973. *Childhood Psychosis: Initial Studies and New Insights.* Washington, DC: V. H. Winston & Sons.

Kaufman, Barry Neil. 1976. *Son-Rise.* New York: Warner Books.

Kaufman, Sharon. 2010. "Regarding the Rise in Autism: Vaccine Safety Doubt, Conditions of Inquiry, and the Shape of Freedom." *Ethos: Journal of the Society for Psychological Anthropology* 38 (1): 8–32.

Kay, Lily E. 1993. *The Molecular Vision of Life: Caltech, the Rockefeller Foundation, and the Rise of the New Biology.* New York: Oxford University Press.

———. 2000. *Who Wrote the Book of Life?: A History of the Genetic Code.* Stanford, CA: Stanford University Press.

Keller, Evelyn Fox. 1983. *A Feeling for the Organism: The Life and Work of Barbara McClintock.* New York: Henry Holt and Co.

———. 1992. *Secrets of Life/Secrets of Death: Essays on Language, Gender, and Science.* New York: Routledge.

———. 1995. *Refiguring Life: Metaphors of Twentieth-Century Biology.* New York: Cambridge University Press.

———. 2000. *The Century of the Gene.* Cambridge, MA: Harvard University Press.

———. 2007. "Whole Bodies, Whole Persons? Cultural Studies, Psychoanalysis, and Biology." In *Subjectivity: Ethnographic Investigations,* eds. Joao Biehl, Byron Good, and Arthur Kleinman, 352–61. Berkeley: University of California Press.

Kennett, Jeanette. 2002. "Autism, Empathy, and Moral Agency," *The Philosophical Quarterly* 52 (208): 340–57.

Kephart, Newell C. 1960. *The Slow Learner in the Classroom.* Columbus, OH: Charles E. Merrill Publishing Company.

Kirby, David. 2005. *Evidence of Harm: Mercury in Vaccines and the Autism Epidemic—A Medical Controversy.* New York: St. Martin's Press.

Kirk, Stuart A., and Herb Kutchins, 1992. *The Selling of DSM: The Rhetoric of Science in Psychiatry*. New York: Aldine de Gruyter.

Kittay, Eva Feder. 1999. *Love's Labor: Essays on Women, Equality, and Dependency*. New York: Routledge.

———. 2001. "When Caring is Just and Justice is Caring: Justice and Mental Retardation." *Public Culture* 13 (3): 557–79.

Kozloff, Martin A. 1973/1998. *Reaching the Autistic Child: A Parent Training Program*. Cambridge, MA: Brookline Books.

Kramer, Peter. 1993/1997. *Listening to Prozac: The Landmark Book about Antidepressants and the Remaking of the Self*, rev. ed. New York: Penguin Books.

Kras, Joseph F. 2010. "The 'Ransom Notes' Affair: When the Neurodiversity Movement Came of Age." *Disability Studies Quarterly* 30 (1). http://www.dsq-sds.org/article/view/1065/1254.

Kroll-Smith, J. Stephen, and H. Hugh Floyd. 2000. *Bodies in Protest: Environmental Illness and the Struggle over Medical Knowledge*. New York: NYU Press.

Kuhn, Roland, and Charles H. Cahn. 2004. "Eugen Bleuler's Concepts of Psychopathology." *History of Psychiatry* 15 (3): 361–66.

Kutchins, Herb, and Stuart A. Kirk. 1997. *Making Us Crazy: DSM, the Psychiatric Bible and the Creation of Mental Disorder*. New York: Free Press.

Ladd-Taylor, Molly, and Lauri Umansky, eds. 1998. *"Bad" Mothers: The Politics of Blame in Twentieth-Century America*. New York: New York University Press.

Lakoff, Andrew. 2005. *Pharmaceutical Reason: Knowledge and Value in Global Psychiatry*. Cambridge, UK: Cambridge University Press.

Landecker, Hannah. 2005. "Living Differently in Time: Plasticity, Temporality and Cellular Biotechnologies." *Culture Machine: Generating Research in Culture and Theory*. http://culturemachine.tees.ac.uk/Cmach/Backissues/j007/Articles/landecker.htm.

Landsman, Gail. 2003. "Emplotting Children's Lives: Developmental Delay vs. Disability." *Social Science and Medicine* 56 (9): 1947–60.

———. 2005. "Mothers and Models of Disability." *Journal of Medical Humanities* 26 (2/3): 121–39.

Landsman, Gail Heidi. 2009. *Reconstructing Motherhood and Disability in the Age of "Perfect" Babies*. New York: Routledge.

Lane, Harlan. 1979. *The Wild Boy of Aveyron*. Harvard University Press.

Latour, Bruno. 1988. *The Pasteurization of France*. Trans. Alan Sheridan and John Law. Cambridge, MA: Harvard University Press.

Leiter, Valerie. 2004. "Parental Activism, Professional Dominance, and Early Childhood Disablity." *Disability Studies Quarterly* 24 (2). http://www.dsq-sds.org/article/view/483/660.

Lemov, Rebecca. 2005. *World as Laboratory: Experiments with Mice, Mazes, and Men*. New York: Hill and Wang.

Lettick, Amy L. 1979a. *Benhaven Then and Now*. New Haven, CT: Benhaven Press.

Lettick, Amy L. 1979b. *Benhaven at Work, May through August, 1978*. New Haven, CT: Benhaven Press.

Lewis, Lisa. 1998. *Special Diets for Special Kids: Understanding and Implementing Special Diets to Aid in the Treatment of Autism and Related Developmental Disorders*. Arlington, TX: Future Horizons.

Lindee, Susan. 2005. *Moments of Truth in Genetic Medicine*. Baltimore, MD: Johns Hopkins University Press.

Lovaas, O. Ivar. 1977. *The Autistic Child: Language Development through Behavior Modification*. New York: Irvington Publishers.

———. 1981. *Teaching Developmentally Disabled Children: The ME Book*. Austin, TX: Pro-Ed.

Luhrmann, Tanya. 2000. *Of Two Minds: An Anthropologist Looks at American Psychiatry*. New York: Vintage Books.

Lunbeck, Elizabeth. 1994. *The Psychiatric Persuasion: Knowledge, Gender and Power in Modern America*. Princeton, NJ: Princeton University Press.

Lyons, Tom Wallace. 1983. *The Pelican and After*. Richmond, VA: Prescott, Durrell, and Company.

MacIntyre, Alasdair. 1999. *Dependent Rational Animals* Peru, IL: Open Court Publishing Company.

Marcus, George. 1998. *Ethnography through Thick and Thin*. Princeton, NJ: Princeton University Press.

Marcus, George, and Michael M. J. Fischer. 1986. *Anthropology as Cultural Critique: An Experimental Moment in the Human Sciences*. Chicago: University of Chicago Press.

Matthews, Fred. 1967. "The Americanization of Sigmund Freud: Adaptations of Psychoanalysis before 1917." *Journal of American Studies* 1: 39–62.

Maurice, Catherine. 1993. *Let Me Hear Your Voice: A Family's Triumph over Autism*. New York: Fawcett Columbine.

McCandless, Jacquelyn. 2003. *Children with Starving Brains: A Medical Treatment Guide for Autism Spectrum Disorder*. Bramble Books.

Mechanic, David, and David A. Rochefort 1990. "Deinstitutionalization: An Appraisal of Reform." *Annual Review of Sociology* 16: 301–27.

Merton, Robert K. 1942/1973. "The Normative Structure of Science." In *The Sociology of Science,* ed N. W. Storer, 267–78. Chicago: University of Chicago Press.

Moon, Elizabeth. 2003. *The Speed of Dark*. New York: Ballantine Books.

Mulkay, Michael. 1976. "Norms and Ideology in Science." *Social Science Information* 15 (45): 637–56.

Murphy, Michelle. 2000. "The 'Elsewhere within Here' and Environmental Illness; or, How to Build Yourself a Body in a Safe Space," *Configurations* 8 (1): 87–120.

Murray, Stuart. 2008. *Representing Autism: Culture, Narrative, Fascination*. Liverpool, UK: Liverpool University Press.

Nader, Laura. 1972. "Up the Anthropologist: Perspectives Gained from Studying Up." In *Reinventing Anthropology,* ed. Dell H. Hymes, 284–311. New York: Pantheon Books.

Nadesan, Majia Holmer. 2005. *Constructing Autism: Unravelling the "Truth" and Understanding the Social.* New York: Routledge.

National Research Council (NRC). 2000. *Toxicological Effects of Methylmercury.* Washington, DC: National Academies Press.

Nelkin, Dorothy, and Lori Andrews. 2001. *Body Bazaar: The Market for Human Tissue in the Biotechnology Age.* New York: Crown Books.

Nelkin, Dorothy, and Lawrence Tancredi. 1994. *Dangerous Diagnostics: The Social Power of Biological Information.* Chicago: University of Chicago Press.

Neumärker, K. J. 2003. "Leo Kanner: His Years in Berlin, 1906–24. The Roots of Autistic Disorder." *History of Psychiatry* 14 (2): 205–18.

Nichols, Shana, with Gina Marie Moravcik and Samara Pulver Tentenbaum. 2009. *Girls Growing Up on the Autism Spectrum: What Parents and Professionals Should Know about the Pre-Teen and Teenage Years.* London: Jessica Kingsley Publishers.

Noll, Steven. 1995. *Feeble-Minded in Our Midst: Institutions for the Mentally Retarded in the South, 1900–1940.* Chapel Hill, NC: University of North Carolina Press.

Nussbaum, Martha. 2006. *Frontiers of Justice: Disability, Nationality, Species Membership.* Cambridge, MA: Belknap Press.

Ochs, Elinor, and Olga Solomon. 2010. "Autistic Sociality." *Ethos: Journal of the Society for Psychological Anthropology* 38 (1): 69–92.

O'Dell, Stan. 1974. "Training Parents in Behavior Modification: A Review." *Psychological Bulletin* 81 (7): 418–33.

Offit, Paul A. 2008. *Autism's False Prophets: Bad Science, Risky Medicine, and the Search for a Cure.* New York: Columbia University Press.

Oppenheim, Rosalind. 1974. *Effective Teaching Methods for Autistic Children.* Springfield, IL: Charles C. Thomas.

Orsini, Michael. 2009. "Contesting the Autistic Subject: Biological Citizenship and the Autism/Autistic Movement." In *Critical Interventions in the Ethics of Healthcare: Challenging the Principle of Autonomy in Bioethics,* eds. Stuart Murray and Dave Holmes, 115–30. Farnham, Surrey, UK: Ashgate.

Ortega, Francisco. 2009. "The Cerebral Subject and the Challenge of Neurodiversity." *BioSocieties* 4 (4): 425–45.

Osteen, Mark. 2008. "Autism and Representation: A Comprehensive Introduction." In *Autism and Representation,* ed. Mark Osteen, 1–48. New York: Routledge.

Pangborn, Jon, and Sidney Baker. 2005. *Autism: Effective Biomedical Treatments. Have We Done Everything We Can for this Child? Individuality in an Epidemic,* 2nd ed. San Diego, CA: Autism Research Institute.

Park, Clara Claiborne. 1967. *The Siege: A Family's Journey into the World of an Autistic Child.* Boston, MA: Little, Brown, and Co.

Park, Clara Claiborne. 1985. Review of *Autism: Nightmare without End*, by Dorothy Johnson Beavers. *Journal of Autism and Developmental Disorders* 15 (1): 113–19.

———. 2001. *Exiting Nirvana: A Daughter's Life with Autism*. Boston: Back Bay Books.

Park, Melissa. 2008. "Making Scenes: Imaginative Practices of a Child with Autism in a Sensory Integration-Based Therapy Session," *Medical Anthropology Quarterly* 22 (3): 234–56.

Pollak, Richard. 1997. *The Creation of Dr. B: A Biography of Bruno Bettelheim*. New York: Simon and Schuster.

Pressman, Jack D. 1998. *Last Resort: Psychosurgery and the Limits of Medicine*. Cambridge, UK: Cambridge University Press.

Prince-Hughes, Dawn. 2005. *Expecting Teryk: An Exceptional Path to Parenthood*. Athens, OH: Swallow Press.

Prussing, Erica, Elisa J. Sobo, Elizabeth Walker, and Paul S. Kurtin. 2005. "Between 'Desperation' and Disability Rights: A Narrative Analysis of Complementary/Alternative Medicine Use by Parents for Children with Down Syndrome." *Social Science and Medicine* 60 (3): 587–98.

Rabinow, Paul. 1996. "Artificiality and Enlightenment: From Sociobiology to Biosociality." In *Essays on the Anthropology of Reason*, 91–111. Princeton, NJ: Princeton University Press.

Raines, Theron. 2002. *Rising to the Light: A Portrait of Bruno Bettelheim*. New York: Knopf.

Rapp, Rayna. 1999. *Testing Women, Testing the Fetus: The Social Impact of Amniocentesis in America*. New York: Routledge.

———. 2000. "Extra Chromosomes and Blue Tulips: Medico-Familial Interpretations." In *Living and Working with the New Medical Technologies: Intersections of Inquiry*, eds. Margaret Lock, Allan Young, and Alberto Cambrosio, 184–207. Cambridge, UK: Cambridge University Press.

Rapp, Rayna, and Faye Ginsburg. 2001. "Enabling Disability: Rewriting Kinship, Reimagining Citizenship." *Public Culture* 13 (3): 533–56.

Rimland, Bernard. 1964. *Infantile Autism: The Syndrome and Its Implications for a Neural Theory of Behavior*. New York: Meredith Publishing Company.

———. 1972. "Operant Conditioning: Breakthrough in the Treatment of Mentally Ill Children." In *Readings on the Exceptional Child: Research and Theory*, 2nd ed., eds. E. P. Traff and P. Himelstein, 573–86. New York: Appleton-Century-Crofts.

———. 1976. "Psychological Treatment versus Megavitamin Therapy." In *Modern Therapies: Noted Practitioners Describe Twelve Different Types of Therapy and the Problems Each Can Help You Solve*, eds. Virginia Binder, Arnold Binder, and Bernard Rimland, 150–65. Englewood Cliffs, NJ: Prentice-Hall.

Roazen, Paul. 1992. "The Rise and Fall of Bruno Bettelheim." *The Psychohistory Review* 20 (3): 221–50.

Robertson, Scott Michael. 2010. "Neurodiversity, Quality of Life, and Autistic Adults: Shifting Research and Professional Focuses onto Real-Life Challenges." *Disability Studies Quarterly* 30 (1). http://www.dsq-sds.org/article/view/1069/1234.

Rose, Hilary. 1983. "Hand, Brain and Heart: A Feminist Epistemology for the Natural Sciences." *Signs* 9 (1): 73–90.

———. 1994. *Love, Power and Knowledge: Towards a Feminist Transformation of the Sciences*. Bloomington and Indianapolis: Indiana University Press.

Rose, Nikolas. 2007. *The Politics of Life Itself: Biomedicine, Power, and Subjectivity in the Twenty-First Century*. Princeton, NJ: Princeton University Press.

Rosenberg, Charles. 1979/1992. "The Therapeutic Revolution: Medicine, Meaning and Social Change in Nineteenth-Century America." In *Explaining Epidemics and Other Studies in the History of Medicine*, 9–31. Cambridge, UK: Cambridge University Press.

Rosenberg, Charles E. 2002. "The Tyranny of Diagnosis: Specific Entities and Individual Experience." *Milbank Quarterly* 80 (2): 237–60.

Rosenberg, Charles, and Janet Golden, eds. 1992. *Framing Disease: Studies in Cultural History*. New Brunswick, NJ: Rutgers University Press.

Rosenhan, David L. 1973. "On Being Sane in Insane Places." *Science* 179 (4070): 250–58.

Ryan, Sara, and Katherine Runswick Cole. 2009. "From Advocate to Activist? Mapping the Experiences of Mothers of Children on the Autism Spectrum." *Journal of Applied Research on Intellectual Disabilities* 22 (1): 43–53.

Sanders, Jacquelyn Seevak. 1989. *A Greenhouse for the Mind*. Chicago and London: University of Chicago Press.

———. 1996. "Autism at the Orthogenic School and in the Field at Large, 1951–1985" *Residential Treatment for Children & Youth*. 14 (2): 1–18

Sanders, Jacquelyn. 2005. "Architecture at the Sonia Shankman Orthogenic School at the University of Chicago." *The Annual of Psychoanalysis* 33: 285–95.

Schopler, Eric, and Gary B. Mesibov. 1984. "Professional Attitudes toward Parents: a Forty-Year Progress Report." In *The Effects of Autism on the Family*, eds. Eric Schopler and Gary Mesibov, 3–17. New York, Plenum Press.

Schopler, Eric, and Robert Reichler. 1971. "Parents as Cotherapists in the Treatment of Psychotic Children." *Journal of Autism and Childhood Schizophrenia* 1 (1): 87–102.

Schreibman, Laura. 2005. *The Science and Fiction of Autism*. Cambridge, MA: Harvard University Press.

Senier, Laura. 2008. " 'It's Your Most Precious Thing': Worst-Case Thinking, Trust, and Parental Decision Making about Vaccinations." *Sociological Inquiry* 78 (2): 207–29.

Seroussi, Karen. 2003. *Unraveling the Mystery of Autism and Pervasive Developmental Disorders: A Mother's Story of Research and Recovery*. New York: Simon & Schuster.

Severson, Katherine DeMaria, James Arnt Aune, and Denise Jodlowski. 2008. "Bruno Bettelheim, Autism, and the Rhetoric of Scientific Authority." In *Autism and Representation*, ed. Mark Osteen, 65–77. New York: Routledge.

Shaked, Michal. 2005. "The Social Trajectory of Illness: Autism in the Ultraorthodox Community in Israel." *Social Science and Medicine* 61 (10): 2190–2230

Shaked, Michal, and Yoram Bilu. 2006. "Grappling with Affliction: Autism in the Jewish Ultraorthodox Community in Israel." *Culture, Medicine, and Psychiatry* 30 (1): 1–27.

Shakespeare, Tom. 2006. "The Social Model of Disability." In *The Disability Studies Reader*, 2nd ed., ed. Lennard Davis, 197–204. New York: Routledge.

Shapin, Steven. 1994. *A Social History of Truth: Civility and Science in Seventeenth-Century Century England*. Chicago: University of Chicago Press.

———. 1999. "The House of Experiment in Seventeenth-Century England." In *The Science Studies Reader*, ed. Mario Biagioli, 479–504. New York: Routledge.

Shapin, Steven, and Simon Schaffer. 1989. *Leviathan and the Air-Pump: Hobbes, Boyle, and the Experimental Life*. Princeton, NJ: Princeton University Press.

Shapiro, Joseph P. 1994. *No Pity: People with Disabilities Forging a New Civil Rights Movement*. New York: Times Books.

Singer, Judy. 1999. "Why Can't You Be Normal for Once in Your Life? From a 'Problem with No Name' to the Emergence of a New Category of Difference." In *Disability Discourse*, eds. Mairian Corker and Sally French, 59–67. Buckingham, UK: Open University Press.

Singh, Jennifer. 2010. "Autism Spectrum Disorders: Parents, Scientists, and the Interpretations of Genetic Knowledge." Ph.D. diss., University of California, San Francisco.

Singh, Jennifer, Joachim Hallmayer, and Judy Illes. 2007. "Interacting and Paradoxical Forces in Neuroscience and Society." *Nature*. 8 (2): 153–60.

Singh, Jennifer, Judy Illes, Laura Lazzeroni, and Joachim Hallmayer. 2009. "Trends in U.S. Autism Research Funding." *Journal of Autism and Developmental Disorders* 39 (5): 788–95.

Solomon, Olga. 2010. "What a Dog Can Do: Children with Autism and Therapy Dogs in Social Interaction," *Ethos: Journal of the Society for Psychological Anthropology* 38 (1): 143–66.

Stacey, Patricia. 2003. *The Boy Who Loved Windows: Opening the Heart and Mind of a Child Threatened with Autism*. Cambridge, MA: Da Capo Press.

Starr, Paul. 1982. *The Social Transformation of American Medicine: The Rise of a Sovereign Profession and the Making of a Vast Industry*. New York: Basic Books.

Stearns, Peter N. 2003. *Anxious Parents: A History of Modern Childrearing in America*. New York: New York University Press.

Stevenson, Sheryl. 2008. "(M)Othering and Autism: Maternal Rhetorics of Self-Revision." In *Autism and Representation*, ed. Mark Osteen, 197–211. New York: Routledge.

Sugarman, Stephen D. 2007. "Cases in Vaccine Court—Legal Battles over Vaccines and Autism." *New England Journal of Medicine* 357 (13): 1275–77.

Sunder Rajan, Kaushik. 2003. "Genomic Capital: Public Cultures and Market Logics of Corporate Biotechnology." *Science as Culture*. 12 (1): 87–121.

Sutton, Nina. 1996. *Bettelheim: A Life and a Legacy*. New York: Basic Books.

Taussig, Karen-Sue. 2005. "The Molecular Revolution in Medicine: Promise, Reality, and Social Organization." In *Complexities: Beyond Nature & Nurture*, eds. Susan McKinnon and Sydel Silverman, 223–47. Chicago: University of Chicago Press.

Tinbergen, Niko, and Elisabeth A. Tinbergen. 1983. *'Autistic' Children: New Hope for a Cure*. London, UK: Allen & Unwin.

Tomes, Nancy. 1981. "A Generous Confidence: Thomas Story Kirkbride's Philosophy of Asylum Construction and Management." In *Madhouses, Mad-Doctors and Madmen: The Social History of Psychiatry in the Victorian Era*, ed. Andrew Scull, 120–43. Philadelphia: University of Pennsylvania Press.

Trent, James. 1994. *Inventing the Feeble Mind: A History of Mental Retardation in the United States*. Berkeley: University of California Press.

Wajcman, Judy. 1991. *Feminism Confronts Technology*. University Park, PA: Penn State University Press.

Waltz, Mitzi, and Paul Shattock. 2004. "Autistic Disorder in Nineteenth-Century London," *Autism*. 8 (1): 7–20.

Warren, Frank. 1984. "The Role of the National Society in Working with Families." In *The Effects of Autism on the Family*, ed. Eric Schopler, 99–115. New York: Plenum Press.

Williams, Roger. 1956/1998. *Biochemical Individuality: The Basis for the Genetotrophic Concept*. New Canaan, CT: Keats Publishing.

Wing, Lorna. 1993. "The Definition and Prevalence of Autism: A Review." *European Child and Adolescent Psychiatry* 2 (2): 61–74.

———. 2001. *The Autistic Spectrum: A Parents' Guide to Understanding and Helping Your Child*. Berkeley, CA: The Ulysses Press.

Wolfensberger, Wolf. 1972. *The Principle of Normalization in Human Services*. Toronto, Ontario, Canada: National Institute on Mental Retardation.

Wolff, Sula. 2004. "The History of Autism." *European Journal of Child and Adolescent Psychiatry* 13 (4): 201–8.

Wolpe, Paul Root. 1990. "The Holistic Heresy: Strategies of Ideological Challenge in the Medical Profession." *Social Science and Medicine* 31 (8): 913–23.

———. 1994. "The Dynamics of Heresy in a Profession." *Social Science & Medicine* 39 (9): 1133–48.

Zaks, Zosia. 2010. "Cultural Commentary: I Have Asperger Syndrome, and I Am a Parent." *Disability Studies Quarterly* 30 (1). http://www.dsq-sds.org/article/view/1057/1243.

Zelan, Karen. 1993. "*Bruno Bettelheim* (1903–1990)," *Prospects: The Quarterly Review of Comparative Education* 23 (1/2): 85–100.

Zelizer, Viviana. 1985. *Pricing the Priceless Child: The Changing Social Value of Children*. New York: Basic Books.

INDEX

ABA. *See* applied behavior analysis
Adams, Christina, 179–80
ADI. *See* Autism Diagnostic Interview
ADOS. *See* Autism Diagnostic Observation Schedule
adults with autism, 234; children of, 162, 286n100; medical problems of, 177; neurodiversity movement among, 234–35, 286nn97–104; self-advocacy by, 7, 11, 15, 125–26, 136, 161–64, 286n88; writings of, 161–62, 249n83, 286nn97–98, 295n57. *See also* self-advocacy movements
advocacy activities, 14–18, 23–24, 49–54; for biomedical treatments, 167–96; biosociality in, 16–18, 142–43, 184–85, 193–96, 240nn50–52, 241n57; for educational rights, 127; embrace of autistic culture in, 143; genetic citizenship debates in, 16–17, 23–24, 241nn57, 59; for genetic research, 149–52, 155–60; internet spaces of, 180–81, 207; for mental patients' rights, 122; moral personhood debates in, 7, 11, 125–26, 143; neurodiversity debates in, 125, 155, 161–65, 176, 234–35, 273nn1, 3, 286n87; parent roles in, 15–16, 23–24, 53–54, 121–23, 267nn66–67, 273n7; political economy of, 17–18, 49–54, 242n62; on vaccines, 200–203, 206–7. *See also* names of specific organizations, e.g. Autism Society of America; self-advocacy movements
affective practices. *See* love
Aichhorn, August, 69, 79
AIDS research, 156–57
Akerley, Mary S., 130–32, 276n30
Allen, Woody, 254n5
allergies/immune dysfunction, 47, 164, 188–92, 204–5

alternative practices. *See* biomedical treatments
Alzheimer's disease, 149, 280n33
amateur therapists. *See* parents' treatment activities
American Academy of Pediatrics, 216
American Psychiatric Association. See *Diagnostic and Statistical Manual of Mental Disorders*
Amsterdamska, Olga, 242n60
amygdala, 153, 155
animal models, 149–53, 209, 281nn42–43
antiviral medication, 178
apoptosis, 208–9
applied behavior analysis (ABA), 95, 108–9, 114, 121, 123–24, 172–73, 267n75. *See also* behavior modification techniques
ARI. *See* Autism Research Institute
Asperger, Hans, 37, 44–45, 50–51, 163, 243n25, 247n64, 278n4
Asperger syndrome, 12, 21, 37, 160, 243n25; diagnostic markers for, 50–52; gendered context of, 44–46, 247n64; self-advocacy in, 52, 161–64
autism (definitions), 2–3, 48–49, 107, 237n4
Autism Biomedical Discussion Group (ABMD), 180–81, 295n54
Autism Birth Cohort (the ABC Project), 288n113
Autism Diagnostic Interview (ADI), 54–55, 59, 60, 194, 252n116
Autism Diagnostic Interview–Revised (ADI–R), 57, 148, 280n25
Autism Diagnostic Observation Schedule (ADOS), 54–57, 59, 60, 148, 194, 252nn116, 119, 280n25